BY THE SAME AUTHOR

WORLD DIARY: 1929–1934 (*1934*)
ENGLAND EXPECTS EVERY AMERICAN TO DO HIS DUTY (*1937*)
BLOOD IS CHEAPER THAN WATER (*1939*)
THE NEWS AND HOW TO UNDERSTAND IT (*1940*)
A WORLD HISTORY OF OUR OWN TIMES
Volume I.
FROM THE TURN OF THE CENTURY TO THE 1918 ARMISTICE (*1949*)
Volume II.
FROM THE 1918 ARMISTICE TO THE MUNICH AGREEMENT (*1953*)

ASHES
OF
VICTORY

WORLD WAR II AND ITS AFTERMATH

Quincy Howe

SIMON AND SCHUSTER · NEW YORK

DEDICATED TO THE MEMORY OF
MARK DEWOLFE HOWE
(1906–1967)

All things are double one against another: and he hath made nothing imperfect.

One thing establisheth the good of another: and who shall be filled with beholding his glory?

Ecclesiasticus 13: 24–25

Acknowledgments

The name of Ellery Sedgwick, editor of *The Atlantic Monthly* from 1908 to 1938, must head this roster of personal acknowledgments. He it was who put me to work in 1922 on *The Living Age*, which he had acquired. There, under the scholarly editorship of Dr. Victor S. Clark, I began to learn the art of reading, selecting, and translating significant material from the foreign press. In 1935, M. Lincoln Schuster plunged me from the somewhat rarefied atmosphere of *The Living Age*—which I had followed from Boston to New York in 1929, to become its editor under a new management—into the mainstream of contemporary American publishing as head of the editorial department of Simon and Schuster. Here he and his partner, Richard L. Simon, assigned me to work on such books as *Mission to Moscow* by Joseph E. Davies and *Ten Years in Japan* by Joseph C. Grew.

Max Schuster's editorial enthusiasms knew no bounds. He not only launched me on what became a twenty-five-year, three-volume plan of contemporary historical journalism. He also launched me on a career of more than thirty years of electronic journalism by commending me, in 1939, to his old friend, Elliott M. Sanger of Radio Station WQXR, New York, who put me in his lifelong debt by giving me my first chance to report and interpret news on the air. The opportunities that Ellery Sedgwick, Max Schuster, and Elliott Sanger had given me between the years 1922 and 1939 underwrote all my subsequent activities of broadcasting news, writing books, teaching journalism, and founding *Atlas*—a replica of the old *Living Age*. This variety of journalistic experience now culminates for me in *Ashes of Victory*.

Here more acknowledgments are in order. The first goes to the late

Samuel J. Hurwitz, professor of history at Brooklyn College, who gave me literally line-by-line advice and assistance in the preparation of the three volumes of contemporary history I have written since 1949. He combined the scholar's rigor, the teacher's zeal, and the craftsman's passion for literary perfection. Next comes the late Jacques Katel, the product of four cultures—Russian, German, French, American—whose wide experience in international journalism made *Atlas* the unique publication it was until the day of his death in May 1965. Our five years of editorial collaboration became for me a seminar such as no institution of higher learning could match. Joseph Barnes, as senior editor for Simon and Schuster until his death in March 1970, guided my labors during the four years this volume was assuming its present scope. After his death, young William H. Simon inherited my manuscript and myself, giving both new impetus by spanning a generation gap of almost fifty years. Finally, the redoubtable Wallace Brockway, with whom I have worked over the years on my own books and on many others, focused his historical scholarship and journalistic experience on an editorial task for which he seemed to me to be foreordained.

Many contemporary historians dwell, in their acknowledgments, on other writers or makers of contemporary history. As one of the first journalists to move from the medium of print to the electronic media, I am at the same time among the last of the all-purpose journalistic jacks of all trades. Hence this emphasis on my debt to those who have helped me mold a lifetime's experience into this, its final form.

QUINCY HOWE

St. James, Long Island
January 1972

CONTENTS

CONTENTS

Prologue: In the First Person

MORE THAN ten years ago this book began as an attempt to show how the Second World War shaped the world we live in today. It now winds up as a reappraisal of that war in the light of its aftermath. Yet each theme has re-enforced the other. The development of the first theme required a journalistic approach; the development of the second theme required a historical approach. Most journalists prefer topical themes; most historians prefer not to deal with periods still in a state of flux. As a journalist who has spent almost half a century reporting and interpreting events of the day in several media, I found myself with one foot in the field of daily journalism, the other in the field of contemporary history. In 1967 I therefore defined, in *The Saturday Review* of May 22, three guiding principles that I had found myself applying to this work, then in progress. Writing under the title "The New Age of the Journalist-Historian," I cited, first, the eternal ironies of history, second, the accelerating pace at which the events of our century have moved, and third, the capacity for transcendence that these ironies and this acceleration demand of the twentieth-century journalist and historian alike.

But how apply these principles to an interpretation of the Second World War and its aftermath? The word "aftermath" provided the key and the Munich Conference the lock that it fitted. For the Munich Conference not only ended the First World War's long aftermath. Hitler at once seized upon the opportunity to continue that war from where it left off twenty years before. The first two chapters of this book tell that story. The last three depict the war's aftermath. Most of these chapters conclude with essays reappraising the story in the light of subsequent events. In the course of a few chapters such essays also appear at the ends of certain sections. The three guiding principles of irony, acceleration, and transcendence, implicit throughout the book, become explicit in the essays, stressing, as they do, the war's continuing impact on the world we now live in.

Every generation rewrites some of its own history and more of the history of earlier times. Every official history begets its own, revisionist counterpart. This volume, however, does not seek to revise any of the history it covers. It aims only to reappraise history—not for reappraisal's sake, but in the light of history's own consequences which even the wisest contemporary cannot, in the nature of things, foresee, but which the wisdom of hindsight gradually reveals. At which point some explanation of this book's three guiding principles becomes in order.

What some people call the ironies of history others call its paradoxes and contradictions and still others call its dialectics. Diplomatic historian Herbert Feis, who has specialized in the period of the Second World War, has noted "how often in the annals of nations, consequences were the opposite of aims and expectations." Yet he also expressed the hope that his grave will not bear the inscription: HISTORY's ONLY IRON LAW IS IRONY. Admiral Samuel Eliot Morison, the United States' official naval historian of the Second World War, wrote in his *Two-Ocean War*, published in 1963: "History is studded with ironies but never were there greater ironies than these: the fundamental reason for America's going to war with Japan was our insistence on the integrity of China, yet all our efforts and sacrifices, instead of strengthening friendly relations with China, have resulted in making her our greatest potential enemy. America in 1939–1941 wanted neither world power nor world responsibility, only to be let alone, but world power and world responsibility were forced upon her by two nations, Germany and Japan, that badly wanted both. And those two nations are now numbered among America's firmest allies."

G. K. Chesterton built a whole literary career on exploiting the paradoxical: he justified his conversion to the Roman Catholic faith by stressing the orthodoxy of his heresy from British Protestantism. Irony gives expression to a positive, even an optimistic view of life. Such clichés as "the irony of life," and "paradoxical as it may seem" sustain the unspoken, unprovable major premise that we live in a rational universe. Just as most humor depends for its effect on the reversal or violation of some accepted code or custom, so irony and paradox involve some departure from an accepted norm. North is more often north than it is south; right is sometimes but not always wrong. Without any codes or customs there can be no humor; without any norms there can be no departures from them. "The exception *probes* the rule."

The so-called "dialectical process" has enshrined irony as the most fundamental of all the facts of life. The Hungarian-born Lajos Egri spells this out in his little modern classic *The Art of Dramatic Writing:* "Everything that moves constantly negates itself. All things change to their opposite through movement. The present becomes the past, the future becomes the present. There is nothing which does not move. Constant change is the very essence of all existence. Everything in time passes into its opposite. Change is the force which compels it to move, and this very movement becomes something different from what it was. The past becomes the present and both determine the future. New life arises from the old, and this new life is the combination of the old with that which destroyed it. The contradiction that causes the change goes on forever."

The activist regards irony as the last refuge of the escapist; the ironist regards the activist as the victim of his own dialectic. The American historian Henry Adams, who wallowed in irony, said of Karl Marx's *Das Kapital:* "I never struck a book which taught me so much and with which I disagreed so radically in its conclusions." But Adams went beyond Marx in singling out the acceleration of history rather than its irony or its dialectics as the hallmark of the twentieth century. In an essay entitled "The Rule of Phase Applied to History," written in 1909, and in a 30,000-word "Letter to American Teachers of History," published the following year, Adams called upon his colleagues to transform history into a science, somewhat akin to physics. His essay and letter contended, in brief, that since 1600 the progress of science had caused history to move, at accelerating speed, through three phases: first, the mechanical phase, which had lasted from 1600 to 1900, second, the electrical phase, which would last until 1917, and, third, the ethereal phase, which would last four years and "bring Thought to the limits of its possibilities in the year 1921." He cited the "law of electrical squares" according to which "the average motion of one phase is the square root of that which preceded." Yet he could not resist the temptation to indulge his love of irony at his own expense. "I'm amusing myself," he wrote in 1910, "by printing a little volume to make fun of my fellow historians. The fun of it is that not one of them will understand the fun."

But the irony of it was that the scientists had the last laugh. Adams knew no more about modern physics than Marx knew about modern economics. William H. Jordy, in *Henry Adams, Scientific Historian,* published by the Yale University Press in 1952, wrote: "Failure is the paradoxical unity in Adams' thought. . . . If he were a failure Adams managed to imply that no one had enjoyed more success. By thus condemning as failure what most meant by success, he chided society for its standards while crediting himself not only for his achievements but also for his perception in seeing its limitations."

The end of Adams' "electrical phase" coincided, in 1917, with America's declaration of war on Germany and with the Russian Revolution. In 1921 thought reached the limits of its possibilities when Harding took office as the President of the United States. But history's accelerating pace not only multiplied history's ironies. The thrust of scientific progress set and kept in motion the half century of world revolution that began with the First World War, accelerated during the battles, sieges, and bombings of the Second World War, and reached its climax at Hiroshima and Nagasaki. The American creators of the first atomic and nuclear weapons then found themselves the prisoners of their own handiwork, whereas their Japanese victims rose like the phoenix from the ashes of defeat. It was Emperor Hirohito who—as this volume will show—offered the first, but surely not the last, example of that transcendence which broke acceleration's spiral.

The victims of history's ironies never knew what hit them. Neither did the victims of history's acceleration. Wilson did not live to see Hitler use the Covenant of the League of Nations to dismember Czechoslovakia, twenty years after the German surrender of 1918. Roosevelt did not live to see Truman use the United Nations Charter, only five years after its adoption, to justify the Korean War. A twenty-year aftermath had separated the two world wars; only five years separated the surrender of Japan in 1945 and the North Korean invasion of South Korea in 1950. No set of principles enables us to discern the future either five years ahead or twenty. But the period of the Second World War saw the acceleration of history steadily overshadowing the ironies of history. In like manner, not until the Second World War's aftermath did the transcendence of history begin to assert itself.

Two centuries ago Goethe summed up the principle of transcendence in four lines of verse:

> *And until you meet this test:*
> *First die, and then transcend,*

You will remain but a dim guest
On this dark earth, my friend.

Stirb und werde—die and become—wrote Goethe in the German original. But the all-purpose German verb *werden* means, in this context, "transcend," which, in its turn, comes from the Latin *trans,* meaning "across" and *scandere,* meaning "climb." During the course of the Second World War, Churchill and Roosevelt transcended themselves in various ways—that is to say, they had clambered above and beyond their own limitations, dying a death and achieving rebirth in the process. In both of them William James would have recognized "twice-born men." Yet man has always transcended himself. That is his truest and highest nature—and, at the same time, his potential nemesis. Hitler transcended downward, Stalin sideways, the populations of Leningrad, Tokyo, London, and other great cities *en masse.* The latter half of the twentieth century now puts an ever higher premium on that capacity—and lays an equally heavy penalty on failure to exercise it.

The Second World War witnessed the fulfillment of Henry Adams' predictions concerning the acceleration of history—and then some. Its aftermath has witnessed the birth of a new postindustrial society in North America and western Europe plus the simultaneous emergence of the Third World of developing Afro-Asian-Latin-American nations. With the decades of the 1950's and 1960's, the history of the twentieth century enters its transcendent phase. The closing chapter of this book cannot do more than establish contact between the Second World War's aftermath and the new age to which it is giving birth, an exercise that lies beyond this Prologue's modest scope.

I

"This Is Where I Came In"

·1·

AT THE MUNICH CONFERENCE, on Sept. 30, 1938, western Europe's four leading statesmen brought a quarter century of war, revolution, and depression full circle. "This is where I came in," muttered many of their contemporaries as they wondered if the world could avoid its prewar mistakes while their offspring wondered if the world could shake off its postwar illusions. The four men of Munich ministered to both moods, each in his own way.

Benito Mussolini, Duce of Fascist Italy, Adolf Hitler, Fuehrer of Nazi Germany, and Edouard Daladier, premier of the Third French Republic, had all fought in the trenches of a war which had claimed the lives of the best and bravest of their generation. In Britain, not even one veteran of the First World War had yet risen to the post of prime minister, which Neville Chamberlain had finally attained, only the previous year, at the age of sixty-seven.

The son of an Italian anarchist blacksmith and a devout schoolteacher mother, Mussolini had boxed the political compass before reaching the age of forty. A prewar socialist and wartime nationalist, he blended elements of both movements in his postwar Fascist party, originally composed of embittered war veterans like himself. Seizing power in 1922 with a march on Rome, Mussolini set an example that later inspired Adolf Hitler. But Hitler's National Socialist movement promoted a racist nihilism that had no more in common with Italian Fascism than Mussolini had with traditional nationalism or socialism.

When the four men of Munich first assembled, Hitler dominated the proceedings. Earlier that year he had annexed Austria; two years before that his troops had occupied the Rhineland. Which hamstrung Daladier from the start. A baker's son from Provence and a brilliant historical scholar, Daladier had served on the Western Front, where he saw his commanders' blind adherence to an offensive strategy wipe out most of his contemporaries and comrades. After the war he entered politics, where his wartime record and solid personal qualities helped him to win the leadership of the Radical Socialist party. Neither radical nor socialist, the members of that party—as the French journalist Pertinax described them in *The Gravediggers of France*—belonged to "that class in French society which has the greatest stability in its interests, its prejudices, and its feelings. It is made up of peasants who are small landowners, of the lower middle-class of the cities, second-rate lawyers and doctors, and most of the retail shopkeepers."

But if Hitler dominated the Munich scene when the curtain went up, it was Chamberlain who became its instant hero, subsequent victim, and ultimate symbol. Moreover, if Daladier, as the leader of the French Radical Socialists, embodied the Third French Republic, Chamberlain, as leader of Britain's Conservatives, spoke for the bulk of his fellow countrymen at that time. After six generations of business, industrial, and political leadership in the life of the city of Birmingham, the Chamberlain family had become a real-life replica of John Galsworthy's fictional Forsytes. Joseph Chamberlain, father of Neville, had led the opposition to Gladstone on the floor of the House of Commons. He called himself a Tory Radical who championed imperial expansion, imperial tariffs, and social reform. He served as colonial secretary during the Boer War.

Neville's older half brother, Sir Austen Chamberlain, had served as foreign secretary under Stanley Baldwin. In 1936 he remarked: "If Austria goes, Czechoslovakia is indefensible." His widow spent much of her time in Rome, where she kept in touch with her late husband's old friend Mussolini. Neville Chamberlain did not enter politics until 1914, when, at the age of forty-six, he was elected alderman in Birmingham and in 1916 its lord mayor, an office that five of his uncles and eleven of his other relatives had held before him. Lloyd George once wrote Neville Chamberlain off as, "A good lord mayor of Birmingham in a lean year." Of himself Chamberlain declared, during the 1920's: "The late Victorian age for me, before the days of motors and telephones." "I was very fond of him," said his personal physician, "I like all unlovable men." His chauffeur commented: "You don't know Mr. Chamberlain until you've been with him for five years."

Without a Chamberlain there would have been no Munich conference. Twice, during the month of September, he took the initiative in flying to consult with Hitler—first at Berchtesgaden in the Bavarian Alps and then at Bad Godesberg on the Rhine—concerning Germany's claim to Czechoslovakia's Sudetenland, based on Woodrow Wilson's principle of national self-determination. By the time of the Munich Conference Chamberlain had already concluded—in his own words—that "with the German troops in the position that they occupied, there was nothing that anybody could do that would prevent invasion unless the right of self-determination were given to the Sudeten Germans, and that quickly." In January 1938, he had written to his stepmother's American cousin that the French "can never keep a secret more than half an hour or a government for more than nine months! Therefore our people see that in the absence of any powerful ally and until our armaments are completed, we must adjust our foreign policy to our circumstances, and even bear with patience and good humor actions which we should like to treat in a very different fashion."

Sir Eric Phipps, British ambassador in Paris, expressed similar views nine months later: "To embark upon what will presumably be the biggest conflict in history with our ally who will fight, if she must, without eyes [air force] and without real heart, must give us furiously to think. I may be asked why I have not reported sooner in the above sense. The answer is that up to the last hour, the French had hypnotized themselves into believing the peace depended upon Great Britain and not upon Hitler. They were convinced, that is to say, that if Great Britain spoke with sufficient firmness, Hitler would collapse."

After the House of Commons had debated the Munich Agreement, with considerable emphasis on the dread features of modern warfare, Chamberlain summed up his own fundamental conviction throughout the crisis: "You cannot ask a people to accept a prospect of that kind, you cannot force them into a position that they have got to accept it, unless you feel yourself and make them feel that the cause for which they are going to fight is a vital cause—a cause that transcends all the human values, a cause to which you can point if, some day, you win the victory, and say, 'That cause is safe.'"

During the twenty years of the Republic of Czechoslovakia's existence, thirteen million Slavs, Teutons, and Magyars of half a dozen different nationalities and of still more different religious sects had built in their mutiracial corner of Europe a miniature world made safe for democracy, such as Woodrow Wilson had depicted on a global scale. Hitler then shattered Czechoslovakia's delicate balance of internal forces by invoking its German minority's right to national self-determination. But Hitler's version of German self-determination called for something quite different from Germany taking her place among the nations of the earth. It called for putting all other nations of the earth in lower places—and this in the name of racial doctrines that had no more bearing on national self-determination than national self-determination had to do with a world made safe for democracy. If it had taken Wilson to defeat Wilsonism, could anything short of Hitler defeat Hitlerism?

In a matter of months, the same question arose about Lenin and Leninism, Stalin and Stalinism. But the four men of Munich had eyes only for its immediate consequences in their immediate neighborhood. To help Hitler destroy Wilson's work in Wilson's name caused Neville Chamberlain no pain. The previous January, Franklin D. Roosevelt, Wilson's successor and former disciple, had tried to avert the crisis that subsequently culminated at Munich by proposing a world conference on raw materials and disarmament. Chamberlain turned him down out of hand, ignoring his foreign secretary, Lord Halifax, and driving Anthony Eden—whom Halifax had recently succeeded—to despair.

In the Munich Agreement Chamberlain saw the vindication of his rebuff to Roosevelt. Indeed, the international conference that Roosevelt had proposed early in 1938 appeared to Chamberlain at the time as futile as the Munich Conference subsequently appeared to his critics. "It is always best and safest to count on nothing from the Americans but words," said Chamberlain, who had felt the same way about Roosevelt's call for a "quarantine" of aggressors in 1937.

It cannot be pointed out too strongly that it was Chamberlain, not Hitler, who set the stage for Munich—and when Hitler and Mussolini sponsored the proposal, Chamberlain embraced it. For, as he saw it, the liquidation of Czechoslovakia had not necessarily freed Hitler to plunge the world—or even Europe—into war. Rather had Munich freed Chamberlain to avoid the two chief errors that his country's leaders had made in 1914. With one hand he therefore offered Hitler such concessions as no prewar British statesman had ever offered to Kaiser Wilhelm while raising the other hand in such warning as no prewar British statesman had ever served on Berlin—a warning not to count on British neutrality in the event of another European war. To Hitler, however, the concessions and warning appeared equally irrelevant. As he saw it, the road now lay open for him to lead Germany to a destiny that would last a thousand years.

· 2 ·

LIKE HITLER and Chamberlain, Mussolini and Daladier also hoped to avoid the mistakes they had seen their countries' leaders make in 1914 —in Daladier's case, blind adherence to an offensive strategy that bled France almost to death; in Mussolini's case, Italian participation in another Anglo-French crusade against Germany. However, all four signers of the Munich Agreement shared one conviction. All had come by different paths to the conviction that personal diplomacy must supplant professional diplomacy. As dictators, Hitler and Mussolini took it for granted that the direction of foreign policy must lie in their hands and theirs alone. Chamberlain believed, with the valor of ignorance, that his common-sense approach to foreign affairs could give the fumbling, professional diplomats lessons in their outmoded game. Daladier, with the caution born of experience, knew just enough more than Chamberlain to recognize his own shortcomings that he saw duplicated in most of the other leaders of the Third French Republic.

Excluded from Munich, Roosevelt and Stalin shared with each other and with the four participants in the conference a similar taste for personal diplomacy. Roosevelt not only swallowed whatever resentment he may have felt at Chamberlain's rebuff in January; he murmured approval of the Munich settlement as he had acquiesced in the Baldwin-Eden policy of nonintervention in Spain's civil war. After Munich, even more than at the time of the Spanish civil war—and in the United States, even more than in Britain—public opinion favored peace at almost any price—which was what Chamberlain appeared to have brought back from Munich.

To Stalin, on the other hand, Munich did not mean peace but war— war against the Soviet Union—a war waged by Germany, with Anglo-French support and America's benevolent neutrality. Certainly Munich had made collective security an illusion and Litvinov's slogan of "peace is indivisible" as irrelevant as Roosevelt's "quarantine the aggressors." Before, during, and after the Munich Conference, Communist propagandists rang changes on the theme of a capitalist-imperialist plot to turn Hitler east, an approach with special appeal to those non-Communists who, before Munich, joined Communists in setting up popular fronts against war and fascism. Now that Chamberlain and Daladier had spurned Stalin and come to terms with Hitler and Mussolini at the expense of Czechoslovakia, a world struggle between communism and fascism seemed close at hand, and millions of non-Communists, the world over, had no doubt about where they—and Stalin—would stand when the showdown came.

But it was not upon Stalin that most of Britain and much of the world pinned their hopes immediately after Munich. It was upon Neville Chamberlain, who had broken sharply with Britain's recent and not-so-recent past. Determined to avoid the prewar mistakes of Sir Edward Grey and the postwar illusions of Anthony Eden, Chamberlain had dealt directly with Adolf Hitler, not in fear and trembling but with hope and confidence. Daladier had his misgivings about Chamberlain, Mussolini had his misgivings about Hitler, and Hitler had his misgivings about their agreement. But Chamberlain had sublime confidence in himself and regarded the Munich agreement as his handiwork and therefore infallible. And it was the influence of Chamberlain's personality on Hitler, not the influence of Hitler's personality on Chamberlain, that made the Munich Agreement what it was. Surely, the proof of the pudding lay in Chamberlain's final proposal to Hitler that they sign a separate Anglo-German Agreement to regard the Munich agreement and the Anglo-German naval agreement "as symbolic of the desire of our two peoples never to go to war with one another again."

Everything that Chamberlain had done and stood for prior to Munich, everything that he had done and said throughout the crisis singled him out as the guarantor of the agreement's integrity. What a welcome contrast between his civilian, starched wing collars and the military uniforms in which Hitler and Mussolini disported themselves. How reassuring his unruffled, British reserve as compared with the chain-smoking Daladier's nervous, Latin temperament. In Chamberlain's role as pilgrim of peace, how appropriate a staff he had chosen—the inevitable, innocuous umbrella. The passage of time and its attendant upheavals have almost obliterated from the pages of history how great a hero Chamberlain appeared not only to his own people but all around the world at the time of Munich and for several months thereafter.

A year later, the pendulum swung so far the other way that the figure of Chamberlain became a kind of foil or contrast to the figure of Churchill. But in politics, as in physics, every action has an equal and contrary reaction. If Chamberlain had not been what he was, could Churchill have risen to the heights he later reached? The answer to that question came during Britain's darkest hours when they worked together with a mutual regard sharpened by past differences. But never had these differences been so sharp as at the time of Munich.

The agreement reached there, which Chamberlain characterized as "peace for our time," Churchill denounced as victory for aggression. "We are in the presence of a disaster of the first magnitude which has befallen Great Britain and France," Churchill told the House of Commons on October 5, 1938. "Do not let us blind ourselves to that. It must now be accepted that all the countries of Central and Eastern Europe will make the best terms they can with the triumphant Nazi power. The system of alliances in Central Europe upon which France relied for her safety has been swept away, and I can see no means by which it can be reconstituted. The road down the Danube Valley to the Black Sea, the road which leads as far as Turkey, has been opened. In fact if not in form, it seems to me that all those countries of Middle Europe, all those Danubian countries, will, one after another, be drawn into this vast system of power politics, not only power military politics but power economic politics—radiating from Berlin, and I believe this can be achieved quite smoothly and swiftly and will not necessarily entail the firing of a single shot."

The small contingent of Liberals in the House of Commons agreed with Churchill. So did most of the Labourites. But the bulk of the Conservatives preferred Chamberlain's hopes to Churchill's fears. No self-respecting Tory had any use for Nazi doctrines, least of all the doctrine that Britain should play second fiddle to Germany. Besides, who could take seriously such a cad and a bounder as Hitler? Clearly the man was mad. And—speaking of madmen—Churchill not only symbolized the Dardanelles disaster of 1915; since then most of his pet schemes had missed fire, most of his predictions had failed to come true. Furthermore, in the eyes of many non-Tories, Churchill had gone on living in a romantic, imperial past while the bulk of the British people gradually came to assume that their empire could never regain the predominance it had enjoyed before 1914 and to fear that another world war would weaken that empire still more. On the other hand, the British people stood in no awe of Hitler. They were prepared to make sacrifices to preserve the freedoms they enjoyed. Whatever the future might hold, they never doubted that they and their island home would survive. On this point Chamberlain and Churchill, the appeasers and the resisters, saw eye to eye.

·3·

ONLY THE CHIEF VICTIM of the Munich conference took immediate note of one facet that the four chief participants chose to overlook. Eduard Benes, cofounder with Thomas G. Masaryk of the Czechoslovak republic and Masaryk's successor as president, had received from Chamberlain a draft of the plans subsequently drawn up at Munich to dismantle the republic that he and Masaryk had established under Woodrow Wilson's sponsorship. Benes neither accepted nor rejected the terms out of hand. Instead, he had the Soviet ambassador at Prague inquire from Moscow what the Soviet government would do in the event of a German attack on Czechoslovakia. The reply stated that the Soviet Union, in accordance with its treaty with Czechoslovakia, would "render immediate and effective aid to Czechoslovakia, if France remains loyal to it and also sends aid." When Benes asked what would happen if France stood aside, Moscow replied that it would submit the matter to the council of the League of Nations and act in accordance with its interpretation of the covenant.

He who lives by the Versailles Treaty and the League of Nations dies by the Versailles Treaty and the League of Nations. There could be no reversal in 1938 of the decisions Masaryk and Benes had reached in 1918 and 1919, when they committed their country to Wilson's program for a world made safe for democracy. Nor had Stalin dictated the reply to Benes in any "I told you so" spirit. In 1934, when Nazi Germany quit the League, Communist Russia joined the "thieves' kitchen at Geneva"—as Lenin used to call it—and Litvinov made frequent use of its rostrum, notably on Sept. 21, 1938, when he announced: "We intend to fulfill our obligations under the pact and together with France to afford assistance to Czechoslovakia by ways open to us." These ways included staff talks with the French. But when the French approved the terms that Hitler had persuaded Chamberlain to endorse, Benes and his cabinet had no choice but to bow to them also.

In sounding out the Soviet ambassador to Prague on the subject of Soviet aid against German aggression, Benes had no thought of selling the pass to Stalin, as no one understood better than Stalin himself. Rather had Benes, in exploring Stalin's intentions, set Chamberlain and Daladier the example that they should have set him. All of them had seen Wilson and Lenin emerge from the First World War as rival messiahs, each offering his own brand of universal salvation: in Wilson's case a world made safe for democracy by the League of Nations, in Lenin's case a world redeemed by revolution, directed by the Third International. Nowhere had the Wilson program so strong an appeal or so effective a leadership as in Czechoslovakia; nowhere had the Lenin program less.

In Thomas G. Masaryk, Woodrow Wilson found a disciple who, in many respects, surpassed his master. Born an Austrian subject of half-Czech, half-Slovak descent, the holder of a Ph.D. in philosophy, a former member of the Austrian Parliament, Masaryk became the very embodiment of the twentieth-century philosopher-statesman, European style. Married to an American wife, he established many ties with many leading Americans, including President Wilson. Masaryk always saw, and helped his young protégé and foreign minister, Eduard Benes, to see that Czechoslovakia could survive and prosper only to the extent that it eschewed narrow nationalism. He and Benes therefore worked for tolerance, compromise, and concession among all the national, racial, and religious groups in their new, polyglot republic. Insofar as they did not make a fetish of national self-determination, but gave priority to the development of a wider community, they succeeded on a small scale where Wilson failed on a large one.

But it was one thing for Benes to plan (as he did) to remain president of a rump Czechoslovakia that had just accepted the subjugation of its non-German inhabitants to the dictates of four of Europe's major powers. A different issue arose when Poland followed up the announcement of the Munich terms with a twelve-hour ultimatum to Prague, demanding, as its share of the spoils, the Czechoslovak district of Tesin, with a population of a quarter of a million, less than one third of them Poles. Benes at once foresaw that Hitler's instant acquiescence to the Polish demand for Tesin had opened a Pandora's box of ever more menacing surprises. Not only had Hitler's award of Tesin to Poland turned Slav against Slav; the Poland that Hitler had favored was the feudal, expansionist, anti-Russian, pro-German Poland of the late General Pilsudski, whose protégé, Colonel Joseph Beck, had served as its foreign minister for the past seven years.

What Masaryk had been to Czechoslovakia, Pilsudski had been to Poland. Pilsudski, an aristocratic soldier turned revolutionary nationalist, had led a wartime and postwar struggle in which he restored national sovereignty to some twenty million Poles over territories their ancestors had inhabited since medieval times. But Pilsudski, like his aristocratic forebears, had wider ambitions. In 1920, under the command of General Weygand, he routed the Red army in a defense of Warsaw that did not end until Polish troops had occupied sixty thousand square miles of the western Ukraine, then inhabited by six million Ukrainians and White Russians. These territories lay east of the so-called Curzon Line and added more than fifty per cent to the area of the newly established Polish Republic.

Pilsudski died in 1935, but not until after he had become the first chief of state to sign a nonaggression pact with Hitler. Beck shared Pilsudski's conviction that Hitler's obsession with the Communist menace guaranteed Poland against German attack. But Benes knew his Germans, Russians, and Poles well enough not to take for granted any alliance that any two of them might enter into against the third. On the morning of September 30, as the terms of the Munich agreement became known, Benes therefore resigned his presidency and chose self-exile in Churchill's London—not asylum in Stalin's Moscow.

·4·

MUSSOLINI KNEW as well as Churchill did that Hitler had won a strategic victory at Munich. He knew as well as Daladier did that Britain and France had suffered a moral defeat. He shared none of Chamberlain's confidence in Hitler's pledged word. When the Germans at once violated the Munich agreement by permitting their own Wehrmacht to determine its own occupation zones, the sole protest came from the Italian member of the four-power inspection team. On November 2, Count Ciano, the Italian foreign minister, played a more active role, when he and Joachim von Ribbentrop the Nazi foreign minister, met at Vienna and awarded Hungary a large slice of Slovakia and a small portion of Ruthenia, with a total population of more than a million (most of them Hungarians), the latest beneficiaries of the Hitlerite version of the Wilsonian doctrine of national self-determination.

Mussolini had returned from Munich less depressed than Daladier, less deluded than Chamberlain, less frustrated than Hitler. At first, Daladier mistakenly assumed that the crowd which welcomed him at the Paris airport had come to bury not to praise him. Chamberlain, on the other hand, had overrated the depth of British popular enthusiasm as much as he had underrated the depth of Hitler's perfidy. As a result, he remained blind to the two major blunders he had committed while seeking to avoid his predecessors' lesser mistakes: the first, his failure to foresee that the breakup of Czechoslovakia would hasten the very upheaval he feared, the second the seal of approval he placed on the false charges Hitler made against the Czechs and the false promises he made in behalf of the Germans.

Inasmuch as Hitler's duplicities at Munich did not differ greatly from the duplicities that Bismarck and Theobald von Bethmann-Hollweg had committed before him, Churchill at once attributed to Hitler expansionist plans similar to those that Bismarck had successfully set in motion but that Bethmann had failed to push any farther. Hitler, however, did not regard himself as a successor to the imperial Hohenzollerns or as a disciple of General Karl Haushofer's streamlined pan-German geopolitics. In 1914, Bethmann dismissed as a mere "scrap of paper" the German pledge to respect Belgian neutrality. Since the 1920's, Hitler had denounced the "Versailles *Diktat*," against which he successfully pitted Wilson's principle of "national self-determination." But only after Munich did Hitler reveal his new and revised interpretation of that honored and widely accepted doctrine.

One month and one day after Churchill described and denounced Hitler's program of conquest before the House of Commons, Herschel Grynszpan, a nineteen-year-old Jewish refugee from Poland, shot and killed Ernst vom Rath, third secretary of the German embassy in Paris. Grynszpan was not a German; Rath was not a Nazi. Nevertheless, on November 10, the day after Rath died, the German Government called for retaliation against Germany's Jews. The order came from Hitler; Propaganda Minister Paul Joseph Goebbels, his one true believer to the very end, carried it out. Crowds in many German cities looted Jewish shops and burned Jewish synagogues. Heinrich Himmler's secret police arrested hundreds of Jews, and on the night of November 10–11 (later known as the Crystal Night) the German government announced that a fine of one billion marks would be collected from the Jews of Germany, partly to compensate for Rath's murder, partly to compensate for Jewish property seized or destroyed by Germans.

New restrictions against Jews at once went into effect throughout Germany. Jews could not attend high schools or universities or engage in many businesses and professions. They were barred from all theaters, movies, and museums as well as from many sections of many towns. All Jews had their driving licenses suspended, along with their automobile and motorcycle registrations. From the United States President Roosevelt announced, "I myself could scarcely believe that such things could happen in a twentieth-century civilization," and ordered Ambassador Hugh R. Wilson to return from Berlin to Washington and give him a firsthand report. Herbert Hoover, recalling the aid that America had sent to Germany after the war, remarked that the United States had "more than the usual right amongst nations of the world to make this protest."

Such statements as Roosevelt's echoed the sentiments of most Americans. But as far as most Germans were concerned, the greater the truth, the greater the libel. By committing atrocities that led to protests from abroad, Hitler turned more and more leaders and peoples in other countries against Germany and the Germans. But even those Germans who agreed with the protests could not turn against Hitler without turning against themselves. The more leaders of other lands protested against Hitler's crimes, the better he liked it. He had always charged that Jewish bankers and Jewish Bolsheviks had organized an international conspiracy against Germany. Now, when his anti-Semitic measures brought protests from abroad, he shouted, "I told you so," thereby identifying the German people still more closely with the Nazis.

Hitler also combined his attacks on the Jews with his attacks on the Versailles Treaty, the League of Nations, and democracy. Chamberlain and Daladier went along with Hitler in tearing up the Versailles Treaty and scuttling the League of Nations. Mussolini had based his whole movement on popular disgust with the war and with the postwar settlements. But all three men feared a new war and tried to prevent or at least postpone it by offering Hitler more and more attractive alternatives. But Hitler not only wanted war for its own sake: he wanted the kind of war he planned to fight more than he wanted the alternatives that the appeasers pressed upon him.

What possessed him? At Munich he turned the tables on Germany's recent enemies and invoked Woodrow Wilson's cherished principle of national self-determination to win for Germany, without war, a stronger position in Europe than Kaiser Wilhelm II ever held. At home, he eliminated all opposition and increased employment from twelve and a half million to twenty-two million. Since three Germans in every four had lived through war, defeat, inflation, and depression they viewed Hitler with awe if not with liking. Burton H. Klein, an economist for the RAND Corporation, in his book, *Germany's Preparations for War*, published in 1959 and based on information gleaned from official German sources, has reported: "In the period of 1933 through 1938 rearmament expenditures absorbed less than 10 per cent of Germany's gross national product, and even as late as 1938, only 15 per cent. The volume of munitions production and the number of divisions which

Germany mobilized was, by comparison with published appraisal, small." As Mr. Klein put it: "The fundamental reason why large war preparations were not undertaken is simply that Hitler's concept of warfare did not require them. Documentary evidence and interrogation of confidants indicate that for the fulfilment of territorial desires Hitler did not expect to fight a protracted war against a coalition of major powers. Rather, he planned to solve Germany's living space problem in piecemeal fashion—by a series of small wars. His strategy, as it developed, was to undermine an enemy's internal and external unity, to intimidate with threat of military destruction, and, if this were not successful, to force a speedy decision by blitz warfare."

Neither at Munich nor during the months that followed did Hitler have the capacity to wage large-scale war. The German war machine of 1938 did not compare with the German war machine of 1914. All the more reason, then, not only to avoid the Kaiser's mistakes of a quarter century ago but to develop a new strategy. It was during the Crystal Night that this new strategy entered a new phase. For more than ten years, Hitler's racist-nationalist propaganda had inflamed millions of Germans—especially among the younger people and the middle classes —whom the war, the defeat, the inflation, and the depression had progressively embittered. Moreover, the very success of this propaganda sent cold shivers down millions of spines in Britain and France where the fruits of the 1918 victory had turned almost as bitter as the fruits of the 1918 defeat had turned in Germany. But the very barbarities of the Crystal Night turned some of those cold shivers to colder recognition that Hitler's new strategy cut two ways. If it tended to rally more Germans around the Nazi regime, it also tended to turn more non-Germans against it. Indeed, it tended to polarize the whole world into pro-German and anti-German camps. Finally, the perpetrators of the Crystal Night gave the world fair warning never again to trust such promises as Hitler had made at Munich.

· 5 ·

ROOSEVELT'S NEW DEAL had brought as many changes to the United States as Hitler's New Order had brought to Germany. But the New Dealers ran into trouble in the November 1938 Congressional elections after Roosevelt tried and failed to purge the Democratic party of senators and representatives who had opposed various New Deal measures, especially his plan to enlarge the Supreme Court. All the Democratic senators whom Roosevelt opposed in the primaries won renomination and re-election. His attempted purge defeated just one congressman, Representative John J. O'Connor of New York, the brother, ironically enough, of Roosevelt's former law partner, Basil O'Connor. James A. Farley, who managed Roosevelt's two presidential campaigns, opposed the purge, and many other conservative Democrats vowed not to forgive or forget the President's action. The party retained control of Congress, though by reduced margins in both Houses. For the first time in ten years, the Republicans showed gains in both Houses and in the popular vote. More important, a bloc of Republicans and anti-New Deal Democrats had begun to take shape and to threaten the Administration's program on the floor of Congress.

While the Munich conference distracted some popular attention from the New Deal's first major setback, the war danger both before and after Munich absorbed more and more of Roosevelt's time. Ambassador William C. Bullitt in Paris established cordial relations with Premier Daladier; Ambassador Joseph P. Kennedy in London developed a personal liking and admiration for Prime Minister Chamberlain, whose appeasement policy he endorsed. Both men kept the President fully and promptly posted on all developments. On the day Chamberlain flew to Munich, Roosevelt asked Kennedy to transmit the two-word message: "Good man."

A month after Munich, Roosevelt told the annual forum of the New York *Herald Tribune:* "It is becoming increasingly clear that peace by fear has no higher nor more enduring quality than peace by the sword. There can be no peace if the reign of law is to be replaced by a recurrent sanctification of sheer force. There can be no peace if national policy adopts as a deliberate instrument the threat of war. There can be no peace if national policy adopts as a deliberate instrument the dispersion all over the world of millions of helpless and persecuted wanderers with no place to lay their heads."

Not all the dangers against which Roosevelt was warning and arming the United States originated at Munich. The Japanese had done more than threaten war. For more than seven years, they had used war itself as an instrument of national policy against China. During the year before the Munich Conference, the Japanese claimed they had occupied 775,000 square miles of Chinese territory and inflicted 1,300,000 casualties upon the Chinese while suffering only 36,000 of their own. Some thirty million Chinese scorched their earth and quit their homes rather than live under Japanese rule. In August 1938, a month before Munich,

Japanese and Russian troops fought a full-scale battle, lasting several days, at Changkufeng on the Manchurian border. The Russians gave such a good account of themselves that the Japanese withdrew from the positions they had tried to seize and called it quits. The Munich conference then relieved the Japanese of any fear of Russian attack. Stalin had too many worries in Europe to take risks in Asia.

Within less than a month after Munich, the Japanese therefore felt free to use one of their armies to capture the south China port of Canton and another to capture Hankow, the temporary Nationalist capital, several hundred miles up the Yangtze River. Chiang Kai-shek then moved his capital another eight hundred miles up the river to Chungking and put ten thousand coolies to work improving the Burma Road to Lashio. On December 22, 1938, Prince Konoye of Japan offered to call off the war and resume diplomatic relations, but demanded in exchange that Nationalist China recognize the independence of Manchukuo and grant special rights to Japanese capital and Japanese troops in the rest of China. Chiang Kai-shek turned the offer down, and Secretary of State Cordell Hull charged that Japan had violated its treaty obligations.

The Munich conference also speeded the fall of the Spanish Republic. Earlier in 1938, Franco's troops had cut the Madrid-Valencia road, thereby splitting Republican Spain and isolating its capital. But the Republican government moved to Barcelona and continued the war from there. In December, Franco announced the opening of a final end-the-war offensive against Barcelona. Russia had long since stopped aiding the Republican side, and Hitler's triumph at Munich had exhilarated the Axis and demoralized the democracies.

Yet the agony of Spain continued. More than two years of fighting had cost close to a million lives, and during the five months between September 1938 and February 1939 another 62,000 persons were estimated to have died in Barcelona, where the Republic made its last stand. Thus, as the year 1939 began, the inhabitants of many other European cities feared that the fate of Barcelona might overtake them, too. Hitler had played upon this fear successfully at Munich. He planned to do more than play upon it again.

During 1938 no chief of state in any European country had stood up to Hitler and dared him to do his worst. Roosevelt's efforts to create a coalition wide enough and firm enough to stop aggression everywhere without war had fallen flat. He therefore seized upon the eighth meeting of the Pan American Union at Lima, Peru, in December 1938 to bind all the American republics together in a regional security pact. But Secretary of State Hull and a strong delegation could not bring back anything better than a declaration of American principles which committed the foreign ministers of the twenty-one American republics to consult with one another in the event of any threat to the peace and security of any one of them, and to take whatever measures each government might consider appropriate. Argentina's Foreign Minister José María Cantillo's warning against "turning our backs on European nations linked to Argentina by traditional bonds" expressed a widely held view.

It was not the view that President Roosevelt expressed on January 4, 1939, in his annual message to the Congress. "A war which threatened to envelop the world in flames has been averted," he began, "but it has become increasingly clear that world peace is not assured." Religion, democracy, and international good faith had all come under attack. "There comes a time in the affairs of men," he continued, "when they must prepare to defend, not their homes alone, but the tenets of faith and humanity on which their churches, their governments, and their very civilizations are founded. The defense of religion, of democracy, of good faith among nations is all the same fight. To save one we must now make up our minds to save all."

Whereas Churchill had addressed himself to "economic power politics" and "military power politics," Roosevelt—like Wilson before him—preferred to deal in abstractions: religion, democracy, good faith. But, as he warmed to his theme, he suggested specific ways and means of promoting these abstractions: "Words may be futile but war is not the only means of commanding respect for the decent opinions of mankind. There are many methods short of war but stronger than mere words, of bringing home to aggressor governments the aggregate sentiments of our people." What aggregate sentiments? Here Roosevelt departed from the Wilson line. Even after the outbreak of war in 1914, Wilson urged the American people to remain "impartial in thought as well as in action." In January 1939, Roosevelt told the American people: "At the very best we can and should avoid any action, or lack of action, which will encourage, assist, or build up an aggressor. We have learned that when we deliberately try to legislate neutrality, our neutrality laws may operate unevenly and unfairly—may actually give aid to an aggressor and deny it to his victim. The instinct of self-preservation should warn us that we ought not to let that happen any more."

But the American people had learned no such lessons from Wilson's efforts to preserve their neutrality during the First World War. Nor did their instinct for self-preservation warn them "not to let that happen any more." Rather were those the prewar mistakes that Roosevelt had learned, from his association with Wilson during the First World War, not to repeat, and the postwar illusions that his own "instinct for self-preservation" warned him to avoid. Roosevelt knew—none better—that he did not yet speak for a united people. But he had confidence that events would soon vindicate him and give him the courage to commit himself accordingly. He therefore rejected the illusion of neutrality to which Wilson had succumbed during the early stages of the First World War and to which Congress had recently succumbed again when it approved legislation outlawing war loans and munitions shipments to belligerents in future conflicts. This legislation had the support of such veteran Republican senators as William E. Borah, and George W. Norris who never had any occasion to regret their opposition to Woodrow Wilson and the League of Nations in 1920, and of Progressive Senator Robert M. LaFollette, Jr., who had made a successful career following in his father's isolationist and Progressive footsteps.

Much of the opposition to Roosevelt's interventionist tendencies, since his "quarantine the aggressors" speech of 1937, had come from the more advanced New Dealers, Republicans and independents as well as Democrats. Yet even in rejecting their isolationist views, he found himself succumbing to an illusion of his own: that the threat of wartime sanctions would frighten aggressors into keeping the peace. For, by 1939, most heads of most European governments had become convinced that economic sanctions, even backed by the League of Nations, would mean war, not peace. Under these circumstances, Roosevelt had little chance of persuading the "peace-loving" peoples of western Europe (not to mention the gun-shy American people) that he had learned to avoid either prewar mistakes or postwar illusions. Subsequent events discredited Roosevelt's critics before they discredited him. In the country of the blind, the one-eyed man is king; Churchill and Roosevelt avoided the mistake that most of their contemporaries made in underestimating Hitler. But the events that Hitler set in motion soon moved with a momentum that swept all before it.

Especially in Asia, where the new threats that Germany posed to Britain, France, and the United States encouraged the Japanese to speed up their invasion of China. They neither consulted nor informed Hitler, nor did Roosevelt bat an eye. For one thing, he considered Germany a greater threat than Japan to the interests of the United States; for another, he knew that many of his fellow citizens took the opposite view. But the same Americans who demanded the kind of neutrality laws that might have kept them out of the kind of war their country fought in Europe in 1917 and 1918 had less fear of involvement in Asia. Indeed, public-opinion polls showed majority support for more aid, short of war, to China and stricter economic sanctions against Japan. Roosevelt therefore used the Munich crisis to bring home to his compatriots the importance of Europe to the whole western hemisphere. If he chose to minimize the war danger in Asia, that did not mean he ignored it.

At the same time, the convictions he held and the efforts he expended to promote them made it easy for him to ignore certain Asian realities, one of them being China's Nationalist-Communist civil war, another being Japan's bid to head a pan-Asian, antiwhite crusade with a potential appeal to two thirds of mankind. Thus, the greater a menace Hitler had become to Europe, as a result of Munich, the greater became Japan's opportunity to seize the leadership of Asia. In addition to laying the groundwork for Hitler's first European victories and for Stalin's subsequent sweep of eastern Europe, the Munich conference also helped set in motion events that eventually convulsed Asia as well.

·6·

IT DID NOT take long for the authors of the Munich Agreement to discover that avoidance of prewar mistakes and postwar illusions was not enough. Only Chamberlain continued, after the beginning of 1939, to believe that Munich had saved the peace. Shortly after Christmas he and Halifax traveled together to Rome for conferences with Mussolini and Ciano. "These men are not made of the same stuff as Francis Drake and the other magnificent adventurers who created the empire," Mussolini commented afterward. "These, after all, are the tired sons of a long line of rich men, and they will lose their empire." Ciano wrote Ribbentrop that the whole meeting amounted to nothing but "a big lemonade."

The Spanish civil war was ending. General Francisco Franco opened his final drive against Barcelona two days before Christmas 1938 and took the city a month later. The remnants of the Republican army and the chief members of the Republican government fled to France. Mussolini warned, "If Paris sends forces, we shall unload thirty battalions at Valencia even if this should provoke a second world war." Mussolini had his eye on the western Mediterranean and North Africa.

He wanted a victorious Franco to take over control of Morocco from a decadent France. He expected Algeria and Tunisia to fall to Italy, along with Corsica, Savoy, and Nice. Distrusting Hitler, despising France, and pitying Chamberlain, Mussolini made up his mind to grab while the grabbing was good. After Chamberlain returned to England, the British ambassador showed Mussolini the outline of a speech Chamberlain planned to deliver before the House of Commons. "I believe this is the first time," Mussolini told Ciano, "that the head of the British government submits to a foreign government the outline of one of his speeches."

While Chamberlain and Halifax dithered at Rome with Mussolini and Ciano, Hitler and Ribbentrop talked turkey in Berlin to Poland's Foreign Minister Beck. Having tossed him a scrap of Czechoslovakia, they had now prepared the bill that they demanded Poland pay for services rendered. Under the Versailles Treaty (which Hitler had already torn up), the League of Nations (which he had just flouted) had administered the ancient German port of Danzig, on the Baltic, as a Free City which Poland had used as a free port. The Versailles Treaty had also awarded Poland a corridor, largely inhabited by Poles, connecting Danzig with the rest of Poland and separating East Prussia from the rest of Germany. To Beck, Hitler and Ribbentrop proposed that he approve the incorporation of Danzig in the Third Reich and cede to Germany a railway and highway corridor across the Polish Corridor, giving Germany access to East Prussia as the Polish Corridor gave Poland access to the Baltic. Hitler was not making any such demand on the semifeudal republic of Poland and on the late Marshal Pilsudki's protégé as he had made on the democratic republic of Czechoslovakia and the protégé of the late Professor Masaryk. Yet, to the astonishment of Hitler and the fury of Ribbentrop, Beck turned them down. Hitler knew that if Beck remained obdurate, Danzig meant war. So did Beck—unless Hitler backed down. Although Hitler had not yet completed his repudiation of the Munich agreement, he had already warned his next intended victim what to expect.

Within another two months, the stone that the builders rejected at Munich had become the keystone of European peace. For if Danzig did indeed mean war between Germany and Poland, Stalin could sell Soviet neutrality to Hitler at a high price. But Stalin had not yet become convinced that Danzig did, necessarily, mean war either to Hitler or to Beck. For one thing, he did not know the details of the Hitler-Beck confrontation. For another, he underestimated Germany's military strength and overrated Poland's. Finally, he not only overrated the military strength of France; the misinformation that his terrified and incompetent aides served up to him and the distorted Marxist-Leninist analysis to which he subjected it encouraged him to accept fantasies as absurd as Chamberlain's vision of "peace for our time."

On March 10, 1938, in Moscow, at the eighteenth congress of the Soviet Communist party, Stalin discussed world affairs in a wide-ranging mishmash of Marxist theory and Leninist practice, best described by the word "Stalinist." According to Stalin, the world recession that began in late 1937 had led to a new imperialist struggle to divide the world through military action. It was not through fear of a "workers' movement"—as some Communists had suggested—that the leading capitalist countries had knuckled under to the aggressors. Nor did Stalin call upon his Communist comrades to foment revolutions inside the aggressor states. Rather (as he saw it) the leading capitalist countries had begun to instigate a war, from which they would hold aloof, a war of aggression, with the Soviet Union as the ultimate victim. "The policy of nonintervention," declared Stalin, "reveals an eagerness, a desire not to hinder the aggressors in their nefarious work; not to hinder Japan, say, from embroiling herself in a war with China, or better still with the Soviet Union; not to hinder Germany, say, from enmeshing herself in European affairs, from embroiling herself in war with the Soviet Union; to allow all the belligerents to sink deeply into the mire of war, to encourage them surreptitiously in this, to allow them to weaken and exhaust each other; and then when they have become weak enough, to appear on the scene with fresh strength, to appear, of course, in the interest of peace, and to dictate conditions to the enfeebled belligerents."

Stalin accused the democracies of using the same tactics that others attributed to him. He ridiculed "certain European and American politicians and pressmen" for wishfully predicting a German "march on the Soviet Ukraine." It seemed to him that "the object of this suspicious hullabaloo was to incite the Soviet Union against Germany, to poison the atmosphere, and to provoke a conflict with Germany without any visible grounds." Stalin closed his speech with a four-point program:

"1. To continue the policy of peace and of strengthening business relations with all countries.

"2. To be cautious and not allow our country to be drawn into conflicts by warmongers who are accustomed to have others pull the chestnuts out of the fire for them.

"3. To strengthen the might of our Red army and Red navy to the uttermost.

"4. To strengthen the international bonds of friendship with the working people of all countries who are interested in peace and friendship among nations."

Having recently charged the defendants in the purge trials with plotting to detach the Ukraine from the Soviet Union, Stalin now declared that only a "lunatic" would make such an attempt, and assailed the foreign press for publicizing such fantasies. Of the signatories to the Munich agreement he said: "One might even think that they gave the German regions of Czechoslovakia for a pledge to begin war against the Soviet Union, and the Germans now refuse to honor their pledge."

Adam B. Ulam, in his exhaustive and authoritative *Expansion and Coexistence: The History of Soviet Policy,* has written: "On March 10 nothing indicated that a bargain with Hitler was a real possibility. Stalin had nothing to sell. For all his dark hints, it was obvious he did not believe in any stories of Hitler's forthcoming attack in the West. In fact, the Soviet leaders had a flattering opinion of Western strength. 'Peaceful democratic states,' said Stalin, lapsing into very strange language for a Communist, 'are without doubt stronger than the fascist ones both militarily and economically.' "

It was not Marxist theory or Leninist practice that had led Stalin astray. It was his own purge of the Old Bolsheviks who had tested their Marxist theories and Leninist practices in the hard school of revolution, civil war, and reconstruction. The principle of national self-determination, as applied in the postwar world, had wrecked Wilson's hopes that the League of Nations could make that world safe for democracy. In like manner, the self-perpetuating dictatorship of the Soviet Communist party destroyed Lenin's hopes for a world redeemed by a revolution led by the Comintern. Wilson did not defeat Lenin; Lenin did not defeat Wilson. Both fell victims to forces they themselves had unleashed.

In Wilson's case, the forces of nationalism gradually prevailed over the forces of internationalism. At Munich, Hitler finished off both the Versailles Treaty and the League of Nations. But in finishing them off, he had also unleashed other forces, notably racist passions directed toward the nihilist goal of destruction for destruction's sake.

In Lenin's case, his anointed heir appeared immediately in the person of Stalin, who gradually fulfilled all of Lenin's worst misgivings by concentrating in his own hands the powers that Lenin had shared with the Central Executive Committee of the Soviet Communist party. But Lenin (as he came to perceive) had invited the very course of events over which Stalin presided, thanks to the lessons he had learned at Lenin's hands. The irony of the fate of Wilson's program lay in the fact that it was Hitler, his antithesis, who turned the contradictions of Wilsonism to his account. The irony of Lenin's fate lay in the fact that Stalin, his official successor, in the name of Leninism built a regime on the fake confessions and real corpses of Lenin's closest collaborators.

The irony of Stalin's fate emerged at once. Overrating Russia's strength and underrating Germany's, his speech of March 10 served notice on Hitler and Chamberlain that neither of them could expect any Soviet aid except on Soviet terms. In spite of his purges—even, perhaps, because of them—Stalin already assumed that Soviet power could swing Europe's destiny this way or that, toward peace or toward war. Twenty-four hours later, the British and French intelligence services learned that Hitler had already crossed his Rubicon and ordered German troops to begin occupying Bohemia and Moravia—the home of the Czech people—on March 15, 1939. Hitler had not only committed himself to destroy Czechoslovakia. In reaching that decision he had set in motion an endless chain of continuing aggression as a permanent, essential feature of the Third Reich's continued existence. Thus Hitler confronted both Chamberlain and Stalin with a new situation. Over the short pull, Stalin occupied a more favorable position than Chamberlain. But what about Hitler? Had he not confronted himself with a new dilemma? He had broken Czechoslovakia with methods short of war. He had outflanked Poland, but could not crush it without war. No doubt it would be the kind of war that he could win in the way he wanted to win it. During the past six months events had moved at accelerating speed. He had not only kept up with them but had also forced their pace. With such momentum, what could stop him?

· · ·

Whatever else the Munich conference may have signified, it did not repeat in any respect any event that had led up to the outbreak of the First World War. Prior to August 1914, no chief of state or head of government in any of the major powers of Europe either threatened or schemed to provoke war as Hitler did, again and again, during the year that followed the Munich conference. Nor did the imminence of the First World War haunt and obsess Europe's statesmen in 1913 and 1914 as the imminence of the Second World War haunted and obsessed the statesmen of 1938 and 1939. Indeed, memories of the First World War served, among other things, to create an utterly different atmosphere a quarter of a century later. No less important: since September 1931, Japanese troops had been attacking, invading, and occupying more and more of China, which had also become the scene of an intermittent civil war between the troops of the Nationalist government and the Communist guerrillas. The Russo-Japanese War of 1904–05 did not merge, ten years later, with the First World War as the Japanese invasion of China, in 1931, merged ten years later with the Second World War.

Parallels between the First World War and the Second World War cast little light on the Munich conference and its aftermath; recollections of the parallel careers of Wilson and Lenin cast much. Indeed, those two careers helped shape the events of the late 1930's, just as the 1930's, in their turn, helped to shape the world of the early 1960's. On the other hand, false analogies between Munich and subsequent conferences at which one party "appeased" the other have distracted attention from Munich's unique significance. The Munich conference became a watershed of contemporary history because it marked the point at which the Third Reich reached and broke through its outermost limits as a predominantly German state. The moment German troops began extending their occupation of the Sudetenland beyond the German-populated regions specified at Munich, they asserted their claim to rule non-Germans—not for their benefit but for Germany's greater glory. In so doing, Hitler flew in the face of experience that extends from the history of the Roman to the history of the British Empire, from Asia to Europe, from the Old World to the New. For history demonstrates that the more different races and nations an empire can assimilate, the longer it endures, the more it prospers. The Roman Empire extended its citizenship throughout its lands; the British in India enlisted the support of native rulers by encouraging local autonomy. The Hapsburg and Ottoman empires could not hold their polyglot populations together, and Hitler, born an Austrian citizen, tried to organize a German Third Reich that would last a thousand years along lines that the most tyrannical Turk or Hapsburg would have spurned.

In the light of hindsight's wisdom, Hitler emerges as a master in the exploitation of the weaknesses of others. In the name of peace, he hustled the credulous Chamberlain along the road to war. He confronted the fatalistic, lethargic Daladier with *fait accompli* after *fait accompli.* He used Wilson's doctrine of national self-determination to destroy the republic of Czechoslovakia only to find himself dependent on Lenin's official successor. By this time, however, Stalin had destroyed and corrupted Leninism almost as completely as Mussolini and Hitler destroyed and corrupted Wilsonism. Almost but not quite, because Stalin knew how to adapt Leninist methods to his own purposes, thus giving him certain advantages over Chamberlain and Daladier, not to mention Hitler and Mussolini, none of whom had any grasp of Leninism or any use for Wilsonism. The ironies that the Munich agreement had brought in its wake arrived at accelerating speed.

II

This Is Where War Came In

·1·

FOR THEIR ISSUE of March 15, 1939, the editors of *Punch* devised a timely full-page cartoon. It bore the title, "The Ides of March," and showed John Bull waking from a bad dream and exclaiming, as a figure labeled "War Scare" flew out the window: "Thank goodness, that's over." Prime Minister Chamberlain, along with millions of his compatriots, eagerly shared that sense of relief, "All the information I get," he had declared on February 19, "points toward peace." As indeed it did since he scorned or ignored any information pointing any other way.

Between October 1938 and March 1939, the British Foreign Office had received a steady stream of reports that Hitler had sent more than one hundred warnings to President Emil Hacha's government at Prague against its terrorist actions "in the populous linguistic islands that the generosity of Germany has left within Czechoslovakia." In point of fact, no such actions had taken place, and no such islands existed. So few Germans remained in what was left of Czechoslovakia that they had no power to act and few grievances to protest. Hitler had therefore adopted a different strategy and began inciting the minority of Roman Catholic Slovak peasants to demonstrate against the city-dwelling Czech majority, finally warning the Slovaks, on March 12, that unless they declared their independence of Prague and sought German recognition of a Slovak state, German troops would invade their country and invite the Hungarians to join them in its partition. Of this information Chamberlain received little and believed none.

On the evening of March 13, 1939, Hitler summoned to Berlin Father Josef Tiso, the prime minister of Slovakia, whom he recognized as the head of a nominally independent Slovak state. The next evening Hitler summoned to Berlin Czechoslovakia's President Hacha, having first taken the precaution of cutting off Prague from contact with the outside world. Hacha had bowed to the Munich agreement because it committed the four men who signed it to respect the continued independence of what remained of his country. Subsequently Hacha also bowed to all of Hitler's interpretations of the agreement's terms. So, when Hitler, charging Hacha with violations of these terms, announced that he had liberated Slovakia from Czech rule and that the two Czech provinces of Bohemia and Moravia must submit themselves to German rule, Hacha collapsed in a faint. For more than half the night, first Hitler and then Hermann Goering bullied, bluffed, and browbeat the half-broken old man until he finally put his name to this statement: "The Czechoslovak President has declared that in order to reach a final pacification, he would place his country confidently in the hands of the Fuehrer of the German Reich." Hitler, on learning of the capitulation, gloated to his secretaries: "Children, this is the greatest day of my life. I shall go down in history as the greatest German."

Hitler had good reason to boast. At Munich he had reversed, without war, the verdict that the victorious allies had imposed on the defeated Germans in 1919. Six months later, he had capped that triumph by reversing, again without war, the Munich settlement that Chamberlain was not alone in hailing as "peace for our time." But could this second triumph also prove a peaceful one? Not if Hitler could help it. Even at the time of Munich he found it hard to believe he had won so much so easily, and with every passing day his conviction grew that only by waging the kind of war he wanted to fight could he gain the kind of victory he wanted to win.

The sequel to the Czech capitulation served only to strengthen this conviction. The Wehrmacht occupation of Bohemia and Moravia proceeded in exemplary fashion. The disciplined but dazed troops could not understand what had become of all the dead and wounded German victims of the civil war that the Nazi radio had reported. Nor could Hitler, who always believed the Goebbels propaganda as deeply as he believed his own. Under the circumstances, the Fuehrer did not arrive in Prague at the head of a conquering army, but in an open automobile. He could not even enjoy a confrontation with his defeated archenemy, Benes, who had flown to London in September 1938. The deflated conqueror left his former foreign minister, Baron Konstantin von Neurath, in the Hradshin Palace, with the title of Protector of Bohemia and Moravia. At the same time Father Tiso proclaimed Slovakia's independence.

Czchoslovakia, as defined in the Munich agreement, no longer existed—at any rate, not in Prime Minister Chamberlain's Europe. "It is natural that I should bitterly regret what has happened," he told the House of Commons on March 15, "but do not let us on that account be deflected from our course. Let us remember that the desire of all the peoples of the world remains concentrated on the hopes of peace and a return to the atmosphere of understanding and good will which has so often been disturbed." The Federation of British Industries shared these hopes. On March 16 a delegation it had dispatched to Düsseldorf signed an agreement with a group of German industrialists "to replace destructive competition with constructive co-operation."

But the Federation of British Industries did not speak for the bulk of the British people nor did Chamberlain speak for the bulk even of his own Conservative party, where anger at Hitler and disgust with the Germans ran strong—especially among those in high places, like Lord Halifax, who felt let down and betrayed, not only by Hitler but even by one of their own. Most Conservatives tried to believe in Munich; few could succeed in believing in Hitler. But neither Halifax nor any other Tory leader felt under any obligation to echo Chamberlain's lame and feeble self-justifications. They could best serve their party and their country, their leader and themselves by persuading him to follow the example that they and the British press and public at once set.

But it was one thing for Halifax to disown a policy that he had little hand in making. It was another matter for Chamberlain to repudiate his own handiwork. Chamberlain's pride in his own opinion always more than counterbalanced his scorn for his detractors. Now that Hitler had just skinned him alive in public, he could not compound his own humiliation with the acknowledgment that he had deceived both himself and the British public. However, by March 17 the stiff upper lip began to tremble, and Chamberlain saw merit in Halifax's appeal to follow the people's lead and beat a dignified retreat to a new position of strength.

Chamberlain's birthday fell on March 18, and he decided to celebrate it the evening before with a broadcast from his native city of Birmingham. "What has become of the assurance, 'We don't want Czechs in the Reich?' " he asked. "What regard has been paid to that principle of self-determination on which Herr Hitler argued so vehemently with me at

Berchtesgaden when he was asking for the severance of the Sudeten-land from Czechoslovakia and its inclusion in the German Reich?" If such questions stirred Chamberlain's indignation, his critics still asked why he had to wait until March 17 to denounce Hitler's action of March 15? "I can never forget," he explained a few days later, "that the ulti-mate decision, the 'Yes,' or 'No,' which may decide the fate not only of this generation but of the British Empire itself lies with me." Here Chamberlain echoed, perhaps unconsciously, his original justification for Munich. To be sure, he conceded to his critics, Hitler had broken many promises. But not this time: "He made them to me."

· 2 ·

THE DISTINCTION meant nothing to Hitler, whose triumph in Czechoslo-vakia had aggravated rather than eased his own situation and impelled him to strike out in two new directions. First, he ordered Ribbentrop to summon Poland's Foreign Minister Beck to Berlin on March 21 and to renew and redouble the pressure they had both applied in January to cede Danzig to the Third Reich. In addition, Ribbentrop proposed a twenty-five-year extension of the Polish-German Nonaggression Pact, which still had more than five years to run. But it was on Danzig that he laid the greatest stress, calling for "a friendly, lasting settlement of Danzig and its corridor." Again Beck turned a deaf ear to a less onerous and more reasonable settlement than Chamberlain had pressured Benes into accepting at Munich.

On the same day that Ribbentrop approached Beck in Berlin, Hitler approached the Lithuanian port of Memel in a German warship and landed there. The Versailles Treaty had assigned Memel and its pre-dominantly German population of 150,000 to Lithuania under a League of Nations administration, but Hitler had long declared it must "come home to the Reich." Instead, he staggered home to Memel, groggy with seasickness, and the Lithuanian government at once capitulated. The word went around in Prague: "Who would have thought at this time last year that we should now have acquired Memel?"

Neither Chamberlain nor Stalin found Hitler's seizure of Memel or his demands on Poland a laughing matter. On the eventful twenty-first of March, unfounded rumors of an imminent German invasion of Ro-mania led the British and French governments, under Chamberlain's prodding, to ask Poland's Foreign Minister Beck to join them and the Russians in a four-power guarantee to defend Romania against German aggression. Beck refused on the ground that the inclusion of Russia would anger Hitler. Chamberlain and Halifax then decided that Britain had more to gain from guaranteeing Poland against German attack than from seeking closer ties with Moscow. The British Imperial General Staff and Chamberlain's own secretary for war warned against extending any such guarantee to Poland, but by playing hard to get Beck bulldozed Chamberlain into offering him a one-way, unconditional pledge of support. "In the event of any action which clearly threatened Polish independence and which the Polish government considered it vital to resist with their national forces," Chamberlain told the House of Commons on March 31, "His Majesty's government would feel themselves at once bound to lend the Polish government all its support in their power."

Having opposed the Munich agreement, Churchill now deplored the guarantee to Poland even more: "There was sense in fighting for Czechoslovakia in 1938 when the German army could scarcely put half a dozen trained divisions on the Western Front, when the French, with nearly sixty or seventy divisions, could most certainly have rolled across the Rhine or into the Ruhr." But in extending a blank-check guarantee to Poland Chamberlain had "accepted an obviously imminent war on far worse conditions and on the greatest scale." On both occasions, however, the prime minister felt that public opinion forced him to act as he had. Nor was this all. On April 4 in London, where Beck had come to hear Chamberlain make his pledge, Britain's "temporary unilateral assurance to Poland" became a "permanent and reciprocal agreement," which Beck carried back with him to Warsaw and which the French felt constrained to endorse.

Munich had not brought "peace for our time." It had brought peace for less than six months, at which point Hitler's occupation of Prague panicked Chamberlain into committing Britain to war under circumstances of Beck's choosing. Beck, a confirmed alcoholic who had recently contracted cancer, talked as belligerently and irresponsibly as Hitler, assuring Chamberlain that Hitler had never contested Poland's right to Danzig while telling Grigore Gafencu, Romania's youthful foreign minister, that if the Germans "touch Danzig, it means war." One simple conviction explained everything: "Hitler knows the reality of the Bolshevik danger. Because of his doctrine, his past, his national and political reason for existence, he cannot come to terms with it. I *know* therein lies the central, primary problem for Hitler's Germany—to which all other problems are secondary." Which accorded with the views Chamberlain had expressed on April 26 in a letter to his sister: "I must confess to the most profound distrust of Russia. I have no belief whatever in her ability to maintain an effective offensive even if she wanted to. And I distrust her motives, which seem to me to have little connection with our ideals of liberty, and seem to be concerned only with getting everybody else by the ears."

Both Churchill and Lloyd George, his wartime chief, credited the Soviet leaders with more serious motives and constructive purposes. So did 92 per cent of the British people, who (according to a Gallup poll taken in mid-May) favored an alliance with Russia. As Winston Churchill told the House of Commons on April 3: "No one can say there is not a solid identity of interest between the Western democracies and Russia. The worst folly would be to chill any international cooperation which Russia can give." At the same time, Lloyd George, who had once hailed Hitler as the man to save Europe from Communism, warned: "If we are to go in without the help of Russia we shall be walking into a trap." He pointed to Russia as the only country in a position to aid Poland: "It is the only country who can get there and who has got an air force which can match Germany's."

Prague, Memel, Danzig. By the early weeks of April 1939, war seemed more certain than it had in the early weeks of July 1914. Once again, conflicts in eastern Europe threatened to spread west. Once again Germany demanded a place in the sun. Once again Britain and France stood side by side—this time, motionless. For Russia, which had stood with them in 1914, now stood apart.

Not so Italy. Shortly after the Germans occupied Prague, Count Galeazzo Ciano, Mussolini's son-in-law and foreign minister, wrote in his diary: "It is useless to deny that all this concerns and humiliates the Italian people. It is necessary to give them a satisfaction and compensation: Albania." Since 1918 Italy had exercised an unofficial protectorate over Albania. On April 7, Mussolini made it official by having Italian troops land in the country and occupy Tirana, its capital city. King Zog and his American-born wife fled to Greece with their newborn son. Ciano arrived a few days later and proclaimed Albania part of the Italian kingdom. Hitler neither approved nor disapproved. The British and French glumly acquiesced, but Mussolini's occupation of the country led them to extend to Greece the same unilateral guarantees that they had granted to Poland, while Hitler's *Drang nach Osten* led them to do the same for Romania.

Less than a month had passed since Hitler marched his troops into

Prague, and the repercussions continued to spread. Where would they end? By April 15 Foreign Minister Georges Bonnet of France had become so disturbed that he went the limit and proposed a far-reaching Anglo-Franco-Soviet treaty of mutual assistance, roughly comparable to the prewar Triple Entente. Paris cynics described Bonnet as being in the pay of every government except his own, but no one acused him of having taken funds from Moscow when he suggested to the Soviet ambassador that Russia join Britain and France in the guarantees they had given Poland and Romania. Nor was this all. Bonnet also went so far as to recommend an Anglo-French pledge to come to the aid of the Soviet Union if such a commitment on its part should lead to a German attack. Chamberlain, however, declined to go so far. On April 17, his government called only for a pledge of Soviet support, "if so desired and in such form as might be suitable," to any neighboring state that might become the victim of aggression.

The French government described Chamberlain's guarded response as "a most terrible diplomatic blunder." The Russians, on the other hand, not only welcomed Bonnet's tougher stance but urged going further and guaranteeing all the Baltic states by name. This counterproposal, dated April 18, called for a three-power pact that "could be embodied in three acts: in the first place, an agreement among the three powers of mutual assistance; in the second place, the conclusion among them of a military convention which would give the mutual security pact real strength; and, finally, a guarantee by the three powers to all states between the Baltic and the Black Sea." The governments of the nations that the Russians wanted to guarantee rejected the offer, and the British and French declined to join the Russians in making it.

The Soviet Foreign Office had not deliberately sabotaged the agreement at the outset by including a provision that the British and French governments could not accept. Rather had the Russians drafted the only kind of agreement with the British and the French acceptable to Stalin, who had no intention of making any deal with one party before finding out what terms he could get from the other. On April 17, the day before the Soviet proposals for a three-power mutual-assistance pact with Britain and France went on its way, the Soviet ambassador to Berlin reminded Baron Ernst von Weizsacker, undersecretary of state in the German Foreign Office, that Russia and Italy had always remained on good terms and asked why Russo-German relations should not follow the same pattern. Summarizing the ambassador's remarks, Weizsacker reported: "Soviet Russia had not exploited the present friction between

Germany and the Western democracies against us, nor did she desire to do so. There exists for Russia no reason why she should not live with us on a normal footing. And from normal, relations might become better and better." It was Hitler's move next.

· 3 ·

STALIN'S DISTRUST of Chamberlain more than matched Chamberlain's distrust of Stalin. But below the mutual distrust lay more dangerous miscalculations—on Stalin's side, a misinformed underestimate of German military might; on Chamberlain's side, an ignorant overestimate of that might, further warped by stubbornly wishful assumptions. Because Stalin's purges had liquidated the bulk of the Soviet diplomatic corps and the bulk of the Red Army's general staff, he knew little of Nazi intentions and less of German capabilities. To the extent that Stalin's purges had carried Lenin's methods further than Lenin himself had ever pushed them, Stalin had only himself to blame for his own and his country's plight. But both he and Lenin before him were the products as well as the progenitors of a Communist dictatorship which devoured its masters and its masses, its rulers and its ruled.

Chamberlain bore a greater personal responsibility for his lesser plight. He could not charge the British Foreign Office with misinforming him or the Imperial General Staff with giving him bad advice. Whereas Stalin fell victim to misinformation, not all of it of his own making, Chamberlain fell victim to his own refusal to accept facts. Parliamentary democracy produced Chamberlains and Churchills; Communist dictatorship produced Lenins and Stalins. Neither Chamberlain nor Churchill could ever have had the other shot, but parliamentary democracy could not save Chamberlain from his own pride or instantly replace him with Churchill. Experience had taught them both how to make the best of their ancient but supple system. Lenin and Stalin had succeeded only in making the worst of their novel and rigid one.

The best that could be said of Stalin and his system is that the desperation of his plight gave him the fortitude to play it cool. Confronted by Colonel Beck, Chamberlain had panicked. Confronted by Hitler, Stalin drew his cards closer to his chest while instructing Ivan Maisky, his ambassador at London, to urge Chamberlain to open military talks with the Poles at once and to extend to Greece and Romania the same guarantees that he had given Poland. Stalin also wanted to have the

Soviet Union included in a still wider network of military pacts. For Stalin had not forgotten the German invasion of Russia during the First World War—not to mention Hitler's traditional anti-Communist, anti-Russian propaganda. Now that German troops had occupied Czechoslovakia, and Hitler had welcomed Memel back into the Reich, the German demand for Danzig could wind up with German troops marching across Poland's plains in the footsteps of Napoleon's and Kaiser Wilhelm's armies.

In line with his dialectical, two-irons-in-the-fire approach to all problems Stalin moved in two directions at once. Recognizing the fearful miscalculations on which he had based his speech of March 10, he dropped his earlier role as Europe's arbitrator. Instead, he began sounding out the British, as the senior members of the Anglo-French alliance, and the Germans. Did his initial sounding out of Chamberlain mean that he preferred to do business with London—or had he chosen this way to stir up Hitler's curiosity and concern? The motives count for less than the results. Since Bismarck's time, many German leaders had favored close relations with Russia, and Russian leaders had responded from czarist times to Lenin's and Stalin's. Had the Munich crisis and its aftermath created a new European balance of power in which yesterday's enemies would become tomorrow's allies? No reversal of alliances had preceded the outbreak of the First World War. Not until its aftermath did the German and Russian pariahs get together. On May 3, 1939, Stalin had Foreign Commissar Maxim Litvinov relieved of his duties and replaced by Vyacheslav Molotov, a member (unlike Litvinov) of the Politburo.

Litvinov embodied the international spirit of the Old Bolsheviks, most of whom Stalin had liquidated long since. Molotov embodied the national spirit of the new Communists who had ridden to power on Stalin's coattails. Born into the Russian *intelligentsia,* a cousin of the composer Scriabin whose family name he bore, Molotov replaced it with the Russian word for "hammer," just as Stalin replaced Djugashvili with the Russian word for "steel." Litvinov—born in the ghetto of a poor Jewish family named Finkelstein—assumed a Slavic surname and spent much of his time doing revolutionary propaganda work abroad. The outbreak of the Revolution found him in London, where he had married Ivy Low, an Englishwoman with excellent official connections. On his return to Russia he went to work in the Foreign Office under Georges Chicherin, whom he eventually replaced as foreign commissar.

In that capacity, he extolled collective security and denounced Musso-lini and Hitler. With the collapse of the Munich agreement his useful-ness to Stalin ended—for the moment.

Molotov lost no time in assuring the Germans that there would be some changes made. On May 5 and May 17 the Soviet Foreign Office raised the question of a new Soviet-German trade agreement. Count von der Schulenberg, the German ambassador, a disciple of Bismarck, Ulrich von Brockdorff-Rantzau, and Walther Rathenau, discussed the matter with Molotov, who suggested creating a "political basis" first. At the end of the month, however, Molotov closed the door to further advances from the German side. As a senior official in the German For-eign Office put it to a group of visiting Soviet officials: "What can Eng-land offer Russia? At best, participation in a European war and the hostility of Germany. What can we offer on the other hand? Neutrality and staying out of a possible European conflict and, if Moscow wished, a Russo-German understanding based on mutual interests which, just as in former times, would work out to the advantage of both countries."

While Stalin kept both his German and Anglo-French irons in the fire, Hitler bound his junior Italian partner to him with hoops of steel but had less luck with the less scrutable Japanese. On May 22, the Ger-man and Italian foreign ministers signed a new agreement that Hitler dubbed a "Pact of Steel" under which the contracting parties pledged themselves to "remain in standing contact in order to come to an under-standing on all questions touching their common interests and the gen-eral situation in Europe," to enter into discussions "should the common interests of the contracting parties be imperiled by international events of any nature whatever," and, if either should become involved in war, "the other contracting party will immediately come to its side as an ally with all its military forces on land, on sea, and in the air." At most, these words bound Italy more tightly to Germany than the Triple Alliance did in 1914. But, on that occasion, it had taken the Italians only a year to declare war against the Germans.

Many Italians felt the Allies had cheated them out of their spoils in the last war. Would Italy fare any better by throwing in its lot with Germany in the next one? In 1936, Germany and Japan had signed an anti-Comintern pact in which the army-dominated government of Pre-mier Koki Hirota pledged itself in vague, bombastic language to stand with Germany against the spread of Communism. In February 1939, Hitler began trying to persuade the new Japanese government, headed by the more moderate Baron Kiichiro Hiranuma, to join Germany and

Italy in a stronger, three-power version of the anti-Comintern pact, but he got nowhere. Both Hitler and Mussolini had counted on the Japanese to worry Stalin and distract Roosevelt, but Hiranuma had more ties with the navy than with the army, and Japan's navy favored expansion in southeastern Asia and good relations with Washington and London; the army favored expansion at China's expense, even at the risk of clashes with the Russians.

Although Hitler had avoided some of the mistakes that Kaiser Wilhelm made in 1914, he found himself living in a different world. And nowhere had the world changed so drastically as in Asia. The leaders of Japan had hastened some of these changes, notably in the way they had industrialized and militarized their own country, but they had opposed others, notably in the way they fought the nationalist movement in China. The Roosevelt administration, on the other hand, had made some effort to aid the Chinese Nationalists while showing more and more hostility to the Japanese militarists. In February 1939, Japanese troops occupied Hainan, an island off the coast of French Indochina. In March they took the Spratly Islands, which France also claimed, and gained control of a chain of coral reefs off the Philippines. In Shanghai, Tientsin, and Amoy, Japanese officials acted more and more belligerently toward Americans and Europeans as Japanese troops marched deeper into China.

On July 24, 1939, the gathering war crisis in Europe led Neville Chamberlain to define a new formula that he wanted Britain and Japan to apply in the Tientsin area. It gave Japan a free hand: "The Japanese forces have special requirements for the safeguarding of their own security and maintaining public order in the regions under their control, and they have to suppress or remove such causes or acts as will obstruct them or benefit the enemy. His Majesty's government have no intention of countenancing any acts or measures prejudicial to the attainment of the above-mentioned objectives by the Japanese forces." At the same time, the British Foreign Office urged the American State Department to persuade Chiang Kai-shek to come to terms with Japan.

On July 26, two days after Chamberlain had proposed that Britain formally recognize Japan's right to subdue parts of China, the State Department invoked a clause in the American-Japanese commercial treaty of 1911, which permitted its termination in six months' time. The move certainly reflected American public opinion. Although the Gallup poll showed that only six per cent of the American people had favored war with Japan in June, 1939, two thirds of them had favored a boycott of all Japanese goods and more than half had wanted an embargo on all exports to Japan. By August, four Americans in five favored stopping all trade with Japan unless its government mended its ways. The American attitude toward the world in general and toward Hitler in particular was taking a different shape.

·4·

IN JANUARY 1939, most Americans expected war in Europe within the year and assumed that they would eventually become involved. But, according to the Gallup poll, seven Americans in ten regretted their country's participation in the last European war and hoped against hope that it could stay out of the next one. That hope their President did not share. For once Roosevelt did not see eye to eye with the mass of his fellow citizens. He agreed with those who expected war but not with those who wanted to stay out. By midsummer most Americans feared that the measures Roosevelt favored to help the victims of aggression would invite rather than discourage war and that the problem was not how to prevent the inevitable but how to keep America at peace when the inevitable happened.

On July 17, Roosevelt and Cordell Hull spent three hours urging a group of leading senators and representatives from both parties to give them the power to raise the mandatory embargo on all trade with all belligerents and thus enable victims of aggression to ship munitions of war from the United States, if they paid for them in cash and shipped them in their own vessels. "Hitler will march in September unless we pass this legislation," warned Hull, but the assembled members of Congress rejected the advice that Senator Borah of Idaho scorned, boasting that he had better information. The dialogue of the deaf ended with the blind continuing to lead the blind.

A similar paralysis immobilized the British and the French. Roosevelt could no more persuade Borah to repeal the Neutrality Act than Churchill could persuade Chamberlain to come to terms with the Russians. Nor could Daladier and Bonnet persuade Chamberlain and Halifax to give agreement with Stalin priority over subservience to Beck. Yet by mid-July the volatile French had come to distrust the Russians more than the phlegmatic British did.

Russian and German initiatives broke the deadlock. On July 18 the Soviet trade representative in Berlin told the Germans that his government strongly desired economic discussions. On July 24, Hitler learned

THIS IS WHERE WAR CAME IN

that the British and French governments had decided to send a military mission to Moscow. On July 29, Hitler gratified Ribbentrop by giving him permission to seek a political agreement with Moscow. On July 31, Chamberlain announced the departure of the Anglo-French military mission; on the same day, the British political mission that had been conducting desultory talks in Moscow for the past two months reported that the Russians had yet to improve on the offer they had made on June 2, at which point in time it so happened that the Germans knew they would have two million men under arms by mid-August.

To head the political mission to Moscow, Chamberlain ignored the renowned and respected Anthony Eden. Instead, he chose William Strang, an able but obscure Foreign Office official. *"Strang nach Osten,"* commented a London wit, but the Russians were not amused. Two months later, when the Russians demanded military talks, it was the same story. Chamberlain did not appoint an outstanding soldier like Lord Gort or General Ironside to conduct them, but the man with the longest name in the Royal Navy: Admiral Sir Reginald Aylmer Ranfurly Plunkett-Ernle-Erle-Drax.

With time running out, the British admiral and his French colleague, General J. E. A. Doumenc, avoided the risks of air travel, preferring a leisurely boat and train trip that consumed several days. On August 11, they arrived in Moscow only to find that Strang had flown back to London for further instructions, and when the meeting opened on August 12 it turned out that the visitors had no written authority to sign any documents and no precise figures on how much aid they could give Poland or how much they expected the Russians to provide. On August 17, General Klementi E. Voroshilov adjourned their discussions until August 21, and General Doumenc agreed to fly home for more instructions and authority. By this time Hitler had ordered full speed ahead on the nonaggression pact with Russia. He had to launch his attack on Poland before the autumn rains.

·5·

MEANWHILE, on August 12, Foreign Minister Ciano of Italy visited Hitler at Obersalzburg, where the two men exchanged some home truths. Back in April Ciano had written in his diary: "No nation wants war today. The most one can say is that they know it is inevitable." Four months later, Hitler confirmed Ciano's pessimism: "Europe will be an impassive spectator to the merciless destruction of Poland by Germany.

France and England will certainly make theatrical anti-German gestures but will not go to war." Ciano's warning that Italy could give Germany no help did not alarm Hitler, who announced that he planned "to annihilate Poland and beat France and England without help." Returning to Italy, Ciano reported to Mussolini: "It is useless to climb two thousand meters up into the clouds. Perhaps we are closer to the Eternal Father up there, if He exists, but we are surely farther from men. This time it means war. And we cannot engage in war because our plight does not permit us to do so." Mussolini finally agreed with his son-in-law that Italy could and should stay neutral.

Hitler spent Monday, August 14, the day after Ciano left, at Obersalzburg, conferring with his generals. "Italy is not interested in a major conflict," he told them. He also declared that "the men of Munich will not take the risk" of going to war to aid Poland. "Why should England fight?" he asked, "You don't let yourself get killed for an ally. Not even England has the money to fight a long war. Nothing can be had on credit." He compared France to "a weak man trying to carry machine guns on his back," and concluded that Poland could expect "no immediate relief by Anglo-French action." Hitler dwelt on Russia's hostility to Poland and Russia's reluctance to "pull chestnuts out of the fire" for Britain and France. "Loose" contacts had been established with the Russians, who still seemed "distrustful," but he had the question of sending a "prominent figure" to Moscow "still under advisement."

It did not remain there long. Immediately after his talk with the generals, Hitler instructed Schulenberg in Moscow to reach a comprehensive Russo-German agreement as soon as possible. Molotov liked the idea but urged careful preparation and asked Schulenberg for specific details on "how the German government was disposed to the idea of concluding a nonaggression pact with the Soviet Union, and further whether the German government was prepared to influence Japan for the purpose of improvement of Soviet-Japanese relations and settlement of border conflicts and whether a possible joint guarantee of the Baltic states was contemplated by Germany." The next day Ribbentrop accepted all three points and suggested that he come to Moscow and confer with Stalin and Molotov before the end of the week. Two days later, Molotov suggested a trade and credit agreement, to be followed by the nonaggression pact that he outlined. On August 20, Hitler wired directly to Stalin, accepting the Russian proposals and suggesting that Ribbentrop arrive in Moscow on August 21 or 22 instead of on the twenty-sixth or twenty-seventh as Molotov had recommended. Stalin set August 22 and the day.

On August 21, *Pravda* announced that Germany and Russia had signed a trade treaty that might become "a significant step towards further improvements not only of economic but also of political relations between the Soviet Union and Germany." That same day General Doumenc informed Voroshilov that he had received the necessary assurances from Paris and that he was prepared to resume discussions that evening. He received no reply until Voroshilov sent for him at seven o'clock and told him that Poland and Romania must give him similar reassurances. Voroshilov might as well have asked for the moon. Marshal Edward Smigly-Rydz, the Premier of Poland, declared at the time: "With the Germans we risk losing our liberty; with the Russians we lose our soul." Later that same evening the Berlin radio announced that Ribbentrop had taken off for Moscow.

By this time, German submarines had taken up positions off the British coast. The German battleship *Graf Spee* sailed for Brazilian waters on August 21. On August 22, Hitler summoned the commanders of the army, navy, and air force to Obersalzburg and told them that until the spring of 1939 he had expected to wait a few years before attacking the west and after that to move eastward. But relations with Poland had become impossible. "Poland would take advantage of any difficult situation to attack us in the back. . . . It has therefore become necessary to dispose of the eastern problem before attacking in the west." He also wanted to exploit his own leadership as fully and rapidly as possible: "All depends on me and my existence because of my political activities. Furthermore, probably no one will ever again have the confidence of the whole German people as I do. There will probably never again be a man in the future with more authority than I have. My existence is therefore a factor of great value, but I can be eliminated at any time by a criminal or an idiot." He went on to praise Mussolini and Franco, from both of whom he expected at least benevolent neutrality.

The British Empire was tottering, the British Isles were stagnating, France was decaying. The Allied coalition that successfully confronted Germany in 1914 had lost its nerve. But Germany must strike soon. As Hitler saw it, "We have nothing to lose. We can only gain. Restrictions have made our economic situation such that we cannot hold out for more than a few years. Goering can confirm this. We have no other choice. We must act." British support had made Poland "unbearable."

There could be no compromise, no arbitration in that quarter. "The Army must see actual battle before the big, final showdown in the west. . . . What we want now is not a general showdown, but the disposition of specific issues: this is the proper procedure not only politically, but also from the military standpoint."

Since "England cannot help Poland," Hitler could not see a long war. "A long war is an untempting prospect. It is nonsense to say that England wants a long war." Then came the climax. Russia was prepared to sign a nonaggression pact with Germany. "Four days ago, I took a special step which brought it about that Russia answered yesterday that she is ready to sign. The personal contact with Stalin is established. The day after tomorrow, Ribbentrop will conclude the treaty. Now Poland is in the position in which I wanted her." He set Saturday morning, August 26, as the probable date for the attack to begin.

The same generals who dreaded the prospect of war with Czechoslovakia in 1938 welcomed the prospect of war with Poland in 1939. General Franz Halder, the chief of staff, saw no reason to fear a French attack on the West Wall or a thrust at Germany through Belgium. General Gerd von Rundstedt more than half expected the Poles to capitulate without a fight. Most of the generals agreed with Hitler. They not only expected war; they wanted war. Did Stalin? Certainly not for its own sake. But since he regarded war as inevitable in any event, only the circumstances of the outbreak mattered, and these could have been much worse from his point of view. He had kept both his irons in the fire to the very end, thus avoiding the worst: a solo confrontation with Hitler. The British and French had not trapped him into fighting their war for them. A year ago he had no reason to believe that Hitler could win so much, so soon, at so small a cost. Nor had he any reason, a year ago, to foresee himself in a position to regain for the Soviet Union almost all former czarist lands in eastern Europe. This could not be done without cost and without risk, but he had delayed so long about closing the deal that Hitler now needed him more than he needed Hitler. Indeed, Ribbentrop had come to Moscow in such a rush that he did not even know the precise Russian demands. Far into the small hours of August 24 he and Molotov hammered out the details and when Stalin joined them in a toast to their completed labors, he declared: "I know how much the German nation loves its Fuehrer. I should therefore like to drink his health."

Hitler had no complaints. Only forty-eight hours before Stalin toasted him in Moscow, Hitler told his generals at Obersalzburg: "I have struck this weapon, the help of Russia, out of the hands of the western powers. The possibility now exists to strike at the heart of Poland." He called the pact the greatest political event of the time. "We need not fear a blockade. The east will supply us with grain, cattle, coal, lead, and zinc. . . . I am only afraid that at the last moment some *Schweinehund* will make a proposal for mediation. . . . Now that I have made the political preparations, the way is open for the soldier."

These political preparations took the form of a seven-point agreement, made public on August 24. The German and Soviet governments pledged themselves not to attack each other for ten years, to consult on mutual problems, and to settle all questions by peaceful means. The treaty made no mention of Poland and contained no such pledges of mutual support as the German-Italian "Pact of Steel." It was a nonaggression, not a mutual-aid pact. "The world stands before a towering fact," Goebbels at once boasted. "Two peoples have placed themselves on the basis of a common foreign policy which, during long and traditional friendship, produced a foundation for a common understanding." Molotov expressed himself in the same vein: "The chief importance of the Soviet-German nonaggression pact lies in the fact that the two largest states of Europe have agreed to put an end to the enmity between them, to eliminate the menace of war, and to live in peace with one another, making narrower thereby the zone of possible military conquests in Europe. Even if military conflicts in Europe should prove unavoidable, the scope of hostilities will now be restricted. Only instigators of a general European war, only those who under the mask of pacifism would like to ignite a general conflagration in Europe, can be dissatisfied with this position of affairs." Although neither of the two parties trusted the other; although each intended to do the other in; although each also knew the other had the same intention, Molotov spoke for them both when he assailed the "instigators of a general European war." The Russians stood to lose as much as the Germans from such a war. Hitler looked forward to fomenting and winning a series of limited blitz campaigns. Stalin cast himself in the role of Hitler's jackal, but counted on being able to turn and rend him when the time was ripe.

What an irony it would be if Litvinov, who had long spoken for Stalin with the authority that Molotov now possessed, should turn out to have been right, after all, when he declared, "Peace is indivisible!" Although Stalin had sacked Litvinov, he did not jail or liquidate him. The assumptions on which he had argued the case for collective security no longer held water. But that did not mean that the Nazi-Soviet pact could win the war for Germany—or lose it for the Soviet Union. At best, the pact offered Germany temporary insurance against having to fight a two-front war and the Soviet Union temporary escape from the risks of isolation. Already, the mere approach of war had resulted in a new European balance of power. What further changes might war itself bring?

For war had now become a certainty. Where and when it might break out remained to be seen. Europe's leading statesmen talked and acted like sleepwalkers. "Better an end to terror than terror without end" summed up the general mood of resignation. Immediately after the announcement of the Nazi-Soviet pact, Chamberlain renewed contact with Hitler by again reminding him, as he had at Munich, not to repeat the Kaiser's mistake of 1914 and take British neutrality for granted. "Whatever may prove to be the nature of the German-Soviet Agreement, it cannot alter Great Britain's obligations to Poland," he wrote Hitler in a personal message. "It had been alleged that, if His Majesty's Government had made their position more clear in 1914, the great catastrophe would have been avoided. Whether or not there is any force in that allegation, His Majesty's Government are resolved that on this occasion there shall be no such tragic misunderstanding." And to prove that he meant business, on August 25 Chamberlain announced that Britain had amplified and fortified its guarantee to Poland into a formal treaty of assistance. The stupefied Hitler, who shared the Kaiser's awe of the British, countermanded his order to attack Poland the next day; instead, he had Ambassador Sir Nevile Henderson flown to London in a German plane with the suggestion that Great Britain sign a nonaggression pact with Germany similar to the pact Ribbentrop had just signed with Molotov in Moscow. Chamberlain turned the proposal down, but according to Joseph P. Kennedy, the United States ambassador in London, the British at this time wanted only one thing— the United States should "bring pressure on the Poles to settle with the Germans."

That was not what the British got from Roosevelt, who sent messages to Hitler and to President Ignacy Mościcki of Poland, urging them to find a peaceful solution. Although Roosevelt knew that the plea would have no effect, he commented: "This puts the bee on Germany, which no one ever did in 1914." That kind of sting did not, however, bother Hitler, who reasoned: "In starting and waging a war, the Right does not matter, only the Victory."

The French government had not shared Chamberlain's confidence in the Munich Agreement; neither did it share his indignation when Hitler destroyed that confidence within six months. "Why die for Danzig?" became a popular slogan, and although Daladier and Bonnet did not ditch their alliance with Poland as they had ditched their alliance with Czechoslovakia, they dreaded the consequences of Chamberlain's bold, new policy. Because their experiences between 1914 and 1918 had taught them the costly folly of offensive warfare, the French had built a system of defenses, known as the Maginot Line, extending from the Swiss to the Belgian border, secure in the belief that the Germans could not break through and content to meet *Blitzkrieg* with *Sitzkrieg*. Yet the attitude of one young monarch in one small country made this whole investment worthless. In 1936, after the Belgians renounced their defensive alliance with France, the French proposed extending the Maginot Line, behind the Belgian border, to the sea, but did nothing when King Leopold III declared that he would consider such a gesture unfriendly.

Although the French wanted no more battles of the Marne or of Verdun, they had not forgotten that Russian armies saved Paris by invading East Prussia in August 1914. Bonnet shared Chamberlain's distrust of Russian Communism, but he recalled more vividly than Chamberlain how much Russia contributed to preventing a German victory in 1914, 1915, and 1916. The Nazi-Soviet pact therefore hit the French harder than it hit the British, and on the day it was announced Bonnet blamed everything on the refusal of the Poles to let the Red army cross their frontiers and defend them against German attack. He went so far as to urge that France reconsider its obligation to defend Poland, but Daladier preferred to stand with Chamberlain.

In Tokyo the Nazi-Soviet pact caused consternation and relief— consternation because Hitler had pleaded so earnestly and so recently for Japan to join the anti-Comintern pact, relief because the plea had been turned down. Experiences during and after the last war had not enhanced the prestige of the white races among the Japanese, who saw in the Russo-German nonaggression pact a confirmation of past suspicions. Premier Hiranuma could only lodge a note of protest with Berlin: Japan would pursue a policy of neutrality and isolation, and he would resign. But just before he quit, on August 28, he rushed more troops to the Soviet-Manchurian border on the basis of a false rumor, just received, that the Russians were sending 300,000 men there. On September 15, the Soviet and Japanese governments signed an armistice agreement. Meanwhile, General Nobuyuki Abe—Hiranuma's successor—relaxed pressure on the British at Tientsin, but showed little inclination to co-operate with the Western powers, Germany least of all. Rather did Japan's new government appear even more determined than the old to avoid close ties with any European power and to continue to expand its influence in Asia. Thus, while Germany turned eastward, Japan turned west.

·6·

ON THE SAME DAY that Sir Nevile Henderson flew to London in a German plane, bearing with him Hitler's offer of a nonaggression pact, Hitler handed to Ambassador Robert Coulondre of France a personal message to Premier Daladier, stressing Germany's desire for the two countries to remain at peace. Had Hitler, who kept raising his demands when he waged his war of nerves over Czechoslovakia a year ago, now lost his own nerve as the moment approached to wage a real war over Poland? Later, in *Failure of a Mission,* Henderson wrote that three schools of opinion existed in Germany during the summer of 1939: "One, far removed from Hitler's entourage and representing the mass of the people, was all for peace and still hopeful that Hitler's wizardry would enable him to achieve his aims without war. A second was equally for war at any price." The third school, to which Hitler belonged, "appeared really to believe that Britain's military preparations were being deliberately undertaken with a view to a preventive war and consequently argued that war in 1939 was better for Germany than war in 1940 or later."

Whatever Hitler's reasons for postponing the attack on Poland, they did not deter him long. Henderson returned from London with a British assurance that Poland would negotiate a settlement of Danzig and the Polish Corridor. The Germans gave the Poles twenty-four hours to send a representative to Berlin to accept whatever plans would be laid before them. And when the British called this an ultimatum and suggested that the Germans establish normal contact with Warsaw, Ribbentrop told Henderson that the time limit had already expired and refused to receive Poland's Ambassador Joseph Lipski in Berlin. Hitler had already decided to provoke war.

As early as mid-August German officials had begun demanding that the Poles withdraw more and more of their customs guards from Danzig, and the more the Germans demanded, the farther the Poles retreated. On August 23 the Germans violated the international statute under which Danzig operated by appointing Albert Förster, the local Nazi gauleiter, "head of state." When the Poles still refused to retaliate, a group of Nazi Schutzstaffel troops, in Polish uniforms furnished by the German army, attacked a German radio station near the Polish border. "Last night for the first time, soldiers of the regular Polish army fired shots on our territory," announced Hitler as seven German armies totaling more than a million and a half men surged across the entire length of the German-Polish border. "Since 5:45 A.M. we have been returning their fire."

The day before German troops invaded Poland, Mussolini proposed another four-power conference to review the bearing of the Versailles Treaty on the current situation. The next day, Chamberlain and Halifax insisted that the Germans first agree to evacuate their troops from Poland, and the Polish Government demanded that all fighting stop before any conference could begin. Bonnet was prepared to leave the Poles in the lurch and sponsor another Munich. Thirty-six hours after the invasion of Poland had begun, the Polish ambassador in Paris protested the failure of the French government to honor its promise to give Poland immediate aid in the event of attack. Bonnet replied, "You don't expect us to have a massacre of women and children in Paris." Across the English Channel, Chamberlain did not invoke Britain's pledge to aid the Poles or propose an immediate declaration of war on Germany. Many of his fellow Conservatives felt such shame at Chamberlain's delay that when Arthur Greenwood, acting leader of the Labour opposition, rose to speak in the House of Commons, Leopold Amery, a diehard Tory, shouted: "Speak for England." Afterward, Duff Cooper, a Churchill supporter, described his fellow Conservatives as having "listened to their own leader in embarrassed silence" and then cheered Greenwood's "robust speech."

Rank and file Members of Parliament, reflecting the views of the voters who had elected them, had now lost confidence in the prime minister and his inner circle. On the other side of the English Channel the French leaders reflected, all too accurately, the doubts and fears of their constituents. Under the circumstances the best that the British and French governments could do for their Polish allies was to give Hitler twenty-four hours to call off his attack and—when he refused to do so—issue their reluctant declarations of war on September 3.

That same afternoon, as Ambassador Henderson left Berlin, he noted the contrast between 1939 and the way he had seen the Berliners respond to the break with Britain on August 4, 1914: "Then a howling mob had surged up in front of the Embassy, had broken its windows, and thrown abuse at its inmates." On September 3, 1939, as reported by Henderson in *Failure of a Mission,* he saw no "discourtesy," not even "a single gesture of hostility." In London, on the other hand, Prime Minister Chamberlain's announcement of Britain's declaration of war on Germany recalled—but did not echo—Foreign Secretary Sir Edward Grey's famous words as he saw the lights of London flicker and die on the evening of August 4, 1914, after Britain's declaration of war on Germany: "The lights are going out all over Europe. We shall not see them lit again in our time." To the House of Commons Chamberlain gave utterance to black despair: "Everything that I have worked for, everything that I have hoped for, everything that I have believed in during my public life has crashed in ruins."

When the German armies marched off to wage war on two fronts in 1914, the Kaiser promised them, "Back before the leaves fall," and they shared his confidence. Neither Hitler nor the German people felt any such confidence, twenty-five years later, as the German armies again marched off to war—this time on one front only. The arrival of the British ultimatum, two days behind schedule, found Hitler in the company of Ribbentrop, who had always insisted that the British would not fight, and of Goering, who had made vain, last-minute appeals to friends in Sweden to save the peace. "Well, what now?" inquired Hitler. Ribbentrop made no reply. Said Goering, "Heaven help us if we lose this war."

. . .

The Nazi-Soviet pact rang down the curtain on the long armistice between the two world wars and provided the backdrop against which much of the history of the next thirty years unrolled. The Czechoslovak crisis had led to the Munich conference, which presided over the breakup of Czechoslovakia. The Polish crisis, which followed immediately, led Chamberlain to extend an instant guarantee to the semifeudal greater Poland of Marshal Pilsudski and Colonel Beck such as he had withheld from the multinational, multiracial republic of Czechoslovakia, sponsored by Woodrow Wilson, founded by Thomas G. Masaryk, and preserved by Eduard Benes. Whereas Chamberlain forbade Benes to accept the aid that he had sought from Moscow, Beck refused to accept the Soviet aid that Daladier had begged him to seek. And Chamberlain and Halifax both endorsed Beck's stand.

This set the stage for the Nazi-Soviet pact which began, but did not end, with a Soviet-German agreement to repartition Poland. Here, as elsewhere, Hitler's Germany and Stalin's Russia needed each other— just as Hitler's and Stalin's successors still do—sometimes as friends, sometimes as enemies, always as complementary, counterbalancing forces. In planning his invasion of Poland, Hitler did not want to have his armies occupy more than the 90,000 square miles of Poland that lay west of the so-called Curzon Line or have to deal with more than the twenty million Poles who lived there. He therefore welcomed a partition of greater Poland that would give Stalin the 60,000 square miles of its territory east of the Curzon Line, territory inhabited chiefly by some six million Ukrainians and Byelorussians who had equal distaste for both Russian and Polish rule.

The consequences of the Nazi-Soviet pact extended in space far beyond the territories of greater Poland and in time far beyond June 22, 1941, when Hitler's invasion tore it to shreds. But inasmuch as the pact played its first role and served its original purpose when Hitler and Stalin agreed to partition Poland, it seems appropriate, at this point, to note that Poland again loomed as large in 1945, when Hitler's Germany went up in smoke, as it did in 1939, when Hitler and Stalin sealed their original agreement at Poland's expense. Poland could no more liberate itself from its Russian liberators in 1945 than it could repulse its German attackers in 1939. Nor could Poland's British allies render any assistance on either occasion. Still more ironic, it was Marshal Pilsudski, the founding father of greater Poland, who had dug his own country's grave back in 1920 when he insisted that it incorporate the western Ukraine and its six million non-Polish inhabitants. For it was this prize that persuaded Stalin to sign his pact with Hitler nineteen years later. Had Pilsudski shown the same respect for the rights of others to national self-determination that he demanded for his own people, he might have made a greater contribution to the Polish national cause.

III

Phony War

·1·

HITLER AT WAR proved as full of surprises as Hitler at peace. At Munich in September 1938, the upstart statesman won more by bluff than Bismarck ever gained by force. A year later in Poland the upstart war lord made the Kaiser look like a little tin soldier. Against the Poles Hitler's generals unleashed a new style of three-dimensional warfare in which high-speed tanks replaced the traditional cavalry charge and screaming dive bombers the traditional artillery barrage. In 1915, as chief of staff to Field Marshal August von Mackensen on the eastern front, General Hans von Seeckt had driven thin, infantry columns deep into Russian territory, where they cut off, encircled, and destroyed masses of infantry on the opposing front lines. Twenty-four years later, German tanks used those same tactics against Polish infantry and artillery while German planes patrolled the skies and bombed Polish supply lines and artillery emplacements. German airmen did not need to shoot down Polish airmen in combat. They had already destroyed Poland's obsolete planes on the ground. Polish troops fought heroically everywhere, but German tanks and planes overwhelmed them.

On September 17, the Soviet Government announced the expiration of all its treaties with the Polish state, because that state had ceased to exist. At the same time, the Red Army poured across Poland's eastern border to protect "the kindred Ukrainian and White Russian peoples" who had been living there since 1920 under Polish rule. The German government announced its approval—as well it might, since its own troops had advanced beyond the limits laid down in a secret clause of its pact with the Soviet Union. Not until seven years later did the world learn that this secret clause also recognized Soviet predominance in

Finland, the Baltic states, and Bessarabia. But the world did not have to wait any time at all to hear the new line that the Soviet leaders laid down for communists everywhere to follow. They assailed the British and French governments as warmongers for refusing to recognize Hitler's conquest of Poland and make peace. But they turned down Hitler's invitation to visit Berlin and discuss the new situation. Instead, they insisted that Ribbentrop again fly to Moscow for another round of talks with Molotov, who now described fascism as "a matter of taste."

During this second round of talks the two men agreed to have the Bug and Vistula rivers form the dividing line between Soviet and German zones of influence in Poland. This gave the Soviet Union a little more territory than the Curzon Line had proposed in 1920 and a little less than the czarist empire had embraced. Within another month the Soviet Union incorporated this territory after its twelve million inhabitants had approved the *fait accompli* by a majority of more than ninety per cent in a Communist-style plebiscite. The Germans incorporated western Poland in the Third Reich without benefit of plebiscite and set up a government general in Warsaw to administer some thirteen million Polish and Jewish inhabitants of central Poland.

When the last fighting ended on October 5, the Germans estimated their own losses at over 91,000 dead, more than 1000 planes, and 1400 tanks. They claimed they had taken almost 700,000 Polish prisoners; the Russians claimed that another 190,000 Poles had fallen into their hands. It was against this backdrop of a defeated, occupied, and partitioned Poland that Hitler arose in the Reichstag, on October 6, and called upon the British and French to make peace. Nor did he speak for himself alone. Soviet propagandists charged the British and French governments with warmongering and endorsed Hitler's Reichstag speech which predicted: "If this war is really to be waged only to give Germany a new regime, that is to say, in order to destroy the present Reich once more and thus create a new Treaty of Versailles, then millions of lives will be sacrificed in vain, for neither will the German Reich go to pieces nor will a second Versailles Treaty be made." He concluded: "One thing only is certain. In the course of history there have never been two victors, but very often only losers. This seems to me to have been the case in the last war. May those people and their leaders who are of the same mind now make their reply. And let those who consider war to be the better solution reject my outstretched hand."

·2·

GENERAL GUSTAVE GAMELIN, the supreme French commander, had seen no reason to synchronize an attack on Germany's West Wall with the German invasion of Poland. The Poles could obviously hold out until spring, by which time the French and British would launch attacks far beyond their present, limited capacities. The British preferred to build up their Royal Air Force rather than expend it by attacking German cities and inviting heavier retaliation by the Luftwaffe. In respect to ground troops they could do even less. By the second week in October, four British divisions, totaling 158,000 men, had landed in France without the loss of a single life, but by this time the Polish campaign had ended.

Chamberlain had already rejected Hitler's "outstretched hand" and within twenty-four hours of the British declaration of war against Germany stretched out his hand to Winston Churchill, who became first lord of the admiralty, the same post he had held in 1914. Lord Hankey, one of Lloyd George's top aides during the First World War, became minister without portfolio. Anthony Eden became dominions secretary. Chamberlain could not persuade a single Labourite or Liberal to serve under him, but welcomed Churchill, Hankey, and Eden to an inner nine-man war cabinet, modeled on the five-man war cabinet formed by Lloyd George in 1916.

Hitler, with half the ground forces the Kaiser possessed in 1914, concentrated the bulk of what he had against a single, weaker opponent, winning a battle of annihilation of limited scope. But the British navy of 1939 enjoyed a command of the seas such as the Kaiser's Germany never approached. On September 3, Admiral Erich Raeder, commander of Germany's vest-pocket navy, composed a gloomy memorandum, blaming Hitler for having started the war five years too soon: "Today the war against England and France broke out, the war which, according to the Fuehrer's previous assertion, we had no reason to expect before 1944. The German navy is obviously in no way adequately equipped for the great struggle with Great Britain."

If Hitler overrated the value of the weapons he did possess, Raeder overrated the value of those he did not possess. Churchill took a more balanced view, always recognizing the limitations of sea power, but sometimes (remembering the four years of carnage on the Western

Front) exaggerating the costs and risks of land warfare. Raeder had only twenty-six submarines when Germany went to war and three 10,000-ton pocket battleships. On October 14, one of his submarines sank the British capital ship *Royal Oak,* at anchor in Scapa Flow, but another—on the opening day of the war—let his country in for a severe propaganda defeat by mistaking the British passenger liner *Athenia* for a cruiser and sending it to the bottom of the Atlantic with a loss of more than one hundred lives, twenty-eight of them American. Goebbels then made matters worse by charging that Churchill had inserted an infernal machine in the *Athenia's* hold in the hope of creating another *Lusitania* incident. The Germans also lost one of their three pocket battleships, and Hitler lost still more face in mid-December when the British bottled up the *Graf Spee* in Montevideo harbor, where the commander scuttled her on Hitler's orders and then committed suicide in shame.

The military and naval involvements that forced Chamberlain to take Churchill into his government also forced that government to widen its diplomatic strategy. Until war came, Chamberlain confined his dealings with Hitler to European problems—and even Czechoslovakia seemed far away. But the outbreak of war forced Chamberlain to tackle world-wide problems with which Churchill had more experience than most British or any German officials. At the turn of the century, Wilhelm II had called upon the peoples of Europe to defend themselves against the yellow peril and had sought new concessions for Germany in China. He had also interested himself in the affairs of the Middle East, pushed the Berlin-Baghdad Railway, and established close relations with Turkey.

Not so Hitler, whose war plans did not extend beyond Europe. The British therefore lost no time exploiting Turkish fear of Russia and Turkish distrust of Germany, and on October 19, 1939, the Turkish Republic signed an eastern Mediterranean treaty of mutual assistance with Britain and France, pledging aid to Greece and Romania if either country should be attacked. Soon afterward Britain and Turkey signed a trade treaty, and British, French, and Turkish officers held military conversations to co-ordinate their defenses in the Balkans and the Near East. Although the Turks did not join the Allied camp, they did not go all the way in the opposite direction as they had in 1914. Thus Britain won a diplomatic and propaganda victory in a critical part of the world, and Germany suffered a setback. By November 7, Churchill felt so confident that he told the British people, "I do not doubt that time is on our side. I go so far as to say that if we come through the winter without any large or important event occurring, we shall in fact have gained the first campaign of the war."

·3·

YET IN MOST RESPECTS, the first two months of the Second World War found the British threatened with as grave a danger as any they had faced since the German submarine blockade of 1917. Nor did Churchill minimize this threat. The purpose of the Dardanelles expedition of 1915 had been to open a supply route to the beleaguered Russians. A quarter of a century later, Britain's former ally seemed to have become Germany's chief accomplice. Churchill put it this way before the House of Commons on October 1, 1939: "I cannot forecast to you the action of Russia. It is a riddle in a mystery inside an enigma: but perhaps there is a key. That key is Russian national interest. It cannot be in accordance with the interest or safety of Russia that Germany should plant herself on the shore of the Black Sea or that she should overrun the Balkan states and subdue the Slavonic peoples of southeastern Europe. That would be contrary to the historic life interests of Russia." Churchill did not mention the Baltic states, for the simple reason that Estonia, Latvia, and Lithuania, taking to heart the lesson of Poland, had all signed the treaties Moscow had drawn up, agreeing in advance to accept Russian protection from possible German attack.

The Nazi-Soviet pact, which put the three little Baltic states in the Soviet zone of influence, did not cover their larger and more important neighbor—Finland. On October 5, Molotov therefore suggested that Finland's foreign minister visit Moscow "to discuss a number of concrete questions." The Finns waited a few days and then sent their top Russian expert, J. K. Paasikivi, who had worked out lasting agreements with the early Bolshevik leaders back in 1920. Now, however, the Russians presented three new demands: a mutual-assistance treaty, the right to occupy and fortify Hangö, a seaport and peninsula at the mouth of the bay of Finland, and the surrender of the Karelian isthmus, up to and including the Mannerheim Line fortifications. The Finns refused to make any real concessions. In exchange, the Russians offered only a valueless stretch of Karelia which the Finns rejected.

The plight of less than four million Finns confronted by some 180 million Russians stirred universal sympathy abroad. But if the Finns had harder heads than the Poles, the Russians had wiser heads than the

Germans. The Russians did not regard the Finns as weak or despicable foes, but as cat's-paws of the Germans and the British. Nor did the Finns regard the Russians as fiends in human form. Under the czars, the grand duchy of Finland had enjoyed more independence than any other part of the Russian Empire, and after the Bolsheviks came to power, the Finns won complete freedom from Moscow. At no point did the Soviet invasion of Finland resemble the Nazi invasion of Poland. To begin with, the Russians did not set out to exterminate the Finns as the Germans set out to exterminate the Poles. Instead, they announced their recognition of a puppet Finnish government set up just across the border by Otto Kuusinen, a Finnish Communist and former secretary of the Comintern who had lived in Russia since 1918. This government at once announced that it had signed a treaty with Moscow, accepting all the Soviet demands. The Moscow government never declared war on the Finnish government at Helsinki, thereby making it possible for any neutral nation to represent Finnish interests in the Soviet Union for the duration of hostilities. Meanwhile, Kuusinen kept denouncing the Helsinki regime and calling upon his compatriots to rally around him.

But instead of embracing Communism, the Finns routed the Russians. The Soviet leaders had misjudged Finland's political mood and military might, thereby making the Red army appear inferior to the invincible Germans. The white-clad Finns, skilled in winter fighting and familiar with their own terrain, let the khaki-clad Russians stumble deep into the snowy forests and then descended upon them, like ghosts on skis, shooting them by the scores and by the hundreds, before vanishing again into the white wastes.

The Russians fared no better on the diplomatic front. When Finland protested the Soviet invasion to the League of Nations, Molotov replied, "The Soviet Union is not at war with Finland, and does not threaten the Finnish people. The Soviet Union maintains peaceful relations with the Democratic Republic of Finland." He added that the Finnish officials who had protested to Geneva "are not the real representatives of the Finnish people." Within two weeks, however, the assembly of the League of Nations voted that the Soviet Union had violated the League Covenant and the Kellogg Pact and urged all League members to do what they could to aid Finland. The next day the League Council unanimously voted that "the USSR is no longer a member of the League."

Neutral Sweden sent more than eight thousand volunteers to fight with the Finnish forces and donated a hundred and twenty-five million dollars' worth of supplies. But when Britain and France asked permission to send an expeditionary force of 100,000 men to Finland via Norway and Sweden both countries refused. "Neutrality is idiocy," said Foreign Minister Richard J. Sandler of Sweden and had to quit forthwith. "Our kingdom will rebuff all attempts upon its neutrality or its territory," commented Prime Minister Per Albin Hansson—and held his job. A Swedish banker, when asked by an American where his country stood in connection with the war between Russia and Finland, replied, "Well, we are still against Russia." The American might well have added, "We, too." Ninety per cent of the money raised for Finland abroad came from the United States, where hatred of Russian Communism ran at least as strong as hatred of German Nazism. But the American people, like the people of all the other neutral countries, feared war more than they hated either Communism or Nazism, and only the British and French, who were already at war with the Germans, made extensive and genuine preparations to send their fighting men to the aid of Finland.

And not without reason. An Anglo-French expeditionary force, operating in Finland from Swedish or Norwegian bases, would at once challenge German control of the Baltic and imperil iron ore shipments from Sweden. It would expose Germany itself to air attack and perhaps invasion from the north. It might even break up the Nazi-Soviet pact. Whatever Stalin's ultimate purposes or Hitler's immediate suspicions, they shared a common interest in terminating the fighting in Finland and forestalling Allied intervention. Hitler therefore stopped the flow of arms that was beginning to move from Italy to Finland across Germany, and Stalin decided to fight an old-fashioned war for an old-fashioned peace. He had no desire to fight side by side with Hitler in a much bigger war, and Hitler had even less desire to see British and French troops setting up bases on the Baltic.

Before the British and French could organize an expeditionary force and before the neutrals could send Finland substantial aid, Stalin put his first military team on the battlefield. The Russian troops who had attacked Finland included no crack divisions and lacked the best weapons. But in February, the Russians sent their best troops against the Finns and smashed the Mannerheim Line with a hub-to-hub artillery barrage of 300,000 shells a day. The Red Air Force resumed its bombings of Helsinki and on March 12 a Finnish delegation that had already spent some weeks in Moscow suddenly agreed to make peace. The Russians got more than they had originally asked for, but they did not impose any such terms on the Finns as the Germans had imposed on the Poles. The Finns reported that they had lost almost 20,000 men killed in action and another 43,500 wounded. Molotov disputed these figures but placed Russian losses at 48,745 dead and 158,863 wounded. Perhaps the Soviet leaders had learned a lesson worth the price. Certainly the example of the Finns inspired millions of their friends and shamed millions more.

· 4 ·

ON THE EVENING of September 3, 1939, a few hours after Britain and France declared war on Germany, President Roosevelt delivered a solemn radio chat to the American people, warning that the United States could not ignore "conflicts taking place thousands of miles from the whole American Hemisphere" and "go about its business. Passionately though we may desire detachment, we are forced to realize that every word that comes through the air, every ship that sails the sea, every battle that is being fought does affect the American future." Having struck this note of warning, he closed on a note of hope: "This nation will remain a neutral nation, but I cannot ask that every American remain neutral in thought as well"—a contrast, this, with Wilson's 1914 injunction to be "impartial in thought as well as in action." Further: "Even a neutral has a right to take account of facts. Even a neutral cannot be asked to close his mind and conscience. I have said not once, but many times, that I have seen war and that I hate war. I say that again and again. I hope the United States will keep out of this war. I believe that it will. And I give you assurance and reassurance that every effort of your government will be directed toward that end. As long as it remains in my power to prevent, there will be no blackout of peace in the United States."

FDR followed through with two decisions both of which went into effect on September 20. The first summoned Congress into special session on that day for the purpose of amending the Neutrality Act. The second called for the dispatch of Undersecretary of State Sumner Welles to Panama to attend a meeting of delegates from the American republics, also set for that date. Eight days later they issued a "general declaration of continental neutrality," affirming a "unanimous intention not to become involved in the European conflict," proclaiming their adherence to recognized principles of international law, and setting up a seven-nation Inter-American Neutrality Committee to make continuing recommendations on neutral rights. They laid plans for closer inter-

American co-operation and defined a three-hundred-mile-wide security belt around the entire Western Hemisphere except Canada and the colonies and possessions of European states. This feature of the declarations the British and French governments rejected, but the delegates to Panama had established a closer solidarity among their nations than they had ever attained in time of peace.

It took less time to commit the American republics to stronger neutrality measures than it did to uncommit the United States from the portion of the Neutrality Act forbidding any shipment of arms to any nation at war. In July, a large bipartisan majority of House and Senate leaders had heeded Senator Borah rather than President Roosevelt and Secretary of State Hull in refusing to amend the Neutrality Act, for fear that such amendment would plunge the United States into war. Now Germany's quick knockout of Poland and the weak responses of Britain and France raised the new and greater danger of German victory. No longer did administration spokesmen urge repeal of the arms embargo as the best means of keeping America out of war. Now they quoted the cable of Ambassador William C. Bullitt in Paris reporting that "every Frenchman in a position to know the facts" had assured him that "German victory would be certain" unless France "could buy arms freely in the United States." The Senate repealed the arms embargo by a vote of 55 to 24 and the House by a vote of 243 to 172. The President signed the repeal on November 4, and Prime Minister Chamberlain called it "not only an assurance that we and our French allies may draw on the great reservoir of American resources; it is also a profound moral encouragement to us in the struggle upon which we are now engaged."

Chamberlain and Churchill, Stalin and Roosevelt, the German generals and the French, America's isolationists and America's interventionists shared one assumption: Germany could not win a quick or easy victory over Britain and France. Finland's showing against the Russians gave new encouragement to the friends of democracy everywhere. The spreading euphoria led Borah to call the deadlock on the Western Front the phony war, Chamberlain to call it the twilight war, and the French to refer to it as the *drôle de guerre*. By February 1940, public-opinion polls showed that less than one third of the American people expected to be drawn into the war and that less than one quarter believed that the country should fight to save Britain and France from sure defeat.

Had Roosevent issued louder warnings against a danger that no longer seemed imminent, he might have alarmed some of his recent, gun-shy converts. Yet to do and say nothing could only encourage the further spread of euphoria. Shortly after the turn of the year he therefore hit upon a course of action that seemed to combine caution with concern and energy with imagination, and dispatched Sumner Welles on a tour of the Italian, German, French, and British capitals to appraise the prospects for peace.

The selection of Sumner Welles gratified many Latin American leaders whose goodwill he had always cultivated and whose concern for the welfare of western Europe he shared. Of the Soviet Union, China, and Japan Mr. Welles knew less, but his itinerary did not include those parts of the world. Here he and the President (both of them the products of Groton School and Harvard College) saw eye to eye. Like most of their compatriots, the President and his undersecretary of state viewed the war, during its opening stages, as a European rather than a global affair. They did not see one chance in a thousand that the various belligerent powers would agree to bring even their limited military operations to an end. Roosevelt's one faint hope lay in the possibility of detaching Mussolini from Hitler.

The President also believed that he might gain new insights from the reports the undersecretary would make on his conversations with Mussolini, Ciano, Hitler, Ribbentrop, Daladier, Paul Reynaud, Chamberlain, and Churchill. "I do not believe," wrote Welles at the end of his final report, "there is the slightest chance of any successful negotiation at this time for a durable peace if the basis is made the problem of political and territorial adjustment." Welles had talked with a Hitler still eager for further conquests, a Chamberlain embittered by his experience at Munich, a Mussolini newly committed to closer co-operation with his Axis partner, and innumerable Frenchmen from only a few of whom did he obtain "the impression of hope, or vigor, or even, tragically enough, of the will to courage."

For the outbreak of war had not dispelled the doubts, fears, and confusions that had paralyzed so many Europeans and that Hitler still exploited with such success. But Hitler needed Stalin's help even to annihilate Poland, and the next thing Stalin knew he had a war with Finland on his hands. Hitler had better luck, even though he did not recognize it as such at the time. Three days before Chamberlain had rejected Hitler's "outstretched hand," the Fuehrer had sent a memorandum to all his commanders: "The German war aim is a final military settlement with the west." The same generals who had talked mutiny during the Austrian and Czech crises again took alarm. Colonel General

Heinrich von Brauchitsch, the commander in chief, and Franz Halder, his chief of staff, told their subordinates on the Western Front to prepare for Hitler's overthrow the moment he ordered an all-out offensive. But Brauchitsch quit the conspiracy before any orders came, and the others kept telling Hitler that bad weather made an offensive impossible. Maybe so. But those generals and Hitler all knew that they could start no offensive against France and the Low Countries unless and until they had protected their northern flank by neutralizing Scandinavia—by bluff if possible, by force if necessary. In view of what presently did occur, the evidence suggests that each new blitz campaign Hitler had planned called for a greater effort than the one before. In the case of Poland, he did not move until he had secured the cooperation of Stalin. Now, as he planned his more extensive operations in the west, he had to execute two maneuvers, not one. Between November 12 and January 20, he announced and postponed the assault on the west sixteen times. But his generals were fooling only themselves if they believed that their plotting forced his postponements.

Chamberlain rightly interpreted this prolonged inaction as a sign of German weakness. But he wrongly assumed that it also revealed, on Hitler's part, a growing fear of Britain's growing strength. On the evening of April 5, 1940, he told a Conservative-party meeting: "After seven months of war, I feel ten times as confident of victory as I did at the beginning." Citing the Germans' failure to take advantage of their head start in war preparations, he not only concluded that Hitler had "missed the bus"; Chamberlain went on to announce that Britain could no longer tolerate a "double standard of neutrality" which benefited the Germans and handicapped the Allies. Three days later, four British destroyers began laying mines in Norway's territorial waters near the northern port of Narvik.

During the First World War, the Norwegians had mined these territorial waters themselves. The Germans had stayed out, and Norway had stayed neutral. But as soon as war broke out in 1939, the Norwegians let German vessels carry Swedish iron ore within their three-mile limit, while German submarines sank Norwegian merchantmen on the broad Atlantic. Progress in undersea and air warfare had given Norway such strategic importance that it could no longer hope to keep out of a general European war. In consequence, Hitler's war plans called for the occupation of Scandinavia and attacks on Belgium, Holland, and Luxembourg as preludes to the conquest of France, the blockade of Britain, and the final struggle with Russia. But Hitler never planned to use Norway as anything more than a base from which his planes and submarines would blockade the British Isles. He saw the decisive campaigns taking place farther south.

On the other hand, the British and French—especially the French—had hoped for great things from the north. Finland's stand against Russia encouraged Daladier to stake his government's existence on the projected invasion to aid Finland. Whereupon the hard-pressed Finns cited the possibility of Allied intervention to get much better terms from Stalin than the Poles got from Hitler. And soon after the Finns and Russians made peace, Daladier fell. The cocky and more conservative Reynaud who replaced him received a one-vote majority on his first appeal to the Chamber of Deputies. In order to increase this majority—and to save France—Reynaud urged that Britain and France mine the coastal waters of Norway and even prepare to open a new front there. The British agreed, and General Gamelin attended a series of conferences in London where he and the British drew up the plans for the campaign. But a copy of them vanished from Gamelin's London hotel room, spirited away, it was learned later, by an Italian servant who transmitted them to the Germans.

Actually, the Germans had planned their occupation of Norway months in advance. On the evening of the same day that the British destroyers appeared off Narvik, German warships shelled Oslo, while German ships and transport planes landed troops all along the Norwegian coast. Hitler called the Allied blockade "a destructive blow at the concept of neutrality" and announced German intervention "to protect peace in the north against every Anglo-French attack." That same night, German ground forces crossed the Danish border and quickly occupied the entire country. As recently as May, 1939, the Germans and Danes had signed a nonaggression pact, promising that they would "in no circumstances resort to war or any other form of violence against each other." Although Hitler broke this promise as he broke so many others, King Christian of Denmark issued a statement, countersigned by his prime minister, accepting the German occupation, under protest. "Germany has assured us that she has no intention of violating Denmark's independence and territorial integrity," said the king. "Our people will doubtless recognize the necessity for the government's attitude." Apparently they did.

King Haakon of Norway and his people chose to fight back, and the British and French governments promised them full aid. Within forty-eight hours, 50,000 German troops had occupied all of Norway's main ports, 2000 of them landing at Narvik. The British got 13,000 men ashore at Namsos to the north and at Andalsnes to the south. Arguments between the Admiralty, supported by Churchill, and the War Office, supported by a majority of the cabinet, led to delays that permitted the Germans to bring their air superiority to bear and force two evacuations. "Too little and too late," said Lloyd George while Churchill pointed out: "An evacuation is not a victory." On June 10, King Haakon, who had found refuge in Britain, advised his people to end a hopeless resistance.

The Norwegians had the will to fight but not the weapons. The British had the weapons and the will but not the leadership. From 1935 to 1937 Churchill had attacked the leadership of his fellow Conservative, Stanley Baldwin; from 1937 until the outbreak of war in 1939 he had attacked the leadership of Neville Chamberlain, upon whose shoulders Baldwin's mantle had fallen. During these years more and more Conservatives turned against that leadership and looked to Churchill to save their party and their country. He not only served loyally under Chamberlain; he succumbed to some of Chamberlain's delusions. Of Hitler's intervention in Norway Churchill assured the House of Commons: "For myself, I consider Hitler's action in invading Scandinavia is as great a strategic and political blunder as that which was committed by Napoleon in 1807 when he invaded Spain." But he faced up frankly to the subsequent British fiasco at Narvik: "The reason for this serious disadvantage of our not having the initiative is one which cannot readily be removed. It was our failure in the last five years to maintain and regain our parity with Germany in the air. That is an old and long story."

In that story, as Churchill and all his hearers knew, he had always called for spending more money on air defenses, which Baldwin opposed more strongly than Chamberlain and which the Labour party had opposed more strongly than Baldwin. By May 8 feeling ran so strongly against Chamberlain in the House of Commons that only 253 of its 365 Conservative members supported him; several outstanding Conservatives even voted nonconfidence, along with the Labour and Liberal opposition. The same Leopold Amery who assailed Chamberlain's failure to denounce the German invasion of Poland at once now flung at him the same words Oliver Cromwell had addressed to the Long Parliament: "You have sat here too long for any good you have been doing. Depart, I say. Let us have done with you. I say: In the name of God, go!"

Chamberlain's attempt to explain and excuse his record fell flat. His plea to the Labour party to join him in a national government fell flatter. He wanted to have Halifax succeed him, but Halifax belonged to the House of Lords, and Labour rejected him on his record. Only Churchill commanded sufficient support in all parties to win approval as the head of the national government that the bulk of the Parliament and the people demanded. His long record of opposition to Hitler, his longer experience with warfare from Cuba to South Africa, from Asia to Europe, on land and sea, and his lifelong immersion in the world of politics at the highest levels made him the man of the hour. Inside Parliament and out, his personal qualities filled a void. He at once brought outstanding members of all parties into responsible positions and created an inner war cabinet of only five members, "with nothing to do but run the war." Members of the House of Commons cheered when he told them he could offer only "blood, toil, tears and sweat." The zero hour in Hitler's war and the hour of destiny in Churchill's life struck together.

· · ·

The Second World War's first, or phony, phase began and ended with lightning German victories. The annihilation of Poland did not rank with the battle of the Marne, nor did the occupation of Norway rank with the battle of Tannenberg. The First World War opened at a furious tempo with scarcely a lull until the gradual Russian collapse of 1917 and the sudden German surrender of 1918. Hitler, on the other hand, initiated the Second World War with a series of lightning moves, both military and diplomatic, that did not result in open war until his blitz campaign in Poland. Germany's professional soldiers had developed their new high-speed tanks and planes side by side with new offensive tactics designed to shatter from the very start the deadlock that had frozen the Western Front for four years. The announcement of the Nazi-Soviet pact, followed as it was by the destruction and repartition of Poland, offered a display of co-ordinated blitz diplomacy and blitz warfare at a speed that gave both the diplomacy and the warfare a new dimension.

But the release of such forces entailed, sooner or later, their recoil on those who released them. To smash Poland in the fall of 1939 with a single knockout blow compelled Hitler to turn to Stalin and to settle on Stalin's terms. Hitler had always marched forward at accelerating speed to a fast-beating drum. He could no more have postponed his decision to annihilate Poland in the fall of 1939 than he could have postponed his decision to break up Czechoslovakia during the spring of that same year. Stalin got from Hitler the terms he wanted, but Stalin underestimated the speed at which Hitler moved, and no sooner had they partitioned Poland than Stalin found it necessary to wage an embarrassing and unwelcome war against Finland. Whereupon Hitler proceeded to occupy Norway as the prelude to his lightning campaigns against France and the Low Countries.

But the repercussions of the Nazi-Soviet pact extended beyond Poland—and Norway, too. It had improved Stalin's position to resist any attack Hitler might launch on the Soviet Union, but that very improvement inclined Hitler to hasten rather than delay it. Moreover, no matter how long or short a time either Hitler or Stalin felt himself bound by their pact, its very existence made each man the other's major concern. Having instigated the war when and as he did, Hitler had given it an eastern orientation; having signed the pact, Stalin had enlisted for the duration, though on which side nobody could then say for sure.

There was less doubt anywhere about what the German occupation of Norway portended. As long ago as 1938 Hitler had explained to his generals that he planned to bombard and blockade Britain from west European bases extending as far north as Norway, thus eliminating the necessity for large-scale invasion. As recently as May 1939, he had told these same generals not to expect war with Britain and France that year; indeed, he did not even alert them to the impending Polish campaign until August. Stalin may have had his qualms about where Hitler intended to go from Norway, but he did not have to wait long to find out. And nowhere—in Paris, London, or Washington—did the blitz campaign that followed cause greater surprise, shock, and consternation than it did to the men in the Kremlin.

It does not require the wisdom of hindsight to appraise the balance of Europe's military and political forces as the German occupation of Norway ended the so-called phony phase of the Second World War. If the British won the battle of Waterloo on the playing fields of Eton, the French lost the battle of France in the Second World War on the battlefields of the Marne and Verdun in the First. It simply took another generation for the losses that the Germans had inflicted on France in those battles to prove fatal. Between 1870 and 1940 the French Third Republic had experienced what Clemenceau called "the grandeur and misery of victory"—victory over the defeat of 1870, victory over the German victory of that year, and finally defeat at the hands of the defeated Germans. But if the French owed their victories to their own qualities, they also owed their defeats to their own defects. The years between the wars produced no Clemenceau—only a flock of Daladiers, Reynauds, and Bonnets; no Foch—only a Gamelin, who soon made way for the 72-year-old Maxime Weygand, former chief of staff to Foch, and finally the 84-year-old Philippe Pétain, the hero of Verdun.

History, geography, and luck put the British in a better position. During the eighteenth and nineteenth centuries wars and revolutions had ravaged France. Since 1688, on the other hand, Britain had undergone no greater cataclysm than its industrial revolution. The sea that cut Britain off from Europe not only gave protection. British control of so many seaways gave it unique advantages over its European neighbors. Finally, as Bismarck had noted, the most important fact of the nineteenth century was that the British and Americans spoke the same language, an observation that has remained as true as ever during most of the century that has followed. During the First World War Anglo-American sea power saved Britain and sealed Germany's doom. The German occupation of Norway thus served timely notice on both London and Washington that the Second World War would make this cooperation more important than ever. By the same token, Hitler's failure to understand the nature of sea power caused his undoing, as it had caused the Kaiser's. Hitler had not made the Kaiser's mistake of squandering efforts on a navy large enough to antagonize Britain but insufficient to give Germany command of the seas. Hitler made the mistake of misusing the sea and air power he did possess and misunderstanding the special Anglo-American relationship.

Chance intervened in that Britain, under the new leadership of Churchill, and the United States, under the renewed leadership of Roosevelt, found themselves in perfect agreement on the nature of the German challenge to both their countries and the role that sea power must play in meeting that challenge. A better-informed Hitler might have recalled that Churchill, during the First World War, had served as first lord of the Admiralty and that Roosevelt had served as assistant secretary of the United States Navy. But neither Hitler nor anybody else could have foreseen the extraordinary qualities that these two men developed, both separately and together, under the stress of war: Churchill as the incarnation of the eccentric British aristocrat, Roosevelt as the patrician embodiment of the American democratic cause. Each complemented the other in his own eyes and in the eyes of the world. The contrast between the Hitler-Stalin combination could not have been more nearly complete.

IV

Fall of France

·1·

DURING THE NIGHT of May 9–10, 1940, two German armies totaling seventy-five divisions invaded Belgium, Holland, and Luxembourg without any declaration of war. A third army, totaling seventeen divisions, remained stationary along the French Maginot Line. "The hour for the decisive battle for the future of the German nation has come," announced Hitler in the opening sentence of his order of the day to the troops. He concluded: "The battle beginning today will decide the future of the German nation for the next thousand years." Flukes and foresight aided the Germans in that battle; fate and folly worked against the French.

It all began with one of those flukes for which no science of history makes any allowance. Originally, Hitler had approved a revised version of the Schlieffen Plan that the Kaiser followed in 1914 and that called for a mighty German sweep across Belgium, followed by a southward drive toward Paris. But the papers setting forth that strategy fell into French hands on January 20, when a German courier, carrying them in a Belgian plane, had to make a forced landing on French soil and hand them over to French officials. Hitler, however, welcomed the misadventure and turned to one of his younger commanders, General Fritz Erich von Manstein, who had long urged the alternative strategy of aiming the heaviest German blow at the rugged Ardennes Forest in northeast Belgium, just above Sedan, where Napoleon III suffered his decisive defeat at the hands of the Prussians in 1870.

Seventy years later the French assumed that the Ardennes Forest plus the Belgian Army would slow the Germans down. The French Maginot Line ended at the Belgian frontier, and the Belgians refused to extend it, but the French overrated Belgian resistance and underrated German armor, German daring, and German trickery. Moreover, the Dutch had refused to co-ordinate their defenses with the Belgians just as the Belgians had refused to co-ordinate theirs with the French. Both had counted on snarling up the advancing Germans by blowing up dikes and bridges, but the Germans took all the Dutch sluices by bribery or surprise and captured two of the four Belgian bridges across the Meuse by main force. The moment the Germans struck, the Belgians invoked a declaration, signed in April 1937, under which the British and French pledged aid against a German attack.

At 6:45, on the morning of May 10, General Gamelin ordered the French and British armies to advance into Belgium, according to plan. All went well until May 13, when German tanks, preceded by dive bombers, broke through the Ardennes Forest and reached Sedan. The French had assigned two professional divisions to this unfortified sector, fifty miles long. The German army had already swamped the Dutch; German planes had demolished a large, defenseless, and heavily populated section of Rotterdam for the sole purpose of spreading terror through Holland and beyond. The Belgians and their British and French allies had all given ground, but it was the breakthrough at Sedan that sealed the doom of France.

On the same day that the Germans reached Sedan, Queen Wilhelmina and the Dutch government fled to England. The next day, the northern four fifths of Holland, including its three chief cities, surrendered. On May 17, the province of Zeeland, which alone had held out, gave in too. In five days of fighting, the Dutch Army of 400,000 men, which insisted on standing alone, had lost one quarter of its effectives, killed or wounded. Belgium's 600,000 soldiers fared little better, but did permit the bulk of the British expeditionary force of 400,000 men and several French divisions to come to their aid. This suited Manstein, whose surprise route through the Ardennes Forest enabled him to slice across the French lines at Sedan, where the second and ninth French armies met. Thus he cut off the entire British expeditionary force, the entire Belgian army, and parts of two French armies from the remainder of the Allied force on the western front. On May 15 Reynaud telephoned Churchill: "We are defeated. We have lost the battle."

The next day the frantic Reynaud summoned 73-year-old Maxime Weygand to leave his post at Beirut as head of the French command in the Middle East and replace General Gamelin as supreme commander on the western front. Daladier, who had already stepped down as premier, now had to quit as defense minister, too, because Gamelin had been his personal choice. Weygand had served as chief of staff to Foch in the First World War and had organized the successful defense of Warsaw against the Red Army in 1920. Reaching still further back and acting on the dubious advice of his ambitious mistress, Hélène de Portes, Reynaud also invited 84-year-old Marshal Pétain to become vice premier. The general, the premier, and the mistress all saw in Pétain a valuable figurehead.

Before 1914, Pétain had held the heretical view that the advantage no longer lay with the attacker but with the defense. Temperament as well as logic dictated this preference, for Pétain had always inclined toward pessimism and caution. He often differed with the British, always disagreed with Foch, but became a national hero because of his defense of Verdun. Weygand, as long as his wartime chief lived, supported Foch against Pétain, but when Foch died in 1929, Weygand transferred his allegiance and in 1934 advised Pétain not to continue as war minister in the cabinet of Pierre Flandin: "You represent a reserve strength. Perhaps some day you will be the Hindenburg of France. You mustn't risk your prestige in Parliament." Already, Weygand saw the French Third Republic going the way of Germany's Weimar Republic. Reynaud, on the other hand, still played both sides of the street. On the same day he took Pétain into his cabinet he also promoted the fifty-year-old Colonel Charles de Gaulle—the one French tank commander to give the Germans any trouble—to the rank of two-star general and the post of undersecretary of defense.

In breaking through the Ardennes Forest and bypassing the Maginot Line, the Germans blitzed France as they had blitzed Poland. It then took Weygand a week to fly from his Beirut headquarters to General Headquarters at Paris. On May 19, he canceled Gamelin's last order of the day, then visited the crumbling front, finally installing himself at Paris on May 22, when he reinstated the order of the day he had canceled three days earlier. During those three days the French armies had received no orders; the British troops had received none in four, by which time German infantrymen were pouring through the holes their tanks had torn in the Allied lines. On May 25, French general headquarters announced that "it had not been possible to establish a continuous line." On the same day Belgium's young King Leopold III, whose father, King Albert, had refused to capitulate to the Germans in 1914, told members of the Belgian cabinet that he planned to surrender unconditionally, even if they withheld their consent. The ministers protested, but on May 28 Leopold, as commander in chief, ordered his soldiers to cease their resistance and lay down their arms. Reynaud at once denounced the King's action; Churchill waited a week before doing the same.

The history of the German invasion of Belgium in 1914 had not reversed itself; neither had the history of the German invasion of Poland in 1939 repeated itself. Hitler's 1940 victories in the west far surpassed the Kaiser's victories of 1914. They also far surpassed the scope of the 1939 Polish campaign. But Hitler had not swept the board as clean in France and the Low Countries as he had in Poland. For one thing, there was more to sweep in France; for another, the German blitz against France and the Low Countries overran so much territory in so short a time that the scope and speed of the victories became self-defeating.

Credit for the strategy that led to the German breakthrough at Sedan belongs to General Fritz Erich von Manstein. Credit for the tactical exploitation of that breakthrough belongs to General Heinz Guderian, who had studied and developed tank warfare since 1918. During the first seventeen days of the fighting, Guderian's ten tank divisions advanced four hundred miles, winding up on the English Channel, outside Dunkirk, the last Channel port still in Allied hands. Hitler, at this point, regarding the battle of Flanders as all but won and the battle of France still to be fought, ordered Guderian's ten divisions to stop in their tracks, where they remained for two days while the British established a well-defended escape corridor leading to Dunkirk. Between May 27 and June 4, more than a thousand ships of all kinds transported 338,000 troops—two thirds of them British—from Dunkirk and the surrounding beaches across the Channel to Britain. More than 30,000 British troops and all the equipment of the whole expedition fell into German hands.

During this time the German generals not only disagreed among themselves; Guderian and most of his colleagues provoked Hitler into one of his temper tantrums as they vainly protested his order to stop just short of Dunkirk. The speed and scope of the blitz campaign staggered Hitler as much as it staggered his enemies. He could not believe that the French would be unable to regroup their forces and fight another battle of the Marne as Joffre had done in 1914. But Guderian, having witnessed the disintegration that his advancing tanks spread through the land, saw more clearly than Hitler how great a victory they had won . . . and how much greater a quick exploitation of their gains could have made it. But General Gerd von Rundstedt, the supreme commander, sensed and even shared some of Hitler's caution; nor could Rundstedt share the enthusiasm of the younger and more impetuous Guderian. Years later, in his memoirs, Guderian also noted: "Hitler and above all Goering believed German air superiority to be strong enough to prevent evacuation of British forces by sea."

In any event, heavy fog kept the German air force grounded for several days and when the fog began to lift, British planes from nearby home bases knocked the Germans out of the sky at the rate of three to one as the evacuation proceeded. Thus, the German drive across Flanders ended, as it began, with a fluke. Hitler had approved the Manstein strategy only after the details of an alternate strategy fell, by accident, into French hands. In like manner, a series of accidents, culminating in a stretch of bad weather, made possible the British evacuation of Dunkirk. If the Germans made the most of the first fluke, the British made a miracle of the second.

·2·

ON JUNE 5, 1940, the day after the Dunkirk evacuation ended, Churchill closed his report to the House of Commons with the words: "We shall defend our island whatever the cost may be; we shall fight on the beaches, we shall fight on the landing grounds, we shall fight in the fields, and in the streets, we shall fight in the hills; we shall never surrender and even if, which I do not for a moment believe, this island or a large part of it were subjugated and starving, then our empire beyond the seas, armed and guarded by the British fleet, will carry on the struggle until in God's good time the New World, with all its power and might, sets forth to the liberation of the Old." The French, no less than the Germans, mistook Churchill's speech for an oratorical tour de force. Most of his compatriots and many Americans, on the other hand, recognized it for what it was: a statement of the case for Anglo-American sea power in terms of contemporary oratory.

Of the British mood at the time, Churchill wrote afterward: "There was a white glow, overpowering, sublime, which ran through our island from end to end." A glow ran through France, too, but there was nothing sublime about it. Many Frenchmen directed their rage against the British for having withheld their heavily armed, high-speed fighter planes for their own defense instead of expending them in the defense of France. Events soon vindicated the British. It took somewhat longer for events to vindicate those Frenchmen who directed their rage against their own leaders. But it was the Germans, from the unbalanced Hitler to the uninspired Rundstedt, who made the gravest miscalculations—not so much because they failed to understand what Churchill was driving at as because they did not understand the situation in which their own leadership had landed them.

Because the Manstein-Guderian blitz had finished off France in a matter of weeks instead of the several months that Hitler and his generals had expected it to take, the Germans found themselves bogged down in a victory for which they had made no preparation. Gamelin had exhausted his reserves even before Weygand replaced him. By June 5, 125 German divisions had crossed the Somme where 65 French divisions and two British divisions opposed them. In another five days, the Germans had advanced almost 100 miles to within 35 miles of Paris. For the first time, their attack began with the classical artillery barrage, followed by masses of infantry. The tanks brought up the rear, making their way through the advancing foot soldiers and then shattering the French front at will.

On that same day—June 10, 1940—Mussolini announced that Italy had entered the war "against the plutocratic and reactionary democracies who had always blocked the march and frequently plotted against the existence of the Italian people." That evening Roosevelt interpolated into a prepared speech on foreign policy: "The hand that held the dagger has struck it into the back of its neighbor." But the hand proved unsteady, the dagger ineffective. Six French divisions stopped thirty-two Italian divisions that moved through the Alpine passes toward the Riviera coast. On June 11 Churchill flew to French general headquarters in the province of Touraine, where he conferred with Reynaud, Weygand, and Pétain. Reynaud had cabled Roosevelt, pleading for more aid and pledging, "We will fight before Paris, we will fight behind Paris; in order to carry on, we will shut ourselves up in one of our provinces and, if we are driven out, we will take our stand to keep up the fight in North Africa or even in our possessions across the Atlantic." Churchill reminded Pétain of Clemenceau's words, during the darkest days of 1918: "I will fight in front of Paris, in Paris, behind Paris." But Pétain pointed out that even in those dark days France had sixty divisions in reserve, Britain had sixty in the front line. On June 11, 1940, France had no reserves, Britain nothing in the front lines.

Weygand then urged the British to throw in all twenty-five of their remaining fighter-plane squadrons: "Here is the decisive point. Now is the decisive moment." Air Marshal Sir Hugh Dowding, who had accompanied Churchill, replied: "This is not the decisive point, and this is not the decisive moment. That moment will come when Hitler hurls his Luftwaffe against Great Britain. If we can keep command of the air and if we can keep the seas open, we can win it all back for you." The next morning Weygand told a meeting of the French cabinet: "As a soldier, it breaks my heart to say it, but we can no longer put off asking for an armistice." Pétain, in the background, nodded agreement.

On June 12 German troops crossed the Marne. The next day the French decided not to defend Paris. On June 14 the Germans moved in. Their government did not want to bomb Paris any more than the French wanted to defend it. But the bulk of the French cabinet wanted to establish a "redoubt" in Brittany and organize a separate government that would move to North Africa with the fleet. But Weygand and Pétain counseled surrender. So did Camille Chautemps, who had served the Third Republic in eighteen cabinets and headed four of them. "You are no longer strong enough," he warned Reynaud, "to put yourself in opposition to those two popular soldiers." At Churchill's suggestion Reynaud cabled two appeals to Roosevelt. In the first, he asked for "clouds of planes," which the Americans did not possess. In the second he warned: "I must tell you at this hour, as grave in our history as in yours, that if you cannot give France in the hours to come the certainty that the United States will come into the war in a very short time, the fate of our world will change. Then you will see France go under like a drowning man and disappear after having cast a look at the land of liberty from which she expected salvation." To which Roosevelt replied that only the Congress had the power to declare war.

From London came an even more desperate proposal to keep France in the fighting. Foreign Secretary Halifax and Sir Robert Vansittart, permanent undersecretary of state for foreign affairs, had worked out with Charles Corbin, the French ambassador to London, and General Charles de Gaulle, the newly appointed undersecretary of defense for France, a proposed declaration of Franco-British Union, calling for joint organs of defense and common foreign, financial, and economic policies. "Every citizen of France will immediately enjoy citizenship of Great Britain; every British subject will become a citizen of France." Churchill described his own, initial response to the. plan as "unfavorable," but felt they must not let themselves be accused of lacking imagination: "Some dramatic announcement is clearly necessary to keep the French going." Reynaud welcomed it. Pétain called it "union with a corpse." Weygand predicted: "In three weeks England will have her neck wrung like a chicken." ("Some chicken; some neck," commented Churchill later.) But the bulk of the French cabinet supported the two professional soldiers, and Reynaud resigned as premier on June 16, saying he preferred to collaborate with his allies rather than with his enemies.

The worldly-wise Chautemps had gone to the heart of the matter when he warned Reynaud not to oppose "two popular soldiers." It was not that the war had enhanced the prestige of Pétain or Weygand; rather had it destroyed the prestige of Daladier and Reynaud, the two civilian heads of the two wartime governments of France. As soon as Reynaud resigned, Pétain therefore organized a new government with Chautemps as vice premier, Weygand as Minister of Defense, and Admiral Jean Louis Darlan as Minister of Marine. Pierre Laval wanted the post of foreign minister, but Weygand and Darlan refused to serve with him. The defeatist Paul Baudouin, minister of state under Reynaud, got the job.

·3·

One month of blitz warfare had given Germany military, political, and economic control of Europe from the Atlantic Ocean to the western borders of the former Russian Empire. But the French army had disintegrated so rapidly and so completely that Pétain found himself still in possession of two trump cards: the French navy and the French overseas empire which that navy protected. The Germans had not yet got their hands on all the French warships in all the French ports—not to mention the bulk of the French navy which lay scattered from North Africa and the Levant to southeastern Asia and the Caribbean. That navy posed no immediate threat to the German Wehrmacht, which, in its turn, posed no immediate threat to the French overseas empire. But that balance could not last long. A time might come when the Anglo-Americans could use some of the French war vessels and some of the French possessions overseas—especially in North Africa—to mount offensives against Hitler's Europe. Moreover, a time might also come, even sooner, when Hitler could mount an invasion of North Africa before the Anglo-Americans could use French ships and French bases to attack him.

It remained, however, for Mussolini to temper catastrophe with an interlude of comic opera. On June 10, when everything seemed to be going Hitler's way, Mussolini informed him and the world that he had joined the fray and awaited instructions as to where in France the Italian Army could help the Wehrmacht most. Two days later Germany's ambassador to Rome, Hans Georg von Mackensen, politely informed him that Hitler rejected any kind of Italian participation in the battle of France. But on June 11, British planes had already bombed Turin and on June 14 a French naval squadron launched a wholly successful aero-naval attack on Genoa. The next day Mussolini ordered Marshal Badoglio to attack the French frontier on June 18. Badoglio replied that he would need twenty-five days to gear his forces to take the offensive and that by that time French resistance would be at an end. "*Signor maresciallo*," retorted Mussolini, "as chief of the general staff you are entitled to advise me on military topics, but not on political topics. Responsibility for those rests entirely with me. If we merely look on while France collapses, we shall have no right to demand our share of the booty. If I do not demand Savoy, which is French, I must have Nice, Corsica, and Tunisia."

Having told off Badoglio, Mussolini telegraphed Hitler: "I need hardly tell you that I will conduct the war with vigor. With regard to the exchange of troops, in token of our comradeship, I suggest that you send me fifty antiaircraft batteries with their crews and ammunition." Later, Mussolini suggested that Italian troops temporarily occupy all of France east of the Rhone and that Italy at once come into permanent possession of Corsica, Tunisia, and French Somaliland. He urged Hitler to occupy all strategic points in France plus the three North African naval bases at Algiers, Oran, and Casablanca and to demand the immediate surrender of the whole French navy and air force. Hitler had different ideas. "It would not be well," he explained to Mussolini, "to demand purely and simply that the French surrender their fleet. France will not agree to that, and against the very slight probability that the French may sink their fleet, there would be a much greater probability that they would send it to join the British fleet."

The German armistice proposals did not, therefore, demand that the French fleet surrender. They provided only that "All French warships outside France are to be recalled to France, with the exception of that portion of the French fleet which shall be designated to represent French interests in the French colonial empire." The Germans demanded no concessions in French North Africa or any other part of the French Empire. They called for German occupation of about three fifths of France, including the northern provinces, a strip of the Atlantic coast, a strip along the Swiss border, and Paris, to which the French government would be given access. This government would continue to function in the unoccupied two fifths of metropolitan France. There was no mention of Alsace-Lorraine.

It took Hitler a few days to formulate these terms; the Pétain Government at Bordeaux accepted them on June 22. Churchill read them "with grief and amazement." Cordell Hull expressed the fear that France had handed Germany "a cocked gun to shoot at us." But if Pétain had compromised the honor of France and jeopardized the security of Britain and the United States, Hitler made no move in the direction of North Africa. Subsequently, Darlan and Laval justified their endorsement of the armistice terms by arguing that Hitler should have moved into North Africa at once. But what with and to what purpose? He not only lacked the necessary sea and air power. He could not then have made the use he did of Pétain. By conceding just enough authority to Pétain, Darlan, Laval, and company, Hitler had forestalled any rival French leaders from attempting to organize a resistance movement that would have compelled the Germans to spread their limited manpower too thin.

Just as the British decision to evacuate Dunkirk compelled Churchill to base all his hopes for British survival on the intervention of the United States, so the French decision to accept the German armistice terms forced Pétain to come to terms with Hitler's Europe. Perhaps neither Churchill nor Pétain had much choice in the matter. Perhaps Hitler made both their choices for them when he halted Guderian's drive toward Dunkirk and ordered the Wehrmacht to throw all its weight against the retreating French. Certainly the miracle of Dunkirk united the British people behind Churchill, who, in his turn, rose to the occasion with the kind of leadership they craved. A dozen Clemenceaus could not have saved France. The same events that had made Churchill the man of the hour in Britain made Pétain the man of the hour in France. But Pétain's hour did not last so long as Churchill's.

Neither Churchill nor Pétain created the situation in which they found themselves. That was entirely of Hitler's making. As a political organizer and revolutionary demagogue he had proved a genius. But the role of war lord which his policies required him to assume called for the reverse of those qualities which had brought him so far: a steadfast rather than a mercurial temperament, the ability to delegate rather than monopolize authority, a passion for practical detail rather than a weakness for uninhibited soliloquy. Within the space of six weeks, during the spring of 1940, the German blitz of France and the Low Countries resulted in the greatest and most rapid military victory in Europe's history. The occupation of Norway, followed by the Wehrmacht's sweep across Belgium, Holland, Luxembourg, and more than half of France, not only gave Germany control of Europe's Atlantic coastline from the North Cape to the bay of Biscay. It left French Indo-China and the Dutch East Indies open to attack by Hitler's Japanese associates. Nor did the repercussions end there. How much longer could occupied France and defeated Belgium rule the richest regions of equatorial Africa? How much longer could beleaguered Britain hold India? At what point would the United States see its vital interests threatened?

To Hitler these questions barely existed as compared to the sudden crisis that threatened his relations with the Soviet Union. On June 6, 1940, four days before Mussolini stumbled to the aid of the victorious Hitler, the Moscow radio warned: "The Soviet government has made it unequivocally clear to Italy that it will not remain passive in the face of a threat to the Balkans." Mussolini at that time posed no threat to the Balkans, as Hitler knew even better than Stalin did. But Italian troops had occupied Albania—Yugoslavia's next-door neighbor—in 1939, and Mussolini and Hitler had both backed the professional assassin, Ante Pavelić, in his subsequent efforts to detach an independent kingdom of Croatia from the rest of Yugoslavia. At the time France fell, neither Mussolini nor Stalin gave top priority to the Balkans. Mussolini had his eyes on Corsica, Nice, and North Africa; Stalin had his eyes on the Baltic states and Romania. But Radio Moscow's warning to Mussolini concerning the Balkans served, among other things, to remind Hitler not to take the Soviet Union for granted. After the words came the actions.

On June 15, Red Army troops occupied Lithuania while the Soviet government charged the Lithuanian government with conspiring against it with Estonia and Latvia. The next day Soviet troops occupied those two countries as well. New governments took office in all three Baltic states, dissolved the existing parliaments, and called for new elections in July, when only the names of Communist candidates appeared on the ballots. None of this violated the letter of the Nazi-Soviet pact—and the less said about its spirit the better. Eleven days later, on June 26, Molotov handed the Romanian minister to Moscow an ultimatum demanding that Romania cede the provinces of Bessarabia and Northern Bukovina within three days. Romania had annexed the former Russian province of Bukovina after the First World War, and the Nazi-Soviet pact had assigned it to the Soviet sphere of influence. On the other hand, the Russian Empire had never included Northern Bukovina, nor did it figure in the Nazi-Soviet pact. But the Soviet ultimatum demanded it anyway on the ground that it belonged with the rest of the Ukraine as part of the Soviet Union.

The Romanian government appealed to both Hitler and Mussolini, but they had their hands full in France. The Italians had no troops near Romania, the Germans only a few. Romania therefore capitulated to Moscow and two of its provinces went the way of the three Baltic states. The Soviet Union thus acquired ten million new inhabitants on top of the thirteen million already gathered in from Poland, and neither Hitler nor Mussolini could do a thing about it. At any rate, not in June 1940.

·4·

ON JUNE 18—the day Pétain sought armistice terms from Hitler—two memorable speeches, both delivered in London, put the new situation in perspective. Winston Churchill, speaking before the House of Commons, put it in universal terms: "What General Weygand called the battle of France is over. I expect that the battle of Britain is about to begin. Upon this battle depends the survival of Christian civilization. Upon it depends our own British life and the long continuity of our institutions and our Empire. The whole fury and might of the enemy must very soon be turned on us. Hitler knows that he will have to break us in this island or lose the war. If we can stand up to him, all Europe may be free and the life of the world may move forward into broad, sunlit uplands. But if we fail, then the whole world, including the United States, including all that we have known and cared for, will sink into the abyss of a new Dark Age, made more sinister, and perhaps more protracted, by the lights of perverted science. Let us therefore brace ourselves to our duties, and so bear ourselves that, if the British Empire and its Commonwealth last for a thousand years, men will still say, 'This was their finest hour.' "

Later that same day, with Churchill's blessing, General Charles de Gaulle stepped before a microphone with the text of a broadcast, prepared to be beamed to France as soon as the anticipated news of Pétain's request for an armistice became known. De Gaulle, like Churchill, depicted the war as a worldwide struggle, but he interpreted it chiefly in French and even personal terms. "The cause of France," he said, "is not lost. The very factors that brought about our defeat may one day lead us to victory." He continued: "The war is not limited to our unfortunate country. The outcome of the struggle has not been decided by the Battle of France. This is a world war. Mistakes have been made, there have been delays and untold suffering, but the fact remains that there still exists in the world everything we need to crush our enemies some day. Today we are crushed by the sheer weight of mechanized force hurled against us, but we still look to a future in which even greater mechanized force will bring us victory. The destiny of the world is at stake.

"I, General de Gaulle, now in London, call on all French officers and men who are at present on British soil, or may be in the future, with or without arms, I call on all engineers and skilled workmen from the armament factories who are at present on British soil, or may be in the future, to get in touch with me. Whatever happens, the flame of French resistance must not and shall not die. France has lost a battle. But France has not lost the war."

Hitler owed his victories to the new technology of war to which General de Gaulle referred. But Hitler had no monopoly on this technology; still less did he have the power to control the victories he had already won. Indeed, the combination of blitz diplomacy and blitz warfare released by Hitler had already destroyed the very foundations of the New Order he had planned for Europe. During the fall of 1939, the Nazi-Soviet pact enabled him to destroy the Polish nation and enslave the Polish people. This neither advanced nor retarded his plans for the rest of Europe but did enable Stalin to strengthen the Soviet Union's position in eastern Europe and make it less vulnerable to German attack. Then, during the spring of 1940, the German blitz campaign in western Europe enabled Stalin to strengthen the Soviet position still further by incorporating the three Baltic states and two Romanian provinces. Stalin did not make these moves with aggressive intent. He made them only to make the Soviet Union better able to defend itself against the eventual and inevitable German attack. Stalin had no illusions about Hitler's intentions. It was Hitler's timing that he misjudged—as who did not?

Who had any inkling when Churchill and de Gaulle spoke as they did from Paris that they spoke from strength? Who had any inkling that it was Hitler who spoke and acted from an indecision born of weakness? Human nature and human history being what they are, great men and great moments often arrive when least expected. Churchill arose in a Britain that had just been ousted from Europe for the first time in centuries; de Gaulle emerged from a France that had just suffered a far more complete and humiliating defeat.

In Churchill's case, he set an example that stirred immediate and overwhelming popular support. In de Gaulle's case, he raised a standard to which more and more of his compatriots later rallied. There was no turning of the other cheek, no attempting to out-Hitler Hitler. Each man drew exclusively on his own resources and traditions, assuming that in speaking for himself he spoke for all.

It was the French request for German armistice terms that set the world stage for General de Gaulle's first appearance upon it. Like Churchill, who sponsored his debut, de Gaulle had attended military school—St. Cyr, the French equivalent of Churchill's Sandhurst. But Churchill had made politics, not soldiering, his profession. There he consistently defied all rules, switching first from Conservative to Liberal, then back to Conservative again and finally into solitary rebellion. His sponsorship of the ill-fated Dardanelles expedition during the First World War almost ended his political career. For all his military training and experience, war itself had brought him ill luck. During the 1920's and 1930's, Churchill excelled as a journalist, historian, and biographer. Ever the political maverick, he made a niche for himself as the outstanding English aristocrat-eccentric of his time.

De Gaulle, sixteen years Churchill's junior, made a niche for himself during the years between the wars as a military maverick of exceptional literary talent. As a prisoner of war in Germany he had mastered the German language; Seeckt and Guderian read, admired, and borrowed from his book, *Vers l'armée de métier*, published in 1934 and translated into English in 1940 as *The Army of the Future*. De Gaulle had already published two essays, the first of which, *Le fil de l'épée*, he dedicated to his first colonel—Pétain. Like Pétain, de Gaulle viewed the Third French Republic with a cold eye, but he rejected Pétain's defensive strategic concepts, and the two men drifted apart. Not until after the Second World War did de Gaulle spell out his political philosophy, the essence of which appears in the opening paragraph of his *War Memoirs:*

"All my life I have thought of France in a certain way. This is inspired by sentiment as much as by reason. The emotional side of me tends to imagine France, like the princess in the fairy stories or the Madonna in the frescoes, as dedicated to an exalted and exceptional destiny. Instinctively I have the feeling that Providence has created her either for complete successes or for exemplary misfortunes. If, in spite of this, mediocrity shows in her acts and deeds, it strikes me as an absurd anomaly, to be imputed to the faults of Frenchmen, not to the genius of the land. But the positive side of my mind also assures me that France is not really herself unless in the front rank; that only vast enterprises are capable of counterbalancing the ferments of dispersal which are inherent in her people; that our country, as it is, surrounded by the others, as they are, must aim high and hold itself straight, on pain of mortal danger. In short, to my mind, France cannot be France without greatness."

The day before de Gaulle delivered his historic radio appeal he had telegraphed his superiors at Bordeaux, offering to continue his efforts to procure more war equipment from the United States. In reply he received orders to return home forthwith. He not only ignored the summons; on June 20, he urged General Weygand to lead a resistance movement and offered to place himself under Weygand's orders. On June 30, the French embassy at London ordered de Gaulle to surrender himself in Toulouse for trial by the Conseil de Guerre. When he failed to appear he was sentenced first to a month in prison and later, on Weygand's demand, to death. Nevertheless, Pétain's collaborationist government at Vichy and de Gaulle's Free French movement, as it later called itself, maintained contacts through the underlings of their irreconcilable leaders. Thus the Gaullists in London kept tabs on the Pétainists in France, who, in their turn, kept tabs on the Gaullists in Britain. It did not take the British long to find out that more top-secret information leaked from London to Vichy than in the other direction, but it did not help their relations with de Gaulle when they withheld their top secrets from him. In war as in peace, in defeat as in victory, the old French saying about the more things change the more they stay the same held true. Frenchmen still squabbled with Frenchmen and still distrusted perfidious Albion as much as honest John Bull distrusted fickle Marianne.

·5·

WHILE THE CORNERED CHURCHILL breathed defiance and the exiled de Gaulle breathed confidence, the conquering Hitler whined that a negotiated settlement with Britain would bring peace. Through the Papal Nuncio at the Swiss capital of Bern he therefore got word to London that he "was prepared to make peace and promise to respect the integrity of the British Empire if Britain would return Germany's former colonies and recognize German predominance in Europe." On June 30, he assured his generals, with a straight face, that "England should be inclined to make peace when she learns she can get it now at relatively little cost." But when Churchill heard the terms from Foreign Secretary Halifax, through whom they had been transmitted, he remarked: "I hope it will be made clear to the Nuncio that we do not desire any inquiries as to terms of peace with Hitler and that all our agents are strictly forbidden to entertain such suggestions."

Nevertheless, for a full month after the fall of France Hitler continued to hope from Britain for the sign that never came. On July 13 he told his commanders that he did not wish to destroy the British Empire: "This would not be to the advantage of Germany. German blood would be shed to accomplish something that would benefit only Japan, the United States, and others." He raged against "Britain's persistent unwillingness to make peace" and blamed Stalin for "flirting with Britain to keep her in the war." In seizing twice as much of Romania as the Nazi-Soviet pact permitted him to occupy, Stalin had struck at Hitler where it hurt most. For Hitler still assumed that his agreement with Stalin guaranteed him against the two-front war into which the Kaiser had led Germany in 1914. In August of that year, the Russian invasion of East Prussia diverted enough German troops from the Western Front to save Paris. Had Stalin's invasion of Romania saved London in 1940? Hardly. But Hitler knew a straw in the east wind when he saw one. Indeed, his obsession with the east and the Soviet Union distracted him from the greater giant he had aroused in the west.

Churchill, on the other hand, had always regarded Roosevelt's America as his ace in the hole. He had never given up the hope that Hitler and Stalin might have a falling-out some day, but he had never lost faith that, under Roosevelt's leadership, the New World would eventually come to the rescue of the Old. The first glimmer of light at the end of the tunnel appeared in late May after the German breakthrough at Sedan but before the final rout of the French armies. For it was then that 71-year-old William Allen White, Republican editor of the Emporia *Gazette* in Kansas, launched the Committee to Defend America by Aiding the Allies. "I never did anything the President didn't ask for, and I always conferred with him on our program," declared Mr. White. By July, the committee had set up three hundred branches all over the United States; it secured radio time for speakers, organized letter-writing campaigns, and produced a book, *Defense of America,* by businessmen, professional people, political figures, and leaders in all walks of life who believed that the freedom and security of the United States depended on Britain's survival and that aid to Britain with methods short of war offered the best guarantee of that survival.

For one thing, it had taken Hitler only six weeks to win such a victory on the Western Front as neither side had been able to win during the more than four years the First World War had lasted. For another thing, that war had lasted almost three years before any American troops appeared on the Western Front, whereas by July 1940 that front had ceased to exist and the regular United States Army numbered less than 300,000 men — half the size of Belgium's and 100,000 less than the Netherlands'. But the United States had a navy second to none, in which President Roosevelt had always taken special pride. Even as France was falling he therefore sanctioned the shipment, to beleaguered Britain, of an assortment of war surplus equipment, including half a million rifles of World War I vintage, 80,000 machine guns, thirty million rounds of ammunition, nine hundred 75-millimeter guns, and a million shells.

With the best will in the world, Roosevelt could not have done more for Britain at this time. With the worst will in the world, Hitler could not do to Britain what he had just done to France. He therefore had no choice but to mount a series of peace offensives—first, discreetly, through the Papal Nuncio in Bern, then openly in his own behalf. Finally, on July 16, he issued War Directive Number 19, ordering all the services to draw up plans, to be known as "Operation Sea Lion," for landings on the English coast, setting September 15 as the date on which a fleet of improvised barges should begin ferrying his invasion army, which never totaled one third of its estimated strength of 250,000 men, across the English Channel. On the day Hitler issued his directive the Royal Navy still enjoyed uncontested control of the seas around the British Isles, and the Luftwaffe had only begun to contest the Royal Air Force's control of the air. Under these circumstances, Operation Sea Lion posed no threat to the British Isles, and if Hitler did not know it, Churchill most certainly did.

Nevertheless, Hitler and Goebbels still believed their own propaganda to such a point that they organized a victory session of the Reichstag on July 19, when Hitler brought his long-prepared victory speech to a climax by repeating his peace offer of the previous month. Three days after having ordered full speed ahead on Operation Sea Lion, he closed his climactic victory speech on this anticlimactic note:

"Mr. Churchill ought perhaps for once to believe me when I prophesy that a great empire will be destroyed—an empire that it was never my intention to destroy or even to harm. I do, however, realize that this struggle, if it continues, can end only in the annihilation of one or the other of the two adversaries. Mr. Churchill may believe that this will be Germany. I know it will be different. In this hour I feel it my duty before my conscience to appeal once more to reason and to common sense in Britain as much as elsewhere. I consider myself in a position to make this appeal, since I am not the vanquished begging for favors,but the victor, speaking in the name of reason. I see no reason why this war must go on."

. . .

It took the fall of France to bring home to Hitler the full scope and significance of the program of eastward expansion to which he had committed himself since the end of 1937. In November of that year, his staff had drawn up for him a "testament," setting forth his conviction that Germany's expanding population could maintain its high living standards only by developing an expanded, self-sufficient living space at the expense of the more thinly settled nearby areas of eastern Europe. As Hitler saw it, "The history of all times—Roman Empire, British Empire—has proved that every space expansion can be effected only by breaking resistance and taking risks." A version of this testament, known as the "Hossbach Memorandum," presently fell into the hands of General Ludwig Beck, then chief of the German General Staff, who at once submitted a countermemorandum in behalf of that body, warning Hitler that the Hossbach program could not but lead to a worldwide war that would end in Germany's ruin. But Hitler had already received Lord Halifax, Chamberlain's second in command, who gave him the impression that the British government would grant him a free hand in eastern Europe. In February 1938, shortly after the resignation of Foreign Secretary Eden, Ambassador Sir Nevile Henderson sought a confidential talk with Hitler to express sympathy for Hitler's desire for "changes in Europe" and to assure him that the Chamberlain government "had a keen sense of reality."

Hitler not only ignored General Beck's subsequent resignation as chief of the general staff; he also set in motion the plans that led, successively, to the annexation of Austria, the breakup of Czechoslovakia, the Nazi-Soviet pact, the invasion of Poland, the occupation of Norway and Denmark, the invasion of France and the Low Countries, and the preparations for the battle of Britain. But Hitler continued to assume that he could have all this and a deal with Britain, too—a deal that would give him the free hand in the east that he had sought from the start. That he had set in motion the general war and the ruination of Germany, predicted by Beck, barely occurred to him. Nor did the German General Staff see how it could stop him in mid-course.

It is one thing to blame the German generals for having done nothing to prevent Hitler from taking over their country in the first place and then having failed to stop him from taking the course that he had spelled out for their benefit in the Hossbach Memorandum. But it is something else again to hold Chamberlain, Halifax, and Henderson equally responsible with Hitler for the war that followed. The origins of that war date back to 1918 and 1919 when the victorious Allies failed, on the one hand, to make a peace of reconciliation or, on the other, to impose a Carthaginian peace on the defeated Germans. The First World War had left enough unfinished business to invite some kind of German effort to reverse the verdict of Versailles.

The late Sir Basil Liddell Hart—Britain's foremost military historian—in his one-volume *History of the Second World War* endorses Churchill's description of that conflict as "the unnecessary war." But how "necessary" was the First World War—or any other? Necessity knows no law. A point arises—in space, in time, in both—when war becomes "inevitable," conflict "irrepressible." Hitler, the chief instigator of the Second World War, was also the last to recognize the scope and significance of what he had started. The Liddell Hart account of the battle of France attaches considerable importance to statements made during and after the war by Field Marshal Gerd von Rundstedt, by General Günther Blumentritt, his operations officer, and by other members of the German General Staff to the effect that, in June and July 1940, Hitler desperately wanted to make peace with Britain on more favorable terms than those he outlined publicly and privately at the time. In a book of postwar interviews with leading German commanders, published in 1951 under the title *The Other Side of the Hill,* Sir Basil quotes Blumentritt's account of Hitler, on the eve of the Dunkirk evacuation, "speaking with admiration of the British Empire, of the necessity for its existence, and of the civilization Britain had brought into the world." Hitler paid tribute to both the British Empire and the Roman Catholic Church as "essential elements of stability in the world," and showed willingness not to press his claims for the return of Germany's former African colonies on the sole condition that Britain "acknowledge Germany's position on the Continent."

Sir Basil, in his own *History of the Second World War,* also recalls that Blumentritt kept harking back to the Dunkirk evacuation when Hitler ordered Guderian's tanks to halt their operations for two days while the British got their troops—but not their equipment—safely away. According to Liddell Hart, Blumentritt "felt that the 'halt' had been called for more than military reasons and that it was part of a political scheme to make peace easier to reach. If the B.E.F. [British Expeditionary Force] had been captured at Dunkirk, the British might have felt that their honor had suffered a stain which they must wipe out. By letting it escape, Hitler hoped to conciliate them." It need scarcely be added that by this time, Churchill, his government, and the bulk of the British Parliament and the British people were in no mood to "acknowledge Germany's position on the Continent." Nor, for that matter, had any such mood existed in Britain at the time of the Munich conference when it was Chamberlain, not Churchill, who spoke for the British people. De Gaulle, in his radio broadcast to the French people, put his finger on what had happened. With the fall of France, the war had become worldwide. Just as it had taken this shock to confirm Churchill's title to lead his people through the greatest crisis in their history, so that same shock sounded Hitler's doom. His program of eastward expansion had already caused Stalin to take protective measures in the Baltic states and Romania. The battle of Britain had begun to widen into the battle of the Atlantic from which the United States could not long remain aloof. And the defeats that the British, French, and Dutch had suffered at German hands on the European mainland could not but weaken the white man's empire in southeastern Asia to the benefit of Japan.

V

The Battle of Britain

·1·

THE SPEED of the French collapse inspired Churchill to instant action and numbed Hitler into immobility. The Royal Air Force still possessed the great bulk of its unexcelled fighter planes, equipment, and personnel. The Royal Navy still controlled the seas around the British Isles, and far beyond. There, Churchill at once took the offensive. The Franco-German armistice terms had left the French navy in French hands. Some of its vessels lay in British ports, some lay under the guns of British ships at Alexandria, some lay at Toulon on the Riviera, one aircraft carrier and two light cruisers lay at Martinique in the Caribbean. The new Algerian base at Mers-el-Kebir, near Oran, harbored two battleships and several light cruisers and destroyers. One battleship lay at the West African port of Dakar. It was the ships at Mers-el-Kabir and Dakar that worried the British and sent Churchill into action.

On the morning of July 3 the British took over all French naval vessels in all British ports. The British commander in the Mediterranean—acting on instructions from London—had already offered the French commander of the vessels at Mers-el-Kebir and Dakar three choices: to sail with Britain against the Axis, to sail with reduced crews to British, American, or Caribbean ports, or to sink all his vessels within six hours. The French commander having refused all three choices, the British opened fire. Their superior numbers gave them almost complete success. One French cruiser escaped to Toulon in battered condition. All other large French war vessels at Mers-el-Kebir were sunk, beached, or disabled with the loss of more than a thousand lives. Two days later the French Government at Vichy broke off relations with London.

Pétain and Weygand rejected the advice of Laval, who demanded a declaration of war.

Roosevelt understood at once the action Churchill had ordered at Mers-el-Kebir and welcomed it as a service to the United States in that it prevented a further, sudden addition to Germany's growing threat to the Atlantic sea-lanes. In May, German planes, submarines, and surface vessels had sunk 75,000 tons of British shipping. The toll mounted to 269,000 in June and to 290,000 in July. The United States also had a stake in the fate of the French overseas empire—notably French Indochina, already under pressure from Japan.

But the same concern for the national interest that led Roosevelt to welcome the British action at Mers-el-Kebir led him to dissociate his country from it. Like Churchill, he recognized that, as the gulf between London and Vichy widened, the necessity for Washington and Vichy to maintain contact increased. From the Caribbean to North Africa, from southeastern Asia to the Middle East, French, British, and American interests coincided or overlapped. But the clash at Mers-el-Kebir had turned most French officials, posted in their country's overseas possessions, against the British. Hence the need for a benevolently neutral United States to remain in touch with French centers of power overseas and with the unoccupied regions of France under the nominal control of Marshal Pétain's Vichy regime.

But the very existence of the Vichy regime testified to the provisional nature of Hitler's new order in Europe. For the war's fast-changing shape had suddenly created a situation in which the scope of Germany's victory in western Europe confronted the triumphant Hitler with a blank wall in other directions, whereas the beleaguered Churchill again found scope for a British initiative in Britain's element—the sea. Under the circumstances, Hitler therefore took to the only remaining element —the air—and assigned the Luftwaffe the impossible task of defying a Royal Navy that still controlled the seas around Britain and a Royal Air Force that he did not know how to knock out of the skies above. In Poland, Norway, and France the Germans proved that they led the world in the use of air power to support tanks, ground troops, and troop transports. They also had long experience in submarine warfare and commerce raiding and were building a new fleet of seagoing submarines and two superbattleships—the *Tirpitz* and the *Bismarck*—to serve as commerce raiders.

Although Hitler had welcomed new men and new ideas in the preparation of the campaigns in Poland, Norway, and France, he turned to a figure of the past when it came to the development of air power as an independent weapon of war. Hermann Goering, an early member of the Nazi party, had flown with Baron Manfred von Richthofen's squadron during the First World War, and what he had learned under Richthofen twenty years before the Second World War began proved worse than useless in the improvisation of Operation Sea Lion. Yet even a better man might have done no better. For never before had any major power even tried to evade and overwhelm the land, sea, and air defenses of a major enemy by means of air power alone.

It remained, however, for the seabound British to prepare themselves for precisely the kind of air assault that Hitler and Goering planned. Back in 1935, Air Chief Marshal Sir Hugh Dowding ordered the British aircraft industry to produce a fighter plane, with eight machine guns, capable of flying more than three hundred miles an hour. During the same year the Germans boasted that British aircraft production could never match theirs. By 1939, the British were producing Spitfires and Hurricanes superior to anything the Germans could put into the air and at a rate that the Germans never equaled. And while Dowding had begun to supply the Royal Air Force with the world's finest fighter planes, the Scottish scientist, Robert Watson-Watt, invented a radio detection and ranging device (known as radar for short) which could determine the distance of approaching planes and detect their speed and direction. With Watson-Watt's radar, Dowding could therefore concentrate his fighter planes at the point of heaviest bomber attack. The British made no attempt to match the German bomber force with an equivalent bombing force of their own. Instead, they concentrated on the development of superior fighter planes capable of repulsing the heaviest bombing attacks the Germans could throw against them.

Although the decisive engagements in the battle of Britain took place in the air, Britain's almost uncontested command of the sea doomed Operation Sea Lion even before it started. By mid-July the air war over Britain had begun. Yet no German naval vessel ever shelled the British coast; no German transport ever carried any troops to British soil. No German planes tried to achieve air superiority over any British beachhead. Until mid-August Dowding's tactics steadily wore down the attacks of German fighters and bombers. Not until the last week of that month and the first week of the next, when Goering shifted his attacks to British fighter-plane bases, did the air war begin to turn in Germany's favor. But impatience and overconfidence got the better of

Goering. On the night of August 24, ten German planes that had wandered off course dropped their first bombs on London. At once Churchill ordered a retaliation raid on Berlin the next night. Of the 105 bombers that set out only twenty-nine hit the German capital, but within the week British bombers hit Berlin four more times. "If they attack our cities," Hitler ranted over the radio, "we will rub out their cities from the map. The hour will come when one of us two will break, and it will not be Nazi Germany."

The hour never came; neither Britain nor Germany broke. But on September 7 Hitler's hysteria infected Goering, who stopped his attacks on British fighter bases; instead, he sent a total of 372 bombers and 642 fighters against London in quick succession. Although the British brought down only 24 fighters and 14 bombers—at a cost of 28 of their own fighter planes—the resistance rattled Goering, who assumed that he had already knocked out the R.A.F. It was also on September 7 that the British had expected the German invasion to begin, but nothing happened. On September 9, Goering had London bombed again, and this time the British put up a more effective defense, bringing down 34 enemy bombers. Two days later Hitler ordered the invasion of Britain postponed indefinitely. For the next six weeks the frustrated Goering could think of nothing better to do than order the Luftwaffe to bomb London every night.

·2·

"NEVER IN the field of human conflict was so much owed by so many to so few." Churchill's tribute, before the House of Commons, to the few thousand R.A.F. pilots who threw back the Luftwaffe in the battle of Britain applied to the whole British people during the year when they stood virtually alone against the Nazi war machine. Another, earlier Churchill dictum also applied: "Courage is rightly esteemed the first of the virtues because it is the one that underwrites all the others." The Second World War witnessed battles of greater scope than the battle of Britain. Nor did the British people display more courage or make greater sacrifices than did the peoples of many other nations. But it fell to the lot of the Royal Air Force and of the British people to inflict on Nazi Germany its first two major setbacks. The R.A.F. not only exploded the myth of German invincibility. It also destroyed the myth of the invincibility of offensive air power. As for the British people, they not only proved that civilians, in time of war, could "take it"; the example they set played the decisive role in persuading the government and the people of the United States to align themselves beside Britain in the battle of the Atlantic. Thus the battle of Britain "underwrote" the battle of the Atlantic, in which Roosevelt saw to it that his nation and his people found themselves increasingly involved.

Having remained in close contact, since early June, with William Allen White and his Committee to Defend America by Aiding the Allies, the President sought its assistance in winning public and Congressional support for a plan to release fifty overage American destroyers to the hard-pressed British in exchange for the right of the United States to use certain British bases in the Western Hemisphere. The project, however, did not take final form until August after the Democratic and Republican parties had held their national conventions to nominate their presidential tickets. Shortly before the Democratic Convention, Roosevelt asked two leading Republicans to join his cabinet—Henry L. Stimson as secretary of war and Frank L. Knox as secretary of the navy. Stimson, a New York lawyer, had served with Taft as secretary of war and with Hoover as secretary of state. Knox, publisher of the *Chicago Daily News*, had served with Teddy Roosevelt's Rough Riders in the Spanish-American War and had run for the vice presidency on the Republican ticket in 1936.

The depression had discredited the Republican party; the New Deal had demoralized it. The fall of France and the Battle of Britain then released new forces in the United States. Business got its biggest boost in living memory as the result of new billions poured into war production. A few days after Roosevelt approved the destroyers-for-bases deal, he arranged to have Senator Edward R. Burke, an anti-New Deal Democrat from Nebraska, and James W. Wadsworth, a conservative Republican from upstate New York, assume joint sponsorship of a bill to draft all young men for a year of military training. It passed both Houses easily and quickly. Not only the state of American public opinion but also the state of the American military establishment ruled out the dispatch of any American expeditionary force anywhere for at least a year. Which made it all the easier for Roosevelt to secure popular and Congressional backing for the moves he had made to commit America's considerable naval power to succor Great Britain at once while beginning to train a mass conscript army on a scale reminiscent of the First World War.

When the Landon-Knox ticket challenged the Roosevelt New Deal in 1936 they carried only two states—Maine and Vermont. In 1940 the war issue overshadowed the New Deal and this time the bewildered, divided Republicans finally nominated Indiana-born Wendell Willkie, an ex-Democrat and anti-New Deal public-utilities lawyer who had successfully challenged the constitutionality of the Tennessee Valley Authority. Willkie supported the White committee but concentrated his campaign oratory on the "third-term candidate." Harold Ickes, Roosevelt's secretary of the interior and a renegade Republican, dubbed Willkie the renegade Democrat, "the barefoot boy of Wall Street." Most of the nation's press supported Willkie, who finally won the nomination—partly because of a divided and clumsy opposition, partly because of the enthusiasm he and his backers generated. The convention then chose conservative Senator Charles McNary of Washington as his running mate. A few weeks later, the Democrats nominated Roosevelt and dropped Vice President Garner, who opposed the third term, replacing him with the President's personal selection, ex-Republican Henry A. Wallace of Iowa, his liberal secretary of agriculture.

By the middle of August, the Gallup poll showed a majority of the American people approving the destroyers-for-bases deal. On September 3, the President announced that he had signed an executive order, prepared by Attorney General Francis Biddle, spelling out the details. Willkie endorsed the action, and the *New York Post* quoted an unnamed senator as having said, "Listen, you can't attack a deal like that. If you jump on the destroyer transfer, you're jumping on the acquisition of bases in the Western Hemisphere. And the voters won't stand for that. Roosevelt outsmarted us all when he tied up the two deals." The isolationist *Daily News* of New York tossed off a characteristic quip: "The United States has one foot in the war and the other on a banana peel."

On top of the fact that public-opinion polls showed majorities of 55 per cent to 95 per cent endorsing Roosevelt's foreign policies, even those who disagreed with him also disagreed among themselves, as did some of his supporters, for that matter. The White committee's sponsors included some strange bedfellows, but so did the America First Committee, which presently took the field against it. New Dealers and Morgan partners, labor leaders and industrialists wanted to defend America by aiding Britain. Most of their money came from eastern seaboard financiers who, in peacetime, commuted between Wall Street and London or Paris. General Robert Wood, chairman of the board of Sears, Roebuck, Socialist Norman Thomas, and Republican Representative Hamilton Fish, Jr., wanted to save America first. Most of their financial backing came from the Middle Western industrialists with headquarters in Chicago. But the America First Committee had no unifying force comparable to what the Roosevelt administration could bring to bear on the White group, and the so-called "great debate" that raged for more than a year between the "interventionists" and the "isolationists" persuaded few of the unconverted that the United States could go it alone forever or that immediate American intervention would bring peace with victory soon.

The moment the Republicans nominated Willkie, the last chance that the course of Roosevelt's foreign policy could be reversed went glimmering. And the moment Hitler canceled Operation Sea Lion, Willkie's last chance of winning the presidency sank without a trace. With Britain's short-term future assured, Willkie dropped his Churchillian pose and began to hint that the boys were already boarding the transports which would carry them to fight overseas. Public-opinion polls showed a slight trend away from Roosevelt, who, taking alarm, told a Boston audience during the final week of the campaign: "And while I am talking to you fathers and mothers, I give you one more assurance. I have said this before, but I say it again and again. Your boys are not going to be sent into any foreign wars." For the first time, he did not add to this pledge the phrase from the Democratic platform, "Except in case of attack."

Charged, later, with this omission, he replied, "If someone attacks us, it isn't a foreign war, is it?" The complete answer would have required more details. From the moment that Hitler invaded Poland in September 1939 until early December 1940, when Churchill asked for more naval aid, Roosevelt had pressed unceasingly for more war credits and more shipments of war equipment to Britain. But he had never suggested that the United States resort to armed intervention or declare war. Political strategy and military strategy went side by side. Public-opinion polls showed overwhelming popular opposition to outright American intervention, but they also showed overwhelming popular support for the Allied cause. Moreover, even an American declaration of war against Germany would not have caused several million Americans to spring to arms, fully trained, overnight. During the phony war, the British and French made little use of the troops they had; with the fall of France there was no place on the European continent where American troops could land or fight, even if such troops had existed. The measures short of war, the repeal of the neutrality measures recommended by Roosevelt, and finally the destroyers-for-bases deal fur-

THE BATTLE OF BRITAIN

nished what the beleaguered British needed most and what the unprepared Americans were best able to supply. No less an authority than Churchill—himself a fellow disciple of Admiral Mahan—had responded in terms that Roosevelt understood and accepted.

Roosevelt's foreign and domestic policies received the popular endorsement he sought when he carried 38 of the 48 states and received more than 55 per cent of the popular vote. His victory thus became a virtual extension of the battle of Britain in that it strengthened the special Anglo-American relationship, thus bringing up to date Bismarck's observation that the most important political fact of the nineteenth century was that the British and Americans spoke the same language.

· 3 ·

THE FALL OF FRANCE and the Battle of Britain produced overnight a new situation with which Roosevelt no less than Churchill had to cope. The first decisions that Roosevelt at once endorsed and implemented came, as a matter of course, from Churchill, both men achieving their purposes with equally paradoxical results. Churchill, who embodied the last, best hopes of Britain's Conservative party, found that the measures he had to take to save the British people from Hitler's onslaught and to steel them for further ordeals entailed the immediate socialization of Britain's social and economic order. Roosevelt, who embodied the last, best hopes of America's populist, progressive, reformist traditions, found that the measures he had to take to meet and master the Hitler menace entailed the gradual transformation of the United States into a total war economy and a garrison state. Yet it was precisely their capacities to transcend the backgrounds from which they came that enabled them to preserve, protect, and defend their countries' vital interests and institutions.

The extraordinary preparations of the Royal Air Force saved Britain from invasion in August and September of 1940. But it required an all-inclusive popular effort to survive the long ordeal of bombing that London endured through the fall, winter, and spring of 1940 and 1941. Each night's bombing left some twenty thousand more Londoners homeless. Sometimes the Germans shifted their attention to other targets, as they did on the night of November 14, when five hundred German planes dropped four hundred tons of bombs on Coventry and its 250,000 inhabitants, gutting the heart of the city but missing most of the new industrial plants on the outskirts. By the beginning of December German air attacks on Britain had killed 19,000 civilians and wounded 27,000 more, nearly four fifths of them in the London area. Hitler had long since abandoned hope of knocking out Britain by air attacks or of launching an early invasion. His new strategy called for attrition from the air.

Britain's defense took three forms—war socialism at home, air attacks on German industrial centers, and limited land, sea, and air offensives in the Mediterranean. And it was the war socialism at home that underwrote the other two. The bombs rained down on rich and poor alike. The Englishman's home, whether hovel or castle, assured him neither privacy nor protection. But by sharing and sharing alike there could be sufficient for all. As a patriotic, class-conscious Tory, Churchill appointed the equally class-conscious, patriotic trade unionist and Labour-party leader, Herbert Morrison, as home secretary, and in that capacity Morrison installed such socialistic practices as he had not even advocated in time of peace. As a result, while those accustomed to the better things of life had to go without their usual pleasures and luxuries, one third of the British people got more of life's necessities in wartime than had ever come their way in times of peace. Unemployment, the scourge of the 1920's and 1930's, no longer existed. War meant work as well as bread for all; what socialism had promised, Toryism—with the connivance of Hitler—brought to pass.

Although the war meant socialism to most of London and to much of Britain, to Churchill it meant military strategy, personal diplomacy, and public oratory. His confidence in British sea power made it impossible for him to take Operation Sea Lion seriously. But because he also recognized the limitations of British sea power he had no such confidence in the outcome of the larger battle of the Atlantic. Here, however, Hitler's obsession with the Slavic-Semitic-Communist conspiracy in eastern Europe blinded him to opportunities and dangers in the west. There, during the last three months of 1940, German planes, submarines, and surface vessels were sinking 80,000 tons of British shipping a week. The fifty overage destroyers received from the United States in mid-September tided Britain over a critical period, but American shipyards still could not make up for the toll the German submarines were taking. For once, Hitler underrated himself and overrated his adversaries, a mistake Churchill never made.

As Churchill saw the prospects, in December 1940: "The decision for 1941 lies upon the seas." In a four-thousand-word memorandum to Roosevelt, he predicted that the British could withstand continued air attacks, but warned that shipping losses had risen to the highest levels of the last war, with the worst still to come. German submarine strength was steadily increasing, and the Germans expected to have their two new superbattleships, the *Bismarck* and the *Tirpitz*, in service by January. "Although we are doing all we can to meet this situation by new methods," Churchill continued, "the difficulty of limiting losses is obviously much greater than in the last war. We lack the assistance of the French Navy, the Italian Navy, the Japanese Navy, and above all of the United States Navy which was of such vital help to us during the culminating years."

Those "culminating years" of the last war had reached their climax during the opening months of 1917, when Germany's unrestricted submarine-warfare campaign almost starved Britain out of the war and at once brought the United States in. In 1940, Hitler wisely refrained from attempting Operation Sea Lion, only to miss an opportunity that never came to Imperial Germany—to bombard and blockade Great Britain into submission. But in Roosevelt he faced an antagonist who rejected Woodrow Wilson's vapid 1916 formula of "peace without victory." The fall of France and the Battle of Britain convinced Roosevelt that the survival of the United States depended on the survival of Britain. Churchill did not talk Roosevelt into this conviction. Churchill did, however, explain to Roosevelt, in the language of Admiral Mahan, that they must arrive at a common strategy in waging the battle of the Atlantic, which had already begun.

Returning to Washington in mid-December from a two-week post-election cruise in Caribbean waters aboard the *Tuscaloosa,* Roosevelt therefore told a press conference that he hoped "to eliminate the dollar-sign" in future dealings with Britain because Americans should aid the British to fight Hitler as they would help a neighbor by lending a length of garden hose to fight a fire. His cruise had given him the opportunity to ponder the memorandum prepared by Churchill, stressing the coming shortage of British shipping and the coming crisis of supply. On December 29, he replied to the Churchill appeal by announcing a new plan that he called "Lend-Lease" to make the United States the "arsenal of democracy." This took the form of the Lend-Lease Bill, drafted by the Treasury Department and approved by the War and Navy departments. It scrapped the last vestiges of the Neutrality Act, eliminated cash and carry, and permitted any "defense article" to be sold, transferred, leased, or lent to any country "whose defense the President deems essential to the defense of the United States." Repayment could be made "in kind, in property, or any other direct or indirect benefit which the President deems satisfactory." Lend-Lease became law on March 10, after the House had passed it by a vote of 317 to 17 and the Senate by a vote of 60 to 31. In explaining it to the Congress on January 6, 1941, the President outlined a series of goals for Americans even more ambitious than the means by which he proposed to attain them:

"In the future days, which we seek to make secure, we look forward to a world founded upon the four essential human freedoms. The first is freedom of speech and expression—everywhere in the world. The second is freedom of every person to worship God in his own way— everywhere in the world. The third is freedom from want—which, translated into world terms, means economic understandings which will secure to every nation a healthy peacetime life for its inhabitants— everywhere in the world. The fourth is freedom from fear—which, translated into world terms, means a worldwide reduction of armaments to such a point and in such thorough fashion that no nation will be in a position to commit an act of physical aggression against any neighbor—anywhere in the world." He went on to describe this as "no vision of a distant millennium," but as "a definite basis for a kind of world attainable in our time and generation."

. . .

The pragmatic Roosevelt defined his "Four Freedoms" in abstractions and generalities that committed him to nothing definite. The idealistic Wilson, in his "Fourteen Points," had put the accent on specifics of which he knew little and about which he could do still less. Two of Roosevelt's four freedoms were negative—freedom *from* want and freedom *from* fear. His two positive freedoms—freedom of speech and freedom of worship—could mean anything or nothing: freedom to proclaim the doctrines of Thomas Jefferson or Karl Marx, freedom to suppress dissenters in God's name or Allah's. But the passage of time left the vacuum of Roosevelt's Four Freedoms undisturbed. Three decades later they mean no more and no less than they did on the day he proclaimed them. Wilson's Fourteen points, on the other hand, have long since "gone to join the ironies with tall King Saul till Judgment Day."

For Wilson's Fourteen Points had included, among other things, the establishment of an independent Poland with access to the sea, national self-determination for all the peoples of the former Ottoman and Hapsburg empires, the evacuation of all foreign troops from Russia, general disarmament, a postwar League of Nations, on terms to be arranged, and—for good measure—two specific freedoms: freedom of the seas and freedom of trade. Five decades later, Russian troops occupy more than half the lands of the former Hapsburg Empire while religious warfare between Arabs and Jews and civil warfare among Arabs and Arabs prevail throughout more than half the lands of the former Ottoman Empire. Wilson's League of Nations lasted less than twenty years and could neither prevent nor survive the Second World War. Roosevelt's United Nations has survived its first quarter century and more than doubled its membership in the process.

Woodrow Wilson's intellectual pretensions did him more harm than good. They distracted him from the great game of politics into which Roosevelt poured far more energy and no less talent. If Roosevelt was too much the politician to become a statesman of the highest rank, Wilson did not possess an intellect so commanding as to compensate for his political and temperamental shortcomings. With Roosevelt, to be sure, self-confidence sometimes led him to take too much for granted and succumb to unworthy fits of pettiness and vanity. But Roosevelt had watched Wilson in action during the First World War and could justifiably assert that experience had taught him negative as well as positive lessons. His very nature also provided a built-in guarantee against repeating most of Wilson's mistakes. The six months between the fall of France and the presidential elections put Roosevelt through a testing time during which the Wilson years loomed large. If only as a timely warning to Roosevelt, Wilson had at last come into his own and —for negative reasons—played a major posthumous role in his country's history.

VI

The Makings of Global War

·1·

FOR MORE THAN nine months after the fall of France, Hitler made little use of the weapons and tactics that had just won Germany an unprecedented succession of military victories. Nor did enemy action account for the long respite that set in. The explanation lay in the nature of the weapons and tactics that the Germans used. Hitler had required both time and good weather before he could bring to bear against France in the spring of 1940 the weapons and tactics he had used to crush Poland in the fall of 1939. Then—when France fell ahead of schedule—he needed still more time to redeploy his forces for the next attack. It did not take him long to find out that he could not invade Britain from across the Channel as easily as he had invaded Poland and France from across his own frontiers. And to unleash blitz campaigns against Sweden, Spain, Switzerland, Romania, Hungary, or Yugoslavia in the summer of 1940 made no kind of sense. One target and one only remained: the Soviet Union. And a campaign there not only required much longer preparation than had gone into all his other campaigns put together but weather conditions required quick victory.

The long period of inaction to which his chosen weapons and tactics condemned Hitler offered the first and perhaps the best evidence of the new phase the war had entered. From the Munich Conference to the fall of France, time had worked on his side. His blitz diplomacy and his blitz warfare complemented each other. But with the fall of France time began to work against Hitler—and in war, as in politics, time is the fourth dimension. Early in the summer of 1940, the war took its first decisive new turn when, as indicated in the previous chapter, the battle of Britain expanded into the battle of the Atlantic, in which Roosevelt enlisted the United States, first through the destroyers-for-bases deal, then in the Lend-Lease Act. From that point on, Hitler found he had committed his country and himself to a global war that involved the United States as well as the Soviet Union and that also spread, almost simultaneously, to Japan, China, and southeast Asia.

Here the wisdom of hindsight plays an essential role—confirming, as it does, some trends that contemporary observers descried while contradicting others. In any event, a tour of the world horizon, during that year of almost suspended military animation, reveals situation after situation, incident after incident, all pointing in the same direction of ever-widening war, that boded the greatest ill for those most responsible for its outbreak. Inasmuch as Hitler heads that sorry company, Romania becomes the starting point of the tour, for it was there that Stalin first violated his pact with Hitler by annexing Northern Bukovina, as well as Bessarabia, to the Soviet Union.

As early as June 26, Stalin confronted Hitler with his annexation plans. One month later—by which time Stalin had carried them out—Hitler and Ribbentrop received a Romanian delegation at Salzburg, where they began preparing their visitors for the worst. On August 7, Hitler demanded that Romania cede the Dobruja to Bulgaria. On August 30 and 31, the Romanian and Hungarian foreign ministers conferred with Ribbentrop at Vienna, with Italy's Ciano sitting in as an observer. When Ribbentrop produced a map ceding half of Transylvania to Hungary, Romania's foreign minister fell in a dead faint across the table. On September 6, Romania's Anglophile King Carol abdicated in favor of his young son, Michael, and fled the country with his Jewish mistress, Magda Lupescu. General Ion Antonescu, one of Hitler's favorite non-Germans, had already received dictatorial powers as premier, and on October 7 twelve German divisions began moving in. By the end of November 200,000 German troops had arrived to protect the Romanians from Hitler's partner in the Nazi-Soviet pact.

The head of a German economic mission to Romania explained that his one aim in that country was "to maintain quiet in the raw-material sphere." Perhaps he believed his own reassurance; certainly, both Hitler and Antonescu knew better. In terms of Russo-German military strategy, only Poland ranked higher than Romania, but Hitler bore a deep racist hatred of the anti-Semitic Poles, while finding the equally anti-Semitic Romanians and Hungarians more sympathetic. To those who already foresaw Hitler's decision to attack the Soviet Union, his treatment of Romania, Hungary, and even Slavic Bulgaria during the summer of 1940 made sense. Germany needed allies if possible, and if not allies, then neutrals, along the Soviet Union's western borders.

Poland, on the other hand, represented a special case. More Poles had lived under Russian rule for many more centuries than any Poles had lived under German rule, and contemporary Poles view both their powerful neighbors with equal distaste. Nevertheless, when Hitler partitioned Poland with Stalin he seized the western two thirds of the prewar Polish state and ninety per cent of its Polish inhabitants, most of the population of eastern Poland having been Ukrainian or Byelorussian. But instead of trying to gain Polish support for his ultimate designs against the Soviet Union, Hitler let his racist, nationalist passions carry him away. After the destruction of the prewar Polish state, Hitler incorporated into the Third Reich those parts of that state which had belonged to the Hohenzollern Empire. The remainder became a limbo, known as the Government General, ruled by a German governor under the directive: "Law is all that which serves the German people. Illegality is that which is harmful to that people." Of the ten million Poles brought into the Third Reich, the Germans drove a million and a half from their homes, replacing them with 400,000 German-speaking persons from other countries, including Germany itself. The Government General had to absorb an additional five or six million Poles, Jews, and other unwanted peoples within its eleven million inhabitants. By the time the Germans fell upon western Europe, they had also transported more than a million able-bodied Poles to slave labor in their fields and factories and unnumbered Polish girls to serve as prostitutes with the German armed forces. Poles who remained in their native towns and cities were so badly fed, clad, housed, and cared for that many of the women, children, and older people died off. Against those who displayed any spirit of resistance the Germans invoked the principle of "mass responsibility" and ordered mass reprisals. Those who showed capacity for leadership were exterminated individually, often after long, sadistic tortures. Jews received still worse treatment. The principle, "There are no decent Poles just as there are no decent Jews," applied everywhere.

During the five years of Germany's wartime occupation, Poland stood out as the most horrible of all examples of Hitler's new order, embodying as it did the principle of selective extermination as well as universal enslavement and exploitation. Hitler, in 1939, had not yet begun to apply the final solution of total extermination to Europe's

THE MAKINGS OF GLOBAL WAR

Jews, but the difference between total and selective extermination is one of degree only and not of kind. The fact that he eventually did adopt the final solution serves, among other things, to underline the lethal and self-defeating character of his whole New Order. Not only did the Nazis finally attempt to exterminate all of Europe's Jews everywhere. Besides, their attitude toward the Jews colored their attitude toward all other non-German peoples. But to conclude from this that all Germans possess a similar inborn tendency is to accept the very essence of Hitler's racial philosophy. During the first few weeks of the German occupation of two thirds of France, Parisians marveled at the good manners of their city's young conquerors. In the countryside, centers of milk distribution appeared with banners offering mothers milk for themselves and their children. But nowhere did this exemplary behavior last more than a few weeks, especially as Nazi officials replaced Wehrmacht officers. First, the occupation troops used paper marks to buy most of the food, clothing, and merchandise in the local shops. Then trainloads of Nazi party members and their wives appeared and bought up all the merchandise that the troops had not mailed home. German businessmen followed, installing themselves in managerial posts. Members of the secret police saw to it that the inhabitants obeyed German orders.

The fate of two million war prisoners stirred the deepest popular bitterness. German officials, immediately violating the agreement their government had just signed, transported a million of these prisoners across the Rhine to work at slave labor like the Poles. During July and August thousands of those lucky enough not to have been shipped to Germany escaped from prison camps in France. An underground resistance organization came into being to help them and others beyond the frontier, thereby undermining German authority and reviving French morale. Among the rank and file of the defeated French Army, hatred of Pétain and the men around him ran as strong as hatred of the Germans. As one of them wrote: "In that shameful pretense at fighting, which taught us more in the three days between the armistices about the petty infamy of certain men than the experiences of a lifetime," the war prisoners recognized those of their fellow countrymen who had betrayed them.

The same national attributes that had undermined the French Third Republic now undermined the regime at Vichy: impatience with authority in any form, extreme individualism, skepticism, cynicism, pride of opinion. The fact of defeat also inspired the leaders of the resistance movement with a courage that the leaders of the Third Republic had rarely displayed.

Few of the Vichy police, soldiery, or civil servants shared Laval's desire for a German victory; more and more of them turned away from Pétain's defeatism. After all, they had entered government service under the Third Republic and shared, perhaps more than most Frenchmen, its democratic aspirations and assumptions. In the two fifths of France unoccupied by the Germans most of the political jobs, except a few at the very top, remained in the hands of solid republicans who clung to the traditional ideals of the French Revolution—*Liberté, Égalité, Fraternité*—scorning Pétain's *Travail, Famille, Patrie*. Foreign refugees fared better in unoccupied than in occupied France, but the lot of the average French citizen remained substantially uniform. The German occupation authorities, like the top Vichy officials, retained the civil servants of the Third Republic.

The cleavage between the rulers and the ruled among a people long accustomed to freedom from restraint encouraged individual dissent on the one hand, counterbalanced by a growing spirit of national unity on the other. On the practical levels of daily life, the men and women of France, the old people and the young, found themselves conspiring against established authority, helping prisoners escape, sheltering foreign refugees.

While more and more Frenchmen came to detest Pétain as a Hitler stooge, Hitler found him increasingly intractable. As for Franco, whom most anti-Fascists viewed with more distaste than they did Pétain, Hitler found him even harder than Pétain to handle. At any rate, after arranging to meet each of the two men on successive days in his private railway car, Hitler emerged, on October 23, 1940, from a nine-hour session with Franco at Hendaye, declaring that he would prefer to have three or four teeth taken out than go through that again. For when Hitler proposed a ten-year alliance and an attack on Gibraltar early in 1941, Franco replied: "Spain would gladly fight at Germany's side," always provided Hitler supplied him in advance with more oil, grain, and military equipment while pledging him all of French Morocco plus part of Algeria afterward.

Just before Pétain joined Hitler in the railway car at Montoire, he had received a lecture from Laval on the merits of collaboration with Germany. Hitler followed through with promises to modify the armistice terms if France would help Germany speed Britain's defeat. After suggesting a "repartition of colonial possessions in Africa" and promising France "territorial compensations" that would leave its colonial domain in Africa "essentially equivalent to what she possesses," Hitler persuaded Pétain to sign a long agreement to that effect. Later that evening Ribbentrop telephoned Ciano that "the program of collaboration is heading toward concrete results," adding that Pétain had promised "to take military measures in Africa," and that the United States had protested the concessions Pétain had made. Pétain himself, however, described the whole agreement as so vague that "it will take six months to discuss this program and another six months to forget it."

Not only had both Franco and Pétain rejected Hitler's new order for Europe. It was at the hands of Mussolini—his first ally and the man he had once taken as his model—that Hitler received the unkindest cut of all. When the two men met at the Brenner Pass on October 4, 1940, Hitler neglected to inform his Axis partner that twelve German divisions would begin moving into Romania in three days' time. The fact that Ribbentrop had permitted Ciano to participate in August as an observer at the Vienna confrontation with representatives of Romania and Hungary made this further slight only that much more galling.

On October 28, Mussolini got his revenge. When Hitler arrived in Florence, fresh from the rebuffs of Franco and Pétain, Mussolini greeted him with the words: "Fuehrer, we are on the march," as he explained to his horrified visitor that he had chosen this moment to stage an invasion of Greece. But Italy's legions marched the wrong way. The three divisions that invaded Greece from Albania turned and ran; another nineteen Italian divisions, drawn up for battle, failed to advance. Hitler did not want even a successful campaign in the Balkans, much less an unsuccessful one. He had expected the Italians to concentrate their limited forces on driving the British from Egypt; now Mussolini's decision to invade Greece for reasons of pique and prestige doomed Marshal Rodolfo Graziani's current thrust across the Libyan and Egyptian desert toward Cairo and Alexandria.

Whereupon the British made things still worse for Italy—and for Hitler. They had divided their navy by attempting to hold the Mediterranean while fighting off German attacks on British shipping in home waters. They had divided their land forces by sending an armored division and two infantry divisions to Egypt and the Middle East. As soon as the Italians attacked Greece, the British navy seized Crete; the British army landed troops on Greek soil; British planes operating from Greek bases attacked the ports of southern Italy. On the night of November 11–12,

Britain's fleet air arm knocked out two Italian cruisers and three of Italy's six battleships in Taranto harbor. These strikes at the Italian homeland and at the heart of Italian sea power gave all the Italian troops in Libya, Eritrea, and Ethiopia reason to fear that they might wither and perish on the vine. More important from Hitler's point of view, the opportunities that Mussolini had opened up to Britain in the Mediterranean and the Middle East jeopardized Germany's *Lebensraum* in the Balkans and beyond.

. . .

First Franco, then Pétain, now Mussolini. Hitler had assumed that his support of their lesser nationalist aspirations would assure their support of his greater aspirations for a greater nation. Instead, their own nationalist pride gave rise to an equally intense suspicion of his. A nationalist international contradicts itself; not so a revolutionary international. Hitler and Stalin found a common ground in their revolutionary pretensions, each one believing that he could subvert the other man's revolution to serve his own. Nationalists, on the other hand, can make common cause only by crusading together against international communism. Thus Hitler sought Japanese and Italian support against Russian Communism, while Stalin sought support of the democracies against any and all varieties of fascism. Such observations reflect the political antagonisms and affinities rampant in Hitler's Europe and beyond during the summer and fall of 1940. It did not take long for them to polarize along two vast and widely separated areas: Germany's expanding *Lebensraum* in eastern Europe and Japan's expanding co-prosperity sphere in eastern Asia. In the first case, control of the Atlantic Ocean played a crucial role; in the second, control of the Pacific.

· 2 ·

As THE YEAR 1940 ran its course, Hitler's commitment to an early and final settlement with the Soviet Union steadily deepened. Europe had always remained his prime concern, and his blueprint for German expansion called for a sweeping victory over the Soviet Union as the basis for Germany's complete and ultimate domination of all Europe—from which still further blessings would automatically flow. Hitler at first did not regard either Britain or the United States as a deadly threat to Germany—or as an essential partner. But between Germany and Russia he envisioned a special relationship in which they jointly launched a localized war one year, the better to wage a wider war against each other two years later.

The destruction of Poland had proceeded according to schedule; the fall of France had proceeded too fast and had led to too many repercussions. Not only had the battle of Britain expanded into the battle of the Atlantic, which the United States had already joined. The fall of France gave new impetus to Japanese expansion in the direction of French Indochina and the Dutch East Indies. Not that Japan's good fortune automatically spelled trouble for Germany. Rather did it face Germany with some of the same dilemmas in Asia that the sudden French collapse had created in Europe.

Over the years, Hitler had made sporadic efforts to use Japan as a counterweight to the Soviet Union, but always as an adjunct to his primary concern: Europe. In 1936, Japan had signed the loosely drawn anti-Comintern pact, but refused, in 1938, to join Germany and Italy in their more binding "Pact of Steel." Hitler got his revenge in the Nazi-Soviet pact of 1939 which led to, among other things, the resignation of Japan's pro-Axis prime minister, Baron Hiranuma. General Abe, Hiranuma's successor, appointed the pro-American Admiral Kichisaburo Nomura as foreign minister and withdrew the Japanese ambassadors to Germany and Italy, both of whom had wanted their country to join the "Pact of Steel."

By the time Hitler invaded western Europe, Japan had a new cabinet, headed by Admiral Mitsumasa Yonai, who took care not to favor either the Axis or the Allies, but seemed to support those Japanese who preferred the British and the Americans to the Germans and the Italians. The fall of France changed all this. On July 16, 1940, Prince Fumimaro Konoye succeeded Admiral Yonai and shook up the government all over again, choosing as his most intimate adviser Yosuke Matsuoka, whose unhappy experiences as Japanese delegate to the League of Nations in 1931 had made him a fanatical nationalist. Konoye dissolved Japan's traditional parties, outlawed the Salvation Army and Rotary clubs and made it plain that now Germany had crushed both France and Holland, Japan expected to add French Indochina and the Netherlands Indies to its "Greater East Asia Co-Prosperity Sphere." Konoye also recognized as the official government of China a puppet regime that Wang Ching-wei, former righthand man to Dr. Sun Yat-sen, had established at Peking. Yet this did not prevent Konoye from unsuccessful advances to Chiang Kai-shek.

Meanwhile, in early August, Hitler sent one of his agents to Tokyo to establish contact with Konoye and on September 22 ordered the Vichy authorities to sign an agreement giving the Japanese rights to establish air bases in northern Indochina. Five days later in Berlin, German, Italian, and Japanese officials signed a new treaty (the so-called "Tripartite Pact"), which had the effect of bringing Japan into the Axis. The Japanese, in their turn, promised to respect Hitler's new order in Europe; the Germans and Italians promised to respect Japan's East Asian co-prosperity sphere; all three undertook "to assist one another with all political, economic, and military means when one of the three contracting parties is attacked by a power not at present involved in the European war or the Chinese-Japanese conflict." Since the agreement also specifically exempted the Soviet Union, it boiled down to a warning to President Roosevelt that if the United States became involved in war with either Japan or Germany, it would have to fight both.

In signing this tripartite pact, Hitler exposed Germany to new risks. No longer could he assume that war in Asia might divert American attention from Europe. Henceforth any American involvement in the Far East would increase the likelihood of American involvement in Europe. As for Hitler's Operation Barbarossa, might it not lead the United States and Japan to intervene? Why not, under these circumstances, merge the tripartite and Nazi-Soviet pacts and call off the invasion of the Soviet Union? Ribbentrop commended this line of thought to Hitler, who let himself be talked into seeking a new settlement with Moscow. Ribbentrop had always valued the Nazi-Soviet pact; his brief stay in London as German Ambassador there gave him an instant anti-British inferiority complex which inspired the dim views he subsequently took of Britain's material and moral powers of resistance. The British also irked Hitler, but he respected them. He feared and hated Churchill but could not believe that some other British leader would not guarantee Germany a free hand in Europe in exchange for a German guarantee to respect the integrity of the British Empire. Ribbentrop, on the other hand, hoped to interest Stalin and Molotov in partitioning the British Empire with Germany—a prospect that made less appeal to the European-minded Hitler. But because Hitler suspected Churchill of secretly scheming with Stalin against Germany, he let Ribbentrop see what headway he could make toward a wider and firmer understanding with Moscow.

A more discerning and experienced statesman than Ribbentrop could hardly have missed the storm signals that the Kremlin kept running up during the summer of 1940. After moving in on the Baltic states and the Balkans in June, the Russians protested the subsequent establishment of virtual German protectorates over Romania and Hungary. They demanded a voice in the control of the Danube River. They protested German deliveries of war materials to Finland at a time when similar deliveries to Russia ceased. They reassured the Turks when the Axis assumed that fear of Russian attack would keep Turkey neutral. The day after Japan joined the Axis, the German radio announced: "Political circles in the Soviet Union who, of course, were informed of the signing of the pact, note with particular attention the fact that it will in no way change the relations between the three powers and the Soviet Union. On the contrary, the pact provides for a further development of these relations." But the Germans had informed the Russians only twenty-four hours in advance, and *Pravda* predicted that the new pact would cause the war to spread.

So thin is the line between tragedy and farce that the naked eye cannot always discern it. But there was more irony than either tragedy or farce in Ribbentrop's attempt to save the Nazi-Soviet pact by persuading Stalin and Molotov to merge it with the tripartite pact. In mid-October Hitler gave Ribbentrop permission to put the question up to Stalin in a letter outlining the history of the Nazi-Soviet pact and proposing closer Russian-Japanese friendship. "In summing up," the letter concluded, "I should like to state that in the opinion of the Fuehrer also it appears to be the historical mission of the four powers—the Soviet Union, Italy, Japan, and Germany—to adopt a long-range policy and to direct the future development of their peoples into the right channels by delimitation of their interests on a worldwide scale." To set such a policy in motion, Ribbentrop proposed that Molotov first visit Berlin and that he pay a return visit to Moscow. Stalin accepted on Molotov's behalf, suggesting November 12 as the date and expressing the hope that Ribbentrop would again visit Moscow soon afterward. "As to joint deliberation on some issues with Japanese and Italian participation," Stalin concluded, "I am of the opinion (without being opposed to the idea in principle) that this question would have to be submitted to a previous examination."

The Nazi-Soviet pact fulfilled Hitler's original purpose when it permitted him to crush Poland with Stalin's connivance. But it became more liability than asset when Stalin took advantage of Hitler's involvement in western Europe to violate its terms by annexing more territory along the Soviet Union's western frontier in eastern Europe.

Nor had this Russian thunderbolt come from a clear, blue sky. It coincided with two other drastic changes in the shape of the whole war: the intervention of the United States in the battle of the Atlantic and the intervention of Japan in southeastern Asia. What had begun as a localized conflict in one corner of Europe had become a global affair.

When Stalin agreed to the original Nazi-Soviet pact, he and Hitler saw eye to eye on the risks and advantages it offered to both of them. But the subsequent expansion of the war had created a new situation that Stalin felt able to take in stride but which caught Hitler unprepared. When Ribbentrop suggested the new approach to Moscow, Hitler jumped at it—not because he saw any chance for success but because he saw in Ribbentrop the ideal emissary for such an assignment. Whereas Hitler remained forever rooted in the lower-middle-class background from which he came, Ribbentrop represented the eternal déclassé cad and bounder. His inferiority complex had an anti-British rather than an anti-Semitic cast. His ambition to improve his social status led him to admire the aristocratic Prussian tradition which called for a special German-Russian relationship. At the same time, he also showed himself susceptible to the infantile appeal of left-wing communism.

Ribbentrop's insecure social status led one of his rich friends to stake him to the cost of having inserted a "von" before his undistinguished family name. Hitler would no more have put a "von" before his surname than he would have terminated it with a "stein." No wonder Stalin welcomed the opportunity to pit Molotov, the revolutionary, intellectual renegade, against the pipsqueak Ribbentrop. Old Bolshevik Molotov had not only survived the Stalinist purges; those purges had wafted him to the innermost circle of Soviet power, and he could take half a dozen Ribbentrops in his stride at any hour of the day or night. Their confrontation at Berlin had all the earmarks of the diplomatic mismatch of the century.

During the Berlin confrontation of November 12, 1940, Ribbentrop spouted vague proposals of four-power agreements to "establish fields of influence along very broad lines." But Molotov got down to cases. The Soviet Union wanted access to the Baltic and the Black seas. "The Soviet Union could not be indifferent to the fate of Romania and Hungary under any circumstances, and what did the Axis contemplate with regard to Yugoslavia and Greece? Paper agreements will not suffice for the Soviet Union; rather will she have to have effective guarantees of her security." When Ribbentrop rambled on about a general four-power agreement to divide the world, Molotov brought up Finland, Romania, Turkey, Bulgaria, the Danube, and the Dardanelles. He also questioned Ribbentrop concerning Yugoslavia, Hungary, and Poland, and Swedish neutrality, but refused to commit himself on the subject of an outlet on the Indian Ocean and informed Ribbentrop that the Soviet Union was making its own arrangements with Japan about a nonaggression pact. At their final session Molotov refused to sign a ten-year agreement with the adherents of the tripartite pact to respect their spheres of influence, to consult them on matters of mutual interest, to co-operate economically, and to refuse to join any coalition directed against any one of them. Only after the settlement, through normal diplomatic channels, of four current Soviet-German issues would the Soviet Government consider adherence to the tripartite pact. On that negative note the conference adjourned.

Hitler took part in some of the discussions and exclaimed, after Molotov left, "Stalin is nothing but a cold-blooded blackmailer." Hitler's translator remarked that no foreigner had ever spoken to the Fuehrer as Molotov had, noting that such treatment made Hitler "meekly polite." Yet it was Molotov who followed through; it was Ribbentrop who let the whole thing drop. On November 25, Molotov transmitted to the German government the four conditions under which Russia would adhere to the tripartite pact. These called for withdrawal of German troops from Finland, the establishment of Russian bases within range of the Bosporus and the Dardanelles, recognition of the area south of Batum and Baku as a center of Soviet aspirations, and renunciation by the Japanese of their coal and oil concessions in northern Sakhalin. To these proposals the Germans never replied. Only in the economic sphere did the Germans and Russians come to any new agreement, and that one, signed on January 10, 1941, led to a considerable increase in trade on both sides.

Although the details of Molotov's visit to Berlin did not become public knowledge until some years later, the silence that followed his return to Moscow told the world that Russia had not joined the Axis. Nor had Molotov and Ribbentrop concluded any new agreements such as they had signed only a year before. This meant that the Germans had not reconciled themselves to Russia's moves into Romania and the Baltic states and that the Russians had not reconciled themselves to the Romanian and Hungarian settlements announced from Vienna by Ribbentrop and Ciano. And as the months passed without a return German visit to Moscow, only the willfully blind could fail to see that the Nazi-Soviet pact had served its purpose.

· 3 ·

Two WEEKS before Molotov arrived in Berlin, Mussolini's reverse invasion of Greece set in motion the first new military campaign since the battle of France. The British at once exploited the self-inflicted Italian disaster by launching air attacks on Italian harbors and ground attacks on Marshal Rodolfo Graziani's desert army in Egypt where it had advanced, without opposition, about one hundred miles beyond the Libyan border. Although outnumbered by the Italians more than two to one, Britain's General Archibald Wavell and his mixed army of British Empire and Polish troops drove the Italians from the Egyptian port of Sidi Barrani on December 9 and 10, and then advanced four hundred miles during the next two weeks, taking 113,000 Italian prisoners and the Libyan ports of Bardia, Tobruk, and Benghazi. Other Italian campaigns in Ethiopia, Eritrea, and Somaliland also fizzled out—for the Italians.

Hitler's war plans had not ignored North Africa and the Middle East, but they gave priority to Operation Barbarossa. In fact, no sooner had Molotov left Berlin than Hitler fixed May 15, 1941, as the day for the attack on Russia to begin. But by February, Mussolini's blundering had caused such confusion in Libya that Hitler had to dispatch four-star General Erwin Rommel and his crack Afrika Korps to Tripoli to "reconnoiter vigorously" but on no account to cross Egypt's border. The Afrika Korps had adapted to desert warfare the same blitz tatics of combined tank and plane operations that Guderian had used to overrun France. Rommel's more modest assignment called only for defending Libya and holding down the largest possible number of British forces in North Africa.

Unaware even of this limited assignment, the British rushed several of Wavell's divisions across the Mediterranean to Greece—not with any thought of repelling a German invasion, but in the hope that this move might encourage other Balkan nations to stand and fight further German encroachments. By the first week of March, the Greeks claimed they had taken 20,000 Italian prisoners and inflicted 120,000 Italian casualties. Before the Italians could hit back, the Greeks struck again, inflicting another 50,000 Italian casualties and cutting up five Italian divisions.

Other difficulties in other parts of southeastern Europe compelled Hitler to send more aid to his Italian partner. In January, the Soviet ambassador in Berlin had described the 200,000 German troops in Romania as being already "prepared to march into Bulgaria, having as their goal the occupation of Bulgaria, Greece, and the Straits." The Soviet ambassador added that his government regarded that whole area as a Soviet "security zone" and predicted that the British would try to open a new front in Bulgaria with Turkish aid. The Soviet government therefore considered "the appearance of any armed forces on the territory of Bulgaria and of the Straits as a violation of the security interests of the USSR." The Germans replied that the British were preparing to land troops in Greece and that German troops had already begun to occupy Bulgaria's airfields to protect Soviet as well as German interests. In January, Churchill had urged President Ismet Inonu of Turkey to let Britain establish at least ten squadrons of bomber and fighter planes on Turkish soil. "Nothing," he argued, "will more restrain Russia from aiding Germany." Inonu remained unconvinced and strictly neutral.

Inonu's neutrality not only cost Britain the one local ally that might have rallied the rest of the Balkan peoples against Germany. On February 17, Inonu also signed a nonaggression pact with Bulgaria, thereby assuring Hitler that the Turks would make no trouble if the Germans took the country over. On March 1, the Bulgarian government drew the logical conclusion and added its signature to the tripartite pact of Berlin as Hungary and Romania had already done in late November. German troops and tanks at once moved in and stationed themselves on Bulgaria's Greek and Yugoslav borders, thus confronting the British with a cruel dilemma. On the one hand they had pledged themselves to defend Greece against attack. On the other hand, Wavell's victorious desert army needed all the available manpower in the eastern Mediterranean region to complete the Italian defeat before Rommel could deploy his Afrika Korps. Churchill gave priority to his pledge to Greece. His decision, dictated at the time by considerations of honor, ultimately proved strategically valid as well, contributing, as it did, to the chain of events that forced Hitler to order a six-week delay in his invasion of the Soviet Union.

At the time, however, the general confusion seemed to play into Hitler's hands. Two weeks before Bulgaria joined the Axis, Yugoslavia's

Prince Regent Paul and Premier Drogisha Cvetković resisted Hitler's pressure to do the same, but they also turned down Churchill's appeal to support Greece and defy the Axis. Young King Peter II and General Dušan Simović, commander of the Yugoslav air force, spearheaded a popular uprising that forced Paul to abdicate in favor of the young king and that replaced Cvetković with Simović. Crowds of Serbs danced in the streets of Belgrade, sang their national anthem, displayed British and French flags, spat on the car of the German minister, and chanted: "Rather war than the Pact; better death than slavery."

Hitler raged. He ordered his commanders to prepare "Operation Punishment" and "to destroy Yugoslavia as a national unit," but to make no move against Greece before attacking Yugoslavia. An April 6, 1941, the Germans struck simultaneously at both. First, they hit enemy airfields. Then came a three-day air bombardment of Belgrade at housetop level, killing 17,000 civilians, and reducing the city to the condition of Warsaw. By April 17, German troops had overrun so much of Yugoslavia that the country surrendered. Greece fared no better. Its surrender came on April 24. On May 1 Churchill told the House of Commons that 48,000 British troops in Greece, totaling 80 per cent of the expeditionary force, had been evacuated. Within the week many of them appeared on the island of Crete, where they began to prepare a base for sea and air operations, all up and down the Mediterranean.

Franco had barred German troops from Spain. Pétain still kept the French flag flying over Morocco, Algeria, and Tunisia. Hitler therefore threw the Luftwaffe into a desperate gamble for Crete, where airborne troops, alone and unaided, wrote a new chapter in military history by seizing the island from Britain's combined land, sea, and air forces. But there they stopped. For Hitler did not view Crete as a steppingstone to the Middle East but as the culmination of his campaign in the Balkans. And this in the face of Rommel's exploits in Libya, where, during the month of April, he and his Afrika Korps recaptured almost everything that the Italians had lost earlier in the year, except the port of Tobruk, where an Australian division barricaded itself behind Italian-built fortifications. Enough supplies had already reached them to maintain them there indefinitely, but they posed no threat to Rommel, before whom dazzling new prospects opened: Alexandria, Cairo, the Suez Canal, the oil of the Middle East.

Hitler saw no such visions. To him the Soviet Union remained, more than ever, the prime objective. Troubles in the Balkans had already compelled him to shorten by six precious weeks the few months during which he expected his troops to complete Operation Barbarossa. The further the war spread, the less his control over it. The German occupation of Crete in mid-May coincided with a *coup d'état*, at Baghdad, the capital of Iraq, engineered by German agents, overthrowing the régime of the youthful pro-British regent and installing Rashid Ali Beg Gailani, a former Iraqi premier with considerable army backing and impeccable anti-Semitic and anti-Zionist credentials. When the Royal Air Force and an Indian division established themselves at an airport sixty-five miles from Baghdad, Rashid Ali appealed to Berlin for aid, but the Germans had too many other commitments and not enough troops. On June 1, the regent and a pro-British government returned to power at Baghdad. So ended a chain of events that began with Mussolini's invasion of Greece in October 1940. Another, that had begun with Japan's adherence to the tripartite pact that same month, kept right on.

·4·

So DID the silence that had enveloped the Molotov-Ribbentrop meeting. After Molotov's return to Moscow, the Soviet news agency Tass found it necessary to deny that the Soviet and Japanese governments had agreed to define their spheres of influence in Asia. Three weeks later the Japanese government found it necessary to deny that the anti-Communist clauses in its treaty with Wang Ching-wei's puppet regime at Peking were directed against the Soviet Union. But nobody issued any denials on January 21, when the Japanese and Soviet governments announced the extension of their fisheries agreement for another year, or on March 20, when the Soviet government extended diplomatic recognition to the pro-Japanese puppet government of Thailand.

On March 20, Foreign Minister Matsuoka, who had brought his country into the Axis, arrived in Moscow for friendly talks with Stalin and Molotov. Three days later in Berlin, he reported to Hitler and Ribbentrop that the Russians had instigated the talks and that he had pointed out to Stalin the common interest Germany, Japan, and the Soviet Union all had in defeating Britain and the United States. Then, with the British Empire liquidated, Japan and Russia could settle any remaining differences between themselves. At this point the ineffable Ribbentrop—the promulgator of the Nazi-Soviet pact—broke in with: "If Germany should feel herself endangered, she would immediately put an end to Bolshevism." On April 5, Ribbentrop warned Matsuoka against making any new commitments with Moscow, where the Japanese foreign minister had already arranged to see Stalin and Molotov again on his way home. By this time, the Germans had lined up most of their armed forces close enough to the Soviet border to be able to strike at any moment. On that same occasion, Hitler promised that if Japan should become involved in war with either Russia or the United States, Germany would fight at its side, in the hope, however, that fear of Japan's military might would ensure the neutrality of both the Soviet Union and the United States.

Matsuoka's subsequent visit to Moscow coincided with the German annihilation of Yugoslavia, which stunned Stalin, who had again underrated the Germans and overrated their victims. By way of appeasing Hitler, he therefore stepped up Soviet deliveries of raw materials to Germany. But, in line with his two-irons-in-the-fire approach to major issues, Stalin sought to use Matsuoka as a counterweight in future negotiations with Berlin. He therefore sanctioned a Soviet-Japanese neutrality pact which left Japanese rights on Sakhalin undisturbed but which contained a secret clause (subsequently ignored by Matsuoka) calling for a settlement within six months. The text of the pact, when published on April 13, caused a sensation comparable to that provoked by the Nazi-Soviet pact of 1939. "Having passed through a multitude of difficult experiences," commented Moscow's *Izvestia*, "Soviet-Japanese relations are now passing through a new phase which promises to bear good fruit." Under the pact, the Russians promised that if Japan became involved in war with the United States, they would not intervene on the American side or take any advantage of Japan's exposed position. The Japanese promised that if the Soviet Union became involved in war with Germany, they would not intervene on the German side or take any advantage of the exposed Soviet position. The Russians also recognized Japan's control of Manchuria; the Japanese recognized Soviet control of Outer Mongolia.

As Matsuoka boarded the Trans-Siberian Express at the Moscow terminal, Stalin paid him the unprecedented compliment of seeing him off at the station platform and declared, for all to hear, "Now that Japan and Russia have fixed their problems, Japan can straighten out the Far East; Russia and Germany will handle Europe. Later, together, all of them will deal with America." No wonder Stalin did not mention China: his pact with Matsuoka had assigned one of its traditional territories to Japan, the other to the Soviet Union. Stalin then sought out Germany's Ambassador von der Schulenberg, threw an arm around his shoulder, and declared: "We must remain friends, and you must do everything to that end." But it was to Matsuoka alone that Stalin confided, "I, too, am an Asiatic."

·5·

DURING 1940 the battle of Britain expanded into the battle of the Atlantic, and with the passage of the Lend-Lease Act of 1941, the United States became a full participant in that wide and vital battleground of the Second World War. But if the United States had not yet committed itself to full belligerence, Germany had not yet committed itself to all-out participation in the battle of the Atlantic. Hitler had lost interest in the battle of Britain even before it began. After canceling Operation Sea Lion and dropping his invasion plans, he reverted to his original strategy of bombardment and blockade. During the first quarter of 1941, new German submarines with cruising ranges of between eleven and fifteen thousand miles were going into action at the rate of ten a month and at eighteen a month thereafter. Operating from bases that extended from Norway to the Bay of Biscay, they often hunted in packs, usually with air reconnaissance to guide them to convoys. The Germans had repaired some of the destroyers and cruisers damaged during the Norway campaign. The superbattleships *Bismarck* and *Tirpitz* neared completion. New planes capable of attacking and sinking merchant vessels on their own caused British shipping losses to rise from 320,000 tons a month in January to 537,000 tons a month in March. Worse yet, at the beginning of March, Britain had accumulated two and a half million tons of damaged shipping, two thirds of it still awaiting repairs. The combined Anglo-American shipping industries could not replace the losses inflicted by the Germans.

Roosevelt did what he could to help. In early April he extended the security zone of the United States to include Greenland and the Azores; a few months later he brought in Iceland, too. This meant that the United States Navy would patrol more than half the waters of the North Atlantic and inform the British of any German surface vessels, submarines, or aircraft encountered there. The American vessels had orders not to shoot at the Germans; the German vessels had similar orders. Admiral Erich Raeder, Germany's first sea lord, and Admiral Karl Doenitz, commander of the German submarine fleet, begged Hitler to let their ships enter the American security zone and sink American vessels there. Hitler forbade any move that might antagonize the

United States. Operation Barbarossa, which called for the annihilation of the Soviet Union within the year, loomed directly ahead. The hostile neutral to the west must not become an active belligerent until the benevolent neutral to the east had been destroyed.

By the middle of May, Operation Barbarossa compelled the Germans to shift the bulk of the Luftwaffe from the unfinished battle of Britain to the approaching battle of Russia. Richard Collier, a survivor of the last great German fire raid on London, during the night of May 10, reached the conclusion in his book *The City That Would Not Die* that if the Germans had continued the attack and had not thrown most of their air force against the Soviet Union, they might have broken British resistance that year. The citizens of London and the Royal Air Force pilots certainly welcomed the respite. The Royal Navy, on the other hand, soon faced a new and formidable adversary in the battle of the Atlantic. On May 21, the new German superbattleship *Bismarck* appeared off the coast of Norway, where it promptly sank Britain's largest and fastest battleship, the *Hood*. The *Bismarck* had longer-range guns, heavier armor, and greater speed than any British battleship. Its sinking of the *Hood* proved its prowess. But instead of slipping away to the safety of one of Norway's many nearby fjords, from which it could have constantly harassed Allied shipping, the *Bismarck* attempted to outmaneuver swarms of seaborne and airborne pursuers. Five days later, the British sent the *Bismarck* to the bottom. Nazi overconfidence in German technology and German inexperience with naval warfare doomed the *Bismarck*. Superior British skill and longer British experience triumphed.

·6·

THE FATE of the *Bismarck* served as an allegory on the fate of a Germany in which Nazi delinquents wrecked a traditional German technological masterpiece in much the same way that juvenile delinquents wreck an automotive masterpiece. But it followed, by two weeks, a reverse allegory in which the number two man in Hitler's gang of Nazi delinquents broke the pattern of reverse transcendence in which his comrades gloried. On the afternoon of Saturday, May 10, Rudolf Hess, Hitler's deputy Fuehrer, flew a Messerschmitt fighter plane, solo, from Augsburg to a Scotch estate of the Duke of Hamilton and Brandon, who, like himself, had dabbled in the Moral Rearmament movement (also known as the Oxford Group), founded by the American evange-

list, Dr. Frank Buchman, whose anti-Communism had led him to proclaim: "Thank God for Hitler." Increasingly horrified by the prospect of
another Anglo-German war, Hess described himself as Hitler's envoy,
come to open Anglo-German peace talks. Hitler knew nothing of Hess'
trip; Hess must have learned something about Operation Barbarossa. In
any event, Hess assured his bewildered British interrogators that Hitler
had found it "indeed difficult" to wage submarine and air warfare on
the British Isles. "It pained him deeply." He then repeated the familiar
Hitler rigamarole about a free hand for Germany in Europe and a free
hand for Britain with her empire. Germany also had certain demands
to make on Russia which Hess described as an Asiatic nation outside
the German *Lebensraum.*

The British authorities did not discourage the wide range of specula-
tion to which the Hess visit at once gave rise. But Hess' replies to their
questions can have brought no surprises, and Hitler's actions, at the
time, seemed as erratic as Hess' words. For several days, the stunned
Goebbels relapsed into silence. Finally, he had only this modest suggestion to offer: "It seemed that Party Member Hess lived in a state of
hallucination, as a result of which he felt he could bring about an understanding between Germany and England." Years later, Churchill
wrote: "Whatever may be the moral guilt of a German who stood near
Hitler, Hess had, in my view, atoned for this by his completely devoted
and frantic deed of lunatic benevolence."

What Hitler put forward in 1940 as a serious bid for peace with Britain, Goebbels called hallucination when Hess proclaimed it in 1941.
And if Hess's "deed of lunatic benevolence" gave him in Churchill's eyes
"something of the quality of an envoy," nothing but "lunatic malevo-
lence" ever possessed Hitler. Like many other Nazi leaders, both Hitler
and Hess had psychotic personalities, but this did not deprive all their
words of meaning or all their deeds of significance. In undertaking his
mad mission, Hess revealed an abiding respect for the British, a growing desire for peace, and a gnawing fear that Hitler's luck had begun to
run out. But had he revealed something more? Did Hitler perhaps
share this same, gnawing fear? Did he wholly deplore the Hess mission
—its purposes as well as its motives, its timing as well as its form? The
journalists who reported the news when it happened at once sensed its
importance; the historians who have analyzed it since have had more
difficulty when it comes to interpretation.

One man who should have known better missed both the importance
and the significance of the Hess mission. Although Stalin had always

distrusted Hitler and never regarded their pact as more than a temporary makeshift with which to buy time and space, the German campaigns in Yugoslavia, Greece, and Crete convinced him that he must make new gestures of appeasement in Hitler's direction. In other words, Stalin decided to appease Hitler at the same moment that Hess felt it necessary for Hitler and Churchill to appease each other. Events did not follow the course they recommended. Hitler spurned Stalin's proferred appeasement; Churchill spurned both Hitler and Hess. But the fears which these would-be appeasers tried to exploit rested on facts, not fancies.

. . .

Do weapons shape the wars that those who use them wage or do the men who use the weapons shape the wars? Long before Hitler came along, the German General Staff developed the weapons and the tactics that the Nazis subsequently used and in doing so locked the Nazis into the kind of campaigns they had fought in Poland and France and now planned to fight in Russia. Perfect co-ordination between tanks and planes summed up the formula for the quick victories that the Germans won against the Poles and the French. The victories quickly turned—as victories do—to dust and ashes, but all the ashes did not at once turn to dust. If few phoenixes rose from any of them, even the Germans could not exterminate the defeated Poles; they focused on exploiting and enslaving those who came under their rule and, in the process, succeeded chiefly in debasing themselves.

The pleasant land of France enjoyed greater natural advantages than the flat Polish plains. The Germans also treated the French somewhat better than they treated the Poles—partly, to be sure, because the surprisingly rapid fall of France gave the Germans less opportunity to exploit the French as cruelly as they exploited the Poles. But in Poland, as in France, the Germans debased themselves, wrecked their new European order even before they had begun to build it, and gave some indication of what they had in mind for the Russians.

Then came the troubles in the Balkans, originally provoked by Hitler's Axis partner and later aggravated by the Yugoslav *coup d'état*. The German invasion of Yugoslavia followed the Polish rather than the French pattern, though Yugoslavia's rugged terrain did not lend itself to blitzkrieg tactics. Large pockets of resistance fighters survived the German invasion. All the more reason, therefore, to launch Operation Barbarossa at the earliest possible moment. No wonder Hitler never even considered canceling Operation Barbarossa in favor of Iraq's

Rashid Ali Beg Gailani. The kind of war machine that the German General Staff built incorporated in it precisely the features to which Hitler's leadership showed itself peculiarly suited.

Born and raised at the turn of the century in a backwater province of German Austria, Hitler had never lifted his eyes above and beyond Europe's frontiers. To him the widest and openest spaces lay in Russia, where his overactive, undereducated imagination saw all manner of Communist, Slavic, and Semitic conspiracies running riot. The maritime British had made a good thing of India and of the Far and Middle East. The French had easy access to North Africa by way of the Mediterranean. For the landlocked Germans, the path of least resistance—and maximum return—lay to the east. Not all the German generals shared all of Hitler's racist, nationalist views. But they stood in awe of his demagogic gifts. They also shared his nineteenth-century geopolitical views: in fact, he had picked some of them up from General Karl Haushofer's geopolitical institute at Munich. But German industry needed more than Russian raw materials; Russia needed more than the products of German industry. Both Germany and the Soviet Union depended more and more (as all other twentieth-century peoples did), on more and more world markets, world trade, and worldwide contacts and communications.

As a Communist, Stalin needed no lessons from anybody on the subject of internationalism. Lenin, in 1921, had described NEP, his New Economic Policy, as one step backward by way of prelude to two steps forward. In like manner, Stalin viewed his policy of socialism in one country as the necessary prelude to a Communist world. The German generals naturally preferred Hitler's National Socialism to Stalin's international Communism. They also felt confident that the weapons and tactics that Hitler had received at their hands would ensure the conquest of the Soviet Union that he and they desired. But the application of these weapons and tactics in Poland and France had not resulted in the creation of the new European order Hitler had promised. Instead, he had succeeded only in spreading the war to the western shores of the Atlantic Ocean and to the eastern and southeastern coasts of Asia. The first year of Hitler's war had looked like an accelerated and improved version of the Kaiser's war of 1914. But the second year took a quite different shape. It entailed much less fighting than had occurred during the second year of the First World War but it set the stage for a conflict of wider scope and greater intensity under conditions less favorable to Germany than those of a quarter of a century before.

VII

War Comes to Russia

·1·

ONE YEAR to the day after the signing of the Franco-German armistice, the greatest battle in history began. During the early morning hours of June 22, 1941, from end to end of a sixteen-hundred-mile front extending from the Baltic to the Black Sea, more than one hundred German divisions surged forward against scattered Soviet forces, approximately equal in numbers but less heavily equipped and armed. Never before had so many men with so great a weight of weapons grappled with each other over so wide a territory. As in the invasions of Poland and France, the Germans struck without warning, without provocation, and in violation of treaty pledges.

The invading Germans divided their armies into three groups. In the north, Field Marshal Ritter von Leeb took off from East Prussia with twenty-one divisions headed for Leningrad. In the northern sector three German tank divisions and two German infantry divisions hit a single Soviet infantry division and in four days advanced one hundred of the two hundred miles that separated them from Leningrad. On the central front, Field Marshal Fedor von Bock took off from northern Poland with thirty-two divisions, headed for Smolensk and Moscow. There, seven full German tank divisions advanced one hundred miles in three days against one incomplete Soviet tank division, one infantry division, and elements of four others. In the south, Field Marshal Gerd von Rundstedt took off from southern Poland with fifty-three divisions, headed for the Ukraine and the Dnieper River. There, six German infantry divisions with six hundred tanks hit two divisions of Soviet infantry that had no tanks. During the first two days, three thousand of the Luftwaffe's four thousand planes shot down five hundred Soviet bomb-

ers and destroyed another fifteen hundred Soviet planes on the ground.
By the end of the first week Rundstedt's forces were beginning to turn the western Ukraine into a replica of western Poland. Bock's forces in the center had not advanced quite so fast; in the north, the Russian lines had begun to hold. Already space and time were beginning to aid the Russians as they had never aided the Poles or the French. Although the Russians had given as much ground as the Poles or the French, they had more men and more equipment as well as more time and space in which to deploy them. Thus, the initial routs became somewhat more orderly retreats. Moreover, no Soviet leader during the first week of the German invasion had echoed the cry of French Premier Reynaud, a week after the Germans invaded his country, that France had already lost the war's first battle.

But Stalin, in adversity, did not echo Churchill. As head of the Soviet government, Stalin assigned the task of breaking the bad news to Foreign Minister Molotov, who announced: "At four o'clock this morning, without declaration of war, and without any claims being made upon the Soviet Union, German troops attacked our country, attacked our frontier in many places and bombed from the air Zhitomir, Kiev, Sebastopol, Kaunas, and some other places." He described the attack as "an unparalleled act of perfidy in the history of civilized nations" and noted that "the German government had never made the slightest complaint of any failure of the Soviet government to live up to its obligations under their nonaggression pact." But when Germany's Ambassador von der Schulenberg, later in the day, handed Molotov a brief message from Ribbentrop announcing that Hitler had ordered the German forces to frustrate a threatened Soviet attack from the rear, Molotov's spontaneous, unrehearsed reply struck a different note: "It is war. Your aircraft have just bombarded some ten open villages. Do you believe we deserved that?"

Molotov's whine spoke volumes, coming as it did from one who had recently treated the upstart Ribbentrop with the same contempt that he showed toward the sanctimonious John Foster Dulles a decade later. Having spent his political life in the shadow and under the spell of Stalin, Molotov surpassed even his protector in his own displays of arrogance and intransigeance. This not only permitted Stalin to play everything cool. It enhanced his dignity and authority. But if Stalin towered over Molotov, he defied comparison with Churchill—and vice versa. It took Stalin until July 3—almost two weeks—to prepare and deliver his first war message to the Soviet people. Churchill, on the other hand, had prepared, well ahead of time, his message to the Russian people concerning a crisis that he had long foreseen. On the evening of the day the German armies struck, Churchill went on the air with his pledge of all-out British support. Frankly acknowledging that "No one has been a more consistent opponent of communism than I have in the last twenty-five years. I will unsay no word I have spoken about it," he went on to pledge: "We have but one aim and one single purpose. We are resolved to destroy Hitler and every vestige of his Nazi regime. From this nothing will turn us. Nothing. We will never parley. We will never negotiate with Hitler or any of his ken. We shall fight him by sea; we shall fight him on the land; we shall fight him in the air until with God's help we shall have rid the earth of his shadow. Any man or state who fights against Nazism will have our aid." Churchill called Hitler's invasion of Russia as "no less than the prelude to the invasion of the British Isles," which Hitler hoped to accomplish before winter and "before the fleet and airpower of the United States will intervene. The Russian danger is our danger and the danger of the United States."

· 2 ·

STALIN'S FIRST WAR MESSAGE to his own people opened with the words: "Comrades, citizens, brothers and sisters, fighters in our Army and Navy. I am speaking to you, my friends!" He needed say no more. All his listeners had heard long since about the German invasion—which all too many of them had already experienced. But for Stalin to address them in such terms as these was "something new"—as Alexander Werth put it in *Russia at War:* "Stalin had never spoken like this before." For him to address the Russian people as his friends, even as his brothers and sisters, caused more astonishment in the Soviet Union than that the anti-Communist Churchill now supported the war effort against Hitler. The bulk of the Stalin speech called upon the Soviet people to wage all-out, total war on the German invader—as soldiers at the front, as factory workers behind their own lines, as partisan fighters behind the enemy's. Of the Churchill broadcast Stalin said, "The historic statement of Mr. Churchill on Britain's help to the Soviet Union and the statement by the United States government on its willingness to help our country can only meet with a feeling of gratitude in the hearts of our people."

For his pact with Hitler, Stalin felt no regrets and offered no apologies: "No peace-loving state could have rejected such a pact with another country, even if such scoundrels as Hitler and Ribbentrop stood at its head. All the more so as this pact did not in any way violate the territorial integrity, independence, or honor of our country." What it did (or what he did) to the territorial integrity, independence, and honor of Poland did not concern him; only the vital interests of his own country mattered. Moreover, Stalin's Russian listeners knew as well as he did that the Poles had no more right to the Soviet-occupied eastern parts of their country than the Germans had to the western regions they seized. At the same time, the enlightened self-interest that Chamberlain in 1939 and Churchill in 1941 displayed in the fate of Poland served them and their country better than Stalin's narrow nationalism served him and the Soviet Union. It was the quixotic British, not the realistic Russians, who took the lead in forming the kind of great coalition which eventually destroyed Hitler and saved Europe. Moreover, that struggle cost the realistic Russians a far heavier price than the quixotic British had to pay.

The very fact that Stalin had only himself to blame for the bind in which Hitler's invasion caught him did little to encourage any magnanimous impulses that he may have harbored. Having tried and failed to gain time and territory at Poland's expense, Stalin became more determined than ever to exploit Poland's weaknesses. Churchill did what little he could to soften the hearts of his new and powerful Russian allies toward his tragic Polish protégés. On July 5, two days after Stalin's first wartime broadcast, British officials in London brought Soviet Ambassador Ivan Maisky together with General Wladyslaw Sikorski, who headed the Polish government in exile there. As Churchill put it in *The Grand Alliance:* "We had gone to war with Germany as the direct result of our guarantee to Poland. We had a strong obligation to support our first ally. At this stage of the struggle we could not admit the legality of the Russian occupation of Polish territory in 1939. . . . There was no way out. The issue of the territorial future of Poland must be postponed to easier times. We had the invidious responsibility of recommending General Sikorski to rely on Russian good faith in the future settlement of Russian-Polish relations."

On July 30, the Polish and Soviet representatives in London did agree to establish diplomatic relations between their two governments. Arrangements were also made that enabled the Poles to enlist the thousands of Polish prisoners in Russia into a Polish army on Russian soil under the Soviet government's supreme command. The agreement included a general statement that the Soviet-German treaties of 1939 concerning territorial changes in Poland "have lost their validity." But there was no mention of any frontiers and on the same day Eden notified the Polish government in exile that his government had "entered into no undertaking towards the USSR which affects the relations between that country and Poland," and did not recognize "any territorial changes which have affected Poland since August 1939."

By this time, Churchill and Stalin had exchanged their first wartime messages and Roosevelt had made his first wartime approach to Moscow. On July 7, Churchill dispatched his first personal communication to Stalin, stressing British air attacks on German targets and expressing the hope that "contact will be established between the British and Russian navies." Shortly afterward, British and Russian military missions exchanged their first visits. On July 19, Churchill received his first personal communication from Stalin. It expressed gratitude for the messages Churchill had already sent, justified the Nazi-Soviet pact on the ground that it had compelled the Germans to fight several hundred more miles before reaching Soviet territory, and called upon the British army to open a front in northern France. "This is the most propitious moment for the establishment of such a front, because now Hitler's forces are diverted to the East, and he has not yet had a chance to consolidate the position occupied by him in the West." Of this and similar subsequent requests, Churchill wrote: "The Russians never understood in the smallest degree the nature of the amphibious operation necessary to disembark and maintain a great army upon a well-defended hostile coast. Even the Americans were at this time largely unaware of the difficulties."

· 3 ·

ONE AMERICAN who did not fall into this or any other category had just arrived in Britain on his second wartime mission to Churchill in Roosevelt's behalf. As chief administrator of the New Deal's program of public works and later as secretary of commerce, Harry Hopkins had carved a unique place for himself as an executive of extraordinary talent, daring, and zeal. As uninstructed as Roosevelt himself in the dismal science of economics, Hopkins administered relief on a pragmatic basis. It was the same story in foreign affairs. There Roosevelt had more practical experience than theoretic knowledge, but it was Bernard Baruch, who, during a weekend in March 1939, at his Hobcaw Barony estate in South Carolina, had spelled out some of the facts of international life to Hopkins, using as his text the horrible example of Neville Chamberlain. Robert Sherwood, in *Roosevelt and Hopkins,* quotes Baruch as having said, years later: "I think it took Harry a long time to realize how greatly we were involved in Europe and Asia—but once he did, he was all-out for total effort."

In another six months doctors at the Mayo Clinic had given up Hopkins as a victim of terminal cancer. Roosevelt, however, refused to accept the doctors' verdict and called in some navy doctors who subjected Hopkins to biochemical treatments used on tropical diseases. He suffered not from cancer but from an inability to absorb fats and proteins. His protein count was one-third normal. The navy doctors pulled him through. He had to quit as secretary of commerce, but he participated in the 1940 presidential campaign and on the night of May 10, 1941, when the German armies marched west, Roosevelt impulsively asked him to spend the night at the White House. He never left. The two men had not only survived similar ordeals; Roosevelt knew that Hopkins, living on borrowed time, could give him service of a kind no other human being could provide. Hopkins' health now precluded what he had hoped for from time to time: high elective office. But he had no allegiance to any party, faction, or faith. He had no ambition for money, power, or social advancement. No son could have—and certainly no son of Roosevelt's did have—a greater claim on the President's affection. Yet it was a claim of personal trust and affection only. The President owed Hopkins nothing; Hopkins had no other obligation to the President than to give the best that was in him to his task.

Those who compared the relationship between the two men with the relationship between Wilson and House during the First World War could not have been more mistaken. Roosevelt had no need of the kind of flattery which House lavished on Wilson nor did Hopkins indulge any such dreams of glory, influence, and power as House entertained. Theory, ideology, the life of the mind, and the world of the imagination made little appeal to either Roosevelt or Hopkins. Politics and the exercise of power fascinated them both, and they had similar instincts for the practical and the pragmatic. But if Roosevelt had the sharper instinct, Hopkins had the more incisive mind; if Roosevelt excelled in making himself all things to all men, Hopkins possessed the killer instinct of the born executive. Roosevelt chose Hopkins as the first, top administrator of the Lend-Lease program to Britain, sending him to London in January 1941, before Congress had a chance to act on the measure. Churchill displayed his satisfaction by dubbing Hopkins "Lord Root-of-the-Matter," and Roosevelt therefore again dispatched him to London in mid-July to discuss the current status of Lend-Lease and to prepare the ground for his forthcoming Atlantic conference with Churchill. But even before Hopkins left, he had become a zealous advocate of Lend-Lease aid to the Soviet Union.

Two weeks after the German invasion of Russia began, and a week before Hopkins left for London, he received a fifteen-hundred-word memorandum from Joseph E. Davies, which closed with this paragraph: "Specifically, I fear that if they [the Soviets] get the impression that the United States is only using them, and if sentiment grows and finds expression that the United States is equally a capitalistic enemy, it would be playing directly into the hands of Hitler and he can be counted upon to use this in his efforts to project either an armistice or peace on the Russian front after he takes the Ukraine and White Russia. Word ought to be gotten to Stalin direct that our attitude is 'all out' to beat Hitler and that our historic policy of friendliness to Russia still exists."

Whether or not Roosevelt ever saw this memorandum, he knew and endorsed the views it expressed. Whether or not he suggested that Hopkins visit Moscow after conferring with Churchill in London, he welcomed the suggestion when Hopkins—with Churchill's approval—cabled for the President's approval. It came at once and, on its heels, the copy of a cabled message to Stalin: "I ask you to treat Mr. Hopkins with the identical confidence you would feel if you were talking to me. He will communicate directly to me the views you express to him and will tell me what you consider are the most pressing individual problems on which we could be of aid." When Hopkins arrived in Moscow on July 30, he became the first top-level British or American official to confer with Stalin since Hitler had struck.

During their two sessions (the first lasting two hours, the second four), Stalin made it clear that he expected the war to last several years and while he seemed confident that Hitler could never conquer Russia, he also felt that only the United States could smash Hitler. "Give us antiaircraft guns and the aluminum," Stalin told Hopkins at one point, "and we can fight for three or four years." In a brief concluding section of the three-part report—a section that only Roosevelt saw—Stalin warned that "the might of Germany was so great that, even though Russia might defend herself, it would be very difficult for both Britain and Russia to crush the German military machine. He said that the one thing that could defeat Hitler and perhaps without firing a shot, would be that the United States was going to war with Germany." But as far as Hopkins was concerned, his stay in Moscow served only to enhance his faith in democracy. "Before my three days in Moscow were ended," he wrote, "the difference between democracy and dictatorship were clearer to me than any words of a philosopher, historian, or journalist could make it."

·4·

BY THE END of July, the battle of Russia had developed into a complex struggle as much political as military and as active behind the Russian lines as behind the German. Although Hitler had lost none of his confidence in the German timetable of victory, his vacillations were already causing his commanders to mutter among themselves about telling him off or even putting him under arrest. They did neither. From the start, they had urged him to concentrate on an all-out drive for Moscow. From the start, he refused to make so firm and final a commitment. On August 3 he ordered a half step in a safer direction and gave priority to Leningrad. Leeb responded halfheartedly but in two weeks had the city surrounded. Whereupon Hitler ordered him only to blockade but not storm it. Meanwhile Bock's drive toward Moscow faltered. Only Rundstedt in the Ukraine kept to his original schedule. In mid-September he took the capital city of Kiev and more than half a million prisoners. But the retreating Russians blew up the Zaporozhe Dam on the Dnieper River, an "engineering masterpiece of the Proletarian Revolution" and sabotaged the factories for which it furnished the power. This fenced off one third of the German forces in the Ukraine at a time when lack of manpower and weapons was delaying the German advances toward Moscow and Leningrad.

The Ukraine also became a vast wasteland of brutality and destruction on the Polish model. But with this difference. Many Ukrainians had long resented Communist Russian rule as bitterly as the Poles had resented the rule of czarist Russia. But the Ukrainians had so little experience with the Germans that they at first greeted them as liberators. Heinrich Himmler's Schutzstaffel organization of secret police and uniformed assassins soon put a stop to that as they tried to make the entire Ukraine into a slave-labor camp along Polish lines. As Goering outlined the program to his protégé, Erich Koch, a former railway clerk from the Rhineland who ruled the Ukraine as he pleased, subject only to Hitler's approval: "Like the skimmed fat at the top of bouillon, there is a thin, intellectual level on the surface of the Ukrainian people; do away with it and the leaderless mass will become an obedient and help-less herd."

It took another quarter of a century for the full story to reach the outside world, but millions of Russians had met similar fates—at Stalin's hands, rather than Hitler's. The outside world knew that in 1931 Stalin's industrialization program had included the starvation of five million of Russia's more prosperous and successful peasants. Between 1934 and 1936 his purge trials of most of Lenin's surviving associates received wide publicity. His execution, in 1937 and 1938, of three of the Red army's five marshals, fourteen of its sixteen army commanders, and all eight of the Red fleet's admirals received less attention. Even the Soviet public (not to mention the world outside) received no official word that between 1934 and 1940 Stalin had almost one million Communist party members arrested or that during 1937 and 1938 he had more than eight and a half million political prisoners thrown into forced-labor camps where one in every ten received immediate death sentences. The death rate in the camps stood at ten per cent a year; most of the sentences ran as long as ten years. As a result only ten per cent of the labor-camp inmates came out alive. Between 1930 and 1936, deaths in the labor camps totaled three and a half million. During the decade prior to the German invasion of Russia, Stalin had therefore liquidated some ten million Soviet citizens, about half of them from among the cream of the peasantry, the other half from the cream of the middle and professional classes. Yet, the rough treatment millions of Russians had received at Stalin's hands did not turn them against him when the Germans struck any more than the Germans turned against Hitler, in revulsion, when he ordered them to commit atrocities against the Poles, Ukrainians, and Russians.

Insofar as the Russian campaign promoted dissension within the German armed forces, the opposition to Hitler came from members of the general staff who objected to his vacillating strategies rather than from any conscientious objectors to his immoral tactics. At the end of September, the supreme command of the German armed forces estimated Russian losses at two and a half million men, 22,000 pieces of artillery, 18,000 tanks, and 14,000 planes. Leeb's troops had isolated Leningrad; Rundstedt's troops had torn the Ukraine away from the Soviet Union, and Nazi officials had begun to administer it as a German colonial domain. On October 3, Hitler told a mass meeting in Berlin: "I declare today and I declare it without any reservation that the enemy in the east has been struck down and will never rise again." The boast coincided with the opening of a new offensive against Moscow. Within three days, General Heinz Guderian announced: "A complete breakthrough has been effected." On October 8 one of his tank divisions entered the city of Orel, some three hundred miles south of Moscow. On October 10, Hitler's press chief, Dr. Otto Dietrich, summoned a press conference at which he announced, "Soviet Russia is done with. The British dream of a two-front war is dead."

By this time the immense scope of the war in Russia had made Nazi propaganda meaningless, irrelevant, and archaic. No longer could Hitler apply his early dictum: the bigger the lie, the more widely it is believed. For the big liar cannot tell his big lie unless he first knows the big truth he wants to distort and misrepresent. The fighting in Russia now covered so much territory and assumed so many forms that Nazis and Communists, Germans and Russians, belligerents and neutrals had to make what they could of bits and pieces of more or less accurate information and more or less expert interpretation. The German High Command had done just that in the estimates of Russian losses it released in late September. Hitler and Dietrich added a few more embellishments, based on the new drive toward Moscow launched by Bock's forces in early October. But when they predicted immediate and total Soviet collapse, they were not telling a deliberate "big lie." They had fallen into the older human error of basing wishful conclusions on insufficient evidence.

During the first few months of the battle of Russia, the sins of Stalin and Molotov were visited upon the Russian people; by October and November, the German people were beginning to pay for the sins of Hitler and Ribbentrop. Gradually, however, the character of the Russian soldier proved the decisive factor. Although the Germans scored many breakthroughs in 1941, they encountered in the Red army soldier a new kind of fighting man. Even in defeat, the Soviet soldier scented future victory; even in victory, the German soldier scented future defeat; never did the morale of Russian troops crack as French morale had. This gave the Germans a shock, but it was the Soviet soldier's contempt for death, his disregard of pain that produced the more shattering effect. As early as June 29, 1941, Hitler's *Völkische Beobachter* was reporting: "The Russian soldier surpasses our adversary in the west in his contempt for death. Endurance and fatalism make him hold out until he is blown up with his trench in hand-to-hand fighting." As Soviet Marshal Nikolai Krylov put it: "The Russian soldier loves a fight and scorns death. He was given the order, 'If you are wounded, pretend to be dead; wait until the Germans come up; then select one of them and kill him! Kill him with gun, bayonet, or knife. Tear his throat open with your teeth. Do not die without leaving behind you a German corpse.' "

Leeb in the north, Rundstedt in the south, and Bock at the center believed their own communiqués as implicitly as Hitler and Dietrich believed their own propaganda. But by November, Leeb could do no better than stabilize the blockade of Leningrad; on November 29, Rundstedt's armies met the first defeat that any German ground troops had suffered since 1918. Having captured Rostov, the "gateway to the Caucasus" on November 19, Rundstedt had to yield to Russian counterattacks and withdraw ten days later. But the decisive battle of the campaign took place on the central front at the gates of Moscow where a new Soviet commander, Marshal Gregori Zhukov, organized a successful defense of the city. Fresh troops from Siberia, using new T-34 tanks that Guderian acknowledged as superior to his own, gradually wore down and eventually threw back the attackers. Seventeen re-equipped Russian armies, most of them led by new commanders, joined the battle. The "last heave" attempted by the Germans on December 2 failed. On December 5, Marshal Zhukov opened a counteroffensive.

·5·

THE NEW WEAPONS and tactics that Hitler had used against Poland and France won victories that shook the world. But the weapons and tactics, new and old, with which the Russians met the German invasion turned Hitler's victories to defeats. Although Stalin had no new weapons or tactics at hand to hurl back the first German onslaught, the time that Hitler lost in starting his campaign and the space in which the Russians deployed their superior manpower robbed the blitzkreig of its distinctive attribute: surprise. Rough terrain, heavy weather, heavier tanks, and superior artillery threw the Germans further and further behind schedule and aggravated tensions between Hitler and his generals, between the Party and the Army.

When the first round of the battle of Russia found the German armies still on the wrong side of Leningrad, Rostov, and Moscow, the German generals had no trouble blaming all their difficulties and defeats on Hitler. It did not occur to them to ask themselves where they would have been without him. Hitler, by the same token, had no difficulty asking and answering that same question to his own entire satisfaction. Only Rundstedt had attained his assigned objective—only to lose it within ten days. And only Rundstedt had regarded the whole Russian gamble as hopeless from the start. A Prussian of the Prussians, he carried out, up to a point, orders in which he had no faith. After the Russians had retaken Rostov on November 29, Rundstedt asked to be allowed to establish winter headquarters on the Mius River, 40 miles to the west. Hitler—accompanied by Brauchitsch, the commander in chief, and Halder, the chief of staff—paid Rundstedt the honor of visiting him at his headquarters instead of summoning him to theirs. When Rundstedt blamed his predicament on those who had planned the campaign, Hitler exploded, and Brauchitsch collapsed with a heart attack. Rundstedt submitted his resignation on the grounds of his failing health. Hitler eventually accepted it, but added that he would never accept a similar request from any other commander, inasmuch as *he* could not go to *his* only superior, God Almighty, with a similar excuse.

For once, Hitler had lapsed into understatement. The strain under which he worked and the drugs he gobbled up to ease that strain had wrecked his nervous system and undermined his health. When Leeb, who wanted to pull the northern armies back into Poland, and Bock, who wanted to shorten the Moscow salient, suffered breakdowns in rapid succession, Hitler gladly let them both go. On December 7, Brauchitsch submitted his resignation as commander in chief; Hitler accepted it on December 19, at once stepping into his shoes. To Halder, who remained as chief of staff, he confided, "This little matter of operational command is something anyone can do. The task of commander in chief is to educate the army in a National Socialist sense. I don't know a single general who can do that the way I want it done."

Nor did he know a single general who approved of his all-purpose, National Socialist strategy of standing firm and fighting to the last man to hold every position everywhere under any and all circumstances. But when he proposed and put through that strategy on the central front, during the winter of 1941–42, it accomplished precisely the results he wanted. First, the Germans held most of their positions; the Russians did not even try to score any major breakthroughs. Second, the achievement restored German morale. Third, spring weather found the Germans hundreds of miles deeper into Russian territory than they would have been had the strategy of the generals prevailed. So, as far as Hitler and his generals were concerned, he had a somewhat better reason to downgrade them than they had to downgrade him.

On the other side of the lines they ordered these matters better. There, Stalin had liquidated the Soviet Union's political and military leaders with fine impartiality, learning, as he did so, more from the defeats the Red Army had suffered during the summer and fall of 1941 than Hitler had learned from the Wehrmacht's victories. Like Hitler, Stalin had fired his older commanders, but on charges of overconfidence, not of insubordination. Unlike Hitler, Stalin did not assume operational command; he promoted younger men while continuing to supervise the war effort as a whole. Unlike Hitler, Stalin kept out of the public eye, especially when things went badly. Loudspeakers carried recordings from his July 3 speech to the front lines, but not until the evening of November 6 and the morning of November 7 did he speak again and on both those occasions he had something new to say.

On the first of them he spoke before the Moscow City Soviet, making the same appeal for a second front in western Europe that he had made in his first message to Churchill. On November 7, the anniversary of the Russian Revolution, Stalin addressed himself to the Red Army troops, to whom he laid down an entirely new line: "'The whole world is looking upon you as the power capable of destroying the German robber hordes! The enslaved peoples of Europe are looking upon you as their liberators. . . . Be worthy of this great mission! The war you are waging is a war of liberation, a just war. May you be inspired in this war by the heroic figures of our great ancestors, Alexander Nevsky, Dimitri Donskoi, Minin and Pozharsky, Alexander Suvorov, Michael Kutuzov. May you be blessed by Lenin's great victorious banner!"

Alexander Nevsky, it should be added, had defeated the Teutonic Knights in 1242, Dmitri Donskoi had repelled the Tatars in 1380, Kozma Minin and Prince Pozharsky had repelled a Polish invasion in the seventeenth century, and Suvorov and Kutuzov had driven out Napoleon. Stalin also invoked the names of such cultural heroes as Pushkin, Tolstoi, and Tchaikovsky. His "Holy Russia" speech described the Soviet Union as waging a "Great Patriotic War" against the German-Fascist imperialists (no reference to Japan) as a member of the new Big Three, Great Coalition of Britain, America, and the Soviet Union.

What a contrast between Stalin's "Holy Russia" speech on the "Great Patriotic War" and his prewar warnings that the Soviet Union would not pull anybody's chestnuts out of the fire. No more talk of socialism—not even in one country. Now the Soviet Union had become one of the Big Three, along with Britain and America, who had formed a Great Coalition capable of outproducing Germany three to one in this new war of machines. Indeed, Stalin announced that an Anglo-American mission headed by Lord Beaverbrook and Averell Harriman would soon arrive with plans to supply the Red Army with planes and tanks plus a billion dollars' worth of Lend-Lease credits from the United States. A new Stalin had a new message for an old Russia—a message that transcended the frontiers of the old Russia and called for the liberation of a new Europe. Sharp as the contrast was between the new Stalin and the old, the contrast between the new Stalin and the old Hitler had become sharper still.

.　.　.

In June 1941, the news of Hitler's invasion of Russia shook the world as it had not been shaken since the news of the Nazi-Soviet pact broke in August 1939. To students of Russo-German relations, the news of the Nazi-Soviet pact came as no surprise. They remembered that the mighty Bismarck in the 1880's and the brilliant Rathenau in the 1920's had both promoted close relations between their country and Russia. Nor did Hitler's violation of the Nazi-Soviet pact come as much surprise to those students of Russo-German relations, who remembered the terrible defeat that imperial Russia suffered at the hands of imperial Germany in the First World War—a defeat that many Russians had neither forgotten nor forgiven.

But events in both Russia and Germany had moved at accelerating speed since the First World War. With the Bolshevik Revolution of 1917, Russian history entered a new era over most of which Stalin had presided. The purges that he set in motion reached their peak during the later 1930's, but the death toll of political prisoners in the forced-labor camps continued until Stalin himself died in March 1953. Robert Conquest, in *The Great Terror*, has estimated that Stalin's purges, executions, and forced-labor camps claimed the lives of twenty million Russians during a twenty-year period. It took longer than that for the full story to become known.

The Nazi Revolution moved at a faster pace than the Bolshevik Revolution did. During the six years between January 1933, when Hitler came to power, and September 1939, when his troops invaded Poland, he had concentrated on building the German war machine and making the concentration camp a national institution. Not until the outbreak of war did the mass killings and atrocities begin. German and Polish Jews and Polish war prisoners and civilians became the first victims. By the end of the war the Germans had exterminated six million European Jews and done away, by various means, with more than twice as many war prisoners, slave laborers, and assorted civilians in Poland, Russia, Yugoslavia, France, and other countries their armies had overrun. Although the full story of the Nazi atrocities did not become known until after the war, it came out soon enough and contained more than enough horrors to stir wider and deeper revulsions than Stalin's killings ever did.

But it was the first six months of the German campaign in Russia that reversed the whole course of the war. After retreating on all fronts, the Russians not only held both Moscow and Leningrad; they brought in fresh troops and equipment that the Germans could not match, either in quantity or in quality. Of course, the soldiers in the Red army thirsted to avenge themselves on the German invaders and pay them back in their own coin. But the very sufferings that each side inflicted on the other offered the most convincing proof that Germans and Russians could never again go for each other as they did between 1941 and 1945. A quarter of a century later the wounds have not yet healed on either side.

VIII
Westward the Star of Empire

·1·

WHAT THE NAZI-SOVIET PACT began in 1939 the Russo-Japanese neutrality pact completed in 1941. Neither pact fulfilled the original expectations of those who signed it. Hitler and Stalin had not expected to fight each other to the death; Matsuoka and Stalin had not expected their nonaggression agreement to ensure American intervention in the war that Germany had started in Europe and the war that Japan had started in Asia. Still less did they foresee these two regional conflicts merging into a single global one. It remained for the Soviet Union, Britain, and the United States to reap what Germany and Japan had sowed and to overextend themselves in the process.

The first weekend of December 1941 saw two climacteric clashes interlock in these two regional conflicts. Before nightfall on Friday, December 5, the Russian defenders of Moscow threw back the last "great heave" of the German attackers. Early in the morning of Sunday, December 7, the surprise attack by a Japanese task force on the American base at Pearl Harbor destroyed more than half of the United States Navy's strength in the Pacific. Six months of the war's hardest fighting preceded the Russian victory at Moscow. From a clear and peaceful sky, Japanese planes knocked out the Pearl Harbor base within a few hours. Yet—thanks to this attack—the Russians could save Moscow, now that Japan posed no threat to their rear.

The events leading up to the grand climax at Moscow began in April 1941 when Matsuoka left that city to the echo of Stalin's boast, "I, too, am an Asiatic." The two men had just agreed to sign a neutrality pact, and Stalin's remark contained less hot air than cold truth as the Japanese foreign minister later learned. For Stalin, in his Asian capacity, had no more reason to identify himself with Japan than he had to identify himself with Germany in his European capacity. Two months later, the payoff began, the day before Hitler's armies invaded the Soviet Union.

It so happened that Washington, on that very day, dispatched a long note to Tokyo restating its refusal to recognize the special position the Japanese claimed for themselves in China and warning them not to stake out similar claims in southeast Asia. The note also insisted that any new Japanese-American agreement must include a Japanese pledge to remain neutral in the event of war between Germany and the United States, a clause that Matsuoka at once seized upon to vindicate his own pro-German, anti-American bias. But Premier Konoye, in his turn, seized upon Hitler's failure to give his Japanese ally advance notice of his invasion of Russia to declare that this violation of the tripartite pact that Matsuoka had just invoked rendered it null and void. Ribbentrop then completed Matsuoka's ruin by proposing a surprise Japanese attack on Siberia as the quickest way to knock the Soviet Union out of the war and to isolate the United States. On July 2, Emperor Hirohito and his privy council, the supreme policymaking group in Japan, ousted Matsuoka and brought the nation's army and navy leaders together in an imperial effort of even greater scope than their turn-of-the-century war with Russia.

So much for the upstart Matsuoka, the pipsqueak Ribbentrop, and their abortive tripartite pact. But the rulers of Japan—civilians and soldiers, generals and admirals—were no more prepared to accommodate themselves to the demands of the United States than the Americans were prepared to recognize Japan's conquests, old or new. Instead of breaking their neutrality pact with the Soviet Union and joining the Germans, who had just violated the tripartite pact, the Japanese leaders decided to take advantage of the Russo-German war to launch their own program of expansion to the south and east. This involved the withdrawal of most of their troops from the Siberian-Manchurian frontier with the Soviet Union, followed by preparations to move in on French Indochina, the Netherlands Indies, and Britain's holdings in the Malay States, Burma, Singapore, and Hong Kong.

In mid-August, two Communist agents, one of whom had penetrated the Japanese Foreign Office, the other the German Embassy at Tokyo, got word to Stalin that Japan would not attack the Soviet Union that year. Two months later they informed him that the Japanese planned to shift their expansionist moves from northwestern to southeastern Asia.

When Stalin learned of the Japanese troop withdrawals from their side of the Manchurian-Siberian frontier, he ordered corresponding withdrawals from his side, shifting from Siberia the troops that saved Moscow in December. Concerning the surprise Japanese attack on Pearl Harbor, which coincided with the final German push on Moscow, Stalin received no information—his Japanese and German informants in Tokyo having received none themselves.

By definition, coincidence occurs by chance. But the great coincidences of history obey a different logic in that sometimes they occur when deeper, calculable forces come into play. Chance did not decree the timing of executing the German decision to invade the Soviet Union. Chance did not decree that the first, crucial stage of that invasion had to reach its last climacteric when and where it did. Nor did chance decree either the timing or the execution of the Japanese decision to embark on their program of southeasterly expansion which reached its first climacteric at Pearl Harbor. The fall of France and the German invasion of Russia offered the Japanese opportunities that might not come again for another thousand years. But sheer coincidence decreed that the Moscow climacteric and the Pearl Harbor climacteric occurred over the same weekend.

These coincidences and climacterics had one common attribute. They occurred at accelerating speed. In February 1941, President Roosevelt remarked to Secretary of the Treasury Morgenthau, "I have got to see Churchill myself in order to explain things to him." At that time, Churchill's Britain alone held the fort against Hitler—the fort that later became the fortress from which the Anglo-American armies liberated western Europe. By August 9, when Roosevelt and Churchill held their first wartime meeting, the battle of Britain had expanded into the battle of the Atlantic, which the battle of Russia already overshadowed. Lend-Lease supplies had begun to flow to Britain, soon to be supplemented by similar shipments to the Soviet Union. A great new hope and a great new fear had arisen: the hope that the battle of Russia might bleed Germany to death; the fear that Japan might take advantage of that battle to spread the war to the Pacific and thereby distract the United States from the battle of the Atlantic and the war against Hitler.

· 2 ·

WHATEVER ROOSEVELT wanted to explain to Churchill back in February had become irrelevant when they met six months later, and, within another four months, when that eventful first weekend in December required them to think, plan, and act anew. At their first meeting, Roosevelt, aboard the cruiser *Augusta,* flagship of the Atlantic fleet, arranged to rendezvous with Churchill aboard the ill-starred *Prince of Wales* off Argentia on the Newfoundland coast. The two statesmen, each accompanied by scores of political and military advisers, remained in close contact from August 9 through August 12. Nobody aboard the *Prince of Wales* or the *Augusta* questioned the importance of aid to the Soviet Union. Russian needs had become so urgent and the difficulties of meeting them so great that the question was not whether to meet them but when and how. Indeed, it was to procure the latest and most reliable information on this subject that Roosevelt and Churchill both sponsored the Hopkins visit to Moscow, which he wound up in time to join them at their Atlantic conference. There, his report on his talks with Stalin so impressed them that they decided on the spot to rush an Anglo-American military mission to Moscow.

On July 26, in a last effort to halt Japanese expansion toward the Netherlands Indies, Roosevelt had frozen all Japanese assets in the United States. When he suggested that the Japanese join the United States in recognizing the neutrality of Indochina and Siam and that they pledge to keep hands off the Netherlands Indies, they turned him down and refused to give up any positions they already held. Roosevelt and Hull wanted to keep on stalling for time. Churchill argued that "only the stiffest warning from the United States could have the slightest counteracting effect"; Roosevelt doubted that Congress would back him and declined to join Churchill in an Anglo-American warning. Finally, it was agreed to have Roosevelt serve a friendly but firm personal warning to Admiral Nomura, Japan's pro-American ambassador in Washington. The most Roosevelt hoped for, at the time, was to be able to "baby the Japs along" for another thirty days.

The termination of the Atlantic conference coincided with the decision of the Japanese government to continue its program of southward expansion and to respect its neutrality pact with the Soviet Union. Nomura knew no more about these decisions than Roosevelt did and therefore took his warning in a friendly, casual spirit. But nobody—least of all the Japanese leaders—had any foreboding of the historic role that their decisions had already assigned to Roosevelt in connection with their country's future. The Atlantic conference had done nothing to restrain or hamper Stalin in his conduct of the battle of Russia—and everything, within its limited range—to aid and comfort him. It had also placed in Roosevelt's hands full and exclusive responsibility for dealing with Japan—up to and beyond the point of open hostilities.

For the record, the participants in the conference expressed satisfaction in the atmosphere of trust and friendliness that prevailed. Yet Roosevelt and Churchill both felt the occasion required some appropriate public gesture. With a minimum of advance preparation and in what time they could snatch from the transaction of other business, they and their aides hammered out an eight-point "Atlantic Charter" setting forth "certain common principles in the national policies of their respective countries on which they base their hopes for a better future of the world." The eight-point declaration that followed (signed only by Roosevelt and Churchill) announced that their countries sought "no aggrandizement, territorial or other." They wanted "no territorial changes that do not accord with the freely expressed wishes of the peoples concerned." They respected "the rights of all peoples to choose the form of government under which they will live." They promised "with due respect to their existing obligations" to promote free trade and equal access to the raw materials of the earth, by all nations. They hoped "after the final destruction of the Nazi tyranny . . . that all men in all the lands may live out their lives in freedom from fear and want." They called for freedom of the seas, disarmament, and eventual establishment of a general system of world security.

A month before the Atlantic conference opened, General Wavell, as supreme British commander in the Middle East, had warned Churchill that the Germans planned to use Iran's self-made monarch, Riza Shah Pahlevi, to set up a pro-Nazi regime in Teheran, where the Grand Mufti of Jerusalem, the foremost pro-Nazi, anti-Jewish, anti-British figure in the Moslem world, had established himself. "It is essential," wrote Wavell, "we should join hands with Russia through Iran and if the present government is not willing to facilitate this, it must give way to one which will." Within the week the British and Soviet governments sent parallel notes to Teheran, demanding that by September 15, it expel all Germans from the country, including some two thousand technicians who had trickled in since 1939, disguised as tourists. The Shah's government refused, and on August 17 the British and Soviet governments warned they would send troops in if the Shah did not send the Germans out.

The Shah appealed to Roosevelt in the name of the newly signed

Atlantic Charter; the State Department stalled for a few days; on August 28, a new Iranian government accepted the Anglo-Soviet demands. The exigencies of war not only overrode the principles of the Atlantic Charter; they threw Churchill and Stalin into each other's arms. Within a few weeks the Shah abdicated in favor of his 22-year-old son. Neither the new government nor the old had any popular mandate. Wilson's Fourteen Points had not made the world safe for democracy, nor did Roosevelt's Four Freedoms so much as promise to do so. But the Atlantic Charter (along with its hodgepodge of generalities, evasions, and reservations) did call specifically for "the final destruction of the Nazi tyranny." From that principle Churchill's Britain had never wavered, nor had Roosevelt, to the extent that his oath of office permitted. Stalin's Russia, on the other hand, embraced the principle only after Hitler violated the nonaggression pact that he and Stalin had signed. That Stalin's attempt to play both ends against the middle had now backfired did not make the predicament in which he found himself any more tolerable.

· 3 ·

THE ANGLO-SOVIET ACCORD on Iran did not reconcile Stalin to the Anglo-American Atlantic Charter. Both left him equally unimpressed. Not until the end of September could be bring himself to receive the Anglo-American mission—decided upon in mid-August—and permit it to start work on a joint schedule for the delivery of weapons. Throughout the summer of 1941, Stalin found himself in the bind to which he had assigned Churchill, who, in his turn, had little sympathy for Stalin's demand that the British at once open a second front in western Europe or—failing that—send twenty-five or thirty divisions, which they did not possess, to fight beside the Red army in the east. "It might almost have been thought," wrote Churchill afterward, with restrained irony, "that the plight in which the Soviets found themselves was our fault."

On the other hand, when Roosevelt returned to Washington, he had such a pleasant conference with Admiral Nomura that it softened the warning he had planned to serve. At the same time, the Argentia meeting inspired Premier Konoye to sound out Roosevelt about holding a similar meeting with him at Honolulu. The President no longer had to worry about "babying the Japs along" for another thirty days. It was for Konoye that time was running out—and faster than he thought, because he assumed that he and the President could hammer out the terms of their agreement after they met, whereas Roosevelt insisted on the traditional diplomatic protocol of agreement first and meeting afterward.

Ambassador Joseph C. Grew, who favored the meeting, cabled from Tokyo on September 12 what he described as "perhaps the most significant message" of his mission, by then in its eighth year. Discussing oil embargoes and other economic sanctions, he warned: "The risks would depend not so much upon the careful calculations of the Japanese Government as upon the uncalculating 'do or die' temper of the Army and Navy should they impute to the United States the responsibility for the failure of their plans for expansion. It may be that such retaliation would take the form of counter-measures by the Government, but it would be more likely that the Navy or Army would strike suddenly without prior authorization or knowledge of the Government." If Konoye were to fall, Grew added, the military would take over and not hesitate to gamble everything on surprise attacks, even at such unlikely targets as Pearl Harbor.

Shortly before the Grew cable arrived, Roosevelt seized a welcome opportunity to commit the United States more deeply to the battle of the Atlantic. A British search plane had informed the American destroyer *Greer*, en route to Iceland with passengers and mail, that a German submarine lay ten miles ahead. The *Greer* located the submarine and gave chase. The submarine, defying Hitler's orders, fired two torpedoes. Both missed the *Greer*, which dropped depth bombs with unknown effect. Roosevelt denounced the action as "piracy, legally and morally," warning that "if German or Italian vessels of war enter into the waters the protection of which is necessary for American defense, they do so at their own peril." He also promised protection to "shipping of any nationality" that cared to join convoys moving between American ports and Iceland."

On the night of October 16–17 a pack of German submarines clashed with a group of American and British destroyers four hundred miles south of Iceland. A German torpedo struck the American destroyer *Kearny*, killing and wounding many members of the crew. The next day the House of Representatives repealed the section of the Neutrality Act forbidding the arming of American merchantmen. A month later both the House and Senate repealed all those sections of the Neutrality Act that had whittled away the freedom-of-the-seas doctrine invoked by Wilson when he declared war on Germany in 1917. The Gallup poll now showed 81 per cent of the American people in favor of arming merchant vessels and 61 per cent in favor of having them carry supplies to England. Yet as recently as July 29, an earlier Gallup poll had shown only 51 per cent of the people in favor of extending the draft for another year and when the matter came before the House of Representatives on August 12 (the day the Atlantic conference ended) 203 voted in favor, 202 against.

· 4 ·

The *Greer* incident occurred one month after the Atlantic conference ended. The *Kearny* incident occurred after another month had passed. On October 15, the day before the *Kearny* incident, Prince Konoye stepped down as premier in favor of General Hideki Tojo, who had held the post of war minister since Japan signed the tripartite pact in September 1940. In 1937 he had become chief of staff of the crack Kwantung army in Manchuria, where his administrative skill and strict execution of orders won him the respect and confidence of the army expansionists. Tojo had no kind of personal or political following. It was his bureaucratic talents that brought him to the top of a bureaucratic army. On replacing Konoye, he promptly rejected any settlement with the United States entailing any troop withdrawals from China. On this issue, as on many others, he and Konoye saw eye to eye. They differed in that Tojo acted and spoke for the army, whereas Konoye, a relative of the Emperor and a man devoted to Western ways, did not even take his politics seriously and went along with the militarists through sheer inertia. Nor had the bureaucratic general Tojo resented serving under Konoye; indeed, he retained the services of Shigenori Togo, Konoye's newly installed and moderate foreign minister.

It came as no surprise to Roosevelt that the rulers of Japan seemed determined to hasten a showdown with the United States in the Pacific at a time when Hitler seemed to be trying to "baby along" the Americans in the Atlantic. But where might this lead? On September 25, the Joint Army-Navy Board in Washington outlined some startling possibilities in a confidential report to the President, regarding the prospects of a German victory in Europe at a time when war with Japan in the Pacific had become his prime concern. According to this report, the prospect of a popular revolt of the German people against the Nazi regime seemed "unlikely in the near future and will not occur until Germany is upon the point of military defeat. It is the opinion of the Joint Board that Germany and her European satellites cannot be defeated by the European powers now fighting against her. Therefore, if our European enemies are to be defeated, it will be necessary for the United States to enter the war and to deploy a part of its armed forces offensively in the Eastern Atlantic and in Europe or Africa." The Joint Board went on to define "the complete military defeat of Germany" as the "number one objective" of the United States. It predicted that this task would require an army of eight million men—an estimate that even Secretary of War Stimson found "staggering." But the Joint Board did not share Secretary Stimson's confidence in America's power in the Pacific. In a subsequent memorandum, dated November 5, the same Joint Board informed the President that the United States fleet in the Pacific was inferior to the Japanese fleet and could not undertake an unlimited offensive in the western part of that ocean. Moreover, if the Pacific fleet were strengthened sufficiently to challenge the Japanese in their own waters, that "might well cause the United Kingdom to lose the Battle of the Atlantic in the near future."

The Japanese had no need of secret agents to know that Roosevelt gave the Atlantic priority over the Pacific, Europe over Asia, and Germany over Japan. They did not need to tap White House telephone lines to know that Roosevelt had told Ickes: "I simply have not got enough navy to go around." In like manner the Roosevelt administration knew that Tojo's promotion from war minister to premier had brought war closer—just how much closer it was hard to say. Tojo was no dictator, no Stalin, no Hitler. He served under an emperor who had inherited a throne that dated back more than two thousand years. But the so-called Meiji Constitution of 1889, named for the grandfather of Emperor Hirohito, had enabled Japan, within the space of a single generation, to make the transition from feudal to representative government, of a sort. Under this constitution all power lay in the hands of a six-man inner cabinet within a ten-man privy council over which the emperor presided. In the Japan of Emperor Hirohito, as in the Japan of his grandfather, the Japanese army had favored expansion on the Asian mainland in Korea, Manchuria, and China; the Japanese navy favored maritime expansion, beyond Formosa and toward the Philippines and southeast Asia. But the army's recent attempt to add the richest regions of overpopulated China to Japan's *Lebensraum* had proved no more successful than Hitler's similar efforts in eastern Europe. On the other hand, the fall of France had opened the door to Japanese penetration of southeastern Asia, while the battle of the Atlantic opened wide vistas on the Pacific.

What the Roosevelt administration did not and could not know was that since January 1, 1941, Admiral Isoroku Yamamoto, commander in chief of the Japanese navy, had headed a group of high army and navy officers in planning a surprise attack on Pearl Harbor, designed to eliminate and exclude American naval power from the western Pacific for a full year. Like many of his naval colleagues Yamamoto opposed a naval showdown with the United States under any circumstances. But the army leaders, frustrated in China, saw in the war that Hitler had launched in Europe, Japan's opportunity to seize southeast Asia and drive the United States from at least half of the Pacific Ocean. Against his better judgment, Yamamoto undertook planning the Pearl Harbor attack on the dubious assumption that if Japan could win and hold control of the western Pacific for an entire year, it could never be dislodged from China or southeast Asia.

The Roosevelt administration had no inkling that Japan planned any such attack. Nor had the Japanese leaders any inkling that American intelligence agents, in the midsummer of 1941, had cracked the secret diplomatic code in which they instructed their ships where to go and their diplomats what to do throughout the world. Thus, on November 19, American radio monitors and decoders picked up a message from Tokyo informing Japanese officials everywhere that a breakdown in Japan's relations with America, Britain, or Russia impended. The message added that when Tokyo knew the break was sure, it would insert a special message in the middle of the daily short-wave, Japanese-language news broadcast. The words "east wind rain" would signify trouble with the United States; "north wind cloudy" trouble with Russia; "west wind clear" trouble with Britain. And on November 22, American officials heard Tokyo inform Ambassador Nomura in Washington that if he did not sign an agreement with the United States by November 29: "After that things are automatically going to happen."

This referred to a foredoomed peace mission that Tojo permitted moderate, civilian Foreign Minister Togo to sponsor. Togo at once dispatched to Washington the professional Japanese diplomat Saburo Kurusu, who, while ambassador in Berlin, had signed the tripartite pact. But the English-speaking Kurusu had closer ties with the United States. He had married his American secretary; their son was an American citizen; Kurusu, on his arrival aboard a Pan-American clipper, told reporters he still hoped "to score a touchdown for peace." Soon he and Nomura began a series of conferences with Hull, culminating on November 26 in a final ten-point American offer. But three of these points made demands unacceptable to the Japanese: evacuation of all Japanese troops from China and Indochina; Japanese abandonment of the Chinese puppet regime at Nanking; Japanese acceptance of Chiang Kai-shek's Nationalist regime as China's only government.

Roosevelt and Hull had not acted carelessly or hastily when they placed these unacceptable proposals before Japan's two envoys. They could not accept anything less and could not see any purpose in further stalling. Nor did Hull expect anything but rejection from Japan. On November 27, the day after presenting his note to the envoys, Hull told Secretary of War Stimson: "I have washed my hands of it and it is now in the hands of you and Knox—the army and the navy." And the army and navy people—like those in the State Department—assumed that the Japanese would hurl their land, sea, and air forces—especially sea and air—against the rich and weakly held territories and islands of southeastern Asia. How could Roosevelt and Hull, Stimson and Knox have known at the time that the intercepted messages in which the naval decoders took such pride revealed only a fraction of Japan's real strategy? What in their experience had made them aware that Japan's leaders might recall and apply the question that every graduate of the Japanese Naval Academy since 1931 had to answer as part of his final examination: "How would you carry out a surprise attack on Pearl Harbor?"

·5·

FOR ADMIRAL YAMAMOTO to carry out what he called "a decision diametrically opposed to my personal opinion" he had assembled, on November 16, a carrier striking force at the mouth of the Inland Sea off the southeastern tip of Honshu Island. It included six carriers, two fast battleships, two heavy cruisers, one light cruiser, eight destroyers, three oilers, one supply ship, and 360 planes. The vessels then rendezvoused a thousand miles north of Tokyo. On November 26, 1941, they weighed anchor and began steaming eastward toward their destination, two hundred miles northwest of Pearl Harbor. Twice they stopped to take on fuel and supplies, the last time on December 4. They had prepared themselves so carefully and proceeded with such caution that they made the entire journey undetected. On December 2, from his flagship on the Inland Sea, Admiral Yamamoto gave his final, irrevocable radio message to attack: "Climb Mount Niikata!" which also went to all other ships of the Japanese navy in Pacific waters.

The American triumph of cracking Japan's diplomatic code then backfired on a scale that nobody in Washington or Tokyo could have anticipated. It simply never occurred to the top American naval brass that the Japanese Navy could organize such a complex and massive operation as a successful surprise attack on Pearl Harbor. The United States Navy had learned through its intercepts that an expeditionary force of 25,000 Japanese troops was steaming toward Indochina at the very moment Secretary Hull was submitting his unacceptable ten-point peace proposal to Japan's two envoys. Because this expedition conformed with American expectations of Japanese intentions and capabilities, the possibility of a simultaneous Japanese strike at Pearl Harbor did not occur to any highly placed American at that moment. The naval decoders not only ignored the possibility of a surprise Japanese attack on Pearl Harbor, they had become so convinced that the Japanese must concentrate their expansionist efforts on southeast Asia that they ignored all other signs and portents that came their way.

The war council of President Roosevelt and Secretaries Hull, Stimson, and Knox met on the morning of November 28. That evening Stimson wrote in his diary: "It was now the opinion of everyone that if this expedition was allowed to get around the southern part of Indochina and to go off and land in the Gulf of Siam, either at Bangkok or further west, it would be a terrific blow at all three powers—Britain at Singapore, the Netherlands, and ourselves at the Philippines. It was the consensus of everybody that this must not be allowed. Then we discussed how to prevent it. It was agreed that if the Japanese got into the Isthmus of Kra the British would fight. It was also agreed that if the British fought, we would have to fight. And it now seems clear that if this expedition was allowed to round the southern point of Indochina, this whole disastrous chain of events would be set on foot or going."

There was talk of drafting two messages—the one, a last-minute personal peace appeal from the President to Emperor Hirohito, the other, a message to Congress reporting and interpreting the threat to southeast Asia. Like everybody else in Washington, the President assumed that the Japanese were planning to take early and large-scale military action in Indochina, Malaya, and Siam. On the other hand, nothing seemed to impend against the Philippines or the Dutch East Indies. Guam, Wake, Midway, and Hawaii lay even farther from the danger zone. In one respect, however, Roosevelt gave what turned out to be a remarkable display of long-distance second sight. The personal message that he finally dispatched to Hirohito one week later focused entirely on French Indochina. Roosevelt urged the Emperor to order immediate withdrawal of every Japanese soldier from Indochina and pledged the United States to do the same on condition that Siam, Malaya, and China follow that example. Perhaps he had overlooked Pearl Harbor, but Vietnam appears already to have impinged on his subconscious, if not on his conscious mind.

The leaders of Japan had no opportunity to take counsel with their subconscious. Their strategy and psychology had little in common with the ways of any other people—East or West. The Japanese had started all their wars suddenly and alone. Their alliance with Britain served them well during the First World War, but during the 1920's the British preferred to cultivate their "special relationship" with the United States. Now Hitler's sweep of western Europe followed by invasion of the Soviet Union opened new opportunities to Japan in southeast Asia and, at the same time, immobilized the Russians in Asia. What an opportunity for Japan to stake everything on a single, all-or-nothing throw of the dice. And Hitler boasted that he had launched Germany on a destiny that would last a thousand years.

But the Japanese were not modeling themselves on any other people —least of all, the Germans. The stakes for which their military and naval leaders had gambled were not world dominion or even the dominion of Asia. Japan's leaders sought only control of the western Pacific and domination of southeast Asia (which, in all conscience, was enough), but they saw no way to win this prize except by shattering American sea and air power in the western Pacific with a single blow. Not until six years after the Nazi dictatorship had come to power in Germany did Hitler dare to go to war and even then he had moved one step, one campaign, at a time. The German General Staff, on whose professional skill he depended to wage that war, remained the only alternative center of power in the country.

How different the situation in Japan. There, even the most fanatical young army officers looked upon Hirohito as divine. For his sake they had murdered generals, admirals, and prime ministers. But they had left the Meiji Constitution undisturbed and attributed to Hirohito supernatural powers in which he himself had no belief. Although Admiral Yamamoto also revered his emperor, he did not believe in the war that General Tojo wanted to fight any more than his emperor did. Nevertheless, both emperor and admiral went through the motions of supporting the war, hoping against hope that somehow, somewhere, sometime the war would end, and Japan and the Japanese would live on. Since most of their people and most of their leaders supported the policies that were now leading them to Pearl Harbor, they could not but play out the parts that their stations in life had assigned them.

At half past eight on the morning of December 4, the big United States Navy receiving station at Cheltenham, Maryland, heard the radio broadcast Japan's message of war with the United States: "east wind rain." But where and when would the blows fall? The decoders had only themselves to blame for their quandary. "A little learning is a dangerous thing." They knew enough Japanese to have decoded messages dealing with the approaching Japanese invasion of Indochina. And because these messages confirmed their fixed ideas about an immediate Japanese invasion of southeast Asia, they relaxed their zeal and neither intercepted nor translated subsequent items dealing with the more important—and therefore more secret—plan to synchronize their invasion of Indochina with the bombing of Pearl Harbor.

From reports filed by their own intelligence officers in Hawaii (Hawaiians of Japanese descent refused to co-operate), the Japanese knew that the bulk of the United States Pacific fleet, notably all eight of its major battleships, was concentrated at Pearl Harbor. The Japanese knew the position of each ship; they knew every detail of the Pearl Harbor installations; they had studied American habits and knew that on a Sunday morning precautions against a surprise attack would be at a minimum. Everything went off according to plan—according to Japanese plan, that is—as wave after wave of Japanese planes, flying from their carrier bases 275 miles north of Hawaii sank five of the eight American battleships in Pearl Harbor and put the other three out of commission. Three destroyers, a mine layer, a repair ship, and a floating dry dock were also sunk. Three light cruisers and a seaplane tender suffered damage. Of 202 navy planes at Hawaii the Japanese destroyed 80 and damaged 70; of 273 army planes they destroyed 93 and damaged almost as many more. Casualties totaled more than two thousand killed, more than a thousand wounded. Nor was this all. Four hours after the Japanese began destroying more than half of America's naval power in the Pacific, a series of surprise air attacks on the Philippines destroyed more than half America's air power in that area. Guam, Wake, and Midway islands had all come under Japanese attack. Bombs had fallen on the British Crown Colony of Hong Kong. Siam had surrendered to an army of invading Japanese who were heading toward Singapore, through the Malayan jungles and down the narrow Kra Peninsula. From Singapore the British at once dispatched their two great battleships, the *Prince of Wales* and the *Repulse,* to stop the armada of

Japanese war vessels and troop ships now sailing up the Gulf of Siam on their way to join the assault on Malaya. On December 10, Japanese air power again asserted itself, as swarms of Japanese torpedo planes and dive bombers sank both the *Prince of Wales* and the *Repulse* within the space of an hour and a half. The Allies had no more capital ships to deny Japan the mastery of the Pacific Ocean.

But the Japanese gamble that began at Pearl Harbor did not end with the sinking of the *Prince of Wales* and the *Repulse*. The decline and fall of the British Empire came next on Japan's agenda, to be accompanied by withdrawal of American power from Asia and the far Pacific. Hitler had already driven British influence from Europe. Japan would do the same in China and in southeastern Asia. And the Japanese program of Asia for the Asiatics must eventually doom British rule in India while Australia and New Zealand would wither on the vine. The United States had suffered too heavily at Hawaii, the Philippines, Guam, Wake, and Midway to be able to prevent the Japanese from consolidating themselves in all of the western Pacific, especially with Roosevelt giving priority to the war in Europe. This was also where Hitler came in. The Japanese had given the Germans no more advance information about their plans for Pearl Harbor and points west than the Germans had given the Japanese about the Nazi-Soviet pact of 1939 or the invasion of Russia two years later. But all's well that ends well. Hitler's delight at the success of Japanese arms in the Pacific made up for any pique he may have felt at having been kept in the dark.

Fourteen hours after the Japanese attack on Pearl Harbor, Japanese Imperial Headquarters declared that a state of war existed with both the United States and the British Empire. The next day, the German navy received orders to attack American ships anywhere, at any time. On December 11, the German government broke off relations with Washington and announced that Germany "as from today considers herself as being in a state of war with the United States." Italy did the same. Hitler preferred to declare war on the United States rather than have the United States declare war on Germany, which suited Roosevelt, too. As for Churchill, he regarded Pearl Harbor as a combination of long-range blessing and short-range curse. "This is what I have dreamed of, aimed at, and worked for, and now it has come to pass," he told the House of Commons. Or, as he put it later in his history of the war: "We had won the war, England would live, Britain would live, the Commonwealth and Empire would live." Two centuries earlier, viewing "On the Prospect of Planting Arts and Learning in America," Bishop

Berkeley had seen a little further and expressed it a little differently: "Westward the course of empire takes its way." Half a century later, the young John Quincy Adams put it this way in an oration delivered at Plymouth, Massachusetts, in 1802: "Westward the star of empire takes its way."

. . .

The Japanese, no less than the Americans, needed to remember Pearl Harbor. Seldom in the history of modern warfare have two major belligerents known less about each other before their conflict began or learned less about each other by the time the conflict ended. Although Admiral Yamamoto did not survive the war, he made a better record than any of his compatriots who did. For he not only masterminded the Pearl Harbor attack. He alone predicted that it could lead only to defeat and disaster for Japan. General Tojo, on the other hand, lived to see the false hopes and assumptions that Pearl Harbor stimulated turn to dust and ashes.

To the Americans Pearl Harbor administered a healthy, long-overdue shock. The sting of defeat gave the war effort the impetus it needed at the start. But the strange pattern set by Pearl Harbor continued to the end. Distance sometimes lends enchantment but rarely breeds hate. Only the closest proximity does that. The six thousand miles of Pacific Ocean that separated Japan and the United States, their different languages, traditions, and surroundings ruled out the kind of love-hate relationship that so long characterized Russo-German relations. Due to events in Europe (notably, the German invasion of the Soviet Union), the expanding Empire of the Rising Sun collided with the American star of empire as it continued along its westward course.

But what did the Empire of the Rising Sun mean to most Americans? Less than the American star of empire meant to most Japanese. Barely ninety years had passed since America's Commodore Perry had opened up the self-isolated Japanese Empire to the outside world. On the other hand, the United States since its very beginnings had cultivated the China trade, and the American missionaries came soon after. Japan's subsequent wars of aggression against China did not improve Japan's image in the United States, which, however, excluded Chinese and Japanese immigration with fine impartiality. It was in behalf of China that Secretary Hull made his unacceptable peace offer to Japan; it was because of their frustrated ambitions in China that the Japanese hit back at Pearl Harbor. But Americans in 1941 did not feel any such identification with the beleaguered Chinese as they felt for the beleaguered

British. Nor did most of them feel so strongly (one way or the other) about the Japanese as they felt about the Germans. In like manner, the Japanese had no such strong feelings about the remote Americans as they did about the nearby Russians and Chinese, with both of whom they had waged recent wars.

The surprise Japanese attack on Pearl Harbor revealed as much Japanese ignorance of America as it revealed American ignorance of Japan. General Tojo had no more understanding of the United States than Stanley K. Hornbeck, the State Department's top expert on the Far East, had of Japan. In Japan, Admiral Yamamoto was a voice crying in the wilderness when he warned his naval and military colleagues that the United States would overwhelm Japan in war; nobody in the White House or the State Department challenged the wisdom of Assistant Secretary Hornbeck when he declared that the Japanese would capitulate rather than wage suicidal war against the United States. Yamamoto was no more a genius than Hornbeck was an idiot. The Japanese and Americans stumbled into war like two blind men. Whereupon it turned out that neither of the two belligerents could carry the war to the heart of the other. The United States could not invade Japan as the Japanese had invaded China; the Japanese could not invade the United States as the Germans had invaded Poland, France, and Russia. Indeed, Japan and the United States could never have gone to war in the first place if both of them had not possessed ships and planes capable of waging long-distance war over wide stretches of the Pacific Ocean. Several of the most important engagements of that war did not involve any exchange of fire between ships of line. Air power played the decisive role throughout.

Thus Pearl Harbor left both the Americans and the Japanese with fewer points of friction than eventually developed between Stalin and the Anglo-Americans or even between Hitler and Mussolini. Nobody could have foreseen this state of affairs the day after the Pearl Harbor attack. But with the passage of time, the wisdom of hindsight brought with it surprises as great as any that the war itself witnessed. The situation, as between the United States and Japan, always remained a special one, but what situation did not? In the case of Pearl Harbor, the Japanese appeared even more deceptive than they had intended to be. The American decoders had not only missed some important details in the intercepts; they had mistranslated some passages by enlivening them with a belligerence absent from the original, colloquial Japanese. But these misunderstandings worked both ways. Emperor Hirohito, for example, never believed in his own divinity before, during, or after Pearl Harbor. American efforts to represent him as a Japanese Hitler never got off the ground. There is a saying that to understand all is to forgive all. Perhaps there is a corollary to the effect that to understand nothing is to assume nothing. Which makes for clean slates on which new beginnings can be inscribed.

IX

From Pearl to Midway

·1·

ALTHOUGH THE ATLANTIC CONFERENCE had neither foreseen nor forestalled the Pearl Harbor disaster, it did anticipate and mitigate some of the consequences. On December 22 Prime Minister Churchill, accompanied by Supply Minister Beaverbrook and the commanders of Britain's army, navy, and air force, arrived in Washington where they spent the next three weeks conferring with their American opposite numbers. They had spent the long sea voyage preparing three papers. The first dealt with immediate military operations in North Africa, the second with "The Pacific Front," the third with "The Campaign of 1943." The Americans had boned up on these and other topics. Going on from where the Atlantic Conference left off, the Arcadia Conference (as Churchill named it) reaffirmed the strategy of beating Germany first. For 1942 that meant keeping open the Pacific supply lines, tightening the noose around Hitler's "Fortress Europa," and restricting new, offensive action to North Africa.

The Americans argued vainly for an immediate invasion of Europe. The British, on whom the brunt of the burden would have fallen, refused. They had already spread their limited resources too thin on too many other fronts, no less vital. The Americans accepted the inevitable and Roosevelt welcomed, as an alternative for 1942, a series of North African landings (to be known as "Torch") that would threaten Rommel's Afrika Korps from the west and provide springboards for future assaults upon what Churchill called "the soft underbelly of the Axis." Such landings would not entail heavy, large-scale fighting and would therefore give the untried American troops the battle experience that President Roosevelt felt they required.

On January 1, 1942, the Arcadia Conference issued a joint declaration, signed in Washington by twenty-six governments and governments-in-exile, endorsing the principles of the Atlantic Charter. The final listing, written in Roosevelt's own hand, led off with the United States, the United Kingdom, the Soviet Union, and China—in that order—followed by the other twenty-two governments in alphabetical order, beginning with Australia and ending with Yugoslavia. Roosevelt, however, vetoed the inclusion of Charles de Gaulle's Free French. The signers pledged themselves to use their full resources against "those members of the Tripartite Pact," with which they were at war and not to sign any separate peace or armistice. Governments of other nations were invited to adhere to these principles and to join "the struggle for victory over Hitlerism," as the Russians insisted on calling it. For the words "Associated Powers" used in the Atlantic Charter, Roosevelt substituted the words "United Nations."

Before the United Nations Declaration appeared, the newly promoted Brigadier General Dwight D. Eisenhower, General Douglas MacArthur's former chief of staff in the Philippines, had completed his first assignment as assistant chief of the War Department's War Plans Division. At the request of General George C. Marshall, the chief of staff, he had prepared a memorandum on the defense of the Philippines, entitled "Plan for an Australian Base," which Marshall approved on December 17. Eisenhower spent the next several weeks vainly seeking ways and means to relieve MacArthur's doomed forces. Finally, the Arcadia meeting improvised a new ABDA Command (American-British-Dutch-Australian), with headquarters on the island of Java, to be headed by Britain's General Wavell. Although the Japanese overran most of the ABDA theater by the end of February 1942, the Wavell appointment set a precedent that proved historic. Churchill and Field Marshal Sir Alan Brooke, who had just replaced Sir John Dill as chief of Britain's Imperial General Staff, opposed the principle of unified command on which Marshall had insisted and to which Roosevelt had to be converted. The principle of unified command called for the creation of a Combined Chiefs of Staff with permanent headquarters in Washington. Field Marshal Dill would represent Britain on this body, which would direct the entire Anglo-American war effort, always subject to the ultimate civilian control exercised by Roosevelt and Churchill. In the case of ABDA, and all other theaters of war subsequently created, a single supreme commander, responsible only to the Combined Chiefs, would have full authority. Marshall got his way and even though the

FROM PEARL TO MIDWAY

ABDA Command lasted less than two months, the Combined Chiefs of Staff which brought it into being continued throughout the war and eventually won the enthusiastic endorsement of both Churchill and Brooke.

At first, the British, with their longer experience and superior military establishment, found it hard to shift the seat of final military decision-making from London to Washington. Whereupon, as time went on and America's military power gradually surpassed Britain's, the Americans found it hard to accept the veto power that the British could always exercise at the very summit and to subordinate themselves to British commanders in certain theaters of war. But the principle of single command in each theater and of unified command at the top spared both parties much of the friction, waste, and frustration that hampered the Allies during the First World War—where Marshall had learned the principles of command he applied in the Second. Of course, the Russians, with growing Anglo-American aid, fought their own, separate war against Germany in the east. The United States also fought its own, separate war against Japan in the Pacific—a war that Roosevelt always subordinated to the struggle against Hitler to which Stalin contributed the lion's share. Nevertheless, to both Roosevelt and Churchill, Hitler always remained the prime enemy and neither of them ever wavered from the beat-Germany-first strategy or from the unified command under which they conducted it.

·2·

THE DECISIONS reached at Washington and the news from the fighting fronts seemed to come from two different worlds. Within a week of the attack on Pearl Harbor, the Japanese appeared to have wrested control of the western Pacific from the Anglo-Americans. On Christmas Day the British governor of the crown colony of Hong Kong and his 12,000 British, Canadian, and Indian troops surrendered to twice as many Japanese, whose planes had bombed the undefended city for two weeks. The surrender came two days after all the local reservoirs fell to the Japanese. Already Japanese troops had begun to close in on the great British naval base at Singapore and to head toward Rangoon, Mandalay, and the southern terminus of the Burma Road, which extended northward to the Chinese Nationalist capital at Chungking. Java, Sumatra, and the rest of the Netherlands Indies lay open to Japanese invasion. Would Australia or India come next on Japan's program of conquest? Churchill understood but deplored the mounting fears of the Australians; the bland indifference of the Indians passed his comprehension.

Yet did Churchill feel, even for Australia, what he felt for England? Did he fear Japan as he feared Germany? Hitler's armies, in overrunning Europe, had isolated Britain and thereby struck at the very heart of its empire. Japan's attack on Pearl Harbor then brought the United States into the war against Hitler, thereby ensuring Germany's defeat and Britain's survival. Roosevelt and Churchill remained as convinced as ever that Anglo-American strategy must proceed on a beat-Germany-first basis, and Roosevelt recognized that this put Churchill in the driver's seat for the next year or two. As for Churchill, he recognized just as clearly that the beat-Germany-first strategy put Roosevelt in the driver's seat as far as the war against Japan was concerned.

It did not take long for the implications of this prospect to emerge. By January, 1942, Churchill was warning Wavell never to forget that in Washington "behind all looms the shadow of Asiatic solidarity," adding, "If I can epitomize in one word the lesson that I learned here in the United States, it was 'China.'" Roosevelt saw in Pearl Harbor the vindication of Admiral Mahan's lifelong insistence that the United States must have a two-ocean navy, second to none. But Roosevelt never shared the imperial doctrine of manifest destiny, preached and practiced by many Republican admirers of the admiral—Theodore Roosevelt, chief among them. Franklin Roosevelt, on the other hand, preferred the Democratic dogma, preached if not practiced by Woodrow Wilson, that democracy could not be safe anywhere until it had been made safe everywhere. In other words the Republican doctrine of manifest destiny and the Democratic dogma of a world made safe for democracy both required the underpinning of a two-ocean United States Navy, second to none.

In warning Wavell against the American obsession with China, Churchill was viewing with alarm Roosevelt's unconcealed sympathy for India and respect for China, neither of which he could bring himself to share. In like manner, Roosevelt viewed with equal alarm Churchill's propensity to identify Britain's nineteenth-century empire with twentieth-century democracy. But what price a democracy underwritten by a two-ocean navy second to none? What price an empire that does not rest on the consent of the governed?

Such questions as these did not appear on the agenda of the Arcadia Conference. Nor did they concern the Japanese who concentrated all their efforts on bringing more and more of the southwest Pacific and of southeast Asia under their control. By January 12, 1942, their troops had advanced more than halfway down the 400-mile-long Malayan peninsula. That was also the day when more than three hundred Japanese bombers and fighters hit Singapore in three daylight raids. *Suez to Singapore*, written at the time and on the spot by the American correspondent Cecil Brown, gives a vivid account of what happened. His bitter CBS broadcasts and dispatches to *Life* cost him his war correspondent's accreditation in that theater, but he had gathered the bulk of his material from British sources which also gave him his warmest support. A British major in the transport service who had spent two years in Singapore told Brown frankly, "I don't think I could be brave out here, but I think I could be back in England. I don't feel inclined to fight for this country. I think the whole place should be blown sky high." When Brown asked how many of his fellow officers shared that view, the major replied, "It isn't a view. It's a reaction. Many of them feel that way. I can't work up any venom against the Japs. They are unimportant blighters." Another British soldier just back from the fighting zone told Brown: "One Britisher is as good as ten Japanese, but unfortunately there are eleven Japanese." G. W. Seabridge, editor of the Singapore *Straits Times*, wrote that while he deplored the shortage of planes and other weapons to defend the city, he found even worse "the many assurances given us over the months that re-enforcements were flowing into Malaya continuously and that the country was ready for anything. . . . Everybody in this country appears to have been lulled into a sense of security by confident statements regarding our armed might. The only people who have not been bluffed are the Japanese."

On February 15, Lieutenant General Arthur Ernest Percival unconditionally surrendered 70,000 British, Australian, and Indian troops to Lieutenant General Tomoyuki Yamashita. The Japanese had used about 100,000 men and some 300 planes. "Singapore was lost in 70 days by bureaucracy, complacency, and a legion of fifth columnists." That was the way the British correspondent Harold Guard writing for United Press, an American news service, summed it up. He continued: "On April 18, 1941, almost eight months before the attack, I wrote a dispatch that the defense of the Malayan peninsula did not in the opinion of military men offer sufficient protection against an attack on Singapore from the rear. The military censor approved the dispatch only because, as he told me, it was so absurd that I would appear ridiculous."

As things turned out, the entire Japanese assault on Singapore Island and its 750,000 inhabitants came from the north, across the narrow Johore Strait. The great naval guns, pointed toward the sea, remained silent because they could not be turned the other way or moved from their emplacements, but it was Japanese air power that proved decisive. Churchill described the fall of Singapore as "the greatest disaster to British arms which our history records." His determination to pursue the beat-Germany-first strategy remained unimpaired. But the fall of Singapore confirmed Roosevelt's expectations rather than Churchill's hopes.

It was the same story in the Netherlands Indies. There, in mid-January, in the five-day naval battle of the Macassar Strait, which separates Borneo and the Celebes, the Japanese lost fifteen warships and 30,000 soldiers and sailors. But the outnumbered ABDA forces could not prevent the Japanese from landing on both islands and by January 25 the defenders suffered such heavy losses they had to withdraw. A month later, the Japanese won the larger naval battle of the Java Sea which separates Borneo and Java. Soon afterward, Java, the richest and most populous of these islands, and Sumatra, the largest, fell to the Japanese, who subdued them with the same tactics they had used in Malaya.

In Malaya and the Netherlands Indies, the Japanese acquired the sources of 46 per cent of the world's tin production and 75 per cent of its rubber production. They also gained access to all the oil they needed for industrial and military purposes. On February 21, in obedience to orders from the Combined Chiefs at Washington, Wavell dissolved his ABDA headquarters on Java and, on Churchill's instructions, proceeded to India to resume the position he had left only two months before as supreme commander. "I admired," wrote Churchill later, "the composure and firmness of mind with which Wavell had faced the cataract of disaster which had been assigned to him with so much formality and precision. Some men would have found reasons for declining, or asked for impossible conditions before accepting a task so baffling and hopeless, failure in which could not but damage their reputation with the public. Wavell's conduct had conformed to the best traditions of the Army."

In another connection it conformed to the worst. Because Wavell set himself such high standards he haughtily refused Chiang Kai-shek's offer of two army corps to help hold Burma where the history of Malaya and Singapore was repeating itself—or going on from where it left off. Japanese ground troops advanced from Thailand; Japanese planes attacked from bases in Thailand and Malaya; finally, Japanese ships landed more troops on Burma's coast. On March 9 the British announced the evacuation of Rangoon, terminus of the railway which had carried supplies to Lashio, the Burma Road, and Chungking. The Japanese conquest of southern Burma thus threatened to cut off China from all outside aid, and the Japanese threat to northern Burma exposed India to invasion. Indeed, Subhas Chandra Bose, a former president of the India Congress party, was already organizing an Indian Liberation army on Burmese soil. The Japanese had paid little attention to Burma until a few years before the war when they invited a group of young Burmese revolutionaries, who took for themselves the title of "Thakin," to visit Tokyo. The British jailed some of these Thakins as well as a former premier of Burma, Ba Maw, whom the conquering Japanese later installed as chief of state. One of the Thakins, named Nu, who later took the more venerable title of "U"—or "uncle"—wrote while in jail in early 1942: "The English claim they entered this great war to protect small countries and defend their independence against aggressors. Burma is a small country. Why not begin by giving it independence? If you cannot grant independence now, promise to grant it as soon as the war is over. If you proclaim this now, we will help the English side against the Fascist brigands who threaten the independence of small nations. If you do not make this proclamation, we will do all we can to hinder your war effort in whatever way we can."

India's leaders felt the same way. Britain had made some concessions both to India and to Burma since the Government of India Act of 1935 separated India and Burma and gave both countries more control over their internal affairs. But it soon proved another case of too little and too late. On March 26, 1942, the editor of the moderate *Calcutta Statesman* wrote: "On the basis of Britain's war, India is as good as lost. She must make it her war, and with Britain aiding her to the utmost, she must save herself."

The editorial appeared in connection with a mission that Stafford Cripps had just undertaken, on Churchill's behalf, to offer India dominion status after the war. Cripps had been ousted from the Labour party before the war because he favored a Popular Front with Communists. Under Churchill, he had served as British ambassador to Moscow, where he made few friends; Communists prefer capitalists to socialists. But Gandhi, Nehru, and the Congress party leaders knew and liked Cripps. He had written in 1936: "I do not myself believe that any British government could in fact consent to India's self-determination in the full sense of that word unless it was so consciously socialist that it was prepared for the break-up of the British Empire. That break-up would involve the most serious problem for the internal British economy, a problem that could be solved only by a complete socialist program."

Eight years later Nehru and the India Congress party refused to accept at Cripps' hands anything short of immediate and complete independence. They had not forgotten that Churchill in 1935 had opposed the moderate Government of India Act and that Chamberlain, in 1939, had brought India into the war without consulting the parliaments of its eleven provinces. Whereupon Cripps, speaking for Churchill, informed them that Britain's viceroy must have the last word in respect to Indian defense and foreign policy until after the war had been won, and only then could real concessions be discussed. Gandhi was reported to have described the Cripps offer as a "postdated check on a bank that is already crashing." But what chiefly worried the Congress party leaders was that Britain's concern for the rights of Indian minorities (notably one hundred million Moslems) implied that the British had set Indian partition as the price that the Hindu majority would ultimately have to pay for Indian freedom.

· 3 ·

WITHIN THREE MONTHS of the attack on Pearl Harbor, the Japanese destroyed the outworn and outmoded foundations of the colonial empires that the British, French, and Dutch had built up, over the centuries, in southeast Asia and beyond. It was a different story in the Philippines. There, in 1935, the United States sponsored a constitution establishing a Philippines commonwealth which granted the peoples of the islands a presidential system of democratic government. It put foreign affairs under the direct supervision and control of the United States, which also had the right to maintain military and other reservations and armed forces. The President of the United States could order the native scouts and constabulary into military service along with the American troops stationed on the islands. The great majority of Filipinos supported the Nationalist party of President Quezon and Vice President Osmena. General MacArthur, who had organized the Filipinos' own armed services, also served as commander in chief of all troops on the islands. These consisted of 18,000 United States Army regulars, 2500 sailors and marines, 8000 Filipino scouts, and 60,000 constabulary.

On December 22, the Japanese put six divisions ashore north of Manila and, the next day, three more to the south. MacArthur withdrew his forces, proclaimed Manila an open city on Christmas Day, and put ten thousand men on heavily fortified Corregidor Island at the entrance of Manila Bay. The remainder took up prepared positions on the peninsula of Bataan to the north. They continued to launch counterattacks against the Japanese; those on Corregidor took a heavy toll of Japanese shipping. But food, ammunition, and medicine gradually gave out. On March 11, on President Roosevelt's orders, General MacArthur, his family, some members of his staff, and the president and vice president of the Philippines left Luzon by motorboat for the north coast of Mindanao, where two flying fortresses picked them up and carried them to Australia. Here the general headed a new Southwest Pacific Command, which had as its first major objective the liberation of the Philippines. "I shall return," predicted MacArthur as he departed, leaving General Jonathan Wainwright, his second in command, in charge. On April 9 Bataan surrendered; on May 6 Corregidor followed suit. But the great bulk of the Filipino people remained loyal to their commonwealth and its exiled leaders. General MacArthur became a national hero. Filipino nationalists looked to Washington, not Tokyo. They preferred the democracy of American imperialism to the Japanese version of Asia for the Asiatics.

Roosevelt being Roosevelt, MacArthur being MacArthur, and the Philippines being the Philippines, the stars in their courses again dictated the course that history took as one of the major consequences of Pearl Harbor. Roosevelt could not turn his back on the battle of the Atlantic or the beat-Germany-first strategy. He recognized sooner than most that nobody was ever going to be able to put together again the British, French, and Dutch colonial empires in Asia that had crumbled, within a few weeks, under the impact of a series of surprise attacks by Japan. For the past forty years, the United States had developed a stake in the Philippines which the Japanese had also overrun, but with greater diffculty and fewer results than they had encountered anywhere else in the area. Compared with the rest of Asia, the Philippine Islands amounted to no more than Norway, Portugal, or Greece did to the rest of Europe. But the Philippines belonged to Asia as much as Norway, Portugal, or Greece belonged to Europe, and while the United

States had no such ties with Asia as it had with Europe, a quite special relationship had long existed between the United States and China. But for that relationship, the United States would not have taken the steps it did during both world wars as well as during the years between those wars to show its concern for China's territorial and administrative integrity in general and for Chiang Kai-shek's Nationalist government in particular. As a timely gesture (if nothing more) in that direction, Roosevelt therefore lost little time after Pearl Harbor in dispatching to Chungking the one senior officer in the United States Army with a speaking and reading knowledge of Chinese.

Major General Joseph W. Stilwell had served many years in China, most recently as military attaché in 1937 and 1938. Roosevelt made him a lieutenant general and commander in chief of United States Army forces in the China-Burma-India war theater. Stilwell also continued to represent the President in all matters connected with Lend-Lease, while acting simultaneously as chief of staff to Chiang Kai-shek. Stilwell flew into Chungking on March 4, 1942, three days before the British evacuated Rangoon. Chiang still had elements of three divisions in or near northern Burma. Stilwell wanted to throw them against the Japanese as soon as possible. Chiang wanted them removed, but went through the motions of accepting Stilwell's plan, while secretly advising his commanders in the field to drag their feet. This resulted in the rout of the Chinese forces and the retreat by Stilwell, on foot, through the mountains and jungles of northern Burma. "We took a hell of a beating," he remarked, when he finally emerged, with his small party, in India.

Even before enduring this ordeal, Stilwell was describing Chiang as "the Peanut," and was filling his diaries with pungent observations. According to Stilwell, "Chiang has been boss so long and has so many yes-men around him that he has the idea he is infallible on any subject. He is, however, determined and forceful, and wants to get on with the war. He is not mentally stable, and he will say things to your face that he doesn't mean fully or exactly. My only concern is to tell him the truth and go about my business. If I can't get by that way, the hell with it: it is patently impossible for me to compete with the swarms of parasites and sycophants around him." Stilwell liked the "Madissima," whom he described as "a clever, brainy woman. Sees Western viewpoint. (By this I mean she can appreciate the mental reactions of a foreigner to the twisting, indirect, under-cover methods of Chinese politics and war-making.) Direct, forceful, energetic, loves power, eats up publicity and flattery, pretty weak on her history. No concessions to the Western viewpoint in all China's foreign relations. The Chinese were always right: the foreigners were always wrong. Writes entertainingly but superficially with plenty of sarcasm for Western failings but without any mention of China's little faults. Can turn on charm at will, and knows it. Great influence on Chiang Kai-shek mostly along right lines, too. A great help on several occasions."

As time passed, Stilwell modified this judgment. In Chungking he saw more and more evidence of "corruption, neglect, hoarding, black market, and trading with the enemy." Casual contacts with Communist leaders led him to take them at their own valuation. "Communist program," he noted in his diary, "reduce taxes, rents, interest. Raise production and standard of living. Participate in government. Practice what they preach." These paper promises looked better than the performance that he witnessed of the Foo Hsing Corporation—"a government-owned trading corporation with monopolistic charter powers that buys bristles locally at $1.40 U.S. a pound, sells them to us at $3.40 U.S. a pound and kicks back 60 cents to the dealer. This leaves a nice little profit of $2.40 a pound for Foo Hsing and the gang who run it." But Stilwell had faith in the qualities of the Chinese soldier, and after nine thousand of them escaped from the Japanese in northern Burma he persuaded Chiang to have them dispatched to a special training center at Ramargh in central India. Here 80,000 Chinese soldiers received instructions from American officers with American arms, along with good pay and food, while another Chinese army inside China received similar training. After the Japanese cut the Burma Road, the Americans developed an alternative air route known as "The Hump," which eventually brought Chiang more tonnage over the Himalayas than he had ever received via the Burma Road. But during the spring and summer of 1942, China's plight became desperate and if the Japanese failed to reach Chungking and force its surrender at that time, it was because they had other obligations, as unexpected as they were urgent, on other fronts.

·4·

THE SLOGAN "Remember Pearl Harbor" helped to bring a united America into an unwanted conflict and keep it there. The United States Navy, which bore the brunt of the surprise attack, delivered the first counterblow. On February 1, in the Marshall Islands, athwart the sea route to

Australia, a task force of cruisers and destroyers commanded by Vice Admiral William F. Halsey on the aircraft carrier *Enterprise* sank seventeen Japanese ships and destroyed more than forty Japanese planes. On February 24, Halsey raided Japanese-held Wake Island and on March 4 Marcus Island, less than a thousand miles from Tokyo. On April 18 he played the key role in a still more spectacular operation, when sixteen United States Army B-25 bombers attacked Tokyo. On that occasion a Halsey-commanded navy task force had sneaked the bombers to within less than 700 miles of Tokyo for which they took off from the deck of the carrier *Hornet.* Lieutenant Colonel James Doolittle led the attack, and fifteen of the planes landed in China, the sixteenth at Vladivostok. The Halsey task force withdrew unscathed, and as a result of the successful strike the Japanese high command speeded up its schedule for further expansion. Originally, the Japanese had assumed that the conquest of the Philippines, Malaya, and the Netherlands Indies would take six months. Having progressed far ahead of schedule and with smaller losses than they had anticipated, they did not wait to consolidate their Greater East Asia Co-Prosperity Sphere; instead, they decided to extend their so-called "ribbon defense" in three directions. First, they planned to dominate the Coral Sea and the approaches to Australia by setting up powerful bases at Tulagi, capital of the Solomon Islands, and at Port Moresby, near the southeast tip of New Guinea. Then they planned to strengthen and extend their positions in the central Pacific by occupying Midway and the Western Aleutians. Third, they planned to cut communications between the United States and Australia by seizing New Caledonia, Fiji, and Samoa. The first effort led to the battle of the Coral Sea, which resulted in a draw. The second led to the battle of Midway, which resulted in the first major American victory in the Pacific. The third plan never got off the ground.

The battle of the Coral Sea on May 7 and 8 and the battle of Midway on June 4 and 5 saw two large fleets engage in major clashes without any exchange of fire among surface vessels. Airplanes inflicted all the damage; the aircraft carrier, not the battleship, proved to be the key to victory. On May 3, planes from the United States carrier *Yorktown* sank twelve of the fifteen Japanese ships in Tulagi harbor and then sailed into the Coral Sea, having joined the carrier *Lexington,* three heavy cruisers, and a destroyer. An Australian heavy and light cruiser completed the task force. The Japanese, instead of concentrating on the two American carriers, dispersed their forces, and, early in the morning of

May 7, carrier-based American planes sank the Japanese cruiser *Ryu-kaku* and all its planes. The next day Japanese bombs hit both the *Yorktown* and the *Lexington*, but the Americans prevented the Japanese from reaching Port Moresby and damaged another Japanese carrier and a heavy cruiser. Several hours after the Japanese withdrew and gave up their attempt to take Port Moresby, the *Lexington* sank as the result of an internal explosion. More than ninety per cent of the ship's company were saved.

The battle of the Coral Sea saved Australia from invasion and halted any further Japanese advance to the southwest. One month later, the battle of Midway not only checked a more serious Japanese drive across the central Pacific. It inflicted heavier losses on the Japanese. Again, the Japanese made the mistake of dispersing their forces too widely. A feint at the Aleutians did not deceive the American commanders, who knew more about Japanese ship movements than the Japanese knew about the Americans'. The Japanese task force heading for Midway Island included occupation troops whom the Japanese expected to put ashore. They did not know how heavily the Americans had fortified the island or how quickly the damage that the *Yorktown* had suffered in the Coral Sea had been repaired. One day decided the battle of Midway. On June 4, American planes sank four Japanese carriers. The next day, they sank one heavy cruiser and disabled another for two years. In destroying the bulk of Japan's remaining aircraft carriers, the United States task force commanded by Admiral Raymond Spruance ended all further hopes of Japanese progress across the Pacific. It had become only a question of time, and the United States could go on the offensive. The Japanese had lost the first decisive battle of the Second World War six months to the day after they had attacked Pearl Harbor.

• • •

The Roosevelt-Churchill strategy of beating Hitler first included a paradoxical corollary. Not only had the attack on Pearl Harbor plunged the United States into war with Japan. The very urgency of the war against Germany compelled the United States to assume prime responsibility for that other war. No President before Roosevelt ever had so great a need for a navy second to none. Never before had the navy so good a friend in the White House as Roosevelt. Even with half the curtailed Pacific fleet out of commission, the ships and planes that remained had inflicted a decisive defeat on Japan only six months after suffering an almost mortal blow at Pearl Harbor. Having caused the tide to turn so soon under such adverse conditions, the navy gave every promise of fulfilling all the hopes it had always inspired in the President.

But the better the account the navy gave of itself in the Pacific, the sooner the Joint Chiefs in Washington had to decide on their strategy in China, where Japan's program of conquest began—and ended. In the Pacific, America's aggressive Japanese enemies had obligingly resorted to the kind of technological warfare where the Americans had all the advantages. On the Asian mainland, on the other hand, the Americans had more to fear from the weakness of their Chinese allies than they had to fear from the strength of their Japanese enemies. The Chinese Communists and Nationalists not only expended as much energy fighting each other as they expended fighting the Japanese, the Americans knew no more about the guerrilla warfare they waged than they knew about the political issues at stake. In pitched battles, the Japanese, with their superior equipment and training, defeated the Nationalists almost at will. Always avoiding pitched battles, the Communists originally concentrated on harassing the Nationalists. Against the Japanese they waged guerrilla warfare and organized resistance groups behind the Japanese lines. By the fall of 1938, the Japanese war of aggression against China had achieved most of its objectives while the Munich Conference and its aftermath finished off Czechoslovakia.

The wisdom of hindsight puts these events in a perspective that few participants in them could foresee. Not that the outcome of the battle of Midway came as any surprise to Admiral Yamamoto or to the members of the Joint Chiefs, who took a calculated risk that paid off. But conditions in China itself did not lend themselves to a land-battle equivalent of the sea-air battle of Midway. For one thing, none of the belligerents possessed tanks and planes comparable to the planes and aircraft carriers that fought the battle of Midway. More important, the military campaigns in China took place under mixed conditions of conventional, guerrilla, and revolutionary warfare.

While the battle of Midway marked the beginning of the end of an outmoded form of warfare, China's civil wars marked the reversion to an earlier type of warfare that did not come into its own until another couple of decades had passed. Just as the Chinese Communists pioneered the guerrilla tactics that the North Korean and North Vietnamese Communists developed during the 1950's and the 1960's, so the United States Navy at Midway foreshadowed the role that the entire American military-industrial complex brought to bear on postwar conflicts in Korea, Vietnam, and other Third World trouble centers. Ever since President Roosevelt entered the White House, he had given the highest priority to maintaining a navy second to none. It was that navy which first turned the tide of war against Japan, then swept Japan's fleet from the face of the Pacific, and—by the time the war ended— emerged stronger than the combined navies of all the other nations in the world.

For this achievement much of the credit belongs to Roosevelt. But he did more than preside proudly over the ever-widening role that the United States Navy played in the Pacific. He, more than any other wartime leader, espoused the cause of precisely those Afro-Asian-Latin American peoples in whose midst the postwar soldiers of American democracy subsequently appeared. But the irony of these events serves to enhance rather than diminish the stature of the man who set them in motion.

X

Second Front Now

·1·

THE BATTLE OF MIDWAY gave almost instant sanction to Roosevelt's strategy of beating Germany first. For within six months of the Pearl Harbor disaster, the United States Navy proved that with more than half its Pacific fleet out of commission, it still had the ships, planes, and men to prevent Japan from dealing their country a mortal blow; whereas the Germans had driven still deeper into the Soviet Union, retained the upper hand in the battle of the Atlantic, and tightened their grip on western Europe. The ultimate consequences of Japan's grand sweep of southeast Asia, of Japan's unbroken hold on most of China's principal cities, highways, and waterways, and America's ultimate role in those theaters of war might still shake the world. But for the foreseeable future—however long or short that might be—Nazi Germany still posed much greater threats to the vital interests of the British Empire, the Soviet Union, and even the United States.

The First World War had remained, from start to finish, a European affair that centered on Germany, although its repercussions spread across the Atlantic Ocean and to parts of the Middle and Far East. But when Roosevelt and Churchill met at Washington in late December, 1941, and most of January, they set about waging global warfare by organizing a United Nations coalition that included all the governments or governments in exile at war with Germany or Japan, and by planning counteroffensives of their own for the coming year. The coalition survived the year; the strategy did not. But the failure of the strategy assured the success of the coalition.

Neither Roosevelt nor Stalin had it in his power, either separately or together, to impose on Churchill the second-front, cross-Channel invasion strategy they both favored. But Roosevelt and Churchill did have it in their power to agree, in principle, on an alternative operation, originally known as Gymnast, to organize predominantly American landings in North Africa in 1942. They neither informed nor consulted Stalin who had no choice but to make do for at least the whole year on his own resources plus whatever the Anglo-Americans might be willing and able to supply.

At any rate, that was the way the Arcadia Conference had left matters when it broke up in mid-January. But by February, Roosevelt was telling Hopkins he had become "more and more interested in plans for the establishment of a new front on the European continent this summer." On March 14 Hopkins wrote in a memorandum to the President: "I doubt if any single thing is so important as setting up some kind of front this summer against Germany." With the memorandum went a project by the War Department's War Plans Division for an invasion of France across the narrowest stretch of the English Channel. "Successful attack in this area," the planners concluded, "will afford maximum support to the Russian front."

Nothing that had happened since the Arcadia Conference had brightened the prospects of an operation that the British had firmly vetoed there. Nor had they lost the right or the power to exercise that veto. The battle of the Atlantic still went from bad to worse. Nor did the turn of the year brighten the Red army's prospects. The winter offensive planned by the Soviet high command had fallen short of its minimum objectives. The bitter winter weather which had helped to save Moscow added to the horrors of Leningrad, where almost one million of that besieged city's three million inhabitants had already died of starvation. The Russians also failed to lift the seige of Sevastopol in the Crimea. Kharkov, due south of Moscow, and Kiev, due west, remained in German hands. Russian losses still exceeded German. German industrial production increased while Soviet production declined; the Germans improved their transport facilities and suffered from no shortages of trucks. With the Russians it was just the other way around.

The American victory at Midway, which did not occur until June, yielded no immediate benefit to the Russians. Meanwhile, in the battle of the Atlantic, the Anglo-American position went from bad to worse. Although the Germans had not been able to cut the Atlantic supply lines, starve out the British, or throw the Russians back on their own resources, the battle of the Atlantic had put Anglo-American shipments of war material to the Soviet Union far behind schedule, slowed down the buildup for an eventual invasion of Europe from the British Isles, and raised the prospect that Rommel might be able to drive all the way to the Middle East and make all of North Africa safe for the Axis. And yet Generals Marshall and Eisenhower joined President Roosevelt and Harry Hopkins in urging the British to scrap the plans for Gymnast and prepare for a cross-Channel invasion of France in 1942.

The military impossibility of such an operation served only to compound the political folly of suggesting it. By early April, the desperate prospects on the Russian front convinced Roosevelt and his advisers that they must scrap, or at any rate modify, the Arcadia decisions and assign top priority to some kind of cross-Channel invasion in 1942. They had not succumbed to Soviet threats or blandishments. The facts (as they saw them) spoke for themselves. As for Stalin, he attached less importance to the victories the Germans had won than he did to the sacrifices the Russians had made. He also expressed the hope that the war might be won in 1942, while raising the unspoken possibility of a deadlock at some future date. Some Anglo-Americans still feared the prospect of another Nazi-Soviet pact. Once bitten, twice shy: the impossible had happened once, why might it not happen again? Because the very fury of the Russo-German conflict had sowed such hatred on both sides as to rule out any kind of compromise.

In opposing a second front, Churchill still dreaded, more than anything else, a repetition of the bloody deadlock on the Western Front between 1914 and 1918. The possibility that the Germans and the Japanese might join hands in the Middle East also haunted him. Not all of Churchill's advisers shared all his views—especially his aversion to the second front. On April 4, when Roosevelt dispatched a special second-front mission to London, headed by General Marshall and Harry Hopkins, the British press and public welcomed the prospect. While the isolationist-Republican *Chicago Tribune* announced, "The second front exists in the Pacific," the semiofficial London *Times* commented editorially, "There is mounting eagerness both in this country and in the U.S. to pass from defense to offense and to make 1942, not 1943 or 1944, the turning point of the war." By April 11 Roosevelt had become so enthusiastic that he cabled Stalin, urging him to send Molotov to Washington in the immediate future to discuss a "very important military proposal involving use of our armed forces in a manner to relieve your critical western front." On the night of April 14, Marshall and Hopkins attended a meeting of the inner British cabinet, to which Churchill submitted the "momentous proposal" that their guests had brought. For himself, however, he warned against a possible German-Japanese pincer movement on the Middle East. It therefore remained for the courtly General Marshall to emphasize that the Americans could make only a modest troop contribution, thus coating with frankness the bitter pill that he and his compatriots might have to swallow.

Meanwhile, Britain's Lord Beaverbrook and the popular Conservative newspapers he owned championed the second front. As minister of munitions, Beaverbrook had headed Britain's first wartime mission to Moscow. He shared Hopkins' confidence in the staying power of the Soviet Union and stood almost as close to Churchill as Hopkins did to Roosevelt. In those two men, the second front had advocates close to the very summit of power in both Washington and London—close, but not at it. As far as public opinion was concerned, Americans tended to assume that the Russians would obligingly complete in 1942 the task they had begun in 1941. The British, grateful to the Red army for the respite it had given them from German bombing, felt a greater sense of urgency about the outcome in 1942 and a greater sense of obligation to help the Russians. Roosevelt, paradoxically, shared the point of view more popular in Britain; Churchill the point of view more popular in the United States. But that was because the realistic Churchill estimated the Anglo-American contribution more modestly than the optimistic Roosevelt did.

· 2 ·

YET IT WAS the realistic Stalin who chose to express the most cheerful and romantic view of all. On May 1, he issued an order of the day, calling upon the Red army to "make 1942 the year of the final defeat of the German-Fascist troops and the liberation of the land of the Soviets from the Hitlerite scoundrels." By the end of the month, Molotov had accepted Roosevelt's invitation and arrived in Washington, stopping at London en route. On May 28 Churchill cabled Roosevelt that he and Eden had carefully avoided making any commitment to open a second front. Roosevelt proved more accommodating. According to Molotov, a second front in Europe, sufficient to engage forty German divisions, might defeat Hitler that year and would ensure his ultimate defeat in any case. Could Roosevelt promise one? Molotov wanted a straight answer. Roosevelt then asked General Marshall whether Stalin could be assured that a second front in Europe was being prepared. The general said yes. Later Molotov asked again, "What answer shall I take back to

London and Moscow on the general question that has been raised? What is the President's answer with respect to the second front?" By way of reassurance Roosevelt let Molotov phrase the answer to his own question: "In the course of the conversations," wrote Molotov, in a statement Roosevelt signed, "full understanding was reached with regard to the urgent tasks of creating a second front in Europe in 1942."

To Molotov, if not to Roosevelt, these words meant that the United States had pledged itself to launch, in 1942, the kind of second front Stalin had demanded. On June 11, after Molotov had laid his case for the second front before a closed session of the House of Commons, Churchill signed a joint communiqué that included the statement Roosevelt had signed in Washington. First, however, he handed to Molotov, in the presence of witnesses, an *aide-mémoire* that included the words, "We can therefore give no promise" to carry out the pledge. The *aide-mémoire* dwelt on Churchill's demand for more landing craft. In addition, Churchill pointed out that the British could furnish only seven divisions and the Americans not more than two. Inasmuch as the Germans already had twenty-five divisions in France, so small a landing force could not divert any forty German divisions from eastern to western Europe, much less establish itself on European soil.

On May 8, one week after Stalin's order of the day called for victory in 1942, Hitler seized the initiative. Checked at Leningrad and frustrated on the critical Moscow front since the end of the previous year, Hitler adopted for 1942 the new strategy of concentrating on a two-pronged offensive in southern Russia where his armies had made their greatest gains during 1941. One of these thrusts began with a costly assault on the fortress city of Sevastopol on the Crimean peninsula. This cost the Germans 300,000 casualties and lasted almost two months, but the Red army could not prevent them from making steady headway, both before and after the Sevastopol campaign, in the Caucasus Mountains, between the Black Sea and the Caspian. The other more important and more successful thrust aimed at the city of Stalingrad on the Volga, where it turns at a right angle, from the southwest to the southeast, to empty into the Caspian Sea. If the Sixth Army, to which Hitler assigned the task, could take Stalingrad, he assumed that the whole Russian front, to Moscow and beyond, could be rolled up in 1942. But if the Red army could hold Stalingrad, the whole German gamble in Russia would fail.

On June 13, when Molotov returned to Moscow, he brought with him the new and wider Lend-Lease agreement he had signed with the

United States and the twenty-year treaty of alliance he had signed with
Britain. The Soviet press featured both documents, and the Supreme
Soviet held a special session to ratify the treaty. In Moscow, hopes for a
second front mounted. Yet, political developments in Washington and
London and military developments in North Africa and southern Rus-
sia soon made the whole question of a second front in 1942 academic.

On June 18, Churchill arrived in Washington for his second wartime
visit. He could not persuade Roosevelt to abandon Sledgehammer (the
cross-Channel invasion) but did revive the President's interest in North
Africa, where Roosevelt himself had suggested landings in 1942. This
Churchill had always favored, and the Arcadia Conference had approved of it in principle. On June 21 the hand of fate intervened. The
news reached Washington that Britain had just suffered its greatest military disaster since Singapore: the surrender of 33,000 seasoned British
Empire troops in the Libyan garrison of Tobruk to half as many Germans. "Defeat is one thing; disgrace is another," wrote Churchill, and
when Roosevelt asked, "What can we do to help?" Churchill replied,
"Give us as many Sherman tanks as you can spare and ship them to the
Middle East as quickly as possible." The British received twice as many
as Roosevelt first promised, even though a German submarine sank one
vessel with seventy tanks aboard.

Returning to Britain, Churchill cabled Roosevelt on July 8: "No responsible British general, admiral, or air marshal is prepared to recommend Sledgehammer." That tore it. Both Hopkins and Marshall had
fought for Sledgehammer. July 22, the day when the Americans recognized that Sledgehammer was dead, Hopkins described himself as
"damn depressed." It seemed to Eisenhower the darkest day of the war.
Only one possibility remained for 1942—the landings in French North
Africa, originally known as Gymnast, now renamed Torch, with General Eisenhower as its top planner in his new capacity as Marshall's
deputy in Europe. For 1943, the Anglo-American planners went through
the motions of reviving Sledgehammer, renaming it Round-Up, which,
they assumed, Marshall would command. But Torch monopolized their
energies for the balance of 1942.

· 3 ·

ROOSEVELT's DECISION to substitute Torch for Sledgehammer did not sit
well with the top navy brass or with the lower levels of command in
the army and air force. Inasmuch as the British refused to attempt an

immediate cross-Channel operation in Europe (so ran the argument), let them fight the German war their way while the United States settles its accounts with Japan. But Roosevelt insisted on Torch as the essential and immediate contribution to the beat-Hitler-first strategy. Churchill agreed but doubted that Stalin would like Torch any better than some of the American admirals did and therefore took it upon himself to fly to Moscow and have it all out, face to face, with Stalin in the Kremlin.

His daring diplomacy paid off. At their first meeting on August 12, 1942, Stalin lashed out "like a snake in heat," as one observer described it. But at their fourth and last meeting on August 15, Stalin accepted the inevitable, made somewhat more palatable by one of Churchill's masterly analyses. The submarine and the airplane, he explained, had revolutionized warfare. To establish a bridgehead on the European coast, the British and Americans needed to win and hold complete control of the air over all the English Channel and much of western Europe. This they might have done, thanks to the rate at which the British were producing planes and training crews. But the Royal Air Force had just launched a series of massive bombing raids on German cities—sometimes as many as a thousand bombers hitting a single city during a single night—many times more destructive than the raids the Germans had made on London two years before. Torch would compel the R.A.F. to abandon these raids.

But German progress in submarine warfare proved the clinching argument against a second front in 1942. As Churchill pointed out, the same German submarines that ruled out Sledgehammer had also cut the flow of war equipment from Britain and the United States to the Soviet Union; German planes based on Norway caused still greater losses. Yet Stalin charged the British and Americans with cowardice and bad faith because they refused to continue, indefinitely, the Murmansk run after their losses climbed to more than fifty per cent per convoy. But when he finally recognized that he could not shake the decision in favor of Torch, he saw its military advantages and could only warn against its political risks. The evening before Churchill left, Stalin suddenly organized an impromptu dinner that lasted from half past eight until half past two. Here they exchanged sharp but friendly jibes and agreed on the text of a joint, friendly communiqué. If neither gave an inch of ground to the other, both went their separate ways with heightened mutual regard.

Churchill, on his way to Moscow, anticipated Stalin's demand for immediate action by stopping off at Cairo and reshuffling Britain's

Middle East Command in the light of the Tobruk disaster. The new commander he installed was General Sir Harold Rupert Leofric George Alexander, whose father, mother, and wife all belonged to the British peerage. Alexander had attended Harrow and Sandhurst, and fought throughout the First World War on the Western Front, where he was wounded three times. By 1937 he had risen to the rank of major general and served as aide to King Edward VIII.

To command the British Eighth Army, under Alexander, Churchill installed General Sir Bernard Law Montgomery, son of an eminent Church of England bishop and of a nonpermissive mother who made his boyhood a misery with such admonitions to visitors as, "Go and find out what Bernard is doing and tell him to stop it." The boy attended and enjoyed one of Britain's stricter schools, St. Paul's of London, and from there in 1907 went to Sandhurst to make the army his career. He served with distinction as an officer on the Western Front throughout the First World War, becoming a general staff officer in 1934. Montgomery resembled Churchill in his dogged eccentricity and flair for showmanship but had as great an aversion to alcoholic stimulants as Churchill had to lemonade.

The more convivial Alexander had commanded the Dunkirk evacuation. Montgomery headed the Southeast Command until Churchill shifted him to the Egyptian desert. Shortly before taking up his new assignment, Montgomery had opposed a reconnaissance in force carried out at Dieppe, on August 19, by some six thousand highly trained men, nearly all of them Canadians. With a passion for perfection that went hand in hand with his horror of useless slaughter, he had helped plan the Dieppe raid, but after two postponements warned against remounting it with new troops. However, Churchill (backed by most of his commanders) decided that such a reconnaissance (the largest of its kind since Gallipoli) must be staged before any full-scale invasion could even be planned. Fortunately, almost everything went wrong: fortunately, because the tragedies and errors of Dieppe taught those who planned the later invasion what not to do. As Field Marshal Sir Alan Brooke, commander of the Imperial General Staff, put it to Churchill in June: "This operation is quite indispensable to the Allied offensive program. If we ever intend to invade France, it is absolutely essential to mount a preliminary operation on a divisional scale."

The Royal Air Force and Royal Navy provided some support—not nearly enough, as things turned out. The attackers threw their greatest strength at the town of Dieppe, where they encountered maximum resistance. All their tanks got ashore; not one got away. One thousand of the Canadian troops could not land; of those who did 68 per cent never returned. German defense in depth and cross fire prevented the invaders from reaching even the minor objectives they had hoped to take. German propagandists announced the repulse of a major Allied invasion.

The high percentage of Canadian losses vindicated British opponents of a second front in 1942; the numbers involved left the Russians unimpressed. But, as Admiral Mountbatten put it two years later, every casualty at Dieppe saved ten lives at Normandy on D Day. The Dieppe raid also made the Normandy landing possible in the first place by proving that with sufficient naval and air support, troops and tanks could get ashore, even on a heavily defended coast. The problem, as Churchill tried to explain to Stalin, was the problem of supply, and that problem plagued the Anglo-Americans everywhere. For instance, the Americans required more than sea and air power to drive the Japanese from the fortified positions they now held in the southwest Pacific. Only massive attacks by ground troops could dislodge the Japanese from the islands they had fortified illegally during the years between the wars or had taken by force during the months since Pearl Harbor.

·4·

ONE WEEK BEFORE the Dieppe raid, the Americans opened the only kind of offensive that could ultimately defeat Japan. On August 7, a task force that included Australian as well as American warships easily seized the small island of Tulagi, with its excellent harbor, in the Solomons. But when two divisions of United States Marines went ashore at the larger, nearby island of Guadalcanal, where the Japanese had begun to build an air strip, it was another story. The subsequent, persistent Japanese attacks on Guadalcanal showed they had planned to make it into an air base from which to cut the supply line between the United States and Australia. By the same token, the Americans wanted Guadalcanal as the base for deeper air strikes at Japanese positions farther north. The battle for Guadalcanal lasted from early August to early December. The Americans and Australians suffered their heaviest naval losses during the first two months, including four cruisers and an aircraft carrier. But by December 9, when the United States Marines, who had seized and held the island, were relieved by the army, the Japanese had lost two battleships, eight cruisers, and six destroyers and had suffered more than 40,000 casualties. American losses came to less than half as much. But these figures cover only a fraction of what the United States paid for the conquest of Guadalcanal. The shipping, fuel, and manpower needed to transport and provision the troops tied up and devoured a large share of the country's limited war-making capacities. Nor could Roosevelt and his advisers, for reasons of morale as well as strategy, ignore other demands of the Pacific war theater.

The British, with more than half a million men in action in Egypt, faced the same problems of large-scale, long-distance supply over sea routes under constant enemy attack. Since the darkest hours of the war, in 1940, Churchill had always maintained several crack, armored divisions in Egypt, where they not only protected the Suez Canal but helped to prevent the Axis from overrunning the Middle East. During the spring and summer of 1942, British fortunes in this theater of war had sunk to their lowest ebb. General Erwin Rommel, commander of Germany's Afrika Korps, had mastered the art of tank warfare in desert country. During the First World War he had won, as an enlisted man, Germany's highest military decoration, and when Hitler came to power the fact that Rommel did not belong to the Prussian aristocracy no longer blocked his advancement. Under his leadership, the Afrika Korps had advanced to El Alamein, less than one hundred miles from Alexandria, where General Alexander, the new head of Britain's Middle East Command, proclaimed in an order of the day, "Thus far and no farther."

By October 1941 the British Eighth Army numbered 230,000 fighting men; Rommel's Afrika Korps had less than 80,000, only 27,000 of them Germans. Montgomery had more than 1400 Grant and Sherman tanks; Rommel had 260 German and 280 Italian tanks, all of them inferior to Montgomery's American armor. Montgomery had at his disposal 1200 serviceable aircraft; Rommel had 350. The crunch came at El Alamein, a narrow stretch of desert, sixty miles west of Alexandria, bounded by the Mediterranean on the north and on the south by the Qattara Depression, an impassable rock canyon. Montgomery opened his attack on October 23. Rommel had flown back to Germany in early September for rest and recuperation. Still ailing, he returned, under orders from Hitler, on October 23, arriving in time to frustrate the attack that Montgomery had already launched. On October 28 Rommel stopped Montgomery, but on both occasions his losses far exceeded Montgomery's. By November 2, Montgomery had a twenty to one superiority; Rommel began to withdraw; Hitler ordered him to stand firm, thereby preventing him from getting out in time to make a stand farther to the rear. But it was the first time Hitler had interfered with Rommel and the last time Rommel paid him any heed. Montgomery renewed his attacks but not in time to cut off and destroy all of Rommel's forces—an opportunity that never came again. By November 11 the Eighth Army had advanced up to fifty miles along a two-hundred-mile front, killing several thousand Germans and Italians and capturing 30,000 more, 20,000 of them Italians. Fifteen thousand Germans got away, two thirds of them without their equipment. Over a thousand guns and 450 tanks fell into British hands. The remainder of Rommel's forces spent the next six months retreating twelve hundred miles to Bizerte, their commander having flouted Hitler's orders to stand and fight to the last man.

Thanks to Rommel's reputation, Montgomery refused to attack until he had overwhelming superiority, and even then he proceeded with care. Although his caution slowed down his own Eighth Army's progress it also prolonged the whole North African campaign, which, in the long run, cost the Germans a far heavier price than the various United Nations forces had to pay. But it's an ill wind that blows nobody good, and Montgomery emerged with an inflated reputation that served him to his entire satisfaction until the end.

Three days after the British won their first major military victory over the Germans since 1918, the first offensive commanded by General Eisenhower got under way. During the night of November 7–8 more than 100,000 American and British troops began landing on a score of beaches along Morocco's Atlantic coast and the Mediterranean coast of Algeria. Allied planners had estimated that Operation Torch required at least half a million men, but they went ahead anyway with what they had available. Roosevelt, with Churchill's concurrence, gambled on the ability of the Americans to persuade the local commanders of 100,000 regular French troops in the area and of some 200,000 reservists, mostly natives, to put up no resistance to the American invaders and later to join in an Allied effort to liberate metropolitan France from German rule. Hitler, unlike some of his associates, attached no great importance to French North Africa and had dispatched no Axis troops there. Roosevelt counted on the good relations he had maintained with the Pétain regime at Vichy and the better relations he had established with Vichyite officials in North Africa to make Torch live up to its name.

By November 12, the light of Torch spread over Algeria and Morocco. "The minimum objective of the North African invasion," as General Eisenhower put it in his *Crusade in Europe*, "was to seize the main ports of Casablanca and Algiers, denying their use to the Axis as bases for submarines, and from them to operate eastward toward the British desert forces. The successful action of the first few days assured attainment of the minimum objective and immediately we turned all our attention to the greater mission assigned us of co-operating with General Sir Harold R. L. G. Alexander's forces, then twelve hundred miles away at the opposite end of the Mediterranean. Between us we would destroy all Axis forces in northern Africa and re-open the sea for the use of Allied shipping." Easier said than done. Not only did six months of hard fighting lie ahead; that fighting left in its wake a series of political crises that compelled Roosevelt and Churchill to appear in person upon the scene.

.   .   .

Until about halfway through 1942, the long-planned military offensives launched by the Germans and Japanese went forward pretty much on schedule. And why not? The aggressors had attacked at times and places of their own choosing with weapons and strategies of their own devising. But before the year had run its course, the military offensives launched by the Axis powers not only gave rise to more than one counteroffensive by more than one member of the United Nations coalition. Their political, social, and economic consequences overshadowed the military repercussions. Japanese troops easily overran the Netherlands Indies, British Burma, British Malaya, and Singapore. On orders from Vichy, the French authorities in Indochina submitted themselves to Tokyo. What price Japan's Greater East Asia Co-Prosperity Sphere? Military conquest did not bring economic prosperity or political stability to southeast Asia. But if southeast Asia never basked in the rays of the Empire of the Rising Sun, neither did it ever swelter again in the rays of any white man's empire.

In western Europe, the unmitigated disaster of the Dieppe raid vindicated all of Churchill's misgivings about a second front in 1942. But two years later, the lessons learned at Dieppe underwrote the Normandy landings. Churchill's 1942 mission to Moscow got off to a poor start, but he did not have to wait two years for Stalin to recognize that he had more to gain by working with Roosevelt and Churchill rather than against them or by himself. And who can say? The two years that Stalin had to wait for his second front may have proved a blessing in disguise. For it gave him time to build up his Red army to such strength that it was able to sweep halfway across Europe and hold all its gains.

Torch, during its first few days, looked as if it were going to be the light that failed. But by the end of the year, General Eisenhower had established himself so firmly in Algiers and the Germans had ferried so many troops into Tunisia that the Anglo-Americans found themselves committed to a Mediterranean strategy that compelled them to postpone the cross-Channel invasion and a second front, worthy of the name, until 1944. Again, nobody had planned it that way, but nobody had planned the fate of southeast Asia its way, either. If 1942 turned out to be the year when military events determined the world's political fate, the years that followed saw the emergent United Nations playing a major role in determining the course of the war.

XI

Overture to Casablanca

·1·

WITH THE NORTH AFRICAN LANDINGS, Roosevelt could take credit for having added a secret, two-year chapter to the long history of Franco-American relations and to the more recent history of the Second World War. To him belongs the credit for having sensed, as early as September 1940, that the United States might, by remaining in contact with the French regime at Vichy, not only bring fallen France back into the war against Germany but also, in the process, bring American troops into action against the Germans. In this connection, the Anglo-French naval clash at Mers-el-Kebir could even have served the useful purpose of strengthening the new, tenuous ties between Washington and Vichy.

Increasingly convinced that North Africa had become "the most likely place where French troops might be brought back into the war against Germany," Roosevelt, in September 1940, summoned to the White House Robert B. Murphy, the chargé d'affaires at the American embassy in Vichy. "The President," as Murphy later wrote in his *Diplomat Among Warriors,* "then said to me that he wanted me to return to Vichy and work unostentatiously to get permission to make a thorough inspection tour of French Africa and to report my findings to him. The French African policy of the United States Government thus became the President's personal policy. He initiated it. He kept it going, and he resisted pressures against it until the autumn of 1942 when North Africa became the first major battleground where Americans fought Germans." The President instructed Murphy to work through General Weygand, whom Pétain had just appointed delegate general to all of French Africa, but "barely mentioned Charles de Gaulle."

Roosevelt had looked into Murphy's background, and found that he was in his mid-forties and had spent twenty years as a foreign-service officer in the State Department. After several years in Germany, he had worked for the next decade in France, where Ambassador Bullitt had promoted him from American consul in Paris to counselor at the embassy. Murphy's father was of Irish and his mother of German extraction. They lived in Milwaukee, where the father had a railroad job. The President felt that Murphy's Roman Catholic faith would commend him to Weygand.

Back in Vichy, Murphy obtained permission to make a three-week tour of French Africa, starting in mid-December. He returned pleasantly surprised to have found most of the Vichyite officials pro-British and anti-Nazi. At Dakar he met General Pierre Boisson, the French high commissioner, who had lost a leg fighting the Germans in the First World War and now prayed for a British victory. On the other hand, Boisson remained embittered by the futile attempt de Gaulle made in mid-September to take Dakar with an Anglo-French expeditionary force.

When Murphy returned to the United States in January 1941, he brought with him an accord he had signed with Weygand permitting Vichyite officials to use French funds, frozen in American banks, to buy limited quantities of nonstrategic American goods and to ship them through the British blockade. The British blew hot and cold, recognizing that the arrangement might bring North Africa back into the war and undercut German propaganda among the native, Arab population, while at the same time fearing that all this might also ease some of Hitler's economic difficulties. According to Murphy, his report and recommendations later became the basis for Roosevelt's African policy.

In any event, they made such a hit with the President that he had Murphy shifted from Vichy to Algiers as American high commissioner for North Africa, still with the rank of counselor to the American embassy. Weygand displayed similar confidence by granting Murphy permission to appoint twelve new American "vice consuls" whose diplomatic privileges enabled them to make contact with French residents of North Africa and thus lay the foundations of an American intelligence service there. Weygand's plotting never caught up with him, but the Red army did. By November 1941, the frustrations of the Russian campaign made Hitler so jittery that he threatened to have German troops occupy all of France and live off its produce unless Pétain dismissed Weygand from his North African post and ordered him home. By this time, however, Murphy had struck oil in the form of a North African resistance group, known as The Five, who were organizing hundreds of followers to support an armed uprising to bring France back into the war.

Here Murphy's long residence in France proved invaluable. He had known socially, and now found himself working professionally, with the most important member of The Five, Jacques Lemaigre-Dubreuil, a financial hustler with Fascistic proclivities and a rich wife, whose financial affairs put her husband into frequent contact with the Germans. Murphy, as a veteran foreign-service officer, made it his business to cultivate the circles in which Lemaigre-Dubreuil moved, just as other members of the foreign service cultivated the Daladiers and the Léon Blums.

Neither Murphy nor The Five got any inkling of the plans discussed at the Arcadia Conference of January 1942, to make North Africa the scene of that year's second front. Nor did they hear any echoes of the backings and fillings that followed. Originally, it will be recalled, Roosevelt and Churchill conceived of Torch as a sop to the Russians. Later, they came to see it as a baptism of military fire for the Americans whose popularity with the French would ensure them a warmer welcome than the British could expect. Churchill, however, came to see Torch as a first step away from a cross-Channel invasion of Europe and then as a long stride toward an assault on the soft underbelly of the Axis. Of all this The Five knew nothing, and it was not until August 30, when Murphy arrived in Washington for top-level talks, that he learned the details.

General Marshall at once warned Murphy against confiding any plans to any Frenchman; Secretary of War Stimson opposed any action in North Africa. He preferred a major, direct assault on western Europe in 1943 to a minor North African sideshow in 1942. On September 4, Murphy spent several hours at Hyde Park with Roosevelt and Hopkins. The President did most of the talking: Torch appealed to his sense of adventure and his love of naval operations, but he recognized its danger and delicacy. He reiterated his wartime policy toward France: "You will restrict your dealings to French officials on the local level, prefects, and the military." In outlining the invasion plans that had only just taken shape he warned: "Don't tell anybody in the State Department about this. That place is a sieve." Of Secretary Hull, he said: "Don't worry about Cordell, I will tell him our plans a day or two before the landings." For his own part Murphy still believed "not too inaccurately," he thought, "that more leaks emanated from the White House in those days than from the State Department." But no leaks reached the French. For all their differences on other matters both Roosevelt and Churchill shared the same total confidence in the total unreliability of General de Gaulle.

· 2 ·

IN LINE with the decisions reached at London on July 22, 1942, the Torch planners had set it up as the largest amphibious force ever assembled up to that time. General Eisenhower served as supreme commander. The Americans provided half the troops, including all those assigned to the initial landings on the Moroccan and Algerian beaches. Americans also assumed responsibility for all political and military arrangements with the French authorities, whose government had broken off relations with the British. But the British troops faced the tougher military opposition farther east in the form of the German soldiers pouring into Tunisia. Roosevelt's enthusiasm for Torch arose, in part, from his conviction that the long tradition of Franco-American friendship would spare the American troops anything more than the merest token resistance from the French. Going one step further, he also saw the entire operation as a political rather than a military one and, for that reason, as great a test for Murphy as for Eisenhower.

The shape that events eventually took began to materialize on April 18 when five-star General Henri Giraud, who had escaped from a German prison camp during the First World War, did it again. On May 19, Lemaigre-Dubreuil and Giraud met in unoccupied France where—according to Lemaigre-Dubreuil—Giraud "was already in possession of a long-matured strategic plan for bringing France back into the war against Germany." Giraud hoped to use the token French forces, still permitted by the armistice, as the nucleus for uprisings that would spread throughout France and even on into Germany. Lemaigre-Dubreuil then talked Giraud into co-operating with the North African conspiracy, but only as a prelude to landings in metropolitan France. Giraud, with the approval of Vichy, named as his man in Algiers General Emmanuel Mast whom the Germans had just released on parole from the same prison from which Giraud had just escaped.

What went on here? Two French generals escape from a German prison—the first under his own steam, the second with the connivance of the Germans. Both then establish ties with Vichy, and Giraud speaks of plans to enlist Germans as well as Frenchmen in an anti-Hitler uprising. But Lemaigre-Dubreuil, who commended Giraud to Murphy, and therefore to Eisenhower, did not appear to take his protégé too seriously. "I chose him from his photographs," he confided to Murphy. "He is the typical French general. Oak-leaf clusters and a lovely moustache, just as they cast them in Hollywood. He was bound to be agreeable to the Americans."

Lemaigre-Dubreuil knew his Giraud no better than he knew his Americans; Murphy knew his Lemaigre-Dubreuil, which did not mean that he admired, respected, or agreed with him. But Murphy concluded, rightly or wrongly, that the time and the place called for the services of such Fascist-minded businessmen as Lemaigre-Dubreuil and such nonpolitical generals as Giraud in the complex game that he and Roosevelt and Eisenhower were about to play in North Africa. As "Personal Representative of the President of the United States," assigned to act as political adviser to General Eisenhower, Murphy held the highest American civilian post in Algiers; as such he described himself "the first civilian in American history to serve on the inner staff of a military commander's headquarters in a war theatre, with access to all military information." Eisenhower, the self-made soldier, and Murphy, the self-made diplomat, both products of the American Midwest, had both risen to the very tops of their chosen, admired professions. But Eisenhower transcended soldiering; Murphy, the diplomat's diplomat, remained the prisoner of his métier. Each respected the other, but Eisenhower, in his humility, perhaps learned more from Murphy than Murphy, in his complacency, learned from a man of wider experience than his own.

According to Murphy, Eisenhower disliked everything about Torch: "its diversion from the central campaign in Europe; its obvious military risks in a vast, untried territory; its dependence upon local forces who were doubtful at best and perhaps treacherous; its bewildering complexities involving deadly quarrels among French factions, and Spanish, Italian, Arab, Berber, German, and Russian politics. Eisenhower listened with a kind of horrified intentness to my description of the possible complications." But Murphy's military innocence matched Eisenhower's political innocence.

On November 1, Giraud wrote Murphy, announcing that his plans for an uprising in metropolitan France would make it impossible for him to arrive in Algiers until November 20. Murphy promptly cabled Roosevelt, recommending a two-week delay in the invasion plans. Eisenhower went through the roof, cabling Marshall that he found it "inconceivable that Murphy can recommend such a delay with his intimate knowledge of the operation and the present location of troops and convoys afloat." Eisenhower's ignorance of Murphy's ignorance matched Murphy's ignorance of Eisenhower's knowledge. Neither one, however, had victimized the other. Roosevelt's passion for secrecy and penchant for the devious had victimized them both.

Later, in his *Crusade in Europe*, Eisenhower summed it up this way: "The Allied invasion of Africa was a most peculiar venture of armed forces into the field of international politics; we were invading a neutral country to create a friend," and in so doing "were asking for what was one of the greatest fighting armadas of all times." Or, as Murphy put it later, when he, too, knew the scope of the operation: "From England and from the United States great convoys of eight hundred ships, carrying 110,000 Americans and Britons were converging upon a score of landing beaches along twelve hundred miles of Atlantic and Mediterranean coasts." For Murphy the supreme crisis arrived during the night of November 7–8, 1942, when the landings began. First, no General Giraud arrived to announce, in person, the landing of the troops. Second, the troops themselves landed late. Third, many of those who went ashore near Algiers did not find on the beaches the weapons they had been promised. Fourth, those who landed on the Atlantic beaches near Casablanca encountered heavy resistance. Last but not least, the full general's uniform that Giraud packed and sent ahead had vanished in transit, and he appeared in civilian clothes. "How to make a *coup d'état* in a bowler hat?" wrote the unflappable Harold Macmillan afterward in *The Blast of War*. "What a problem! A new uniform had to be procured of five-star general rank and a precious day was lost."

Although General Giraud, whom Murphy had expected, did not appear, Admiral Darlan, whom he had not expected, did. Darlan's son, a victim of polio, faced emergency treatment in an Algiers hospital, and the father hastened to his bedside. Meanwhile, two experienced American diplomats, sensing that Giraud expected to assume immediate command of the entire operation, had taken the precaution of having him visit General Eisenhower, at Gibraltar, en route. There Eisenhower encountered his baptism of political fire—fortunately at the hands of another and far less political general than himself. Between nightfall on November 7 and the morning of November 9, temporary three-star General Eisenhower persuaded permanent five-star General Giraud to accept the subordinate role of commander of French forces only. By the time Giraud and General Mark W. Clark, as Eisenhower's deputy, arrived later that day at Algiers, the situation had changed again, to Giraud's further disadvantage. For no sooner did Giraud drop out of the skies from Gibraltar than Darlan emerged from nowhere to outrank him. Yet, even Darlan now needed Pétain's permission before he could order the French forces in Morocco to hold their fire.

The deadlock ended the next day with the news that the Germans had violated the armistice by invading unoccupied France, thus freeing Darlan to issue orders in his own behalf. But General Charles Noguès, the top Vichy official in Morocco, whose troops were still resisting General George S. Patton's II Corps at Casablanca, continued fighting until November 12, when Noguès flew to Algiers, where he agreed with the supporters of Giraud and Darlan on a formula for a French command similar to one that Eisenhower had proposed three weeks earlier, before the Vichyite defections began. Giraud gladly agreed to serve under Darlan as commander in chief of the French forces; Noguès remained resident general of Morocco; General Alphonse Juin, Vichyite commander in chief of all French ground forces in North Africa, took command of the French forces in Tunisia, where the Germans had begun pouring troops, weapons, and planes through Bizerte.

· 3 ·

The unthinking crowd to majesty may bow,
Exalt the proud and idolize success;
But more to innocence their safety owe
Than power or genius e'er conspired to bless.

Thomas Gray. Lines deleted from his *Elegy*

No AMERICAN PRESIDENT before or since Woodrow Wilson had wielded so much power as Franklin D. Roosevelt. He issued the orders; the Marshalls, MacArthurs, and Kings, the Hulls, Stimsons, and Knoxes, and scores of specialists—Robert Murphy among them—carried them out. Roosevelt had avoided some of Wilson's mistakes, but already his secret diplomacy was proving no more successful than Wilson's open covenants openly arrived at had been. Unlike Wilson, Roosevelt could not depend upon himself alone; he had also to delegate to others many of his greater and more complex powers. But Murphy had showed himself something less than an American Talleyrand when he turned to Lemaigre-Dubreuil, who, in turn, promptly came up with Giraud, who shortly gave way to Darlan. It was Murphy's business, not Roosevelt's or Eisenhower's, to know what manner of men these were. Thus Roosevelt's power depended on Murphy's genius. Yet, in spite of Murphy's ignorance of the complexities of triphibious warfare, the landings did not founder; nor did Eisenhower's ignorance of the complexities of French politics prevent the formation of an effective center of military and civil power at Algiers. The transcendent innocence of the Eisenhower personality swept all before it.

In and of themselves, the North African landings had no effect on the continued progress that the British Eighth Army made across the Libyan Desert. Nor had General Eisenhower yet begun to cope with the streams of German troops that continued to pour into Bizerte and drive across Tunisia toward Algeria. Political warfare also continued at Eisenhower's Algiers headquarters where Frenchman fought Frenchman with no holds or weapons barred. As a result neither Admiral Darlan nor his political cause survived the year. Roosevelt presently described him as a "temporary expedient," only to find him more temporary than expedient on November 27, when German troops occupied the Toulon naval base while the officers and crews scuttled their own vessels. Darlan assured both Churchill and Roosevelt that this justified his policy because the fleet had not passed into German hands. But it had not passed into Allied hands either—and Hitler had no crews to man the ships and no plans that required their use. So it looked like a half victory for the Axis. But Eisenhower recalled that Churchill once told him: "If I could meet Darlan, much as I hate him, I would cheerfully crawl on my hands and knees a mile if by doing so I could get him to bring that fleet of his into the circle of Allied forces." And, until the scuttling of that fleet, this always seemed to Eisenhower a possibility he could not ignore.

Meanwhile, in Tunisia, too, the Germans went on the offensive. By November 13, when all resistance had ended in Morocco, the Germans had landed enough men and equipment at Bizerte to launch an offensive which carried them well into Algeria by Christmas, when only the bad weather stopped them. General Eisenhower had made a trip to the front in the hope that he might be able to order a Christmas offensive. But on December 24, the rain, snow, and mud convinced him that the Allied forces—British, American, and French—could not do more than hold their own, if that. No sooner had he reached that decision than still worse political news came from the rear. Admiral Darlan had been assassinated. Thirty hours of nonstop driving through mud and sleet brought Eisenhower back to Algiers, where he promptly succumbed to an attack of flu which kept him in bed for a week.

On the afternoon of December 23, Darlan had told Murphy in private: "You know, there are four plots to assassinate me. Suppose one of these plots is successful. What will you Americans do then?" The son of a local law reporter who had separated from his Italian wife shot Darlan dead just outside the same office where Murphy and the admiral had their last talk. The boy, who was seized on the spot, said he had "brought justice to a traitor who stood in the way of the union of France" and swore that he had acted alone and without accomplices. In another forty-eight hours, a firing squad executed the assassin. As one reporter put it later, the war council in whose hands the boy's fate lay consisted of "octogenarian reactionaries with no hope in the world but to hold their present positions." Fearful of what a full investigation might disclose, they preferred to move fast and "bury the Admiral, bury the boy, and bury the story." Another twenty-three years passed before Peter Tompkins dug up and reassembled the details in *The Murder of Admiral Darlan* (1965).

Those details do not belong here. Suffice it to say that the young assassin had acted in behalf of a group of French royalists who had occasionally made trouble for the Third Republic. That a plot of theirs had eliminated Darlan spoke volumes on the utter disorganization that prevailed in Algiers at the time of the American landings. Just as the shock of Darlan's sudden end overshadowed his no less sudden rise to power, so the consequences of the murder now overshadowed the murder itself. Friends of the admiral circulated false rumors of new assassination plots against Murphy and Giraud. For six weeks, General Eisenhower imposed a censorship on all political news from Algiers. Prime Minister Churchill became so disturbed that he asked and obtained permission to send a political officer of his own to General Eisenhower's headquarters. He chose his old friend and political supporter, Harold Macmillan. The fact that Mr. Macmillan's mother was Kentucky-born would surely commend him to the Americans.

It was an inspired choice. Macmillan's personal charm and diplomatic aplomb captivated Murphy. Eisenhower's simpler virtues won Macmillan's admiration. "I can't understand why these long-haired starry-eyed guys keep gunning for me," Eisenhower blurted out to Macmillan when liberal Anglo-American journalists assailed his dealings with Darlan, "I'm no reactionary. Christ on the mountain! I'm as

idealistic as Hell." More than two decades later, in *The Blast of War,*
Macmillan summed up the Eisenhower whom he had first come to
know in Algiers: "When big decisions had to be taken Eisenhower
never flinched. The landings in North Africa, when the conflicting news
might have made a small man hesitate; the attack on Sicily, when an
unexpected storm seemed to put the whole operation at risk; finally the
frightful weather at the time of the invasion of metropolitan France: on
all these vital occasions the terrible decision rested with him—postponement and perhaps chaos, or to pursue the plan with the prospect of
frightful casualties and perhaps defeat. Eisenhower, at all crises, military or political, showed supreme courage."

Twenty-four hours after the Darlan murder the White House cabled
General Eisenhower to put General Giraud in charge of French military and civil affairs in North Africa. At the same time a cable went to
General de Gaulle, instructing him to postpone his projected visit to the
United States. But de Gaulle had already cabled Giraud that the Darlan murder made it more necessary than ever to establish a single, national French authority and followed through with a letter proposing
they meet in Algeria or Chad to study ways and means of setting up "a
provisional central power" that would bring metropolitan France and
its overseas territories together in "the struggle for the liberation and
welfare of France." Giraud replied that in his view the murder of Darlan made delay preferable to haste but suggested that de Gaulle send "a
qualified representative" to Algiers to discuss the matter further. De
Gaulle welcomed this as a "first exchange of views" between them,
while continuing to insist on his own.

The matter did not rest there long. On January 2, 1943, in a letter to
Eisenhower and Murphy, Roosevelt spelled out the details. He described North Africa as a "military occupation zone" in which the
American commanding general had "complete control of all affairs,
both civilian and military. Our French friends," he continued, "must not
be allowed to forget this for a moment. In the same way, they must not
be led to believe that we are going to recognize any one group or committee as representing the French Empire or the French government.
The French people will be able to settle their own affairs when the war
ends with victory for us. Until that time, whenever our armies are in
occupation of former French territory, we will deal on a local basis with
local Frenchmen, and if these local officials will not co-operate, they
will have to be replaced." It was with these aims in mind that Roosevelt
arrived at Casablanca on January 12 for a two-week conference with

Churchill and their Joint Chiefs concerning their next military moves
on the Atlantic, the Pacific, and the Mediterranean, their next political
moves toward the Soviet Union, China, and North Africa, and air operations over Germany, the rest of Europe, and the Himalayas. As the
final item on this agenda they added their hoped-for reconciliation between de Gaulle and Giraud. Thus, the Casablanca Conference consisted of a review of the first year of combined Anglo-American operations against the Axis on all fronts and a schedule for the year ahead.
The North African meeting place also made it certain that the chief
military operations would occur in the Mediterranean and that the future of France would stand high on the political agenda.

·   ·   ·

The second chapter of the second volume of de Gaulle's *War Memoirs*, covering the period of Darlan's stewardship at Algiers, bears the
title "Tragedy." The third, covering the Casablanca Conference, bears
the title "Comedy." Here de Gaulle reappraised his passions as a participant in these events in the light of the wisdom imparted by thirteen
years of hindsight. Perhaps the passage of still another thirteen years
lends further weight to some of his judgments, notably those bearing on
the United States in general and on President Roosevelt in particular:

"Franklin Roosevelt was governed by the loftiest ambitions. His intelligence, his knowledge, and his audacity gave him the ability, the powerful state he headed afforded him the means, and the war offered him
the occasion to realize them. If the great nation he headed had been
long inclined to isolate itself from distant enterprises and to distrust a
Europe ceaselessly lacerated by wars and revolutions, a kind of mes-
sianic impulse now swelled the American spirit and oriented it toward
large undertakings.

"The United States, delighting in her resources, feeling that she had
no longer within herself sufficient scope for her energies, wishing to
help those who were in misery and bondage the world over, yielded
in her turn to that taste for intervention in which the instinct for
domination cloaked itself."

XII

Unconditional Surrender

·1·

WHEN ROOSEVELT ARRIVED at Casablanca on January 12, the Anglo-American Combined Chiefs of Staff had begun their strategy sessions, at which the Americans found themselves stymied from the start. To begin with, General Marshall still demanded priority for the cross-Channel invasion, over which the British had the veto power, since it would be up to them to provide the bulk of the troops. Admiral Ernest J. King, who commanded the United States Navy in all oceans, and General Henry H. Arnold, head of the United States Army Air Force, favored doubling the war effort in the Pacific as long as the British refused to launch a cross-Channel invasion. But neither Roosevelt nor Marshall would have any part of any strategy that gave the war in the Pacific priority over the strategy of defeating Germany first.

Under these circumstances, Field Marshal Sir Alan Brooke, Chief of the Imperial General Staff, had no difficulty in imposing his views on all concerned. Brooke did not suffer fools—or Americans—gladly. Too clever by half to foresee that the time would come when the Americans could dictate strategy to him as he now dictated strategy to them, he sowed a whirlwind. But the sowing yielded the Axis no benefits during the summer of 1943. Churchill, Brooke, and all the other British representatives at Casablanca agreed that a Mediterranean strategy offered the best—indeed, the only—area for early offensive action against Germany. They had therefore brought with them to Casablanca plans to invade Sicily, as soon as they had cleared the Axis forces from Tunisia, and to knock Italy out of the war immediately afterward.

But these plans for offensive operations remained subordinate to logistics—that is, where, when, and how to keep the global supply lines open and send the necessary troops and equipment over them. The Casablanca agenda therefore called for the defeat of the U-boat as "a first charge upon the resources of the United Nations." The second item also stressed defense: "The Soviet force must be sustained by the greatest volume of supplies that can be transported to the Soviet Union." Although Stalin had viewed the prospects of Torch with misgivings—and worse—he confessed on November 13 to Henry Cassidy, Moscow correspondent of the Associated Press: "The African campaign again refutes the skeptics who affirm that the Anglo-Americans cannot organize a serious war campaign." A month later he wrote Roosevelt: "In view of all sorts of rumors about the attitude of the Soviet Union toward the use of Darlan and other men like him, it may not be unnecessary for me to tell you that in my opinion as well as in that of my colleagues, Eisenhower's policy with regard to Darlan, Boisson, Giraud, and others is perfectly correct." After all, Hitler's former political bedfellow could not be too squeamish about the company that the Anglo-Americans kept.

Before receiving this letter from Stalin, Roosevelt had written Churchill in early November: "I feel very strongly that we have got to sit down at the table with the Russians." Churchill agreed but felt equally strongly that the British and Americans must confer first on a common policy. Roosevelt said, "No." He feared that would "give Stalin the impression that we are settling everything between ourselves before we meet him." In January, Stalin needled Churchill with the reminder: "I am awaiting your reply to the paragraph of my preceding letter regarding the establishment of the second front in Western Europe in the spring of 1943." But the Casablanca Conference had already decided otherwise—for logistical rather than political reasons. Brooke, like Churchill, never excluded the Soviet Union from his calculations. Later, he described Anglo-American policy toward the Russians as "wrong from the very start." "We have bowed and scraped to them, and never asked them for a single fact or figure concerning their production, strength, dispositions, etc. As a result they despise us and have no use for us except for what they can get out of us."

Brook, at Casablanca, made little if anything of the effect that Britain's Mediterranean strategy might have on Stalin's ambitions in eastern Europe and the Balkans. At that time the Red army posed no threat to the Anglo-Americans. Everything still hinged on the hope that the Red army might drive the Germans from Soviet territory. Indeed, some of the Americans who clamored in 1943 for a cross-Channel invasion came by 1944 to favor the British Mediterranean strategy as a barrier to Soviet expansion in that part of the world. Roosevelt—like Churchill— saw further ahead. Although the two did not see eye to eye, neither of them permitted this latent clash to mar their relationship at Casablanca. Churchill played the military cards Britain still held to impose his country's Mediterranean policy on Roosevelt, who, in his turn, did not advertise his determination to mount the cross-Channel invasion in 1944, when he would hold such cards as Churchill could never trump at any future time.

·2·

AFTER THE AMERICAN JOINT CHIEFS agreed at Casablanca to accept Britain's Mediterranean strategy for the 1943 campaign against their prime, German enemy, the British Joint Chiefs accepted the American strategy of stepping up the Pacific campaign against their secondary, Japanese enemy. All plans for 1944 went to the back of the stove. However, one more piece of unfinished business required attention: what to do about General de Gaulle. The murder of Admiral Darlan had made it, in the American idiom, a new ball game, which required de Gaulle's presence on the playing field. Originally de Gaulle had owed everything to Churchill. Now, with Darlan suddenly removed from play, Churchill needed de Gaulle as much as de Gaulle needed Churchill. But Roosevelt, in his determination to dominate the play, had discovered that expedience required the services of Darlan. This at once exposed him to such attacks as he had never suffered before from his New Deal supporters at home and his anti-Fascist admirers abroad. His old friend and secretary of the treasury, Henry Morgenthau, Jr., denounced Darlan for having sold thousands of people into slavery, and Stimson described Morgenthau as so "sunk" that he almost wanted to give up the war. The more equable Judge Sam Rosenman could not remember a time when the President had taken any political attack so hard. The fact was that Roosevelt shared his critics' distaste for Darlan. Whereas Churchill was able, at the height of the furor over Darlan, to explode: "Well, Darlan is not as bad as de Gaulle, anyway," Roosevelt's anguish testified to the gnawing suspicion that he had let his supporters down and in so doing betrayed himself as well. The long shadow of General de Gaulle lay heavy on the last act of the Casablanca drama.

Not until Friday, January 22, when that drama had only two more days to run, did the man who cast that shadow finally consent to appear upon the scene. Even Churchill had not been able to cajole or threaten de Gaulle into flying from London to Casablanca and there make his peace with Giraud under the eyes of Giraud's French and American sponsors. But when the French sponsors of de Gaulle's own committee unanimously demanded that he take part in the Casablanca proceedings with the single commitment of seeking to promote the interests of France, he reluctantly gave way.

At Casablanca de Gaulle found an angry Churchill and an imperturbable Roosevelt, who had not improved the mood of his British friends by giving a nonalcoholic dinner in honor of the sultan of Morocco. "The President talked a great deal about colonial aspirations toward independence and the approaching end of 'imperialism,' " wrote Macmillan in *The Blast of War*. "All this was equally embarrassing to the British and to the French. He dwelt at some length on possible economic co-operation between America and Morocco." To his son Elliott the President explained: "Imperialists don't realize what they can do, what they can create. They've robbed this continent of billions and all because they are too shortsighted to understand that their billions were pennies, pennies compared to the possibilities! Possibilities that *must* include a better life for the people who inhabit this land."

If Roosevelt could echo the anti-imperialist clichés of Vice President Wallace—then the darling of the New Dealers—he could also echo the anti-Gaullist clichés of Secretary Hull, who wrote off de Gaulle as "a polecat." "Elliott, de Gaulle is out to achieve one-man government in France," the President explained to his son. "I can't imagine a man I would distrust more. His whole Free French movement is honeycombed with police spies. To him freedom of speech means freedom from criticism—of him." But Roosevelt had no better an opinion of Giraud, only a different one. "This is the man," he pointed out to his son, "that Bob Murphy said the French would rally around. He's a dud as an administrator, he'll be a dud as a leader."

The day after de Gaulle arrived at Casablanca from London, Lemaigre-Dubreuil arrived from Washington, bearing a one-page memorandum from Hull for Giraud to present to Roosevelt. It included a clause establishing a generous fifty to one ratio between the dollar and the franc. The President initialed the memorandum as it stood, but Churchill withheld approval of a settlement that would have lodged dictatorial economic power in Giraud's hands. James MacGregor Burns, in *Roosevelt: The Soldier of Freedom*, has supplied a revealing footnote to this incident. It seems that Giraud had brought Roosevelt "two documents that dealt in part with military and economic matters, the product of much earlier discussion, but contained political provisions that promised every facility to Giraud to unite 'all' Frenchmen fighting against Germany and gave Giraud 'the right and duty of preserving all French interests in the military, economic, financial, and moral plane' until the French people could ultimately set up a constitutional government of their own. The President looked rapidly through these documents and signed them. Thereby he upset the elaborate matrimonial negotiations that he and Churchill had been conducting between Giraud and de Gaulle and he committed Churchill to Giraud without the Prime Minister's approval or even knowledge. Consternation resulted when Washington learned of Roosevelt's action later; Churchill had to alter the agreement quietly to restore the balance between the two Frenchmen."

How account for Roosevelt's behavior? Perhaps the answer lies in his own nature and in the nature of the political drama in which he found himself playing a leading role. A political showman of the first order, Roosevelt could not permit the upstart de Gaulle to frustrate him or Churchill, the old master, to upstage him. Roosevelt therefore threw himself into playing the part he played best—the part of himself, the great improviser. The Casablanca drama had to end with a joint Roosevelt-Churchill press conference at noon on Sunday, January 24. Suffice it to say that the two principals contrived to bring de Gaulle and Giraud together shortly before noon in the President's villa, where the President and the prime minister had scheduled their joint press conference. There Giraud agreed and de Gaulle refused to sign a joint communiqué that the Anglo-Americans had prepared for them during the previous night. But when the reporters, photographers, and newsreel cameramen arrived outside the villa, Roosevelt addressed a last appeal to de Gaulle: "In human affairs the public must be offered a drama. The news of your meeting with General Giraud in the midst of a conference in which both Churchill and I were taking part, if this news were to be accompanied by a joint declaration of the French leaders— even if it concerned only a theoretical agreement—would produce the dramatic effect we need."

"Let me handle it," replied de Gaulle. "There will be a communiqué, even though it cannot be yours." De Gaulle then presented his aides to the President, who presented his to de Gaulle. Churchill, Giraud, and their aides joined them as Churchill continued to rail against de Gaulle for having refused to sign the communiqué while Roosevelt made one last request on which he had set his heart. "Will you agree to being photographed beside me and the British prime minister along with General Giraud?"

"Of course, for I have the highest regard for this great soldier."

"Will you go so far as to shake General Giraud's hand before the camera?" To which de Gaulle replied, in English: "I shall do that for you."

De Gaulle, in his *War Memoirs*, from which this account is drawn, derived as much enjoyment from what seemed to him the President's vanity and naïveté as the President got from his triumph in public relations. De Gaulle and Giraud subsequently signed a short communiqué, written by de Gaulle. "We have seen each other, we have spoken together," it began. They reaffirmed their faith in the victory of France and the triumph of human liberties, and announced the establishment of permanent liaison. At Giraud's request, de Gaulle substituted the words "human liberties" for the "democratic principles," which he had originally written. The Roosevelt-Churchill press conference then followed in due course.

According to a memorandum written by Harry Hopkins at the time and on the spot, Roosevelt told him immediately afterward: "We had so much trouble getting those two French generals together that I thought this was as difficult as arranging the meeting of Grant and Lee—and then suddenly the press conference was on and Winston and I had no time to prepare for it, and the thought popped into my mind that they had called Grant 'Old Unconditional Surrender' and the next thing I knew I had said it." The thought that popped into his mind rang around the world in words that still reverberate: "Peace can come to the world only by the elimination of German and Japanese war power. . . . The elimination of German, Japanese, and Italian war power means the unconditional surrender by Germany, Italy, and Japan. That means a reasonable assurance of future world peace. It does not mean the destruction of Germany, Italy, or Japan, but it does mean the destruction of the philosophies in those countries which are based on the conquest and subjection of other people."

The time and place that Roosevelt chose for his unconditional-surrender announcement underscored its importance in his eyes. Its style and content revealed its nature. Those who had attacked the deal with Darlan now attacked the President's refusal to deal with de Gaulle. It had been bad enough to base the deal with Darlan on expedience. But what kind of expedience is it that at once spells death to its key figure? From the moment the landings began (several hours behind schedule), anticlimax followed anticlimax. Yet, if Roosevelt had told the full truth he would have had to admit that the landings owed what success they did achieve to Frenchmen who had rallied around Pétain when he capitulated to Hitler. Worse yet, he would have had to add that these same reactionary opportunists had now become the prime candidates for leadership in their country's liberation. Neither Roosevelt nor Churchill had any appetite for the crow pie that they would have to eat at de Gaulle's hands if they now sat at his table. On the other hand, Giraud looked like a nontemporary inexpedience.

The sudden proclamation of "unconditional surrender" as the war aim of the United Nations coalition on all fronts provided at least a temporary distraction from North Africa, de Gaulle, and Giraud. In more positive terms unconditional surrender also marked an improvement over Wilson's Fourteen Points which, in 1918, had committed the victorious Allies to grant the defeated Germans certain peace terms as the *quid pro quo* for the armistice of that year. The weakest feature of Roosevelt's unconditional-surrender statement lay in its careless phrasing and extemporaneous presentation. He had played the de Gaulle-Giraud reconciliation the only way it could be played and the way he could play it best—by ear. But under circumstances that compelled him to play his unconditional-surrender announcement the same way.

His reference to "Unconditional Surrender" Grant revived one of the favorite fallacies of American history—on a par with George Washington having cut down the cherry tree. In point of fact, Grant had not demanded unconditional surrender of Lee at Appomattox. He had allowed, on his own initiative, Lee's troops to keep their horses and side arms. It was of General Simon B. Buckner at Fort Donelson, two years earlier, that Grant had demanded unconditional surrender. Nor did Roosevelt compose his unconditional-surrender terms on the spur of the moment at Casablanca. He had often used the words before, and they appeared again in the notes from which he spoke at Casablanca. Churchill and his cabinet had all heard and approved them long before that. But Roosevelt had not given anybody any warning of the time, circumstances, or form of the announcement.

Had he, perhaps, put his worst foot forward? Unconditional surrender conceded nothing to Hitler or to any other Axis leader. It left the United Nations coalition free to impose its own terms. But Goebbels lost no time in telling the German people that unconditional surrender meant national destruction—and voices were raised in the United

States, Britain, and the Soviet Union criticizing the impression the President had made. He lost no time in seeking to repair the damage. On February 12, before the White House Correspondents Association, he restated his unconditional-surrender terms, laying as much emphasis on the humane aspect of unconditional surrender as on its unilateral aspect: "In our uncompromising policy we mean no harm to the common people of the Axis nations. But we do mean to impose punishment and retribution in full upon their barbaric leaders." And he also called attention to another feature of unconditional surrender that he had not mentioned at Casablanca, pointing out that it foreclosed in advance any attempt the Axis might make to "create the idea that if we win the war, Russia and England and China and the United States are going to get into a cat-and-dog fight." If Roosevelt had felt it necessary to point out both at Casablanca and at Washington that unconditional surrender cut two ways, why had he waited three weeks to point out that it also contained a built-in guarantee against a rift in the United Nations coalition? Had he perhaps hoped that, with the passage of time, that point would make itself, or had he feared, in the confusion and strain of Casablanca, even to hint at the possibility of such a rift?

· · ·

Of course those questions yielded no clear answers. That was why Roosevelt had balanced retribution with mercy. But, almost as if by way of afterthought, he included the reminder that a rift in the United Nations could prove an even greater threat to the future peace than a postwar resurgence of the Axis or of any Axis partner. Indeed, such a rift would almost automatically precede such a resurgence. And yet to suggest the possibility of such a rift could also backfire. Roosevelt therefore took in stride the attacks on his unconditional-surrender formula, irrespective of the motives or nationalities of the attackers.

But history contrived an outcome that confounded both the President and his critics. For at the very moment Roosevelt proclaimed his war aims, the fighting on the eastern front took a turn that made any other aims academic. Hitler and Stalin, having concluded the nonaggression pact that started the war, found themselves in less than two years committed to a fight to the finish between their two systems. Roosevelt's proclamation of unconditional surrender as the basic war aim of the United Nations coalition had drawn the logical—if belated—conclusion that eighteen months of unprecedented destruction had long since imposed on the German and Russian antagonists in that struggle. The question had now become: After unconditional surrender—what? For that question Roosevelt had begun to hope and even to plan that the United Nations coalition could eventually devise the answers. Meanwhile, the war itself must go on.

Especially on the eastern front. There the worst destruction had not occurred on the battlefield but behind the lines, where the Germans had enslaved, starved, and slaughtered many more millions of Russians than they had killed in combat—and where the Russians had also waged increasingly effective partisan warfare on the Germans. Moreover, as a counterpart to the destruction that the Germans spread across all the Russian lands they occupied, they set in motion their "final solution" of the "Jewish problem," which called for the extermination of more than six million European Jews—men, women, and children, Germans and non-Germans. From the east, like the echo of Roosevelt's Casablanca formula, came two other words that made unconditional surrender obsolete and irrelevant—Stalingrad and Auschwitz.

XIII

Stalingrad and Auschwitz

·1·

ROOSEVELT'S IMPULSIVE DECISION to release his long-prepared unconditional-surrender statement missed its mark. It did not distract attention
from the confusions and delays that followed the Allied landings in
North Africa. Nor did it impress Stalin, especially after February 2,
1943, when the German Sixth Army did the unconditional surrendering
at Stalingrad under conditions that made North Africa look like a picnic
ground. Thanks to Hitler's stand-and-fight tactics of December 1941,
Germany's 1942 offensives went on almost from where the previous
year's offensives had left off. Thus, by August 1942, the German Sixth
Army's quarter of a million, newly equipped veterans were rapidly approaching Stalingrad across the fifty-mile plain between the Don and
the Volga rivers. Hitler's troops had overrun more than twice as much
Russian territory as the troops of Napoleon or the Kaiser did and had
held most of that territory more than twice as long.

From late August to mid-November German planes and artillery
bombed Stalingrad to rubble. On August 23, six hundred German
planes killed 40,000 of its residents. But the retreating Russians turned
the wreckage created by the advancing Germans into barricades and
shelters. From the far side of the Volga Soviet artillery and mortar fire
made further havoc of the positions the Germans slowly gained. Soviet
propaganda dinned away at the old Russian saying: "Russia can be
conquered only if the enemy crosses the Volga." The German enemy
did not cross. Indeed, the Germans never drove all the Russians from
all of Stalingrad.

On September 29 Hitler dismissed Halder as chief of staff. "To settle
matters in the east," he explained, "we do not now need professional

ASHES OF VICTORY

ability but National Socialist ardor, and this I cannot expect of you."
General Kurt Zeitzler, the professional soldier who replaced Halder,
warned of impending disaster and eventually persuaded Hitler to pull
back the Fourth Panzer Army which had failed to penetrate the Caucasus. But of Stalingrad Hitler still said: "Where the German soldier sets
foot, there he remains." Most German soldiers had remained where
they had set foot in 1941 and then received enough re-enforcements in
1942 to resume their advance toward Stalingrad and the Caucasus. But
in driving to Stalingrad they had extended their supply lines and weakened themselves on other fronts while the Russians had shortened their
supply lines and brought up fresh troops and equipment. According to
General Vasili Chuikov who commanded the defense of Stalingrad, it
remained touch and go until the middle of October, and the Germans
did not launch their last, vain offensive until November 7, at which
point Hitler again promoted devout Nazis and demoted professional
soldiers.

On November 19, the Russians threw two new armies against the
Germans, one north, the other south of Stalingrad, breaking through
lines held mainly by Hungarians, Romanians, and Italians. Within a
week Hitler admitted that the Russians had "temporarily" surrounded
the Sixth Army, but he promised early relief. Although Goering had
assured him that the Luftwaffe could transport the necessary supplies,
the emergency deepened. Hitler then sought the advice of Field Marshal Fritz von Manstein, outside Leningrad, who told him: "The whole
eastern front must be stabilized with the object of shortening it. The
Sixth Army must break out of Stalingrad." Its commander, General
Friedrich von Paulus, told one of his aides that he regarded withdrawal
as "the more useful course to follow," but added, "We lack the facts on
which to base such a presumption."

With the encirclement came winter and subzero cold. On December
12, Paulus ordered: "When a unit has been overrun, it is the right and
duty of an officer to shoot himself." A battalion commander told Paulus:
"I regard suicide as the ultimate act of cowardice," adding he would
"choose captivity first." The Moscow radio kept repeating: "Every
seven seconds a German soldier dies in Russia—Stalingrad, mass
grave." On the morning of January 8, three Soviet officers, carrying a
flag of truce, offered to accept a German surrender, guaranteeing
safety, medical treatment, normal rations, and ultimate repatriation to
all. Hitler's headquarters, hundreds of miles west, rejected the offer:

· 218 ·

"All units are to be instructed that in the future enemy emissaries are to be fired upon."

On January 9, with a twenty-to-one artillery advantage, the Russians opened their final assault on the German-held sector of the city. By the end of the month, the end had come. On January 30, Hitler told Field Marshal Keitel: "There is no record in German military history of a German field marshal being taken prisoner." The next day he promoted Paulus to that rank. But when Soviet envoys appeared at Paulus' Stalingrad headquarters demanding unconditional surrender, he did not take his own earlier advice to officers of lesser grade and kill himself. He merely instructed his chief of staff to transmit this message to the Russians: "The commander in chief wishes to be regarded as a private person and does not wish to go on foot through the town." By this time, all isolated German outposts had capitulated, one by one, after the troops had destroyed their equipment. Paulus never signed any surrender document, but he did confer with the Soviet emissary, a Lieutenant Elchenko, who permitted him to be conveyed in a German car to General Konstantin Rokossovsky. The formal surrender came on February 2.

"I cannot believe that Paulus has been taken prisoner," said Hitler when he heard the news. "He had the choice between life and immortality; how could he, standing on the threshold of immortality, have preferred to live? I cannot see how a field marshal could make such a choice."

· 2 ·

A BALANCE SHEET showing what the battle of Stalingrad meant to the Russians on the one hand and to the Germans on the other explains why it stands out as the decisive military engagement of the Second World War. In all history, only the battle of Verdun surpassed Stalingrad in its scope. In importance Stalingrad more than matched the two battles of the Marne rolled into one.

Stalin learned more from the grave defeats that the Red army had suffered in 1941 than Hitler learned from the Wehrmacht's limited victories. The Russian people had paid heavily for Stalin's double folly— first, when he made his pact with Hitler; second, when he fell into the trap that he thought he had set for the western democracies. For twenty years the Red army's political commissars had indoctrinated the Red army troops with Communism and saw to it that officers toed the party line. But even this did not satisfy Stalin, who wound up his cycle of purges by liquidating Marshal Mikhail Tukhachevsky and most of the Red army's other outstanding professional soldiers. As a result, the Red army's military performance during the first few months of the war matched Stalin's political performance during the first few years before the German attack. But, as casualties mounted, Stalin enlarged the military duties of the political commissars whom he renamed war commissars as he merged their functions with the functions of the regular officers, until the officers corps absorbed them—for the duration. The Communist party still kept tabs on the army through its political generals and higher officials, and Stalin took unto himself the title of marshal along with the duties that the rank entailed. Here he mastered the intricacies of military command with a patience and thoroughness quite alien to Hitler's temperament. Unlike Hitler, Stalin also granted a new generation of field commanders an ever-widening range of operational authority.

While Stalin curtailed the powers of the political commissars and permitted his field commanders wider scope, Hitler moved in the opposite direction. After firing his top commanders in 1941 and assuming personal command of the Wehrmacht, he began to tackle what he considered his real task—"to educate the Army in National Socialism." This entailed the creation of a new "People's Officers Corps," the abolition of traditional educational requirements, no more regard for "family, education, and financial standing," but sole reliance on "unconditional readiness for action for the Fuehrer, the People, and the Fatherland." Throughout the battle of Stalingrad, Hitler kept insisting to General Zeitzler, his new chief of staff, that the sacrifices made by the Sixth Army were compelling the Russians to take heavier losses in other sectors. It was just the opposite. The longer the Germans held Stalingrad, the more they lost elsewhere and the more the Russians gained. Finally, the German surrender at Stalingrad coincided with the lifting of the siege of Leningrad. By this time, half of its original three million inhabitants had died of starvation and disease. The German army never recovered from the ordeal of Stalingrad; the Russian people took the greater ordeal of Leningrad in stride.

In 1942, as in 1941, the Germans tried to do too much with too little too fast. They had also lost their most valuable asset: surprise. Finally, just as Hitler's determination to invade Russia in 1941 cost him whatever chance he ever had of winning the battle of the Atlantic, so his 1942 offensives in Russia cost him all the gains that Rommel had made in the Egyptian desert and enabled the Anglo-Americans to establish themselves in Morocco and Algeria almost by default. Indeed, just as Stalin's decision to come to terms with Hitler in 1939 swung the European balance of military power in Germany's favor, so Hitler's violation of that pledge, in 1941, reversed that balance in Stalin's favor by 1943.

At this point, Hitler assigned to Goebbels the task of telling the German people the bitter truth. Having predicted inevitable German triumph throughout the war, Goebbels crowned his propaganda career by grimly warning his people that they must redouble their efforts or suffer total disaster. The moment the news of the Stalingrad surrender reached Berlin, Goebbels had all the radio stations play funeral marches, climaxed by a roll of drums and the strains of the soldier's lament, "Ich hat' einen Kamaraden," while he intoned the details. Black borders surrounded the front pages of the next morning's newspapers. "The army of the fallen has not surrendered its arms," declared Goebbels. "In reality, it is marching in the ranks of the soldiers."

On February 18, 1943, Hitler still could not bring himself to face a German audience. It was Goebbels who told a Sportspalast mass meeting in Berlin that "Stalingrad was and is the great alarm call of fate to the German nation. . . . Two thousand years of Occidental civilization are at stake. . . . No one in Germany today thinks of a foul compromise; the only thing the people want is a hard war." He wound up with a dialogue in which he asked his listeners, if they did not want to make sacrifices. "Am I right? Yes or no?" he asked, and when the crowd roared, "*Ja!*" he ticked off a ten-point program: Did they still believe in the Fuehrer? Were they prepared to work ten, twelve, fourteen, sixteen hours a day? Would the women of Germany submit themselves to the same discipline as the men? And so on. For the fact was that the Nazis had not, even at this late date, installed so drastic a war economy as the British adopted after Dunkirk. Hitler had never dared to warn the German people that they might face a long war; Churchill had never dared to lead the British people to believe that they faced anything else.

War by its very nature destroys wealth. To the victors belong the spoils and in obedience to that principle, German occupation of conquered territories began with the looting of private property by individual Nazi officials, privileged soldiers and civilians, and their wives. Wholesale plunder of public wealth followed. From the banks, factories, warehouses, museums, docks, and depots of western Europe—chiefly France—trainloads of art treasures, gold, foreign exchange, finished and unfinished goods, raw materials and foodstuffs worth millions of dollars flowed into Germany. To loot wealth means only to move it from place to place, from owner to owner, to tie up transportation, to expend labor, fuel, time, and resources on unproductive effort. Bad enough in all conscience. But how about those racist, nationalist appeals which first attracted millions of Germans to the Nazi party and then boomeranged when Hitler turned from political theory to economic practice? The Nazis' increasing reliance on slave labor led to increasingly inefficient production and to a still sharper decline in living standards and public health. The Nazis' "final solution" of the Jewish question then carried their racial theories to their logical conclusions. The extermination of six million Jews liquidated, at great cost, the most precious asset any nation or community possesses—its own people.

Yet not until after the Stalingrad disaster did Hitler dare to impose a total war economy on German workers and peasants, manufacturers and industrialists. Before the North African landings, the Germans charged the French budget 300 million francs a day for the occupation; after the landings the figure went up to 500 million. The Germans also commandeered from 20 to 100 per cent of all the goods various French industries produced.

What a travesty the Nazi New Order in Europe presented. The French novelist and academician Jean Guéhenno noted in his diary, in July 1940: "The defeat of France is only one episode of the European civil war. Beneath the conflict between nations lies a deeper social conflict. Each nation is so sharply divided within itself that some of the parties that compose it can think that their country's loss is their gain." Charles Maurras, editor of the royalist *Action française,* had hailed Hitler's victory as a "divine surprise." Guéhenno never shared that view. At first he had hated the German soldiers who swarmed through the streets of Paris. In 1943 he wrote: "I do not hate you. I no longer hate you. I pretend not to see you. I act as if you did not exist."

But in 1944 a painter named Jean Bruller, who turned to writing for the underground press under the name of Vercors, declared: "The enemy by his abominable acts has made hatred almost a duty." Addressing himself to that enemy, he added: "Of all the reasons for hating you, oh you that I cannot call my fellow man, this single one would suffice: I hate you because of what you have made of me. Because you sowed and cultivated in me, with the diabolical persistence that is yours, sentiments for which I feel only disgust and scorn."

·3·

IT TOOK FOUR YEARS of German occupation to make one French intellectual feel degraded to his enemy's level. It was a different story in the Soviet Union, especially the Ukraine, where many inhabitants hoped that German occupation might bring them a better life, if not liberation. But Hitler's anti-Slavic prejudices, which many Germans shared, blinded him and them to their opportunities. Everywhere in the Soviet Union the German invaders at once treated the people of the territories they occupied like slaves, animals, or vermin, thus swelling the ranks of the resistance movement and assuring the Soviet authorities of loyal support as they ordered all dams, bridges, and power stations blown up along with such factories and equipment as could not be shipped to improvised installations beyond the Urals. Many of the fleeing peasants scorched their farms. The Germans shipped the more able-bodied of those who remained to slave labor, starvation, and death in Poland and Germany. City dwellers underwent similar ordeals.

After Stalingrad the process of retribution began. As the Red army troops liberated the cities and villages that the Germans had wrecked, desecrated, and destroyed, a growing desire for revenge possessed them. Kharkov, in the Ukraine, had a prewar population of 900,000. When the Germans arrived, 700,000 remained; when the Russians returned 350,000 had vanished. The Russians established that 120,000 of them had been shipped to slave labor in Germany; between 70,000 and 80,000 had died of privation; the Germans had killed 30,000, more than half of them Jews. The Russian city of Viazma had consisted of 5500 buildings before the war; only 51 remained. Rzhev had shrunk from 5433 buildings to 495. Else Wendele, in *Hausfrau at War,* quoted her husband, on his return from the eastern front, as having blurted out: "Do you know how we behaved to the civilians? Shall I tell you? We behaved like devils out of hell. We left those villagers to starve to death behind us, thousands and thousands of them. How can you win a war this way? Don't think they won't avenge themselves some day. Of course they will."

Heinz Schroeter, the Sixth Army correspondent at Stalingrad, described the 91,000 troops of that army, taken prisoners there, as having "marched into oblivion." But where did the five million Russian prisoners who had fallen into German hands by the end of 1942 march? At least two million died of starvation, exposure, and disease while in German captivity. One million gained release during the war; another million remained unaccounted for. Most of them found death, soon or late, performing some kind of forced labor in one or another of the various work camps, concentration camps, and death camps that the Germans set up in Poland. When the Germans marched into Poland in 1939, the systematic extermination of Poles and Jews began. But it was not until the Germans invaded Russia during the summer of 1941 that their extermination program assumed mass proportions and permanent status, for only then did Hitler and Goering pass on word to Himmler and to his deputy Heydrich to have their S.S. troops prepare to set the "final solution" of the Jewish question in motion.

The Einsatzgruppen, first organized in Poland by Himmler and Reinhard Heydrich to round up the Jews, later extended operations to the occupied countries of western Europe and then to the Soviet Union. Many of the Jews whom they shipped to concentration camps in Poland and Germany were starved, worked to death, or executed; total extermination did not begin until after the flood of Russian war prisoners arrived. In June 1941, the convicted murderer Rudolf Hoess received orders from his superiors in the S.S. to set up an extermination camp at the Polish town of Oświecim (better known by its German name of Auschwitz), which had excellent railroad facilities. Within another year Auschwitz had become, and remained throughout the war, by far the largest of all the death camps. Its gas chambers and four crematoria possessed a capacity of six thousand Jews a day. Commandant Hoess, in an affidavit, estimated "2,500,000 victims executed and exterminated, and at least another half million who succumbed to starvation and disease, making a total of about 3,000,000." The Russians estimated that Auschwitz alone accounted for four million victims. In any event, by 1945 some six million European Jews went to their deaths in Auschwitz and more than a dozen other camps, large and small, in Poland and Germany.

Before setting up the extermination camp at Auschwitz, Hoess visited Treblinka where 80,000 Jews, including all those from the Warsaw ghetto, had been exterminated in six months. Among the improvements over Treblinka of which Hoess boasted was that "at Treblinka the victims almost always knew they were to be exterminated while at Auschwitz we endeavored to fool the victims into thinking that they would go through a delousing process. Of course, frequently they realized our true intention, and we sometimes had riots and difficulties. Very frequently women would hide their children under their clothes but of course when we found them we would send the children in to be exterminated. We were required to carry out these exterminations in mercy, but of course the foul and nauseating stench from the continuous burning of bodies permeated the entire area and all of the people living in the surrounding communities knew that exterminations were going on at Auschwitz."

Gerald Reitlinger, in *The Final Solution—The Attempt to Exterminate the Jews of Europe,* described "the most ghastly job of all," performed by Jewish inmates who had been promised their lives for performing it, only to be exterminated in their turn. Naked prisoners who had expected a delousing shower found themselves in a gas chamber and stampeded away from the gas vents toward a metal door where "they piled up in one blue, clammy, blood-spattered pyramid, clawing and mauling each other even in death." Twenty minutes later, the special commandos, wearing gas masks and rubber boots and carrying hoses, appeared: "Their first task was to remove the blood and defecations before dragging and clawing the dead apart with nooses and hooks, the prelude to the ghastly search for gold and the removal of teeth and hair which were regarded by the Germans as strategic materials. Then the journey by lift or railroad to the furnaces, the mill that ground the clinker to fine ash, and the truck that scattered the ashes in the stream of the Sola."

Lord Russell of Liverpool, in *The Scourge of the Swastika,* quotes a former prisoner in the Ravensbrueck concentration camp for women who gave this account of the end all these factories of death served: "The whole system in this camp had but one purpose and that was to destroy our humanity and our human conscience; the weaker individuals fell into the very bottom of moral and physical existence; all the lower bestial instincts developed while the better instincts were stifled and had no chance to show themselves. Even the stronger ones who came out of the camp alive are marked with unnatural characteristics which will never be erased: they have lost all faith in goodness and justice."

Near Auschwitz, which claimed more victims than all the other death camps put together, the I. G. Farben chemical trust and the Krupp Industries erected factories, submitting competitive bids. Here the doomed inmates of the camp worked as slave laborers until their strength gave out. On the other hand, the children of Jewish families were dispatched at once because—as Hoess put it—"by reason of their youth, they were unable to work." German doctors conducted fatal experiments on some of the Auschwitz inmates; camp guards tortured and murdered others. As the thousands of victims lined up outside the gas chambers they were regaled by Strauss waltzes and Viennese operettas played through loudspeakers. According to Hoess, so-called "special prisoners"—presumably Russian war prisoners—were killed with injections of benzine.

But the bulk of the Russian war prisoners had already succumbed to more brutal treatment. The Nazis regarded all Slavs as subhuman beasts of burden and had no compunctions about working or starving them to death. Polish intellectuals they executed out of hand. "The Slav peoples," as Hitler remarked during the battle of Stalingrad, "are not destined to lead a cleanly life. They know it and it would be wrong to persuade them to the contrary." But it was only the Jews whom the Nazis sought out and singled out for complete extermination.

. . .

The Stalingrad surrender marked a turning point in the tangled histories of the Russian, German, and Jewish peoples. Insofar as the Russians were concerned, it confronted Stalin with another of his two-irons-in-the-fire alternatives. At first, he showed some signs of following Lenin's example and using his victory over the Germans as his first step toward the export of Communist revolution to German soil. Hence the January surrender appeal to the Sixth Army and the subsequent effort to use Field Marshal von Paulus to head a Soviet-sponsored committee of German officers. But Hitler and Goebbels began beating him at his own revolutionary game when they responded to the Stalingrad surrender with renewed and redoubled anti-Communist, anti-Russian propaganda and with a summons to the German people to wage revolutionary war of their own, Nazi style, in defense of Germany and the West. And, as time went on, it seemed more design than accident that Hitler set in motion his "Final Solution" of the "Jewish Problem" to coincide with the Stalingrad surrender.

It took another two years for Hitler to complete what became known as "The Holocaust," and it took longer than that for the full story to reach the outside world. During the first few postwar years, as Auschwitz came to connote the ultimate horror, most Germans had to struggle so hard to stay alive that they could do little in the way of restitution or penance. But during those same years, those Jews who had chosen Palestine as their sanctuary from Hitler threw themselves into building the new state of Israel there. Large, affluent, and generous Jewish communities in the United States provided financial, political, and administrative support on a scale that enabled the Jewish emigrants to Palestine to establish a new nation—or, rather, to re-establish an old one—two years after the German surrender, building, of course, on foundations laid by the Zionist movement before and after the First World War. But it was the very horror of the holocaust that provided the impetus which ensured the creation and development of Israel. It would be too much to say that its survival and prosperity require permanent and substantial German contributions, of which Chancellor Adenauer became one of the early sponsors. But it would not be too much to note that unless the Germans continue to regard the survival and prosperity of Israel as an essential feature of their own survival and prosperity, they may find they have forgotten where their own vital interests lie.

If the state of Israel might be regarded as the first, tangible monument to the German surrender at Stalingrad, the consequences of that battle on the Germans and Russians went deeper and took longer to reveal themselves. The Russian agony during the first eighteen months of the German invasion far surpassed the German agony during the two years that followed. But if the Russians, during the Second World War, suffered greater losses at German hands than any other people endured, the Soviet Union emerged from that war the chief beneficiary of Germany's defeat. Not until Stalingrad did German suffering at Russian hands reach mass dimensions, but German suffering at Russian hands did not end there any more than Russian suffering at German hands did. Yet precisely this community of suffering at each others' hands served, among other things, to intensify that mixture of hatred and fear, of horror and awe that had characterized their relations over the centuries. The Germans—notably Hitler and Goebbels—had never respected the Russians so much as after Stalingrad. To the Russians, Stalin had never appeared more impressive.

What's in a name? In the case of Stalingrad, plenty. During Russia's postrevolutionary civil war when the city still bore the name Tsaritsyn (City of the Czars), Stalin won a battle there by substituting his own plans for Trotsky's. Later, he had the city renamed in his honor. To Hitler the symbolic importance of Stalingrad came to outweigh even its strategic importance, and it was by Hitler's decision that it later became the symbol of Russia's approaching victory over Germany in the Second World War. Whether the fall of Stalingrad would have led to the fall of

Stalin nobody can ever know. But the German surrender at Stalingrad not only saved Stalin from the ruin that his purges so nearly brought upon him. It enabled his supporters to argue that his purges had helped him steel himself and his people for the ordeal that culminated there.

XIV

1943's Long, Hot Summer

·1·

FOUR WEEKS AFTER CASABLANCA and two weeks after Stalingrad, Stalin dispatched a sarcastic letter to Roosevelt and Churchill, repeating his "understanding that by the decisions you have taken you have set yourselves the task of crushing Germany in 1943 and I should be very much obliged for information concerning the actual operations planned for the operation and on the schedule for carrying them out." The Casablanca decisions, which they had communicated several weeks before, contained no references to any such operations, but before Roosevelt or Churchill could make reply, Stalin celebrated Red Army Day on February 23 with the announcement that the Soviet Union was now "bearing the whole brunt of the war" on the eastern front, where the real struggle had only just begun.

In another month, the Soviet authorities announced that their forces had liberated almost 200,000 square miles of Russian territory, advanced as much as 445 miles in some sectors, killed over 850,000 Axis troops, and taken more than 340,000 Axis prisoners. But the Anglo-Americans also had a tale to tell. General Eisenhower, as supreme commander, had transferred the field command to his deputy, General Alexander, who at once made effective use of Montgomery's Eighth British Army and of Patton's enlarged II Corps, to which 5400 army trucks had been rushed under special naval convoy. By the middle of May, Eisenhower's polyglot forces—French, Polish, Indian, South African, as well as British and American—had swept the Axis from North Africa, at a cost of 70,000 casualties. Axis casualties totaled more than a million, including 240,000 prisoners taken by the Allies during the final week. Goebbels called it the worst German defeat since Stalingrad and quoted Roosevelt's unconditional-surrender formula to justify bitter-end German resistance.

At this juncture, Goebbels' propaganda sounded like music to Roosevelt's ears, especially in contrast to Stalin's sarcasm, snubs, and smugness. But instead of turning to his senior military advisers or to the younger generation of New Dealers who had served him well on many fronts, Roosevelt reached back into his political past to two men who, like himself, had come to Washington in 1913 as supporters of Woodrow Wilson and who, like himself, had remained disciples of the master: Secretary of State Cordell Hull and Joseph E. Davies, the ambassador to Russia. All three men had backed Wilson in his fight for the League of Nations; all three had modified some of their convictions of a quarter century before; but all three shared the same determination to start planning and even building a postwar security organization before rather than after victory had been won. If Stalin had already begun to make trouble, if Churchill and Brooke already distrusted the Russians, all the more reason for Roosevelt and his colleagues to establish closer ties with Stalin while each depended so much upon the other. Roosevelt had no interest in trying to talk to the peoples of the Axis nations over the heads of their rulers. He wanted to establish contact with Stalin not only in order to speed the defeat of the Axis, but to discuss postwar plans.

With this in mind, Roosevelt first turned to Ambassador Davies, whose recent book, *Mission to Moscow*, had become a best seller. In it, with the President's blessings, the State Department had cleared many of the dispatches and much of the correspondence that Davies had sent from the Moscow embassy in 1937 and 1938, plus additional dispatches, letters, and diary entries. Davies had served as Wilson's Midwest campaign manager in 1912; later he headed the Federal Trade Commission; he came within a whisker of winning election as a pro-League Senate Democrat from Wisconsin in 1918. Since then he had practiced law in Washington. While ambassador to Moscow in 1937 and 1938, Davies had established good relations with Foreign Minister Litvinov and even with Stalin, representing himself as a progressive capitalist.

After the German attack on Russia, Davies found himself one of the few men close to the White House who had remained on friendly, personal terms with the Soviet leadership, without involving himself in their affairs, interests, or beliefs. Unable, for reasons of health, to comply with Roosevelt's first request that he return to his Moscow post, Davies did the next best thing and flew there in late May bearing with him a letter from the President to Stalin, together with a motion-picture version of his book, of which the less said the better. After a brief, warm, and somewhat confused reception, Davies returned with Stalin's tentative agreement to meet Roosevelt at Fairbanks, Alaska, on July 15, 1943.

While laying plans for the Davies flight to Moscow, Roosevelt began to bone up on the main subject he hoped to discuss. To this end, he prevailed upon Britain's Foreign Secretary Eden (always *persona grata* at Moscow) to spend the first two weeks of March in Washington discussing, with Secretary Hull and others, "the most effective methods of preparing for meetings of all the United Nations to consider questions arising out of the war." As a Democratic congressman from Tennessee, Hull had supported Wilson's fight for the League of Nations. As senator during the 1920's and as secretary of state since 1933—the longest time any one man occupied that office—Hull had remained an unreconstructed internationalist and free trader. But the war and the events that had led up to it convinced him and Roosevelt, as the President himself put it, "that the real decisions should be made by the United States, Britain, Russia, and China who would be the powers for many years to come that would have to police the world."

Churchill and Stalin always treated as a harmless whim Roosevelt's insistence on great-power status for postwar China. During the spring of 1943, the Washington discussions therefore included China and the Far East but laid greater stress on Germany and most emphasis of all on Soviet postwar claims to territories from the Baltic to the Black Sea. As unofficial White House representative in the State Department, Undersecretary Sumner Welles devoted more time than Hull did to these discussions, but it was Hull who summarized them to Ambassador Litvinov on March 31. The widening rift between him and Welles, which finally led to Welles' resignation in early November, served only to strengthen Hull's position, especially among members of the House and Senate with whom he had served so long.

· 2 ·

BY THE SPRING OF 1943 both Roosevelt and Churchill recognized that German aggression in Europe and Japanese aggression in Asia had convinced Stalin that the security of the Soviet Union required the acquisition of more territory in Europe and Asia than czarist Russia ever possessed. By the same token, Stalin recognized that the territorial extension of Soviet power offered the Soviet Union greater security than it could achieve by reverting to Lenin's policy of world revolution. On May 22, 1943, the Presidium of the Executive Committee of the Communist International therefore declared the entire Comintern "out of date" and even "an obstacle in the way of the further strengthening of the national working-class parties." The war had confronted the working class in the Axis countries with the task of overthrowing their governments; in the United Nations, on the other hand, the working class had the duty "to support the governments' war effort." Roosevelt and Churchill had both urged some such gesture and welcomed this one when it came. Both also expected that insofar as Stalin had renounced the Comintern as an instrument of Soviet policy, such traditional devices as spheres of influence, balances of power, and naval and military bases might come to the fore. Churchill assumed that these traditional devices would serve their traditional purposes; Roosevelt hoped they might serve the purposes in which Wilson had believed. And he found support from an unexpected quarter. Wendell Willkie, the renegade Democrat whom he had defeated for the presidency in 1940, also reverted to his Wilsonian past and wrote a best-selling book, One World, based on a wartime trip around the world, made possible by Roosevelt's good offices. One World sold over a million copies and helped to swing many Republicans away from their prewar isolationism and toward Roosevelt's revised standard version of the internationalist gospel first preached by Woodrow Wilson. Indeed, Willkie's belated discovery that the world had become one made him, in some respects, a better Wilsonian than Roosevelt.

But the mere fact that the world had become one did not make it any safer for democracy or for communism either. Roosevelt perceived this; Churchill understood it; Stalin took action. But it was Germany's Propaganda Minister Goebbels who gave Stalin the final prod. On April 13, 1943, the German radio announced the discovery at Katyn Forest, near Smolensk, of the dead bodies of "about ten thousand" Polish officers, apparently murdered by the Russians three years before. A press conference at the German Foreign Ministry supplied the details. Representatives of the Polish government in exile in London visited the spot where four thousand bodies had been unearthed. The Moscow radio at once dismissed the story as "vile fabrications." The London Poles responded with a long account of 180,000 Polish war prisoners, including 10,000 Polish officers who had fallen into Soviet hands on September 17, 1939 and disappeared without a trace. They suggested that the International Red Cross investigate the matter further. That tore it. On April 27, 1943, the Soviet government "suspended relations" with the Polish government in exile.

This government had come into being in Paris on September 30, 1939, when it won almost instant recognition by Britain and the United States. After the fall of France it moved its headquarters to London. On July 30, 1941, it opened diplomatic relations with the Soviet Union which had absorbed eastern Poland, with its predominantly Ukrainian and Bylorussian population, after Hitler had absorbed or laid waste the country's central and western regions. On October 31, 1939, Molotov had told the Supreme Soviet: "Nothing is left of that monstrous bastard of the Versailles Treaty." More than a million Poles who had fled into Soviet territory at the time of the German-Russian invasion had also vanished.

But after the Germans, in their turn, invaded the Soviet Union some of these Poles reappeared, and the Russians equipped 73,000 of them to fight the Germans. On December 4, 1941, in Moscow, Stalin gave a dinner for General Wladyslaw Sikorski, prime minister of the Polish government in exile, with whom he openly raised the question of the post-war Russo-Polish frontier. Sikorski said he had no authority to discuss the matter but did remark: "Poland assumes that the prewar boundaries will prevail once the war is won." Stalin at once objected and shortly thereafter began to lay the foundation of what first emerged, early in 1943, as the Union of Polish Patriots. Whatever Goebbels may have intended in 1943 with his charge that the Russians had murdered ten thousand Polish officers in the Katyn Forest in 1940, he had set the stage for Stalin to break relations with the London Poles and to create behind the Soviet lines a rival Communist regime which the Soviet Union later recognized as the sole legal government of Poland. The Soviet victories that followed Stalingrad and the subsequent German atrocities, symbolized by Auschwitz, then created an atmosphere that Stalin found helpful to his postwar designs on Poland. Indeed, it was precisely the victory at Stalingrad that ensured Soviet domination of Poland and most of the rest of those east European lands the Germans had overrun.

· 3 ·

THE KATYN massacre story broke less than a month before Roosevelt, Churchill, and their top military aides held their most comprehensive strategy session to date. From May 11 to May 25, more than fifty Anglo-American leaders, only ten of them civilians, gathered in Washington at what they called the Trident Conference, to discuss global strategy. For the first time, members of the top military brass from the Far East in the persons of Field Marshal Wavell from India and General Stilwell and General Claire L. Chennault from China spoke their pieces to their colleagues from other theaters and before their commanders in chief. Mme. Chiang Kai-shek had visited the White House early in March and charmed a joint session of the Congress with an appeal to give aid to China priority over the defeat of Germany, but she made no converts among Roosevelt's or Churchill's entourage. The beat-Hitler-first strategy remained in force, but how, when, and where to beat him put Anglo-American unity under a constant strain.

On the second day of the Trident Conference came General Eisenhower's announcement of the great Allied victory in Tunisia. The Casablanca Conference had already scheduled the invasion of Sicily. Now the case was clinched for the subsequent invasion of Italy and the way barred toward a cross-Channel invasion until 1944 at the earliest. But the postponement of the kind of second front demanded by Stalin permitted the Trident Conference to sanction speedier advances by General MacArthur's forces in the southwest Pacific and Admiral Chester W. Nimitz' in the central Pacific. More supplies would be flown in to Chiang Kai-shek at Chungking.

The most important and specific decision reached by Trident instructed General Eisenhower, as Allied commander in chief in North Africa, to "plan such operations in exploitation of Husky [the invasion of Sicily] as are best calculated to remove Italy from the war and to contain the maximum number of German forces." It also decided to establish "forces and equipment" in Britain "with the object of mounting an operation with target date of May 1, 1944, to secure a lodgement on the Continent from which further offensive operations can be carried out." The Americans interpreted this as a firm commitment to invade Europe on that date. The British interpreted the words "target date" to mean an intention, not a commitment to invade. But by June 5, when the details reached Stalin (the same day that Roosevelt thanked him for his friendly treatment of Davies) he had no doubt about what the Trident Conference decisions meant. To him they signified (as Robert Sherwood put it in *Roosevelt and Hopkins*) "deliberate bad faith by the Western Allies." The Roosevelt-Stalin meeting at Fairbanks never took place. In July, Stalin recalled Maisky from the London embassy and in August he recalled Litvinov from Washington.

These hostile gestures coincided with two favorable military developments, one in Russia, the other in the Mediterranean. On July 5, 1943, the Germans launched their long-prepared and widely publicized offensive against the Soviet-held Kursk salient, which stretched more than two hundred miles between the German-held cities of Kharkov and Orel, some five hundred miles northwest of Stalingrad. The Germans threw thirty-seven divisions, more than two thousand tanks, and almost two thousand planes against four Russian armies. In four days the Germans gained some ten miles at one part of the Kursk salient and thirty miles at another. But the Russians hit back with such force that Hitler had to call off the battle on July 15. The Germans had lost almost all their tanks and 70,000 men killed in action. Walter Goerlitz, one of modern Germany's leading historians, has described Stalingrad as the political-psychological turning point of the Russo-German war and Kursk as the military turning point. In any event, Kursk marked the mightiest single offensive ever launched by the Germans against the Russians. It was also the last. The fact that the Russians not only stopped it in ten days, but went on an offensive that eventually carried them to Berlin suggested that they had come through their terrible ordeal more powerful than they had been when it began.

Although no such masses of men, planes, and armor clashed in the Mediterranean, an armada of almost three hundred ships began landing an invasion force of 160,000 men in Sicily on July 9. According to its commander in chief, General Eisenhower: "Up to that moment, no such amphibious attack in history had approached this one in size." The preliminary action against the little island of Pantelleria had gone off without a hitch. It took the United States Seventh Army, commanded by General Patton, and the British Eighth Army, commanded by General Montgomery, twenty-eight days to occupy all of Sicily and drive all German troops from the island. And on July 25, halfway through this operation, the Italian radio announced that King Victor Emmanuel III had ousted Mussolini and assumed command of all of Italy's armed forces. Clearly, the war had entered a new stage. The Soviet victory at Kursk had opened eastern Europe to Soviet invasion. The Allied landings on Sicily portended no such military reversal in western Europe, yet new and more brilliant opportunities for political warfare had suddenly opened on Hitler's southern doorstep. Unhappily, these new opportunities also provoked a new outburst of truculence on Stalin's part. But if victory had brought forth such bitter fruit, what would have followed defeat?

·4·

THE SUMMER OF 1943 witnessed a double climax in the Mediterranean —first in Algiers, where General de Gaulle swiftly organized and presently controlled a seven-man French Committee of National Liberation; then in Italy, where the Fascist Grand Council handed Mussolini a 19 to 7 vote of nonconfidence, thus setting the stage for King Victor Emmanuel III to dismiss him from office and place him in protective custody. The French Committee of National Liberation announced its birth on June 3, with Generals de Gaulle and Giraud as joint chairmen. But when Giraud casually signed, without reading, certain papers de Gaulle had handed him, he eliminated himself as a major factor. It was also at this point that the shrewd and distinguished Jean Monnet, a diplomat of the first order, who had previously worked with the British, the Americans, and Giraud, switched his allegiance to de Gaulle. Monnet, a private banker, had helped finance France during the First World War and served as first deputy general of the League of Nations during the years between the wars. With the outbreak of the Second World War, he again threw himself into the task of financing his country's war effort, spending much of his time in London, where he remained after the French defeat. He did not align himself with de Gaulle, but established contacts in Washington, notably with Harry Hopkins, who—at Casablanca—persuaded Roosevelt to approve of Monnet as political adviser to General Giraud. The State Department, already suspecting that Monnet harbored Gaullist sympathies, blocked the appointment but could not prevent Hopkins from writing, in Roosevelt's behalf, to both Eisenhower and Murphy, asking them to lend Monnet all possible assistance.

When de Gaulle arrived in Algiers he found that Monnet had won Giraud's confidence. Monnet not only attended all meetings of the seven-man committee, to which be belonged; he reported back to Macmillan and Murphy. Of Giraud Monnet said, "When the general looks at you with those eyes of a porcelain cat, he understands nothing." Not so Monnet, whom Murphy has described as "in many respects more remarkable than de Gaulle himself. It can be plausibly argued," he continues in *Diplomat Among Warriors*, "that Monnet has been the most influential man in France of his generation, and he also has exerted a major influence upon the affairs of the United States, Great Britain, and other countries. He is the kind of international figure who avoids publicity, preferring to remain in the background no matter how much power he is wielding. It is characteristic of Monnet that he has never claimed credit for his part in de Gaulle's elevation to power in Algiers in June 1943."

It would be hard to find a public figure more unlike Monnet than Mussolini—the man whose fall from power distracted attention from the no less momentous emergence of General de Gaulle. As de Gaulle himself tells the story in his *War Memoirs,* the fall of Mussolini on July 25 confirmed the claims of the committee (and of its leader) to speak for France: "Speaking on the radio, I declared that Mussolini's fall, the sign of the certain defeat of the Axis and a proof of the failure of the Fascist system, was for France the first of justice's revenges. 'Mussolini's example,' I said, 'is now added to the history of all those who have outraged the majesty of France and whom destiny has now punished.' Having stressed the fact that we must redouble our efforts to achieve victory, I stated, 'The collapse of Italian Fascism may very soon lead to a new settlement of accounts. And it is quite obvious that despite the terrible situation in which our country still finds herself, such a settlement can be neither valid nor lasting without France.'" He went on to call for Franco-Italian reconciliation based on "the interdependence of the two great Latin peoples" and to reaffirm his committee's claim to possess "the ardent confidence of the overwhelming French majority . . . as a body responsible for the sacred interests of the nation."

The political role that de Gaulle took unto himself at Algiers marked him as the first major European leader to emerge from the Second World War. By the same token, the fall of Mussolini removed from Europe's political stage the first major European leader to emerge from the backwash of the First World War. At the age of fifty-three, de Gaulle could look back on more than a quarter of a century's service with the French army. During that time he had evolved from a loyal disciple of Philippe Pétain, now the embodiment of French reaction, into the old marshal's deadliest enemy. At the age of sixty, Mussolini could look back on more than forty years of political activity, during which he had evolved from a clamorous supporter of the revolutionary extremists who abounded in Europe at the turn of the century to the founding father of the century's first successful counterrevolution, to which he gave the name of Fascism. Into this counterrevolutionary movement Mussolini poured all the lessons he had learned as a professional revolutionary whereas de Gaulle brought to his self-appointed role as the liberator of France the disciplines he had learned as a professional soldier. In both cases, however, character, not fate, proved decisive.

·5·

IN 1922 MUSSOLINI had accepted all his powers from the willing hands of Victor Emmanuel III. In 1943, the willing hands of Mussolini turned back those powers to the reluctant monarch. "I don't want it to be said," muttered the king before he summoned Mussolini to their final interview, "that I have laid a trap for the head of my government by having him arrested in my own house." After the shattered Mussolini left the shattered king, he and his secretary meekly entered the waiting ambulance, into which two *carabinieri* captains, three armed noncommissioned officers, and two plainclothesmen propelled them. "That was not at all nice," Queen Elena, a fiery Montenegrin, remarked to her husband afterward. "They could have arrested him anywhere they liked, but not here. Mussolini was our guest. They have violated the rules of royal hospitality."

General Enzo Galbiati, commander of the Fascist militia, quickly concluded that his oath to the reigning king's army took precedence over his oath to the fallen Duce's militia. Through the army, Galbiati ordered the militia dissolved and as soon as he learned that the king had appointed Marshal Pietro Badoglio to replace Mussolini as head of government with all of Mussolini's powers, he resigned his army post. Badoglio proudly linked himself with Pétain and Mackensen as one of the three field marshals of the First World War period who had lived to witness the Second. But Badoglio occupied the unique distinction of having suffered total defeats in both world wars—at Caporetto during the First and in Greece during the Second. Of his record under Fascism, he said to Macmillan: "I was a Fascist because the King was a Fascist. When the King ordered me to organize an anti-Fascist Government, I agreed to do so. I do what the King tells me." At the age of seventy-one, so durable and adaptable a figure seemed ideally equipped to continue in the service of his seventy-three-year-old monarch.

On the evening of the day Mussolini fell, Hitler wanted to order the only German division in central Italy "to drive into Rome with a special detachment and arrest the whole government, the King, all that scum, but primarily the Crown Prince, to get hold of this rabble, principally Badoglio, and the whole gang. And then you watch them creep and crawl." But his generals persuaded him to accept the friendly gestures that the new government began making, notably when it permitted two more German divisions to enter Italy by the Brenner Pass. At this point —it was late July—the Germans had three divisions on the Italian mainland, one in Sardinia, and four more fighting in Sicily. By the end of the first week in August, another ten German divisions had entered Italy by the Brenner. By the end of the month nine more had arrived. The Italians had sixteen divisions that might jump either way—and then refuse to stay put.

Against these known and unknown quantities, the Anglo-Americans, who had not yet invaded any part of the Italian mainland, could throw only eight divisions, and they still needed until early September to assemble the necessary landing craft, air cover, and other equipment. While supporting Roosevelt's unconditional-surrender formula, the Americans stressed the liberation of Italy—from the king and Badoglio as well as from Mussolini. The British, following Churchill's lead, favored unconditional support of the king and Badoglio. Inasmuch as the British had three times as many ground troops, four times as many warships, and about as many planes as the Americans in the Mediterranean theater, their word carried weight and their General Alexander commanded all the ground troops assigned to the Sicilian and Italian campaigns.

But everything about Italy cut at least two ways, and some cut three or four. As far as Churchill was concerned, the king—any king, whether Italian or British—could do no wrong. In 1943, Churchill supported the squalid Victor Emmanuel III as loyally as he had supported the star-crossed Edward VIII in 1936. He would have no truck with Italy's former foreign minister, the anti-Fascist Count Carlo Sforza, whom Roosevelt and the Americans favored. But a stronger case could be made, in terms of political and military expedience, for the king and Badoglio. As temporary stopgaps, they seemed well equipped to guide their weary, confused, and excitable people from the wreckage of Fascism and war to a more peaceful and democratic order. Italy, in its three-thousand-year history, had survived native tyrants and foreign invaders before and could do so again. Moreover, Italy's Nazi invaders —although more diabolical than any of their forerunners—were as divided among themselves as were the Anglo-American liberators. Finally, just as the British and Americans could not agree on how to deal with the king and Badoglio, Hitler and his generals disagreed on how to handle Mussolini. The generals had prevented Hitler from ordering a German division to seize the king and Badoglio in Rome.

Meanwhile the Anglo-Americans bickered over when and where to attack their German enemy and how to co-ordinate this attack with the plans of their Soviet ally. In July General Marshall dispatched Secretary of War Stimson to Britain to see Churchill and to the Mediterranean to see Alexander in order to nip in the bud any long-range plans they might have to expand the 1943 Italian campaign into a 1944 assault on the celebrated "soft underbelly of the Axis," and thus beat the Russians to the Balkans and to Vienna. For just as Churchill dreaded the cross-Channel invasion as the prelude to another bloody deadlock on the Western Front, Marshall and Stimson dreaded a wider Mediterranean campaign as another inadequate substitute for the essential and long-deferred second front.

On the basis of the North African campaigns, the Casablanca and Trident conferences reached decisions that led to the invasion of Sicily and the fall of Mussolini. But events in Italy did not follow the North African pattern—or any other. The differences between Italy and North Africa far outweighed the similarities. Italy was full of Italians, most of whom had had a surfeit of Mussolini. North Africa was full of Arabs, few of whom saw much to choose between Hitler and Churchill or Pétain and de Gaulle. Issues that set German against Englishman or Frenchman against Frenchman left most Arabs unmoved. Nor did the French settlers in Algeria—known as *colons*—have much in common with Italy's anti-Fascist masses. The French administrators throughout North Africa and Algeria's privileged French residents rallied to Pétain and the Vichyites as a matter of course. But with the expulsion of the Axis from North Africa and the German occupation of all metropolitan France, Pétain's authority evaporated and de Gaulle's soared. Instead of kowtowing to Roosevelt and Churchill, as they planned grand strategy and sought to improve their relations with Stalin, de Gaulle improved his contacts with the French resistance movement, strengthened his own committee, and established close relations with the Soviet diplomat Alexander Bogomolov, one of Stalin's most trusted troubleshooters and his chosen envoy to de Gaulle.

While de Gaulle made political hay at Algiers, Roosevelt and Churchill journeyed to Quebec, where they held their third full-dress conference of the year, lasting from August 14 to August 24 and dubbed "Quadrant." It went on from where Trident had left off in that it called for more triphibious operations in the central and south Pacific and set May 1, 1944, as the target date and 29 divisions as the scope of the cross-Channel invasion of western Europe. By the time the conference ended, Stalin's sulks had so irritated Roosevelt and Churchill that they sought neither his advice nor consent in connection with the cross-Channel invasion. "This operation will be the primary American and British air and ground action against the Axis," they reported, and let it go at that.

Already, however, events in Italy had begun to mollify Stalin. By the middle of August Badoglio offered not only to surrender to the Anglo-Americans but to enter the war as their fighting ally. Weeks of negotiation, intrigue, feints, and deceptions followed. On September 3, after Montgomery had sneaked two of his Eighth Army divisions across the Messina Straits from Sicily to the toe of Italy, Badoglio's deputy and Eisenhower's deputy signed an abbreviated surrender document that remained a secret until the evening of September 8, when four divisions of General Mark W. Clark's Fifth Army prepared to land at Salerno, forty miles southeast of Naples. At that time General Eisenhower broadcast the same document, preceded by the statement: "The Italian Government has surrendered its armed forces unconditionally." Two other events made that same September 8 still more memorable: German troops occupied Rome, and Stalin informed Roosevelt and Churchill that he would meet them in Iran between November 15 and December 15. Arrangements had already been made, during the Quadrant Conference, for a preliminary foreign ministers' conference at Moscow in mid-October.

·6·

THE ALLIED LANDINGS in Italy gave Stalin a pleasant surprise and Hitler a nasty one. Not until mid-August did it begin to dawn on Stalin that perhaps Roosevelt and Churchill had not deliberately double-crossed him, but that they had both the capacity and the determination to create at least a reasonable facsimile of a second front in Italy. Already, the fall of Mussolini had opened Stalin's eyes to new possibilities, as they opened Hitler's to new dangers. By the end of August, Anglo-American operations in Italy had diverted to that country and the Balkans the forty crack German divisions that Stalin had pleaded to have taken off his back the year before. On August 24, Stalin therefore called upon Roosevelt and Churchill to transfer General Eisenhower's powers as supreme commander to a United Nations military-political commission on which the Soviet Union would have a representative—perhaps armed with the veto power. Ask a foolish question and you get a foolish answer. On September 5, Roosevelt responded with the suggestion that Stalin send a Soviet officer to General Eisenhower's headquarters where he could sit in on the Anglo-American discussions. Three days later, the exchanges turned serious as Stalin agreed to the Big Three conference in Iran, and on September 10 Roosevelt and Churchill showed their appreciation by announcing that they would, indeed, set up a military-political commission for Italy on which they invited Stalin to appoint a representative. He accepted with alacrity, naming Andrei Vishinsky as the Soviet representative with General de Gaulle's friend, Bogomolov, as his deputy.

A safety-first Menshevik, Vishinsky had not joined the Bolshevik party until it had the revolution safely won. From then on his instinct for personal survival made him more Stalinist than Stalin. He served as chief prosecutor at the later purge trials at Moscow. Unlike his two predecessors—Genrik G. Yagoda and Nikolai Yezhov—Vishinsky did not pay for this honor with his life; instead, he won promotion to the post of assistant commissar of foreign affairs. That Stalin assigned Vishinsky to the military-political commission on Italy showed the importance he attached to the position and to the man he chose to fill it. He had sent a leading troubleshooter to a leading trouble spot.

Two days later another troubleshooter appeared, suitably armed, at another trouble spot. On July 26—the day after Mussolini fell—Hitler assigned Colonel Otto Skorzeny, one of the leading parachutists and secret agents in the S.S., to liberate Mussolini whenever and however he could. Skorzeny and his parachutists completed their mission on September 12 by whisking Mussolini from the hotel in the Gran Sasso mountain ski resort near Rome where he had recently been moved from farther south. Just how this came to pass remains a mystery. This much does not: neither the king nor Badoglio, neither Eisenhower nor Alexander, shed any tears. Dead or alive, Mussolini in their hands would have done none of them any good. Nor did he yield Hitler any political mileage either in Germany, where he spent the next ten days, or in his native northern province of Romagna, where he tried to raise an Italian republican army.

Both Generals Keitel and Rommel opposed the Mussolini kidnaping. They urged Hitler to occupy whatever parts of Italy he wanted and let it go at that. Goebbels wrote in his diary: "However much I may be touched by the human side of the Duce's liberation, I am nevertheless skeptical about its political advantages. With the Duce out of the way, we had a chance to wipe the slate clean in Italy. Without any restraint and basing our actions on the grandiose treachery of the Badoglio regime, we could force a solution of all our problems in regard to Italy. . . . Under the leadership of the Duce, assuming he becomes active again, Italy will attempt to start a national rump government toward which we shall have some obligations in many respects."

Mussolini's inertia plunged the true-believing Hitler into the depths of gloom: "What is this sort of Fascism that melts like the snow before the sun?" he expostulated to Mussolini at the time. "For years I have explained to my generals that Fascism is the soundest alliance for the German people. I have never concealed my distrust of the Italian monarchy; at your instance, however, I did nothing to obstruct the work which you carried out to the advantage of the king. But I confess we Germans never understood your attitude in this respect." Hitler not only believed his own propaganda; he also believed Mussolini's—which the Duce himself seldom did.

·   ·   ·

During the summer of 1943, the Second World War twice reversed the course that the First World War had taken. At Stalingrad and Kursk the Red army inflicted defeats on Hitler's Wehrmacht as decisive as those that the Kaiser's armies inflicted on the Russians at Tannenberg in Russia in 1914 and between Tarnow and Gorlice in Austria in 1915. German victories over Russia in 1914 and 1915 paved the way for the Russian Revolution of 1917 and the Brest-Litovsk Treaty of 1918. In 1943, at Stalingrad and Kursk, the Red army won victories that paved the way for its occupation of eastern Europe in 1944 and its conquest of Berlin in 1945. The first major victim of the First World War became the first major victor in the Second.

At the same time, a similar reversal occurred in Italy, which staged, in 1922, a counterrevolution against the democratic cause for which it had gone to war in 1915. Then, in 1943, the fall of Mussolini and the subsequent first steps that the king and Badoglio took to restore Italian democracy marked another reversal of history. Hitler at once saw (more clearly than Stalin, Roosevelt, or Churchill did) that the fall of Mussolini had struck a mortal blow at his own Nazi order. Throughout the war, Mussolini's efforts to aid Hitler backfired repeatedly. Now—as a result of Mussolini's fall—the Italians embarked on a course that later made their country a bastion of democracy during western Europe's first and most anxious postwar years.

The Trident and Quadrant conferences showed which way the tides of war were already sweeping the world. On both occasions, Roosevelt, Churchill, and their Joint Chiefs of Staff treated the war against Germany and the war against Japan as a single whole. On both occasions, only three months apart, they brought their commanders halfway around the world to sit down together at a single table. For not until Quadrant had the war reached the stage at which the United Nations coalition could fight it as well as talk it on a global scale. Before Roosevelt and Churchill left Quebec, they therefore found it necessary to agree with Stalin to hold the Moscow Foreign Ministers' Conference that led to the subsequent Big Three meeting at Teheran. What Roosevelt had once described as a crusade for the Four Freedoms for everybody, everywhere, always, had become a worldwide struggle to impose unconditional surrender on the Axis powers and then to entrust the peace of the world to the United Nations' "Four Policemen": Britain, Russia, China, and the United States. But imperialist powers fighting an imperialist war? Unthinkable.

During the mid-1890's, the aristocratic Sir William Harcourt, successor to Gladstone as leader of Britain's Liberal party, observed: "We are all socialists now." Neither then nor half a century later did Churchill agree. But by the mid-1940's, Churchill, Roosevelt, and Stalin could all have brought Harcourt's observation up to date: "We are all imperialists now": Churchill an obsolete British imperialist, Roosevelt an up-to-date American imperialist, Stalin a throwback to Russian imperialism, Communist style. After de Gaulle fought to restore a French Empire as obsolete as Britain's, his successors—who had surrendered to the Germans—tried and failed to restore that empire by main force while Churchill's successors (who had never surrendered to the Germans) let theirs go without a fight. What's in a name? Imperialism is as imperialism does.

XV

Damn Clever, Those Chinese

·1·

ADMIRAL ISOROKU YAMAMOTO, commander in chief of the Japanese navy, occupies a unique niche in the history of the Second World War. In January 1941, he publicly warned the leaders of one of Japan's supernationalistic patriotic societies that war with the United States would become a life-or-death struggle, with the odds heavily against Japan: "If hostilities were to break out between Japan and the United States, it would not be enough for us to take Guam and the Philippines or even Hawaii and San Francisco. We should have to march into Washington and sign a treaty in the White House. I wonder if our politicians who speak so lightly of a Japanese-American war have confidence in the outcome and are prepared to make the necessary sacrifices." Poor Admiral Yamamoto. While he supervised the plans for the attack on Pearl Harbor, his superpatriotic compatriots denounced him as a traitor, and after Pearl Harbor, a few words of his ironic warning, taken out of context, made excellent war propaganda for the United States. Early in 1943, he met his death at the hands of an American aerial ambush over the Solomon Islands.

Not only had his warning against the war that he gave his life to prosecuting backfired among his own people, it also fanned the flames of anti-Japanese propaganda among his country's enemies. Yet—in the longer run—the double irony yielded a doubly transcendent dividend. For by his example, Admiral Yamamoto gave advance sanction to America's demand of unconditional surrender and to Emperor Hirohito's transcendent decision to accept it, thus diminishing the toll of Japanese-American casualties and hastening the day of Japanese-American reconciliation. Neither Yamamoto in 1941 nor Hirohito in

1945 needed any occult powers or secret information to decide and act as they did. In Yamamoto's case, he not only transcended most of his countrymen in recognizing that they needed more than the banzai spirit to win the war on which they had embarked; he also recognized, almost a year before the attack that he had planned on Pearl Harbor, that the Americans possessed both the power and the will to strike back with devastating effect.

By the summer of 1943 (less than two years after Pearl Harbor and less than six months after Yamamoto's death) the United States Navy and United States industry, working hand in hand, had produced, equipped, and trained a modern fleet, larger and more deadly than the combined navies of all the other belligerent powers. Five of the eight battleships damaged at Pearl Harbor had been restored and renovated. To them had been added seven bigger and better ones plus hundreds of modern carriers, destroyers, destroyer escorts, landing craft, submarines, and planes of all shapes and sizes. The Japanese spent these same two years fortifying the Pacific islands they had seized since Pearl Harbor as they had already fortified the islands over which the League of Nations had assigned them mandates after the First World War. Here they created an oceanic security belt 4000 miles long and 2000 miles wide dotted with hundreds of islands and atolls, many of which they transformed into heavily armed, unsinkable, immovable aircraft carriers behind which they began to exploit the Philippines, the Malay States, French Indochina, the Dutch East Indies, Thailand, and Burma as they had successively exploited Korea, Formosa, Manchuria, and much of China itself.

But Japan's security belt provided no more security than its co-prosperity sphere provided prosperity. American sea power, air power, and assault troops pulverized every Japanese-held island bastion that they had received orders to attack. During the summer of 1943, Admiral William F. Halsey's Seventh Fleet, operating in General MacArthur's southwest Pacific theater, carried on from where the fighting on Guadalcanal had left off. One high point in a series of engagements known as Operation Watchtower came on July 23, when Marshall suggested that MacArthur leapfrog the big Japanese-held base of Rabaul at the eastern end of New Britain. The following month the Quadrant Conference ordered MacArthur and Halsey to occupy Kavieng in New Ireland and Manus in the Admiralties, several hundred miles to the northwest. The completion of this mission in April 1944 completed Watchtower.

By this time the center of gravity in the Pacific war had shifted still further to the northwest. Quadrant also designated the Philippines as the next objective for MacArthur and Halsey, while directing modest, meticulous Admiral Raymond T. Spruance, the newly named commander in chief of the central Pacific, to head his mighty Task Force 58 toward Tokyo. On December 3, the Combined Chiefs approved of the plan by Admiral Nimitz—now commander in chief of the entire Pacific —for a two-pronged attack on Japan, one by MacArthur and Halsey along the New Guinea-Philippines axis in the southwest Pacific, the other by Nimitz and Spruance via Guam, Tinian, and Saipan across the central Pacific. The navy supported the Nimitz strategy; MacArthur disagreed. He had always advocated a single command (presumably but not necessarily headed by himself) to direct the entire Pacific strategy of the war against Japan.

In mid-November, Tarawa Island in the Gilberts, 2500 miles west of Hawaii and 1200 miles east of Guadalcanal fell to the Second Division of the United States Marines. Other marines—all in the central Pacific theater—took Kwajalein, the world's largest atoll on February 27, and Eniwetok, three hundred miles eastward, two weeks later. Already carrier-based planes had bombed the great Japanese base at Truk, in the Carolines, five hundred miles southeast of Guam. Meanwhile General MacArthur completed the conquest of New Guinea. After occupying Manus Island he leapfrogged Wewak and seized Hollandia on May 3, 1944. It took him another three months to reach the western tip of New Guinea and to set November 15 as the day he expected to reach Mindanao in the Philippines. By that time Nimitz hoped to have established air bases in the central Pacific within bombing range of Tokyo.

·2·

GLORY ENOUGH and to spare for MacArthur and Halsey, for Nimitz and Spruance, for the soldiers, sailors, marines, and airmen under their commands and for their suppliers half a world away. They had made a unique and almost wholly American contribution to the military defeat of Hitler's Asiatic partner. But some of the most serious defeats the Japanese suffered at this time did not occur on any kind of battlefield. Some had occurred in the southeast Asian sector of Japan's co-prosperity sphere. More had occurred in the most important of all regions that had come under Japanese rule—China.

The Quadrant Conference had designated the southwest and central

Pacific theaters as regions of exclusive American responsibility. The Americans also had representation in two other Far Eastern theaters where the Combined Chiefs ordered a few changes made. Admiral Lord Mountbatten replaced Field Marshal Wavell as commander in chief of the southeast Asia theater, embracing Burma, Ceylon, and Sumatra, with General Stilwell as his deputy. Stilwell also wore a second hat as chief of staff to Generalissimo Chiang Kai-shek in the China theater, which now embraced Indochina and Siam as well. These two theaters received lower priorities than the southwest or central Pacific. Chiang felt even more slighted than General MacArthur did, and Roosevelt sought to mollify him by setting up a special meeting with him and the reluctant Churchill at Cairo, just before the Big Three session at Teheran.

Even as early as Quadrant, the war in the Pacific had become more than a test of strength between the American and Japanese war machines. Symptoms of economic anemia and political fever already gripped most of the lands and peoples that had come so recently and so suddenly under Japanese rule. The departure of the white man caused the anemia; the arrival of the Japanese caused the fever. Prior to the Second World War southeast Asia had depended on its exports of foodstuffs and raw materials to Europe and the United States and on its imports of European and American factory products. The war not only put an end to this two-way trade. Japan could neither absorb southeastern Asia's exports nor provide southeastern Asia with the imports (not to mention the capital investments) that Europe and the United States had furnished for generations. Finally, American submarine and air attacks took a fast-growing toll on Japanese shipping to and from southeastern Asia, thereby transforming the dream of co-prosperity into the nightmare of co-poverty.

The war that the Japanese waged to create a Greater East Asia Co-Prosperity Sphere at once defeated itself on the economic front. Not until November 1, 1942, did Prime Minister Tojo institute a Greater East Asian Ministry with four separate bureaus for General Affairs, Manchurian Affairs, China Affairs, and Southern Region Affairs. On December 11, he celebrated the first anniversary of the German-Italian-Japanese pact by declaring: "The current war is not merely hostilities for the possession of natural resources, but it is a sacred campaign for the moral idea of creating a new order whereunder all nations will have what they are entitled to and whereunder the lasting peace of the world will be ensured."

By the summer of 1943, the turn of the tide in the Pacific war and the deepening economic difficulties in southeast Asia compelled Tojo and the men around him to move from words to action. During the spring and summer of 1943 they began to relax some of the controls they had imposed on British Malaya and the Dutch East Indies. On August 15, the Japanese occupation forces proclaimed the nominal independence of Burma and the Philippines, after having found in both countries some local nationalists willing to work with them. Two months later, the Malay States and the Dutch East Indies received promises of ultimate independence. The Indonesian Nationalist leader, Sukarno, whom the Dutch had imprisoned, collaborated with the Japanese but returned empty-handed from Tokyo when he went there at the end of 1943 seeking independence. Siam, the one independent nation in southeast Asia, continued during the war the same policy of pro-Japanese neutrality that it had pursued since 1932, when a military oligarchy seized power. In June 1942, the Japanese army, which had established many prisoner-of-war camps in Siam, began constructing a 250-mile railway to Burma in the hope of relieving shipping losses. Its completion in October 1943 cost the lives of some 10,000 Japanese troops, another 12,000 prisoners of war, and 250,000 Asian coolies. Japanese officers took special satisfaction in humiliating their white prisoners, but the huge death rate among the Asian workers made no friends for Japan in Siam.

French Indochina presented as special a case as Siam. Admiral Jean Decoux, the French governor general, had no love for de Gaulle or Churchill and remained loyal to Pétain as long as Pétain remained at Vichy. Pétain rewarded this loyalty by giving Decoux wide discretion that he exercised when he defied Vichy's ambassador at Chungking by refusing to break relations with Chiang Kai-shek. Decoux also established secret contact with the French Committee of National Liberation at Algiers, and though he would not join it, he persuaded de Gaulle not to support any Chinese or Anglo-American invasion of Indochina. It was not that Decoux hated de Gaulle any the less; he and de Gaulle simply hated Roosevelt and Churchill more than they hated each other. During 1944, de Gaulle and Decoux worked together to forestall a Japanese *coup d'état* in Indochina—not, however, because they objected to the Japanese as such, but because such a *coup d'état* might open the door to an eventual take-over by the native nationalists, who would then defy French postwar claims to Indochina. As long as the Greater East Asia Co-Prosperity Sphere held together, the Japanese turned to Admiral Decoux as a lesser evil than the native nationalists. Not until

March 1945, when the Japanese had to pull up stakes and go home, did they turn their backs on Decoux and turn over power to native leaders, including the French-trained Communist, Ho Chi Minh.

Because the Japanese invaders could not begin to fill the vacuum left by southeast Asia's departing British, French, and Dutch overlords, more and more native leaders found themselves projected into positions of new and widening responsibility. Those who collaborated with the Japanese gained experience in administration; the noncollaborators gained experience in guerrilla warfare, all of which came in handy after the Japanese left and when some of the prewar officials and other residents of European origin tried to return. Only in the Philippines had these native nationalists received encouragement and support from the prewar occupying power. There, American and Filipino troops fought the Japanese, side by side, to the very end, and the native resistance leaders never gave up, sustained as they were by pledges of postwar independence from the United States.

· 3 ·

BEFORE, DURING, AND AFTER the Second World War, the Philippine Islands and two General MacArthurs—father and son—played crucial roles in the affairs of the United States, the Far East, and the whole world. In the Philippines, General Arthur MacArthur, one of its first military governors, set the world an example when he followed up his pacification of the islands by granting an amnesty to Aguinaldo, the insurgent leader, and by helping to lay the foundations on which the Philippines built their independence.

General MacArthur's son Douglas had just been graduated from West Point at the top of his class with the best academic record in a quarter of a century. More than half a century later, the son, in his *Reminiscences,* quoted from a speech delivered in 1900 by President McKinley, of which he wrote: "I cannot tell you how profound an impression this speech made upon me. Little did I dream, however, that nearly fifty years later it was to guide my conduct in the occupation of a defeated enemy's country." A single sentence of President McKinley's must suffice: "The present is all-absorbing to me, but I cannot bound my visions by the blood-stained trenches around Manila, where every red drop, whether from the veins of an American soldier or a Filipino, is anguish to my heart; but by the broad range of the future years when that group of islands, under the impulse of the year just passed, shall have become one of the gems and glories of those tropical seas, a land of plenty and of increasing possibilities, a people devoted to the arts of peace, in touch with the commerce and trade of all nations, enjoying the blessings of freedom, of civil and religious liberty, of education and of homes, and whose children and children's children for ages hence bless the American Republic because it redeemed their fatherland and set them in the pathway of the world's best civilization."

In 1903, Douglas MacArthur's first assignment took him to the Philippines. Early in 1905 he was ordered to Japan to join his father, who had been sent there to observe the Russo-Japanese War. Here the son met the leading Japanese generals and admirals and after the war accompanied his father on a nine-month trip that took them from Japan to India via southeast Asia and that included several months in China. "We were nine months in travel," he wrote in his *Reminiscences*, "covering countless miles of lands so rich in color, so fabled in legend, so vital to history that the experience was without doubt the most important factor of preparation of my entire life."

During the First World War—already a one-star general—MacArthur served with distinction on the Western Front. After the war he served as commandant at West Point and then, under the Coolidge, Hoover, and Roosevelt administrations, as army chief of staff. In 1936 he returned to the Philippines as the organizer of its first army. Most of the first year after Pearl Harbor he spent in Australia. To seven million Australians, MacArthur came to symbolize their white protector against the Yellow Peril; to eighteen million Filipinos, he came to symbolize American democracy. Thus, by 1943, he possessed two large popular constituencies in his southwest Pacific theater. In addition to his personal popularity and military prestige among America's only viable allies in the Far East, MacArthur also enjoyed substantial popular support among those Republicans who regarded Japan rather than Germany as America's number one enemy.

A benign Providence could not have chosen a commander better equipped than MacArthur to head the United Nations war effort in the southwest Pacific. His compelling personality inspired the people of Australia during 1942 as Churchill's had inspired the people of Britain during 1940, for MacArthur was as authentic a survival of the McKinley era as Churchill was of the Victorian age. Moreover, by 1943 MacArthur had transformed Australia from a beleaguered, defensive bastion into a continental base for offensive operations against the Philippines and points north. If MacArthur was a natural actor playing the part of a general, he was also a soldier, born and bred, who had mastered the actor's art of holding and winning public attention. Alone of all commanders in all nations and all theaters of war, he saw to it that all communiqués from his theater bore his name: "MacArthur's Headquarters."

In Brooke, Georgi Zhukov, and Marshall, the Second World War had produced strategists equal to MacArthur and in Erik von Manstein, Montgomery, and Vasili Chuikov equally able field commanders. Had any of these men—whether in Communist Russia, Nazi Germany, or democratic Britain—set himself above and apart from his military peers and his civilian superiors, he would have vanished quickly from the scene. MacArthur, however, got away with it—not because his ego was bigger than theirs, but because America's professional soldiers had never loomed so large in the nation's political life as to pose a threat to its institutions. Nor did MacArthur ever pose such a threat. During the war against Japan MacArthur served the Roosevelt administration loyally and well. He had never concealed his doubts about the beat-Germany-first strategy. Indeed, it was precisely because he opposed that strategy that Roosevelt assigned him to the war against Japan.

Had Roosevelt been a Republican and MacArthur an admiral, they might have worked together more closely. But there were Republicans and Republicans, Democrats and Democrats, admirals and admirals, generals and generals, few of whom stayed put. Since the turn of the century, the more vigorous Republican leaders had quoted the writings of Admiral Mahan to justify the construction of a navy second to none and a matching expansionist policy in the Far East. Democrat Franklin Roosevelt shared his Republican cousin Theodore's admiration for Admiral Mahan and for the navy in which they had all served, while MacArthur, whose ties with the Republicans were as close as F.D.R.'s ties with the Democrats, opposed the navy's strategy for victory over Japan. Admirals King and Nimitz urged the heaviest possible assault on Japan at the earliest possible moment. General MacArthur gave priority to the liberation of the Philippines, which he viewed as the perfect springboard from which to invade Japan. Roosevelt and Marshall backed MacArthur's Philippines strategy, but as a prelude to the liberation of China from its Japanese invaders. King and Nimitz saw no further than Japan. It overshadowed the Philippines, and after Japan's defeat the United States had nothing to fear from China. Nor could MacArthur see beyond the Philippines. His horizon, too, ended on Asia's Pacific coastline.

Not so General Marshall, who wrote in his *War Records:* "If the armies and government of Chiang Kai-shek had been finally defeated, Japan would have been left free to exploit the tremendous resources of China without harassment. It might have been possible when the United States and Britain finished the job in Europe and assailed the Japanese homeland for the government to flee and continue the war on a great rich land mass." Neither Roosevelt nor Marshall ever had any reason to regret their original grand strategy of seeking to defeat Germany before Japan. But that decision had a fateful corollary that took time to emerge. To defeat Germany first meant to help China last.

·4·

IF GENERAL MACARTHUR took the beat-Germany-first strategy as an almost personal affront, how much more reason Chiang Kai-shek had to consider himself, his government, and his country the victims of a more deadly, deliberate, and duplicitous policy of "help China last." Japan had attacked China ten years before it attacked Pearl Harbor, and eight years before Germany had attacked Poland. Moreover, during most of those years Chiang also found himself waging—and losing—a civil war to the Chinese Communists. A few figures tell the story. In 1937, 100,-000 Chinese Communist troops occupied 35,000 square miles of Chinese territory with a population of 1,500,000. By the end of 1943, 250,-000 Communist troops controlled 155,000 square miles with a population of 54,000,000.

Between the middle of 1937 and the end of 1938, Japanese troops occupied more than a million square miles of China (comprising almost all the territory worth having), with a population of 170,000,000. When the fighting ended, one million Japanese troops occupied the area; four million Chinese Nationalist troops faced them. In 1943, four million Chinese Nationalists still faced them, although Chiang had steadily conscripted new troops at the rate of a million and a half a year throughout the period, during which time Chinese casualties totaled less than half a million. But some seven million Chinese had deserted to the enemy, escaped to their homes, or died in training. Inasmuch as the Chinese arms industry could provide its troops with only four bullets per month per man, the Japanese suffered fewer casualties, but maintenance of their occupation forces in China cost them more than their conquest yielded.

Only Mao Tse-tung's balance sheet showed a credit balance. Every

Nationalist defeat became a Communist victory; every Japanese advance gave the Communists that much more territory in which to wage guerrilla warfare. The more desperate China's plight became, the more grist that brought to Mao Tse-tung's mill. It took General Stilwell a little more than a year to devise a strategy designed to break this vicious circle. On September 6, 1943, he suggested that the Chinese Nationalist and Communist troops confronting each other in the northwest join forces and invade Burma in the southeast. Chiang hit the roof. His wife, her sister, the wife of Finance Minister H. H. Kung, and her brother, Foreign Minister T. V. Soong, formed a Soong Dynasty united front and warned Chiang to heed Stilwell as the authentic voice of an America where they had all lived and learned and with which Chiang had no firsthand experience. Chiang not only ignored them; he sidelined T. V. Soong for several months, thus excluding him from the Cairo meeting with Roosevelt in late November. Yet the Stilwell warning did not fall on completely deaf ears. On September 13, the Chinese Communists at Yenan rejected Chiang's proposal that they dissolve their government and put their army under his command. But, after flouting the letter of General Stilwell's warning, Chiang paid lip service to its spirit when some Kuomintang members defied Stilwell and demanded that Chiang invade the Communist-controlled northwest. Even Chiang refused to go to that extreme and brought its proponents to heel with the statement: "I am aware of the opinion that first of all we should clearly recognize that the Chinese Communist problem is a purely political problem and should be solved by purely political means."

Chiang's statement took some wind out of the extremists' sails and led the Kuomintang's executive committee to pass a resolution in the same vein. Meanwhile word had also come from the American embassy in Moscow that Soviet officials, for the first time, had backed the Chinese Communists and assailed the Nationalist regime at Chungking. British officials also warned against anti-Communist moves by the Kuomintang. All of which the Americans brought to the attention of Chiang, who had no hesitation about defying Stilwell, but respected the pressure that London and Moscow had also begun to apply. In British and Russian eyes, Chiang had proved himself, at best, a weak ally. Now his quarrel with the Chinese Communists made him look like an unreliable one as well. On October 18, 1943, the American embassy at Chungking reported, in detail, the continuing Nationalist-Communist friction, summing things up with this concluding sentence: "All these factors point to but one conclusion, to the continued struggle between the two rival parties—civil war at some future time."

·5·

DURING THE NINETEENTH CENTURY, American traders and missionaries established many ties with China. But after the war with Spain had planted the Stars and Stripes on the Philippines, Secretary of State John Hay heeded the advice of his British friends and unilaterally proclaimed the new American doctrine of the Open Door in China which called upon all the other major powers to follow the American example and guarantee the territorial and administrative integrity of China while foreswearing any special privileges there. After the fall of the Manchu Empire in 1912 and the emergence of Dr. Sun Yat-sen's Republic of China, the United States played a greater part than any other Western power in China's political and economic development. During the First World War, American pressure blocked Japanese efforts to impose on China "Twenty-One Demands" that would have put Japan in position at least to hamstring China's unification and at most to dominate its richest regions. Shortly after the First World War, the British termination of their alliance with Japan and their support of the American naval disarmament program made Japan's navy invincible in its own waters and the Anglo-Americans supreme almost everywhere else. With Japanese sea power held in check by the Anglo-Americans and Russia weakened by seven years of war and revolution, China entered a new era as the 1920's began.

During the first half of that decade Sun Yat-sen turned to Lenin, under whose guidance a handful of Soviet officials and agents reorganized the Kuomintang along Communist lines, at the same time establishing close ties with the newly formed Chinese Communist party. But the death of Dr. Sun in 1925 and the rise of his forty-year-old brother-in-law, Chiang Kai-shek, drove the Communists from the Kuomintang. At this point the Chinese Communists themselves split as the pro-Russian faction in the party tried and failed to organize a revolution based on the industrial workers. The showdown came at Canton in 1927, when Chiang's troops crushed a Communist-led uprising there. The thirty-year-old Mao Tse-tung, one of the founders of the Chinese Communist party, then began to emerge as the leader of the dominant, new faction which, in defiance of Stalin's orders, proceeded to organize a revolution based on China's peasant masses.

It took until 1931 for Mao Tse-tung and his anti-Stalinist opposition to win control of the Chinese Communist party. By this time Chiang had completed a more drastic purge of the Left opposition (most of it pro-Russian) in the Kuomintang. Before the First World War, Chiang himself had attended military school in Japan. In 1923 he spent six months studying military and political tactics in Moscow, where a son, by his first marriage, remained and married a Russian wife. As commander of the Kuomintang's armies, Chiang also assumed Dr. Sun's position of leadership in the party, which still conformed with the Communist pattern, though it had long since abandoned Communist purposes. Chiang had ties with Shanghai industrialists and with various secret societies in his nearby native province of Chekiang. He also had important connections with the United States through his father-in-law, Charles James Soong, an American-educated, Christian Chinese businessman who had financed the Chinese Revolution for twenty years. His three daughters had attended Wellesley College; his son, T. V. Soong, was graduated from Harvard with the class of 1915.

Of Charlie Soong's three daughters, the eldest married Dr. H. H. Kung, who claimed descent from Confucius and proved it by becoming director of Nationalist China's central bank and the richest Chinese of his time; the middle daughter became the second wife of Dr. Sun Yat-sen and lived on to become the grand old lady of Communist China; the youngest became the second wife of Chiang Kai-shek and lived on to become the mainspring of his long political career. "T.V." served as Chiang's foreign minister until after the war, when he faded into the background. But the "Soong Dynasty," which had swallowed Chiang Kai-shek, found itself swallowed in its turn by Chiang Kai-shek and the Kuomintang, who had made themselves the most effective available instrument to give China its first strong, central government in more than a century.

By 1931, the Japanese saw which way the wind was blowing and set their sails accordingly. "The Second World War is here!" wrote the Soviet propagandist L. Magyar at the time: "Japanese imperialism has begun it." The world depression had hit Japan even harder than it had hit the Western democracies, thus playing into the hands of the Japanese extremists while demoralizing the more moderate Western leaders. But the Japanese had more nearly complete plans to conquer China by stages, beginning in Manchuria, than Hitler had to dominate Europe, and the very desperation of Japan's plight permitted no delay. But Japan's leaders in 1931 resembled Germany's leaders in 1914 and again in

1939 in that they challenged the existing division of the world by force of arms. They differed in that they challenged that division in Asia, not in Europe, and as Asians not Europeans.

·6·

WHEN THE NEWS of Pearl Harbor reached Nationalist China's isolated mountain capital of Chungking, a cynical American remarked, "Pearl Harbor Day in Washington was Armistice Day out here." To which a realistic Chinese might have replied: "Pearl Harbor Day marked the tenth anniversary of Japan's invasion of China. What were you doing all that time?" The Americans had done little for China until they took the steps that led to Pearl Harbor, by which time the Chinese Nationalists could do little for themselves. They had their hands full, holding off the Communists with one of them, holding off the Japanese with the other. As for the Communists, they needed three hands: one with which to fight the Nationalists, one with which to fight the Japanese, and a third with which to organize and maintain resistance throughout the Japanese-occupied areas. For the kind of war the Chinese had waged sporadically since 1931 bore little resemblance to the battles of France, Britain, Russia, or the Atlantic. From the time of the German invasion of Poland, the Second World War had consisted of a series of military clashes between the armed forces of sovereign states—sometimes sharp and decisive, sometimes long-drawn-out and inconclusive, but all of them fought in the assumption that there was no substitute for victory, no greater disaster than defeat.

Not so to Chiang Kai-shek's Nationalists or Mao Tse-tung's Communists. Neither of them ever assumed that any single clash must lead either to victory or defeat. To them both, the kind of war they fought signified an endless period of inconclusive strife, sometimes involving large or small forces of Chinese and Japanese, more often consisting of indecisive clashes among rival Chinese factions. As Chiang Kai-shek had written in his diary in 1941: "Rapprochement and estrangement, gain and loss in diplomatic relations cannot be everlasting and without change. For love and hate, separation and unity do not depend upon sentiments but upon power. Given a prolonged period of time and with power in one's grasp, international maneuvering can be all in one's hands. Joy and sorrow, love and hate all depend upon me."

In this philosophy of opposites East met East; Chiang met Mao. In this same philosophy of opposites East also met West. Just as Mao Tse-tung had learned from China's philosophers how to think dialectically before he had heard of Hegel or Marx, Dr. C. G. Jung derived his own "philosophy of opposites" from the Chinese. In the Winter 1969 issue of the quarterly *Quadrant*, published by the C. G. Jung Foundation for Analytical Psychology, Barbara Hanna notes that the Chinese and the whole East "have a very different attitude toward the opposites than we have in the West." She recalls that "as Jung frequently pointed out, it is not pursuing perfection but holding the balance between opposites that is the vital thing now," and she quotes from "Late Thoughts" in his *Memories:* "Evil has become a determinant reality. We must learn from it since it is here to stay. How we can live with it without terrible consequences cannot for the present be conceived."

But Jung continued: "Touching evil brings with it the grave evil of succumbing to it. We must, therefore, no longer succumb to anything at all, not even to good. A so-called good to which we succumb loses its ethical character. Not that there is anything bad on that score, but evil results develop because we succumb to it. Every form of addiction is bad, no matter whether the narcotic be alcohol or morphine or idealism. . . . Recognition of the reality of evil necessarily relativizes the good, and the evil likewise, converting both halves of a paradoxical whole."

To which Barbara Hanna adds: "I have just reminded you of how Jung himself regarded the opposites, because it leads the way into the whole Chinese philosophy of life which—in contrast to the West—is all based on the equality of opposites. Those of us who use the *I Ching* are well acquainted with the equal opposites of Yang and Yin, masculine and feminine, but perhaps we are less aware that Chinese philosophy regards life and death also as a pair of opposites on which all human beings are based. In fact, if it tends to favor one of these opposites, it is rather death." In the case, however, of those Chinese opposites, Chiang and Mao, it became a war to the death in which Chiang's corrupt revolution of middle-class Nationalists steadily lost ground to Mao's Communist revolution of peasant masses who had no more use for Chiang than they had for Stalin.

The Japanese invasion strengthened the Communists still further and drove Chiang Kai-shek to hole up at Chungking. After Pearl Harbor, Chiang got more supplies from the United States and reverted to the traditional Chinese policy of "using barbarians to fight barbarians." But Mao found that it paid revolutionary dividends to fight both the Japanese invaders and the native nationalists. Both Chiang and Mao viewed the Second World War as primarily one more crisis in China's long history, but Mao recognized more clearly than Chiang that war is the mother of revolution and that in time of war revolution prospers. Chiang's career had reached its zenith during the years between the wars. It hit the skids before the Second World War ended. Mao's red star entered its ascendant even before the Second World War began. In 1949 Mao's Communist revolution triumphed over Chiang's Nationalist revolution only to enter a new revolutionary cycle of its own. Within another ten years, Mao's Great Leap Forward, designed to hasten China's industrialization all but wrecked its economy. In 1966 he launched his far more extensive Great Proletarian Cultural Revolution, with almost fatal consequences to himself and his regime. But China's traditional law of opposites still held good. The Leap Forward and the Cultural Revolution carried within themselves the seeds of their own regeneration. From the ashes of both defeat and victory rose China's eternal phoenix, the bird of paradox. Thus the very backwardness of China's Communist-controlled regions made them self-sufficient; their poverty left them with little to lose; their inaccessibility made them almost immune to invasion, blockade, or bombardment. Japan's conquests in China also played into the hands of the Communists, whose guerrilla warfare yielded maximum results in the Japanese-occupied areas. By 1943, the Chinese Communists had brought to near perfection those techniques of guerrilla warfare that the Vietnamese used with such effectiveness against the Americans a quarter of a century later. Indeed, even a quarter of a century turns out to have been too short a time for the rest of the world to learn how damn clever these Chinese really are.

XVI

Moscow—Cairo—Teheran

·1·

THE SUMMER OF 1943 had seen so much action on so many fronts that Roosevelt, Churchill, and Stalin felt it necessary to meet face to face and co-ordinate their 1944 strategies before 1943 had run its course. Plans for a Roosevelt-Stalin meeting at Fairbanks, Alaska, in mid-July disintegrated, but Secretary of State Hull had developed a sense of mission that enabled him to overcome a claustrophobic dread of air travel and fly to Moscow on October 7 for three weeks of meetings with Molotov and Eden to arrange a Roosevelt-Churchill-Stalin meeting within the next two months, With him Hull brought various resolutions that he and Eden had already drafted, one of which called for Foo Ping-sheung, the Chinese ambassador in Moscow, to join them in signing a "Declaration of Four Nations on General Security." The so-called "Moscow Declaration" that finally emerged announced that the British, American, Soviet, and Chinese governments would continue their united prosecution of the war "for the organization and maintenance of peace and security."

The Declaration pledged them "to act together in all matters relating to the surrender and disarmament" of their common enemies. It recognized "the necessity of establishing at the earliest practicable date a general international organization, based on the sovereign equality of all peace-loving states, and open to membership by all states, large and small, for the maintenance of international peace and security." The Chinese took special comfort in the sixth and final point: "That after the termination of hostilities they will not employ their military forces within the territories of other states except for the purposes envisaged in this declaration and after joint consultation."

On his return to Washington, Secretary Hull informed an unprecedented session of both Houses of Congress: "As the provisions of the four-nation declaration are carried into effect, there will no longer be need for spheres of influences, for alliances, for balance of power, or any arrangements through which, in the unhappy past, the nations strove to safeguard their security or promote their interests." The cynic —as romantic as any idealist—sees Hull, the true believer in Woodrow Wilson, soaring above the realms of reality on the wings of his own rhetoric. Stalin and Molotov—unencumbered by memories of the Wilson era—respected Hull for a toughness equal to their own and for an idealism sufficiently realistic (as Wilson's was not) to adjust itself to their necessities as they adjusted themselves to his. Thus, when Hull told Molotov privately that for the United States to join the Soviet Union in excluding China from the Big Four would shock the American public so deeply as to compel drastic policy changes in the Pacific area, Molotov saw the point and capitulated. With equal realism, Hull accepted the omission of Poland and other specific bones of Anglo-Soviet-American contention from the Moscow Declaration.

Stalin waited until October 30, the final night of the conference, to crown Hull's mission with complete success. On that occasion, Stalin, as Hull put it, "astonished and delighted me by saying clearly and unequivocally that, when the Allies succeeded in defeating Germany, the Soviet Union would then join in defeating Japan." How Roosevelt, Hull, and so many other American policymakers could have expected Stalin, Molotov, and their colleagues not to insist on entering the war against Japan as soon as possible after the defeat of Hitler remains a mystery, so quickly and so easily do so many of us forget the innocence of those times. Oddly enough, the Soviet war effort against Germany loomed so large in American eyes that Roosevelt and Hull forgot—as Stalin and Molotov assuredly did not—that the Soviet Union had interests in the Far East no less vital than those in Europe; indeed, for centuries the Russian star of empire had taken an eastward, not a westward course.

Stalin and Molotov respected Roosevelt and Hull more than they understood them—a compliment that Roosevelt and Hull returned. But Roosevelt's political instincts served him well when he entrusted to Hull, one of the last of a vanishing breed of homespun, American idealists, the delicate and vital task of setting up the first wartime Big Three conference. Hull and Roosevelt both believed, as Wilson had before them, in the collective organization of postwar peace and security. But while Hull abhorred the words "spheres of influence" and "balance of power" as much as many of his contemporaries abhorred "Fascism" or "Nazism," the words "areas of responsibility" bothered him not at all, especially when the signatories of the four-power declaration used them. Hull also saw eye to eye with Roosevelt concerning China's postwar role, of which Churchill and Stalin took a different and dimmer view.

If the inclusion of China in the four-power declaration testified to the war's global scope, the limits that each major power set on the areas of its own responsibility testified to their regional approach toward a postwar settlement. Britain had to recognize the east coast of Asia as an area of future Chinese responsibility; the United States had to recognize eastern Europe as an area of future Russian responsibility; the Soviet Union had to recognize the Atlantic and Pacific oceans as areas of Anglo-American responsibility. Only China assumed no responsibilities beyond its traditional frontiers. A global war that had divided itself into more than a dozen separate military theaters was preparing the ground for a global settlement, in which each of the four victorious major powers would become responsible for the regions in which they had borne the major military burden.

If this emerging four-power world followed a different blueprint from the one Cordell Hull brought back from Moscow, it is not less true that the world which had shaped Hull had little in common with the world that had shaped Molotov. Unless the Roosevelts and the Hulls could learn to understand the Stalins and the Molotovs, no world in which they could all exist would be likely to emerge from the war. Insofar as the Moscow conference of foreign ministers speeded the Big Three on the road to Teheran, it strengthened the United Nations coalition at its most vital spot. But insofar as the foreign ministers left Moscow more divided and suspicious than they were when they arrived, the dimmer were the prospects for agreement among the Big Three heads of government at Teheran. Thanks largely, but not entirely, to Cordell Hull, the Moscow conference more than fulfilled the hopes of its organizers. In the atmosphere they had created there, Stalin could not fail to sit down with Roosevelt and Churchill at Teheran, where no one of them could afford to block agreement with the other two. But the Chinese, in their weakness, no less than the Russians, in their strength, posed two different challenges to the four-power declaration. In the case of China, what kind of Chiang Kai-shek and Mao

Tse-tung would its civil war bring forth? In the case of Russia, what kind of Stalin would emerge from its victory?

·2·

ON OCTOBER 31, the day Hull started home from Moscow, Roosevelt arranged to meet Churchill in Cairo, on or about November 20, and to have Chiang Kai-shek join them there a few days later. Not until November 12 did Roosevelt, in his role as middleman, notify Churchill that Stalin had agreed to meet them at Teheran between November 27 and November 30. "Thus endeth a very difficult situation," Roosevelt informed Churchill, "and I think we can be happy about it. In regard to Cairo I have held all along, as I know you have, that it would be a terrible mistake if Uncle J thought we had ganged up on him on his military action. . . . It will not hurt you or me if Molotov and a Russian military representative are in Cairo too. They will not feel they are being given the 'run-around.' "

But no Russian appeared. Runaround or no runaround, the Russians still had a neutrality pact with Japan, and for a high Soviet military official and the Soviet foreign minister to attend military talks with the political and military leaders of three of their enemies did not accord with the ideas of neutrality held by that self-styled Asiatic, Joseph Stalin. But all was well that ended with Roosevelt, Churchill, Chiang Kai-shek, and their chiefs of staff meeting at Cairo on November 22 and with Roosevelt, Churchill, and Stalin conferring in the same way at Teheran on November 27.

To the military problems that Chiang and his military advisers had come to Cairo to discuss they contributed not a word. They had not mentioned the subject even among themselves until they boarded their plane. After the Anglo-Americans outlined plans for an invasion of Burma, General Brooke, as the presiding officer, invited the Chinese to outline theirs. "We wish to listen to your deliberations," their spokesmen declared. The Anglo-Americans went into further detail, and when Brooke again asked the Chinese for their ideas, he received the same reply: "We wish to listen to your deliberations."

What they then heard were more hours of increasingly angry talk in which Admiral King, General Stilwell, and General Brooke all took part. The Americans advocated two separate operations—one of them Buccaneer, a two-pronged British naval attack on the coast of South

Burma and on the offshore Andaman Islands, further north; the other, Tarzan, a ground invasion of northern Burma in which three Chinese divisions, trained by Stilwell, would fight side by side with British Empire troops. The prospect of Chinese troops liberating Burma from Japanese rule sickened Churchill; the prospect of British naval forces playing any part in the enterprise maddened him. On the other hand, the prospect of Operation Tarzan delighted Stilwell's soul; Buccaneer filled him with a scorn that Brooke not only shared but that he also infuriated most of the Americans present by expressing.

But even as the Joint Chiefs wrangled at Cairo, General MacArthur and Admiral Halsey, in the southwest Pacific, and Admirals Nimitz and Spruance, in the central Pacific, launched sweeping, island-hopping offensives that threatened Japan's home islands with two-pronged invasions from the south and east. As a result, few men and fewer supplies remained available for Burma, especially with plans for the cross-Channel invasion of Europe receiving priority over the campaigns in the Pacific. Chiang Kai-shek shed no tears over the prospective downgrading of Buccaneer and Tarzan, both of which he regarded as dangerous diversions from the Chinese Communist threat to the north. The one military benefit that the Cairo Conference bestowed upon Chiang took the form of a stepped-up schedule of air shipments to Chungking. Time, however, transformed this overreliance on air power from a manifest blessing into a disguised curse.

Chiang's increasing dependence on air power dated back to the summer of 1937, when physical disability forced Captain Claire L. Chennault to resign from the United States Army Air Corps and accept a position as civilian adviser to the Chinese Nationalists. By 1940 Chennault had organized a volunteer force of American fighter-pilots, known as the Flying Tigers, who—though heavily outnumbered—consistently outfought and outmaneuvered the Japanese. In 1942, now restored to active duty as a major general, Chennault claimed that starting with 105 fighter planes, 50 medium bombers, and 12 heavy bombers he could expand his forces and eventually destroy all of Japan's China-based planes and bomb the Japanese islands into submission. A year later, at Cairo, Roosevelt backed Chennault and Chiang in their appeal for an independent Chinese air force—this in the face of General Marshall's warning that Japanese ground troops could always overrun Chinese air bases. But the President's determination to remain on good terms with Chiang made him susceptible to wartime delusions concerning the omnipotence of air power which had just begun to turn the tide of the Pacific war—but only when used in conjunction with sea power and only when directed against the vulnerable Japanese archipelago. In addition, Roosevelt found it just as easy to underrate China's chronic civil war and the chronic corruption of Chiang's regime as it was to overrate the role that air power might play in that rugged and remote theater of war.

Chiang and Chennault had entered into a promising marriage of military and political convenience that might or might not endure. Chennault's obsession with air power distracted him from the necessity of coming to terms with the Chinese Communists or at least compelling Chiang to modernize and reform his ground troops along the lines laid down by Stilwell. The wisdom of hindsight now reveals the Chiang-Chennault nuptials as a disaster for all concerned, notably the principals. It doomed Chiang to defeat in the showdown he himself sought with the Communists. It riveted Chennault to the lost cause of Chiang Kai-shek. Mercifully, Roosevelt did not live to see the consequences of his decision to choose the easiest way out of a cruel dilemma.

It took no time at all, however, for the conference itself to produce its most important result. Nobody could wipe from history's page the fact that the British and United States governments had, for the first time, dealt with the head of a Chinese government as their equal. But Chiang's own weaknesses and his refusal to face up to them soon undermined his newly attained status. In order to send him back to China with something to show for his long journey, Roosevelt and Churchill prepared a "Cairo Declaration" to which they and Chiang all put their names. Here they announced it as "their purpose that Japan shall be stripped of all the islands in the Pacific which she has seized or occupied since the beginning of the First World War in 1914, and that all the territories stolen from the Chinese, such as Manchuria, Formosa, and the Pescadores, shall be restored to the Republic of China." Those last four words, referring as they did, specifically and exclusively, to Chiang's regime at Chungking, gave him all that Roosevelt or Churchill could then give him to justify his claim to speak and act for all of China. The signers of the Cairo Declaration also affirmed their determination that "in due course Korea shall become free and independent." The declaration made no reference to any Russian claim to any territory then under Japanese or Chinese control. Chiang had come empty-handed to Cairo. He did not return in that same condition. Could Stalin, in his strength, do better at Teheran than Chiang in his weakness had done at Cairo?

·3·

THE SUCCESSION of conferences at Moscow, Cairo, and Teheran linked for the first time the two separate wars that the United Nations coalition and the Axis powers had been fighting simultaneously since the Arcadia Conference of January 1942 proclaimed the United Nations' existence. Ever since the Japanese invaded Manchuria in September 1931, they had been waging their own, separate, undeclared war against China. In December 1941, they expanded that war to include more than half the Pacific Ocean and all of southeast Asia, plunging themselves into war with the United States and Britain in the process. Meanwhile Hitler, since invading Poland in September 1939, had resumed the First World War where it had left off in November 1918. In overrunning western Europe in the spring of 1940, he laid the British, French, and Dutch colonial empires in southeast Asia open to easy conquest by Japan. But it was the Japanese attack on Pearl Harbor that merged the two wars by bringing the United States into both of them simultaneously.

Hitler's invasion of the Soviet Union committed him to a two-front war in Europe, but the Russo-Japanese neutrality pact, in the spring of 1941, insured the Russians against war with the Japanese—and vice versa. However, the weapons and tactics which the British, Russians, and Americans successively brought to bear against the Germans prevented Hitler from turning his quick, early conquests into the sweeping victory he sought. By the end of 1943 when the Moscow, Cairo, and Teheran conferences took place, the United States had become more than democracy's arsenal. It had become democracy's army, navy, and air force, democracy's prime industrial supplier, source of raw materials, and financial stabilizer. It had also become the sole outside support of Nationalist China's nondemocratic regime, which had been fighting the Japanese five times as long as the nondemocratic Soviet Union had been fighting the Germans.

Churchill's rhetoric, Roosevelt's ghost writers, Hitler's Goebbels, and Stalin's Politburo had their functions, but it was to their war machines that they owed their very existence, and nowhere had this war machine grown so fast or reached such proportions as it had in the United States. It was this war machine that gave credibility to Roosevelt's demand of unconditional surrender; indeed, it was this war machine which, by its very function and power, dictated that demand. For the

American war machine, sustained and fortified as it had been by earlier and essential Chinese, British, and Russian efforts, emerged at the Cairo and Teheran conferences as the controlling factor in the war's final phase and—as such—the controlling factor during the first postwar years. For the kind of victory that Roosevelt and his generals decided to win could not but play a major role in determining the kind of peace they wanted to make.

But the scope of the Teheran Conference did not extend beyond the war against Germany, and in that war the Red army could at once play a larger role in eastern Europe than the Anglo-American forces could play in the west. The Russian campaigns had put Stalin in position to impose his own settlements on his neighbors to the west and thereby veto any attempt Roosevelt might make to impose his own settlement on Germany. On the other hand, the worldwide fronts on which the United States had deployed its land, sea, and air forces put Roosevelt in position to embark on a truly global foreign policy such as Stalin could not even attempt. Thus, Teheran marked more than the beginning of Hitler's end. It marked the emergence of two new superpowers: the United States and the Soviet Union. Roosevelt based his hopes for that new era on the evolution of the United Nations wartime coalition into a postwar organization for world security. Stalin approved in theory; in practice, he viewed the future of the Soviet Union in terms of its own security from external attack. At Teheran, he was the man from Missouri, who had to be shown. On one point he and Roosevelt agreed entirely: their meeting could not fail to change the course of history.

Within fifteen minutes after Roosevelt's arrival in Teheran at the comfortable villa in the convenient Soviet compound where the Russians insisted that the American President stay, Stalin paid a call. For the next three quarters of an hour the two men exchanged views. Roosevelt got his first surprise when Stalin described Pétain rather than de Gaulle as "the real physical France." At the opening three-and-a-half hour session that followed immediately, Roosevelt took advantage of his position as chairman to indicate, with the aid of maps, the course of the war in the Pacific. Stalin soon interrupted to lay two ghosts. First: "We shall be able by our common front to beat Japan." He then laid the second ghost of a separate Soviet-German peace by producing a memorandum on the treatment of postwar Germany, depicting "all measures proposed by either the President or Churchill for the subjugation of Germans as inadequate."

Churchill had proposed splitting off Prussia from the rest of Germany. Roosevelt wanted to split Germany into five fragments. Stalin called for substantial transfers of prewar Polish territory to the Soviet Union and of prewar German territory to Poland. He also opposed Roosevelt's unconditional-surrender policy on the ground that it undercut defeatist Soviet propaganda and aided Goebbels in rallying support to the Nazi regime. The next day, November 29, Roosevelt refused Churchill's invitation to a private lunch, but conferred alone with Stalin during the afternoon when he outlined his plan to make the United Nations a permanent world-security organization. He suggested a forty-nation General Assembly, a ten-nation executive board, and a smaller body of "Four Policemen"—Britain, Russia, China, and the United States—with sole authority to use force against any disturber of the peace. Stalin boggled at China as one of the four policemen and called for special precautions against German aggression.

The following morning, the Anglo-American military leaders spent three hours discussing the details of "Overlord"—code name for the cross-Channel invasion of western Europe. Since this called for the buildup of an expeditionary force in which the Americans would eventually outnumber the British five to one, the supreme commander had to be an American, to be named by Roosevelt and approved by Churchill. Stalin therefore opened the afternoon's plenary session with the question: "Who will command Overlord?" Judging others by himself, Stalin assumed that Roosevelt had of course reached his decision and that Churchill had presumably approved. How little the Old Bolshevik from the Caucasus understood the Anglo-Americans and their muddling ways. Some time before, the impulsive Churchill, assuming an authority he never possessed, had promised the job to Brooke. Although both Churchill and Brooke knew, by the time of Teheran, that this could not be, Roosevelt had not yet decided whom to name and so informed Stalin, who thereupon turned on Churchill with the question of whether or not the British wanted Overlord in the first place. Churchill's own convictions and attitude justified Stalin's suspicions. But the realistic Brooke had long accepted (as the romantic Churchill could not yet bring himself to do) the inevitability of Overlord, which enjoyed wide popular support in Britain, especially after the 1942 and 1943 postponements of the second front. By December 1, when the Teheran Conference ended, it reached agreement to launch Overlord during May 1944, to be quickly followed by smaller landings, known as Anvil, in the south of France. The Russians, for their part, agreed to launch offensives in the east on a scale that would prevent the Germans from shifting any troops to the west.

But military agreement did not lead to political agreement. Unable to match the co-ordinated military measures they planned to take against Germany with corresponding political measures, Roosevelt, Churchill, and Stalin proceeded to improvise a new technique of summit diplomacy to which they and their successors reverted on more than one subsequent occasion. They made their first try at an off-the-record state dinner given by Stalin on the evening of November 29, when Roosevelt truckled to his host's sense of humor by ribbing Churchill about the British Empire—no laughing matter to Churchill or, for that matter, to Stalin either, who praised Britain's war effort and went on to express the hope that the British Empire might be able to gain still more territory. When Churchill responded by asking what territorial claims the Soviet Union might press, Stalin replied, "There is no need to speak at the present time about any Soviet desires—but when the time comes, we shall speak."

·4·

ROOSEVELT's's first foray into summit diplomacy had backfired—and he knew it. Indeed, he afterward confessed, to his old friend Frances Perkins, that he had come back from Teheran as perplexed as he was when he set forth. In 1942 Roosevelt had thought he could instruct Churchill and the British Foreign Office on how to deal with the Russians. Now he was not so sure. "I wish someone would tell me about the Russians," he confided to Frances Perkins. "I don't know a good Russian from a bad Russian. I can tell a good Frenchman from a bad Frenchman. I know a good Greek when I see one. [Roosevelt seldom sold himself short.] But I don't understand the Russians. I just don't know what makes them tick. I wish I could study them. Frances, see if you can find out what makes them tick."

"Do you mean that seriously?" she asked.

"Yes, find out all you can and tell me from time to time. I like them, and I want to understand them." Later she told him that one American who had lived in Russia a long time gave her this answer to the "tick" question: "The desire to do the Holy Will."

On November 30, Churchill played host at the second and last summit session, which happened to fall on his sixty-ninth birthday. All went better than well. Brooke, who had arrived at Teheran announcing that Stalin had hoped to make Overlord into a trap that would bring military disaster to Britain and the United States, won Stalin's approval by suggesting that the best friendships sometimes arise from misunderstandings. For these words, Stalin threw his arms around Brooke, who afterward described the evening as "wonderful." Stalin attributed the very survival of Britain and the Soviet Union to American production, which he thereupon toasted. Churchill toasted "Stalin, the Great." The goodwill generated by this second dinner more than counterbalanced the misunderstandings that arose at the first. But neither at the two dinners nor at any of the three plenary sessions did the Big Three reach any political agreement about postwar policy toward Germany or toward Germany's east-European neighbors whom the Red army planned to liberate.

Roosevelt and Stalin held their third and last conversation on the afternoon of Wednesday, December 1, shortly before the final plenary session, that evening. Roosevelt spent most of the afternoon session cautioning Stalin and Molotov not to accept at face value some of the wishful reports the American Communist leaders sent them. He also reminded them of the large ethnic blocs—notably some seven million Americans of Polish extraction—whose opinions he had to take into account. At the subsequent plenary session he set them the example of making no comment on Polish matters but did repeat his suggestion of the dismemberment of Germany into five, autonomous states. Stalin called for stronger measures against the German General Staff, and the whole question was turned over to the European Advisory Committee in London.

Stalin had read and approved the Cairo Declaration, but he offered no suggestions and declined to sign it. Nor did he give any written promise to join the war against Japan. He did put his name to a Teheran declaration which the Big Three released on December 6. "We express our determination that our nations shall work together in war and in the peace that will follow," the Teheran declaration began. "The common understanding which we have here reached guarantees that victory will be won," it continued. "And as to peace—we are sure that our concord will make an enduring peace. We recognize fully the supreme responsibility resting upon us and all the United Nations to make a peace which will command the good will of the overwhelming mass of the peoples of the world, and banish the scourge and terror of war for many generations." The three signatories concluded: "We came here with hope and determination. We leave here friends in fact, in spirit, and in purpose." No wonder Robert Sherwood wrote in *Roosevelt and Hopkins:* "If there was any supreme peak in Roosevelt's career, I believe it might be fixed at this moment, at the end of the Teheran Conference. It certainly represented the peak for Harry Hopkins." But not for Winston Churchill. The Teheran declaration's political, postwar generalities, contributed by Roosevelt, seemed to Churchill worse than useless. The euphoria of the state dinners soon wore off. Now Churchill saw a Red army stronger than the Wehrmacht had ever been, in position to overrun an exhausted, demoralized eastern Europe. His experience before, between, and during both world wars had given him insights that neither Roosevelt nor Stalin could match into the workings of twentieth-century European power politics. By 1943, however, Britain's power no longer matched Churchill's insights. Even in the war against Hitler Britain had become America's junior partner, and Churchill could only fret and fume as Roosevelt vacillated between his plans to build a peaceful postwar world around the wartime Big Four and his hopes for a postwar United Nations Organization for world security. As for Stalin, he concentrated on the territorial expansion of the Soviet Union, not by means of a Leninist world revolution but along traditional lines that Churchill understood all too well.

·5·

WHEN THE ANGLO-AMERICAN Combined Chiefs of Staff arrived back in Cairo from Teheran, they at once reviewed their previous commitments to Chiang in the light of their subsequent commitments to Stalin. They also took a longer, harder look at Anvil, the diversionary assault on southern France, originally designed to coincide with Overlord. Although Churchill had fought Overlord all the way, it won sudden, if temporary, merit in his eyes: the landing craft it required ruled out Buccaneer. The Combined Chiefs also found they might have to postpone Overlord from the last week in May to the first week in June, and that Anvil must come still later. Having decided to fudge a little on the promises made to Stalin at Teheran, they reneged completely on Buccaneer, the projected British naval attack on southern Burma. On December 6, Roosevelt accepted its cancellation but tried to save face for Chiang by offering him the choice between Tarzan in early February and stepped-up air deliveries over the hump. General Stilwell, with whom the President conferred, welcomed the cancellation of Buccaneer as much as he welcomed the prospect of Tarzan, and he hastened back to Chungking to sell the latter to Chiang.

But Chiang was not buying. Instead, he wrote Roosevelt, demanding that the United States government "assure the Chinese people and army of your serious concern in the Chinese theater of war," extend a billion-dollar loan to China, supply double the number of planes previously agreed upon, and increase the airlift of supplies into China to at least twenty thousand tons a month by February 1944. Chiang had tried once too often to turn military weakness into political strength. His airfields could not begin to handle the increased planes and shipments he demanded. The United States Treasury—with wartime spendings at all-time highs—could not spare China a billion-dollar loan. The armed forces of the United States already had the Japanese on the run in the Pacific. Stalin had made it plain that he would help drive them from the Asian mainland as soon as Germany went down to defeat. Roosevelt, Churchill, and Stalin had no urgent need for Chiang's aid against Japan. His temporary and limited association with the Big Three had lasted barely two weeks.

Whereupon the Americans added insult to injury. Not content with rejecting Chiang's demands for clouds of planes and mountains of supplies, Roosevelt assigned to Stilwell the mission of winning Chiang's support for Tarzan. Stilwell saw in Tarzan potential vindication of his own high regard for the military capabilities of well-trained, well-equipped, well-led Chinese ground troops. By the same token, Chiang saw in Tarzan potential vindication of Mao Tse-tung's guerrilla tactics and potential exposure of his own efforts to glorify himself by corrupting, exploiting, and demeaning the very people he pretended to serve. Although Roosevelt had denied Chiang any additional credits, planes, or supplies, he had already granted Chiang's request to give General Chennault and a separate Chinese air force priority over General Stilwell and the ground troops Tarzan required. What an irony that the impulsive decision taken at Quebec in August 1943 by the hard-pressed Roosevelt and the ill-informed Hopkins, to back Chiang and Chennault against Stilwell and Marshall, made so mighty a contribution to the ultimate defeat of the Chinese Nationalists by the Chinese Communists. No sooner did the Teheran Conference set in motion the events that led, in less than a year and a half, to the Russian conquest of half of Europe, including half of Germany, than the Cairo Conference set in motion the events that led, in six years' time, to the Communist conquest of all of China.

·6·

THE TEHERAN CONFERENCE had an instant, sharp, and far-reaching impact on all three of its chief participants. Throughout its course a heavy cold sapped much of Churchill's strength and required the constant ministrations of Dr. Charles Moran Wilson [later Lord Moran], who noted that his patient's failing health led to a corresponding decline in his mental and emotional condition. Stalin and the Russians bothered him more and more; Hitler and the Germans less and less. "A bloody lot has gone wrong," Churchill confided to Wilson after the first day's session. By the time the Teheran Conference ended Churchill pinned all his hopes on a meeting that he and Roosevelt had arranged to hold with Turkey's President Inonu at Cairo, where they hoped to talk him into bringing Turkey into the war. But Roosevelt, suspecting that Churchill hoped to use Turkey to divert attention from Overlord, found himself sympathizing with Inonu for not wanting "to be caught with his pants down"—in other words, not wanting to help the Russians make Bulgaria a Soviet satellite. More distraught than ever by Roosevelt's virtual connivance in Inonu's turndown, Churchill then planned to confer with General Alexander in Italy. "I am not going to see Alex for fun," he informed Wilson. "He may be our last hope. We've got to do something about those bloody Russians."

At Cairo, Churchill's anti-Russian maneuvers got no support from the British members of the Combined Chiefs, all of whom joined Brooke in trying to convince the Americans of the need to maintain pressure on the Germans in Italy, to cancel Buccaneer, and to postpone the long-deferred Overlord a few more weeks. Britain's top professional soldiers had no more use for the diversions Churchill favored in the Balkans and the Middle East than he had for Buccaneer. On December 13, Dr. Wilson's worst fears came true as Churchill contracted a serious case of pneumonia, complicated by a recurrence of the heart attack that first hit him during his first wartime visit to Washington. Two nurses and a pathologist flew on from London to help care for him, and within another three weeks their rugged patient had himself moved to Marrakesh in Morocco, there recuperating while again trying to run the war. As therapy, the change of scene worked wonders, but the war had entered a stage far beyond Churchill's power to direct or control.

Churchill's near collapse after the Teheran and Cairo meetings reflected his despair when Roosevelt and Stalin overruled his opposition to Overlord. But Stalin had not threatened, bluffed, or blackmailed Roosevelt into insisting on an early, definite commitment to Overlord. Rather had Roosevelt's insistence, since Casablanca, on unconditional surrender left the Big Three with no alternative. As Stalin himself pointed out, American war production had reached such a peak that the Anglo-Soviet-American coalition now had it in their power to fight their wars against both Germany and Japan to the bitter end of unconditional surrender. The Anglo-Franco-American alliance had not been able to end the First World War on any such terms in the fall of 1918, even though imperial Germany had lost all hope of victory and even though the war was ending in Europe, where it had begun.

By the time of the Moscow, Cairo, and Teheran meetings, the Second World War had not only spread to the four corners of the earth; American technology, American resources, and American manpower had put the Anglo-Soviet-American coalition in position to impose unconditional surrender on all its enemies on all fronts. It was Stalin (not Roosevelt or Churchill) who had pointed out that it was one thing to prevent Hitler from winning the war, but that it was something else again to compel him to surrender on the victors' terms. And this could not have happened when and as it did without the miracle of American war production.

What neither Stalin nor anybody else could foresee at Teheran was the consequences of the American war effort on the Americans themselves. By the end of 1943, the Second World War had become a transcendent affair in that it had broken all limits set by previous wars. If it extended over twice as much territory and involved twice as many people as the First World War had involved, it had also resulted in four times as much destruction. Its planes flew at three times the speed of planes in the First World War; its tanks traveled six times as fast; the range of its bombers and their capacity had increased tenfold. Civilian casualties from all causes exceeded casualties in the armed services as battlefields overleaped all limits. Limited wars like those waged in times past could not result in more than limited victory or limited defeat. Total war, by definition and its very nature, meant total victory or total defeat. And this before the development of atomic and nuclear weapons.

When Roosevelt at Casablanca proclaimed the war aim of unconditional surrender, he did so in the hope of forestalling another German resurgence such as occurred during the twenty years between the 1918

Armistice and the Munich Conference. Every year that has passed since 1943 has made such a repetition of history less likely as the science of war itself has become ever more self-defeating. But even in 1943 the war machine itself had reached such dimensions as to have become a power in its own right—and nowhere more so than in the United States, which had responded to the challenge of the Second World War with so vast a national effort. Seen in perspective, President Roosevelt and the military hierarchy that he, Secretary Stimson, General Marshall, and a succession of other officials in and out of uniform organized during the Second World War left a self-perpetuating legacy for which the war and its aftermath could always supply justifications and functions. Different motives and intentions inspired them, but the results of their labors have created a juggernaut just as capable of terrorizing the world into total peace as it is of plunging the world into total war.

XVII

Breakthrough 1944: Germany First

· 1 ·

FROM STALIN, in January 1944, came the first major application of the Teheran decisions as three Russian armies broke the siege of Leningrad, freeing 600,000 of the city's inhabitants and advancing along a 300-mile front. In February and March two more Russian armies attacked along a front that wound almost a thousand miles across the Ukraine, starting 150 miles north of Kiev and ending at the Crimea. Some of these troops liberated Odessa in April and cleared the Crimea in May. In an order of the day issued May 1, Stalin announced that the Red army had reached the Soviet Union's western border on a 250-mile front and had liberated more than three quarters of all German-occupied territories. He praised the British and Americans for the supplies they had sent during the past year, for their air attacks on Germany, and for their diversionary campaign in Italy. But he also noted: "The liberation of Europe and the smashing of Germany on her own soil can be done only on the basis of joint efforts from the Soviet Union, Great Britain, and the United States as they strike from the east and the west."

His kind words about the Italian campaign came as a surprising and welcome contrast to the disapproval emanating from British and American sources. Churchill and Brooke saw it as the necessary prelude to Overlord and chided their American allies for not pressing it hard enough. Roosevelt and Marshall viewed it as a dangerous distraction from the all-important cross-Channel invasion. On January 22, under pressure from Churchill, Brooke, and Alexander (who had now succeeded Eisenhower as supreme commander in the Mediterranean), the Anglo-Americans committed 36,000 men and 3000 vehicles to Operation Shingle, an amphibious landing on the Anzio beaches, thirty miles from Rome and sixty miles behind the German lines. It was as close a thing as the first landings at Salerno during the previous September, and the Anglo-Americans had to rush more than twice as many men and weapons to Anzio even to hold the beachhead. Nor did their troops enter Rome until June 4.

As the British and Russians saw these Italian campaigns, they had succeeded: Hitler had responded just as Field Marshal Brooke predicted he would, rushing more divisions to Italy and thereby weakening German defenses in both Russia and France. In May, the story repeated itself in the Crimea, where Hitler again ordered the German forces to stand and fight to the last man, thereby again weakening future German resistance at more vital spots. The Anglo-American operations in Italy did not compare in scope with Russian campaigns in the Ukraine and beyond Leningrad, but all conformed with the strategy of regional responsibility laid down at Teheran.

These and other developments during the first half of 1944 added only slightly to Russian understanding of Anglo-American strategy. Never having grasped the scope or the importance of the battle of the Atlantic, the Russians had no idea of the physical obstacles to an invasion of western Europe. Only gradually did they perceive that just as the output of American shipyards laid the foundations of victory on the Atlantic, so the output of American aircraft factories laid the foundations of Anglo-American control of the air over western Europe. To land their armies on Europe's mainland, the Anglo-Americans had to win the naval battle of the Atlantic. To drive these armies to the heart of Germany they also had to win the battle of the air over Europe itself.

In conformity with the Teheran decisions, the Anglo-Americans devoted the opening months of 1944 to launching a crescendo of air attacks at railways, bridges, and factories in Germany and the German-occupied countries of western Europe. Not until then had America's aircraft industry developed the capacity to produce planes in such numbers as to be able, for the first time, to clear the Luftwaffe from the skies of Europe and thus to create conditions under which Anglo-American ground troops could land in western Europe and proceed against Germany without fear of German air attack. What ways and means might have been used to implement Britain's Mediterranean strategy must remain in the realm of conjecture, but it is hard, in retrospect, to see how America's enormous industrial potential could have been turned to more efficient account than it was.

·2·

THE UNEXPECTED DIFFICULTIES of the Italian campaign forced the Anglo-Americans to postpone, for one month, the cross-Channel invasion that they had promised to launch in early May. They also had to postpone even longer the landings that they had planned in the south of France to coincide with the landings in Normandy. But neither postponement altered the decisions reached at Teheran. The fighting in Italy had weakened the Germans more than it had weakened the Anglo-Americans, who took Rome just twenty-four hours before General Eisenhower took the greatest military gamble in history and set June 6, 1944, as D Day for the Normandy landings.

Originally he had chosen June 5, but on June 4 the worst storm in twenty years hit the English Channel, and the invasion had to be postponed. At 9:30 that evening, the forecasters predicted clearing weather during the night, getting worse by morning, followed by barely tolerable conditions for not more than another twenty-four hours. This compelled Eisenhower to choose June 6 because not until early July would a late-rising moon again coincide with a low tide at dawn. To have delayed the invasion a second month would have meant landing in a season of shortening daylight and losing a whole month of dry weather and summer campaigning. Encouraged by General Bernard Law Montgomery, the British commander of all the ground troops, and by his own chief of staff, General Bedell Smith, General Eisenhower set his jaw and decided to make it June 6. At the same time—recognizing the risks the circumstances forced him to assume—he wrote in his own hand the following communiqué which he stuffed in his pocket and carried throughout the next day: "Our landings in the Cherbourg-Havre area have failed to gain a successful foothold and I have withdrawn the troops. My decision to attack at this time was based upon the best information available. The troops, the air, and the Navy did all that bravery and devotion to duty could do. If any blame or fault attaches to the attempt it is mine alone." These words do more than testify to General Eisenhower's supreme fitness for his position as supreme Allied commander. They also serve as a reminder that in the most complex military operation in history, all the courage in the world, all the technology, skill, and power still remained subject to the laws of chance.

Yet it had taken more than luck to get those six divisions—three American, two British, and one Canadian—plus 14,500 tons of equipment ashore along a thirty-mile stretch of the Normandy coast within the space of forty-eight hours. On that first thrust everything else depended: the establishment of the beachhead virtually assured its extension. More than two years of Anglo-American planning had gone into the preparations for D Day; more than three months of Anglo-American air bombardment had preceded the actual landings. On D Day itself, the Tactical Air Command flew more than 10,000 sorties; the Air Transport Command more than 1700. By midafternoon, more than three thousand landing craft and five hundred warships had sailed from sixteen British ports. By nightfall they had put 170,000 troops ashore, with casualties approximating 10 per cent.

Generations of maritime experience underlay the broad strategy and enhanced the Anglo-Americans' understanding of air power, its limitations as well as its possibilities. Churchill, who had promoted the tank during the First World War, threw himself with comparable energy behind a type of floating, artificial harbor known as the Mulberry. Scores of obsolete warships and merchant vessels were towed across the Channel and then sunk to form breakwaters, or Gooseberries. Thanks to this improvisation, supplies began to arrive at the Normandy beachheads within four days of the landings and continued to pour in during the weeks required for the capture and repair of the ports of Cherbourg and Le Havre. For all practical purposes, German sea and air power did not exist on D Day. Had the invasion come sooner, it could not have proceeded with such precision and force. Had Eisenhower waited another month, he could not have scored so complete a surprise.

But, on June 10—perhaps to make up for the good luck Eisenhower had on D Day—nature came to the aid of the Germans as the worst gale to strike the English Channel in forty years raged for four days, wrecking the Mulberry on which the Americans had planned to land most of their supplies and severely crippling the one the British used. Deliveries of supplies at once dropped ninety-five per cent behind schedule. Had General Eisenhower delayed the invasion even a few days longer, there is no telling what effects, both psychological and physical, the storm would have had on his beachheads, his buildup, and the entire course that the war in the west followed. Even as it was, the storm delayed the progress of the Allied armies to such a point that they found themselves on June 23 on the line they had hoped to reach by June 11.

Nor was this all. In June the Germans had attacked London with their first pilotless planes or "buzz bombs." On July 6, Churchill told the House of Commons that the 2754 flying bombs the Germans had launched up to that time caused 2752 fatal casualties. Within another two months the British had learned to knock them out of the sky with fighter planes. They had also established air bases on the Continent from which they were able to destroy most of the bases and factories from which the buzz bombs came.

The Normandy landings marked as great a defeat for Germany in 1944 as France suffered in 1940 when the Germans broke through the Ardennes Forest and outflanked the Maginot Line. Indeed, Hitler believed in his impregnable Atlantic Wall as blindly as Gamelin had believed in his impregnable Maginot Line. It was a belief that few of Germany's professional soldiers shared. The Atlantic Wall, which extended from Le Havre to the Dutch border, consisted of concrete gun emplacements, underwater mines at low tide level, and land mines above the high-water mark, all of which half a million slave laborers spent two years in building. Rommel called it the Fuehrer's "Cloud-Cuckoo-Land." Anglo-American air power, guile, and luck made it useless—first when the R.A.F. bombed the Pas-de-Calais area so heavily that the Germans assumed it had to be the invasion target; later, when General Eisenhower ordered up D Day under such bad weather conditions that the time as well as the place of the landings took the Germans by surprise.

On the eastern front, the time for surprise had long since passed, and there was no longer any place where either side could even attempt it. The third anniversary of Hitler's surprise attack on the Soviet Union fell two weeks after D Day but it was no surprise to anybody when four Russian armies opened their summer offensive on a 450-mile front that extended from the southeast corner of Estonia to central Poland. They scored six breakthroughs, and on July 3 Russian troops entered Minsk, the capital of Byelorussia, surrounding 100,000 Germans and taking 57,000 of them prisoners in "a defeat worse than Stalingrad." By this time, the Red army had ten per cent more men under arms than in November 1942, and these men had thirty per cent more tanks, eighty per cent more guns and mortars, and twice as many planes.

Nevertheless, as the Germans saw it, the Normandy landings overshadowed the Soviet summer offensive. For one thing, since Stalingrad more and more Germans had become more and more convinced that Hitler's Russian gamble had failed. For another thing, most of these same Germans saw Hitler making the same mistake in France that he had made in both Russia and Italy. Instead of ordering his troops to retreat to prepared positions and take a heavy toll from the enemy before retreating again and repeating the process, he demanded that they stand and fight everywhere for every position they held. What took two years to happen in Russia and one year to happen in Italy took less than two months in France. On orders from Hitler, the Germans delayed Montgomery's capture of Caen for several weeks, thereby causing some Anglo-American friction. But when Caen did fall, it had served its purpose as a pivot from which the Americans under Omar N. Bradley and Patton swung south, across the Normandy peninsula and then drove eastward to Orléans, Chartres, and Paris.

·3·

BY THIS TIME those Germans who had long known that Hitler had lost his Russian gamble saw that he had now lost the war. On the night of July 1, Field Marshal Keitel, the supreme commander of all German forces, asked Rundstedt: "What shall we do? What shall we do?" "Make peace, you fools," replied Rundstedt. "What else can you do?" How this might be done Rundstedt did not explain, but some of his aristocratic friends had ideas on the subject. They had supported Hitler's war longer than they—or their fathers—had supported the Kaiser's war, but now they wanted out. At the time of the Munich crisis and again when war came a year later, the strongest opposition to Hitler came from within the Army High Command. Since then, General Ludwig Beck, former army chief of staff, Admiral Wilhelm Canaris, head of the German Counter-Intelligence Service, and Count Klaus von Stauffenberg, chief of staff to the deputy commander of the German home army, who had lost his right arm, his right eye, and two fingers of his left hand in North Africa, had maintained contacts with Dr. Hjalmar Schacht, former president of the Reichsbank, Ulrich von Hassell, former ambassador to Italy, and Dr. Karl Goerdeler, former mayor of Leipzig. As soon as the Anglo-American armies landed in Normandy, these men resolved to assassinate Hitler and set up a new government of their own which would seek a separate, compromise peace with Roosevelt and Churchill while continuing the war in the east.

How little could Germany's would-be leaders learn from their country's participation in two world wars and from the impact of those wars on the peoples and leaders of the Old World and the New? Roosevelt and Churchill had just successfully honored, in Normandy, the most difficult and important part of the pledge they had made to Stalin at Teheran to synchronize their long-deferred invasion of western Europe with the Red army's summer offensive. Was this the time to dishonor that pledge and cast away its benefits by signing a separate peace with a government of German generals? The plotters understood Germany no better than they understood the world outside. On July 11, Stauffenberg, who had occasional access to conferences attended by Hitler, turned up at one of them in Berchtesgaden, bearing a briefcase with a bomb inside, but he did not set it off because the plotters had decided that Goering and Himmler, to whom some of the armed forces owed a personal allegiance, must be eliminated at the same time, and neither one of them attended this meeting. Four days later Stauffenberg passed up a still better chance at Hitler's headquarters in the East Prussian town of Rastenberg, where Goering appeared but Himmler did not. On June 20 a third opportunity presented itself, again at Rastenberg, where Hitler had scheduled a conference with about twenty military leaders. Neither Goering nor Himmler attended this meeting, but the plotters decided to go ahead anyway.

Shortly after noon, Hitler left his re-enforced concrete bunker and entered the wooden conference shed, followed by the conferees who had gathered outside. Stauffenberg waited another five minutes in his nearby car, opened his briefcase which he held against his body with his one arm, put his head inside, pulled out the bomb fuse with his teeth, closed the briefcase, and walked quickly to the conference room, where he joined the group standing about the table. He made his way to the head of the table, at Hitler's right, put the briefcase on the floor, leaning it against a beam that ran up to one corner, and whispered to one of the conferees, "I must go and telephone. Keep an eye on my briefcase. It has secret papers inside." He then walked from the conference room toward his car. After he had covered about sixty yards, he heard a loud explosion behind him, turned only long enough to see the hut enveloped in a cloud of dust and debris, and continued on his way. In his car he drove to the airport; from the airport he flew his personal plane to Berlin, where he arrived three hours later.

The bomb, which would surely have killed Hitler and those around the table had the conference taken place in the usual reinforced concrete bunker, dispersed most of its force by blowing the flimsy hut to bits. It killed four men at the table. Hitler, however, suffered only minor injuries; a nearby heavy beam saved his life. Some of the conspirators assumed, as did Stauffenberg, that the plot had succeeded. But they did not begin spreading the word over the system of military communications that they controlled until after Stauffenberg arrived in Berlin. By this time, Goebbels had sized up the situation, commandeered the Berlin radio and the whole communications network radiating from it, and flashed the news that an attempt on Hitler's life had failed. In the mistaken assumption that the attempt had succeeded, Stauffenberg and his fellow conspirators spread a false version of the events at Rastenburg, thus exposing themselves.

The failure of so ambitious a plot suggested that Hitler led a charmed life. But perhaps the wonder was not that the plot failed but that it came as close as it did to success. The military men on whom everything depended remained, throughout, prisoners of their own rigid framework of operation and of their insistence on meticulous detail. Personal character and professional habit made it impossible for them to improvise. Thus Stauffenberg missed two opportunities to do away with Hitler because the original plan called for eliminating Goering and Himmler too. By the time Stauffenberg recognized that he must concentrate on Hitler, he made the attempt under singularly unfortunate conditions. But he could no more call off an ill-starred effort, partway through, than he could seize the unexpected opportunities that had offered themselves before. The same Prussian military tradition, the same German sense of duty that Hitler had exploited when he first came to power still served his interest, and he turned the full fury of his fanatical nature against the plotters. Not only did he have all the ringleaders executed. His People's Courts sent another estimated five thousand persons to their deaths and ten thousand more to concentration camps. Most of these had no connection with the plot. Many were Social Democrats, Liberals, and assorted anti-Nazis who could have helped build a different and better Germany after the war. Some were Nazis with whom other Nazis had scores to settle. The net result: Hitler emerged more nearly unassailable than ever.

The failure of the July 20 plot against Hitler vindicated Roosevelt's unconditional-surrender policy by shifting responsibility for its execution from the President's shoulders to Hitler's. The survival of Hitler, the execution of the plotters, and the widespread purge of oppositionists now ensured a German fight to the finish of unconditional surrender. It also ruled out a repetition of the events of November 1918, when Woodrow Wilson speeded the end of the First World War by offering the Germans an armistice on the basis of his Fourteen Points, which combined concessions to the defeated Germans with obligations upon the victorious Allies. The 1918 armistice and the subsequent peace treaties may not have caused but they certainly did not prevent the rise of Hitler, the liquidation of the Weimar Republic, or the outbreak of the Second World War. But Roosevelt's unconditional-surrender policy and the failure of the July 20 plot can hardly be said to have invited a repetition of the events that followed the German defeat of 1918.

The failure of the July 20 plot did, however, suggest a reverse parallel between the events that preceded the outbreak of the First World War and the events that preceded the end of the Second. The successful bomb plot against Archduke Franz Ferdinand of Austria at Sarajevo in June 1914 led, by August, to the outbreak of the First World War. The failure of the bomb plot against Hitler, in July 1944, led to the prolongation of the Second. What might have happened if the 1914 plot had failed we cannot know any more than we can know what might have happened if the 1944 plot had succeeded. What happened as the result of those two accidents of history we do know all too well.

· 4 ·

DURING THE SUMMER OF 1944, the Anglo-Americans—like the Germans in 1940—swept across France so fast that they became victims of their own success. The original plan for the liberation of France assumed that four months after D Day, the Channel ports would remain in the hands of the Germans, who would also still occupy Paris. Nowhere had the Allies expected to advance more than two hundred miles. As things turned out, within three months of D Day, General Courtney H. Hodges' First American Army had liberated Paris while General Patton's Third American Army had swept across France, where it made contact at Dijon with the Sixth Army Group, commanded by General Jacob L. Devers, which had landed in the south of France on August 15. By this time, American troops outnumbered the British and Canadians by more than two to one. Montgomery, who had commanded all the Allied ground forces in France until August 1, now commanded only the sixteen divisions that made up the British Second and the Canadian First armies with the rank of field marshal, as of September 1. After a month of hard fighting, they took the Channel ports and liberated Brussels.

Hitler's stand-and-die tactics had delayed the initial progress of the Anglo-Americans by only a few weeks, after which time the Eisenhower broad-front strategy led to a series of Anglo-American breakthroughs that cost the Germans some 200,000 casualties and another 200,000 prisoners. By early September, the Anglo-Americans found themselves several months ahead of schedule, but not within several months of victory. For Hitler's stand-and-die tactics had now begun to pay off at the mouth of the river Scheldt and at Arnhem, while the American armies to the east and south had stretched their supply lines so long and thin that their offensive lost its momentum. Both the tempestuous Patton in the southeast and the headstrong Mongomery in the northwest found the situation intolerable. Each assumed that he and his troops could quickly win a war that the fumbling supreme commander simply did not know how to fight. Patton called Eisenhower "the best general the British have got," and told him: "We'll win your goddam' war for you if you keep the Third Army going,"—while demanding another 400,000 gallons of gasoline. At the same time Montgomery offered to serve under Bradley if Eisenhower would only back his plan to break into the Ruhr Valley, where the Germans manufactured half their war equipment.

All well and good. But Eisenhower's second-guessing critics chose to forget that on June 12, the Germans had launched the first of more than 2700 pilotless planes, or "buzz bombs," which they showered upon London for the next two months, inflicting almost exactly one casualty per plane. Two months later they followed through with rocket bombs that flew faster than the speed of sound. British fighter planes presently mastered the buzz bombs, and British bombers destroyed most of their launching sites near the Channel coast. But it took longer-range pinpoint bombing to destroy the rocket-launching pads near Peenemunde on the Baltic. According to General Eisenhower, "It seemed likely that, if the German had succeeded in perfecting and using these new weapons six months earlier than he did, our invasion of Europe would have proved exceedingly difficult if not impossible." Thanks, however, to the Eisenhower broad-front strategy during the summer months, his critics were able to indulge in the luxury of second guessing when autumn came.

As for Hitler, on September 5, he appointed Rundstedt supreme commander in the West, with orders to launch a major offensive in mid-December against the lightly held Ardennes Forest, scene of the great German breakthrough of 1940. Rundstedt and the younger Walter

Model, whom he had replaced as supreme commander, warned Hitler that their available resources were "much too weak for such far-reaching objectives" as Antwerp, Brussels, and the Channel coast that Hitler had set. They urged the kind of operation that General Bradley, who bore responsibility for the Ardennes sector, feared: a spoiling attack that might pinch out the salient that the Americans had won at Aachen, where they had breached the Siegfried Line.

Political, not military, considerations governed Hitler's thinking. "Never in history was there a coalition like that of our enemies, composed of such heterogeneous elements with such divergent aims," he explained to his generals on December 12. "Even now these states are at loggerheads, and he who, like a spider sitting in the middle of his web, can watch developments, observes how these antagonisms grow stronger from hour to hour. If we now can deliver a few more heavy blows, then at any moment this whole artificially bolstered common front may collapse with a gigantic clap of thunder."

Suffice it to say that the German attack which came on December 16 shook up the Anglo-Americans and drove a salient more than forty miles deep on a front about thirty miles wide. It also provoked a sharp but temporary Anglo-American rift as Field Marshal Montgomery claimed responsibility for a victory in which, as Churchill told the House of Commons, "The United States troops have done almost all the fighting and have suffered almost all the losses." By December 26, the German drive lost its momentum.

. . .

After the German defeat in the so-called "Battle of the Bulge," the overwhelming military and economic presence of the United States in western Europe could not but lead to a corresponding political presence. No high American official from President Roosevelt and General Eisenhower down had the authority, intention, or capacity to impose American political institutions—much less American political rule—on any of the highly sophisticated peoples of western Europe. First in North Africa and later in Italy, the Anglo-Americans had their disagreements with each other and with the local population. But they never sought to subjugate any people or take permanent control of any territory. In France and the Low Countries, General Eisenhower's forces included political officers and military-government teams charged with helping the citizenry of the liberated regions restore their own political institutions. In Italy anti-Fascist partisans and in France

Gaullist resistance fighters co-operated with the Anglo-American soldiery.

By the end of 1944, General Eisenhower's decision to spread his armed forces across the face of France and the west-European approaches to Germany opened the broad highway of military, economic, and political penetration that bound the North American continent to western Europe for the next quarter of a century. The same General Marshall who served as chief of staff of the United States Army throughout the Second World War served as secretary of state from 1947 to 1949, when the European recovery program that bore his name set western Europe on the path to postwar prosperity. The same General Eisenhower who commanded the Allied Forces in Europe from 1944 through 1945 also served as first commander of the North Atlantic Treaty Organization's armed forces from 1950 to 1952. The military strategies that these two men shaped and executed during 1944 laid the foundations of the restored western Europe that began to emerge in 1945. The military strategies that Stalin and his associates shaped and executed during that same year laid the foundations of a new eastern Europe that presently began to replace the old.

·5·

ALTHOUGH STALIN'S RED ARMY in the east and Eisenhower's Allied Expeditionary Force in the west shared the common purpose of crushing the armed forces of Nazi Germany, the different strategies they followed sought different postwar goals. In Italy, Britain's Field Marshal Alexander, the supreme Allied commander in the Mediterranean, sought to restore the democratic system Mussolini had overthrown in 1922. In western Europe, General Eisenhower sought to restore the democratic regime that Hitler had driven out in 1940. But Stalin had no plan to implant democracy where it had never existed or to restore it where it had never taken root. Between January and May 1944, five Soviet armies had liberated Leningrad and Odessa and driven the Germans from the Crimea and the Ukraine. Two weeks after the Normandy landings, four Russian armies began to surge across Poland.

By July 28, the Red army and the Red air force had brought Praga, the industrial quarter of Warsaw, under fire. The next day, Moscow's Polish-language radio called upon "the sons of Warsaw" to join the Red army and some of its Russian-trained troops in its ranks in "wiping out the Hiterlite vermin from the Polish land." The Polish inhabitants of Warsaw, who had spent the previous four years organizing an underground government, including an army of 40,000 troops, responded on August 1 when their commander, General Tadeusz Bor-Komorowski, ordered them to strike at the hour of the day when the largest crowd filled the Warsaw streets. As usual, he had taken his orders from the Polish government in exile in London, representing Poland's six major, prewar political parties.

Five German divisions struck back instantly. From Italy, Norway, and nearby Lublin came elements of three more crack German divisions. But no help came from the Red army. When asked to supply the uprising with tanks and artillery, Stalin replied: "The trouble with the underground army is that it does not want to fight the Germans." Stanislaw Mikolajcyk—the member of the government in exile to whom Stalin made the remark—offered this postmortem in *The Rape of Poland:* "The cream of our remaining youth in Poland had been virtually wiped out by German guns in league with Russian compliance. A million people were living in Warsaw when the rising against the Germans began. A quarter of these, including the bulk of the 40,000 incredibly valiant men who came up to fight the enemy on August 1, 1944, were killed, wounded, or missing by the time of the capitulation (on October 2). Some 350,000 people of Warsaw were forcibly evacuated, mostly to slave labor and to murder. In January 1945, when the Russians entered the city, they found only death."

The abortive July 20 plot against Hitler had made it virtually impossible for Roosevelt and Churchill not to continue the fight against Germany to the bitter end of unconditional surrender. Now, the abortive two-month Warsaw uprising had bogged the Red army down in eastern Europe. Before the war, Soviet living standards lagged behind Europe's —east or west. During the war Soviet losses of life and property also exceeded Europe's. But the German retreat from the Soviet Union left eastern Europe at the mercy of the Red army, thus putting Stalin in a better position to impose Communist rule on eastern Europe than Hitler had been to impose the Nazi New Order there. But to say that is not to say much. The Red army had no such industries, no such resources, no such transport facilities behind it as the United States placed at the disposal of General Eisenhower's armies in western Europe. The Anglo-Americans brought liberation, freedom, better living standards to western Europe. The Red army brought occupation, Communism, and lower living standards to eastern Europe.

In permitting the Germans to lay waste Warsaw, Stalin perpetuated Polish hatred of Germany. In choosing the city of Berlin as his final objective, he prolonged the German will to resist. Indeed, the combined results of Warsaw's prolonged death agonies and the Red army's prolonged drive to Berlin left that army so exhausted and the Soviet economy so weakened that Stalin and his successors had their hands full for the next quarter of a century trying to digest the large hunks of eastern Europe that the Red army had bitten off during the war.

·6·

THE FARTHER the broad front of General Eisenhower's Allied Expeditionary Force swept across western Europe, the higher the morale of the people it liberated rose. English-speaking armies appealed to a west-European sense of community that few east Europeans shared. Stalin and his associates could no more treat Poland as the Anglo-Americans treated France than he could deal with eastern Europe as the Anglo-Americans dealt with western Europe. In addition to having to put all his eggs in the one basket of the Red army, Stalin also faced an infinite variety of problems in the various nations his armies overran.

On June 20, the Finns stopped fighting and asked for Soviet surrender terms. Stalin demanded surrender first, talks afterward. Ribbentrop flew to Helsinki, where he persuaded Foreign Minister Rysto Heikki Ryti to accept his offer of German troops to defend the city. On June 30 the United States broke off diplomatic relations with Finland; on August 1 Ryti canceled his pact with Ribbentrop and resigned. On August 25 the Finns offered to surrender. Hostilities ceased on September 5, and they signed the armistice two weeks later. The Russians halved their reparations demand and gave Finland six years instead of five to pay up; they canceled their lease on the Hango peninsula in the Baltic and restored their 1940 Soviet border except for the Arctic port of Petsamo and one naval base. No Soviet troops occupied Finland. The national administration remained in Finnish hands. Stalin and his associates saw no more reason to treat Finland as they had treated Poland than they saw to treat Hungary, Romania, or Bulgaria—when their time came—as they had treated Finland.

That time came soon. During the month of August, the Soviet embassy at Stockholm, through which the Russians and Finns had established contact, made preliminary arrangements for the Russians and Romanians to do the same. Young King Michael declared war on Germany; a new pro-Ally government that included Iuliu Maniu, the leader of the Peasant party, Dinu Bratianu, the leader of the landowning Liberals, and Lucretiu Patrascanu, leader of the hitherto outlawed Communists, signed a formal surrender whereby Romania withdrew from Bessarabia and Northern Bukovina in exchange for Soviet recognition of its title to all of Transylvania, half of which the Axis had awarded to Hungary. The Red army at once marched to Budapest, where some Hungarians turned against the Germans, while others fought beside the Germans against the Russians to the end. On October 17, General Bela Miklos, the Hungarian commander in chief, went over to the Russians with his chief of staff. But it took until 1945 for a new Hungarian government to sign an armistice with the Soviet authorities in Moscow, and the last German soldier did not leave Hungary until April 4 of that year.

Events in Slavic Bulgaria followed a different course. Although a member of the German house of Saxe-Coburg-Gotha, King Boris never declared war on the Soviet Union, while the Soviet minister to Sofia never lost touch with the local Communists. Like Hungary, Bulgaria signed the anti-Comintern pact and declared war on Britain and the United States on December 13, 1941, but sent no troops to the Russian front and maintained normal relations with Moscow. On August 25, 1943, King Boris visited Hitler. Three days later the Germans had him done away with under mysterious circumstances, and his pro-German brother, Cyril, became regent on behalf of Boris' six-year-old son Simeon. A year of internal struggle followed. Bulgaria's pro-German government had the halfhearted backing of the army; the pro-Ally Fatherland Front had the open backing of the Communists and their Partisan guerrillas, many of them army deserters. On September 5, 1944, Red army troops reached the Bulgarian frontier. The Soviet government declared war; the Bulgarian government did the same. Three days later, the Fatherland Front staged a coup d'état, declared war on Germany, and asked the Russians for an armistice. The residents of Sofia greeted the troops of the invading Red army as their liberators and avengers.

Both in Romania and Bulgaria, Soviet officials adopted what they described as the same procedure the Anglo-Americans had followed in Italy where they included a Russian member on the Allied Control Commission, informing him of all their decisions, but not consulting him in advance. In like manner, Soviet Foreign Minister Molotov gave Ambassadors Sir Archibald Clerk-Kerr and Averell Harriman in Moscow advance information on steps the Soviet government and its high

command had decided to take in Romania and Bulgaria. By October, however, Churchill could stand it no longer. The Pacific war and the campaign for a fourth White House term absorbed Roosevelt, who re-
ʃluctantly approved of Churchill's plan to seek a face-to-face encounter with Stalin, similar to their showdown meeting of August 1942. It was the fate being prepared for Poland, not the steps already taken in Romania and Bulgaria, that concerned Churchill most deeply. He also feared for the future of Greece and Yugoslavia.

In connection with Poland, Churchill got nowhere, but at his first private session with Stalin he had an inspiration. "Let us settle our affairs in the Balkans," he quoted himself as having told Stalin. "Your armies are in Romania and Bulgaria. We have interests, missions, and agents there. Don't let us get at cross-purposes in small ways. So far as Britain and Russia are concerned, how would it be for you to have ninety per cent predominance in Romania, for us to have ninety per cent of the way in Greece, and go fifty-fifty about Yugoslavia?" There were to be fifty-fifty splits in Yugoslavia and Hungary and a seventy-five per cent Soviet predominance in Bulgaria.

The percentage approach set a pattern to which events in Romania and Bulgaria had already conformed. In Hungary the fifty-fifty split could not stand up against Soviet possession. In Yugoslavia, on the other hand, possession did not lie in Stalin's hands—or Churchill's ei-
ther. The veteran Croatian Communist Josip Broz, who—under the nom de guerre of Tito—received his baptism of fire in the Spanish Civil War, went on to apply what he had learned against all and sundry. First his Partisan army of guerrilla fighters disposed of Colonel Draza Mihailovich and the remnants of the defeated Yugoslav army that sometimes collaborated with the Germans and Italians against the Partisans. Churchill had welcomed King Peter's royal Yugoslav government in exile in London, but showed his respect for Tito by having his son Randolph dropped by parachute on Tito's headquarters. By the sum-
mer of 1944 Tito was charging Alexander, now a field marshal and the supreme Allied commander in the Mediterranean, with conniving in a German air attack on Partisan headquarters; by October 20 Tito's sus-
picions extended to Stalin, whose efforts to pose as the liberator of Yugoslavia Tito frustrated by seeing to it that his Partisans, not the Red army, marched into Belgrade on the heels of the departing Germans. Although Tito, on December 7, signed an agreement with Dr. Ivan Subasic, to respect the regency council in London and to abide by the free elections that the council would supervise three months after Yu-

goslavia's final liberation, Tito's anti-Fascist council assumed the functions of Parliament, and Subasic followed King Peter into the shadows. So did most of the provisions of the Churchill-Stalin agreement. Churchill's eyes proved bigger than his stomach, and Stalin's stomach ‡ bigger than his eyes. Before the end of 1944 civil war had broken out in Greece between the Communist National Liberation army, known by its initials as ELAS, and the National Republican Greek League's rival army, known by its initials as EDES, which consisted of only a few thousand troops, operating in the northeast. The British kept them well supplied, and as more officers from the regular army joined them they became increasingly anti-Communist. Although the British maintained liaison with both groups, the Communists had no use for the king, whom they called George Glücksburg, the name with which he had been born. Few Greeks felt that outsiders had liberated their country by landing on their soil. As most Greeks saw it, the Red army's sweep through the Balkans had done more to get the Germans out of their country than the British and Americans had been able to do from North Africa. But even the ELAS forces did not know at the time that Tito had played at least as large a part as Stalin in their liberation.

As the last German troops left Greece in October, the first British troops appeared. By December 60,000 of them had arrived, only to find themselves battling partisans who had fought the Germans for three and a half years. Churchill and Eden flew to Athens for Christmas, where Churchill told the commanding British general to treat the city like a conquered capital. Churchill and Eden also brought an end to the civil war by imposing a provisional government under Archbishop Damaskinos, whom Churchill called, in private, "a scheming medieval prelate," as temporary regent. By this time Roosevelt's health had entered its final period of decline. Visibly exhausted, he took a December vacation, leaving the newly appointed neophyte, Edward L. Stettinius, Jr., in charge of the State Department. Although Stalin had accepted all of Churchill's moves in Greece without a murmur, Stettinius at once established his amateur status by publicly deploring these departures from the principles of the Atlantic Charter. Thus, Anglo-American relations (already strained by the brief German flare-up in the Ardennes) ended the year on a note of nontriumph.

· · ·

During 1944 the Anglo-American campaigns in western Europe and the Red army's campaigns in eastern Europe began laying down the lines that the subsequent divisions of Germany and of Europe followed.

In conformity with his broad-front strategy, Eisenhower had advanced with all deliberate speed—but never so fast as to get ahead of his supply lines that provisioned the ever-growing masses of west Europeans whom his armies liberated. Not so the Red army. The farther it advanced across eastern Europe, the more occupation troops it had to leave behind to install and protect the native Communist officials who gradually ousted, replaced, and gave orders to whatever local officials might remain. A Russian-dominated Romania, Hungary, or Bulgaria might enjoy slightly better living standards and stabler government than the pro-Nazi regimes which preceded them had provided. But their Russian liberators understood their problems no better than their German overlords had. Yugoslavia represented a special case. There, Tito considered himself a better Communist than Stalin and by 1948 took his country out of the Soviet bloc into a new, nonaligned status that proved an inspiration to many leaders of the so-called Third World of developing nations that began emerging during the 1950's and 1960's.

As professed Communists, both Stalin and Tito had long since accepted as a fact of life that every victory contains within itself the seeds of future defeat and every defeat the seeds of future victory. What some call the dialectics of history others call its ironies. But the practicing, true-believing Communist of whatever stripe finds it almost impossible to recognize that he is no less subject than the Fascist or the Nazi, the liberal or the conservative, the capitalist or the socialist to history's iron laws. Thus, in 1944, Stalin could not see that precisely those military weapons, that patriotic spirit, that Communist discipline which had enabled the Soviet Union to rout its German invaders had become self-defeating as soon as the Red army crossed its own frontiers. In eastern Europe Stalin and his associates not only encountered more difficult problems of more different kinds than those with which Roosevelt, Churchill, and Eisenhower had to deal in western Europe, but the Russians had fewer resources with which to meet them.

Having handled Finland with kid gloves and Poland with a meat-ax, Stalin played the Romanians off against the Hungarians, only to find the Communist Tito giving him three times as much trouble as the three monarchs of Yugoslavia, Greece, and Romania all put together. Meanwhile the Anglo-Americans had put themselves in position not only to reap richer rewards from their victories in western Europe than Stalin could hope to win in the east. By 1945 their armies easily overran Germany's most populous and productive regions in the west, while the

Red army needed all its troops, arms, and supplies to consolidate Soviet power in Poland, Austria, Czechoslovakia, East Prussia, and—last but not least—Berlin. But long before these ironies of history caught up with the Russians in eastern Europe and eastern Germany, history's acceleration swept the United States into an Asian maelstrom that, within the next half dozen years, reversed the direction in which the whole world had moved during the previous five centuries.

XVIII
Breakthrough 1944: Japan Next

·1·

DURING 1944 the war that Hitler and Stalin had launched in Europe and the war that Japan had launched in Asia both turned against their instigators. In Europe Hitler found himself caught in a two-front war against the Anglo-Americans in the west and against the Russians in the east, a predicament that he had brought upon himself when he invaded the Soviet Union before settling accounts with Britain. Stalin, too, found himself his own worst enemy as the retribution he tried to wreak on Hitler plunged him into an east-European adventure that had already begun to cost him more than it was worth.

Similar reversals occurred in the war that Japan had launched against the United States. Far from distracting Roosevelt from Europe, the Japanese attack on Pearl Harbor enabled Roosevelt to pursue his beat-Germany-first strategy with redoubled vigor. Indeed, by 1944 the United States seemed to be having it both ways. The shock of Pearl Harbor propelled the American economy into a war effort of such scope that within two years General Eisenhower could launch a cross-Channel invasion of western Europe while at the same time Admiral Nimitz in the central Pacific and General MacArthur in the southwest Pacific launched campaigns of comparable scope against Japan.

The Japanese had spent more than half a century building the warships and naval bases and more than two decades building the war planes and air bases that enabled them to assert their ascendancy over the far Pacific and southeastern Asia. But within less than two years after Pearl Harbor the Americans had developed their naval and air power at such a rate that the Japanese could no more stand up against them than the Chinese had been able to stand up against Japan at the turn of the century. Nor was this all. The absolute superiority of American naval and air power also doomed Japanese hopes for permanent ascendancy over China. But whether American naval and air ascendancy over Japan also assured American ascendancy over Japan's crumbling Co-Prosperity Sphere in southeastern Asia—not to mention China—remained to be seen.

The fall of Tarawa, in the central Pacific, to the Americans in November 1943, marked the first breakthrough in the final stage of the Pacific war. By this time the Pacific Fleet had been divided into two commands, the Fifth Fleet, to the north, under Admiral Spruance, the Third Fleet, to the south, under Admiral Halsey, both under Admiral Nimitz. Task Force 58—now known as Fast Carrier Force and commanded by Admiral Marc A. Mitscher, an aviation pioneer—operated almost continually between them. On June 18, 1944, elements of the Fifth Fleet took Saipan, killing 24,000 Japanese and taking 1780 prisoners, more than half of them Koreans. American losses totaled 3426 marines and infantrymen. The news shocked General Tojo and his cabinet into quitting. The new, long-range B-29 bombers had just begun to hit Japan from bases in southeastern China. The acquisition of Saipan now enabled them to bomb Japan from the central Pacific as well.

The next day Admiral Marc A. Mitscher's Fast Carrier Force had its turn, as it clashed in the Philippine Sea with Japan's mobile fleet in the greatest carrier battle of the war. More than three times as many forces participated as did at Midway. By June 23, when the four-day battle ended, the Japanese had lost all but thirty-five of the 430 planes with which they had started, plus two of their carriers. The Americans lost thirty planes. One battleship had suffered damage. Quality as well as quantity accounted for the outcome: every United States naval aviator had two years of training and three hundred hours of flying time. The Japanese flyers had between two and six months of training, after which they went stale from long waiting.

Although Admirals King, Nimitz, Spruance, Halsey, and Mitscher had put on a stunning demonstration of American naval and air superiority in regions where Japan lay most vulnerable to attack, their breakthrough strategy faced a formidable obstacle in the person of General MacArthur. In the first place, he had the backing of three large popular constituencies—seven million Australians, eighteen million Filipinos, and a good many more million Americans whose imaginations he had captured and held. In 1943, with only 100,000 of the one million soldiers then stationed outside the United States and with the same proportion of planes and a smaller proportion of naval forces, General MacArthur pioneered the leapfrogging technique of bypassing most of the Japanese-held bases along his line of advance. But by June, 1944, it was the admirals, not MacArthur, who had the ships, the planes, the men, the supplies, and the bases to hit Japan's home islands hardest and soonest.

MacArthur and the admirals differed not only on strategy and tactics but on the political and military objectives that their strategies and tactics sought. Inasmuch as the Philippines lay less than a thousand miles from his great Australian base, MacArthur saw them as the ideal springboard from which to launch the invasion of Japan. The admirals, on the other hand, urged bypassing the Philippines in favor of an assault upon Formosa, to be followed by assaults on Iwo Jima and Okinawa which lay only half as far from Japan as the Philippines did. But these smaller islands, for all their proximity to Japan, lay five times as far from their bases in Hawaii as the Philippines lay from Australia. Thus, the smaller islands, being closer to Japan, also would become more vulnerable than the Philippines to Japanese counterattack. But it was the moral and political case for the Philippines that finally decided the argument in MacArthur's favor. The United States in the Philippines (unlike Britain, France, and the Netherlands in southeast Asia) had won the support of the native population, in this case eighteen million Christian Filipinos, to whom Roosevelt had pledged independence after the defeat of Japan.

The showdown came on July 27–28 at Honolulu, where the President's authority started a long chain of events in motion. Bypassing both General Marshall, the army chief of staff, and Admiral King, chief of naval operations, Roosevelt arranged to have Admiral Nimitz, as commander in chief of the Pacific fleet, present the case for bypassing the Philippines, followed by General MacArthur, as supreme commander in the southwest Pacific, making the case for bypassing Formosa and liberating the Philippines as the necessary first step before the invasion of Japan's home islands. Suffice it to say that MacArthur won hands down. "We will not bypass the Philippines," Roosevelt assured him. "Carry on your existing plans. And may God protect you."

While giving MacArthur the green light to proceed toward the Philippines, the President at the same time withheld the still wider authority MacArthur had so long sought. The Honolulu showdown left the military command of the war against Japan as divided as ever, but the assignment of MacArthur to the Philippines ensured his emergence as the hero of the Pacific war just as the assignment of Eisenhower to the supreme command of Overlord assured his emergence as the hero of the war in western Europe. There, however, the parallel ended. The Pacific theaters of war did not include mainland China any more than the west-European theaters of war included the east-European theaters, not to mention the Soviet Union itself. In the war against Japan, China had become more a liability than an asset; in the war against Germany, the Red army had inflicted the heaviest defeats on the Germans, and scored the greatest victories over them. China, in its weakness, posed as serious a problem to the Americans in Asia as the Soviet Union, in its strength, posed to them in Europe.

One incident, however, affecting the Philippines illuminated some of the complexities that America's Asian commitments entailed. In May, 1942, some 75,000 soldiers—12,000 of them Americans, the rest Filipinos—had surrendered to the Japanese at Bataan after receiving promises of good treatment. Several months earlier, 70,000 British Empire troops had surrendered under similar circumstances at Singapore. Partly in the dim hope of forestalling reprisals, but chiefly in the grim determination to persist in the beat-Germany-first strategy from start to finish, the British and American authorities waited until January 1944 before the Americans released an eyewitness account of the Bataan death march by Colonel William E. Dyess. He not only survived it but escaped from the Philippines to describe how 21,000 men perished on the march itself and how another forty per cent of the survivors died of malnutrition and maltreatment during the first three months of their subsequent imprisonment. Made public sooner, the story might have stimulated a popular outcry in the United States for a beat-Japan-first stategy; made public when it was, the story stirred fresh sympathy for the Filipinos and for the American troops who shared their fate, thus serving the MacArthur rather than the Nimitz strategy.

There is some truth, but not much, in Bernard Shaw's quip about the American and British people being divided by the common language they speak. The history of Japanese-American relations, on the other hand, suggests that differences in language, culture, and surroundings seldom make for peace and understanding among nations and peoples. At Pearl Harbor the Japanese took brilliant advantage of American ignorance of their ways to score one of the great military upsets in history only to succumb, in their turn, to their ignorance of American striking power and the will to hit back. The long-distance, remote-control type of war that the Japanese and Americans then waged against each other for the next two years enhanced the mutual misunderstanding which had surrounded its outbreak. The closer, fiercer combat in which the Russians and Germans had been locked during the same period tended to confirm rather than contradict that mixture of hate and fear, suspicion and awe, which each had long felt toward the other. But Japan's military hotheads who had plotted the Pearl Harbor attack still had no idea of how disastrously they had underrated the American war potential, while at the same time most Americans continued to overrate Japan's powers of resistance.

By 1944, Japanese ship losses were averaging five times the rate of new ship construction. Plane construction remained meager: 8208 in 1942, 16,295 in 1943, 28,220 in 1944, of which only thirty per cent could fly in combat. Japanese steel production never reached more than 4,300,000 tons a year before the war or more than 4,500,000 tons during it; American steel production ranged between sixty to one hundred million tons a year. During the same month of July, 1944, when President Roosevelt made the decision that gave MacArthur's drive to liberate the Philippines priority over the navy's drive toward Japan, the Japanese had to evacuate Guam which they had held for two and a half years, while the new American B-29's, based on newly gained Pacific islands, began dropping bombs on Tokyo. But the Japanese defenders of these islands still believed they could break American morale by shouting, as they charged: "God damn Babe Ruth!" Japanese officers disemboweled themselves with their swords rather than surrender. The few Japanese whom the Americans took prisoners turned against their captors, stabbing doctors, shooting orderlies. The Americans therefore shot most Japanese who fell into their hands as they would shoot mad dogs. The Japanese who gave no quarter themselves expected none.

Just as British bombing of German cities surpassed German bombing of London, American bombing of Tokyo surpassed the bombing in Europe. The Japanese lacked any such system of air defenses as both the British and the Germans developed, and the shacks and shanties in which so many of them lived and worked burned like straw. Unable to provide shelter or protection, the leaders of Japan's air-defense program taught the people songs with which to bolster their courage:

> Why should we be afraid of air raids?
> The big sky is protected with iron defenses.

For young and old it is time to stand up;
We are loaded with the honor of defending the homeland.
Come on, enemy planes. Come on many times.

American fire bombings of Tokyo more than matched British fire bombings of Hamburg and Dresden—and Japanese morale more than matched the morale of the Germans. During the first two years of the war, the Japanese people—again like the Germans—lived better than they ever had. But this did not last long; by 1944 the wartime diet of the average Japanese had dropped from 2400 calories a day to 1500—or ten per cent less than the German diet during the worst period of the First World War. Yet Napoleon's apothegm assigning to the moral factor in time of war three times the value of the material factor eventually broke down, even in Japan, all as a result of the mistake its leaders made of trying to beat the Americans at their own industrial, technological game.

·2·

Six weeks after President Roosevelt at Honolulu gave General MacArthur the nod over Admiral Nimitz, the Combined Chiefs of Staff—then meeting at the second Quebec Conference—quickly approved a new American timetable in the Pacific. The navy had made so much headway in the direction of Japan, and MacArthur had made so much headway in the direction of the Philippines that the Combined Chiefs recommended a divided command operation to liberate the Philippines at once. General MacArthur's Southwest Pacific Command would embrace General Walter Krueger's Sixth United States Army and Admiral Thomas C. Kinkaid's Seventh United States Fleet. Nimitz's command, on the other hand, would not extend beyond Spruance's Third Fleet, Halsey's Fifth Fleet, and Mitscher's Fast Carrier Force, which shuttled between the two. "The team remains about the same, but the drivers change," said Nimitz. It remained, however, a divided two-theater MacArthur-Nimitz operation.

At dawn on October 20, 1944, seven hundred ships of the United States Navy arrived at Leyte Gulf in the Philippines. Elements of the Seventh Fleet led the way. After them came freighters, transports, and landing craft. By October 25 they had put 132,400 men and 200,000 tons of supplies ashore, and the greatest naval battle in history was nearing its end. On sea as on land, the greater the battle, the greater the confusion. The battle for Leyte Gulf had included four separate naval actions, comprising every known type of naval warfare and every naval weapon except the mine. The Japanese had assembled 64 vessels carrying 42,800 men against 218 vessels, all but two of them American, carrying 143,668 American and Australian sailors. The Japanese had deliberately let Admiral Kinkaid's Seventh Fleet get General Krueger's Sixth Army ashore. The "great decisive battle" that the Japanese planned to fight called for Admiral Jisaburo Ozawa's mobile force to lure Halsey's fleet north at which point Admiral Takeo Kurita's central force was to hit Leyte Gulf, break through the American ships in the area, and annihilate General Krueger's expeditionary force. Ozawa did lure Halsey north, but submarines sank three of Kurita's heavy cruisers en route and carrier-based planes sank his superbattleship *Musashi*. A sudden thrust by Halsey in one direction and a sudden Japanese disengagement in another set the stage for one of the Escort Carrier groups of the Seventh Fleet to force Kurita to withdraw. Admiral Toyoda directed the Japanese naval forces from Tokyo. Admiral Nimitz directed the Third and Fifth Fleets from Pearl Harbor, where a misunderstanding of one of Halsey's messages enabled Kurita to get most of his central force away.

Japanese losses totaled four carriers, two battleships, six heavy cruisers, three light cruisers, and six destroyers, plus at least thirty-five more ships sunk or damaged. The first battle of the Philippine Sea in mid-June, when the Japanese lost more than four hundred planes, virtually foredoomed them to defeat at Leyte Gulf. Nevertheless, that battle hardly qualifies as a decisive American victory. Many Japanese lived to fight again. It was also at Leyte Gulf that Japan's suicide flyers made their first appearance, crashing their obsolete planes into enemy vessels which they set afire with gasoline and exploded with bombs. Eventually thousands of youthful Japanese fanatics enlisted for these fatal missions which required little training. Their *corps d'élite* received the name kamikaze, which means "Heavenly Wind," and dates back to 1570, when a typhoon scattered a Chinese invasion fleet headed for Japan.

The secret of the kamikazes' success, which began at Leyte Gulf but did not end there, dated back to long before the sixteenth century. Outstripped by the Americans in the technology of war, the Japanese reverted to one of their earliest traditions, imparting the suicidal fervor of their ancient warriors to the most effective military weapon that the twentieth century had yet produced. Although they hit upon that combination of the old and the new too late to save themselves from eventual defeat, they had revived a spirit which, harnessed to weapons yet to come, might doom the whole world to the kamikazes' fate.

·3·

THE JAPANESE DID NOT WAIT for June and the fall of Saipan—not to mention October and the battle of Leyte Gulf—to begin preparing for the worst. With the Americans advancing across the Pacific and the Southeast Asia Co-Prosperity Sphere disintegrating, Japan's army leaders chose the month of May as the time to launch an overland drive from the Chinese river port of Hankow on the Yangtze to the Indochinese border, five hundred miles to the south. On the way, they also planned to overrun the American air base at Kweilin, headquarters of General Chennault's Fourteenth Air Force, which had sunk one million tons of Japanese shipping—one fifth of the entire Japanese merchant fleet. If the Japanese could knock out Kweilin, establish a land route to southeast Asia, and annihilate Chiang Kai-shek's ground forces in the area, the Americans might drop their demand for unconditional surrender and settle for a negotiated peace.

The Japanese offensive opened in early May with instant victory at Changsha, some four hundred miles south of Hankow and more than five hundred miles east of Chungking. General Hsueh Yueh, self-styled "Tiger of Changsha," disliked and distrusted Chiang Kai-shek but had only 12,000 troops of his own to hold the city against twice as many Japanese attackers. Chiang had kept for himself—primarily for use against the Communists—most of the military supplies he had received from the United States, and it was another month before his Sixty-second Army arrived, several hundred miles south of Changsha, to help Hsueh and several other generals and their 15,000 troops stop the Japanese there. But the two Chinese armies and their generals could not agree on a common strategy; Chiang's men held back; Hsueh's suffered another setback. The campaign ended in August almost a thousand miles south of where it had started. In a five-day battle at the gateway to South China's Kwangsi Province and to Kweilin, its capital, Chiang Kai-shek's Ninety-third Army disappeared from the face of the earth. Its commander had made such a botch of the battle, and his troops had looted so many supplies, that Chiang ordered him and several other high officers shot.

Chiang's troubles came from two directions: General Stilwell in

Chungking and the Chinese Communists in the northwest. Ever since the summer of 1942, after his ignominious retreat from Burma, Stilwell had striven to break the Japanese blockade of the Burma Road. This called for simultaneous infantry drives from Ledo in India and from Kunming in China, converging upon Myitkyina in north Burma. At the same time, a third force was to advance eastward from Kunming to Kweilin and drive from there to the sea. It came as no surprise to Stilwell when the British, in the spring of 1944, found it impossible to mount Buccaneer, the amphibious invasion of Burma that they had half promised at Cairo. But that did not prevent the three Chinese divisions that Stilwell had trained at Ledo, plus an assortment of crack British and American forces, from fighting their way through two hundred miles of jungle, between December 1943 and August 1944, when they reached Myitkyina. Chiang had never approved of the campaign, but in April he agreed to sanction a second offensive from Kunming, crossing the Salween River and joining Stilwell's troops in the final stage of their drive to Myitkyina. For the first time in eight years of warfare, a predominantly Chinese army had won an extended campaign against the Japanese.

By this time the British-Indian Fourteenth Army under General William J. Slim also appeared in Burma. At the end of June, 1944, it shattered the Japanese Fifteenth Army's attempt to invade India, driving the Japanese beyond the Chindwin River in northwestern Burma. Stilwell referred to Slim as "slick Slim" who nevertheless recognized Stilwell's virtues more clearly than Stilwell recognized his. Like Churchill, Slim wrote history as brilliantly as he made it, and his *From Defeat into Victory* is one of the few first-person accounts of the Second World War worthy to stand beside Churchill's. Of Stilwell Slim wrote: "He was two people, one when he had an audience and a quite different person when talking to you alone. I think it amused him to keep up in public the 'Vinegar Joe, Tough Guy' attitude, especially in front of his staff. Americans, whether they liked him or not—and he had more enemies among them than among the British—were all scared of him. He had courage to an extent few people have, and determination, which, as he usually concentrated it along narrow lines, had a dynamic force. He was not a great soldier in the highest sense, but he was a real leader in the field; no one else I knew could have made his Chinese do what they did. He was, undoubtedly, the most colorful character in Southeast Asia —and I liked him"—words never echoed by Stilwell concerning Slim.

During August and September 1944, Stilwell paid several visits to eastern China, where he gave the final orders to blow up the American installations at Kweilin. The contrast between the campaign just won by the Chinese troops he had trained and the performance of the Chinese Nationalist forces at Changsha and Kweilin lost Chiang some more face: Stilwell had not only proved himself a more effective commander than Chiang of Chiang's own troops. The success of the Myitkyina campaign added further weight to Stilwell's repeated demands that Chiang use fewer troops blockading the Communists in the northwest and more fighting the Japanese in the southeast.

Clarence Gauss, United States ambassador at Chungking, shared Stilwell's nonconfidence in Chiang. But, instead of spelling out his gripes to Chiang, Gauss communicated them to the State Department and to President Roosevelt, who dispatched Vice President Wallace, during May and June, on a China mission that took him first to the Communist-controlled areas and then to the Nationalist capital of Chungking. When Wallace returned in July he quoted Chiang as having told him that the Communists were working for the collapse of the Kuomintang before the end of the war, because the Kuomintang needed only to survive the war to be able to turn and rend the Communists afterward. But Averell Harriman quoted Stalin as having remarked to him in June: "The Chinese Communists are not real Communists. They are margarine Communists."

Roosevelt, however, did not wait for Wallace's return to cut the ground out from under both Chiang and Stilwell. This he had already done on July 28 at Honolulu, when he gave MacArthur the green light to proceed at once with the invasion of the Philippines, a decision that not only favored MacArthur over Nimitz but also gave the triphibious invasion of Japan priority over large-scale operations on the Chinese mainland. However, as a sop to Chiang, Roosevelt, in early August, sent two personal emissaries to Chungking fully authorized to deal with every detail of the situation there. Donald M. Nelson, head of the War Production Board, had the assignment of surveying China's economic needs for war and peace and of recommending what kind of American specialists and how many American supplies would be required to meet those needs. Nelson, a former top executive at Sears, Roebuck, had won Roosevelt's confidence because of his ability to work smoothly with labor leaders, New Dealers, professional military men, and the business community. The more delicate and protracted assignment in China went to General Patrick J. Hurley, Hoover's former secretary of war, who had proved himself an equally effective political troubleshooter in Australia and at the Kremlin. Inasmuch as Nelson had also enjoyed doing business with Stalin, both he and Hurley flew to Moscow, where they discussed China with Molotov, Nelson directing the questioning and Molotov leading his two American visitors down the garden path with assurances that the Soviet Union of course wanted friendly relations with a unified China—the main difficulty being that Chiang spent so much time fighting the Communists that he had none left to make friends with the Russians. As for the Communists, Molotov downgraded them, just as Stalin had done in his conversation with Harriman two months before. All of which gratified Roosevelt, who liked nothing better than a Republican businessman who found that Stalin talked his language—except, perhaps, a Republican politician who saw eye to eye with Stalin on foreign affairs.

·4·

By MID-SEPTEMBER, when Nelson and Hurley arrived at Chungking, the campaigns in the Pacific promised so much and conditions in China had deteriorated so fast that Chiang had little difficulty in having Stilwell relieved of his command and sent home. Wallace had advised as much in June; by September Stilwell was telling his cronies: "The cure for China's troubles is the elimination of Chiang Kai-shek." On October 13, Hurley cabled the President: "There is no issue between you and Chiang Kai-shek except Stilwell. . . . My opinion is that if you sustain Stilwell in this controversy, you will lose Chiang Kai-shek and you will probably lose China with him." Roosevelt took Hurley's advice and within a few days also lost the services of Ambassador Gauss, who responded to the removal of Stilwell by submitting his own resignation. Whether for better or worse, things could never be the same again. While relieving Stilwell of his command, the Joint Chiefs split the former China-India-Burma theater in two, shifting General Albert C. Wedemeyer from the post he had held for a year as chief of staff to Lord Mountbatten, at the Ceylon headquarters of the Southeast Asia Command, to Chungking as commanding general of the United States forces in the new, separate China theater. The Joint Chiefs also authorized Wedemeyer to accept the post of chief of staff to Chiang Kai-shek, who had already approved. General Daniel Sultan became commanding general of the United States forces in the India-Burma theater, replacing General Wedemeyer there.

·5·

IT WAS BAD ENOUGH for Chiang to demand the replacement of the one American commander with the courage and experience to save him, his government, and their country. To make matters worse, Chiang's timing ensured his own destruction. By the latter half of 1944 the campaigns of MacArthur in the southwest Pacific and of Nimitz in the central Pacific had developed such momentum that their appeals for more manpower and more fire power had an urgency that no spokesman for the China theater could match. Marshall and Stimson had pleaded Stilwell's case to the end, but only as against Chiang and Chennault, never in behalf of the China theater as against the two Pacific theaters. Eventually, it was Marshall who again proved himself a shrewd judge of men and events by backing Wedemeyer as Stilwell's ideal replacement.

Born at Omaha, Nebraska, in 1897, the son of a German father and a French Huguenot mother, Albert Coady Wedemeyer was graduated from West Point in 1919 and from the General Staff College at Leavenworth in 1936, followed by two years at the German War College in Berlin. His family background, the generation to which he belonged, and his military education disposed him to take a critical view of United States policy during both world wars and the years between. In his *Wedemeyer Reports!*, Wedemeyer reports that his study of history convinced him that the British bore as much responsibility as the Germans for the First World War. Of the Second World War he wrote: "If we had followed the policy advocated by ex-President Hoover, Senator Taft, and other patriotic Americans, we probably would have stood aside until our intervention could enforce a just, and therefore enduring, peace instead of giving unconditional aid to Communist Russia. And if, after we became involved in the war, Roosevelt and Churchill had not sought to obliterate Germany, which was tantamount to destroying the power equilibrium on the Continent, we might not have fought in vain."

Ever the activistic extrovert, General Wedemeyer possessed a talent for military planning, a charm of manner, an equilibrium of temperament, and a capacity for hard work that caused General Marshall to select him, as early as July, 1941, to serve as secretary to General Leonard T. Gerow, chief of the War Plans Division. In this capacity, Wedemeyer helped to frame the Victory Program that became the first blue-print for American strategy during the Second World War. Although a noninterventionist prior to Pearl Harbor, Wedemeyer—like Marshall and Stimson—always favored a cross-Channel invasion of Europe at the earliest possible moment and opposed, root and branch, Churchill's Mediterranean strategy. The first irony in Wedemeyer's wartime career came in 1942 when he favored a second front as urgently as Stalin. The second came in 1943 when Marshall reluctantly released him from the war-planning staff in Washington to serve as chief of staff to that most British of Britishers, the half-German Lord Mountbatten who, in his turn, released Wedemeyer with equal reluctance to Chiang Kai-shek a year later.

At Chungking the bitter tea in General Wedemeyer's cup of ironies overflowed. Here the prewar nointerventionist, the wartime propo-nent of the second front first, the tireless critic of unconditional surren-der found himself charged with redeeming pledges that the policies he had opposed left him helpless to fulfill. Yet, it was his friend and pro-tector, General Marshall, who had chosen him for this impossible task —and the better he performed it, the better a figure his *bête noire*, President Roosevelt, would cut in history. Stilwell did not remain at Chungking even to greet his successor—much less to brief him. On Oc-tober 31, Ambassador Gauss welcomed Wedemeyer with the remark: "We should have pulled the plug and let the whole Chinese Govern-ment go down the drain." A week later, Gauss' successor, General Hur-ley, flew to Yenan to celebrate the anniversary of the Bolshevik Revolu-tion with Mao Tse-tung and Chou En-lai.

For the next month, Wedemeyer found himself up to his neck reor-ganizing his staff and organizing some of the Chinese forces under Chiang's command to block another Japanese advance that threatened Kunming and even Chungking. Hurley's effusive personality more than filled the vacuum left by the saturnine Stilwell's departure. Hurley and Chiang hit it off at once and with Wedemeyer's arrival things went still better. Wedemeyer's new military duties filled all his time, and he gladly left the politicking to Hurley, an old hand at the game. Or-phaned in childhood, he had long since learned to cultivate his abun-dant energies and his overflowing talents. He learned to speak the lan-guage of the Choctaw Indians in his native Oklahoma, worked his way through law school, sometimes as a coal miner, sometimes as a cowboy. He served as an officer in the First World War and as Hoover's secretary of war ten years later. By the time he came to China, Hurley's hair had turned white, but his bristling moustache and tall, erect figure made him every inch a soldier.

Arriving at Yenan's primitive airfield on November 7 (the anniversary of the Bolshevik seizure of power), Hurley greeted Mao Tse-tung (whom he later called Moose-dung) with a Choctaw war cry. His hosts reminded him of armed, Oklahoma Republicans. At the dinner in his (and Lenin's) honor he presented the terms on which Chiang proposed co-operation between Chungking and Yenan. They called for Mao, his party, and the regions they occupied to submit themselves to Kuomintang control. Mao at once denounced the terms and the men who had proposed them. Hurley lashed back. The evening ended in a deadlock.

The next day, however, Hurley drew up what seemed to him a fair solution. It called for a coalition government with Communist participation, instead of a Kuomintang government, in which the Communists would hold one seat, and an integration of Communist with Nationalist armies, under control of the central coalition government, instead of the subjection of the Communist armies to Nationalist control. And, for good measure, Hurley added a Chinese equivalent of the United States Bill of Rights. The Communists welcomed the Hurley proposals, to which he signed his name as a token of good faith. But he made it plain he could not speak for Chiang; he could only urge Chiang to put his own name on the dotted line. The Communists delegated Chou En-lai to accompany Hurley back to Chungking to discuss matters with Chiang, who, on account of illness, refused to see Chou for several days, and then saw him only briefly, and rejected all the Hurley proposals. Chiang stood pat on the terms he had sent the Communists through Hurley. When Hurley suggested that Chou accept Chiang's offer, with the hope of getting more concessions later, Chou charged Hurley with trying to sell him out to Chiang. A plea by General Wedemeyer proved futile.

·6·

MEANWHILE IN WASHINGTON, ill health had forced Cordell Hull to step down as secretary of state. Into his shoes stepped Edward R. Stettinius, Jr., former board chairman of the United States Steel Corporation and improbable protégé of Harry Hopkins. The new secretary's almost complete ignorance of the Far East created a vacuum that Joseph C.

Grew, the new undersecretary, could not entirely fill. Grew's ten years in the Tokyo embassy made him uniquely qualified to pass judgment on matters relating to Japan, but, by the same token, caused him to view China, as many other Americans did, from a somewhat distorted perspective.

By the end of 1944, the Chinese Communists had lost faith in Hurley but he had not lost hope in them. On December 24, he wrote to the new secretary of state: "There is little, if any, difference between the avowed principles of the National Government, the Kuomintang, and the avowed principles of the Chinese Communist Party." (True enough, to those who recognized "avowed" as the operative word.) Later he added: "The Communists are not, in fact, Communist, they are striving for democratic principles; and the one-party, one-man personal government is not, in fact, Fascist, it is striving for democratic principles. Both the Communists and the Kuomintang have a long way to go, but, if we know the way, if we are clear-minded, tolerant, and patient, we can be helpful." But time had already run out. T. V. Soong made a last attempt to bridge the gap between Chungking and Yenan by offering the Communists membership on a political affairs committee, under the Supreme National Defense Council, which Chiang dominated. The Communists refused. They had already launched offensive operations in eastern China, with a view to controlling its coast by the time the Americans might arrive. They scorned Chiang for the disasters his armies had suffered in 1944. They knew he could contribute nothing important to the final assault on Japan. At one time, they had resented his assumption that he alone could speak for all China. Now they regarded him with contempt and would have no part of any arrangement giving him the complete authority he still demanded.

Foreseeing the decline of Chiang and the rise of the Communists, Stilwell and Gauss had tried to serve as intermediaries between the two. Their very understanding of the realities antagonized Chiang, and Stilwell's acid personality did not make his views any more acceptable at Chungking. Hurley knew little about the background, but made up in assurance for what he lacked in knowledge. When the Communists refused to subordinate themselves to Chiang, that finished them as far as Hurley was concerned. But it did not finish Hurley as far as Roosevelt was concerned. Roosevelt had now backed Chiang for so long that he could afford no more generals like Stilwell, no more ambassadors like Gauss. As a good soldier, Wedemeyer accepted his new command at Chungking; as a good soldier of fortune, Hurley welcomed the profferred ambassadorship a few weeks later. Not that either man had any inkling at the time of what lay in store. But the more they shunned the examples their predecessors had set and accommodated themselves to Chiang Kai-shek, the more deeply they committed themselves to share his doom.

• • •

While the Americans converted much of their wartime economy into a peacetime one that enabled them to speed recovery and prosperity in western Europe, the Russians had to maintain much of their Red Army and their war industries in order to fasten their control on the lands and peoples of eastern Europe. The weapons and methods that they had used to smash Germany and the Germans became the instruments with which they not only enslaved their neighbors but shackled themselves. The Americans could point to a more constructive record in western Europe than the Russians could point to in the east. But the war in the Pacific swept the Americans into an adventure of another kind. In eastern Europe, the Russians became their own worst enemies. In eastern Asia, the Americans fell victims to the accelerated technology that enabled them to smash Japan and the Japanese far ahead of schedule and at a fraction of the estimated cost. The ships and planes, the landing craft and tanks that sped the Americans on their way across the Pacific enabled them not only to reduce Asia's one industrialized nation to rubble. The industrial-military complex that brought the Americans mastery over the Pacific and victory over Japan gave them an advantage over China and all the other preindustrial nations of Asia far greater than the British, French, or Dutch colonialists had ever enjoyed in that part of the world.

This narrative will cover, in due course, the role that America's atomic weapons played in ending the war against Japan and in shaping the postwar world. But more than six months before the midsummer of 1945 when the atomic age began, American technology had already brought the Japanese almost to their knees and had laid the foundations on which the United States built its postwar industrial supremacy. Nor did it take the atomic bomb to convince the peoples of China, India, Indochina, or Indonesia that their hour had come. Although the Japanese had driven the British from the Malay peninsula and from Burma, the French from Indochina, and the Dutch from the East Indies, they had done no better in China or in southern Asia than the Germans had done in Russia or in southeast Europe.

President Roosevelt had long sensed the crucial role that the Soviet

Union had to play in the war against Germany. That Stalin, through his pact with Hitler, would almost do himself and the Soviet Union in, Roosevelt did not foresee. Nor was Roosevelt alone, at the end of 1944, in not perceiving that Stalin had again miscalculated (this time compensating for his excessive prewar trust in Nazi Germany with his excessive postwar fear of all Germans and of their wartime allies in eastern Europe). With the moment of Germany's unconditional surrender drawing ever nearer, Churchill and Roosevelt felt it necessary to meet again with Stalin to discuss that prospect. In addition, Roosevelt attached equal importance to conferring with Stalin on the final stages of the war against Japan, for which the United States bore the chief responsibility. Indeed, as Roosevelt saw it, the future of Asia posed even more questions than the future of Europe.

At the time of the Japanese attack on Pearl Harbor, the future of Germany and Europe loomed larger in Roosevelt's mind than the future of China and Asia. But by the end of 1944 the priorities had begun to shift. China and Japan now concerned even Stalin as much as Germany and France did. Regarding the future of the British, French, and Dutch colonial empires, Roosevelt had good reason at the time to feel that his views resembled Stalin's more closely than they did Churchill's. But what neither Roosevelt nor Stalin nor Churchill could calculate with any accuracy was the rate at which events were moving. Already —before either Germany or Japan yet seemed on the verge of surrender —the war's center of gravity had begun to shift from Europe to Asia, a process that seemed likely to continue into the indefinite future.

XIX
Yalta

·1·

BEFORE 1944 RAN ITS COURSE, the military decisions reached at Teheran had proved so successful that the three men who made them had to meet again to deal with the political consequences. They fixed upon early February 1945 as the time, and the Crimean town of Yalta as the place at which to foregather. Going on from where they had left off at Teheran, they found at the top of their agenda combined Anglo-Soviet-American operations against Germany.

On February 4, 1945, at the first plenary session, Colonel General Alexei Antonov, deputy chief of the Soviet General Staff, stole the show with a prepared paper on the Soviet winter offensive. Here he reported that on January 12 four Russian armies, totaling three million men, began advancing against three quarters of a million Germans along a four-hundred-mile front that extended from the Baltic clear across Poland to Czechoslovakia. The northernmost army cut off East Prussia from the rest of Germany and headed for Königsberg; the second drove for Danzig; the third, commanded by Marshal Zhukov, took Warsaw in three days, surrounded Posen, and headed for Berlin; the fourth, commanded by Marshal Ivan Koniev, overran Silesia and headed for Breslau. By the time the Yalta Conference opened, the Russians had advanced as much as three hundred miles at one point and had come to within forty miles of Berlin at another. Thanks largely to their artillery fire, they had put forty-five German divisions out of action. But Antonov also spoke of stiffening German resistance and warned that the Germans might bolster their defenses with as many as thirty or thirty-five crack divisions from France, Italy, and Norway.

Stalin and the Soviet delegation applauded Antonov's paper. They saw in it a sharp and timely reminder to the Anglo-Americans of the swift Soviet response to Churchill's urgent appeal of January 6 for immediate Soviet action to draw off German troops from the Ardennes. Because of that appeal, the Russians launched their winter offensive, under less than ideal conditions, only six days later. And when Churchill turned out to have exaggerated Eisenhower's setback in the Ardennes, Stalin had all the more reason to resent the way General Marshall and Field Marshal Brooke followed up Antonov's masterly report of the massive Soviet winter campaign with their crisp, smug accounts of the compromise they had reached between the Eisenhower broad-front strategy and Montgomery's preference for a concentrated attack on the heart of Germany's war industries in the north. Moreover, the best that Marshall and Brooke could do to match Soviet performance was to outline their plans to drive the Germans from the west bank of the Rhine by the end of February and to start their crossings of the Rhine by early March. Only then would Montgomery and his British and Canadian armies possess irresistible strength in the north, while American troops would be responsible for the remaining ninety percentage of the Western Front, except for a narrow sector, held by a single French army, in the south.

.   .   .

Stalin knew little and cared less about the Eisenhower-Montgomery split. But the Anglo-Americans had to wait almost twenty years to get the full details concerning a deeper split between Stalin and several of the most successful Soviet commanders. According to Erich Kuby, one of West Germany's most respected journalists, "Stalin [at Yalta] held a trump card that might easily have won him the game for Germany: he was in a position to order the occupation of Berlin by Soviet forces. But Stalin chose not to play it." Kuby made the statement in his book *The Russians and Berlin 1945*, published in the United States in English translation in 1968. Two years later, Diane Shaver Clemens, in her comprehensive and meticulously researched *Yalta*, added: "Kuby was right," and quoted articles by Marshal Vasili Chuikov, former supreme commander of the Soviet Land Forces, from Soviet publications in 1964 and 1965. Chuikov had served under Marshal Zhukov, whose First Byelorussian Army Group had fought its way from Stalingrad in February 1943 to within 40 miles of Berlin, exactly two years later when the Yalta Conference began.

In October and November, 1944, Chuikov, Zhukov, Antonov, and other Soviet commanders had worked out the details of a Soviet win-the-war offensive to open on January 20, 1945, to capture Berlin in fifteen days, and to defeat Germany in another month. But Stalin's "overly cautious" supreme command turned them down. In retrospect, however, Stalin's discretion makes at least as much sense as his generals' valor. In tying up more than half of Germany's armed forces, the Soviet summer offensive of 1944 had not only made possible the success of the Normandy landings. In overrunning Romania, Hungary, and most of the Balkans, the Red army had brought the eastern half of Europe under its control at minimum cost. Had Stalin driven the bulk of the Red army straight to Berlin, he would have encountered much heavier resistance than the Germans could put up farther south and thereby perhaps have forfeited his last, best chance to make all of eastern Europe a permanent buffer zone against future aggression from the west.

But, speaking of permanent, neither Stalin nor his generals, neither the friends nor the enemies of the Soviet Union in Britain and the United States, took sufficient account at the time of the permanent damage Stalin's purges of the 1930's and his forced-labor camps of the 1940's inflicted on the Soviet Union. By the end of the war, Soviet officials publicly and even proudly acknowledged that their wartime losses ran as high as twenty million killed. But not until another twenty years had passed did the outside world discover what neither Stalin nor his successors—even including Khrushchev—had ever publicly revealed, that almost as many Russians met their deaths at Stalin's hands as at Hitler's. These unacknowledged losses not only went a long way toward accounting for Stalin's "overly cautious" Berlin strategy. A generation later they still contribute to that air of mystery that remains a permanent fixture of Soviet policy, both foreign and domestic.

· 2 ·

THAT OPENING CLASH between the Soviet and Anglo-American military strategists at Yalta reflected the same mutual mistrust and anxiety that permeated the dispute over Poland and consumed more of the conference's time than any other subject. But the Soviet winter offensive of 1945 described by Antonov had done more than put the Red army in position to take Berlin. It meant that the fate of Poland now lay entirely in Stalin's hands. The final text of the Yalta Declaration could therefore express no more than an aspiration that Stalin had repeatedly assailed and that Roosevelt had never more than half supported: "The provisional government which is now functioning in Poland should therefore be reorganized on a broader democratic basis, with the inclusion of democratic leaders from Poland itself and from Poles abroad. This new government should then be called the Polish Provisional Government of National Unity." The words "democratic leaders" and "broader democratic basis" could mean whatever each one of the high contracting parties chose to make them mean. The communiqué bound none of the signatories either to take or renounce any specific action toward Poland; it merely described what "should" happen and "authorized" the British and American ambassadors in Moscow to "consult" with Molotov and with "members of the present Provisional Government and other democratic leaders from within Poland and from abroad with a view to the reorganization along the above lines."

Roosevelt and Churchill had done what they could—each in his own way—to persuade Stalin to make Poland safer for their kind of democracy. But Stalin had the power and the will to disregard their pleas and to proceed with the imposition of his own settlement on the Soviet-occupied zone of Germany. All three had accepted the procedure of unconditional surrender. All three had agreed that the German war machine and the industries that supported it were to be delivered to the victors or destroyed. After unconditional surrender, as Herbert Feis put it in *Roosevelt, Churchill, and Stalin:* "Supreme authority was to be exercised by the American, British, and Soviet Commanders in Chief, each in his own zone of occupation, and also jointly in matters affecting Germany as a whole. They were to act together as members of a top organ called the Control Council." These zones of occupation had been settled but not ratified. At the time of Yalta, France had no specific role. In December, de Gaulle had conferred at Moscow with Stalin, who described him as an "awkward and stubborn man," but not a very complicated one. De Gaulle's estimates of the contribution France had made to winning the war seemed to Stalin unrealistic. Not until the seventh and last meeting of the Big Three on February 11 did Hopkins finally persuade Roosevelt to go along with Churchill and give France an occupation zone in West Germany and a seat on the Control Council. Stalin as suddenly, and even more unexpectedly, concurred.

Because the two-front battle of Germany had barely begun, the military leaders at Yalta focused on the co-ordination of their two efforts. As Herbert Feis put it: "The record of the talk about co-ordinating efforts against Germany gives no signal of competition between the Western Allies and the Soviet Union for renown or political advantage to be won by advancing the farthest possible. . . . Thus no attempt was made to reach agreement as to the places or lines along which the armies coming from the east and from the west should stop. Their destination was to be decided by the course of battle; the question of where and how long the armies of each should *remain* was left to the makers of political arrangements."

In the assignment of the ultimate zones of occupation, the Greater Berlin district fell deep within the Soviet area. But the agreement on control machinery stipulated that a Kommandatura, appointed by the commanders in chief of the four zones, should administer Berlin. At Yalta, the American military planners proposed that "the general principle be accepted of freedom of transit by each nation concerned between the main occupied area and the forces occupying Berlin and similar isolated areas." The British military planners concurred; the Russians hung back. The matter was deferred.

Although the fluid military situation compelled the postponement of such political decisions, certain economic decisions, of prime political importance, could not wait. In September 1944, at the second Quebec Conference, Roosevelt and Churchill set off a series of fireworks among their military and political advisers by giving casual and tentative endorsement to a plan by Henry Morgenthau, Jr., the United States Secretary of the Treasury, to transform Germany from an industrial into a pastoral country. Secretary of State Hull and Secretary of War Stimson strongly disapproved, arguing that a deindustrialized Germany would impoverish all of Europe. "Henry pulled a boner," commented Roosevelt, and the "Morgenthau plan" was shelved. But its very drawbacks drew attention to Germany's economic importance to Europe. Already, at Teheran, Stalin had approved of Roosevelt's suggestion to break up Germany into five independent states; a year later Churchill proposed splitting Germany into two parts (Bavaria and Prussia) and placing the Ruhr and Westphalia under international control.

At Yalta, however, Churchill argued for the wisdom of deferring any decision as long as possible. Whereupon Stalin produced, from the Soviet delegation, Ivan Maisky, his wartime ambassador to Britain, who presented a mass of facts and figures justifying the imposition on Germany of a twenty-billion-dollar war indemnity, in kind, half of it to go to the Soviet Union, forty per cent to Britain and the United States, and the remainder to other victims of German aggression. Churchill objected, recalling that the imposition of excessive reparations on Germany after the last war had led to a cycle of depression, Fascism, and war, which he did not want to see repeated. Hopkins urged Roosevelt to support Stalin against Churchill to the extent of passing the buck to the Reparations Commission, along with the minutes showing British disagreement. Although Stalin had easily blocked Churchill's efforts to rescind, at the conference table, the political consequences of the Red army's sweep across Poland, he had not been able to prevent Churchill from taking more of the conference's time with Poland than he and Maisky had been able to consume arguing for twenty billion dollars in German reparations. More important, however, Stalin had no such means of forcing these reparations from Germany as he had of forcing most of eastern Europe into the Soviet postwar empire. So it ended in a draw, as Stalin left Yalta with no more chance of getting ten billion dollars' worth of reparations from Germany than Churchill had of getting free elections in Poland.

·3·

ALTHOUGH THE BATTLE OF GERMANY had barely begun at the time of the Yalta Conference, the Red army found itself playing the same role in western Poland and eastern Germany as it had already played in Romania, Hungary, and Bulgaria, this time extending Soviet territories westward at the expense of eastern Poland and then extending Polish territories westward at the expense of eastern Germany. While Roosevelt, at Casablanca, had offered the Germans no alternative to unconditional surrender, Stalin followed the examples of Lenin and Wilson to the extent of appealing to the German people over the heads of their wartime leaders. But he did this in his own way, which had hardly more in common with Lenin's than it had with Wilson's.

Lenin had expressed willingness to give a Communist revolution that had not yet occurred in industrialized Germany priority over the Communist revolution that had already occurred in backward Russia. Stalin, on the other hand, assigned to the Red army the task of spreading Soviet Communism to eastern Europe, culminating in Germany. But he did not call upon the German people to make their own Communist revolution, as Lenin had, much less their own democratic revolution, as Wilson had. Although Hitler had smashed the Communist party in Germany as completely as he had smashed the Socialist party, one or two hundred hard-core German Communists had made their way to Moscow before and during the war. More, however, stayed in Germany, where most of them remained faithful to Stalin in their varying fashions. But their headquarters had shifted from German to Russian soil.

After Stalingrad, Stalin began to make serious efforts to bring German war prisoners and captured German officers into Communist-controlled, anti-Nazi organizations, one of which Field Marshal von Paulus consented to head. But no comparable organization made any headway among the German armed forces on the other side of the lines, where Communist propaganda carried little more weight than Nazi propaganda carried among the Russians. By the time of the Yalta Conference, the German collapse had gone so far that Stalin had to reappraise his German policy, which had never depended solely on organizing anti-Nazi prisoners of war. When he did not get the reparations windfall he demanded at Yalta, he lost interest in trying to crush Germany with one hand while milking it with the other. Now, however, that a German revolution no longer offered a serious alternative to unconditional surrender, the victors could choose between a dismembered and a partitioned Germany. The dismembered Germany might in time become either a unified democratic Germany, a unified Communist Germany, or a permanent vacuum in the heart of Europe. The partitioned Germany might in time result in a democratic West German state and a Communist East German state. Subsequent events followed the second course.

·4·

THE CONDITIONS of wartime secrecy under which the Yalta Conference took place precluded any recourse to the "open diplomacy" that Wilson often preached but did not always practice. At Yalta it had to be secret agreements secretly arrived at until the release of the official communiqué on February 11. But it took several months for the most momentous decision taken at Yalta to become known. This had to do with the timing and circumstances of the Soviet Union's declaration of war on Japan. Whereas the Yalta Conference spent a maximum amount of time and reached a minimum amount of agreement on Poland, it took Roosevelt, Stalin, and their aides only a few hours to agree on the conditions under which the Soviet Union would declare war on Japan. Churchill did not even attend the meeting but simply endorsed its decisions, which stipulated that within three months of the German surrender, the Soviet Union would enter the war against Japan on condition that the *status quo* of the Mongolian People's Republic be preserved and that the rights lost by Russia to Japan after their turn-of-the-century war be restored. This meant that Japan had to turn over the Kurile Islands and the southern half of Sakhalin Island to the Soviet Union.

The most important provisions in the agreement dealt with China and called for concessions from Chiang Kai-shek, whom Roosevelt had neither consulted nor informed. These included internationalization of the Chinese port of Dairen, where the pre-eminent interests of the Soviet Union would be safeguarded, and the reinstatement of Port Arthur as a Soviet naval base. The Chinese Eastern and South Manchurian Railroads would come under joint Soviet-Chinese operation, "the pre-eminent interests of the Soviet Union" being safeguarded and Chinese sovereignty over Manchuria restored. Roosevelt agreed to obtain Chiang's concurrence for all matters bearing on China; the Soviet Union expressed willingness to conclude a pact of friendship and alliance with China's National government and to assist it and its armed forces in liberating China from the Japanese yoke. Finally, all details of the agreement were to be withheld for one year.

·5·

IF THE SECRET decisions reached by Roosevelt and Stalin, spelling out the terms on which the Soviet Union would enter the war against Japan, overshadowed all other agreements reached at Yalta, the plans to transform the United Nations from the greatest war coalition in history to the most formidable international peace organization ever assembled stand out as Yalta's greatest single achievement. Stalin got his way in Poland. Churchill blocked Stalin's efforts to dismember Germany and then collect ten billion dollars in reparations, in kind and in labor. But Stalin settled for the partition of Germany, forty per cent of its territory, including the bulk of Prussia, passing into Soviet control. Roosevelt, having originally favored almost as drastic a German settlement as Stalin, preferred to concentrate his ebbing energies on the establishment of the postwar United Nations before the fighting had ended.

To Lord Moran, Churchill's politically-minded personal physician, this came as no surprise. "To a doctor's eye," he wrote in his diary during the course of the conference, "the President appears a very sick man. He has all the symptoms of hardening of the arteries of the brain in an advanced stage, so I give him only a few months to live." Hopkins he found in even worse condition. A fatally defective digestive condition known as hemochromatosis confined him to bed half the time. "Physically, he is only half in this world." When Hopkins told Moran that Roosevelt did not want to fall out with Stalin and felt confident of Russian co-operation after the war, Roosevelt did not, in Moran's view, "seem to see that he had invented a Russia that did not exist."

But had not Moran, perhaps, invented a Roosevelt who did not exist? His observations on both Roosevelt and Hopkins have the ring of medical truth, but hardly the ring of political and psychological truth. Although Moran noted that "in American eyes the first purpose of this conference is to lay the foundation of an international peace organization," he underrated the exaltation and tenacity with which those two dying men flung their ebbing energies into the fight for the earliest possible establishment of a world security organization—with the accent on the "earliest possible." The one lesson that Wilson's career had burned most deeply into Roosevelt's memory was the necessity of setting up his postwar security organization while the waging of war still held the allied coalition together, and before final victory could sow the seeds of dissension. The postwar settlements would not last forever; the charter of the permanent, postwar United Nations envisaged by Roosevelt could be amended. But the more rapidly the collapse of Germany approached, the more urgent it became to commit the Anglo-Soviet-American military coalition to build a postwar international organization to secure the peace that had at last come into view.

Stalin had already made it clear that the Soviet Union was not prepared to swallow any compromises in eastern Europe. In connection with the international peace organization, he then demanded sixteen seats on its General Assembly (one for each Soviet republic) in addition to the Soviet Union's permanent seat on the Security Council. Roosevelt found this wholly unacceptable, and he and Hopkins and Stettinius regarded it as a major concession when Stalin settled for only three seats on the General Assembly—one for the Soviet Union and one each for the Ukrainian and Byelorussian Republics. Stalin also accepted two slight modifications in the Security Council's voting procedure, one to the effect that "decisions of the Security Council on procedural matters should be made by an affirmative vote of seven members" and the other providing that "a party to a dispute should abstain from voting." The Yalta communiqué and the subsequent protocol merely offered these as suggestions to a conference of the United Nations, to be held on April 25 in the United States, to prepare a charter for the General International Organization.

The first and longest item in the protocol dealt with the "World Organization," and it was here that Roosevelt, Hopkins, and the American delegation to Yalta scored their outstanding triumph. Owing mainly to the Americans, and to some extent to Britain's Foreign Secretary Eden, the most precise, specific, and binding decisions reached at Yalta dealt with the unwritten charter of a nonexistent organization. Stalin, in his enthusiasm for decisions rather than discussions, for tangibles rather than abstractions, made firmer commitments concerning the unborn United Nations than he did concerning allies or enemies, reparations or boundaries. As for Roosevelt, his relative indifference to German and Polish questions commended him to Stalin, rather than the reverse. Nor did his consuming passion for a world security organization pose any immediate or inherent threat to the Soviet Union: it might even lend itself to the promotion of Soviet interests in the postwar world. Thus Roosevelt, who first transcended himself when the affliction of polio led to his spiritual rebirth, prepared to close his career by winning, before the Second World War had ended, the fight that Wilson lost after the First World War had been won.

. . .

The Yalta Conference bore out the old saying that no stream can rise higher than its source. Each of the three participants used different means to gain different ends—some of them self-defeating, some of them in conflict with one another, some of them reconcilable. Operating on the principle that possession is nine points of the law, Stalin sought primarily to hold those territories that the Red army had gained in eastern Europe and to regain some of the positions that the czars had once held in the Far East. But the methods he used to gain these ends backfired. Now here now there, now sooner now later, he found that he had overextended himself in all directions. Most of his troubles dated back to his purges of the 1930's, which went a long way toward accounting for his pact with Hitler. That he had dug the pit into which he later fell did not make that fate any more acceptable.

Churchill at Yalta refused to reconcile himself to the approaching liquidation of the British Empire and therefore did not at once foresee that the rearguard actions he fought against Roosevelt and Stalin served the interests of the British people no better than Stalin's forays into eastern Europe served the Russian people. With a longer and more consistent anti-Nazi record than Stalin's, Churchill also emerged from Yalta the best friend of the people of West Germany by saving them for western Europe. In so doing, Churchill also emerged from the Yalta

Conference as the best friend of General de Gaulle—or, at any rate, a better friend than either Roosevelt or Stalin proved himself. "Why was more to be demanded of Poland than of France?" asked Stalin, who could not see France playing any other postwar role than that of Britain's Poland, a reflection on Britain as much as on France.

"When a thing has become unavoidable, one should adapt oneself to it." Nobody has summed up Roosevelt's performance at Yalta better than he did himself in those words. Or as Lord Moran put it: "He doesn't like thinking things out, but waits for situations to develop and then adapts himself to them." Mrs. Clemens quotes both these remarks in her book Yalta, which she closes with the words: "It is perhaps relevant to ask what the world would have been like if the spirit of Yalta had triumphed." Her own pages answer her own question. Neither Hopkins nor Sherwood regarded Yalta as Roosevelt's finest hour, but to Roosevelt himself Yalta seemed, at the time, to mark the high point of his career—if only because it came near the end of a life during which events seldom stood still. At Yalta, Roosevelt accepted as unavoidable Stalin's domination of Poland and the extension of Soviet power halfway across Europe. But he did not accept as unavoidable a repetition of the mistakes Woodrow Wilson had made in connection with the League of Nations and if he could escape those mistakes only by accepting Stalin's rough treatment of Poland and Churchill's more forebearing attitude toward Germany, so be it.

Nobody had planned to have the Yalta Conference come out the way it did—or, indeed, any other particular way. Nobody could know at the time of Yalta what, if anything, would come of Roosevelt's supersecret Manhattan Project to produce an atomic bomb. But even before the first successful test explosion, Chiang Kai-shek wanted to make more— not fewer—concessions to Stalin in return for more assurances of Soviet support against Mao Tse-tung. "The significance of the Conference," Mrs. Clemens has written in the opening paragraph of Yalta, "lies partly in the fact that, although agreements made at Yalta were subsequently abandoned, the decisions made there portended a different course than relationships took after the war." But, of course, is it not the rule rather than the exception for human decisions to take a different course than they portended at the time they were taken, especially as events of the twentieth century continue along their accelerating course?

XX

Yalta Postscript

·1·

WHEN THE YALTA CONFERENCE assembled, the war against Japan still loomed large in Roosevelt's mind. On February 3, at his first meeting with Stalin, the President opened the conversation by offering to bet that MacArthur would take Manila before the Russians would take Berlin. Stalin replied with a laugh that those who bet on Manila would win. Could the laugh have expressed his delight with Roosevelt's apparent assumption that Berlin lay within the Russian sphere of operations just as clearly as Manila lay within the American? MacArthur's spectacular Philippine campaign provided no laughing matter to any well-informed Russian.

Back in October, the Japanese navy had fought and lost its last major engagement: the battle of Leyte Gulf. MacArthur at once followed through with a series of decisive land battles, first on Leyte Island, then on Mindoro, and finally on Luzon. In his *Reminiscences,* he has described the Leyte campaign, which ended on December 27, 1944, as "perhaps the greatest defeat in the annals of the Japanese Army." The enemy dead numbered 80,557; only 798 Japanese fell into American hands alive. American casualties totaled 3320 killed and 12,000 wounded.

After Leyte came Mindoro, where MacArthur's Eighth Army established a beachhead without the loss of a single life. The swift buildup that followed led the Japanese to rush most of their forces on Luzon from Lingayen Gulf in the north to the southern end of the island, which the Eighth Army now seemed in position to invade. But MacArthur had prepared his Sixth Army to land on Luzon's northern shore, where it could cut the Japanese supply route to their home islands.

While the Japanese prepared to repel MacArthur's Eighth Army at the southern end of Luzon, he landed the Sixth Army in the north, on the Lingayen beachhead, where he waded ashore on January 9, quickly establishing a beachhead twelve miles deep. By February 1, his troops had enveloped Manila, but it took them almost another month to occupy the whole city plus the Bataan peninsula, where the Americans had made their last stand three years before. On February 27, MacArthur announced the restoration of full constitutional government in the Philippines. Concerning the campaign as a whole, he wrote: "The enemy, during the operations, employed 23 divisions, approximately 450,000 men, all of which were practically annihilated. Our force comprised 17 divisions. This was one of the rare instances when, in a long campaign, a ground force of superior numbers was entirely destroyed by a numerically inferior opponent."

Having vindicated Roosevelt's decision to give the Philippine strategy priority over the Nimitz strategy of an immediate all-out assault on Japan, MacArthur renewed and redoubled his efforts to have all United States forces in the Pacific brought under his command. But the President could not again fly the Pacific to make an on-the-spot, face-to-face decision as he had in July. He therefore anticipated MacArthur's request for another meeting by assigning Robert Sherwood to undertake a wider and deeper study of the whole Pacific area than the President himself could make. Sherwood visited MacArthur at the general's temporary headquarters in Manila shortly after the city's occupation. The two men talked for almost three hours, and Sherwood "came away enormously impressed with his understanding and the breadth of his views" but "shocked by the inaccuracy of the information" held by the general and his immediate entourage. "To hear some of the staff officers talk, one would think that the War Department, the State Department, the Joint Chiefs of Staff—and, possibly, the White House itself—are under the domination of Communists and British imperialists."

These comments appeared in a memorandum prepared by Sherwood for the President—a memorandum that concluded with an extraordinary tribute to General MacArthur, whose "views on the future handling of Japan" not only impressed Sherwood but seem to have had the same effect upon his chief. Sherwood's interpretation of General MacArthur's views merits reproduction on three counts: first, because, as a professional writer, he summarizes these views in a clearer, more succinct prose than General MacArthur's own; second, because Sherwood's statement of MacArthur's views persuaded the President and his advisers and successors to select General MacArthur as the supreme allied commander in postwar Japan; finally, because these views suggest that on the subject of Asia in general and Japan in particular Roosevelt and MacArthur saw almost eye to eye.

"Tracing the history of Japan, particularly in the past century," Sherwood wrote the President, "the General expressed the conviction that the 'imperial sanctity' idea is a myth fabricated by the military for their own purposes. Essential to the continuance of this myth, he said, is the legend of invincibility; the Emperor remains a god only as long as the Army and Navy are all-conquering. The total destruction of Japanese military power, therefore, can involve (for the Japanese civil population) destruction of the concept of Hirohito's divinity. This will result in a spiritual vacuum and an opportunity for the introduction of new concepts. The Japanese people will have inevitable respect for as well as fear of the instruments of their own defeat. Believing that might makes right, they will conclude that we of the U.S.A. must be right. Furthermore the prestige throughout Asia that we have established by our Philippine policy and which will be vastly increased by conquest of Japan will make us the greatest instrument on the future development of Asia. If we exert that influence in an imperialistic manner, or for the sole purpose of commercial advantage, then we shall lose our golden opportunity; but if our influence and our strength are expressed in terms of essential liberalism, we shall have the friendship and co-operation of the Asiatic peoples far into the future.

"It seemed to be General MacArthur's view that the Japanese population if treated with stern justice and strength would be more capable of redemption than are the Germans."

.   .   .

General MacArthur's *Reminiscences* illuminate what Sherwood described at one point as his "persecution mania." At the height of the Philippines campaign, MacArthur received what he called "a shocking order" to release seventy of his transports to carry munitions from San Francisco to Vladivostok. He "protested violently," only to be "instructed to return most of the Pacific fleet to Admiral Nimitz to be used in the attack on Okinawa." That attack began on April 5. On April 6 a new directive went out from Washington, giving MacArthur command of all ground troops in the Pacific and Nimitz command of all naval units, while Arnold's Twentieth Air Force became a separate strategic command with headquarters at Washington. At Okinawa, Japanese planes—most of them kamikazes—sank 36 American ships, damaged

368 others, and destroyed more than 800 American planes. American casualties totaled 50,000. Iwo Jima cost 22,000 more. Perhaps a unified command under General MacArthur would have cut these losses in two; perhaps it would have doubled them; perhaps it would have made no difference. Who can say?

· 2 ·

THE MACARTHUR CAMPAIGN in the Philippines, which marked the high point of ground conflict in the war against Japan, had all but ended before the Yalta Conference began. Forty-eight hours after the adjournment at Yalta came the high point in the air war against Germany as 750 British bombing planes and one wave of more than 300 American bombers leveled sixteen hundred acres of the virtually undefended city of Dresden, in east Germany, killing an estimated 135,000 persons. The exploding bombs and the fires they set created an updraft, heating the air to temperatures as high as 1100 degrees Fahrenheit. A city with one sixth of London's population had suffered three times as much damage as London suffered during the entire course of the war.

It must be recorded, to the eternal credit of the British people, that even after five years of war, such a public outcry arose that Churchill addressed this memorandum to General Sir Hastings Ismay, his chief of staff, and to Air Marshal Sir Charles Portal, chief of staff of the R.A.F.: "It seems to me that the moment has come when the question of bombing cities simply for the sake of increasing the terror, though under other pretexts, has to be reviewed. Otherwise we shall come into the control of an utterly exhausted land. We shall not, for instance, be able to get housing materials out of Germany because some temporary provisions would have to be made for the Germans themselves. The destruction of Dresden remains a serious query against the conduct of Allied bombing. I am of the opinion that military objectives must henceforward be more strictly studied in our own interests rather than in that of the enemy."

As long ago as August, 1944, Britain's Joint Intelligence Committee had opposed area bombing of German cities as being unlikely "to achieve any worthwhile degree of success." But in view of the Soviet offensive of January 1945, that Committee recommended the bombing of east Germany, partly to snarl up German troop movements, partly to help the Russians, and partly for its "political value in demonstrating to the Russians, in the best way open to us, a desire on the part of the

British and Americans to assist them in the present battle."

Originally, Berlin headed the list of potential targets for a series of Anglo-American, round-the-clock, area bombings, to be known as "Thunderclap," but the United States could not provide adequate, long-range fighter cover. Because Chemnitz, Leipzig, and Dresden possessed no such antiaircraft defenses as Berlin, they were substituted for the German capital. Sir Arthur ("Bomber") Harris, the chief air marshal who headed Britain's Bomber Command, had pleaded incessantly for heavier bombing as the key to quick and total victory over Germany. His arguments appealed alike to the national pride of the British, arising from the victory their Royal Air Force had won over the Luftwaffe in 1940, and to the Americans' propensity to maximum reliance upon the latest advances in military technology. On both sides of the Atlantic "Victory Through Air Power" became a popular slogan that neither Roosevelt nor Churchill could entirely resist.

At the last moment, Harris' deputy, Air Marshal Sir Robert Saundby, suggested scratching Dresden as a target on the ground that it had little importance either as an industrial city or as a railroad center. American planes had launched but two minor attacks on Dresden—the first on October 7, 1944, the second on January 16, 1945. The German authorities had therefore skimped to the vanishing point on Dresden's antiaircraft defenses while almost doubling its normal population of 630,000 by flooding the city with refugees, wounded soldiers, war prisoners, and slave laborers. Having spared Oxford (but not Coventry), the Nazi leaders assumed that the British would reciprocate by sparing Dresden with its churches, museums, and baroque public buildings.

. . .

With the British bombing of Dresden the role of air power in the Second World War came full circle. In 1938 at Munich, Hitler used the threat of the Luftwaffe to extract concessions from Chamberlain. By 1945, the Royal Air Force had attained such superiority over the Luftwaffe as German air power had never gained over Britain, only to find, as Churchill now saw it, that absolute air power had wound up defeating itself absolutely. Churchill had always insisted on standing up to Hitler, while insisting that Britain in its own self-interest could not afford to wipe Germany and the Germans off the map. More and more of his own people also opposed indiscriminate area bombing, but not so much for pragmatic reasons as for reasons of principle.

Only the British had never stopped fighting the Germans since Hitler invaded Poland. Unlike the French, who had lost the war before it began, the British never capitulated. Unlike the Russians, the British had gone to war with Germany on principle and from the start. Of course, the Russians had suffered and sacrificed more than the British at Hitler's hands and had dealt him heavier blows. And it was the late-coming Americans who supplied the overwhelming power that Roosevelt's policy of unconditional surrender demanded. But the British people, in their moral shock at their own R.A.F.'s bombing of Dresden, set a unique example. Their long ordeal had not left them cynical, embittered, or thirsting for revenge. Rather had experience confirmed their faith in the principles of freedom, tolerance, and justice for which they fought. Within six more months, the bombing of Hiroshima and Nagasaki confronted the American people with a similar challenge.

· 3 ·

THE BOMBING of Dresden foreshadowed the fate of Germany as clearly as the rout in the Philippines foreshadowed the fate of Japan. Both also conformed with the war aim of unconditional surrender that Roosevelt had proclaimed to both Germany and Japan. During the course of the Yalta Conference, he had already chosen San Francisco as the place and late April as the time at which the United Nations wartime coalition would transform itself into a worldwide security organization that would come into being before the fighting ceased, whereas the League of Nations did not even reach the discussion stage until after the First World War had ended.

Roosevelt never betrayed the slightest fear that any mere physical ailment could frustrate the completion of his life's work. Still less did it occur to him that his own passing from the scene might complicate rather than simplify matters. But as the strain of the Yalta Conference increased, so did the President's determination to get away from it all at the earliest possible moment. No sooner had the final session of the Yalta Conference and the deadline for the official Big Three communiqué been set for Sunday, February 11, than the President confirmed the tentative arrangements he had already made to receive King Fuad of Egypt, Emperor Haile Selassie of Ethiopia, and King Ibn Saud of Saudi Arabia for separate, private conversations aboard the cruiser *Quincy* at the northern entrance of the Suez Canal on the following Tuesday and Wednesday. Prime Minister Churchill vainly urged the President to linger for another day or two of personal talks. Disappointment gave way to suspicion as Churchill, greatly disturbed and eager to know the President's intentions, sought out Hopkins.

"Fortunately I could not tell him," wrote Hopkins in a subsequent memorandum, "because I had asked the President the same thing. I had made up my mind that it was, in the main, a lot of horseplay and that the President was going to enjoy the colorful pageantry of the sovereigns of this part of the world who thought that President Roosevelt of the United States could probably cure all their troubles." In Ibn Saud, the last of his three visitors, the President had taken on more than he bargained for. According to the Hopkins memorandum, it came as a shock to the President when he found out that Ibn Saud not only disliked the Jews but refused to admit even a small number of them to Palestine, arguing that "the Jews in Palestine were successful only because British and American capital had been poured in in millions of dollars and said that if those millions had been given to the Arabs they could have done quite as well. . . . There is no doubt that Ibn Saud made a great impression on the President that the Arabs meant business. None of this had anything to do with the merits of the case. I know the conference in relation to Palestine never came to grips with the real issues but developed into a monologue by Ibn Saud and I gathered that the President was overly impressed with what Ibn Saud said. And I never could reconcile the President's statement at a press conference later that he had learned more from Ibn Saud about Palestine in five minutes than he had learned in a lifetime because the only thing he learned which all people well acquainted with the Palestine cause know is that the Arabs don't want any more Jews in Palestine."

The President's meetings with the "Three Kings of Orient" revived his spirits, but all else remained unchanged, including his own enfeebled state of health. Nor was this all. As soon as the *Quincy* left Ismailia, Harry Hopkins had to take to his cabin while arrangements were made to have Judge Samuel Rosenman, another speech-writer and adviser, flown from London to join the party at Algiers for the nine-day homeward trip. Roosevelt had counted on Hopkins, during those nine days, to help him put the finishing touches on his climactic report to Congress and the American people concerning the Yalta meeting. The weakened President did not take this change of plan with his customary grace, nor did Hopkins, who had already served far above and beyond the call of duty, make sufficient allowance for the President's condition. After a four-day rest at Marrakech in Morocco, Hopkins flew back to Washington on February 24 but had to leave two days later for emergency treatment at the Mayo Clinic in Rochester, Minnesota, where he remained until the day after Roosevelt himself died.

Two days out of Algiers tragedy struck again. The President's be-loved military aide, General Edwin W. ("Pa") Watson, who had suffered a mild stroke at Sevastopol, died on the voyage. Burial serv-ices took place at sea. "The President seemed unusually depressed, and exhausted," wrote James MacGregor Burns in *Roosevelt: The Soldier of Freedom.* "For days Rosenman could not get him to work on his report to the Congress and the people." While Hopkins recovered enough stamina to carry out, several months later, a major assignment from Roosevelt's successor, Rosenman carried on, bringing new energies and perspectives to Hopkins' unfinished task.

Meanwhile Churchill had returned from Yalta, echoing Roosevelt's enthusiasm for the United Nations Organization as he had never echoed Roosevelt's enthusiasm for the cross-Channel invasion after Teheran. And because Churchill could see no other cause worthy of total commitment, he also found it necessary to sing Stalin's praises with as whole a heart as Roosevelt. "The impression that I brought back from the Crimea, and from all my other contacts, is that Marshal Stalin and the Soviet leaders wish to live in honorable friendship and equality with the Western democracies. I also feel that their word is their bond. I know of no Government which stands to its obligations, even in its own despite, more solidly than the Soviet Russian Government. I de-cline absolutely to embark here on a discussion of Russian good faith."

·4·

CHURCHILL MADE this statement before the House of Commons on Feb-ruary 27, 1945, in the course of a long report on the Yalta Conference. Two days later Roosevelt made a similar report before a joint session of the House and Senate. The British press and the BBC always carried such reports by Churchill after he had made them in Parliament, and this one followed that pattern. But Roosevelt's report on Yalta not only went out live by radio; what he said on that occasion and the way he said it changed the course of history. For the President seized upon this as his first major opportunity to win bipartisan Congressional and popu-lar support for an effort still in its preliminary stage. With a character-istic blend of imagination and conviction, courage and grace, he en-listed his liabilities to enhance his appeal. Instead of standing before the Congress behind the lectern on the raised rostrum, the President was wheeled, seated in his wheelchair, into the well of the House. Before him lay the manuscript of the address on which he and Judge Rosenman had labored so long, but he began with this impromptu statement, spoken in conversational tones: "I hope you will pardon me for this unusual posture of sitting down, but I know you will realize it makes it easier for me not to have to carry about ten pounds of steel around at the bottom of my legs; and because of the fact that I have just completed a fourteen-thousand-mile trip." Never, since the 1924 Democratic Convention when Roosevelt delivered his "Happy Warrior" nomination speech for Al Smith, had he made any public reference to the effects of his polio ordeal, and it took as much courage to break that silence as it had taken to keep it for so long:

There were two main purposes in the Crimean Conference. The first was to bring defeat to Germany with the greatest possible speed and the smallest possible loss of Allied men. That purpose is now being carried out in great force. . . .

The second purpose was to continue to build the foundation for an international accord which would bring order and security after the chaos of war, and would give some assurance of lasting peace among the nations of the world. . . .

Never before have the major Allies been more closely united— not only in their war aims but in their peace aims. And they are determined to be united with each other—and with all peace-loving nations—so that the ideal of lasting peace will become a reality . . .

Our objective in handling Germany is simple—it is to secure the peace of the future world. Too much experience has shown that that objective is impossible if Germany is allowed to retain any ability to wage aggressive war. . . .

A Conference of all the United Nations of the world will meet at San Francisco on April 25th, 1945. There, we all hope, and confidently expect, to execute a definite charter of organization under which the peace of the world will be preserved and the forces of aggression permanently outlawed.

This time we shall not make the mistake of waiting until the end of the war to set up the machinery of peace. This time, as we fight together to get the war over quickly, we work together to keep it from happening again. . . .

There have been instances of political confusion and unrest in these liberated areas—as in Greece and Poland and Yugoslavia and other places. Worse than that there actually have come to grow up in some of them vaguely defined "spheres of influence" which were incompatible with the basic principles of international collaboration. . . .

I am convinced that the agreement on Poland, under the circumstances, is the most hopeful agreement possible for a free, independent, and prosperous Polish state. . . .

It is still a long, tough road to Tokyo. The defeat of Germany will not mean the end of the war against Japan. On the contrary, America must be prepared for a long and costly struggle in the Pacific.

But the unconditional surrender of Japan is as essential as the defeat of Germany—if our plans for world peace are to succeed. For Japanese militarism must be wiped out as thoroughly as German militarism. . . .

The Conference in the Crimea was a turning point in American history. There will soon be presented to the Senate and the American people a great decision which will determine the fate of the United States—and of the world—for generations to come.

There can be no middle ground here. We shall have to take the responsibility for world collaboration or we shall have to bear the responsibility for another world conflict. . . .

Twenty-five years ago, American fighting men looked to the statesmen of the world to finish the work of peace for which they had fought and suffered. We failed them then. We cannot fail them again and expect the world to survive.

. . .

Some twenty-five years later, the remarkable feature of Roosevelt's last, major public utterance is not that it contained many accurate predictions—or many false ones. The United Nations has not entirely fulfilled nor completely betrayed his hopes. Two of America's most formidable wartime allies—Russia and China—have become, in American eyes, the twin enemies of western civilization. America's two most formidable wartime enemies have become America's most formidable European and Asian bastions. Roosevelt's 5000-word report on the Yalta Conference contained no criticism of Communism, Russian or Chinese, no criticism of colonialism, British, French, or any other kind. Roosevelt may have taken too sanguine a view of the prospects for freedom in eastern Europe; his obituary on "spheres of influence" seems to have been premature. But who, in March, 1945, saw the future more clearly?

Certum est quia impossibile est. Events may have proved some of his beliefs absurd, but the courage with which he set them forth gave hope to millions and if no millennium dawned, neither did the apocalypse descend. The spirit of Yalta that he invoked and created banished, in advance, the atmosphere of partisan politics and moral arrogance with which the Wilson-Lodge controversy had poisoned American foreign policy for a generation. Roosevelt minimized his differences with Stalin over Poland not only in order to ensure full Soviet participation in the San Francisco meeting but also to lull American suspicion of Soviet methods and motives. Roosevelt also kept to himself his misgivings about British, French, and Dutch colonialism. Again, it was not only a question of subordinating his differences with some of his allies to his plans for San Francisco; he also wanted to lull American criticism of Churchill's and de Gaulle's determination to maintain and reconstitute their prewar holdings overseas.

Roosevelt may have underrated Stalin's capacity to make trouble and overrated Churchill's capacity to prevent the liquidation of the British Empire. But his own hopes for a postwar United Nations overrode all doubts, uncertainties, and misgivings. Moreover, it did not take any twenty-five years for Roosevelt's idealism to prove a better guide to the course of events than the realism of either Churchill or Stalin. No sooner had Churchill and Roosevelt made their optimistic reports on the Yalta Conference than Stalin used the power of the Red army to flout the clear spirit of the agreements he had reached at Yalta, if not their imprecise letter. Whereupon Roosevelt proved himself a greater realist than Churchill by accepting, with what grace he could muster, the settlements that Stalin imposed on Poland and elsewhere, while continuing to give the highest priority to his hopes for the San Francisco Conference. But Stalin's determination to hold every square inch of territory that the Red army had occupied under the terms of the Teheran and Yalta meetings bound the Soviet Union to a chain of obligations that have become increasingly burdensome and frustrating with the years. As for the United Nations, to which Roosevelt attached supreme importance, that has become the last, best hope on earth for the Third World of developing countries, for which Roosevelt had always hoped so much. But China—the one great nation for which Roosevelt hoped the most—remained for more than two decades the one pariah that the United Nations excluded.

XXI

F.D.R. Transcendent

·1·

DURING THE TWO YEARS between the Casablanca and Yalta conferences Roosevelt's insistence on unconditional surrender held the Anglo-Soviet-American military coalition together. The military strategy of beating Germany first plus the political decision to rule out a negotiated peace did the trick. Because the defeat of Germany had now become certain, the participants in the Yalta Conference felt compelled to reach an understanding on the fate of Germany and the future of Europe. The conduct of the war against Japan also acquired new urgency. Faced with new situations both in connection with Germany and in connection with Japan, President Roosevelt felt compelled to give top priority to the transformation of the United Nations from a military wartime coalition into an international body to preserve the peace in the postwar world. At Casablanca he had stressed unconditional surrender as the best means of holding the Anglo-Soviet-American coalition together long enough to organize a postwar security organization before the fighting came to an end. At Yalta the end for Germany seemed so near at hand that Roosevelt and Hopkins concentrated their diminishing energies on postwar planning.

Both at Teheran and Yalta, Roosevelt had withheld support from Churchill's efforts to block the settlements that Stalin and the Red army sought to impose on Poland and Germany. Without ever approving the ends Stalin sought or the means by which he tried to attain them, Roosevelt never supported Churchill's countermoves—to say nothing of making any countermoves himself. For one thing, he could no more have prevented Stalin from occupying most of eastern Europe and almost half of Germany than Stalin could have prevented the Anglo-

Americans from proceeding as they did in western Europe and in western Germany. But second, and more important, Roosevelt saw little to be gained and much to be lost in even appearing to oppose Stalin at the very moment when the Anglo-Soviet-American coalition at last had Hitler just where they wanted him after all these years. Finally, Roosevelt's concentration on a postwar United Nations security organization raised no immediate obstacles in the way of Stalin's ambitions in eastern Europe or Germany.

In one respect, Stalin and Churchill saw eye to eye. Both based the hopes and fears that dictated their decisions on traditional territorial assumptions. Like Hitler and the Kaiser, like the Austrian emperors and the Russian czars, they saw Europe (past, present, and future) in terms of who owns what lands. To be sure, Churchill's ambitions for Britain did not run to real estate in Europe. Churchill's fears of Stalin's ambitions caused the trouble. For Stalin, as Churchill well remembered, had seen the victorious Allies after the First World War quarantine the Soviet Union behind a sanitary cordon of small nations and had then seen Hitler enlist these same, small nations in his efforts to build a thousand-year Reich, primarily at the expense of the Soviet Union. In Churchill's view, Stalin therefore emerged from the Second World War as a menace second only to Hitler, in Hitler's prime.

Field Marshal Montgomery shared the prime minister's fears and did what he could to allay them. "Berlin was lost to us when we failed to make a sound operational plan after the victory in Normandy," wrote Montgomery in his *Memoirs* ten years later. "The Americans could not understand that it was of little avail to win the war strategically if we lost it politically; because of this curious viewpoint we suffered accordingly from VE Day onwards, and we are still suffering. War is a political instrument; once it is clear you are going to win, political considerations must influence its future course. It became obvious to me in the autumn of 1944 that the way things were being handled was going to have repercussions; it looked to me as if we were going to 'muck it up.' I reckon we did."

Montgomery's dogmatic clichés contained some truth, but not much. Of course, the way things were handled had repercussions; of course, much was mucked up. But Montgomery's political horizons later proved as narrow as Eisenhower's military horizons proved wide. Ten years later, Montgomery still could not see that Stalin, in 1945, had overreached himself—not quite so badly, to be sure, as Hitler had overreached himself in 1941, but in the same war and in the same part of the world. Nor had Montgomery yet perceived that the partition of Germany and the division of Europe had long since made the final stage of the battle of Germany irrelevant. The three million Red army troops who appeared on the scene had their hands full, not only defeating the Germans but occupying all the lands between Germany and the Soviet Union where they foisted Soviet Communism on the reluctant inhabitants. Eisenhower's broad-front strategy, on the other hand, enabled four million Anglo-American troops to help the nations and peoples of western Europe re-establish democracy in their lands. These four million Anglo-American troops could no more challenge the three million Red army troops in eastern Europe than the Red army could spread Communism to the English Channel.

· 2 ·

NEITHER AS NEGOTIATOR at Yalta nor as commander in chief of the armed forces of the United States could Roosevelt deny Stalin whatever east-European territories the Red army chose to occupy. At most the President could best "husband out life's taper at its close" by doing his utmost to engage the Soviet leaders as deeply as possible in the postwar United Nations Organization. In the Pacific war, the final assault on Japan clearly took precedence over large-scale aid to China. But the best news the President received after his return from Yalta arrived on March 7, when German folly, negligence, and disintegration enabled the alert Ninth Armored Division of General William H. Simpson's Ninth American Army to seize almost intact the Ludendorff Bridge which crossed the Rhine at Remagen, fifteen miles south of Bonn and thirty miles south of Cologne. Within two days, five divisions of General Hodges' First Army had joined the Ninth Armored on the Rhine's east bank, where they expanded the bridgehead to a depth of five miles. Within another three days pontoon bridges were carrying all the traffic. General Bradley's Sixth Army Group, which now included Hodges' First Army and Patton's Third, found itself in position to launch rapid advances southeast toward Prague and Vienna or northeast toward Berlin.

But on March 13, General Eisenhower foreclosed these possibilities by ordering the First Army to advance no more than ten miles beyond Remagen. Instead of using the Remagen bridgehead as the springboard for an American eastward thrust, he used it as a means of drawing German troops away from the defense of the Ruhr Valley, which Field

Marshal Montgomery's Twenty-first Army Group of British, Canadian, and American troops had been scheduled to invade on March 23. For months Montgomery had urged Eisenhower to scrap his broad-front strategy and throw all available resources behind a Twenty-first Army Group drive through the Ruhr Valley and on to Berlin. Eisenhower rejected Montgomery's northern-front strategy just as he had rejected the earlier pleas of Bradley, Hodges, and Patton to concentrate on a similar breakthrough farther south. Now that the shoe was on the other foot, Montgomery and Brooke berated Bradley and the men around him for demanding that their Sixth Army Group receive the same privileged treatment that the British had demanded for their Twenty-first. On this occasion, the British generals praised Eisenhower for having stuck to his broad-front strategy through thick and thin.

Now, Eisenhower and his broad-front strategy may have been as mistaken as the British charged, but Eisenhower knew as well as Montgomery did that military decisions have political consequences. He also knew (better, it seems, than Montgomery did) that political decisions also have military consequences. The broad-front strategy had not sprung, fully armed, from the military genius of Dwight Eisenhower. It had gradually taken shape as a result of the military and political decisions reached by the Big Three at Teheran and Yalta. As General Eisenhower himself pointed out in his *Crusade in Europe,* Prime Minister Churchill knew that "regardless of the distance the Allies might have to advance eastward, he and the American President had already agreed that the British and American occupation zones would be limited on the east by a line two hundred miles west of Berlin."

Here General Eisenhower not only justified the broad-front strategy he imposed on the reluctant Montgomery before the Remagen crossing and on the reluctant Bradley afterward. He also justified the action he took when he communicated to Stalin the next two parts of his general plan. Churchill objected to the plan itself and objected even more to Eisenhower's communication of the details to Stalin. Churchill, in Eisenhower's words, "held that because the campaign was now approaching its end, troop maneuvers had acquired a political significance that demanded the intervention of political leaders in the development of broad operational plans. He apparently believed that my message to the Generalissimo had exceeded my authority to communicate with Moscow only on purely military matters. He was greatly disappointed and disturbed because my plan did not first throw Montgomery forward with all the strength I could give him from the American forces, in the

desperate attempt to capture Berlin before the Russians could do so."
In the course of a letter to General Marshall, dated March 30, 1945,
Eisenhower wrote: "May I point out that Berlin itself is no longer a
particularly important objective? Its usefulness to the German has been
largely destroyed and even his government is preparing to move to another area."

. . .

From mid-February to the the end of March, 1945, General Eisenhower served his commander in chief well as soldier, diplomat, and
politician. As soldier, he continued beyond the Rhine the same broad-
front strategy that had brought his armies across it. As a result, Allied
troops poured across the most productive and populous regions of
western Germany in a single, solid wave, encircling the industrial Ruhr
Valley and approaching from the rear the great North Sea ports of
Hamburg and Bremen and the Baltic ports of Kiel and Lübeck. In central Germany they advanced beyond the line, two hundred miles west
of Berlin, that the Big Three at Yalta had laid down as the eastern limit
of the Anglo-American occupation zone.

It was here that Eisenhower's diplomatic inexperience undercut his
strategic commitment. But Eisenhower knew that Churchill, Brooke,
and Montgomery had favored racing the Russians to Berlin, as they had
favored a breakthrough rather than a broad-front strategy during the
earlier stages of the invasion. For his part, the supreme commander felt
it incumbent upon himself to pursue a strategy that carried forward the
military and political decisions that Roosevelt had already made at
Teheran and Yalta. But it had simply not occurred to Eisenhower that
his transmission of these plans to Stalin would cause such an explosion
in the highest British political and military circles. Soon enough afterward, both Stalin and Churchill gave him further lessons in the practice
—as contrasted with the theory—of military diplomacy among fighting
allies.

Yet, Eisenhower's diplomatic innocence did more good than harm in
the long run. For it was this very innocence that presently spotlighted
the most important of all postwar political issues, now that the conver-
gence of the Allied armies from the west and the Red army from the
east had sealed Germany's military doom. Roosevelt, Marshall, and Eisenhower all knew that their insistence on Operation Overlord had not
only filled the military vacuum that the collapse of Germany had left in
western Europe. By the same token, the Soviet leaders, through the
Red army, were also filling the military vacuum that the collapse of

Germany created in eastern Europe. The question now had become how these two converging forces would adjust themselves to the new situation—and to each other.

General Eisenhower's innocence had served the Anglo-American cause better than Prime Minister Churchill's guile, having all unknowingly lured Stalin into unforeseen and unending difficulties. The Anglo-Americans lacked the military means and the political incentive to halt Stalin's crude and brutal program of westward expansion, but it did not take long for the new Stalinist order (like the new Nazi order before it) to prove its own worst enemy. The ills of eastern Europe dated back further and ran deeper than the ills of western Europe. At the same time, the Red army and the Stalinist regimes it imposed on eastern Europe set the hands of the clock back, whereas General Eisenhower's Allied Forces not only liberated western Europe from Nazi rule, they also set the stage for the postwar Marshall Plan to usher in a new era of peace and prosperity.

· 3 ·

ROOSEVELT'S REPORT on the Yalta Conference opened the month of March on a note of triumph. Already, his projected United Nations Organization gave promise of succeeding where Woodrow Wilson's League of Nations had failed. Yet before the month ended, almost everything seemed to have turned to dust and ashes. Stalin made no bones about his own decision to put a new and different interpretation on his agreement, made at Yalta, to have a three-man commission of Molotov and the British and American ambassadors at Moscow supervise the reorganization of the provisional Polish government on a new and broader basis. Now Stalin insisted that Communists occupy all the key posts while Roosevelt still resisted Churchill's proposal to join him in a stiff protest to Moscow. Not until Roosevelt learned, late in the month, that Andrei Gromyko, then Soviet ambassador in Washington, rather than Foreign Minister Molotov, would represent the Soviet government at the first United Nations Conference at San Francisco in April, did he cable Stalin that "a thinly disguised continuation of the present Warsaw regime would be unacceptable."

The worst was yet to come. March 8 had marked three simultaneous turning points in the history of the Second World War. First, the American capture of the Ludendorff Bridge at Remagen; second, Hitler's dismissal of the defeatist General von Rundstedt as commander in chief in the west and his replacement by "Smiling Albert" Kesselring, who had performed brilliantly in Italy; third, the meeting between Allen W. Dulles of the Office of Strategic Services, at his office in Bern, Switzerland, with Major General Karl Wolff, the top S.S. officer in Italy, to discuss the surrender of one million Axis troops in that theater. Wolff, a hard-core Nazi who had risen from the ranks, had simultaneously repented his Nazi past and reached the conclusion that Germany had lost the war. Unlike the aristocratic participants in the July 20 plot against Hitler, Wolff favored unconditional surrender—the sooner the better, for he had reason to believe that Kesselring agreed with him. Both men feared that a German collapse would lead to a Communist sweep across northern Italy and the south of France and therefore urged the unconditional surrender of all Axis forces in Italy as the prelude to ending the war on those same terms.

Wolff had made his contact with Dulles, who reported their conversation to Washington, London, and General Alexander's headquarters at Caserta, near Naples. Two representatives of Alexander then went to Switzerland for further talks with Wolff. On March 12 the British and American ambassadors at Moscow sent Molotov a report that they had just received from Alexander, reminding them that any talks with Wolff would deal only with the unconditional surrender of all German forces in Italy and Yugoslavia. Molotov referred to the talks as "negotiations" and demanded that representatives of the Soviet High Command attend any further meetings. On March 15, Alexander and the Combined Chiefs refused; the next day Molotov demanded that the talks break off at once. The talks continued without the Russians and on March 22 Molotov charged that the Anglo-Americans had been negotiating with the German High Command for the past two weeks. The next day Roosevelt wrote Stalin: "There can be in such a surrender of enemy forces in the field no violation of our agreed principle of unconditional surrender and no political implications whatsoever." Stalin replied that the Germans had taken advantage of the talks to move three divisions from Italy to the eastern front. On April 3 Stalin wrote Roosevelt that negotiations had indeed taken place and that the President had been misinformed. According to Stalin, his "military colleagues" had told him that Kesselring, now the German commander in the west, had "agreed to open the front and permit the Anglo-American troops to advance to the east, and the Anglo-Americans have promised in return to ease the peace terms for the Germans. I think that my colleagues are close to the truth."

Roosevelt flatly denied the charges, concluding that "it would be one of the great tragedies of history if at the very moment of victory now within our grasp, such distrust, such lack of faith, should prejudice the entire undertaking after the colossal losses of life, materials, and treasure involved. Frankly, I cannot avoid a feeling of bitter resentment toward your informers, whoever they are, for such vile misrepresentations of my actions or those of my trusted subordinates." In his reply of April 7, Stalin did acknowledge: "I have never doubted your integrity or trustworthiness, just as I have never questioned the integrity or trustworthiness of Mr. Churchill." But he added: "I still think the Russian point of view to be the only correct one, as it precludes all possibility of mutual suspicions and makes it impossible for the enemy to sow distrust between us."

Yet even among these qualified assurances, Roosevelt found some crumbs of comfort. "Thank you," he replied to Stalin, "for your frank explanation of the Soviet point of view of the Bern incident, which now appears to have faded into the past without having accomplished any useful purpose. There must not, in any event, be mutual mistrust and minor misunderstandings of this character should not arise in the future. I feel sure that when our armies make contact in Germany and join in a fully co-ordinated offensive the Nazi armies will disintegrate." When Ambassador Harriman suggested omitting the word "minor" before "misunderstandings," the President turned thumbs down. What had happened seemed minor to him. To Churchill, to whom he also sent a copy of the message, he cabled: "I would minimize the general Soviet problem as much as possible, because these problems, in one form or another, seem to arise every day, and most of them seem to straighten out, as in the case of the Bern meeting. We must be firm, however, and our course thus far is correct."

The President's own course had almost ended. This copy of his last message to Stalin, together with his last words to Churchill, went out on the morning of April 12 from Warm Springs, Georgia, where Roosevelt had gone on March 31 for a two-week vacation. Shortly before his departure from Washington, his personal physician, Admiral Ross T. McIntire, Navy Surgeon General, reassured the press about his patient's health and saw no reason to accompany him south, but his assistant, Commodore Howard Bruenn, did go along. Mrs. Roosevelt, since her husband's return from Yalta, had found him increasingly reluctant to discuss politics and world affairs, as had long been their custom, and therefore welcomed his decision to invite two of his favorite relations to join him—his near cousin, Laura Delano, and his more distant cousin, Daisy Stuckley, both spinsters in their mid-forties. Mrs. Roosevelt also welcomed the opportunity to give more of her time to preparations for the approaching San Francisco Conference.

On the morning of April 12, Commander Bruenn checked the President's heart and blood pressure, which he found normal. At noon, the morning mail arrived, and Roosevelt spent the next hour going through it. Shortly after one o'clock, he inserted a cigarette in his holder, raised his hand to his forehead. "Did you drop something?" asked Miss Stuckley. "I have a terrific headache," he replied, as his body sank between the arms of his chair. A massive cerebral hemorrhage had wiped out consciousness. Commander Bruenn and two servants bore him, unconscious but breathing, to his nearby room where they changed him to pajamas and put him to bed. Inoculations brought little response. Heavy breathing continued for another two hours until the heart stopped beating, and silence fell.

·4·

THREE DAYS LATER it was Churchill who, as usual, rose to the occasion in his eulogy before the House of Commons: "Not one man in ten millions, stricken and crippled as he was, would have attempted to plunge into a life of physical and mental exertion and of hard, ceaseless political activity. Not one in ten millions would have tried, not one in a generation would have succeeded, not only in entering this sphere, not only in acting vehemently in it, but in becoming the indubitable master of the scene. In this extraordinary effort of the spirit over the flesh, of will power over physical infirmity, he was sustained by that noble woman, his wife, whose high ideals marched with his own, and to whom the deep and respectful sympathy of the House of Commons flows out today in all fullness."

Time's fullness confirmed the prime minister's tribute to the President's widow. Eleanor Roosevelt's devotion, ambition, and resolution had pulled her husband through that dark night of the soul which followed his crippling battle against polio. From that shared ordeal emerged the outstanding political partnership of their generation. For one thing, no other husband could have installed Eleanor Roosevelt as First Lady of the Land in her Uncle Ted's White House; for another, no other wife could have kept Franklin Roosevelt there through three successive terms and four victorious election campaigns.

Her husband's death, which ended her wifely political career, launched her on a whole new career which went on from where her duties as First Lady had left off. President Truman at once appointed her a member of the American delegation to the United Nations. Later, she produced a daily, syndicated newspaper column, magazine articles, books, and lectures. There she told enough about herself, her husband, and her family to suggest that much of the goodness and kindness she radiated to others sprang from private griefs to which she could never give utterance. Until her death in 1962, Mrs. Roosevelt led an active, rewarding life.

What of Roosevelt? What legacies did he leave and what became of them? His private life could be described as an exercise in sublimation, his public life as an achievement in transcendence. To sublimate is merely to deflect one's energies. Almost everybody does it almost all the time. To transcend is to surpass one's own capacities. Some of us can do it some of the time; few can do it all the time. It was in his public capacity that Roosevelt made a habit of transcendence. To him belongs nearly all the credit for having established the United Nations as a going concern before the war ended. Which by no means ensured its success. Roosevelt and the United Nations could no more establish peace on earth than Wilson and the League of Nations had been able to do so. But in the very process of establishing the United Nations, Roosevelt had brought his career to an appropriate grand climax. Just as his insistence on unconditional surrender held the Anglo-Soviet-American military coalition together during its most critical years, so the subsequent priority he gave to the inclusion of the Soviet Union in the United Nations went a long way toward preventing that same coalition from falling apart even before the final stage of the war against Japan had begun.

Nothing had darkened the last weeks of Roosevelt's life so much as the prospect that Molotov would not attend the San Francisco Conference. Roosevelt had preferred to split with Churchill rather than oppose Stalin on the Polish issue. He had minimized Stalin's charges of bad faith in connection with General Wolff's offer of unconditional surrender on the Italian and Yugoslav fronts. But with his death came triumph. When Harriman broke the news to Stalin and Molotov, it moved Stalin to such a point that he asked what contribution he could make to Allied unity. The loyal Harriman, following the priorities set by Roosevelt rather than his own inclinations at the time, ignored Poland and suggested that Molotov attend the San Francisco Conference, to which Stalin at once agreed. This also accorded with the wishes of Roosevelt's successor. "My first act as President of the United States," wrote Harry Truman in his *Year of Decision*, "had been to reaffirm the American desire for a world organization to keep the peace. Within a few minutes of taking the oath of office I announced that the United States would take part in the San Francisco Conference with no delay in the schedule or change in the arrangements." Roosevelt had already taken the Republican opposition into camp with his appointment of Senator Vandenberg of Michigan, a former isolationist and senior Republican member of the Senate Foreign Relations Committee, and former Governor Harold Stassen of Minnesota, nominator of Wendell Willkie at the 1940 Republican National Convention, to the American delegation to San Francisco.

As the years went by, however, the means that Roosevelt used to speed the establishment of the United Nations Organization overshadowed the ends he sought. A quarter of a century later is still too early to pass final judgment on the success or failure of the United Nations. But it has not taken that long for Roosevelt to emerge as the man whose death restored and preserved the wartime practice of Soviet-American consultation that he had worked so hard to inaugurate. Sometimes these sporadic consultations increased Soviet-American tensions; sometimes they eased them. But neither the rigid Molotov nor the fumbling Dulles could break them off; neither the mercurial Khrushchev nor the supple Kennedy could stabilize them. Roosevelt not only foresaw the Soviet-American relationship as the major fact of world politics during the third quarter of the twentieth century. He helped to create the framework in which this relationship exists. He left a legacy in perfect tune with his own temperament. But nothing so enhanced that legacy as that moment in time at which he passed it on.

XXII

Deutschland Kaputt

·1·

ROOSEVELT'S POLITICAL INSTINCT served him well when he based his plans for a peaceful postwar world on the development of a Soviet-American axis. So did his sense of timing when he insisted on the immediate establishment of a United Nations Organization, in which both the United States and the Soviet Union would play commanding roles. Moreover, in shaping American military strategy, Roosevelt attached as much importance to these political considerations as Churchill attached to the political importance of beating the Russians to Berlin and meeting the Red army as far east as possible. Nor did General Eisenhower ignore or underrate the political importance of military decisions. Although he had not even sat in on the Teheran or Yalta Conference, he accepted, as a good soldier, the decisions reached by the participants concerning zones of military occupation in Germany. But General Eisenhower was also a wise enough diplomat to make his case in military terms. As Stephen E. Ambrose has put it in his authoritative volume *The Supreme Commander:* "One way to avoid placing a strain on the alliance, and the one Eisenhower usually tried to adopt, was to act as if there were only objective, military considerations at stake. This would work, however, only if the British agreed to limit discussions to military objectives."

In his capacity as supreme commander of the Allied Expeditionary Force, Eisenhower had to do more than carry out political and military decisions. He had to maintain his authority over the clashing personalities and nationalities under his command. As long as Roosevelt lived, Eisenhower saw to it that his heart and the President's beat as one. But Roosevelt's heartbeat weakened steadily and perceptibly after his return from Yalta, and his departure from Washington for Warm Springs at the end of March coincided with Eisenhower's telegram to Stalin. With Marshall in Washington and Roosevelt at death's door, Eisenhower had only the personal, professional, and moral authority of his own immediate subordinate, General Omar N. Bradley, to uphold him against the combined efforts of Churchill, Brooke, and Montgomery to wear him down.

At this time, more than a million and a half Red army troops stood on German soil along an 800-mile front that followed the course of the Neisse and then of the Oder River from the Czechoslovak border to the Baltic. Marshal Zhukov's First Byelorussian Army Group of 768,000 men held the center of that line. In late March some of these troops had crossed the Oder at Küstrin and established a beachhead on the west bank, thirty-eight miles from Berlin. Marshal Konev's First Ukrainian Army Group of five armies and 511,000 men held the southern sector. At no point were they closer than seventy-five miles to Berlin. But each of the two commanders assured Stalin that he and his men could take the city. Declaring that time was of the essence, Stalin gave them forty-eight hours to draw up their plans and submit them to the High Command. He then ordered them to depart for the front lines, to set their plans in motion, and to await instructions. They left Moscow on April 3.

Immediately thereafter Stalin replied to Eisenhower's communication of March 28. According to Stalin, the supreme Allied commander's plan to cut Germany in two by linking up with Soviet forces in the Leipzig-Dresden area "entirely coincides with the plan of the Soviet High Command," which would go into effect "approximately the second half of May." Stalin also informed Eisenhower that "Berlin has lost its former strategic importance" and that the Soviet High Command would therefore send only "secondary forces" in that direction. At four o'clock in the morning of Monday, April 16, Zhukov's forces subjected the German-held portion of the Küstrin bridgehead to the heaviest artillery attack ever mounted on the eastern front. Two hours later Konev's forces opened a more selective but no less deadly attack on the western, German-held bank of the Neisse.

At the northern end of the line stood Marshal Konstantin Rokossovsky's Second Byelorussian Army Group of 314,000 men, who did not participate in this drive on Berlin. They counted on an eventual linkup with Montgomery's Twenty-first Army Group which took the North Sea ports of Bremen and Hamburg, the Baltic port of Lübeck, and finally liberated Denmark before the Russians could arrive. Konev's armies cracked Berlin's southern defenses on April 22, twenty-four hours ahead of Zhukov. On April 23, Stalin issued an order of the day dividing Berlin into two occupation zones, the larger of which went to Zhukov. On the afternoon of April 25, two units of General Hodges' First U.S. Army and two units of Marshal Konev's First Ukrainians linked up on the River Elbe, seventy miles south of Berlin, thus cutting Germany in two.

When Stalin assured Eisenhower that "Berlin has lost its former strategic importance," he lied in his teeth. He had gone through the motions of accepting Roosevelt's assurances about the Bern discussions with General Wolff, but he did not share Roosevelt's trust in Roosevelt's informants, and even assumed that Eisenhower was lying to him as he had lied to Eisenhower. But the truth that Eisenhower told—and that Stalin doubted—vindicated Eisenhower's long-standing resolve not to race for Berlin and reflected little credit on Churchill's insistence on trying to meet the Russians as far east as possible—in other words, as deeply as possible inside the Soviet occupation zone of Germany. For one thing, Eisenhower had always favored a prearranged meeting with the Russians at some river or other definite natural frontier as prudent insurance against sudden, unexpected collision between Soviet and Anglo-American troops. For another thing, agreement had already been reached at Teheran for the Soviet occupation zone of Germany to extend two hundred miles west of Berlin. In the third place, as Eisenhower put it to General Marshall in a message dated April 15: "Frankly, if I should have forces in the Russian occupation zone and be faced with an order or 'request' to retire so that they may advance to the points they choose, I see no recourse except to comply. To do otherwise would probably provoke an incident with the logic of the situation all on the side of the Soviets."

Under the conditions that did, in fact, develop, Stalin's decision to hurl Zhukov's and Konev's armies against Berlin in mid-April set in motion a train of military clashes that led to the total collapse of Germany within two weeks. These clashes raged around, about, and inside Berlin, which Stalin had long since regarded as the Red army's supreme objective and which had now become Hitler's last stronghold. The two men, each of whom needed the other's help to liquidate Poland and usher in the Second World War, still needed each other as desperately as ever—but this time as enemies, not allies. By taking Berlin and toppling Hitler, Stalin and the Red army would not only gain for the Soviet Union much of the credit for Germany's defeat; they would also place themselves in position to retain whatever territories and strong points they might hold at the time of Germany's unconditional surrender. Stalin therefore attached the highest priority to gaining undisputed possession of Berlin and next highest priorities to Vienna and Prague.

Hitler's determination to hold Berlin to the end and at all costs accorded perfectly with Stalin's determination to establish Soviet power there. As a matter of ideology, Hitler stood for anti-Semitism, anti-Slavism, and anti-Communism. As a matter of power politics, he stood for the eastward expansion of German living space and had always refused to consider unconditional surrender to anybody. He insisted on the extermination of his enemies to the east. Now that he could see the jig might be up, he had no stomach for any kind of settlement with the Anglo-Americans; he preferred to drag as much of Germany as possible down to defeat with him at the hands of the Russians, and at their hands alone. There lay his final opportunity to prove to Germany, to the world, and to posterity that he and his Nazi movement had fought to the end for its racist, nationalist, anti-Communist principles.

On the day that ended with the news of Roosevelt's death, Eisenhower saw what he called, in *Crusade in Europe*, "my first horror camp," near the town of Gotha. "I have never been able," he wrote, "to describe my emotional reactions when I first came face to face with indisputable evidence of Nazi brutality and ruthless disregard of every shred of decency." General Patton, on his first visit to a similar camp, vomited, then burst into tears. Eisenhower followed up his visit to the Gotha camp by urging the United States and British governments "to send instantly to Germany a random group of newspaper editors and representative groups from the national legislatures. I felt that the evidence should be immediately placed before the American and British publics in a fashion that would leave no room for cynical doubt."

Neither Hitler's bitterest enemies nor Stalin's best friends could have timed the concentration-camp disclosure at a more effective moment. Stalin's past crimes and present prevarications faded into insignificance. To speed Hitler's defeat became all-important. A week had passed since Stalin had acknowledged the receipt of Eisenhower's plan to finish off Germany and his pledge to link up with the Americans in the Dresden-Leipzig area and bypass Berlin. On April 15—the day before Zhukov and Konev violated these pledges by launching their two drives on Berlin—instructions went out from Eisenhower to Bradley to hold General Simpson's Ninth Army on the Elbe River and abandon a recent plan to dash for Berlin—not unlike the plan that Stalin had suspected. But Eisenhower not only took Stalin at his word; he also took seriously current Nazi propaganda describing a mythical "National Redoubt" that a self-styled "Werewolf" organization of Nazi diehards boasted they would assemble in the mountains of southern Bavaria to wage partisan guerrilla warfare.

The death throes that seized the Nazi movement and wracked all of Germany bore no resemblance to the revolutionary underground warfare that speeded the departing German guests from the countries they had overrun. In Germany the summons to partisan warfare came, not from the enemies of Hitler, but from Hitler himself, who called upon all good Germans to join him in a pact of national self-destruction. On March 18, he told Albert Speer, his close associate and minister of armament and war production, "If the war is to be lost, the nation will also perish. There is no reason to consider the necessity even of a most primitive existence any longer. On the contrary, it is better to destroy even that and destroy ourselves. The nation has proved itself weak, and the future belongs only to the stronger, eastern nation." Speer not only answered back: "We have no right to carry out demolitions which might affect the life of the people." He went up and down the land, in the course of his duties, countermanding Hitler's orders to destroy German industry, transport, and resources before they could fall into enemy hands. But as Hitler saw defeat drawing closer, he demanded that the Germans inflict such death and destruction on themselves as even they had never inflicted on their enemies. His revolution of nihilism had come full circle.

·2·

"My FUEHRER, I congratulate you! Roosevelt is dead! It is written in the stars. The last half of April will be the turning point for us. This is Friday, April 13. It *is* the turning point." Thus Goebbels to Hitler. But it was the turning point against, not for. That "Last Battle," as Cornelius Ryan entitled his detailed account of Berlin's last days, not only compelled the Germans to surrender on all other major fronts; it transformed Europe from a field of battle on which Anglo-Soviet-American armies fought the Germans into a field of political maneuver where the Anglo-Americans and the Russians competed for postwar positions in Germany and the neighboring nations of eastern Europe.

In March, Stalin had compelled the Anglo-Americans to suspend negotiations aimed at the unconditional surrender of all Axis troops in the

Italian theater of war. By April, however, his plans for the battle of Berlin had reached the stage at which he not only sanctioned negotiations that led to the unconditional surrender of a million Axis troops to Field Marshal Alexander at Caserta on April 29. Stalin also approved negotiations that led on May 4 to the unconditional surrender of two and a half million Germans to Field Marshal Montgomery, thirty miles southeast of Hamburg, on May 4. The territories covered by this surrender included northwest Germany, Schleswig-Holstein, Denmark, Holland, Friesland, and various offshore islands.

On the same day that Field Marshal Montgomery won the most sweeping victory in Britain's military history, Field Marshal Zhukov won the battle to which the Soviet leaders in the Second World War attached supreme importance. On May 4, German resistance in Berlin ceased. The Red army had gained complete and uncontested control of the city. According to Cornelius Ryan, civilian deaths during the battle of Berlin probably came close to 100,000. Soviet authorities estimate their military casualties at more than that same number killed. Estimates of rape ran from 20,000 to 100,000. The Germans have no separate figures on military casualties but lump them in with the four million killed in action during the entire course of the war.

The battle of Berlin does not rank with Stalingrad or Alamein, with Midway or Leyte Gulf, as one of the decisive military clashes of the Second World War. Nor, since its outcome had never been in doubt, can it be said to have marked a military turning point in the war's history. And yet no battle in the war's history gave rise to so many important by-products. For one thing, it gave the Russians an immediate psychological advantage. For another, it brought Soviet power into the heart of Europe—to stay. But Stalin, in winning veto power over Anglo-American plans for all of Germany, had to grant them that same veto power, while also allowing them to establish themselves in the most populous and productive parts of the country. With the passage of time, the Soviet conquest of Berlin and the advance of Soviet troops to the Oder-Neisse—in accordance with decisions reached at Teheran— made the partition of Germany and the division of Europe inevitable.

Events during April 1945 happened too fast for almost everybody concerned, especially Hitler. Before he could put through his plan to move his headquarters from his bunker beneath the Berlin Chancellery, to his favorite retreat at Berchtesgaden, the Russians had the city surrounded, and Hitler decided to await the end there. On April 20, he presided over a grim, confused birthday celebration that lasted from noon until the small hours of the following morning. He received and bade farewell to Field Marshal Keitel, supreme army commander, and Grand Admiral Doenitz whom—as a rebuke to the army—he appointed commander of all of Germany's armed forces. Goering, as head of the air force and next in the line of Nazi succession, and Himmler, who had succeeded Goering as head of the Gestapo, also put in their appearances, but both men knew their numbers were up. They left early, Himmler heading north and Goering south. Himmler made a futile bid to serve as intermediary in a surrender bid to General Eisenhower, via Count Bernadotte, head of the Swedish Red Cross. Goering cut his last tie with Hitler by filing a memorandum-ultimatum, demanding confirmation of his status as deputy Fuehrer. Had they not made these moves on their own, Hitler would have charged both men with treason and betrayal because a drama that he and Goebbels were already preparing called for just that.

The first act of this drama opened on April 22, when Hitler staged a three-hour tantrum in the presence of some of the same army and party bigwigs who had attended his birthday celebration. This time he blamed the disasters now engulfing the Third Reich on all ranks of all the armed services, charging them with betrayal, treason, desertion, insubordination, and cowardice. For the first time, he made it plain that if Berlin were to die, he would die with it. The second act came on April 29, when news reached the bunker that a patrol of Italian partisans had seized and shot Mussolini and his mistress, Claretta Petacci. On April 25, after the last remnants of Mussolini's own armed forces had disintegrated, he and a few of his supporters joined a small German convoy heading from Como toward the Swiss frontier. He met with an appropriate death. The professional Italian revolutionary who had begun his career as a Socialist, only to turn against his former Socialist comrades, ended his days at the hands of a new generation of Italian revolutionaries who recognized the former Duce, in spite of the German helmet and German greatcoat in which he tried to disguise himself. Twenty-four hours later they shot both him and his mistress and rushed their bodies to Milan to be displayed, hung head down from meat hooks, at the same spot on a public square where the Germans had recently shot a group of Italian partisans. Crowds jeered at the dead bodies and pelted them with refuse.

From Mussolini's death Hitler learned more than he had from Mussolini's life. The night of April 28–29 he spent drawing up a last will and testament in which he set forth his final instructions for the succession of power. All German officials, military and civilian, Nazi and non-Nazi, had to accept these orders. So did the political and military leaders of the Anglo-Soviet-American coalition. For no other German source existed from which such orders could come. Never had Hitler commanded such absolute power in Germany as he did at the very moment when—by his own decision and action—he blew that power to kingdom come. And under the terms of Hitler's last will and testament its provisions could come into operation only after he had taken his own life.

The first portion of the will ended with the announcement that Hitler had decided to remain in Berlin where he would "choose death voluntarily at the moment when I believe that the residence of the Fuehrer and Chancellor can no longer be held." The second portion appointed Doenitz Reich president and supreme commander of the armed forces and Goebbels Reich chancellor. The shadowy Martin Borman, who lurked in the background, wound up as executor of the will "with full authority to make all decisions." While dictating these instructions to his secretary, Hitler married Eva Braun in a civil ceremony, conducted by a Berlin municipal inspector, appointed by Goebbels, who also served as a witness along with Borman. The will concluded, "My wife and I choose to die in order to escape the shame of overthrow and capitulation. It is our wish that our bodies be burned immediately in the place where I have performed the greater part of my daily work during the course of my twelve years' service to my people."

In preparation for the final act of the drama, servants in the chancellery had managed to rustle up, during the morning of April 29, some fifty gallons of gasoline for the cremation. After a two o'clock lunch, Hitler and Eva Braun shook hands with the fifteen other residents of the bunker, including Goebbels and Borman, and returned to their suite. One shot rang out. Hitler had fired his pistol into his mouth; Eva Braun had swallowed poison. Hitler's body, wrapped in a blanket to conceal the shattered head, and the fully clothed body of Eva Braun, followed by six mourners, were laid in a shallow trench in the chancellery's garden, and soaked in gasoline. A tossed match set them in flames, and they burned for more than an hour, filling the ventilating system of the bunker with a smell like burned bacon. At eleven o'clock that night, three men buried the bodies, which the flames had not entirely consumed, in a shell crater nearby.

Within twenty-four hours of Hitler's death, his only surviving true disciple chose the same way out. After giving their six children poison rather than sentence them to life in a Hitlerless Germany, Goebbels and his wife had themselves shot by S.S. men and ordered their bodies to be burned, as Hitler's and Eva Braun's had been. Within the month Himmler swallowed a phial of cyanide, such as Hitler had in his mouth when he shot himself; two years later, Goering cheated the hangman at the Nuremberg war-crimes trial the same way.

But unconditional surrender came into play only after the Germans had fought to the point of total exhaustion, and the British, Russian, and American forces prevailed everywhere. The surrender formalities therefore entailed no discussion and a bare minimum of formalities. With the fall of Berlin on May 4, the fighting came to a virtual halt. On May 7, at General Eisenhower's headquarters at Reims, General Bedell Smith, chief of staff to General Eisenhower, and General Alfred Jodl, chief of staff to Field Marshal Keitel, held the instrument of unconditional surrender which French and Soviet officers witnessed. Hostilities ceased at midnight, May 8. On May 9, at Marshal Zhukov's headquarters in Berlin, he and Field Marshal Keitel signed the formal ratification, along with General Eisenhower's deputy, Air Chief Marshal Arthur William Tedder. *Deutschland kaputt.*

·3·

"I AM SIXTY-ONE this morning, and I slept in the President's room in the White House last night." Thus, at about 6 A.M. on May 8, 1945, did Harry Truman begin one of the frequent letters that he wrote during the first weeks of his presidency to his 92-year-old mother and to his sister, Mary Jane. "My expensive gold pen doesn't work as well as it should," he complained, but he looked forward to a "historical day." The Germans had signed the unconditional-surrender papers at General Eisenhower's headquarters the day before. The President would broadcast the announcement at 9 A.M. Hostilities would cease on all fronts at midnight. "Isn't that some birthday present?"

Truman continued in the same vein: "Have had one heck of a time with the Prime Minister of Great Britain. He, Stalin, and the U. S. President made an agreement to release the news all at once from the three capitals at an hour that would fit us all. We agreed on 9 A.M. Washington time which is 3 P.M. London and 4 P.M. Moscow time. Mr. Churchill began calling me at daylight to know if we shouldn't make an immediate release without considering the Russians. He was refused and then he kept pushing me to talk to Stalin. He finally had to stick to the agreed plan—but he was as mad as a wet hen. Things have moved at a terrific pace here since April 12. Never a day has gone by that some momentous decision didn't have to be made. So far luck has been with me. I hope it keeps up. It can't stay with us forever however and I hope when the mistake comes it won't be too great to remedy."

Franklin Roosevelt had brought to the White House assurance and a sense of *noblesse oblige*, the legacy, in short, of his feudal, Hudson River Valley background. Harry Truman then brought to the White House the democratic pride of a son of the middle border. Poor eyesight kept him from attending school until he was fitted for glasses at the age of eight. His mother had taught him to read; the necessity of wearing glasses prevented him from engaging in boyhood sports. But dependence on eyeglasses did not prevent him from joining the Missouri National Guard in 1905. After holding desultory clerical jobs as a bank clerk, mailing-room clerk, and railroad timekeeper, he managed one of his father's farms from 1904 until 1917, when he and his regiment, which had elected him a second lieutenant of artillery, went to France. Unlike Generals Marshall and Eisenhower, Harry Truman had commanded troops in combat, rising to the rank of captain.

After the war, he and one of his comrades-in-arms, Eddie Jacobson, with whom he had operated a successful wartime canteen, formed a partnership and set up a men's haberdashery shop that soon failed. Jacobson went into bankruptcy; it took Truman until 1932 to pay off his debts. By this time he had behind him more than ten years in Missouri politics on local and state levels. He had lost but one election and in 1934 won his seat in the United States Senate. During his first term, Truman backed most of the New Deal legislation as well as Roosevelt's plan to enlarge the Supreme Court. He voted for the Neutrality Act but lived to regret it and to vote for its repeal. Not until his second term did he make his mark as chairman of a special Committee to Investigate the National Defense Program. His Senate colleagues and the leaders of the industries under investigation respected his judgment, grasp, and fair-mindedness. The press always liked him. He led a happy family life, being the devoted husband of his high-school sweetheart and the fond father of a delightful daughter.

Roosevelt won the Democratic presidential nomination in 1932, when he agreed to accept as his running mate crusty John Nance Garner—favorite son of Texas, favorite candidate of William Randolph Hearst, of William G. McAdoo, and of the California delegation to the Democratic Convention. In 1940, after Garner broke with Roosevelt over the third term, Roosevelt broke with the professional politicians and picked as his running mate Henry A. Wallace, his secretary of agriculture, who had never run for public office. By 1944, Roosevelt found himself all too happy to accept the advice of a new generation of politicians who insisted on a Roosevelt-Truman ticket. Henry Wallace proclaimed the Century of the Common Man; Harry Truman turned out to be that man—in person.

·4·

NOT SURPRISINGLY, it was Churchill who put Truman to his first major test. The day after Roosevelt died Churchill dispatched two messages to the new man in the White House. The first expressed his "personal sympathy in the loss you and the American people have suffered" and his hope that he might be "privileged to renew with you the intimate comradeship in the great cause we all served." The second message proposed that the British and American governments issue an immediate, joint public statement concerning their difficulties with the Russians, citing the compulsion he felt to speak on this subject before the House of Commons at an early date.

Truman's reply to the first message expressed gratitude for the sympathy extended and pledged continuation of the "loyal and close collaboration which to the benefit of the whole world existed between you and our great President." But the reply to the second message marked a measurable shift away from Roosevelt's tendency to conciliate Stalin and toward Churchill's tendency to stand firm. Yet Truman did not go all the way over to Churchill or slam the door on one last effort at conciliation. "I felt," he wrote in *Year of Decision,* "that military and political collaboration with Russia was still so important that the time was not ripe for a statement on this difficult and unsettling Polish situation," and before the day had ended, he followed through with a draft of his counterproposal: "a joint British-American message . . . to Stalin, putting definite proposals to him and setting them forth in direct language."

By the end of the afternoon of April 13 Truman had learned something of which he knew nothing before and of which Roosevelt had never received all the details. On April 7, Stalin had sent a message charging the Americans and British with having departed from the Yalta agreement, thus bringing the Polish question to what he called "really a dead end." He therefore now proposed following in Poland the example set by Tito in Yugoslavia, where the Communists received the twenty-one most important posts in the twenty-seven-member government, leaving six minor posts to non-Communists. Truman at once had Secretary of State Stettinius and Charles E. Bohlen, the State Department's top Russian expert and Roosevelt's interpreter at Yalta, draw up counterproposals that conformed to the Yalta specifications. Churchill promptly approved, forwarding them to Stalin, who again turned thumbs down.

But Truman, like Roosevelt, attached more importance to the San Francisco Conference than he did to Poland and regarded Molotov's attendance there as vital to its success. By this time, Stalin—in tribute to Roosevelt—had agreed to send Molotov to San Francisco and to have him stop off at Washington en route for a meeting with the new President. For this occasion Truman had himself briefed by experts, turning first to his old friend and former Senate colleague, James F. Byrnes, who had gone from the Senate to the Supreme Court and from there to the White House as "Assistant President" in charge of the home front. Soon Roosevelt gave Byrnes reason to believe that he would support him for the vice-presidential nomination, for which Truman headed up his old friend's pre-Convention campaign. But Roosevelt had not only dropped Wallace; he went on to pull the rug out from under Byrnes, and it was partly in the hope of helping "to balance things up" that Truman turned to Byrnes at his first opportunity.

He could easily have done worse and could hardly have done better. Byrnes had returned from the Yalta Conference, which Roosevelt insisted he attend, with an almost complete transcript of its sessions. This at once made him invaluable to the new President, who also told Byrnes he wanted him to replace Stettinius as secretary of state immediately after the San Francisco Conference, at which Stettinius had earned the right to serve as head of the American delegation. Truman also believed that the secretary of state (now being the man next in line for the presidency) should have won high elective office, as Byrnes had, many times.

Truman and Byrnes held their first meeting on April 13, only an hour before Stettinius and Bohlen appeared with their memorandum on Poland. Late that afternoon, the new President held his first meeting with the Roosevelt cabinet, to all of whom he expressed the hope that they would remain at their posts for the time being. Their silence seemed to mean consent, and all those present filed quietly away, except for Secretary of War Stimson, who asked for an early opportunity to describe to the new President an urgent project, concerning the secret development "of a new explosive of almost unbelievable destructive power." They made a date for April 25.

The next morning—April 14—Harry Hopkins arrived after more than a month in the Mayo Clinic. "One reason I am glad to be here," Hopkins told Truman in the course of their two-hour conversation, "and am glad to offer all the assistance I can is because I'm confident that you will carry out the policies of Franklin Roosevelt. And I know you know how to carry them out." Hopkins described Stalin as "a forthright, rough, tough Russian. He is a Russian partisan through and through, thinking always first of Russia. But he can be talked to frankly."

Ambassador Averell Harriman had waited until Stalin agreed to send Molotov to San Francisco before betaking himself to Washington, a few days ahead of the Soviet foreign minister. On April 20 he told Truman that "certain elements around Stalin misinterpreted our generosity and our desire to cooperate as an indication of softness, so that the Soviet Union could do as it pleased without risking challenge from the United States." At the same time, Harriman saw the Russians in such need of American help to reconstruct war damage that the United States could "stand firm on important issues without running serious risks." When Harriman ridiculed those Americans who "believed it was a matter of life and death to American business to increase our exports to Russia," Truman remarked that he did not fear the Russians, that he intended to be firm and fair, and that "the Russians needed us more than we needed them."

Harriman then went further, warning against a "barbarian invasion of Europe" and predicting that the establishment of Soviet control over any country meant its ultimate and total communization. Yet he did not consider himself a pessimist provided the United States abandoned "any illusion that the Soviet government was likely soon to act in accordance with the principles which the rest of the world held in regard to international affairs." Harriman called for give and take, with concessions on both sides. "I agreed," wrote Truman in his *Memoirs*, "saying I understood this, and that I would not expect one hundred per cent of what we propose. But I felt we should be able to get eighty-five per cent." When Harriman asked Truman how much importance he attached to the Polish question at San Francisco, the President "replied emphatically that it was my considered opinion that, unless settlement of the Polish question was achieved along the lines of the Crimea decision, the treaty of American adherence to a world organization would not get through the Senate. I said I intended to tell Molotov that in words of one syllable." When Harriman asked what would happen if Russia dropped out, Truman replied that without Russia there would be no world organization.

It goes without saying that Truman's reply to Harriman did not accord with other statements he had made at the same time or with the decisions he had made in conformity with them. But it also goes without saying that Harriman could not have been more pleased. No doubt he, too, had expressed similar sentiments, from time to time, to Roosevelt, whose silence he had mistaken for agreement. For if Truman suffered from an occasional propensity to blurt out whatever happened to come to the top of his head, Roosevelt sometimes followed the more dangerous practice of encouraging his aides to speak their minds while he nodded his head in what they mistook for agreement. In any event, Hopkins and Harriman both came away from their first encounters with Truman convinced that he saw eye to eye with both of them concerning the Soviet Union. "Frankly," said Harriman, as they parted, "one of the reasons that made me rush back to Washington was the fear that you did not understand, as I had seen Roosevelt understand, that Stalin is breaking his agreements. My fear was inspired by the fact that you could not have enough time to catch up with all the cables. But I must say that I am greatly relieved to discover that you have read them all and that we see eye to eye on the situation."

The most important "agreement" that Stalin, Churchill, and Roosevelt had tried to negotiate dealt with Poland, and Roosevelt did not live to see it completed. But the first agreement Stalin breached had to do with Romania and the accident happened sixteen days after the Yalta Conference adjourned. Young King Michael of Romania had declared war on Germany during August 1944, when a pro-Ally coalition government ousted General Antonescu's pro-Axis military regime. The new government also included Constantin Bratianu, leader of the Liberal party, representing the landowners, Juliu Maniu, leader of the Peasant party, the nation's largest, and Dr. Lucretiu Patrasceanu, veteran leader of the Communist party, one of the nation's smallest. Thirteen days after the Yalta Conference, the Soviet member of the Control Commission refused the requests of other members of that body to call a meeting. Three days later Soviet Deputy Foreign Minister Vishinsky appeared on the scene, demanding the resignation of the new coalition and ordering King Michael to appoint still another one, headed by Petru Groza, a former landowner and industrialist, who had no more trouble working with the Communists than they had working with him. Thirteen of the seventeen cabinet members obeyed any orders Groza might give, and he obeyed any orders given him by Patrasceanu who joined the new government along with Bratianu and Maniu.

Economically rich, politically unstable, militarily weak, Romania lay well inside the Soviet "area of responsibility" and Stalin did not dare not to make it a satellite, whether or not the British, Americans, or Romanians liked it. That old saying about Romanian being a profession not a nationality still held good.

Poland amounted to much more than Romania writ large. Historically, geographically, culturally, Poland had played a major role in the affairs of eastern Europe for a thousand years, and enjoyed a great resurgence during the years between the wars. Never a major power on the scale of Germany, Russia, France, or even Italy, Poland had played almost as great a part in the history of eastern Europe as Spain had played in the history of western Europe. The major powers of Europe always had to take Poland into account; they could never leave Poland outside their calculations. Even Chamberlain had never described Poland as he had described Czechoslovakia: "A far-away country of which we know little."

Never in Europe's history did Poland loom so large as it did in 1945. Since 1939 the war had exterminated six million of its twenty million Polish inhabitants. In that year the Germans invaded western Poland and laid it waste, while Red army troops occupied eastern Poland, a region in which Ukrainian and Byelorussian inhabitants predominated. By October, Ribbentrop and Molotov were able to announce that the Polish state no longer existed. In 1941, German troops again invaded Poland—this time on their way to the Soviet Union. In 1944 and 1945, Red army troops invaded Poland from the east, driving across its entire territory on their way to Berlin and points west. To most Poles liberation by the Russians represented little improvement over invasion by the Germans. But the survival of Poland in any form, even as a Soviet satellite, posed as difficult a problem to the victorious Russians as it did to the defeated Germans, and almost as much of a problem to the Anglo-Americans as well. The imprecise letter of the agreements reached at Yalta meant what their signatories were willing and able to make them mean, and the spirit of the signatories could not but reflect irreconcilable clashes of interest and sentiment. Thus, the Truman-Molotov confrontation on the specifics of the Polish problem continued the dialogue of the deaf that the death of Roosevelt had interrupted. Not until another ten years had passed did the authentically Polish voices of the anti-Stalinist Wladyslaw Gomulka and the Roman Catholic Cardinal Stefan Wyshynski make themselves heard.

·6·

TRUMAN AND HARRIMAN had met on April 20. Molotov arrived in Washington on Sunday, April 22, and Truman received him that evening. Stettinius, Harriman, and Bohlen sat in, as did Molotov's interpreter, Pavlov. Truman opened the discussion with the assurance that he "stood squarely behind all commitments and agreements entered into by our late, great President and I would do everything I could to follow along that path." Molotov echoed these observations and specifically endorsed the Yalta Agreement, which Truman assured him that he, too, intended to carry out.

But when Truman raised the specific issue of Poland and how deeply the American public felt about it, Molotov replied that the Russian public felt even more strongly and considered Poland a vital issue because it lay on their border. Truman agreed but pointed out that Poland had acquired great symbolic importance. He then expressed the hope that the Soviet, British, and American foreign ministers could reach agreement on various minor matters, and Molotov declared agreements could easily be reached, provided the views of the Soviet Union received consideration. He added that his government attached the greatest importance to the San Francisco Conference, especially in the light of recent military developments. Did the agreements reached at Yalta concerning the Far East still stand? "They did," replied Truman and repeated his opening assurance that he intended to carry out all agreements made by his predecessor.

Before their second and final meeting at five o'clock the following afternoon, Truman had engaged in a freewheeling conference with ten of his top military and political advisers. Stimson and Marshall argued that the Russians had a more realistic view of their interests in Poland than the Anglo-Americans did and that, in any case, they would not back down. Marshall added that the Russians had it in their power to delay their entry into the war against Japan until the United States had done all the dirty work. On the other hand, Secretary of the Navy James V. Forrestal argued that if the showdown had to come, the sooner the better. He attached prime importance to disabusing the Russians of any notion they might have of taking over eastern Europe without objection by the United States.

During the discussion, Truman (as he described it later) "explained that I had no intention of delivering an ultimatum to Mr. Molotov— that my purpose was merely to make clear the position of this government." Stettinius, Harriman, Bohlen, and Admiral Leahy, Roosevelt's chief of staff, who continued in the same capacity with Truman, remained with the President, helping him prepare himself for the second Molotov meeting. When Molotov arrived he brought with him his translator, Pavlov, and Andrei Gromyko, Soviet ambassador to the United States.

President Truman opened the meeting with an expression of regret, which Molotov immediately echoed, that no progress had been made toward a solution of the Polish question. The President declared that he and Churchill could not go beyond the new concessions they had made in their joint statement to which neither Stalin nor Molotov had paid any heed. Indeed, the Soviet government had just signed a military treaty with the provisional Polish government, thus according it further approval and enhancing its prestige. Truman continued to insist that he stood four-square behind Roosevelt and the Yalta agreements and that refusal by any of the Big Three powers to carry out the agreement on Poland would jeopardize their postwar unity of purpose. The United States not only planned to organize a postwar United Nations. It planned to appropriate large sums to help other nations repair wartime destruction and rebuild their economies. But Congress would not be likely to vote such appropriations to aid a recalcitrant Soviet Union.

Truman then handed Molotov a message for immediate transmission to Stalin, repeating the terms of the recent joint Churchill-Truman statement on Poland. Molotov replied with an authorized two-point statement of the Soviet point of view. First, he stated that the three governments, in spite of difficulties, had found a common language on the basis of which they had been settling their differences. Second, he noted that the three governments had always treated one another as equals and that at no point had any two of them tried to impose their views on the others. Truman replied that he asked only for Soviet compliance with the Yalta decisions on Poland. Molotov said his government, too, stood by the Yalta decisions as a matter of honor and that all difficulties could be overcome if the three governments continued to work together. Twice again Truman demanded Soviet compliance with the Yalta agreement. But Molotov hedged. First, he argued that Stalin could not see why the Yugoslav formula could not be applied to Poland. Then he said that while his government still supported the Yalta decisions it also insisted that any one of the Big Three could unilaterally reverse any one of these decisions at any time especially when—as in the case of Poland—it dealt with the affairs of a neighboring nation. Truman again declared that the United States was prepared to carry out the Yalta decisions and asked only that the Soviet Union do the same. The United States still wanted friendship with Russia but only on the basis of mutual observation of agreements, not on a one-way-street basis. "I have never been talked to like that in my life," said Molotov. "Carry out your agreements and you won't get talked to like that," Truman replied.

Yet, Truman never let his disgust with Soviet tactics toward Poland deflect him from his predecessor's major purpose of getting Molotov to San Francisco and the Soviet Union into the United Nations. What happens when an irresistible force collides with an immovable body? Truman, after Roosevelt's death, found himself in command of the irresistible force of the United States. Stalin, at the same time, had brought the Soviet Union out of its war against Germany an immovable body that even the irresistible force of the United States could not dislodge from eastern Europe or eastern Germany. Moreover, Truman had an incalculable unfinished task to complete in the Pacific war where Stalin carried little more weight than Truman carried in eastern Europe. Neither at the time of the German surrender, nor indeed at any other later date, did either of the two men dare risk challenging this standoff.

·7·

TWO DAYS AFTER Truman's second confrontation with Molotov came the most shattering confrontation of them all as Secretary of War Stimson laid before him more details on the supersecret, two-billion-dollar Manhattan Project, then nearing completion. As long ago as December 31, 1944, General Marshall had informed President Roosevelt that a bomb capable of producing "the equivalent of a ten-thousand-ton TNT explosion" should be ready about August 1. Not until April 13, after his first meeting with the Roosevelt cabinet, did Truman first hear of the project. The next day Byrnes expressed the belief that the new weapon "might well put us in position to dictate our own terms at the end of the war." Soon afterward, Dr. Vannevar Bush, head of the Office of Scientific Research and Development, explained to the new President the rudimentary principles of atomic energy and the consequences of its release. Whereupon Admiral Leahy blurted out: "That is the biggest fool thing we have ever done. The bomb will never go off, and I speak as an expert in explosives."

But not as an expert in physics, of which he knew no more than Truman or Stimson did. But the well-educated Stimson and the self-educated Truman possessed the kind of education that Leahy, Byrnes, and many other know-it-alls never sought or mastered—the capacity to recognize the authentic expert when they saw one. Whereas Leahy saw in the atomic bomb only another explosive that could not work, while Byrnes saw in it only a means of imposing a *pax americana* on the world, Stimson, as Truman put it, "seemed at least as much concerned with the role of the atomic bomb in the shaping of history as in its capacity to shorten the war."

At this point in time, the more a presidential adviser knew about the Manhattan Project, the greater his awe for its potential and the greater the caution he urged in exploiting it, militarily, politically, or any other way. Roosevelt, who died on the eve of Germany's unconditional surrender, lived to within less than three months of the first successful atomic-bomb test. Until the completion of that test, Roosevelt's successor could make no firm decision about the atomic bomb one way or the other. But those who had reason to believe that it would play a role in the final stage of the war against Japan could not but consider its impact on the Soviet Union and on the emerging United Nations Organization.

On no single individual did this responsibility weigh so heavily as it did on the President of the United States. Furthermore, even before the German surrender, Truman was getting one kind of advice from Secretary Stimson and General Marshall, another kind from his old crony Jimmy Byrnes, and still another from his predecessor's personal chief of staff, Admiral Leahy. At the same time, Harry Hopkins—the closest of all Roosevelt's aides and the American official whom Stalin trusted most —had offered his services (indeed his very life) to try to improve relations in that quarter. But the deaths of Roosevelt and Hitler, the succession of Truman, the opening of the San Francisco Conference, Truman's confrontation with Molotov, Germany's unconditional surrender, and the lengthening shadow thrown by the atomic bomb on the fate of Japan followed one another in such rapid succession that the very pace of events shook the world as much as did the events themselves.

• • •

At the time of the German surrender, some American troops occupied parts of central Germany and western Czechoslovakia, which Stalin considered earmarked for the Red army. Churchill, Montgomery, and some American officials, in and out of uniform, urged Eisenhower to disregard this arrangement, at least until Stalin stopped violating his agreements in other parts of Europe. But Eisenhower followed the letter of the agreements and the spirit of Roosevelt's policies, as did Truman after him. Only in Berlin had the Red army occupied German territory to which the Teheran and Yalta agreements granted the Anglo-Americans joint occupation rights. Not without truculence, the Russians respected these rights and agreed to similar arrangements for the temporary partition of Austria and the temporary joint occupation of Vienna.

The death of Roosevelt and the succession of Truman neither speeded nor delayed these developments, which simply followed the course the war itself had taken. Germany's surrender had not set the stage for an early peace conference; rather had it ushered in a brief period of Anglo-American bickering and a longer period of jockeying for position between the Anglo-Americans on the one hand and the Russians on the other. But it soon began to dawn on Stalin that the Red army could not extend its iron controls beyond the territories it already occupied. He found it more and more to his interest to stabilize a *status quo* that the Anglo-Americans, in like fashion, found it more and more dangerous to upset. The war against Germany had ended—not in a peace between victors and vanquished, but in a condition of total collapse on the German side, and, among the victors an east-west division that Churchill subsequently labeled the cold war.

XXIII

Hoist by Their Own Petards

·1·

THE INTERLUDE between Roosevelt's death and Germany's surrender became for Harry Truman a twenty-five-day crash course in his new presidential duties. The ten-week period between the German surrender in early May and the final conference of the Anglo-Soviet-American Big Three at Potsdam gave Stalin more than twice the time to apply his version of Marxist-Leninist dialectics to the new opportunities that the defeat of Germany had presented to the Soviet Union. President Truman, during his first twenty-five days in the White House, helped to organize the mechanics of the German surrender and of the United Nations Conference at San Francisco by the simple process of stepping into Franklin Roosevelt's shoes. But when the time came to deal with Molotov on Poland, he tried on a new pair of his own, which fitted him no better than Roosevelt's had fitted Roosevelt. But Churchill could not fault Truman with undue softness toward Stalin, who, in turn, could not fault Truman for kowtowing to Churchill. Nor could Roosevelt's closest advisers charge Truman with letting F.D.R. down. Yet no sooner had Germany surrendered than Truman succeeded in affronting both Churchill and Stalin.

On May 7, Leo Crowley, foreign economic administrator in charge of Lend-Lease, and Acting Secretary of State Joseph C. Grew advised President Truman to sign an order they had prepared putting an immediate end to Lend-Lease shipments to America's European allies in the war that had just been won against Germany. Crowley, a business executive drafted into wartime bureaucratic service, saw no alternative to following the precise stipulations of the Lend-Lease Act. Grew, a professional diplomat with forty years in the foreign service behind him, should have known better. "What they told me," Truman wrote later, "made good sense to me; with Germany out of the war, Lend-Lease should be reduced. They asked me to sign it, I reached for my pen and without reading the document I signed it." The order hit the British harder than it hit the Russians, but the Russians made the loudest outcry. Truman later had the order rescinded and learned his first lesson: not to sign anything he had not read. But to read everything he had to sign would have taken all his time. Thus he learned his second and more important lesson: "It is necessary for a President to delegate authority."

The third lesson took a longer time. Eventually Truman summed it up in the motto that stood on his desk: "The buck stops here," and it took the combined efforts of Churchill and Stalin to teach it to him for the first time. Since the middle of April, Churchill had been urging him to persuade Stalin to set an early date for another Big Three meeting, but the new President had his hands full conferring with Congressional leaders as well as with Roosevelt's former associates in the executive branch of government and in the armed forces of which he had now become the commander in chief. On May 7, a few hours before the German surrender to General Eisenhower at Reims, Churchill quoted Stalin's latest and toughest message on Poland as further evidence of the need for an early meeting. Two days later, Truman replied that he would rather have the request come from Stalin. Churchill argued that time was on Stalin's side; Truman replied that he wanted to wait until the San Francisco Conference had run its course. By this time, however, General Marshall, Admiral Leahy, and Joseph E. Davies had warned the President against Churchill's propensity to think first, last, and all the time of British Empire interests. Time might well be running in favor of the Soviet Union, but it was running still more strongly against British interests—as Churchill saw them.

The presence of Harry Hopkins in Washington provided the solution. Hopkins stood almost as high in Churchill's book as he did in Stalin's. On May 19, after Harriman had attended the opening weeks of the San Francisco Conference, he checked in at Washington with Truman and with the secretaries of war and navy. They all approved of sending Hopkins on a mission to Moscow to discuss with Stalin the details of a Big Three meeting and other matters of mutual concern. After the State Department gave its grudging consent, Truman informed Churchill of the Hopkins mission, which Stalin had already approved. Truman also arranged to have Harriman—for whom Churchill had a warm regard—

stop off in London and explain the Hopkins mission face to face. Churchill took it all in good part, even the exclusion of any British representative from the Stalin-Hopkins talks. Subsequently, Truman also sent Davies—the most pro-Stalin and anti-Churchill member of his inner circle—on what he considered a parallel mission to London to discuss with Churchill the projected Big Three conference and other matters of Anglo-Soviet-American concern.

In *Triumph and Tragedy,* the final volume in his history of the Second World War, Churchill recaptured the mood into which he sank immediately after the German surrender: "Apprehension filled my mind as I moved about among the cheering throngs of Londoners in their hours of well-won rejoicing after all they had gone through. The Hitler peril, with all its ordeals, seemed to most of them to have vanished in a blaze of glory." But not to Churchill: "The main bond of common danger which had united the Great Allies had vanished. The Soviet menace, to my eyes, had already replaced the Nazi foe. But no comradeship against it existed. . . . I could not rid my mind of the fear that the victorious armies of democracy would soon disperse and that the real and hardest test still lay before us. I had seen it all before."

Seen all what before? Nazi Germany, in May 1945, had fallen into such an abyss as never swallowed up the Kaiser's Germany in November 1918. Stalin's Russia, in May 1945, bore even less resemblance to Lenin's Russia a year after the Bolshevik Revolution. Or did Churchill in 1945 see in Stalin a greater threat to the British Empire than Hitler had been in 1939? Perhaps the fact that Churchill had rightly seen in Hitler a greater threat than the Kaiser led him to see in Stalin an even more terrible version of Hitler.

Churchill's historical analogies throw more light on himself and the British Empire than they do on Stalin and the Soviet Union. For light on Stalin, Milovan Djilas, former Yugoslav foreign minister and Tito's number two man, offers striking, firsthand evidence in his *Conversations with Stalin.* Here he quotes Stalin as having told him in April 1945, while concluding a treaty with Yugoslavia's new Communist government: "This war is not as in the past; whoever occupies a territory also imposes on it his own social system. Everyone imposes his own system as far as his army will reach. It cannot be otherwise." Nor did Stalin agree with those who foresaw no German revival for another fifty years. With their highly developed industry, their large working class, and their intellectual elite: "Give them twelve to fifteen years and they'll be on their feet again. And this is why the unity of the Slavs is important. But even apart from this, if the unity of the Slavs exists, no one will dare move a finger." Churchill made a deep impression on Stalin as a farsighted and dangerous bourgeois statesman. As for Stalin's own plans, they seemed to confirm Churchill's suspicions: "The war shall soon be over. We shall recover in another fifteen or twenty years, and then we'll have another go at it."

Djilas' impression of Molotov also bears repeating, especially in view of the impact he made on Truman—and that Truman made on him. From Molotov Djilas got the impression that he "looked upon everything—even upon Communism and its final aims—as relative, as something to which he had to rather than ought to subordinate his own fate. It was as though for him there was nothing permanent, as though there were only a transitory and unideal reality which presented itself differently every day and to which he had to offer himself and his whole life."

"Whoever occupies a territory also imposes on it his own social system." There spoke the Georgian seminarian whom Lenin had converted into a Russian Bolshevik. Lenin's Marxism effected the Bolshevik part of Stalin's conversion. But it was as Lenin's first Commissar for Nationalities that the young Georgian desperado who spoke Russian with a regional accent received his first indoctrination as a Russian nationalist. As Commissar for Nationalities Stalin bore the responsibility of organizing the non-Russian Soviet Socialist Republics and bringing them into the Russian-dominated Union of Soviet Socialist Republics. Some twenty years later, when Red army troops, under the terms of the Nazi-Soviet pact, brought Estonia, Latvia, Lithuania, and parts of Poland and Romania into the Soviet Union, Stalin found himself reverting to his earlier National-Bolshevik phase.

But the doctrine that Stalin expounded to Djilas in April 1945 went further and became the leitmotiv of the third and final period of his dictatorship. First had come industrialization of the Soviet Union under the slogan "Socialism in One Country," culminating in the great purges. The second period, which began with the Nazi-Soviet pact, culminated in the Great Patriotic War, with its twenty million Russian victims—the same number estimated to have died in the purges. But even before the German surrender ushered in the third and final period of Stalin's rule, he had proved himself as Russian as any czar and as relentless a scourge of his Old Bolshevik comrades as any Cossack.

.   .   .

The passage of time did not add to Stalin's stature. During the months of May and June 1945, Churchill lacked the power to match his convictions. Truman needed all the power he possessed to finish off Japan. This left Stalin free to do as he pleased in Romania, Hungary, Bulgaria, Yugoslavia, Poland, Czechoslovakia, and those parts of eastern Germany liberated by the Red army. His worst enemy could hardly have propelled him on a more disastrous course than the one he freely chose. While many Anglo-American officials, in and out of uniform, persuaded themselves and their compatriots that the Red army could march to the English Channel with less trouble than it had marched to the Baltic Sea, Stalin convinced himself that this same Red army could impose the social order of Soviet Communism on all the territories it had occupied beyond its prewar, western frontiers.

Neither Churchill nor Truman had planned it this way. It was Stalin who had incorporated the Baltic states, East Prussia, and parts of Romania and Poland into the Soviet Union and called them "Socialist Republics." It was Stalin who installed puppet Communist regimes in Hungary, Romania, Bulgaria, Czechoslovakia, and East Germany and called them "People's Democracies." But, as time passed, this widespread application of Stalin's postwar doctrine not only set the hands of the clock back in the very territory on which the Red army had imposed it. The maintenance of a satellite empire in eastern Europe proved no boon to the Soviet Union—economically, politically, or militarily. The German menace, which had inspired it, never emerged. Instead, the partition of Germany, on which Stalin and his successors always insisted, led in due course to the creation of a new and lopsided double Germany—the weaker, eastern Communist half a constant source of trouble and expense to Moscow, while the burgeoning German Federal Republic in the west became, within another quarter century, the most powerful nation in western Europe and as such the logical political and economic partner of its mighty neighbor to the east.

·2·

WHEN HOPKINS, on April 14, assured Truman that Stalin could be "talked to frankly," he had no idea that before the end of May he would be doing the talking. It was Truman's idea, with which Churchill concurred and which Stalin embraced, to have Hopkins fly to Moscow for a series of wide-ranging talks with Stalin. After all, it was Hopkins who, in Roosevelt's behalf, initiated the Lend-Lease shipments to Britain in the spring of 1940 and to the Soviet Union in the summer of 1941, shipments that Truman casually canceled after the German surrender but resumed soon afterward.

Between May 27 and June 6, Stalin and Hopkins met six times. At their first session, Hopkins seized the initiative and persuaded Stalin to head their agenda with the recent deterioration in Soviet-American relations, including the determination of the Truman administration to get those relations back on the same basis that had existed under Roosevelt, to whose policies Truman remained completely devoted. Stalin took the initiative at their second meeting, ticking off his five chief complaints: Argentina's admission to the United Nations, the participation of France as an equal with the Soviet Union on the German Reparations Commission, the American attitude toward Poland, the abrupt American termination of Lend-Lease, and the disposition of the German navy and merchant marine. The session closed with Stalin's suggestion to take up three more topics: future occupation policies in Germany and Japan and another Big Three meeting.

The third session dealt with Soviet participation in the war against Japan, the future of China, Japan's unconditional surrender, and the Soviet Union's role in the Far East. The postwar treatment of Germany wound up the session. The fourth session reverted in still more detail to the Polish question, which Stalin agreed to discuss with Truman and Churchill at Potsdam. The fifth meeting began with more of the same but ended with a conversation between Stalin and Hopkins only, Pavlov serving as interpreter for both. Here Hopkins pleaded at length for the fourteen Polish representatives who had come from London to Moscow to discuss their country's future, only to be clapped into jail. "I told Stalin further," wrote Hopkins of the interview, "that I personally felt that our relations were threatened and that I frankly had many doubts about it and with my intimate knowledge of the situation I was, frankly, bewildered with some of the things that were going on." He got nowhere. "Marshal Stalin stated that he did not intend to have the British manage the affairs of Poland and that is exactly what they want to do." At the sixth and final meeting on June 6 Stalin said he "wished to thank Mr. Hopkins for his great assistance in moving forward the Polish question." Stalin also "stated that he was prepared to accept the American position on the point at issue at San Francisco in regard to voting procedure."

At the time the two men met, Stalin's demands on Poland and his opposition to some provisions of the United Nations Charter threatened to break up the San Francisco Conference and to prevent Big Three agreement on how to make peace with Germany and war on Japan. Hopkins obtained no concessions on Germany or Poland, but his Moscow mission did result in a compromise at San Francisco whereby the Soviet Union did not veto Argentina's bid for membership and the United States did not veto Poland's. The Latin American republics consented to admit two of the Soviet republics to membership in the United Nations General Assembly, and the Soviet Union accepted an American formula under which the Soviet Union eased some of its veto power in connection with the subjects the Security Council might discuss but not the action it might take. Stalin had more to gain from supporting the creation of the United Nations than he had to gain from sabotaging it at the start. He had more to gain from agreeing to discuss a German settlement with Truman and Churchill than he had to gain from open defiance. He had more to gain from entering the war against Japan than from remaining neutral. The Hopkins-Stalin talks had not broken down any old barriers or raised any new ones. They had cleared the way for future diplomatic contacts and political arrangements. A peace treaty with Germany still lay in the far future. First, however, the victorious great coalition had to make peace with itself.

The Hopkins mission to Moscow did not change Stalin's spots or Stalin's policies. But the sheer guts that Hopkins brought to his assignment could not but win Stalin's admiration. The give and take between them added to the regard in which each held the other. Afterward, Acting Secretary of State Grew transcended the ingrained suspicions of the career diplomat and heaped praises on Hopkins, who, in his handling of Stalin, served Truman as well as he had served Roosevelt. By speaking bluntly to both Truman and Stalin, Hopkins moved the two men closer to mutual understanding—if not to mutual agreement—than Roosevelt and Stalin had ever come. Stalin never forgave nor forgot Truman's cancellation of Lend-Lease; Truman remained as suspicious as ever of Stalin's methods and motives in Poland. But Hopkins made it a little easier for Stalin to bring the Soviet Union into the United Nations and to confer with Truman and Churchill at Potsdam.

The Hopkins mission to Moscow brought the two principals together six times during a two-week period. The Davies mission to London lasted only a week end and brought him and Churchill together for a total of eight hours. Stalin and Hopkins had discussed issues: Poland, China, Japan, Soviet-American trade, the United Nations. Churchill and Davies talked politics and philosophy. It was quite a contrast. Describing one of Churchill's diatribes, Davies wrote the President that as he was listening to Churchill "inveighing so heavily against the threat of Soviet domination and the threat of Communist domination in Europe, and disclosing such a lack of confidence in the professions of good faith of Soviet leadership, I wondered whether he, the Prime Minister, was now willing to declare to the world that he and Britain had made a mistake in not supporting Hitler for, as I understood him, he was now proclaiming the doctrine which Hitler and Goebbels had been proclaiming and reiterating for the past four years in an effort to break up Allied unity and 'Divide and Conquer.' "

What purpose did the Davies mission serve? In *Between War and Peace* Herbert Feis suggests that it "may have served to make Churchill aware of the way in which his proposals were disturbing the civilian members of the American government who thought continued co-operation with Russia essential for peace; and how keenly they were worrying the military members who wanted such co-operation in order to bring the war against Japan to the quickest possible end." Such may —or may not—have been Truman's intention. Certainly the war against Japan had become his first order of business. But different motives animated Davies, and Churchill took his visit in the spirit that his visitor paid it. As the prime minister saw it, his prestige had suffered another setback, and Stalin now threw an ever-darkening shadow across Europe.

· 3 ·

THE ACCELERATING PACE of events justified these misgivings—at any rate for the moment. One week before the Potsdam Conference, scheduled to open on July 16, Truman wrote his wife: "Wish I didn't have to go, but I do and it can't be stopped now." The previous week Byrnes had taken the oath of office as secretary of state, and on July 6 the presidential party sailed for Antwerp aboard the cruiser *Augusta*. To fortify himself against Churchill's powerful personality and against the anti-Soviet elements in the American delegation, Truman arranged to have Davies sit beside him at the conference table and then had to be reminded that the American delegation also included Averell Harriman, Roosevelt's wartime envoy to Moscow, who did not share the hopes that Stalin had inspired in both Roosevelt and Davies.

Davies before the war and Harriman during it had both served Roosevelt as ambassador to Moscow. Davies returned convinced that Stalin, for all his ruthlessness, could be persuaded in his own self-interest to co-operate with the United States during and after the war. But the burden of proof lay with the United States, as the stronger party, to show the same respect for and understanding of the Soviet Union as it expected the Soviet Union to show for the United States. Like Davies, Harriman believed that Stalin could be persuaded, in his own self-interest, to co-operate with the United States during and after the war. But Harriman argued that Stalin respected nothing but force and that the United States, as the stronger party, could best win and hold Stalin's respect by standing up for its interests as firmly as Stalin stood up for Soviet interests. Roosevelt found merit in both points of view and while he listened sympathetically to the advice of Davies, and even accepted it about as often as not, he gave Harriman a free hand to conduct his day-to-day dealings with Stalin and Molotov as he saw fit. Thus Truman, at Potsdam, found himself in the position of having to reconcile the divergent views of two of Roosevelt's most trusted advisers on Soviet affairs.

The day before the American delegation sailed, the United States and British governments made a decision more in line with the views of Davies than with the views of Harriman. This took the form of joint Anglo-American recognition of an enlarged and reorganized Polish provisional government of national unity, thus placing their seal of approval on Stalin's settlement of Soviet relations with both Poland and Germany. The new Polish government contained twenty-one posts, of which thirteen of the most important fourteen went to Communists— Bierut remaining as president, Osubka-Morawski as premier, and Gomulka as vice premier. One non-Communist, Stanislaw Mikolajczyk, former leader of the Peasant party, the largest in prewar Poland, and former president of the Polish government in exile in London, became minister of agriculture and land reform and held the rank of second deputy premier.

To Poland's non-Communists this single concession to Mikolajczyk meant nothing. But Stalin had only to support their demand to push Poland's postwar western frontier from the eastern to the western Neisse River to win their approval of the reorganized provisional government. This still did not give postwar Poland as much German territory in the west as the Russians had taken away from prewar Poland in the east, and it caused Stalin no pain at all. The new Poland would now include the former German cities of Breslau and Stettin, and ten million

Germans (three million of them from between the two Neisse rivers) would have to quit their prewar homes and lands for permanent abodes further west.

Historian Herbert Feis, like many other pliers of his craft, has often speculated on the ironies of history—a theme to which the Soviet settlement of postwar Poland's frontier with postwar Germany lent itself: "Suppose the Americans and British had their way, instead of the Poles and the Russians, and the line between Germany had been drawn further to the east. In that event, the eastern part of Germany—the area that was the Soviet zone—would presumably now be larger and more populous, and have greater coal, industrial, and land resources. Thus it would be able to challenge the effort of West Germany—formed out of the American, British, and French zones—to represent all Germany. Poland would have been weaker, perhaps less afraid of future German attempts to regain its territory, but perhaps more dependent than it is upon the Soviet Union. The way the situation has worked out up to now is one of those numberless incidents in history which show how often results are different from anticipations."

History's ironies often arise from the inherent propensity of men and events to bring forth their own opposites. "All things are double one against another," as the Apocryphal Book of Ecclesiasticus has it. Stalin's efforts to secure the Soviet Union's frontiers by expanding Soviet rule beyond them increased the insecurity that they were designed to diminish. Worse yet, this reversion to the crudest type of imperial expansion backfired against its initiator in an increasingly anti-imperialist world. Whereupon the source of that backfire proved as ironical as the backfire itself.

Thanks to the broad-front strategy—which Eisenhower, not Stalin, originated—the unconditional surrender of Germany found that country and the rest of Europe split in two along the Stettin-Trieste line. Nor did the first threat to the integrity of that line come from Stalin; it came from Tito and it affected Trieste, not Stettin. For Tito had designs not only on the ports of Trieste and Fiume, at opposite sides of the base of the Istrian peninsula. He also wanted the entire peninsula, with its predominantly Italian population, which had been awarded to Italy after the First World War. Because Croatian and Slovene minorities inhabited some of Trieste's suburbs they refused to leave other regions which Yugoslav troops occupied after driving out the Germans. After considerable backing and filling, Truman and Churchill finally authorized Field Marshal Alexander and his Anglo-American forces to secure

Trieste and finally the whole peninsula for Italy. No clashes occurred and while Stalin always backed Tito, he did so only in words, and Tito quietly accepted the inevitable.

Tito's intransigence seemed, at the time, a grim augury of deeper divisions and sharper conflicts still to come, but subsequent events have put the whole episode in a different light. Stalin did not lift a finger to help Tito at Trieste or press any of his claims anywhere beyond the Stettin-Trieste line. On June 24, Churchill glumly but frankly acknowledged that the division of Europe had come to stay when he wound up a message to Stalin with the observation: "It seems that a Russianized frontier running from Lübeck through Eisenach to Trieste and down to Albania is a matter which requires a very great deal of argument conducted between good friends." The argument continues, sometimes subjecting the friendship to considerable strain. But the longer the argument has gone on, the stronger a factor the Stettin-Trieste line has become in the stabilization of postwar Europe.

Originally, that line conformed to agreements reached at Quebec in 1944, at Yalta in 1945, or to positions held by the Soviet and Anglo-American forces at the time of the German surrender. Churchill, Stalin, Roosevelt—and Truman after him—all assumed that all these positions remained subject to changes that an eventual peace conference would decree. But, as time went on, the temporary congealed into the permanent; whatever existed became its own excuse for continued existence. The French have some words for it: only the provisional endures. Unsatisfactory as each twist and turn in the Stettin-Trieste line might be, any alternative appeared increasingly impractical and unworkable. Nobody planned it that way, but, in doing what came natural, Stalin found himself consolidating the positions the Red army already held in eastern Europe while Truman found it just as natural to seek the earliest possible end to the war against Japan by shifting more and more American ships, planes, and troops to the far Pacific—and points still further west.

. . .

Stalin lived to see himself hoist, in eastern Europe, by his own dialectical petard; Roosevelt did not live to see his United Nations Organization hoist by the atomic petard he had fashioned. The previous chapter has described Secretary of War Stimson's explanation of the Manhattan Project to President Truman. The next chapter will describe the impact of the first successful atomic test on the Potsdam Conference. The following chapter will describe the impact of the first atomic bombings on the war itself. But no reappraisal of the events before and after Potsdam can ignore the mood that the imminent probability of a successful test explosion generated in President Truman's official family. It took, however, another twenty years for this mood and its consequences to emerge in clear perspective.

In 1965, twenty-eight-year-old Gar Alperovitz brought six years of research at the universities of Wisconsin, California, and Cambridge, England, and in Washington, D.C., to bear on the completion of his book *Atomic Diplomacy: Hiroshima and Potsdam. The Use of the Atomic Bomb and the American Confrontation with Soviet Power.* "I now believe," wrote the author in his introduction, "new evidence proves not only that the atomic bomb influenced diplomacy, but that it determined much of Truman's shift to a tough policy aimed at forcing Soviet acquiescence to American plans for Eastern and Central Europe." And not in eastern and central Europe only. In briefing Truman on the Manhattan Project, Stimson urged delaying the Potsdam meeting until such time as he could attend with the "master card" of a tested atomic weapon in hand. Stalin also favored delay, but for a different reason. The longer he could postpone the Potsdam meeting, the stronger the Red army's hold on eastern Europe would become. And because Churchill dreaded that prospect, he pleaded for a meeting with Stalin before July at the latest.

Whereupon Truman—with his eyes on Japan—used the Hopkins mission to Moscow to pin Stalin down to meet at Potsdam on July 15, by which time the President believed that the Manhattan Project would also have completed its mission. Even that left Stimson less than satisfied, as he warned Truman of "the greatest complication" if the bomb itself were not "laid on" Japan before the meeting with Stalin. But Truman could wait no longer about breaking the news to Chiang Kai-shek and his brother-in-law and foreign minister, T. V. Soong, concerning the deal that Roosevelt had made with Stalin at Yalta at Chiang's expense. Far from resenting the arrangement, Soong jumped at the opportunity to open his talks with Stalin at Moscow in June, leading as they did to new pledges of Soviet support to Chiang Kai-shek. Indeed, Soong wanted to conclude the talks at the earliest possible date and was prepared to make further concessions to Stalin in exchange for further Soviet reassurances. But Truman did not dare to go so far or to explain the reasons for his caution, partly because he did not trust Soong to keep the details of the Manhattan Project to himself and partly because he did not yet know whether or not the test explosion would prove successful.

Fifteen years later, Dr. Leo Szilard, one of the European physicists closest to the Manhattan Project, described a conversation he had with Byrnes on May 28, 1945: "Byrnes was concerned about Russia's having taken over Poland, Romania, and Hungary, and so was I. Byrnes thought the possession of the bomb by America would render the Russians more manageable in Europe. I failed to see how." Of all the men around Truman, only the ailing Joseph E. Davies and the seventy-eight-year-old Stimson agreed with Dr. Szilard. All the others regarded the atomic bomb as a club to be held over Stalin's head. And Stimson alone went so far as to regard it as the new foundation on which a stable, realistic settlement with the Soviet Union could be gradually erected. In a farewell memorandum to Truman, dated September 11, 1945, Stimson warned that Soviet-American relations "may be perhaps irretrievably embittered by the way we approach the solution of the bomb with Russia. For if we fail to approach them now and merely continue to negotiate with them, having this weapon ostentatiously on our hip, their suspicions and their distrust of our purposes will increase." And Stimson added: "The chief lesson I have learned from a long life is that the only way you can make a man trustworthy is to trust him; and the surest way to make him untrustworthy is to distrust him and show him your distrust."

The Soviet Union produced few Stimsons and fewer Alperovitzes. Even in the United States they were the exceptions rather than the rule. In the United States it is the Trumans, in the Soviet Union it is the Stalins who make history. But the Soviet Union has no Alperovitzes who write, revise, and reappraise history. And so much the worse for the Soviet Union. For the very strength of the case that Gar Alperovitz has drawn up against American atomic diplomacy suggests (among other things) what a case a Russian Alperovitz could make against the use to which Stalin put the Red army in eastern Europe, while Truman was using atomic diplomacy to frustrate Stalin in the Far East. Whether Roosevelt could have put America's atomic monopoly, which he helped to create, in the service of the United Nations Organization, which he also helped to bring into being, we can never know. But Stalin and Truman wound up the slaves rather than the masters of the weapons that had won them the greatest war in history.

XXIV

Potsdam Watershed

·1·

By July 17, 1945, when the Potsdam Conference opened, Stalin had seen to it that his army's red star of Soviet empire would cast its beams as far westward across Europe as the Stettin-Trieste line—but no farther. Not so the American star of empire which still pursued its westward course beyond the waters of the Pacific Ocean to the mainland of Asia from which the British, French, Dutch, and Japanese empire builders were all withdrawing. No longer did coalition warfare based on a beat-Germany-first strategy hold the Anglo-Soviet-American alliance together. Now the future of a defeated Germany, an undefeated Japan, and a China torn by civil war created more division than harmony. At first the death of Roosevelt shocked Stalin into bringing the Soviet Union into the United Nations, while permitting him at the same time to frustrate Churchill and gratify Truman by postponing their Potsdam meeting until mid-July. But the stars in their courses, obeying their own laws, caught up with everybody concerned.

Stalin's opportunity came first—more than a week before the Potsdam meeting—when he agreed to a Polish settlement, a redivision of Europe, and a new balance of power that froze the Red army occupation zones. This caused Truman less pain than it caused Churchill, who feared that the red star of empire would resume its westward course while Britain's star of empire would fade away. Truman did not welcome either prospect, but he now gave top priority to the war against Japan and if he could make the Potsdam Conference serve that aim, so much the better.

At Potsdam the man who carried most weight with Truman was neither Davies nor Churchill, Harriman nor Stimson, but his old personal friend and political ally Jimmy Byrnes, whose experience and versatility provided those secondary but essential qualities for which Truman's rarer and simpler virtues left ample scope. On first meeting Truman, Churchill described himself as "impressed with his gay, precise, sparkling manner and obvious power of decision." Field Marshal Brooke, less responsive than Churchill to American ways, entered this first impression in his diary at Potsdam: "On the whole I liked him: not the same personality as his predecessor, but a quick brain, a feeling of honesty, a good businessman, and a pleasant personality. Last night, in one of his quick remarks, Stalin had said about him, 'Honesty adorns the man,' and he was not far wrong."

Herbert Feis, in *Between War and Peace*, described Truman as having been "impressed" by Stalin and "pleased by traits that ease the work of the Conference, by Stalin's directness, by the way in which he stuck to the main point, by his signs of wanting to do business quickly, and even by his off and on geniality." Byrnes went further. "The truth is he is a very likable person." Thus, Roosevelt's successor made his diplomatic bow under propitious circumstances. For one thing, he could always rely on the quick-thinking, fast-talking, well-briefed Jimmy Byrnes to exploit any defensive or offensive opening that either the British or the Russians might develop. Moreover, who, better than Truman, could start the ball rolling in the first place? Fate having chosen him as the man to carry on the Roosevelt tradition, he could not wait to start reorganizing Europe for peace and redeploying the armed forces of the United States to bring the war against Japan to an early and victorious close. The first plenary session sought only to agree on an agenda based on suggestions made by the principals. Truman bluntly advised the conference to learn from the experience of the peacemakers of 1919 and establish at once a Council of Foreign Ministers to draw up peace treaties with Italy, Romania, Hungary, Finland, and Bulgaria. He postponed consideration of peace terms with Germany as too controversial. The first plenary session paid him the compliment of passing this as its first motion.

Three more proposals followed: the political and economic principles to govern the occupation of Germany; plans for implementing the Yalta Declaration on Liberated Europe; a new approach to German reparations. Never at Teheran or Yalta had Roosevelt presented so well-prepared or comprehensive a program. But this cut little ice with Churchill and none with Stalin. The inclusion of China, already a permanent member of the United Nations Security Council, as one of the five nations to be represented on the Council of Foreign Ministers drew an immediate objection from Stalin, who argued that the Chinese foreign minister had no competence or interest in European affairs. Churchill then wanted more time to study the Yalta Declaration on Liberated Europe. He also cautioned against undue haste in drawing up peace terms for Italy, which had made a lot of trouble for Britain in 1940.

When it came Stalin's turn to speak, he listed eight topics: 1. Disposition of the German navy and merchant marine. 2. Reparations. 3. Trusteeships for the Soviet Union under the United Nations Charter. 4. Status of the former Axis satellites. 5. The future of the Franco regime in Spain. 6. Tangier. 7. Syria and Lebanon. 8. Poland. The head spun. Especially Truman's. "I told Stalin and Churchill that we should discuss the next day some of those points on which we could come to a conclusion," wrote Truman in *Year of Decision*. "Churchill replied that the secretaries could give us three or four points—enough to keep us busy. I said I did not want just to discuss. I wanted to decide. Churchill asked if I wanted something in the bag each day.

"He was as right as could be. I was there to get something accomplished, and if we could not do that I meant to go back home. I proposed we meet at four o'clock instead of five in order to get more done during the time we would be meeting. The others agreed to this. I then proposed we adjourn. Stalin agreed to the adjournment, but said there was one question he would like to raise first: Why did Churchill refuse to give Russia her share of the German fleet? Churchill replied that he thought the fleet should be destroyed or shared, saying that weapons of war are horrible things and that captured vessels should be sunk. Whereupon Stalin said, 'Let us divide it,' adding, 'If Mr. Churchill wishes he can sink his share.' With that the first meeting of the Potsdam Conference adjourned."

· 2 ·

THESE OPENING-DAY EXCHANGES echoed the discussions at Teheran and Yalta. But the whole tone at Potsdam soon changed. At Teheran, Roosevelt and Stalin had pressured Churchill into agreeing to open the long-delayed second front the following year. At Yalta Roosevelt and Churchill had pressured Stalin into pledging Soviet support to a post-war United Nations, while Roosevelt and Stalin drew up a secret agreement, later approved by Churchill, calling for Soviet intervention in the war against Japan within three months of Germany's surrender. In short, the first two Big Three meetings tried to speed the course of events that the war had set in motion, whereas at Potsdam, the longer the conference lasted, the greater the outside pressure on the participants to catch up with events that threatened to get beyond their control.

On July 17, the day of the first session, Secretary of War Stimson received a cable-memorandum from home, announcing that on July 16 the first full-scale test of an implosion-type atomic-fission bomb had been successfully completed at Alamogordo Air Base in New Mexico. The British had been in on Manhattan Project from the start, and on July 18 Stimson gave further details, that he had just received, to Truman and to Churchill, who strongly opposed informing the Russians. Back in 1943, Roosevelt and Churchill privately agreed to reject any suggestion "that the world should be informed about the Tube Alloys, with a view to international agreement regarding its control and use," but that "it might perhaps, after mature consideration, be used against the Japanese, who should be warned that the bombardment will be repeated until they surrender." An interim committee, headed by Stimson and charged with setting policies concerning the bomb's production and use, subsequently and independently reached the same conclusion. On May 14 Stimson in his diary described the atomic bomb—then known to be nearing completion—as "a master card in our hand," specifically in the event of difficulties with the Russians in the Far East.

But after the German surrender, after the preparations for the test at Alamogordo, and after the agreement to hold the Potsdam Conference, the matter of informing the Russians acquired new urgency. Foreseeing this predicament, Truman had suggested and Stimson had approved that they say nothing until after the successful test explosion. "On July 24," wrote Truman afterward, "I casually mentioned to Stalin that we had a new weapon of unusually destructive force." To which Stalin replied: "That's fine. I hope you make good use of it against Japan." Two days before this, after Churchill had read the full text of a 2000-word memorandum on the Alamogordo test by General Leslie R. Groves, head of the whole Manhattan Project, he exclaimed as he laid down its pages: "Stimson, what was gunpowder? Trivial. What was electricity? Meaningless. This atomic bomb is the second coming in wrath."

But Field Marshal Brooke had responded as phlegmatically to the Groves memorandum as Stalin had responded to his chat with Truman.

"He had absorbed all the minor American exaggerations," wrote Brooke in his diary concerning Churchill, "and as a result was completely carried away. It was now no longer necessary for the Russians to come into the Japanese war; the new explosive alone was sufficient to settle the matter. Furthermore, we now had something in our hands which would redress the balance with the Russians. The secret of this explosive and the power to use it would completely alter the diplomatic equilibrium which was adrift since the defeat of Germany. Now we had a new value which redressed our position (pushing out his chin and scowling); now we could say, 'If you insist on doing this or that, well . . .' and where are the Russians!"

True to form, Brooke dismissed, out of hand, any and every innovation that bore the "Made in U.S.A." label. In like fashion, Stalin, whose agents had given him at least as thorough a briefing as Brooke had received, could no more reconcile the atomic breakthrough with his closed Marxist-Leninist universe than Brooke could reconcile it with his equally irrelevant Anglo-centered universe. In point of fact, the first atomic explosion had shattered the prejudices of Brooke, the preconceptions of Stalin, the hopes of Churchill, and the dreams of Stimson, who differed from most of their fellow pilgrims to Potsdam in that they had brought with them assorted visions, dreams, ideologies, and aspirations that had served them well throughout their lives. The world-weary Brooke may not have entertained such high hopes for the superannuated British Empire as the cynical Stalin cherished for the brash Soviet Union. The irrepressible Churchill saw an atomic miracle guaranteeing the consolidation and preservation of an English-speaking millennium. Stimson clung to the Emersonian formula that to make a friend you must be a friend, hoping that through bestowal of atomic and other favors on the Russians the United States could bribe Stalin into renouncing Communism and embracing democracy.

The once-born, two-dimensional Truman took a more direct approach. Unlike his predecessor he neither sought to charm Stalin nor to needle Churchill. He had stood firm on every commitment Roosevelt made to Stalin, he had supported Churchill's stand on Poland to the end, while always rejecting Churchill's advice to match every treaty violation of Stalin's with a counterviolation of his own. Although Truman became progressively disillusioned about the Russians and found the proceedings at Potsdam increasingly irksome and futile, he "often felt that Molotov kept some facts from Stalin, or that he would not give him all the facts until he had to. It was always harder to get agreement out of

Molotov than out of Stalin. Where Stalin could smile and relax at times, Molotov always gave the impression that he was constantly pressing."

Yet, Truman came home from his face-to-face confrontation with Stalin with a conviction that he could never have reached by any other route than the one that took him to Potsdam: "Anxious as we were to have Russia in the war against Japan," he wrote in *Year of Decision,* "the experience at Potsdam now made me determined that I would not allow the Russians any part in the control of Japan. Our experience with them in Germany and in Bulgaria, Hungary, Romania, and Poland was such that I decided to take no chances in a joint setup with the Russians. As I reflected on the situation during my trip home, I made up my mind that General MacArthur would be given complete command and control after victory in Japan. We were not going to be disturbed by Russian tactics in the Pacific.

"Force is the only thing the Russians understand. And while I was hopeful that Russia might someday be persuaded to work in cooperation for peace, I knew that the Russians should not be allowed to get into any control of Japan."

·3·

A FORTNIGHT BEFORE Truman had reached these conclusions, further reports from New Mexico and from the Pacific theater of war convinced him and his military, scientific, and political advisers that the time had come to explain to the leaders of Japan just how much more they had to gain from surrendering unconditionally at once rather than continuing a long-drawn-out fight to the finish. On July 26, Truman, Chiang Kai-shek, and Churchill therefore put their names to a thirteen-point Potsdam Proclamation calling for Japan's immediate, unconditional surrender. Its first three points stressed that the United States, Britain, China, and their allies could now bring much greater military force to bear against Japan than the military force that had just destroyed Germany and warned the Japanese to take careful note of the Germans' fate. "The time has come," read points four and five, "for Japan to decide whether she will continue to be controlled by those self-willed militaristic advisers whose unintelligent calculations have brought the Empire of Japan to the threshold of annihilation, or whether she will follow the path of reason. The following are our terms. We shall not deviate from them. There are no alternatives. We shall brook no delay."

The points that followed called for the elimination "of those who have deceived and led the people of Japan into embarking on world conquest." It reaffirmed the terms of the Cairo Declaration, which limited the area of postwar Japan to its home islands. Points nine and ten read: "The Japanese military forces, after being completely disarmed, shall be permitted to return to their homes with the opportunity of leading peaceful and productive lives. We do not intend that the Japanese shall be enslaved as a race or destroyed as a nation, but stern justice will be meted out to all war criminals, including those who have visited cruelties upon our prisoners. The Japanese Government shall remove all obstacles to the revival and strengthening of democratic tendencies among the Japanese people. Freedom of speech, of religion, and of thought, as well as respect for fundamental human rights, shall be established."

The next two points assured the Japanese that they could develop peacetime industry and engage in peacetime world trade and that the Allied occupation forces would be withdrawn when the terms of the ultimatum had been fulfilled. Point 13 read: "We call upon the Government of Japan to proclaim now the unconditional surrender of all Japan's armed forces, and to provide proper and adequate assurances of their good faith in such action. The alternative for Japan is complete and utter destruction." The proclamation did not mention the emperor or demand his elimination or liquidation. Neither did it offer any assurances of respect for his person or his powers. For the next forty-eight hours, American radio transmitters broadcast the full text of the proclamation world wide. The ambassadors of neutral nations also received copies of the full text to transmit to the Japanese. After two days American listening stations reported that Radio Tokyo had begun referring to the proclamation as "absurd," "presumptuous," "unworthy of consideration." During those two days no meetings had taken place at Potsdam. The eyes of the world had turned to London where Churchill had flown to hear the results of the general election of three weeks before.

Since the Teheran Conference of November, 1943, Churchill had seen Roosevelt and the Americans playing greater and greater parts in determining and executing grand strategy. At the same time, his own efforts, even his own style, antagonized more and more of his compatriots. Having promised, when he organized the national government in May 1940, to call a general election after the defeat of Germany, he set July 5 as the day on which the British electorate would choose a new House of Commons for the first time in ten years. It took until July 26 to gather complete returns, notably from two million servicemen all around the world. On July 25, Churchill and Eden therefore flew from Potsdam to London, accompanied by Clement Attlee, leader of the Labour party and, as such, deputy prime minister, who had attended all the Potsdam sessions. The next day they watched the ballot count give Labour an unprecedented majority of more than one hundred seats in the House of Commons and five years in which to exercise it.

On July 28, Prime Minister Clement R. Attlee and Foreign Secretary Ernest Bevin arrived in the Cecilienhof Palace at 10:30 P.M. when the tenth plenary session of the Potsdam Conference opened. Before the regular session started, Stalin read a communication that Japan's Ambassador Sato had received on July 13 from Tokyo recommending that Prince Konoye visit Moscow in the hope that the Soviet government would mediate the war between the United States and Japan and negotiate a new agreement with the Soviet Union. Stalin had already told Truman that the Japanese had suggested the possibility of such mediation by Konoye before and that now they had suggested nothing new. On both occasions he turned them down.

The account of the events that led up to this mediation offer and that followed its rejection belongs with the rest of the account of the war in the Pacific, in which the Potsdam Conference played a role as important as it was unexpected. The fact that the American atomic breakthrough at Alamogordo coincided with the final Big Three meeting served to link the war that had just ended in Europe with the war that was about to end in the Pacific. Stalin, having focused all his attention for the past ten weeks on the partition of Germany, the division of Europe, and the creation of a Soviet satellite empire in eastern Europe, failed to grasp the military and political consequences of the American atomic breakthrough, especially in connection with the war against Japan. He assumed that in a matter of months the Red army would overrun so much of Manchuria and Korea that it would be able to share, as a matter of course, in the occupation of Japan itself and in the settlement of the Chinese civil war. Churchill may have overreacted to the American atomic breakthrough, but he had erred in the right direction. Stalin's underreaction erred in the wrong one.

At this juncture, the entire British nation found itself living in what amounted to a collectivist, socialist society. The outcome of the voting suggested that most Britons wanted more of the same and less of what

Churchill and his fellow Conservatives represented. In December 1944, under the title "Churchill Must Go," H. G. Wells wrote in the pro-Labour weekly *Tribune:* "Winston Churchill, the present would-be British Führer, is a person with a range of ideas limited to the adventures and opportunities of British political life. He has never given evidence of thinking extensively or of any scientific or literary capacity. Now he seems to have lost his head completely. When the British people were blistered with humiliation by the currish policy of the old Conservative gang in power, the pugnacity of Winston brought him to the fore. The country liked fighting and he delighted in fighting. For want of a better reason, he became the symbol of our national will for conflict, a role he has now outlived."

Bernard Shaw, writing in the Socialist *Forward,* ridiculed both Churchill and Roosevelt at Yalta: "As to rebridging the rivers the Allies have made impassable, rebuilding the cities they have reduced to heaps of rubble, replacing the locomotives they have smashed, training craftsmen and professionals to do the work of those they have slain, feeding the millions they have left destitute; in short, repairing the damage by war which has reduced itself to absurdity, not a blessed word. Nothing but fairy tales.

"Pass on to something real. We know the names of the Three in One. But who was the One in Three? Clearly Uncle Joe. On the Polish question he was the first and the rest nowhere. Lublin has beaten London hands down; and Washington has looked on, not knowing what to say."

Captain B. H. Liddell Hart, Britain's leading military expert since the early 1920's, offered this analysis of the world of 1945 in a speech before a Liberal party rally: "This war was won—in the only real sense of the word—when the Germans' aggressive power was crippled. That result was achieved over two years ago. Since then we have been fighting on, blindly, to smash the Germans' defensive power—and with it, their power to act as a buffer for the West. That result brought glory at a heavy price, but meant losing the peace. Britain's leader was too excited by the battle to look ahead, and see the inevitable consequence of the smashing victory for which he thirsted. It makes no sense."

· · ·

These comments from three of Churchill's most eminent contemporaries give authoritative expression to the doubts that he had stirred not only among his political adversaries but within the military establishment that he had served so long. When Mrs. Churchill said to her husband after the election returns arrived, "It may well be a blessing in disguise," he replied: "At the moment it seems quite effectively disguised." That moment did not last long. The pendulum of public opinion had swung so far against Churchill that his days of political leadership seemed to have gone forever. But history's acceleration not only restored him to power in another six years. He spent most of his time writing his six-volume masterpiece, *The Second World War*. Only those readers who know nothing of the subject will regard it as the last word. But on no reader can even a brief exposure to its pages fail to leave a lasting impression.

The postwar years brought Churchill a happier fate than befell Stalin. The ballots that deprived Churchill of the immense (but fading) powers that he had wielded for five years liberated him from increasing frustrations. Since the turn of the century his life had oscillated between periods when he made history and periods when he wrote it. He therefore had long and firsthand experience with history's ironies and contradictions as well as with what Clemenceau had called its grandeurs and miseries. None savored more keenly than Churchill the irony of his wartime role as the imperialist who presided over the liquidation of the British Empire and the Tory who transformed Great Britain into a socialist, welfare state. Churchill had not transcended himself; he had fulfilled himself. He had led a double life—part statesman and part historian—and in so doing proved that the whole can be greater than the sum of its parts.

·4·

WITH NO CHURCHILL to bait and no Roosevelt to delude, Marshal Stalin found himself confronted at Potsdam by former Captain Harry Truman and former Major Clement R. Attlee, both of them veterans of the Western Front in the First World War, but members of the awkward squad when it came to the new diplomacy of World War II. But it was quite a different story as far as Soviet Foreign Minister Molotov was concerned. In James F. Byrnes he found a tougher, rougher, more experienced antagonist than Secretary of State Stettinius, and in Foreign Secretary Ernest Bevin, leader of Britain's rough, tough transport workers' union, a ruder opposite number than the well-groomed, aristocratic Anthony Eden.

On Saturday, July 28, when Attlee and Bevin replaced Churchill and Eden at the eleventh plenary session, the discussion dealt first with extending diplomatic recognition to Bulgaria, Romania, and Hungary; it closed with more discussion of reparations from Germany and Italy. At one point Secretary Byrnes remarked: "The United States has unfortunately found that if it agrees with the Soviet delegation, the British delegation does not agree, and if it agrees with the British that the Soviet disagrees." But the American delegation did agree with Foreign Secretary Bevin when he questioned Stalin more sharply than Eden had ever done on the question of German reparations. Yet all to no purpose. The session adjourned, agreeing only to continue the discussion and postpone the decision. President Truman raised his voice to report the news he had received the day before that the United States Senate had ratified the United Nations Charter by a vote of 89 to 2.

On the afternoon of Sunday, July 29, Molotov called on Truman in Stalin's behalf to report that his chief had come down with a cold which would compel him to postpone the twelfth plenary session until Tuesday, July 31. Meanwhile Stalin also wanted Truman to know that the Soviet government now considered that it could best enter the war against Japan when and if the United States, Britain, and the other Allied governments addressed a formal request to the Soviet government to do so. Molotov argued that this would shorten the war and save lives, adding, however, that the Soviet formal declaration of war still had to await the conclusion of an agreement with China. It did not seem to bother Molotov that only as a result of pressure by the United States had the Chinese agreed even to discuss such an agreement with the Russians in the first place.

Needless to say, that consideration had not escaped Truman's attention, and did not disguise his displeasure. As he wrote afterward in *Year of Decision,* he saw in Molotov's proposal "a cynical diplomatic move to make Russia's entry at this time appear to be the decisive factor to bring about victory." He continued: "At Yalta Russia had agreed, and here at Potsdam she reaffirmed her commitment, to enter the war three months after V-E Day, provided that Russia and China had previously concluded a treaty of mutual assistance. There were no other conditions, and certainly none obliging the United States and the Allies to provide Russia with a reason for breaking with Japan. Our military advisers had strongly urged that Russia should be brought into the war in order to neutralize the large Japanese forces on the China mainland and thus save thousands of American and Allied lives. But I was not willing to let Russia reap the fruits of a long and bitter and gallant effort in which she had no part."

In a more politely phrased letter to Marshal Stalin, Truman also quoted three passages from the charter of the United Nations (to which both the Soviet Union and the United States now adhered), citing violations of its principles by Japan and obligations, under that charter, that the United States and Soviet governments should fulfill. Molotov also repeated the Soviet case in favor of fixing Poland's western frontier along the course of the Oder and western Niesse rivers and again pressed the Soviet claim to ten billion dollars' worth of German reparations. Secretary Byrnes, Admiral Leahy, and Charles E. Bohlen joined the discussion which Truman and Byrnes recapitulated later in the day to Attlee, Bevin, and Sir Alexander Cadogan, the permanent Foreign Office representative at Potsdam.

Stalin's request that the Allies appeal to Moscow for a declaration of war against Japan got even shorter shrift than his requests for Italian colonies, exclusive rights at the Dardanelles, and quarantines of Franco's Spain and Perón's Argentina. But it differed from these other political fishing expeditions in two respects. For one thing, it marked a first, not a last step. In the second place, the power of decision rested exclusively in the hands of the United States. Stalin accepted American control of the Far Pacific with the same realism that he expected the United States to show toward Soviet control of eastern Europe. But he found it as hard to reconcile himself to this state of affairs as Truman did to reconcile himself to the state of affairs east of the Stettin-Trieste line.

Secretary Byrnes, on the other hand, saw some scope for maneuver, based on a give-and-take "package deal." As he explained it in *Speaking Frankly*, published in 1947: "On July 31, I told Mr. Molotov there were three outstanding issues: reparations, Poland's administration of a part of the Soviet zone, and our paper entitled 'Admission to the United Nations' dealing with Italy and the Balkan states. I submitted a proposal containing the only concessions we were willing to make and requested that Mr. Molotov present the three proposals to Generalissimo Stalin so that they might be discussed at the afternoon session. I told him we would agree to all three or none and that the President and I would leave for the United States the next day."

That same afternoon, Truman opened the plenary session with Stalin by suggesting that Byrnes present his "package deal" for discussion. After expressing shocked disapproval of Byrnes' tactics, Stalin adopted them himself with all the gusto of a veteran bargainer at Oriental bazaars. "First," wrote the author of *Speaking Frankly*, "he suggested a fantastic increase in reparations. Then, he proposed that the amount of capital equipment to be removed from the western zone in return for such products as food, coal, timber, and so on, be increased from 12 per cent to 15 per cent. I said if he would withdraw his other demands and agree to the other two proposals in dispute, we would agree to the 15 per cent. He agreed and the conference ended shortly thereafter."

At the friendly, closing session on August 1, Stalin, who had "disliked the tactics of Mr. Byrnes" the day before, asked permission, just before the gavel fell, to say a few words about "Mr. Byrnes who has worked harder perhaps than any of us," adding, "He has brought us together in reaching so many important decisions." When President Truman then expressed the hope that the next Big Three meeting might occur in Washington, Stalin muttered, "God willing." Had the sardonic Old Bolshevik, who, as a youth, studied briefly for the priesthood in a Tiflis seminary, chosen this means of expressing doubt?

•   •   •

The participants in the Potsdam Conference suffered their worst defeats in those areas in which they had prepared themselves most thoroughly and to which they had devoted the most time: Germany's future and Europe's. But their greatest achievements lay in those areas in which they could neither prepare nor commit themselves: Japan's future and China's. Thanks to Stalin and his determination to impose his Communist social order on all the lands and peoples of eastern Europe beyond the Stettin-Trieste line, the Anglo-Americans and the French subordinated their suspicions of one another and their fears of the Germans to the task of making West Germany safe for democracy and integrating it with its west-European neighbors. Wartime illusions of a united Germany and a united Europe helping to build one world gave way to the postwar realities of a partitioned Germany and a divided Europe seeking some stability in a new postwar balance of world power. Which sent the achievements of the Potsdam Conference up in smoke.

For these achievements had taken the form of a twenty-one-point protocol of its proceedings, more than two thirds of it devoted to the establishment of a Council of Foreign Ministers—Soviet, American, British, French, and Chinese—to make preparations for early peace treaties with Italy, Romania, Bulgaria, Hungary, and Finland and an eventual settlement with an eventual government of Germany, plus a statement of "The Principles to Govern the Treatment of Germany in the Initial Control." Here the authority would lie with the commanders in chief of the Soviet, American, British, and French armed forces in their different occupation zones. The "package deal" devised by Secretary of State Byrnes saved the Potsdam Conference from disintegrating before it had adjourned and helped to pave the way toward peace treaties with the former German satellites and their admission to United Nations membership. But disagreements over the control of Germany ruled out any possibility for a peace treaty with a government representing all of Germany—or even the existence of such a Germany. Stalin on the one hand and the Anglo-Franco-American leaders on the other agreed to disagree on the future of Germany and of Europe. Stalin persisted in his determination to impose his social order on one half of Europe and one half of Germany. The western Allies thus found themselves compelled to build a new order in western Europe and West Germany.

This did not, however, mean that the Potsdam Conference had led only to negative results. For one thing, it permitted Truman, Churchill, and Chiang Kai-shek to serve an unconditional-surrender warning on Japan in terms that presently applied to the new atomic weapons the Americans could bring to bear. In the second place, the Potsdam Conference enabled Truman to make personal contact with Stalin and thereby steel himself for situations that might well have proved too much for the weary and troubled Roosevelt. More important—as things turned out—Truman, at Potsdam, also made the acquaintance of Attlee, with whom he had important and productive dealings for the next five years. Finally, the very disappointments that Truman encountered at Potsdam renewed and redoubled his determination to concentrate on the defeat of Japan, a consummation not, perhaps, devoutly to be wished for, but surely to be welcomed as one more initiation to the inevitable consequences of unconditional surrender.

The death of Roosevelt in mid-April had removed from the scene the most important member of the wartime Big Three. The fall of Churchill, three months later, conformed with the accelerating tempo of events. Although China had no representative at Potsdam, Chiang Kai-shek's name appeared on the Potsdam Declaration. Although Stalin asserted himself throughout the Potsdam talks, he did not sign the Potsdam warning to Japan. Stalin had boasted to Japan's Foreign Minister Matsuoka, in 1941, "I, too, am an Asiatic." Lenin, in 1920, had unilaterally canceled the "unequal treaties" that the Russian czars had forced upon the Chinese and followed through by establishing close ties with

Dr. Sun Yat-sen's Republic of China. Stalin continued the good work, turning to the Chinese Communists after they had broken with Chiang Kai-shek.

None of this came to the fore at the time of the Potsdam Conference, but as far as Stalin was concerned, he could never afford to ignore Japan, China, or almost any other part of Asia. Russia's star of empire had taken an eastward course for a longer time and over a wider area than it had taken in a westward one. Indeed, Russians had settled in parts of Alaska before any Americans had arrived. But America's star of empire, at the time of the Potsdam Conference, suddenly radiated an atomic glow, and nothing could ever again be quite the same as it had been before.

XXV

The Second Coming in Wrath

· 1 ·

WITH THE FALL OF MANILA, on February 25, 1945, General MacArthur wound up the one major land campaign fought by American ground troops in the Pacific war. On the night of March 9–10, General Curtis LeMay opened the final campaign of that war, when he sent 279 low-flying B-29's over Tokyo, where the fire bombs they dropped destroyed over 250,000 of its flimsy buildings, killing more than eighty thousand persons, leaving more than a million others homeless, and leveling more than sixteen square miles of the city, with a loss of fourteen planes and 140 airmen. The Washington headquarters of the Twentieth Strategic Force, of which LeMay headed the XXI Bombing Command, promptly marked thirty-three Japanese urban centers—Osaka, Kobe, and Nagoya, among them—for similar treatment. The attacks continued until the atomic bombings of Hiroshima on August 6 and Nagasaki, two days later.

The Yalta Conference followed the fall of Warsaw to the Red army and coincided with the Soviet occupation of Budapest. General LeMay's first bombing of Tokyo came two days after the first American troops crossed the Rhine at Remagen. As far as the war against Germany was concerned, the Yalta Conference set the stage for the post-war arrangements later made by the victorious Anglo-Soviet-American coalition on the one hand and the defeated Germans and their former satellites on the other. As far as the war against Japan was concerned, the Yalta Conference set the stage for subsequent Soviet participation in that war—at China's expense.

While General LeMay's B-29's subjected Japan's fragile cities to the most intensive air bombing of the war, the Joint Chiefs at Washington decided to take another long step toward Tokyo by throwing seven crack army and marine corps divisions against sixty-mile-long Okinawa, largest of the Ryukyu Islands, 350 miles south of Japan, and less than that from the China coast. The Imperial General Staff at Tokyo saw in this decision their opportunity to do on Okinawa what Hitler had tried and failed to do in his 1944 Ardennes offensive: that is, throw the American drive for final victory into reverse. For one thing, the Japanese had already discovered on Iwo Jima that they could cut their own losses and increase American casualties by abandoning their traditional banzai charge. Instead of hitting the attacker at the water's edge, they let him "come to them." In the second place, they took advantage of Okinawa's rocky terrain to construct the heaviest concentration of artillery they had ever assembled on any Pacific island. In the third place, Japan's Imperial General Staff assigned General Mitsuri Ushijima, a veteran of the Burma campaign, and more than 100,000 men to throw back the American attackers, while more than a thousand kamikaze flyers would sink the bulk of the American naval vessels on which the expansion of any American beachhead would depend. Finally, in connection with that beachhead, the Japanese battle plan called for their last remaining—and the world's largest—battleship, the 72,920-ton *Yamato*, which did not have enough fuel to make the round trip, to run itself aground close enough to shell the American ground troops with its nine batteries of 18-inch guns.

From April 1 to April 5, General Ushijima permitted the Americans to occupy Okinawa's offshore atolls and to land on some of its beaches. On April 5, his artillery fire brought the advancing Americans to a swift and bloody halt. The next day came the kamikazes, followed by the *Yamato*. Within a little more than twenty-four hours, American planes had sunk the *Yamato* before she could get within range of the beachhead; the kamikazes had sunk or disabled twenty-four American vessels, including one destroyer, the *Bush*, sunk. Within another few days, the Japanese lost most of the rest of their kamikazes, but the ground fighting continued until June 22, when General Ushijima chose to die under American gunfire outside his dugout. American losses totaled 12,000 killed; Japanese totaled 100,000. But for the first time in any battle on any Pacific island the unheard-of total of more than 7000 Japanese troops chose to surrender.

Five days after the Americans landed on Okinawa, Stalin and Molotov drew their conclusions and took appropriate action. Four years had passed since the spring of 1941, when Stalin had signed a neutrality pact of mutual nonaggression with Japan. On paper, it meant that neither country could make war on the other until three months after renouncing the agreement. In fact, it served notice on the Japanese to expect to have the Russians on their necks as soon as the Russians got the Germans off theirs. Since February, the Russians had been shipping troops and weapons to Siberia at the rate of thirty carloads a day. But Molotov waited until April 5 to inform the Japanese ambassador at Moscow that the Soviet government was renouncing their neutrality pact. By the end of May, the Russians had shipped 160,000 men, 1200 tanks, and 1300 planes to Siberia. After that, they speeded up their deliveries. Thus the Japanese could expect a Russian attack any time after July 5. The Japanese had access to information about Germany not readily available to the Russians, who (in their turn) had information about the United States not readily available to the Japanese. By early April both the German and the Japanese governments had only to put two and two together.

·2·

EMPEROR HIROHITO's resemblance to Hitler did not extend beyond the first two letters of their names. As Japan's allegedly 124th emperor and the legendary descendant of the sun goddess, Ama-Terasu, Hirohito embodied his country's most ancient and treasured traditions. He chose the word *Showa,* meaning peace, to characterize his era and his reign. In contrast to the loudmouthed German demagogue, the shy Japanese emperor spoke in a high-pitched voice. Hitler based his racist, nationalist propaganda (which he firmly believed) on a distorted mishmash of tribal legends and modern quackery. Hirohito, while still a youth, rejected the myth of his divine origin. His horrified teacher referred the recalcitrant pupil to Prince Kimmochi Saionji, eldest of Japan's elder statesmen and a former prime minister, who assured Hirohito that he agreed with him completely, that he himself came of as good a lineage, if not a better one, but that while Hirohito had no obligation to believe in the myth of his divinity, he did have an obligation to perpetuate that myth among the Japanese people, who needed a superhuman God of the Sun and Son of Heaven to rally around, worship, and die for. Saionji therefore urged Hirohito to drop the study of so controversial a subject as history and to take up one of the sciences, in any event steering clear of politics. Hirohito took the advice to the extent of becoming an outstanding marine biologist. Born in 1901, he came to maturity during the peaceful 1920's and acceded to the throne on the death of his mentally deranged father in 1926, having already acted as prince regent for several years. But when war came, and things went from bad to worse, he found that the name he had chosen for his reign and the ancestral exercise of his ceremonial duties—far from isolating him from politics—laid upon him an inescapable obligation to his country, his station, and himself.

Japan's Supreme Council for the Direction of the War, consisting of the war and navy ministers, the army and navy chiefs of staff, and the prime minister and foreign minister, wielded almost absolute power in wartime Japan. Almost but not quite. On two occasions—the fall of Saipan in July 1944 and the American landing on Okinawa in April 1945—a council of former prime ministers, known as the Juishin, exercised its authority to meet and advise the emperor to dismiss the incumbent prime minister and to replace him with another. As prime minister, General Tojo had ruled with a strong hand, but much good that did him in the light of the defeats to which his leadership had brought his country, culminating in the fall of Saipan. The Juishin recommended the replacement of Tojo with the more moderate General Kuniaki Koiso, who made no secret of his belief that Japan had lost the Pacific war. Hirohito welcomed the replacement, but the American landing on Okinawa convinced him that the time had come to sue for peace. His closest confidant, Marquis Koicho Kido, Lord Keeper of the Privy Seal, agreed. So did the eighty-year-old retired Admiral Kantaro Suzuki, a hero of the Russo-Japanese War, who had also served for ten years as majordomo of the Imperial Court, when he approved of the 5–5–3 naval ratio among the American, British, and Japanese navies. But Suzuki had no desire to step into Koiso's shoes until Kido made this personal appeal: "Japan's position is so critical that I, as Lord Keeper, must implore you to make a firm decision to save the nation." When the forty-four-year-old emperor called the eighty-year-old admiral into his presence, Suzuki felt obliged to mention his political inexperience, his advanced age, and his impaired hearing. Hirohito replied: "Your unfamiliarity with politics is of no concern nor does it matter that you are hard of hearing." Later, Hirohito revealed, "I was aware of Suzuki's sentiments from the very beginning of his appointment and likewise I was convinced that Suzuki understood my sentiments. Consequently I was not in a hurry to express to him my desire for peace."

Nor was Suzuki in any hurry to let the Japanese public in on his secret. "The current war is a war for the liberation of Asia," he told the

Diet in his first speech. "We have no alternative but to fight. . . . We can never tell what a fatal blow the fighting spirit of the Japanese soldiers on Iwo Jima and Okinawa has given the enemy. . . . We can conclude that we are not losing the war." But Suzuki put his finger on the nub of the matter when he predicted that any impairment of the imperial system would deprive life of all its meaning for one hundred million Japanese.

Japan differed from all the other major belligerents in the Second World War in that at no point did any single Japanese wield any such power as Roosevelt or Stalin, Churchill or Hitler, Chiang Kai-shek or Mussolini. On the other hand, in no other warring nation did the armed services count for so much as they did in Japan or the political leaders and political parties count for so little. But the two meetings of the Juishin—the first after the fall of Saipan, the second after the landings on Okinawa—suddenly revealed the bankruptcy of Japan's military and naval establishments, even in their own field. In July 1944, the emperor accepted the Juishin's recommendation and approved the appointment of General Kuniaki Koiso to replace General Tojo as premier. In May 1945, the emperor accepted the Juishin's recommendation of Admiral Suzuki as Koiso's successor. The delicate Japanese balance of power among army, navy, parliament, Juishin, and emperor had shifted steadily, measurably, decisively in the emperor's favor.

On May 11, 12, and 13, 1945, immediately after the final German surrender to the Russians in Berlin, Japan's Supreme War Council focused its attention on the Russians. Either in spite of or because of Molotov's denunciation of the neutrality pact there was talk of inviting the Russians to mediate the war in the Far East, of persuading them to resume their neutrality, or even of requesting Russian supplies. General Korechika Anami, war minister, army spokesman, and strong man of the Council, argued: "As the Soviet Union will be in confrontation with the United States after the war and therefore will not want to see Japan too much weakened, the Soviet attitude toward us may not be severe." Foreign Minister Togo shared Anami's delusions about the Russians but not his determination to fight the war to a finish. Admiral Yonai, the navy minister, took a much darker view of Japan's prospects. "I think the turning point of the war was the start," he declared. "I felt from the beginning there was no chance of success." Admiral Teijiro Toyoda, the navy chief of staff, still agreed with Anami. General Umezu, the army chief of staff, under whom Anami had served in Manchuria, was even more determined than Anami to fight to the finish. With the Council split 3–3, neither faction had the upper hand, and the forces of inertia prevailed. Something, somewhere had to give.

·3·

STALIN HAD LEARNED at Yalta how much the Americans could increase their war effort against Japan once Germany had gone down to defeat. He also learned from Japan's Ambassador Naotake Sato that more and more Japanese leaders feared the worst—at an early date. Sato, for his part, learned from Soviet sources about Soviet troop movements against Japan, and he included in his reports along these lines the advice to Foreign Minister Togo to seek peace before the worst happened. Having cracked the Japanese code, American officials picked all this up from the wireless messages through which Tokyo and Moscow communicated. Lester J. Brooks, in *Behind Japan's Surrender: The Secret Struggle That Ended an Empire*, has written: "This should have been sufficient to bring about a crash program to end the war. Instead, plans and preparations for the Potsdam Conference proceeded as scheduled and other efforts went ahead on a 'war as usual' basis."

During the month that passed between the fall of Okinawa on June 22 and the release of the Potsdam Declaration on July 26, conditions in Japan went from bad to worse. The men at the top knew that Molotov's termination of the Soviet-Japanese neutrality pact and the Soviet troop concentrations foreshadowed Russian intervention. Only some fire-eating generals and the fanatical kamikaze flyers saw any prospect of military victory. Air attacks had destroyed eighty Japanese cities. The population of Tokyo had dropped from 6,800,000 to 2,400,000. Fire bombs had burned out the city's fire-fighting equipment.

Nevertheless, three members of the six-man Supreme Council for the Direction of the War—War Minister Anami, Army Chief of Staff Umezu, and Navy Chief of Staff Toyoda—clung to their faith in the inherent invincibility of Japan and the inevitable doom that must overtake Japan's enemies. To them, the example set by a few thousand kamikaze suicide flyers could not fail to inspire millions of Japanese soldiers and tens of millions of the Japanese people to hurl themselves, with the same disregard of death, into a final battle from which the divinity of their emperor would ensure their victorious emergence and the frustration of their foes. They had not underestimated the importance of their emperor in their country's scheme of things. Their mistake had been to assume that their divine emperor would think and act as they did. But so deeply did they revere their emperor that, when the moment of truth came, they followed the dictates of his intelligence and conscience rather than their own.

Nobody in Japan, and only a select few in the United States, knew at this time that the Americans had already successfully tested a plutonium bomb, of which they had one in readiness, plus another uranium bomb which required no testing. But the fire bombs already dropped on eighty Japanese cities had made the Declaration's warning of "prompt and utter destruction" entirely credible. Japan's six-man Supreme Council had no doubts about the military superiority of the United States. It was the Declaration's unconditional-surrender clause that half the members of that Council found unacceptable. But the Americans knew no more about the deadlocked Council than the Japanese knew about the plutonium and uranium bombs. It did not take the Americans much longer to let the Japanese in on their secret.

·4·

ON OCTOBER 11, 1939, Alexander Sachs of the Lehman Corporation brought President Roosevelt a letter from Albert Einstein informing him that two outstanding physicists, the Italian, Enrico Fermi, and the Hungarian, Leo Szilard, had sent him a manuscript that led him "to expect that the element uranium may be turned into a new and important source of energy in the near future." The letter continued: "It may become possible to set up a nuclear chain reaction in a large mass of uranium, by which vast amounts of power and large quantities of new radium-like elements would be generated. . . . It is conceivable— though much less certain—that extremely powerful bombs of a new type may thus be constructed." The Einstein letter and further conversation with Alexander Sachs led Roosevelt to say, "Alex, what you are after is to see that the Nazis don't blow us up." To his secretary Roosevelt added: "This requires action." The action, in which both Fermi and Szilard participated, followed and further research led Roosevelt two years later to order Dr. Vannevar Bush, head of the Office of Scientific Research and Development, to organize the production of an atomic bomb as soon as possible, with secret funds provided for under the budget.

Two months later came the Japanese attack on Pearl Harbor after which the President ordered the release of still more funds for the unit, eventually known as the Manhattan Project, with General Leslie R.

Groves, a forty-six-year-old West Point graduate with an engineering degree, as the co-ordinator. For the next three years, under the supervision of a four-man committee of Dr. Bush, President James M. Conant of Harvard, General William Styer, and Admiral William Purnell, General Groves put together a scientific-industrial complex, combining research and development. Such theoretical physicists as Enrico Fermi, Szilard, the brothers Arthur and Karl Compton, and J. Robert Oppenheimer headed the research. A far more numerous but less highly specialized assortment of engineering and industrial personnel reduced vast piles of metallic raw materials into tiny concentrations of atomic and nuclear energy and made the bomb-casings that contained them.

In September, 1944, General Groves brought the Manhattan Project into its final phase which began on the Utah desert and ended with the dropping of the first bomb itself. From Utah he moved, in January 1945, to Cuba for another two months, and finally to the northeastern corner of Tinian Island in the Mariannas, one hundred miles southwest of Guam and seventeen hundred miles from Tokyo. Here the fifteen hundred picked airmen whose training had begun in Utah continued to fly secret, practice missions in the course of which, at heights of 30,000 feet, they dropped replicas of the narrow uranium bombs and the thicker plutonium bombs which they would drop at some future, unknown date on an unspecified target, one bomb per mission.

On June 18, more than two months after the death of President Roosevelt and more than one month after the German surrender, President Truman summoned a meeting in Washington of his so-called Interim Committee of top military and civilian officials to discuss and decide how to compel Japan to surrender in the shortest possible time with a minimum loss of American lives. "As I understand it," said the President in summation, "the Joint Chiefs of Staff, after weighing all the possibilities of the situation and considering all possible alternative plans, are still of the unanimous opinion that the Kyushu operation is the best solution under the circumstances." The President here referred to a preliminary invasion of Kyushu Island prior to the major operation across the Tokyo plain on the larger island of Honshu. Secretary of War Stimson agreed that there could be no other choice, adding only that he thought "a large submerged class in Japan" opposed the war and that "something should be done to influence them." Admiral Leahy, long a skeptic concerning the whole Manhattan Project, could never justify the unconditional-surrender formula and again deplored it: "I do not agree with those who say that unless we obtain the unconditional surrender of Japan that we will have lost the war. I fear no menace from Japan in the foreseeable future, even if we are unsuccessful in forcing unconditional surrender. What I do fear is that our insistence on unconditional surrender will only result in making the Japanese more desperate and thereby increase our casualty lists. I don't think this is at all necessary."

After the meeting President Truman asked Assistant Secretary of War John McCloy for his opinion. He called the talk of invading Japan "fantastic." "Why not drop the atomic bomb?" he asked. Truman reassembled the meeting, but further discussion got nowhere because nobody knew whether the test explosion in New Mexico would succeed. One month later they got their answer. Thus, the Second World War that Hitler deliberately set in motion had set in countermotion a chain reaction of its own. More than one hundred thousand persons of many nationalities and skills had worked together for more than four years at a cost of two and a half billion dollars to achieve a military, industrial, and scientific breakthrough that overshadowed the very war that had inspired it from the start. To the Second World War belonged the dubious credit for having hastened the dawn of the atomic age with all its implications for peace as well as war, for the future as well as the present, for the world as well as for the United States.

On June 1, 1945, Secretary of War Stimson had informed President Truman that the scientists who had developed the bomb recommended that it "be used against the enemy as soon as it could be done. They recommended further that it should be used without specific warning and against a target that would show its devastating strength." The quotation appears in Truman's Year of Decision. "We can propose no technical demonstration likely to bring an end to the war"; the scientists added. "We see no acceptable alternative to its direct military use." The scientists included Dr. J. Robert Oppenheimer, Dr. Arthur Compton, Dr. Ernest O. Lawrence, and Dr. Enrico Fermi. On July 24, under instructions from President Truman, General Thomas T. Handy, as the U. S. Army's acting chief of staff, directed General Carl Spaatz, as commander of the U. S. Army Strategic Air Forces, to have the 509th Composite Group of the Twentieth Air Force on Tinian "deliver its first special bomb as soon as weather will permit visual bombing after about 3 August 1945, on one of the targets: Hiroshima, Kokura, Nigata, and Nagasaki."

Although the Potsdam Declaration of July 26 made no reference to the atomic bomb, Secretary Stimson spoke for all his colleagues when he described it as "an eminently suitable weapon." As for Japan's six-man Supreme War Council, they knew no more about the bomb after July 26 than they knew before and therefore remained deadlocked, 3–3, over acceptance of the Declaration. Due to the mistranslation of a press-conference comment, Prime Minister Suzuki—who privately favored acceptance of the ultimatum—had gone on record as regarding the Declaration unworthy of comment. Foreign Minister Togo, a more outspoken member of the peace faction, had no objection to the Declaration, but still hoped for Soviet mediation of the war with the United States, even in the face of warnings to the contrary from the Japanese ambassador at Moscow.

Stalin's inert response to news of the American atomic breakthrough puzzled Truman only mildly at the time; had he known that Stalin had received more information than had come his way, and over a longer period in time, that, too, he could have taken in stride. For Truman had quickly inured himself to the slings and arrows that assail any President of the United States, especially one who had assumed the responsibilities of that office when and as he did. To Roosevelt's lively imagination and active mind Stalin had appeared as large as life and twice as natural. The two-dimensional Truman saw him in simpler, earthier terms. Stalin may have overrated Roosevelt's IQ and underrated Truman's. Yet, Truman—for all his limitations, if not because of them—saw through Stalin farther and faster than Roosevelt had. "I was not altogether disillusioned," wrote Truman of his mood as he left Potsdam, "to find that the Russians were not in earnest about peace. It was clear that Russian foreign policy was based on the conclusion we were headed for a major depression, and they were already planning to take advantage of our setback." Truman left Potsdam in the early morning hours of August 2 and boarded the *Augusta* at Antwerp. This enabled him to stop at Plymouth, where he spent six hours exchanging visits with King George VI of England. On August 5, in mid-Atlantic, he received word from Stimson: "Big bomb dropped on Hirsohima. . . . First reports indicate complete success which was even more conspicuous than earlier test." "This is the greatest thing in history," the President told Byrnes and a few others gathered around him. "It's time for us to get home."

·5·

By JULY 24, when Truman specified the time and the targets for the dropping of the first, newly developed superbombs, so many men of so many high abilities had worked so long and so closely together toward a single objective that the Manhattan Project had become almost its own excuse for being. It represented a capital investment larger than many great universities, foundations, or commercial enterprises could boast. Its *esprit de corps* rivaled that of the United States Marine Corps. Its secrecy enhanced its prestige, notably among the armed services. As events soon proved, it could no more vacillate or reverse itself than the Red army could have abandoned its drive on Berlin or the Allied Expeditionary Forces have settled for anything less than Overlord.

During the cloudless predawn hours of August 6, twenty-nine-year-old Colonel Paul Tibbets, commander of the 509th Composite Group on Tinian, set forth at the controls of the *Enola Gay*, followed by two other modified B-29's, on their long-prepared mission which had as its target the Japanese military base of Hiroshima. The *Enola Gay* carried the five-ton uranium bomb. Close behind flew its instrument ship, *The Great Artiste*, piloted by Colonel Charles Sweeney, an expert on the B-29, and manned by Crew 15, which he had trained for months. A third, camera plane, Number 91, brought up the rear. Hiroshima, near the southeastern tip of Honshu, the largest island in the Japanese archipelago, lay some fifteen hundred miles northwest of Tinian. It was sighted at 7:50 in the clear morning sunshine. Less than an hour later, from a height of almost six miles, the *Enola Gay* released the bomb, then banked at a sixty-degree angle while dropping a cluster of instruments to measure the force of the explosion. That came automatically when the bomb had fallen to a little more than a mile above ground. The plane had dropped the bomb seventeen seconds behind schedule and directly over the assigned target.

The men who had taken part in the mission and those who had directed it knew that everything had gone off without a hitch. The plane crews who had witnessed the sunburst blaze and the mushroom cloud of the explosion itself returned stricken with awe. What it had done to the inhabitants, the city, and the factories of Hiroshima they could not even surmise. They knew only that this new weapon had a destructive power many times greater than any weapon they had ever released.

The Hiroshima performance had dwarfed the New Mexico rehearsal, confirming the hopes of most of the military men and the fears of most of the scientists. But for all of those connected with the Manhattan Project there could be no turning back now. Indeed Admiral Purnell had always insisted, and General Groves had always agreed, that the dropping of the first atomic bomb had to be followed up as soon as possible with the dropping of a second—partly to prove that the United States had more than one such weapon in its arsenal, partly to suggest that they might already be in production. President Truman, Secretaries Byrnes and Stimson, and all the other responsible officials, civilian and military, concurred.

Three days later, Colonel Sweeney, who had piloted the instrument plane over Hiroshima, headed the lead plane, *Bock's Car,* for the prime-target city of Kokura at the northern end of Kyushu Island. Fred Bock, for whom the plane had been named, piloted the instrument plane—again *The Great Artiste.* But rainy weather obscured Kokura, and the third, photograph plane failed to rendezvous with the other two over Yokashima Island. However, it arrived in time to follow them over the secondary-target city of Nagasaki, one hundred miles further west, where a break in the clouds enabled Colonel Sweeney to drop his plutonium bomb on target. With only enough fuel for a single run, all three planes made emergency landings on Okinawa, after a tempestuous day, the photograph plane arriving an hour after the other two. Finally, they all made it back to Tinian, twenty hours after they had set forth.

As a technical exploit, successfully completed under adverse conditions, the bombing of Nagasaki surpassed the bombing of Hiroshima. But it was Hiroshima that went straight from the news tickers, news broadcasts, and newspapers into the history books. It will be recalled that Truman at once described it as "the greatest thing in history." He followed this up with instructions to Stimson, in Washington, to release several statements he had prepared at Potsdam, giving some of the background on Manhattan Project, and some indication of future American policy. These repeated with increased urgency his warning to the Japanese leaders to accept the Potsdam terms or "expect a rain of ruin from the air, the like of which has never been seen on this earth." The statements also announced that while "under present circumstances it is not expected to divulge the technical processes of production or all the military applications" of the new weapon, he would "recommend that the Congress of the United States consider promptly the establishment of an appropriate commission to control the production and use of atomic power in the United States."

Nowhere did the bombing of Hiroshima create so great a sensation or produce such rapid results as in the Kremlin, where Stalin had not shown himself in any particular hurry to reach, with China's Foreign Minister T. V. Soong, the agreement that was to precede the Soviet declaration of war on Japan. But on the evening of August 8, before the second bomb had exploded over Nagasaki, Stalin summoned the British and American ambassadors to inform them that on August 9, the Soviet Union would consider itself at war with Japan. "Stalin reported," cabled Harriman the next day, "that his advance troops had already crossed the frontiers of Manchuria both from the east and from the west, not meeting heavy resistance on any front, and had advanced ten or twelve kilometers in some sections. The main forces were starting across the frontier as we spoke." A column of Russian cavalry had also entered South Manchuria from the Gobi Desert. All three attacks aimed at the cities of Harbin and Changchun.

For centuries the Chinese Empire had embraced Mongolia, Manchuria, and Korea, but as that empire began to weaken at its core, the Russians and Japanese began to move in on its outlying regions. Now that the Japanese Empire seemed on the verge of collapse, the Russians were getting in position to claim some parts of it, while Chinese were preparing to reclaim others. The approaching breakup in Asia bore some resemblance to the breakup that had just occurred in eastern Europe. Imperial Japan bore some resemblance to Nazi Germany, but Chiang Kai-shek's China had no more resemblance to the empires of the Hohenzollerns, Hapsburgs, or Romanovs than Mongolia bore to Poland, Manchuria to Romania, or Korea to Hungary. Viewed from London or Washington, Stalin might look like Mao Tse-tung's Big Brother —but not from Moscow, and still less from Mao's hide-out in the caves of Yenan.

. . .

The atomic bombing of Hiroshima destroyed more than that one Japanese city. It also finished off those disciples of Karl Marx who defined their Communist creed as "scientific socialism," just as it also destroyed the subsequent claim of Henry Adams to have outlined a "science of history." Marx's dialectical approach still illuminates some of history's pages. Adams' emphasis on history's acceleration makes more sense than his attempt to reduce history to a fixed rate of acceleration, which Einstein's theory of relativity had discredited more than twenty years before Hiroshima. But Marx's dialectics did catch up with Albert Einstein—the former apostle of Gandhi and the founder, in the 1920's, of the War Resisters League—when his letter to Roosevelt set off the chain reaction that resulted in Hiroshima and Nagasaki. Moreover, both Roosevelt and Einstein had planned the atomic bomb either to anticipate or to destroy Hitler, only to have him surrender unconditionally without their having to employ those atomic weapons which he had not even tried to build. Instead, the atomic bomb became the decisive weapon in the war against Japan, which Roosevelt, Churchill, and Stalin all regarded as secondary to the war against Germany. However, a quarter of a century later, these bombings loom larger than ever, reminding the world, as they do, that the white race had used this terrible, new weapon it developed only against the yellow race of Japanese.

The matter need not, will not, and cannot stand here. For the ironies and contradictions of the atomic age fade into insignificance as compared with its acceleration. The fact that war happened to be the mother of this particular invention may be regarded as par for the course. But war is not the only game played on that course, and wars bring forth strange fruit. Jet planes and computers may be by-products of war, but the contraceptive pill, the Salk vaccine, and other recent medical and biological breakthroughs have set in motion changes as drastic as the changes brought by war itself. Wartime research and development accelerated the progress of peacetime research and development. More ominous, however, the whole military-industrial juggernaut, which does not devote all its energies to preparations for nuclear war, has become by far the largest, as it has also become the most dangerous, of all of war's by-products.

As far as Hiroshima and Nagasaki are concerned, nothing brings out the transformation that followed the dawn of the atomic age so clearly as the new meaning that unconditional surrender suddenly acquired. Both Roosevelt and Hitler died three months before the dawn of the atomic age. To both of them unconditional surrender meant complete subjugation of the vanquished to the will of the victor. Roosevelt insisted on fighting until the enemy capitulated. He refused to commit himself to any specific surrender terms beyond his reassurance that he did not demand the enemy's destruction or enslavement. Hitler, who boasted that he did not trust Roosevelt any further than Roosevelt trusted him, preferred to have the war end with Germany's destruction and his own death rather than accept surrender on Roosevelt's terms. Only on the one occasion, when Churchill warned against any more bombing attacks like the one on Dresden, did any Allied leader suggest that total victory might cost a price that even the winner could not afford to pay.

It took the destruction of Hiroshima—which Roosevelt and Hitler did not live to witness—to bring home to all belligerents the fatal consequences to which the unrestricted use of atomic weapons could lead. Indeed, the successful atomic test-bomb explosion had already suggested such a possibility to President Truman and his advisers, leading them to soften the terms in which the Potsdam Declaration defined unconditional surrender. Although the Japanese at that time knew nothing about the atomic bomb or its destructive power, more and more of them were finding the unrestricted fire bombings unendurable. But after the atomic bombs had fallen on Hirsohima and Nagasaki many more Japanese began to understand far better than any Americans could the awful possibilities of this new weapon. The outcome of the war thus did not depend so much on the Americans as on that small group of Japanese leaders who alone possessed the authority either to accept or reject the Potsdam Declaration.

XXVI

We Are Gentlemen of Japan

·1·

NEWS OF THE HIROSHIMA BOMBING reached Emperor Hirohito in his imperial garden on the morning of August 6, one hour after it happened. He had spent the night before in the air-raid shelter under the imperial palace, and there he remained most of the time during the next several days. But when the news of the Soviet Union's entry into the war arrived early in the morning of August 9, the emperor conferred with Premier Suzuki, Foreign Minister Togo, and Marquis Kido, who all agreed that the Potsdam Declaration had to be accepted before the day was out. Suzuki laid down the strategy: "I will make sure there is no final vote taken in any meeting in the morning or afternoon." In order to avoid a showdown in the deadlocked Supreme War Council, Suzuki would promote a discussion that only the emperor could resolve.

Suzuki at this time had a morbid fear of assassination aggravated by a genuine concern for the emperor and by an old man's inherent caution. Like many Japanese, Suzuki eased his nerves, while muddling his mind, with frequent sips of sake. He also preferred, when dealing with great issues, to take the devious rather than the direct approach. He could see the logic, even the necessity, of unconditional surrender. He knew that the Potsdam Declaration contained specific promises of good treatment not mentioned at Cairo. He knew that Potsdam went far beyond Roosevelt's unconditional-surrender formula issued from Casablanca and directed primarily against Germany. He knew it contained no reference to Japan's imperial family. He knew all of these things because his country's intelligent, well-informed foreign minister had told him so.

The emperor and his three advisers then arranged to have eighty-year-old Baron Kiichiro Hiranuma join the discussion as observer and interrogator. Originally an extreme nationalist, Hiranuma had mellowed with the years and in 1939 headed Japan's last moderate government. He had no right to attend—much less to direct—the day's discussions, but the two diehard generals, Anami and Umezu, and Admiral Toyoda found themselves outmaneuvered by such wily and experienced political operators as Suzuki, Togo, and Hiranuma, especially with the emperor in the background.

Suzuki summoned the Supreme War Council to meet in the morning and the cabinet to meet in the afternoon, after lunch. The Supreme Council had already split twice, 3–3. On both occasions War Minister Anami, Army Chief of Staff Umezu, and Navy Chief of Staff Toyoda had rejected the Potsdam terms and insisted that Japan try its own war criminals, disarm its own troops, and receive pledges that no Allied troops occupy any of Japan's home islands. They also insisted that any surrender by Japan must include the condition that the emperor's position remain untouched. With this stipulation, the other three members of the Council—Premier Suzuki, Foreign Minister Togo, and Admiral Yonai—agreed. Although the Potsdam Declaration made no reference to the emperor, both factions in the Supreme Council also called for a specific clarification and modification in the Potsdam Declaration on that point.

In a statement phrased by the Foreign Office and approved by Togo, the Japanese government described itself as "ready to accept the terms of the joint declaration which was issued at Potsdam on July 26, 1945 . . . *with the understanding that the said declaration does not comprise any demand which prejudices the prerogatives of His Majesty as a Sovereign Ruler*" (italics added). Subject to this reservation, the peace faction on the Supreme Council accepted every word of the Potsdam Declaration. Both factions agreed with equal fervor that under no circumstances could Japan renounce its empire system and its emperor. Nothing in the Potsdam Declaration either affirmed or rejected this interpretation. But the war faction demanded three specific concessions from the victorious Allies.

After lunch the fourteen-member cabinet voted and split down the middle, as before. Suzuki took no vote from the Supreme Council, where all lines still held. The bare news of the Nagasaki bombing served only to harden the positions of both sides. During the late afternoon and evening, Hiranuma's questioning made it clear that Japan no longer had a navy or an air force, that the army lacked arms, and that there was no defense against any more atomic bombs that might fall. "How on earth can you believe it is still possible to continue the war under existing circumstances?" inquired Hiranuma. Anami, Umezu, and Toyoda had no answers.

As midnight approached, Suzuki brought matters to a head by proposing "to seek Imperial guidance and substitute it for the decision of this conference." In other words, he suggested that the Supreme Council, rather than make any further effort to reach a decision by vote or by consensus, abdicate its power of decision to the emperor. Called upon to break a precedent more than two thousand years old, Hirohito rose to the occasion and joined the conference, where Prime Minister Suzuki turned to him with these words: "Your Imperial Decision is requested as to which proposal should be adopted, the foreign minister's or the one with the four conditions." Hirohito came to the point at once. "I agree with the foreign minister's plan." He then described Japan's hopeless military situation. "I cannot bear to see my innocent people struggle any longer. Ending the war is the only way to restore world peace and to relieve the nation from the terrible distress with which it is burdened." He continued: "It goes without saying that it is unbearable for me to see the brave and loyal fighting men of Japan disarmed. It is equally unbearable that others who have rendered me devoted service should now be punished as instigators of war. Nevertheless, the time has come when we must bear the unbearable." After a pause, he concluded: "When I think of the feelings of my Imperial grandfather, Emperor Meiji, at the time of the Triple Intervention, I cannot but swallow my tears and sanction the proposal to accept the Allied Proclamation on the basis outlined by the foreign minister."

The emperor's reference to his grandfather recalled his revered predecessor under whose reign from 1867 to 1912 Japan had moved from medieval to modern times. The Triple Intervention had occurred in 1895 when the Emperor Meiji, commonly known as Mutsuhito, under pressure from Britain, France, and Germany, relinquished the claim Japan had just made to China's Liaotung peninsula. Now Hirohito, in Japan's hour of defeat, recalled that his grandfather, even at Japan's moment of triumph, had preferred to live with the inevitable rather than die in a vain struggle against it.

Suzuki's strategy recognized and conformed to this delicate and dangerous state of affairs. Instead of replying to the Potsdam Declaration with an unacceptable counterproposal or the dead silence of a deadlocked leadership, Suzuki arranged matters so that the one man who could speak for all Japan dealt with the unprecedented crisis the country now faced by invoking those precedents that his own grandfather had set fifty years before. Later, Prime Minister Suzuki, in discussing the situation, pointed out how well the Japanese warrior's Bushido code applied: "My position was this: we were defeated and as long as we admitted our defeat, the only manly thing to do was to leave everything to the victor. Such had been the military tradition from ancient times. Only I had one absolute conviction as to what to do. That was to trust the enemy commander. The 'Bushido' is not a Japanese monopoly. It is a universal code. To protect your adversary, who has surrendered, as one on your side is the way of the warrior."

Official announcement of the decisions arrived at by the Japanese government at Tokyo during the early hours of August 10 reached Washington via Sweden and Switzerland at half past seven the same morning. Exactly three months had passed between Germany's surrender in early May and Japan's response to the Potsdam Declaration. The Tokyo government still retained more power of decision than Germany's distraught leaders possessed after the death of Hitler. In addition, Washington could now handle Japan with more authority than any single Allied capital could bring to bear on Germany at the time of that country's surrender. In early May Stalin's writ ran strong in eastern Europe; in early August Truman's writ ran strong across the Pacific. The Red army had put itself in position to overrun much of Manchuria, but the rest of China had reverted to the chaos that had prevailed since the turn of the century when the breakup of its empire began.

On August 10 it was therefore toward Washington that all eyes turned as President Truman summoned Secretary of State Byrnes, Secretary of the Navy Forrestal, Secretary of War Stimson, and Presidential Chief of Staff Admiral Leahy to the White House to consider the first official Japanese reply to the Potsdam Declaration. Could the message, asked the President, be considered even a "conditional acceptance" of the Potsdam terms? How reconcile the retention of Hirohito with unconditional surrender and the elimination of militarism from Japan? Stimson and Leahy recommended acceptance of the condition set by the Japanese on the ground that without the authority of the emperor no surrender terms of any kind—conditional or unconditional—could be enforced. Because Byrnes felt that the United States, not Japan, should set the terms, he found it hard to reconcile himself to anything short of unequivocal surrender. Forrestal suggested that the

American reply indicate willingness to accept but that it define the surrender terms to conform with the intents and purposes of the Potsdam Declaration. Again, as at Potsdam, Truman turned to Byrnes, the master craftsman of compromise, requesting him to draft a reply along those lines.

At a cabinet meeting that afternoon Byrnes presented such a draft, containing this key passage: "From the moment of surrender the authority of the Emperor and the Japanese Government shall be subject to the Supreme Commander of the Allied Powers, who will take such steps as he deems proper to effectuate the surrender terms." The cabinet approved the Byrnes text, which went to Attlee in London, Chiang Kai-shek in Chungking, and Stalin in Moscow. Attlee and Chiang approved at once, Attlee suggesting that the Byrnes provision requiring the emperor and the Japanese High Command to sign the surrender terms be changed to read: "The Emperor shall authorize and ensure the signature by the Government of Japan and Japanese General Headquarters." Chiang also approved, singling out for special commendation the passage that Attlee had suggested amending. Truman accepted the Attlee amendment.

From Moscow Harriman cabled that Molotov wanted twenty-four hours to think it over. He doubted that the Byrnes text conformed to the unconditional-surrender formula. Presently, however, he dropped that question only to raise another: "that the Allied Powers should reach an agreement on the candidacy and candidacies for representation on the Allied High Command to which the Japanese Emperor and the Japanese Government are to be subordinated." That sent Harriman through the roof. He pointed out to Molotov that the proposal would give the Soviet government veto power over the selection of the supreme Allied commander. That sent Molotov running to Stalin, who quickly agreed to withdraw the suggestion, asking only that all the Allied Powers be "consulted." The incident speaks for itself.

·2·

THE HIROSHIMA AND NAGASAKI EXPLOSIONS, which had shocked even Stalin and Molotov into compliance with American dictates, had considerably greater impact on the people among whom the two bombs had fallen. On both cities, the explosions had released sudden blasts of heat, greater than the sun's, obliterating two large sections of two great cities and instantly incinerating tens of thousands of persons. In addition, the explosions subsequently released deadly radiation that caused many more thousands of persons to drop dead in their tracks during the next few days while others lingered on for weeks in helpless pain. At this point a generation gap developed between Japan's exuberant fifty-seven-year-old War Minister Anami and his fanatical young officers, who could not see even yet that the game was up.

By August 13 the tide of opinion in the cabinet and in the Supreme Council had turned in the peace faction's favor. That morning, General Umezu, the army chief of staff, blurted out: "I'm sorry. I accept the Potsdam Declaration." Admiral Yonai, the navy minister, who favored surrender, was able to shame most of the younger naval officers and fliers who wanted to continue the war into submission. It took until that evening for Anami to persuade a larger and more belligerent group of young army officers to call off an uprising they had planned. For the past several days, American planes had been dropping millions of leaflets on Japan, explaining to civilians that the war was lost and that only acceptance of the Potsdam terms could bring it to an end. When one of these pamphlets fell into Marquis Kido's hands he showed it to the emperor, who at once ordered him: "Do whatever you wish to speed the end of this war." Kido suggested summoning all the principals to attend a conference on accepting the surrender terms that very day.

Once again, as in the small hours of August 10, Emperor Hirohito forced the issue. At two o'clock in the afternoon of August 14 he told an audience of twenty-four persons, chiefly members of the cabinet, the Supreme War Council and their various secretaries: "I have studied the terms of the Allied reply and have decided that they constitute a virtually complete acknowledgment of the position we maintained in the note we dispatched several days ago. In short, I consider the reply to be acceptable." His own sobs twice compelled him to interrupt the reading of his brief statement. When he ended, all those present dissolved in sobs, tears, and embraces. The emperor then recorded the speech for an unprecedented broadcast to his people the following day.

Just as Suzuki's decision to accept the post of premier made the emperor's first speech possible, so Anami's decision to wheedle his own subordinates in the War Ministry made the second speech possible. After the broadcast of Hirohito's recorded speech on August 15 Suzuki stepped down as premier. Prince Naruhiko Higashi-Kuni, the emperor's uncle, replaced him. But General Anami did not wait so long to leave the stage. During the night of August 14 he slit his stomach open and plunged a dagger into his neck. But his hand had faltered; he continued to breathe for three hours of agony until a compassionate doctor ended it with a hypodermic needle. A bloodstained paper near his body read: "Believing firmly that our sacred land shall never perish I—with my death—humbly apologize to the Emperor for my great crime." The crime, that is, of having lost the war. In taking his own life, General Anami had not only made his personal amends to his emperor; in shouldering sole responsibility for the defeat he relieved his colleagues of their obligation to follow his example. He had acted for all.

·3·

THE AMERICAN ATOMIC BREAKTHROUGH at Alamogordo in mid-July and the subsequent atomic bombings of Hiroshima and Nagasaki in early August offered a near-perfect example of accelerated history in action. By the same token Emperor Hirohito's instant response to these events offered the near-perfect example of historical transcendence when he pledged the thousands of years of his country's imperial history that he embodied to acceptance of the Potsdam Declaration of unconditional surrender, at the same time subordinating himself to his country's conquerors in the task of rebuilding a new and peaceful Japan. General MacArthur, who received the appointment of supreme commander for the Allied Powers on August 15, then assumed his essential role in the same spirit.

The emperor had met the challenge of the atomic bomb by exploiting his own people's widespread belief (which he did not share) in his own divinity; General MacArthur, with a belief (which all of his compatriots did not share) in his own infallibility, threw himself into his role as magnanimous conqueror with the same fervor that the emperor brought to his role as the defeated warrior who trusts the victorious enemy commander. Not all Japanese accepted at once the role their emperor assumed; not all Americans (not to mention some of their allies) applauded the selection of General MacArthur as their first post-war proconsul in Japan. But the war-weary people of Japan and the rank and file of Japan's armed forces had never supported their emperor more strongly than they did when he called upon them to surrender rather than resist. All but an insignificant faction of fanatics soon accepted their emperor's decision. Nor did it take long for the American people to accept President Truman's choice of their country's outstanding military commander as the right one for the task at hand.

General MacArthur lost no time in justifying the confidence he inspired among Americans and Japanese alike. Recognizing that the Japanese authorities would require a few weeks rather than a few days to prepare their people to accept the fact of unconditional surrender, the American authorities arranged to have the final ceremonies held on September 2 aboard the recently commissioned battleship *Missouri* in Tokyo Bay, where General MacArthur, flanked by British, Chinese, Soviet, Australian, French, and Dutch officers, stood over Japan's Foreign Minister Mamoru Shigemitsu and General Umezu, chief of the Japanese General Staff, while they signed the surrender instrument.

MacArthur's account of that occasion throws light on the man who wrote it as well as on the occasion itself: "Trying to recall my emotions and impressions as I prepared to receive the surrender of the mighty warlords of the Far East, I wish that my pen were wielded by one on such intimate terms with words—those immortal heralds of thought which at the touch of genius become radiant—that at my call they would convey my feelings in terms that would satisfy the ultimate sources of reason, history, and interpretation. For I have a consciousness that in the events culminating in this immortal moment lie those truths which at last are transplanted into epics and lyrics, and those exalted terms which we find on the lips of the great seers and prophets.

"I had received no instructions as to what to say or do," the MacArthur account continues, "I was on my own, standing on the quarter-deck with only God and my own conscience to guide me." In a brief, simple address he called upon both victors and vanquished "to rise to that higher dignity which alone befits the higher purposes we are about to serve, committing all our people unreservedly to faithful compliance with the obligation they are here formally to assume." As for himself: "As Supreme Commander of the Allied Powers, I announce it my firm purpose in the traditions of the countries I represent, to proceed in the discharge of my responsibilities with justice and tolerance, while taking all necessary dispositions to insure that the terms of the surrender are fully, promptly, and faithfully complied with." After all the representatives had signed the documents, MacArthur added: "Let us pray that peace may now be restored to the world and that God will preserve it always. These proceedings are closed."

•   •   •

For the next five years, General MacArthur found himself administering more power in more directions than ever before in his experience. "I had to be an economist, a political scientist, a teacher, even a theologian of sorts. I had to rebuild a nation that had been almost completely destroyed by the war." He listed in this order the reforms he planned: "First destroy the military power. Punish the war criminals. Build the structure of representative government. Modernize the constitution. Hold free elections. Enfranchise the women. Release the political prisoners. Liberate the farmers. Establish a free labor movement. Encourage a free economy. Abolish police repression. Develop a free and responsible press. Liberalize education. Decentralize the political power. Separate church from state." The New Deal that MacArthur proudly imposed on Japan went beyond the New Deal that he sadly deplored when Franklin Roosevelt introduced it to the United States.

The Japanese people readily accepted MacArthur's New Deal, partly because of the enthusiasm and skill with which he administered it and partly, as Edwin O. Reischauer has put it in *Japan Past and Present*, because: "It was based in part on old Japanese habits of acceptance of authority, re-enforced by the preceding fifteen years of growing authoritarian control." Thus the authoritarian MacArthur and the submissive people of Japan democratized the nation and its institutions at breakneck speed. By 1947 five million Japanese workers had joined 25,000 trade unions. In 1945 tenants farmed half of Japan's arable land. By 1950 freeholders farmed ninety per cent. During the year 1946 Japan's gross national product totaled 1.3 billion dollars or $17 per capita. By 1950 the figures had increased almost tenfold.

One incident during the first month of General MacArthur's stewardship at Tokyo reveals one of the secrets behind this success story. When his staff members urged him to summon the emperor to his headquarters as a show of power, he would have none of it: "To do so would be to outrage the feelings of the Japanese people and make a martyr of the Emperor in their eyes. No, I shall wait and in time the Emperor will voluntarily come to see me. In this case the patience of the East rather than the haste of the West will best serve our purpose." And so it proved. The emperor shortly requested an interview. "In cutaway, striped trousers and top hat, riding in his Daimler with his imperial grand chamberlain facing him on the jump seat, Hirohito arrived at the Embassy." There he received the full imperial treatment, including, at MacArthur's hands, the offer of an American cigarette, which he took with thanks. "I noticed how his hands shook when I lighted it for him. I tried to make it as easy for him as I could, but I knew how deep and dreadful must be his agony of humiliation. I had an uneasy feeling he might plead his own case against the indictment as a war criminal."

WE ARE GENTLEMEN OF JAPAN

But these fears proved groundless. "What he said was this: 'I come to you, General MacArthur, to offer myself to the judgment of the powers you represent as the one to bear the sole responsibility for every political and military decision made and action taken by my people in the conduct of war.' A tremendous impression swept me. This courageous assumption of responsibility implicit with death, a responsibility clearly belied by facts of which I was fully aware, moved me to the very marrow of my bones. He was an Emperor by inherent birth, but in that instant I knew I faced the First Gentleman of Japan in his own right."

General MacArthur at once laid down a purely American "Initial Post-Surrender Policy," which Molotov made permanent by attempting to sabotage it at the December 1945 session of the Foreign Ministers' Conference in Moscow. Unwilling and unable to devise alternative proposals, the Russians wound up perpetuating the benign, authoritarian rule that MacArthur exercised with as much fervor as the Japanese accepted it. His strength lay in his unquestioning faith in the copybook maxims of late-nineteenth-century Americanism. Born to the purple of the American military aristocracy (a color reflected by his prose), MacArthur found himself preordained by temperament, nurtured by environment, and conditioned by experience to function in Japan as the very embodiment of the magnanimous American conqueror. But the same tangibles and intangibles that transformed a great military commander into a transcendent helpmeet to Japan's rebirth doomed him to eventual frustration and failure—first, when he assumed that the knowledge and experience he had gathered in the Philippines and Japan made him equally knowledgeable and expert in Chinese affairs; second, when he assumed that the same uncompromising opposition he brought to bear against Stalin's designs on Japan would prove no less effective against Mao Tse-tung's designs on China and its Asian neighbors.

"Too good to be true" sums up the double, postwar apotheosis of MacArthur—and Hirohito, with whom fate eventually caught up, as it did with all the other major figures in all the other major belligerent powers. The diabolic Hitler and the subservient German people reaped as they had sown. Stalin suffered the no less ironic and no less deserved fate of hoisting himself and the Soviet Union by their own petard. Churchill lost the British Empire, first by saving the British people and then, in political retirement, by writing an imperishable version of the history he had made, ending his days pleading for an end to the cold war that he himself had declared. Roosevelt cheated fate by dying at the peak of his power and his glory. His successor followed in his footsteps, as best he could, ending his political career on a note of triumph in his dismissal of General MacArthur, who had finally succumbed to his own *hubris*. Which leads to the unfinished final chapter of the Second World War—a chapter that also opens the story of that war's aftermath.

XXVII

Aftermath: China First and Last

· 1 ·

IF THE FIRST SHALL BE LAST and the last first, China had it both ways: first victim of Japanese aggression in 1931; last member of the Great Alliance to taste any of the sweets of the 1945 victory, sweets that, in true Chinese style, had a sour taste as well. To Chiang Kai-shek and his Chinese Nationalists, the Japanese surrender promised fulfillment of long-deferred hopes. At last they saw themselves leading their country to its rightful place among the nations of the earth. Mao Tse-tung, on the other hand, needed only the Soviet declaration of war against Japan to follow through with a declaration of all-out civil war against the Chinese Nationalists.

This declaration of civil war coincided with the appearance of Red army troops on Chinese soil, where they drove the Japanese from western Manchuria and shared some of their spoils of war with some of their Chinese Communist comrades. But the Red army never clashed with the Chinese Nationalists, nor did American land, sea, and air forces, which arrived at the same time to evacuate Japanese soldiers and civilians, ever clash with any Chinese.

The precedents set by the Russian Revolution and the practices that it followed had driven Stalin and Mao Tse-tung ever further apart. Russia's Stalinized Communists of 1945 bore no more resemblance to the little band of Bolsheviks who followed Lenin in 1917 than they bore to Mao Tse-tung and his massed Communist millions, armed and unarmed, peasants, workers, students, middle classes who had been rallying to his support for twenty years. Stalin's Russia, having emerged in 1945 as one of the two chief victors in the century's greatest war, thus faced in the China of Mao Tse-tung a possibility that had yet to become a fact: the possibility that Mao Tse-tung might emerge from the war's aftermath as the leader of a revolution that would rank with Lenin's.

More than a year before Japan's surrender, Roosevelt's decision to follow the MacArthur strategy against Japan relegated Chiang to a subsidiary role during the final stage of the Pacific war, thereby opening a new stage in Mao Tse-tung's revolutionary career. For Mao had long foreseen the Sino-Japanese war passing through three stages: first, Japense offensives against Chinese strategic defenses; second, Chinese counteroffensives against the strategic position seized by the Japanese; third, a "favorable international situation" which would make possible a final, general Communist offensive against the Japanese everywhere. By the summer of 1944, the fighting in China had reached the second stage. By the end of the year Mao's "favorable international situation" began to materialize. Stalin, who respected Mao but feared him, neither feared nor respected Chiang. But, since Stalin preferred a weak and divided non-Communist China to a strong and united Communist one, he favored the Nationalists over the Communists. So did Roosevelt, though for different reasons. He knew that Chiang headed a corrupt regime and Mao an honest one. But he preferred the Nationalist crook he knew to the honest Communist he did not know.

When Stilwell arrived at Chungking in 1942, the State Department assigned John Paton Davies, one of its top China experts, to accompany him. Stilwell admired Davies' reports so much that he asked the State Department to supplement the Chungking staff with another China expert, John Stewart Service, who had a wide acquaintance among Chinese officials and spoke their language fluently. After General Stilwell and Ambassador Gauss returned to Washington in the fall of 1944, Davies and Service continued to report to Wedemeyer and Hurley as they had reported to their predecessors. On November 15, 1944, Davies warned: "We must not indefinitely underwrite a politically bankrupt regime. And if the Russians are going to enter the Pacific war, we must make a determined effort to capture those Chinese Communists rather than let them go by default wholly to the Russians. Furthermore, we must fully understand that by reason of our recognition of the Chiang Kai-shek government as now constituted, we are committed to a steadily decaying regime and severely restricted in working out military and political co-operation with the Chinese Communists.

"A coalition Chinese Government in which Communists find satisfactory place is the solution of this impasse most desirable to us. It provides our greatest assurance of a strong, united, democratic, independent, and friendly China—our basic strategic aim in Asia and the Pacific. . . .

"In seeking to determine which faction we should support, we must keep in mind these basic considerations: Power in China is on the verge of shifting from Chiang to the Communists."

Davies stressed the weaknesses and shortcomings of the Kuomintang; Service accentuated the positive elements in the Chinese Communist movement: "The conclusion therefore seems justified that the peasants support, join, and fight with the Communist armies because they have been convinced that the Communists are fighting for their interests, and because the Communists have created this conviction by producing some tangible benefits for the peasants."

A third State Department official—John Carter Vincent—head of its China Affairs Division, also played a leading part in this dispute. He had accompanied Vice President Wallace on his China mission in the summer of 1944 and saw eye to eye with Davies and Service on the Kuomintang and the Communists—as, of course, did Stilwell. On January 4, 1945, Secretary of State Stettinius sent President Roosevelt this memorandum from Vincent: "Chiang is in a dilemma. Coalition would mean the end of the Conservative Kuomintang domination and open the way for the more virile and popular Communists to extend their influence to the point perhaps of controlling the Government. Failure to settle with the Communists, who are daily growing stronger, would invite the danger of an eventual overthrow of the Kuomintang. Chiang could, it is felt, rise above party selfishness and anti-Communist prejudice to head a new coalition government which might bring new life into the war and insure unity after hostilities."

But on December 24, before Vincent's views reached the White House, Hurley informed Stettinius that he had already flouted the recommendations of the head of the State Department's China Affairs Division. "In all my negotiations," wrote Hurley, "it has been my understanding that the policy of the United States in China is (1) to prevent the collapse of the National Government; (2) to sustain Chiang Kai-shek as President of the Republic and Generalissimo of the Armies." It was not Chiang's opposition to Mao Tse-tung that commended him to Hurley; it was the kind words that Stalin and Molotov had spoken in his behalf. Hurley viewed with suspicion and alarm the reports filed by Davies and Service. As his amused friend and comrade-in-arms General Wedemeyer put it, "Whereas many Americans were deluded by clever propaganda into believing that the Chinese Communists were not real Communists but agrarian reformers, Pat Hurley would seem to have fallen for another and equally pernicious myth. To him it seemed that Stalin, Molotov, and Co. could be relied upon or their words believed, and that the villains of the piece were the Chinese Communists and the State Department in the persons of the political advisers on my staff whom I had inherited from Stilwell."

· 2 ·

THE INDESTRUCTIBLE MOLOTOV and the irreplaceable Chou En-lai: how perfectly each of those super number two men embodied the characters and projected the images of the Communist parties they served. What Molotov had done for Stalin, Chou En-lai had done for Mao Tse-tung: acted the part of himself. Molotov had changed his name from Scriabin to the proletarian cognomen "Hammer," rejecting the intellectual-esthetic traditions to which he had been born in order to assume the lifelong role of the immovable "Stone-Bottom." Chou En-lai, on the other hand, prided himself on the mandarin descent that his name proclaimed. Abandoning his original ambition to become an actor, he found greater satisfaction in the real-life role of aristocrat turned revolutionary. Chou En-lai maintained his family ties and pre-Communist friendships. He ingratiated himself with his opposite numbers at the negotiating table and enjoyed speaking French and English to non-Chinese. The multilingual Molotov spoke only Russian to everybody, thriving on his hatred of himself and others. Concealing a background as cosmopolitan and tastes as sophisticated as Chou's, he took the offensive (in every sense of the word) everywhere always. Chou En-lai practiced Mao Tse-tung's subtle, Chinese style of Communism with the same perfection that Molotov adopted the hammer-and-tongs tactics of Lenin and Stalin.

Molotov's golden years began with the negotiation of the Nazi-Soviet pact in August 1939. Chou's golden years began in October 1944, when he brought a new political weapon and an old political strategy to bear on his Nationalist adversaries in the statement issued from Yenan: "We demand that the government and the army be reorganized to permit coalition government and joint control of the armed forces." As far as Chiang Kai-shek was concerned, that tore it. To him "coalition government"—Communist style—meant a built-in veto power that would enable the Communists to rule or ruin any coalition to which they belonged. Hurley had witnessed the November confrontation between Chiang Kai-shek and Chou En-lai at Chungking where the Communists refused to subordinate themselves to the Nationalists, who, in their turn, refused to share power with the Communists. Yet, in the very teeth of this experience, Hurley sponsored a second round of National-ist-Communist talks at Chungking in January. By this time, with the Yalta Conference coming up, the dying Roosevelt, the preoccupied Stalin, and the frustrated Churchill could not even attempt to fill the vacuum that the Japanese collapse had created in China.

Neither Mao Tse-tung nor Chou En-lai had any illusions about the limitations of their military, political, and economic power. But their alternating fight-fight, talk-talk tactics threw the Nationalists into such disarray that Ambassador Hurley and General Wedemeyer found it necessary to fly to Washington in late February to bring themselves and their superiors into harmony on developments in the China theater. Prior to his trip to Washington, Hurley had Davies transferred from Chungking to Moscow and before he returned he had Service shifted, too. Because their reports did not confirm Hurley's preconceptions, he questioned their patriotism, at the same time trumpeting his faith in the veracity of Stalin and Molotov and his confidence in the staying power of Chiang Kai-shek. Hurley had undermined his commander in chief better than he knew—or, indeed, intended. Because the reports of Da-vies and Service offended his vanity, he made unsupported charges against them, charges that the irresponsible Senator Joseph R. McCar-thy and the sanctimonious John Foster Dulles later endorsed on nothing more substantial than Hurley's almost worthless word and wholly reckless judgment.

Hurley's visit to Washington in early March reached its tragicomic climax when he called on Roosevelt who showed him a copy of his agreement with Stalin, which Hurley deplored. A few days later, ac-cording to Hurley, the President confessed that he, too, had some doubts and suggested that Hurley arrange to confer with both Church-ill and Stalin about modifying the terms of the Yalta accords on China. At any rate, that was Hurley's story, and it lost nothing in his telling of it: "When the President reached up that fine, firm, strong hand of his to shake hands with me, what I found in my hand was a very loose bag of bones. Then I looked at him closely and the skin seemed to be pasted down on his cheekbones; and you know, all the fight I had in me went out." But not for long. Hurley's subsequent visits to Churchill and Stalin took on some of the aspects of the travels of Baron Munchhausen. His own account of them makes no mention of what he had described as their ostensible purpose: to secure modification of the Yalta terms on

China. Churchill dismissed American China policy as "the great American illusion," and when Hurley spoke of invoking the Atlantic Charter in connection with Hong Kong, Churchill reminded him it did not apply there. It wound up with Churchill reaffirming previous pledges to support unification of China's armed forces and the creation of a free, unified, and democratic China. The parallel with Poland can hardly have escaped Churchill's notice, but he made nothing of it.

From Stalin Hurley received unqualified endorsement of American policy toward China—at any rate in the form Hurley himself outlined it. Stalin also assured Hurley that the Soviet government attached special importance to the immediate unification of China's armed forces and to full Soviet recognition of Chiang's Nationalist regime. Harriman, who sat in on the conversation, said of Hurley afterward: "At no time did he indicate to me that President Roosevelt was disturbed about the understanding reached at Yalta or that he desired that this understanding be ameliorated. On the contrary, the purpose of Ambassador Hurley's visit to Moscow, as he stated it to me and to Stalin, was to find out from Stalin when Chiang could be told about the Yalta understanding and to help further cement the relations between the Soviet Union and the Chinese National Government."

At the time Hurley and Wedemeyer had arrived in Washington, the communication lines of the Chinese Communists extended from the Yangtze Valley in central China to the Great Wall in the northwest. During March and April, they began to advance eastward across Hunan Province, in south central China, and in May they drove south of Nanking, across the Yangtze, and headed for the coast. Anticipating American landings, the Communists planned to get there ahead of the Nationalists. They made still greater efforts north of Shanghai, where they had considerable support among the fishing villages, but in Shanghai itself, the Kuomintang remained strong with the business and professional classes. Shanghai had a prewar Japanese colony of 150,000. The prewar wealth of the Shanghai Municipal Council had been estimated at thirty million pounds; the value of foreign-owned assets in Shanghai came to an estimated five billion dollars.

Although this Chinese Communist offensive which continued before, during, and after the Yalta Conference lay within General Wedemeyer's China theater, neither he nor Chiang Kai-shek could take any part in it. Wedemeyer, however, differed from Stilwell in that he used honey rather than vinegar on Chiang; he also differed from Hurley in that he considered himself a professional soldier and not a practitioner of personality-cult diplomacy. As such, Wedeymer therefore concentrated on persuading Chiang to start disbanding his 320 unequipped, untrained, underfed divisions and to start building up a Praetorian Guard of some forty divisions into which Wedemeyer had some five hundred American officers and five hundred enlisted men incorporated. Partly as a result of this buildup, Japanese ground troops launched no more offensives in China after May, and for the first time in three years Nationalist troops went on the offensive in the south. By July they were planning operations against Liuchow and Kweilin and by August against Port Bayard and Canton. But here they encountered their unbeaten Communist compatriots as well as their defeated Japanese enemies.

· 3 ·

DURING THIS PERIOD of transition from the Roosevelt to the Truman presidency, the Anglo-Soviet-American coalition wound up the fighting in Europe and drew up a postwar settlement of sorts at Potsdam. In Asia, on the other hand, maximum confusion prevailed among and even within the various nations waging declared or undeclared war on Japan. From Hopkins, Harriman, and others, Truman had received guidelines, originally laid down by Roosevelt, on how to handle Stalin and the Soviet Union. These he had faithfully followed. But he had received no corresponding guidelines on how to handle China with its endemic civil war between the ruling Nationalist party, which showed signs of battle fatigue, and the rival Communist party, which openly challenged the Nationalists' claim to continue their one-party leadership. The closest and most recent equivalent to a Roosevelt directive in Truman's possession took the form of the deal that Roosevelt had worked out with Stalin, listing the conditions under which the Soviet Union would enter the war against Japan. In this agreement both Roosevelt and Stalin assumed that Chiang Kai-shek and his Nationalist government would speak for China after the war just as Roosevelt and Stalin had spoken for their two countries during it. While Roosevelt had indeed committed Chiang to turn over to Stalin certain Manchurian ports and railways that the Russians had wrested from the Chinese during the previous century, the agreement included Stalin's guarantee to recognize Chiang Kai-shek's Nationalist regime as China's sole, legal, postwar government. At the time Roosevelt and Stalin came to this agreement neither man had any reason to believe that two American atomic bombs would force Japan to surrender unconditionally within another six months. Both assumed that Stalin had undertaken a large-scale military obligation from which he expected to derive corresponding political and economic benefits.

That still remained the prospect when Harry Hopkins undertook his mission to Moscow in late May and early June 1945, shortly after Truman had succeeded Roosevelt. Poland headed the Moscow agenda, but Soviet participation in the war against Japan came second. When Hopkins returned to Washington, he reported to Truman that Stalin had stepped up his demands to include the return of Port Arthur, Dairen, and the two Manchuria railways to virtual Soviet control as his price for approving a Sino-Soviet treaty. To Truman's surprise, Hurley had already given Chiang the details of the deal that Roosevelt had made with Stalin at Yalta at Chiang's expense; to Truman's astonishment Chiang had not only approved the terms—including, as they did, Stalin's promise to support Chiang rather than Mao during and after the Soviet declaration of war on Japan. Now, Chiang and Soong hoped to be able to widen this agreement by offering Stalin more concessions. Soong therefore wanted to fly to Moscow at once, where he also hoped to widen the Sino-Soviet treaty into a four-power pact, including Britain and the United States. The State Department not only turned thumbs down but held up Soong's departure for Moscow several days and finally sanctioned the journey and the meeting with Stalin on the understanding that any agreement they reached remained subject to approval by the Big Three at Potsdam.

But by the time the Potsdam meeting began, Truman had received word of the successful atomic test explosion at Alamogordo. When he casually mentioned the matter at Potsdam, Stalin's attitude seemed satisfactory, but he asked for no details and Truman vouchsafed none. Not until after the first bomb had been "laid on" Japan at Hiroshima did Truman consent to a continuation of the Stalin-Soong talks. The next day Molotov made it known that the Soviet Union considered itself at war with Japan, whereupon Mao Tse-tung announced, in his turn, that the Chinese People's War against Japan had entered its third and final stage and commanded all his forces—regular and irregular—to attack everywhere, forthwith.

·   ·   ·

During President Truman's first three weeks in office, he and Generals Marshall and Eisenhower followed faithfully in Roosevelt's footsteps as they rejected the pressures of Churchill, Brooke, and Montgomery to try to beat the Russians to Berlin and to other parts of eastern Europe that the Teheran Conference had assigned to Soviet occupation. But within the same three weeks, as the Manhattan Project approached the point of breakthrough, nearly all the advisers whom Truman had inherited from Roosevelt urged him to plan to use this new weapon to redress, in eastern Asia, the balance of power that the Red army had swung in the Soviet Union's favor in eastern Europe. Whereupon it took another ten years for the Soviet occupation of eastern Europe, the American atomic breakthrough, and the final stage of the Chinese Revolution to come into focus as three links in a single chain. Having developed the bombs that atomized Hiroshima and Nagasaki, Truman could no more refrain from using them to discourage a Russian take-over in eastern Europe than Stalin had been able to refrain from using the Red army to execute that take-over in the first place. As things turned out, however, Stalin's Red army overextended itself in eastern Europe from which Truman's atomic threats could no more expel it than that army could submit western Europe to eastern Europe's fate. Thus, Mao Tse-tung emerged as the first beneficiary of the atomic age and of its prolonged Soviet-American "balance of terror" during which neither the Russians nor the Americans could prevent him from making his kind of revolution in China.

·4·

NOT ALL OF THESE EVENTS took all of the Americans concerned in them entirely by surprise. As early as July 20, 1945, orders had gone from Potsdam to the Joint War Planning Commission in Washington to drop everything and concentrate on planning for the situation that the sudden collapse of Japan would create in China. By July 30, the Joint Chiefs had plans for American planes and ships to rush troops and supplies to the ports of Shanghai, Chefoo, Chuangho (just below Manchuria), and Pusan in Korea. It was assumed that Russian and Chinese Nationalist troops would handle most of the ground fighting—the Russians in Manchuria, the Chinese Nationalists at points south.

The atomic bombing of Hiroshima changed all this. Mao knew little and cared less about the scientific aspects of America's atomic breakthrough. Stalin's decision to invade Manchuria gave him all the political and military information he needed. Simultaneously, Chu Teh, as "Commander in Chief of the Resist-Japanese Armies in the Liberated

Areas of China," jumped the gun with orders to seven of his field commanders to seize enemy-held territories. Four of his armed groups, commanded by two of his best generals, marched from the south into three Manchurian provinces. Another 100,000 men, commanded by Lin Piao, Mao's "comrade in arms on the Long March," followed the course of the Peking-Mukden railroad into Manchuria, where they acquired from the Japanese 300,000 rifles, 138,000 machine guns, and 2700 pieces of field artillery.

Chiang Kai-shek did not take this in silence or lying down. On August 10, he charged Chu Teh with taking "abrupt and illegal action" and told him to order his forces to "remain in their posts and wait for further instruction" and "never again to take independent action." The Communist radio at Yenan branded Chiang as a "fascist chieftain" who "treated enemies as friends and friends as enemies." On August 13, Chu Teh called Chiang's orders "contrary to the national interest" and "only beneficial to the Japanese invaders and traitors." He also cabled the Japanese commander, General Yasuji Okamura, demanding that the Japanese surrender only to the Communists. Not until two days later —August 15—did the Japanese in fact begin surrendering to anybody, and then General MacArthur's General Order Number One instructed the Japanese in Manchuria to surrender to the Russians and the Japanese in the rest of China to surrender to the Chinese Nationalists.

On August 13, Mao again announced that the Soviet Union's entry into the war ensured the surrender of Japan (no mention of the atomic bomb) and that the domestic struggle had now become the supreme task, the issue being, "To whom should the fruits of victory in the war of resistance belong?" Mao predicted that the major cities of Shanghai, Nanking, and Hankow would fall to the Nationalists, that both sides would contest for the medium and small cities of north and central China, and that the Communists would control the rural, northern regions. Mao had not waited even for the Japanese surrender to issue a Communist declaration of civil war against the National government. Two days later a spokesman for that government told a news conference at Chungking that Chiang's orders must be obeyed: "Those who violate them are the enemies of the people." To which Mao replied: "This shows that Chiang Kai-shek has declared war against the Chinese people."

Not for the first time, the Chinese Communist leaders had talk-talked bigger than they could fight-fight. For they could not, at this juncture, match the troops or equipment, the planes or the transport, that the

Nationalists either possessed or could obtain from the Americans. When Chiang Kai-shek sent telegrams to Mao Tse-tung, Chou En-lai, and others suggesting that they again shift their battlefield to the negotiating table at Chungking, the Communists accepted and arrived on August 28, escorted by Ambassador Hurley. The Nationalists now controlled all transport lines and major cities in Manchuria and north China; the Communists controlled the countryside. In central and eastern China the Nationalists encircled Communist enclaves.

But China had fallen into such chaos that neither party dared to risk a showdown. Chiang counted on American military, economic, and financial aid to enable him to bring all of China under Nationalist control. Mao had no expectation of corresponding Soviet aid. Nationalist collapse remained his last, best hope—all the brighter in the wake of the atomic thunderclap that had led to Japan's instant surrender. Although the bombing of Hiroshima had not come quite soon enough to forestall a Soviet declaration of war on Japan or to prevent Red army troops from invading Manchuria, the fighting ended so abruptly that the Red army found itself in no position to prevent General MacArthur from becoming supreme Allied commander in the occupation of Japan and from keeping the Russians on the outside, looking in.

On August 7, Stalin and Soong resumed the talks they had broken off on July 14, when Stalin left Moscow for Potsdam. Now Stalin demanded more concessions than Roosevelt had made to him at Yalta, but Harriman intervened, demanding a written Soviet commitment to maintain the Open Door in all regions where the Russians were moving in on the Chinese. By August 14 Stalin and Soong had initialed a Sino-Soviet treaty in which Stalin conceded many points over which he had quibbled before Japan's surrender. In the course of the nine documents that finally emerged the Soviet Union agreed "to render China moral support and aid in military supplies and other material sources . . . to be entirely given to the central government of China." In another document, the Soviet Union "regarded the Three Eastern Provinces as part of China and reaffirmed its respect for China's full sovereignty over the Three Provinces and recognized their territorial and administrative integrity." Both Truman and Harriman thus had reason to feel that the Stalin-Soong agreement met the specifications that Roosevelt and Stalin had laid down in their secret understanding at Yalta. On August 29 President Truman told a press conference that Madame Chiang Kai-shek had just thanked him for his support: "She was very happy over the Russian-Chinese treaty, just as all of us are."

·5·

EVERYTHING COMES to him who waits. During most of his political career, Mao Tse-tung had seen events follow a zigzag course, quite in keeping with his dialectical view of them. He had always based his calculations on China's peasant masses—first to wage the kind of war and then to make the kind of revolution that he favored. During early 1945, the Chinese Communists still fought that kind of war. General Stilwell not only shared Mao's faith in China's soldier-peasants. He had taught them to fight the kind of war Mao had been waging for years. Stilwell shared Mao's distaste for Chiang Kai-shek, but on personal grounds rather than on political ones. General Wedemeyer, an airman in his mid-forties, regarded Stilwell—an infantryman in his mid-sixties —as a military has-been. No doubt. But it so happened that the Chinese Communst guerrillas trained by Mao and the Chinese infantrymen trained by Stilwell turned out to be Asia's soldiers of the future. Their ground tactics not only took the measure of the Japanese; they repeatedly took the measure of Chiang Kai-shek's Nationalists.

Chinese troops trained by Stilwell had already defeated the Japanese during 1944—a fact that nobody appreciated more keenly or praised more warmly than Britain's General Slim, who had done with the Indian troops of the Fourteenth British Army what Stilwell had done with five of Chiang's Chinese divisions. Stilwell's troops and Stilwell's example also served Wedemeyer well in the defensive measures he had the Chinese take at Kunming and Kweilin in 1944. Then, at the end of January, 1945, America's General Daniel Sultan, with three Stilwell-trained Chinese divisions, plus his own American "Mars" brigade and the 36th British Division, made contact at Namhkam on the old Burma Road with Chinese forces from the east and British forces from the west. On January 28, 1945, the first convoy from the Indian province of Annam reached the Chinese frontier. Several months after Chiang contrived to have Stilwell recalled, Chinese troops that Stilwell had trained took successful offensive action against the Japanese and helped open the door to Britain's long-deferred return to southeast Asia.

Thus Lord Mountbatten, from the Ceylon headquarters of his Southeast Asia Command, was able to usher in the year 1945 with an order to General Slim to liberate Burma, first by capturing Mandalay in the center of the country, and then by driving south to Rangoon. General Sultan could not provide the help on which Mountbatten had counted especially after Chiang Kai-shek called home three Chinese divisions. However, enough American planes remained to enable Britain's Fourteenth Army to capture Rangoon with the aid of a two-day bombing attack, a parachute division, and an amphibious assault. The city fell on the morning of May 2, a few hours before a monsoon halted all further operations.

With the fall of Rangoon, General Slim's polyglot army completed what Mountbatten and Churchill called the "liberation" of Burma. But Burma was not France, Mountbatten was not Eisenhower, and Churchill—in another three months—was no longer prime minister. In 1942, the Burmese had welcomed the Japanese as the French had never welcomed the Germans in 1940, or any other year, and if the Burmese became disillusioned with their Japanese overlords, the Japanese became no less disillusioned in their new role as empire builders in a far, strange land. It had taken the British considerably longer to learn the same lesson, but the outcome of the British election soon suggested, among other things, that a majority of the British people wanted to have Attlee divest them of the empire that Churchill had not become His Majesty's first minister to liquidate.

On May 1, the 18th Australian Division landed at Tarakan on the Dutch island of Borneo, supported by American naval and air forces. On July 1 the 7th Australian Division, with similar naval and air support, also landed on Borneo and took Balikpapan. But the Dutch could no more repossess their former East Indian territories than the French could repossess Indochina. And neither the Americans nor the Australians could carry out their missions for them. In other words, Admiral Leahy and General Hurley had barked up the wrong tree, back in January, when they warned Roosevelt against Anglo-Franco-Dutch intrigues in southeast Asia and China.

Especially China. "The China question was on Roosevelt's mind constantly during the month preceding our departure for the Yalta meeting because of the growing seriousness of opposition to the National Government of Chiang Kai-shek," wrote Admiral Leahy in *I Was There*. "The dissident elements were said to be Communist-inspired." But reports from Hurley convinced Leahy and the President that "the activities of the British French, and Dutch in Southeast Asia" also opposed "America's attempts to unify Chinese forces against the Japanese." The Leahy account continued: "The British ambassador to China told Hurley that the American policy to unify China was detrimental if not destructive to the position of the white man in Asia. None of the imperial nations took any interest in the war being fought by China against Japan."

Leahy then added: "Obstacles to the unification of China seemed to be: a standpat element in the Kuomintang Party; stubborn resistance of the Communists; underhand tactics of the British-French-Dutch representatives; and constant opposition from some of our own diplomatic and military officers." Of all these obstacles, the long-drawn-out civil war between Chiang Kai-shek's Kuomintang and Mao Tse-tung's Communists headed the list, and it was this war which, in its turn, led some American military men to favor Chiang and some State Department officials to urge more concessions to the Communists. Few, if any, then perceived that the Nationalist-Communist conflict had long since become irreconcilable. No doubt, some British, French, and Dutch agents had spun some plots. But the Japanese occupation of British Burma and the Dutch East Indies as well as the Japanese protectorate over the Vichy French regime in Indochina had shaken all those colonial empires as profoundly as the Nationalist-Communist civil war was shaking China. Whatever regions the Japanese had occupied, whether in China, Indochina, or the adjacent islands, things could never be the same again.

While Roosevelt before, during, and after the Yalta Conference saw British, French, and Dutch imperialists under every bed in the Far East, others saw Russian and Chinese Communists under these same beds. But they all missed the wider panorama of national revolution which flew Communism's red flag over many parts of China that the Japanese had occupied and a variety of national colors over other regions. Roosevelt, Stalin, and Chiang Kai-shek all overrated the recuperative powers of the British, French, and Dutch empire builders. In recalling Stilwell from Chungking, Roosevelt had therefore done Churchill no favor. Indeed, it was to Chiang's five Stilwell-trained divisions that Lord Mountbatten owed the momentum that launched his Burma campaign which, in its turn, did not end until the Union Jack flew again over Singapore. Neither Stilwell nor Chiang—united, for once, in their common dislike of Britain—had planned it that way, but Britain's General William J. Slim had. Thus, the recovery of Singapore also gave Churchill a fleeting triumph over the dead Roosevelt, who had never been able to regard Singapore as one of democracy's chief citadels.

At the same time and in the same region, Roosevelt's successor handed the late President another posthumous defeat: this one at the hands of General de Gaulle. During the Japanese occupation of French

Indochina, French Vichyites collaborated with Japan and at the same time maintained contact with the Gaullists. Although the Anglo-Americans had not been able to mount any campaigns in Indochina until the summer of 1945, they had helped the popular Communist leader Ho Chi Minh wage guerrilla warfare in Indochina against the Japanese and their Vichyite collaborators and had supported his Vietminh movement to establish a native, nationalist regime after the defeat of Japan. But on August 24, Truman suddenly yielded to the pressure of General de Gaulle and endorsed his efforts to restore French rule. In January 1946, the Communist Vietminh won a popular majority in Indochina's first postwar election, but by this time French troops had appeared and tried to reimpose French rule in Vietnam, Cambodia, and Laos. Thus Truman's decision of August 24 to withdraw support from Ho Chi Minh and back General de Gaulle marked not only his first but perhaps his most critical departure from Roosevelt's grand design for the postwar world.

Maybe Truman had done the wrong thing, but he had two right reasons for having done it. First, he welcomed the opportunity to make a goodwill gesture toward de Gaulle. Second, he felt it important to show the world that he favored what he called "the establishment by China of close and friendly relations with Korea, Burma, Thailand, Indochina, and other neighboring areas, *without Chinese domination over such areas*" (italics added). As far as Indochina was concerned, before it had been under Japanese domination, it had been under French rule and before that under Chinese. With the departure of the Japanese, the native nationalists felt their time had come—and not in Indochina only, especially with China in no position to pose a clear or present danger to any of these smaller nations along its borders. The danger to China came from its own civil war which caused as much confusion in Chungking and Yenan as it did in Washington and Moscow.

·6·

ALTHOUGH STALIN knew more about the Manhattan Project than he had let on at Potsdam, even the Americans could not then foresee all its consequences. Ever since, there has been the usual huffing and puffing about the ifs of history (as if the Soviet Union could have been kept out of the war against Japan), while some of the facts of history have received less attention. Fact number one: the shock of atomic warfare brought about the surrender of Japan at least a year before the Russians or Americans expected it. Fact number two: the American occupation of Japan kept the Russians on the outside, looking in. But it also distracted American attention and diverted American resources from China. Fact number three: Japan's sudden surrender compelled Stalin to make a hasty settlement with Nationalist China's Foreign Minister Soong, a settlement that he later violated but that left the Communists free to do the same. Fact number four took the form of the closing sentence in a report submitted by Colonel Ivan Yeaton, former U.S. military attaché at Moscow, whom General Wedemeyer selected, in mid-August 1945, to appraise Chinese Communist military and political capabilities in north China: "The Communist army does not possess enough strength militarily to directly oppose the Kuomintang armies in position warfare; but over a long period of time as an occupying force the Kuomintang cannot hold out even with American help."

Colonel Yeaton's appraisal took into account the chain reaction that began with the atomic bombing of Hiroshima on August 6 and culminated in the release of the text of the Sino-Soviet treaty of friendship and alliance, made public on August 27. The next day, in the company of Ambassador Hurley, Mao Tse-tung flew from Yenan to Chungking for his first face-to-face meeting with Chiang Kai-shek since their paths had crossed at Canton back in 1925 and 1926. "These two principal figures of the negotiations formed a sharp contrast of personalities," Jerome Ch'ên has written in *Mao and the Chinese Revolution*. "Alert, quick-witted, and unyielding on matters of their respective principles, both were being hailed as sagacious leaders by their respective followers, and therefore each had a popular image to live up to. Emotionally Chiang was quick-tempered, while Mao was calm; morally Chiang was rigid and self-righteous, while Mao was more flexible and less fastidious; politically Chiang was the less coherent, while Mao was an unadulterated Marxist. The meeting of the two enthralled the nation while it raised hopes for peace."

But the destruction and chaos that China had suffered since the 1926 meeting between Chiang and Mao had left its people too exhausted to organize themselves for peace, war, or revolution. Chiang's arguments left Mao unmoved; Mao's arguments left Chiang unmoved; neither could budge the other. "The most important condition for national unity is the nationalization of all the armed forces of the nation," Chiang declared in his VJ Day message. Mao demanded a "new-democratic coalition Government" to which both the Communists and the Kuomintang must hand over all their troops. Chiang insisted on continuation of the Kuomintang's one-party rule; Mao's "new-democratic" coalition would usher in one-party rule, Communist style.

After more than three weeks of negotiation only Ambassador Hurley remained undiscouraged. The Sino-Soviet treaty had reconfirmed his faith in Stalin. He could not believe that Mao, having made the journey from Yenan to Chungking, would refuse to see the light and subordinate himself to Chiang. After postponing his departure from Chungking, originally set for September 18, to September 22, Ambassador Hurley took off for Washington. His final report, dispatched as he left, concluded: "The spirit shown by the negotiators is good, the rapprochement between the two leading parties in China seems to be progressing, and the discussion and rumors of civil war recede as the conference continues."

Chiang and Mao did not wind up their talks until October 10 when they agreed to proceed with the peaceful reconstruction of China and to call a Political Consultative Conference on January 10, 1946, to be attended by delegates from the Kuomintang, the Communist party, the Democratic League, the Youth party, and nine smaller groups. For the first time, the Kuomintang had acknowledged the equal status of all these parties, which, in their turn, had recognized Chiang as the leader of the nation. But for how long? The Communists' tantalizing tactics drove the Nationalists to distraction. For years Chiang Kai-shek and his Soong family in-laws had starved their own troops and demoralized their own people while fattening their own bank accounts. Now, the ashes of victory which choked the Nationalists half to death nourished the steady growth and eventual triumph of Communist China. For the kind of war the Communists fought, they could draw on the vast reserves of China's peasantry. For the kind of war the Nationalists fought, they had to depend on the limited resources and diminishing enthusiasm of the rapidly vanishing Americans.

·7·

BETWEEN MID-AUGUST and early November, 1945, American planes and ships carried a total of between 400,000 and 500,000 Nationalist troops to key regions in north and east China and landed another 53,000 United States Marines in the north where they occupied Peking, Tientsin, the Kailan coal mines, and the Peking-Linyu railway system. The Americans had come only to speed the evacuation of almost a million

Japanese troops, secure their arms and reserve stocks, and receive their surrender. But the Chinese Nationalists had come to stay. Or so their commanders thought.

But they presently found they had several other thinks coming. By early November the Nationalists ran out of the troops they needed to take over Manchuria, and the Soviet troops whom they had been replacing agreed to postpone their withdrawal, originally set for November 15, to December 3. On November 14, General Wedemeyer notified Washington that the Nationalists could not occupy Manchuria in the face of continuing Communist opposition and urged Chiang to consolidate his positions and communication lines south of the Great Wall before advancing any further into Manchuria. The next day, Chiang's troops seized Shanhaikwan at the sea end of the Great Wall and continued north. As O. Edmund Clubb tersely put it in his history, *Twentieth-Century China:* "The contest for Manchuria had been taken to the battlefield."

But no American troops appeared on that battlefield. The day of Japan's surrender found only 60,000 American servicemen in the China theater of war and within another month 16,000 of them had been shipped home, and the remainder followed at that same rate (the 53,000 United States Marines came and went later). When General Wedemeyer in November asked the War Department for seven American divisions "to create a barrier through north China and Manchuria against Soviet Russia," the Joint Chiefs informed him that the divisions he called for were not available.

Nobody can prove that seven American divisions could have done the job General Wedemeyer wanted done, with or without war. Nobody can prove that just a little more American resolution could have turned the tide in China's civil war. But few can deny that those tens of thousands of Americans whose "Bring the Boys Home" propaganda swept the American public, the halls of Congress, and the armed services deserved well of their country. The officers in the Pacific and China theaters of war and the political leaders at home had no alternative but to follow the demands of the men and women in the armed services and their families. For by the time that Chiang Kai-shek asked for American help in his civil war against his Communist compatriots, he had already shot his bolt—as the Americans had shot theirs, in reverse, when the westward wartime flow of American fighting men turned, with redoubled force, to an eastward ebb. That westward flow had provided the striking power that defeated the Japanese enemy against whom Chiang's troops had seldom fought with such vigor as they had shown against the Communists. With Japan laid low, what new threat to the vital interests of the United States could arise, in any foreseeable future, and from that part of the world? Only a suicidal determination by the United States to attempt to assume in China and southeast Asia the white man's burden from which the war had freed the British, French, and Dutch.

The United States had not declared war on Japan in order to restore the British, French, and Dutch colonial empires in southeast Asia to their prewar European overlords. Indeed, President Roosevelt's aversion to these colonial empires amounted almost to an obsession. But that obsession never got the better of his determination to follow a beat-Germany-first strategy in fighting the war into which the attack on Pearl Harbor had forced him. With Germany's unconditional surrender, President Truman faced two dilemmas that had never confronted Roosevelt: first, how to use his new atomic weapons against Japan; second, how to handle the final stage of China's civil war. The very fact that the bombing of Hiroshima and Nagasaki hastened Japan's unconditional surrender, leaving that country at the mercy of the United States, instantly transformed the situation in China from which the Americans withdrew their few troops as the Red army moved in *en masse*. But Stalin had no more stomach than Truman did for intervening in China's civil war.

Nobody had anticipated—much less planned—the course that China's civil war followed during the three months between mid-August and mid-November, 1945. But how appropriate, how characteristic a role General Patrick J. Hurley, the man Roosevelt handpicked for the impossible assignment as United States Ambassador to the court of Chiang Kai-shek, played to the bitter-sweet end. From the time of his arrival in China in the fall of 1944 until he returned to the United States one year later, Hurley had followed (all unintentionally) the advice of Lewis Carroll's White Queen, who advised Alice to believe six impossible things each morning before breakfast. Hurley settled for half as many: first, that Stalin and Molotov told him the truth, the whole truth, and nothing but the truth; second, that the dictates of common sense and enlightened self-interest ensured agreement between Chiang Kai-shek and Mao Tse-tung; and third, that the root of China's postwar troubles lay in the subversive recommendations of the State Department's foreign-service specialists in Chinese affairs. For General Wedemeyer's military advice Hurley had no more use than he had for the political advice of John Paton Davies and John Stewart Service. He also found it possible to believe that the hearts of Stalin, Chiang Kai-shek, and Mao Tse-tung all beat as one.

Even after Chiang's troops overran the Manchurian ports of Linyu, 125 miles east of Peking, on November 15, and Hulutao, 125 miles to the northeast, on November 22, thereby causing another breakdown in the Nationalist-Communist talks, Hurley still laid the whole blame on the State Department's foreign-service officers. Not until the afternoon of November 26, when Democratic Congressman E. H. deLacy criticized both Hurley and Chiang before the House of Representatives, did Hurley quit. Within twenty-four hours, President Truman announced his replacement by General Marshall.

Ten days later, the indomitable Hurley insisted: "Russia—and this is my own analysis; it is not a quotation—does not recognize the armed Communist Party as Communist at all." He pointed to the Stalin-Soong agreement, adding, "I have read that the Soviet has transgressed certain matters that involve the territorial and independent sovereignty of China, but frankly I have no evidence that would convince me that it is true. I believe that the United States and Russia are still together on policy in China."

It took another three years for the cream of the jest to surface: and Stalin and Molotov came out looking as foolish as Truman, Marshall, MacArthur, and many another of Hurley's compatriots. In 1948 Yugoslavia's former Vice Premier and Foreign Minister Edvard Kardelj quoted Stalin as having confided to him: "After the war, we invited the Chinese Comrades to come to Moscow. We told them bluntly that we considered an uprising in China had no prospects, that the Chinese Communists should seek a *modus vivendi* with Chiang Kai-shek and dissolve their army. The Chinese Communists agreed here in Moscow with the views of the Soviet comrades but went back to China and acted quite otherwise. They mustered their forces, organized their armies and now, as we see, they are beating Chiang Kai-shek's army. Now, in the case of China, we admit we were wrong."

·8·

MAO TSE-TUNG'S DECLARATION of war to the death against Chiang Kai-shek's Chinese Nationalists, announced on August 8, 1945, opened the final, major campaign of the Second World War. But with the passage of time, what began as the last campaign of World War Two developed into the first campaign of what might be called the Third-World War in that it involved a series of armed clashes—some of a revolutionary nature, some along nationalist lines, and some a mixture of the two—all of which have occurred in the Third World of developing Afro-Asian-Latin-American nations, China being incontestably the first among them. Now comes that war's Third-World aftermath in which the Chinese Revolution overshadows the Russian Revolution as much as the Second World War overshadowed the First. Whereas the events of the Second World War set in motion many forces that shaped the world of the 1970's, the course of China's civil war, which the Second World War greatly accelerated, foreshadowed subsequent patterns of conflict from Korea and Indochina to India, Pakistan, Indonesia, Egypt, Algeria, Cuba, equatorial Africa and the Middle East. The Russian Revolution ended with Lenin proclaiming his New Economic Policy and Stalin installing socialism in one country only. The Chinese Revolution, on the other hand, coincided with a widespread outburst of similar upheavals affecting two thirds of mankind.

A full account of the Second World War can no more ignore the events in China during the last five months of 1945 than it can find space for a full account of what happened in China during the next five years. Just as 1945 ended with the farce of General Hurley's return from his abortive mission to China, 1946 ended with the tragedy of General Marshall's equally futile efforts to mediate China's civil war. The first two months of that year also saw Soviet troops completing their withdrawal from China four months behind schedule with the removal of almost nine hundred million dollars' worth of industrial equipment from Manchuria. Not to be outdone at that game, Chiang and the Soong Dynasty looted the island of Formosa, recovered from eastern China all National government properties that Wang Ching-wei's puppet regime had appropriated, and went on to appropriate for themselves substantial Japanese-owned enterprises in the area. During the first half of the year, the Export-Import Bank in Washington had made more than six hundred million dollars in new credits available to the Chinese Nationalists and in August sold them nine hundred million dollars' worth of war surplus materials at a fraction of their value.

But all this American sustenance served only to fortify Chiang's determination to make no concessions to the Communists. Instead of strengthening his hold on northern China, Chiang demanded a free hand in Manchuria, where his writ did not run beyond a few of its cities. By September, a disillusioned Truman had withdrawn the 53,000

United States Marines from northern China, leaving only 12,000 American troops there, as compared with 113,000 the year before. The Nationalists responded by overextending themselves still further both in northern China and Manchuria. With the turn of the year, the Communists went on the offensive, never seeking to hold their gains, but always leaving the Nationalists badly weakened. By summer, however, the Communists were able to mount an offensive that isolated the Nationalists in their Manchurian strongholds of Chungchun, Kirin, and Mukden. Dispatched by President Truman to make an on-the-spot report, General Wedemeyer returned in September 1947, convinced that the Communists' new People's Liberation Army had gained both the tactical and strategic initiative and could now launch a new counter-offensive. When the United States suggested in November aiding the Chinese Nationalists with another $300 million foreign-aid appropriation, Madame Chiang Kai-shek flew to Washington, where her appeal for a three-billion-dollar appropriation to be spread over three years fell flat.

By this time official American estimates placed Nationalist troop strength at 2,700,000 men and Communist strength at 1,150,000. This estimate not only ignored 2,200,000 militiamen claimed by Mao Tse-tung; it underestimated the strength of his regulars by 850,000. In March 1947, American Ambassador J. Leighton Stuart—General Marshall's personal choice for that post—reported from Chungking: "There is an increasing realization, shared even by the Generalissimo, that military victory over the Communists is impossible and that some other solution must be reached if Communist-domination of all China is to be avoided."

What had happened? A comparison between the Russian and Chinese revolutions goes to the heart of the matter. Lenin and his little band of Bolsheviks had based their revolutionary strategy on seizing a propitious moment of general breakdown to organize an uprising of industrial workers and improvise a dictatorship of professional revolutionaries. Lenin's Bolsheviks therefore seized power first and fought their civil war afterward. Mao and his little band of Communists reversed this process. They began by building up mass support among the peasantry, drawing their leadership from all classes. In the process of fighting their civil war, Mao's Communists created a professional army, a still larger force of peasant guerrilla fighters, and ever-growing popular support over ever-widening areas. Four years of civil war followed the Bolshevik Revolution of November 1917. Four years of civil war preceded the establishment of Communist rule over all of mainland China.

The decisive battle in this war began at the end of its third year, on November 7, 1948, and continued for sixty-seven days into 1949. Between November 1 and November 5, the Communists had captured the last Nationalist strongholds in Manchuria—Mukden, Chinchow, Yingtao, and the Hulutao beachhead. Two days later, six hundred miles to the south, they launched their *coup de grâce* that became known as the battle of the Hwai-Hai because it took place on a vast plain between the Hwai River and the Lunghai Railway which ran from the coast to Shensi province. The flat plain lent itself perfectly to the campaign of maneuver, planned by Mao Tse-tung, and doomed Chiang Kai-shek's static, defensive warfare to disaster. More than a million men took part in the fighting, which bore little resemblance to Hitler's campaigns in Poland and France or to the battles of Stalingrad and Kursk. The victorious Communists fought with Japanese and American weapons that had fallen into their hands, but it was their own guerrilla tactics that enabled them to prevail over the more modern weapons and conventional tactics of the Nationalists. Sometimes the Communists staged frontal, human-sea attacks; more often they resorted to the nibbling tactics of harassment; most of all, they bore down on cutting Nationalist supply lines and chopping up defending forces, piecemeal. The final result, however, took the form of a battle of annihilation as complete as the German victory of Tannenberg during the First World War or the Russian victory at Stalingrad during the Second. For the Communists adapted their tactics to their weapons just as the Germans and Russians had done, before them.

The Nationalist capital of Nanking fell to the Communists on April 22, 1949. Not until October 1, after they had established their rule over almost all of China, did they proclaim the Central People's Government of the Chinese People's Republic of China at Peking. In December, Chiang Kai-shek established a rump Nationalist government in exile on the island of Formosa, which became in due course the home of the Republic of China. The Second World War had brought forth the Chinese Revolution. Less than a year later came the Korean war—preceded and followed by warfare in Indochina. World War III: No. Third-World War: Yes.

XXVIII

From Cold-War Myth to Third-World War

·1·

THE SECOND WORLD WAR's aftermath took two forms. First, the China theater of that war again became the scene of a civil war which culminated, in four years' time, in China's Communist Revolution. By this time similar outbreaks of war and revolution had broken out in other nations of the so-called Third World that had begun emerging from the ashes of Japan's defeat. Meanwhile, the atomic breakthrough that had brought the Second World War to such a sudden end also led to a sharp increase in Soviet-American tensions. The atomic bombings that brought revolutionary developments to China and other Third World nations plunged the Soviet Union and its wartime allies into a postwar state of chronic tension that presently became known as the cold war.

It all began at Potsdam, where Truman's confidence in the atomic bomb led him to assume—rightly, as it proved—that the Red army could never reach Tokyo and that he could install General MacArthur there as Japan's new Mikado. But the President had also assumed—wrongly, as it proved—that his possession of the atomic bomb would compel Stalin to grant free elections and set up new governments in Romania and Bulgaria. Secretary Byrnes's rude awakening came in London at the first Foreign Ministers' meeting in September, when he had no more success in persuading Molotov to accept the American formula for an east-European settlement than Molotov had in reconciling Byrnes to the Soviet *fait accompli*. This London meeting not only confirmed the failure of Potsdam to make any headway toward a German settlement. It also alerted Truman to the fact that America's temporary atomic monopoly had not given irresistible power to his demands or invincible strength to his position. Three months later at the

Foreign Ministers' meeting in Moscow, just before Christmas, Byrnes made some slight headway, but angered Truman by delivering a radio report on the meeting without clearing it first with the White House. "Unless Russia is faced with an iron fist and strong language another war is in the making," Truman wrote Byrnes at the time, "Only one language do they understand—'how many divisions have you?'. . . . I'm tired of babying the Soviets."

Byrnes needed no prodding from Truman on this score, and their hard responses to unyielding Soviet tactics did not turn away Stalin's wrath. In January 1946, the Kremlin refused to withdraw Soviet troops from Iran's northern, border province of Azerbaijan on schedule, thus setting the stage for the first Soviet veto in the United Nations Security Council and the walkout by Andrei Gromkyo, head of the Soviet delegation. On February 9, 1946, Stalin described the "capitalist world" as splitting into two hostile camps and lurching toward inevitable war. But the immovable Molotov at London and Moscow and the all-too-mobile Gromyko at the United Nations served chiefly to unify and antagonize the western allies.

It therefore came as no surprise when Winston Churchill on March 5, at Truman's invitation, delivered a momentous address at Westminster College in Fulton, Missouri. America's atomic breakthrough had stirred Churchill to even higher hopes than those which possessed Truman, who introduced the former prime minister and nodded approval from the speaker's platform as Churchill proclaimed: "From Stettin in the Baltic to Trieste in the Adriatic, an iron curtain has descended across the Continent. Behind lie all the capitals of Central and Eastern Europe. Warsaw, Berlin, Prague, Vienna, Budapest, Belgrade, Bucharest, and Sofia, all those famous cities and populations lie in what I must call the Soviet sphere and all are subject to very high and, in many cases, increasing measure of control from Moscow."

That laid it on the line—on the Stettin-Trieste line, that is, which Churchill had glumly accepted at Potsdam. Since then, however, the *coup de grâce* that the bombings of Hiroshima and Nagasaki had administered to the war in the Pacific had persuaded Churchill as well as Truman that the American atomic breakthrough had shifted the balance of military power in eastern Europe as well as on the far Pacific. By March 1946, the Anglo-Americans had indeed encouraged the reestablishment of democratic rule in western Europe on a firmer basis than the Russians were establishing pro-Communist regimes in eastern Europe, where Stalin's attitude had been described as "What's mine is mine and what's yours is negotiable." Over the long pull, Stalin and Molotov had probably overreached themselves in eastern Europe. But over the short pull Truman and Churchill were certainly overreaching themselves in challenging the Soviet position east of the Stettin-Trieste line.

In any case, Churchill's Fulton speech sounded like martial music to Stalin's ears. "A setup for war, a call to war against the Soviet Union," he called it. Although Stalin knew much better than Churchill did that the men in the Kremlin neither planned, wanted, nor expected war, he also knew how to turn the Fulton speech to his purpose of casting Truman and Churchill in the roles of warmongers. As for Churchill's qualifying phrase that what the Russians desired was not war but "the fruits of war and the indefinite expansion of their powers and doctrines," Stalin said nothing.

But the actions he took spoke louder than the words that he neither spoke nor quoted. On March 13, the Soviet Union announced its first postwar Five-Year Plan as Molotov suddenly rejected the billion-dollar postwar loan for which he had been importuning Washington ever since the sudden cessation of Lend-Lease shipments in May 1945. The Soviet authorities also refused to join the World Bank and the International Monetary Fund, at the same time tightening their economic bonds with the East Germans by suspending further removals of machinery from that quarter. On May 3, 1946, General Lucius D. Clay, in his capacity as deputy military governor of the U.S.-occupied portion of West Germany, stopped the flow of reparations to the Soviet Union. On September 7, Secretary of State Byrnes delivered a major foreign-policy speech at Stuttgart in West Germany, where he announced that the British and United States governments had agreed to administer their two occupation zones as a single whole, thereby easing Britain's financial burden, increasing America's, and strengthening West Germany's economy: "Germany must be given a chance to export goods in order to import enough to make her economy self-sustaining. Germany is part of Europe, and European recovery, particularly in Belgium, the Netherlands, and other adjoining states will be slow indeed if Germany with her great resources of iron and steel is turned into a poor house."

While the peripatetic Byrnes harried Stalin by threatening to build up West Germany, Truman, from his White House vantage point, continued to give the highest postwar priority to rushing immediate aid to millions of displaced persons—six million of them in Germany alone, but many more millions in many other lands. By the end of 1946, the United Nations Relief and Rehabilitation Administration had distributed three and a half billion dollars' worth of supplies, most of them from the United States, to displaced persons in hundreds of UNRRA camps all around the world. For this the United States could reap nothing but goodwill from the recipients—and little but suspicion from the Kremlin.

Nor did that suspicion diminish in March 1946 when President Truman persuaded ex-President Hoover to head a Famine Emergency Committee that, within six months, shipped six million tons of bread grains to feed hungry people almost everywhere. With the single exception of the United States, all the major belligerents in the Second World War—the victorious British and Russians, as well as the defeated Germans, Italians, and Japanese—emerged weaker, poorer, and hungrier than they had gone in. The Americans, and only the Americans, emerged richer, stronger, better fed, and more than twice as productive as before. While the President, from time to time, bewailed the speed at which Congress and the public had compelled him to "bring the boys home," only this rapid demobilization enabled the United States to begin reconverting its economy to peacetime production and peacetime needs—abroad, even more than at home—as great as the needs of war itself.

Byrnes, however, lacked the experience and the talents to deal with the economics and politics of the postwar world. Although his fast diplomatic footwork at Potsdam, London, and Moscow had impressed Stalin, his high-handed methods irked Truman, who gave him a dressing down after the Moscow conference for having played his cards too close to his chest. Byrnes at once submitted his resignation, but agreed, at the President's request, to stay on through 1946 in order to allow General Marshall time to complete his mission to China before taking over as his successor. Nobody welcomed the prospect more than Dean Acheson, who had served as undersecretary since the summer of 1945 when he replaced Joseph C. Grew. Early in the Roosevelt administration, Acheson had left a leading Washington law firm to serve in the Treasury Department, but found the President's departure from the gold standard too whimsical for his taste and resigned. During the battle of Britain, however, Acheson joined the State Department, where he made an instant success. His old friend Felix Frankfurter once described him as a "frustrated school teacher, persisting against overwhelming evidence to the contrary, in the belief that the human mind could be moved by facts and reason."

Acheson served Truman with a loyalty and devotion that the President unfailingly reciprocated. In connection with Truman's "epoch-making series of decisions," Acheson has written: "In later years the prevailing doctrine of 'preserving options' precluded this continuity of action so typical of the Truman years." But in General Marshall, Acheson saw a "man for all seasons" and quoted with approval the words President Conant of Harvard used in conferring an honorary doctorate on Marshall in 1950: "An American to whom freedom owes an enduring debt of gratitude, a soldier and statesman whose ability and character brook only one comparison in the history of this nation." Shortly after taking office on January 21, 1947, Marshall created a new Policy Planning Staff and appointed as its chief George F. Kennan, who had served in the State Department since 1925, winding up as its top expert on Soviet affairs.

Truman, Marshall, and Acheson endorsed and embraced what Kennan called a policy of "long-term, patient, but firm containment." As Kennan saw it, the United States "has it in its power to increase enormously the strains under which Soviet policy must operate, to force upon the Kremlin a far greater degree of moderation and circumspection than it has had to observe in recent years and in this way to promote tendencies which must eventually find their outlet in either the breakup or the mellowing of Soviet power." On the one hand, Kennan cautioned against the assumption that the Soviet leaders could mend their ways, much less change their beliefs. On the other hand: "The Kremlin is under no ideological compunction to accomplish its purposes in a hurry. . . . Its main concern is to make sure that it has filled every nook and cranny available to it in the basin of world power. But if it finds unassailable barriers in its path, it accepts these philosophically and accommodates itself to them."

· 2 ·

IF CHURCHILL, TRUMAN, AND STALIN had not invented a mythical cold war, a real cold war would have had to exist. But a real cold war would not have served their purposes. For a real cold war (being a contradiction in terms, a paradox, like hot peace, cold heat, nonviolent violence) would have quickly and automatically resulted in compromise. No such deplorable fate could soon overtake the cold-war myth invented by its supreme commanders, who, instead of having to compromise something somewhere at once, now had everything—both ways for an indefinite period. Thus they could accuse one another of preparing atomic and nuclear weapons to wage total war, fanning the war spirit of their own people, and charging their adversaries with equally belligerent intentions and behavior. Churchill saw the cold-war myth justifying himself in the eyes of posterity, if not in the eyes of his contemporaries. Truman saw the cold-war myth as the regrettable but inevitable end result of the policies he had inherited from his predecessor. Stalin saw the cold-war myth enabling him to win the rewards of a hot war that he neither intended nor expected to fight. Neither stone-cold nor totally warlike, the cold-war myth encouraged Churchill to try to call Stalin's bluff, Truman to rally bipartisan support behind an anti-Communist foreign policy, and Stalin to perpetuate his dictatorship by justifying a permanent war economy.

During the 1930's, the French used the expressions *guerre à froid* and *guerre blanche* to describe Hitler's war of nerves, but the phrase "cold war," used to describe Soviet-American relations, bore a "Made in U.S.A." label. Herbert Bayard Swope, former Democratic editor of the New York *World,* coined it during the spring of 1946 in his capacity as ghost-writer for Bernard M. Baruch. President Truman had requested Acheson and David Lilienthal, former chairman of the Tennessee Valley Authority, to prepare a report on the international control of atomic energy for Baruch to present to the United Nations. But Baruch scorned the step-by-step approach taken by Acheson and Lilienthal and insisted that the final version not only rule out any possible recourse to a Soviet veto but also assure the United States of a permanent, built-in majority behind its own control proposals. When finally submitted on June 14, 1946, the report also included the provision that the United Nations must accept it without change.

That sunk the Baruch Report without a trace, at the same time leaving the Congress free to establish a United States Atomic Energy Commission under the Atomic Energy Act of 1946, which, in turn, contained a provision demanded by the armed services that prohibited the exchange of information on the use of atomic energy with any other nation until Congress had decreed that "effective" international controls did indeed exist. By way of footnote, it should be added that while Baruch, the pioneer cold warrior, cautiously waited a year before using Swope's phrase, Walter Lippmann, the first journalist to give it wide circulation, always deplored the "cold war," not so much because of its mythical as because of its militant character.

"A rose by any other name . . ." The origins of the phrase "cold war" are not without interest, but whether they describe a real myth or a mythical reality has less importance than the all too solid fact of the Congressional elections of November, 1946, when the Republicans won a 51–45 majority in the Senate, where only one third of the seats were at stake, but a 248–118 majority in the House, where contests were held for all seats. If a wise Supreme Court follows the election returns, a wise President anticipates them. Harry Truman—like Franklin Roosevelt before him—had every reason to expect that the Second World War would be followed by the kind of "back to normalcy" reaction that led in 1920 to twelve years of Republican rule followed by the Wall Street crash, the world depression, the Second World War, and twenty years of Democratic rule.

But during those twenty Democratic years, the pace of history accelerated at a greater rate than it had during the twelve preceding years of Republican rule. The Second World War, in its turn, caused greater convulsions than the First and gave rise to a stormier aftermath. Moreover, the Second World War merged imperceptibly into a Chinese civil war that drove the Americans from that country, finally culminating in a revolution that involved one fifth of the human race and threatened to spread to more than half.

Nor did the Second World War's aftermath engulf Europe in the kind of chaos that four years of civil war and revolution spread across China. Droughts, floods, storms, and excessive cold made the winter of 1946–47 Europe's bitterest in living memory. At the same time, owing to war damage, economic recovery lagged, inflation raged, and farm production and factory output sank. In December 1946, British production fell to prewar levels, and bread had to be rationed. By February, cold weather forced more than half the factories in Britain to close. They ordered these matters no better in France, where one quarter of the electorate voted Communist and eighty per cent of all workers belonged to the Communist-controlled General Federation of Labor. One third of all the Italian electorate voted Communist, and in both France and Italy, Communist parties had more members than any other. In Germany conditions became so bad that nobody had any energy for politics of any kind. Ten million refugees from the east had poured into the western occupation zones. Even in 1947, cigarettes remained West Germany's chief currency. One package equaled one man's labor for one month. Rations dropped to barely 1000 calories a day. During the winter of 1946–47 two hundred people froze to death in Berlin.

But natural disasters are not the stuff of which revolutions are made.

Western Europe and the western occupation zones of Germany posed opportunities as well as dangers. The sharpest immediate crisis lay in Greece, where Communist guerrillas, supplied by Tito's Yugoslavia, were proving more than the British could handle. Stalin still kept the promise he had made to Churchill, in October, 1944, to recognize Greece as a zone of British responsibility, but Attlee a year and a half later, had to give it up as a bad job. On February 21, 1947, the British notified Washington that they would have to stop sending military and economic aid to Greece and Turkey to the tune of some $250 million a year. Three weeks later Truman called upon the Congress to appropriate $400 million to supply such aid. In another two months, bipartisan majorities in both Houses of Congress approved the so-called Truman Doctrine and the necessary funds.

In his address delivered before a joint session of the two Houses of Congress on March 12, 1947, the President declared: "At the present moment in world history, nearly every nation must choose between alternative ways of life." One he described as being "based upon the will of the majority . . . free institutions, representative government, free elections, guarantees of individual liberty, freedom of speech and religion from political oppression." The other "based upon the will of a minority forcibly imposed upon the majority" and relying upon terror and oppression, a controlled press and radio, fixed elections, and the suppression of personal freedoms.

"I believe that it must be the policy of the United States to support free peoples who are resisting attempted subjugation by armed minorities or by outside pressures.

"I believe that we must assist free peoples to work out their own destinies in their own way. . . . I believe that our help should be primarily through economic and financial aid which is essential to economic stability and orderly political processes."

Senator Vandenberg had advised the President to "scare the hell out of the American people" and to judge from the speech and its effect he had done just that.

·3·

PRESIDENT TRUMAN, in the doctrine that bore his name, had applied to the eastern Mediterranean the principles of the cold-war myth that Winston Churchill had expounded at Fulton, Missouri, just a year before. But within another three months Secretary of State Marshall and

Undersecretary Acheson launched a bold attempt to transcend that myth. On May 8, at the President's instigation, Acheson outlined to the Delta Council at Cleveland, Mississippi, a long-range foreign-aid program ten or twenty times as great as the emergency-aid program for Greece and Turkey. On June 5, at Harvard University's commencement, General Marshall took all Europe as his province, inviting all nations on both sides of the Stettin-Trieste line to list their economic recovery needs which the United States would then do its best to fulfill. Marshall named no dates to be met, no services to be rendered, no goods to be supplied—or denied. "Our policy is not directed against any country or doctrine, but against hunger, poverty, desperation, and chaos. . . . Any government that is willing to assist in the task of recovery will find the full co-operation, I am sure, of the United States Government. Any government which maneuvers to block the recovery of other countries cannot expect help from us." The "Marshall Plan"— as it came to be called—included no military equipment. It amounted to a blank American check, good for whatever the recipient might require to repair the wreckage that war, weather, and time had wrought the length and breadth of Europe.

At a series of meetings in Paris during late June and early July the foreign ministers of Britain, France, and fourteen other west-European nations met American officials with whom they quickly made arrangements that reversed, almost overnight, the rising tide of misery, chaos, and unrest that threatened, less than two years after the German surrender, to demoralize them all. Within another two years, recovery if not prosperity had begun to make western Europe look like itself again.

Not so the Europe that lay behind the Iron Curtain. On June 26, 1947, Molotov and an eighty-nine-member delegation had arrived in Paris, where they spent most of the next three days telephoning Moscow. Molotov then proposed that each nation present its own recovery program to Washington, whereas the British and French, on June 30, proposed that all the nations of Europe present a single program listing all the needs of all. Molotov at once walked out, charging the Americans with "trying to divide Europe into two groups of states" and then "creating new difficulties between them."

Before his departure for Moscow on July 2, he also charged the Americans with intending "to restore the economy of Germany and Japan, on the old basis, provided it is subordinated to the interests of American capital." Within another week, he followed through with his own "Molotov Plan" that tightened Moscow's control over its east-European satellites by stimulating the flow of trade and investments. Suiting their actions to Molotov's words, the Poles and Czechs, who had shown interest in making their own arrangements with Washington, informed the conferees at Paris that they, too, had to withdraw because their attendance "might be construed as an action against the Soviet Union."

Far from transcending the cold-war myth, the Marshall Plan gave it a new lease on life. Four days after Molotov's return to Moscow, Stalin ordered A. A. Zhdanov, one of his favorite strong-arm men, to summon the leaders of the Communist parties of the Soviet Union, Yugoslavia, France, Italy, Poland, Bulgaria, Czechoslovakia, and Hungary to forgather in Polish Silesia and organize a streamlined version of the Communist International, which had been dissolved in 1943. As secretary of the new organization, Zhdanov assailed "the aggressive and frankly imperialist course to which American imperialism has committed itself since the end of World War Two." G. M. Malenkov, as Stalin's personal representative at the scene, charged Truman and Marshall with hatching "plans of fresh aggression, plans for a new war against the Soviet Union and the new democracies. . . . Imitating the Hitlerites, the new aggressors are using blackmail and extortion." The new organization that replaced the extinct Comintern became known as the Communist Information Bureau, or Cominform.

Hot or cold, war is war, and anything goes. When Stalin waged hot war, he went the limit; when Roosevelt waged hot war, he demanded unconditional surrender. But when it came to cold war, Stalin, Truman, and their henchmen did not even believe the phrases they hurled at one another. In *The Cold War as History* Louis Halle noted that "the Cold War presented itself as a worldwide contest between liberal democracy and Communism." But he also went on to describe such an ideological contest, waged in ideological terms, as "in its essence mythical." When the Truman Doctrine proclaimed that "it must be the policy of the United States to support free peoples who are resisting subjugation by armed minority or by outside pressures," Stalin and his associates denounced Truman and the men around him as a bunch of Hitlerites. And they, in their turn, construed the Soviet occupation of eastern Europe as the mere prelude to a program of further expansion embracing not only western Europe but the great globe itself.

Louis Halle urged his fellow Americans to distinguish "between the conflict represented by ideology and rhetoric, which was global and at best secondary, and the real conflict, which was over the balance of power that had its fulcrum in Europe. What the United States set out to do in 1947 was simply to defend what was left of Europe against an expanding Russia." No doubt. But what the United States set out to do was one thing; what it found itself doing turned out to be something else again. In the Truman Doctrine and the Marshall Plan the United States had indeed taken new initiatives—the first military, the second economic—both in regions of Europe where Soviet power had already failed to penetrate. But Molotov, on November 7, went off on another tack when he celebrated the twentieth anniversary of the Russian Revolution with the terse announcement: "The atomic bomb is no longer a secret," thus stirring deeper concerns about wider areas than those at which the Cominform had directed its fire. And yet, even when the Russians exploded their first atomic bomb two years later, they still had a long way to go to acquire atomic parity with the United States and thus establish that "balance of terror" which—in Churchill's eyes—later improved the prospects for world peace.

Whether Stalin chose to bear down on atomic or conventional weapons, on production for peace or production for war, on industry or agriculture, it would still take decades, not years, to build a Soviet economy comparable to the American economy. The Americans, of course, might wind up riding for a fall, but as far as the 1940's were concerned, their destiny lay in their own hands and the Truman-Marshall-Acheson-Kennan foreign policy pursued precisely that Europe-first line of which Louis Halle approved. Moreover, China's civil war and Stalin's decision to concentrate his limited resources on the development of his newly acquired east-European domain left the Americans almost no choice but to make west-European recovery their prime, postwar concern.

· 4 ·

ON MARCH 17, 1948, President Truman sent a message to the Congress asking it to restore the draft: "Since the close of hostilities, the Soviet Union and its agents have destroyed the independence and democratic character of a whole series of nations in Eastern and Central Europe. It is this ruthless course of action, and the clear design to extend it to the remaining nations of Europe that have brought about the critical situation in Europe today." At the same moment, representatives of Britain, France, Belgium, Luxembourg, and Holland met at Brussels where, at the suggestion of Britain's Foreign Secretary Bevin, they signed a treaty providing that "if any of the Parties should be the subject of an armed attack in Europe, the other Parties . . . will afford the Party attacked all military and other aid and assistance within their power." On April 14, at Washington, the five members of this new "Western Union" group joined Denmark, Iceland, Norway, Portugal, Canada, and the United States in forming the North Atlantic Treaty Organization (NATO), pledging themselves to consider an armed attack on any one of them as an attack upon all and to assist the party or parties under attack.

Three days later, the Russians responded by withdrawing their representative from the Allied Control Council in Berlin and pronouncing that body dead and buried. If Germany remained the keystone of Europe, Berlin remained the keystone of Germany. The Truman administration and its west-European allies had announced their determination to fuse the western occupied zones of Germany into a single "federal form of government" that, in its turn, would co-operate in the "economic reconstruction of western Europe." On April 1, the Russians temporarily halted the movement of military supplies from western Germany to west Berlin; on June 4, the British, French, and American occupation authorities gave the west Germans the signal to start organizing a German Federal Republic for which the three western allies began issuing a new currency, good in their occupation zones but not in Berlin. On June 23, the Anglo-Americans began issuing these new marks in their sectors of West Berlin. The next day, the Russians halted all surface traffic between West Germany and West Berlin.

On June 28, 1948, President Truman informed a few of his advisers: "We are going to stay, period." General Marshall later added: "We had the alternative of following a firm policy in Berlin or accepting the consequences of failure of the rest of our European policy." The loosely drawn statute concerning the rights of access to Berlin did not forbid the Russians to do what they did and cut all road, rail, river, and canal traffic to the city. But the statute did not forbid the western allies to do what they did and fall back on the air corridors. The United States at once organized a massive airlift which was soon delivering thirteen thousand tons of supplies a day. In a month, the Russians agreed to discuss the whole problem, but insisted on tying a Berlin settlement to "the general question of four-power control of Germany." The western allies refused to make such high stakes a negotiable matter and the airlift continued for 324 days. Stalin used all of them to crack down on his east-European satellites. The western allies used them to hasten the development of a West German Federal Republic as a member in good standing of the North Atlantic community.

·5·

To SPEAK OF the creation of the West German Federal Republic is to speak in the next breath of the creation of the state of Israel. Upon all the nations that had waged war against Nazi Germany, the Nazi wartime holocaust of Europe's Jews imposed the moral obligation to work with the World Zionist Congress and the United Nations to transform Britain's prewar mandate to establish a national home for the Jewish people in Palestine into the new and independent state of Israel. But a far heavier obligation lay upon the German people whose Third Reich had organized this holocaust. For several years, the consequences of unconditional surrender had reduced all Germany and all Germans to total dependence on their conquerors. But neither the British government, which still held its prewar mandate to administer Palestine, nor the Zionist Congress could wait for West Germany's postwar economic miracle to come along before seeking restitution for the crimes that the Third Reich had committed against world Jewry. At the end of 1945, at the instigation of the British government, an Anglo-American Committee of Inquiry therefore undertook a joint study of the Zionist demand for the admission of another one hundred thousand Jews into Palestine, where enough Jewish emigrants from other lands had already settled to form a national community. On April 3, 1946, the Committee of Inquiry accepted the Zionist demand on two conditions: "First, that Jew shall not dominate Arab and Arab shall not dominate Jew in Palestine. Second, that Palestine shall be neither a Jewish state nor an Arab state."

Easier said than done. The Palestine Jews and Arabs refused even to sit down together. The British government favored and the United States government opposed provincial autonomy. In February 1947, the British government placed the issue before the United Nations General Assembly, where a Special Committee on Palestine came up with majority and minority reports. The majority report recommended partition of Palestine into Arab and Jewish states and an international regime for Jerusalem—Britain to remain responsible for the administration of Palestine under the United Nations until September 1, when both states would become independent.

The British never accepted the report, and when the Assembly approved a slightly modified version, the British abstained from voting, and their government announced that it would not share its responsibilities with anybody, but would terminate its mandate on May 15, 1947. This left the Palestine Jews and Arabs with five months to work out their own settlement. Fighting at once broke out, but the neighboring Arabs gave the Palestine Arabs little help, and Jewish troops occupied more territory than the Anglo-American and United Nations committees had recommended. On May 14 the Jewish leaders in Palestine proclaimed the existence of the state of Israel; within fifteen minutes, Truman announced its recognition by the United States, rejecting the advice of the State and Defense departments, but receiving overwhelming bipartisan support from the Congress. There can be no doubt that he had acted in full accord with the wishes of the American people and of most of the people in most of the nations of Europe. But virtually all the Palestine Arabs and most of their Arab neighbors opposed the President's action.

There are those who ascribe Truman's zeal for the cause of Israel to his friendship for his wartime comrade and peacetime business partner, Eddie Jacobson, an enthusiastic Zionist. Others note the preponderance of Jewish over Arab voters in the American electorate. Yet in 1948, the anti-Jewish Stalin supported the action of the pro-Zionist Truman. Did this signify a thaw in the mythical Soviet-American cold war? Not a bit of it. At that time, even Stalin had not recovered from the shock of the holocaust that Hitler had unleashed on Europe's Jews. At that time, not even the Arabs of the Middle East rallied around the dispossessed Arabs of Palestine. In the nature of the case, that mood could not last; in the nature of the case, the Zionists and their friends made the most of an opportunity for which their people had been waiting for more than nineteen hundred years.

How the mood and the world changed in the next twenty years. By the mid-1960's a series of real Third-World wars had spread from Indochina to Indonesia, to Korea, Algeria, Cuba, India, the Congo. To the Arabs of the Middle East and to more and more of the other developing nations of the Third World, the Arab-Israeli struggle had become part of a steadily widening conflict that involved them all. What was the Soviet-American cold war to them or they to the Soviet-American cold war? Not so much as the Third World had become to Dr. Adenauer's Germany or Dr. Adenauer's Germany to the Third World. For the importance of the Third World to Dr. Adenauer arose from the fact that Israel lay at the geographical heart of it. The importance of Dr. Adenauer to the Third World arose from the fact that the German Federal Republic could supply it with economic aid of superior quality at reasonable prices and with a minimum of political, economic, or military strings attached.

A Roman Catholic Rhinelander, born in 1875, under the reign of Emperor William II's grandfather and during the chancellorship of Bismarck, Adenauer had always regarded the Prussians as the worst enemies of the best Germans and the Nazis as the worst enemies of the best Christians. Unlike most members of the Catholic Center party, Adenauer supported the Weimar Republic to the end and opposed Hitler from the beginning. He preferred ties with France to subservience to Prussia, and served as Cologne's lord mayor until ousted by Hitler. After the war, the British at first distrusted Adenauer's ultraconservative background (which subsequently proved his great source of strength), but the Americans reinstated him as mayor of his native city, and he presently gave all persons and parties concerned lessons in political infighting as he made himself the leader of the Christian Democratic Union which had inherited the Catholic supporters of the prewar Center party and welcomed Protestants to its fold. But he always viewed, as Germany's prime postwar obligation, the debt of blood it owed to the Jewish victims of the Nazi holocaust.

Adenauer's sympathy for Israel enhanced rather than exhausted his claims to Anglo-Franco-American support. For Adenauer's sympathy for Israel had its roots in his fundamental conviction that Germany's best hopes for the future lay with a west-European community of nations. He therefore saw in the German Federal Republic a golden opportunity for West Germany to detach itself from its previous dependence on Prussia and to align itself more closely with France and its other west-European neighbors. His conservative political views and his Roman Catholic faith caused some misgivings in Britain and the United States, just as his Germanic temperament caused some misgivings among the French. But Adenauer's genius lay in the fact that he brought to the cause of European peace and reconciliation those personal attributes with which many of his compatriots had pursued aggressive, imperialistic aims, and he therefore may be said to belong to that small company of contemporary statesmen who transcended themselves. But he could not begin moving in his chosen direction of European unity until September 7, 1949, when the three western-occupied zones of Germany became the German Federal Republic under his chancellorship.

·6·

By this time, Stalin found himself in deeper trouble with his own east-European satellites than he was with the cold warriors of the west. In February 1948, four months before the Berlin blockade began, he took advance, protective action against Czechoslovakia where, in the free election of May 1946, Communist candidates won 38 per cent of the vote—the largest that went to any party. Several Communists therefore held seats in the coalition cabinet of President Benes and his half-American Foreign Minister Jan Masaryk, son of the founder of the Czechoslovak Republic. But what was good enough for Benes and Masaryk was not good enough for Stalin who ordered Red army troops to mass along the Czechoslovak border while a Soviet mission flew to Prague demanding that Benes quit forthwith and turn over all power to an all-Communist regime. Benes, who had been through it all before with Hitler, now bowed to Hitler's conqueror. But with the younger, tougher Masaryk, the Communists took no chances. They murdered him under contrived circumstances that made it look like suicide.

Next on Stalin's list came Yugoslavia, where he expected trouble, though nothing like the trouble he got. Because he had succeeded, before the war, in establishing Communist rule over one sixth of the earth's surface, Stalin saw every reason to believe that he could extend Soviet rule after the war to almost all those regions of eastern Europe which his armies had occupied during it. But the Red army had not liberated and occupied Yugoslavia, as it had liberated and occupied Romania, Hungary, and Bulgaria. Moreover, in Tito Stalin faced a Communist leader who might not be able to beat him at his own game, but knew how to play and win a different one. For Tito's experience in Yugoslavia and his observation of Stalinist policies elsewhere convinced him that Stalin had already bitten off more than he could chew and that the future of the Communist movement lay with looser federations of smaller nations rather than with the one Soviet world that Stalin and the Stalinists still seemed determined to build.

Stalin always assumed that what was good for the Soviet Union was also good for the Soviet satellites. Tito, on the other hand, not only refused to build Yugoslav Communism according to Soviet specifications. All of his own tried and tested comrades agreed with him. On top of this, Tito joined forces with his old friend Georgi Dimitrov—former secretary of the original Cominform, secretary of the Bulgarian Communist party, and central figure of the Reichstag fire trial, at which his baiting of Goering made him an international hero—in projecting a Balkan federation.

That tore it. In June 1948, the Cominform ruled that the leaders of Yugoslavia's Communist party "had placed themselves in opposition to the Communist Parties affiliated with the Information Bureau." Back in April, Tito and his Foreign Minister Kardelj had written Moscow: "No matter how much each of us loves the land of socialism, the U.S.S.R., he can, in no case, love his country less." To which the Cominform replied in December: "The attitude toward the Soviet Union is now the test of devotion toward the cause of proletarian internationalism."

Stalin took no overt action against Tito. He simply declared that Tito had separated himself from the Cominform. Moscow and Belgrade did not break diplomatic relations. Moscow, however, ordered an 85 per cent cut in its trade with Yugoslavia and ordered its satellites to follow suit. By September 1948, the Export-Import Bank had extended a twenty-million-dollar credit to Yugoslavia to purchase machinery for its copper industry. In Washington, the National Security Council revised its commercial policy to permit Yugoslavia to buy whatever it needed to maintain a "peacetime economy." Yugoslav officials at the United Nations invoked the principles of national self-determination and denounced outside interference in the internal affairs of other countries. Tito not only challenged Stalin's pretensions to dominate eastern Europe. He challenged the myth of the cold war which these pretensions had encouraged. This myth, in its turn, rested on the assumption that the Second World War had created a two-power world that the development of atomic and nuclear weapons threatened to polarize still more sharply. The fact that a dissident Communist from little Yugoslavia's Croatian minority had defied Stalin without yielding an inch to Stalin's enemies shrank not only Stalin but Stalin's enemies down to size.

The fact of America's atomic monopoly plus the myth of the cold war led some extremists—Bertrand Russell, the British philosopher, among them—to urge the Truman administration to exploit that monopoly, while time remained, by confronting the men in the Kremlin with the choice between capitulation or atomic destruction. The suggestion fell on deaf ears. Some of the moderate American majority favored George

Kennan's policy of containment; others preferred the logic of Walter Lippmann, who argued that if only the Americans would withdraw their troops from western Europe while the Russians withdrew theirs from eastern Europe, the world might settle down to a generation of peace. Both Stalin and Tito, however, knew better. Stalin clung to his conviction that he who occupies a country must rule it forever more, Tito to his vision of an emerging Third World, of which he saw a miniature preview in the Balkan peninsula.

Hamilton Fish Armstrong, editor of *Foreign Affairs,* had similar premonitions based on immediate firsthand experience. His book *Tito and Goliath,* published in 1951, written in 1950, and researched on the spot in 1949, called the dice while they were still rolling, along with the heads of Stalin's east-European victims. On the basis of interviews with Tito and other Yugoslav leaders in the spring and early summer of 1949, Armstrong concluded: "Stalin erred as he had not done since he sent Trotsky out of the Soviet Union alive—and the results on this occasion were even more momentous. He struck at his antagonist and failed to kill him." (He had not made that mistake with Trotsky in 1940.)

Having failed to eliminate his most formidable heretic east of the Stettin-Trieste line, Stalin compounded his troubles by arresting, jailing, and liquidating some of his own most efficient henchmen in the satellite nations of eastern Europe: Poland's Deputy Premier Wladyslaw Gomulka, ousted, jailed, and stripped of his Communist party membership; Czechoslovakia's Rudolf Slansky, secretary general of the party, tried and executed; Albania's General Koci Xoxe, deputy prime minister and minister of the interior, tried and executed; Hungary's Laszlo Rajk, foreign minister and former minister of the interior, tried and executed; Romania's Lucretiu Patrasceanu, minister of justice and veteran member of the party's political bureau, jailed for six years and then shot in the back of the head after a two-day trial on charges of treason. Shades of Bukharin, Rykov, Zinoviev, Radek, Krestinsky and other members of the Anti-Soviet Bloc of Rights and Trotskyites and of the Anti-Soviet Trotskyite Center who suffered similar fates at Moscow during the 1930's.

Similar but far from identical. Stalin's purges of the Old Bolsheviks during the 1930's wiped out all potential rivals and established a dictatorship as absolute as any in the world. His purges of the east-European Communist leaders between 1948 and 1950 assured the Stalinization of all the east-European nations that the Red army had occupied. But, far from strengthening or stabilizing their regimes, Stalin had weakened them still further. While denouncing the political cold warriers of the west, he waged hot political war against his east-European neighbors. Only in east Germany did he temper the wind to such super-Stalinists as President Wilhelm Pieck and Deputy Premier Walther Ulbricht, while retaining as the inspector general of East Germany's armed forces the former Nazi General Vincenz Mueller. But in West Germany he had Max Reimann, deputy chairman of the underground Communist party, kidnapped and jailed on charges of Titoism. All of which could not have caused much surprise among Stalin's intimates, for his daughter subsequently quoted him as having repeatedly declared, shortly after the war, "Ech, together with the Germans we would have been invincible."

·7·

WHILE THE DIALECTICS OF HISTORY, as embodied by Stalin, heaped contradiction on paradox and irony on both in eastern Europe, the acceleration of history did not slacken during the unexpired three years and nine months of Roosevelt's unexpired fourth term that Truman served out. In Europe, the doubled postwar productivity of the American economy assured the success of the Truman Doctrine and the Marshall Plan. Whereas the aftermath of war in China took the form of civil war and revolution, the aftermath of war in Europe, as in Japan, brought unexampled prosperity, thanks to the contributions of the United States. Yet it caused little surprise, in November 1946, when the Republicans won control of both Houses of the Congress for the first time since 1930. "It's time for a change," summed up the mood and the Republicans were not alone in their assumption that the country had entered a long period of reaction against Democratic rule.

Whereupon the events of 1947 and 1948 knocked this assumption into a cocked hat. Four years of war and three years of aftermath had created a host of new issues that atomized the American electorate. The simple fact that Truman had sat in the driver's seat from the time of the German surrender through the MacArthur occupation of Japan, the Marshall Plan, the economic recovery of Europe, and the Russian blockade of Berlin gave the incumbent President and his administration an authority that Governor Dewey and the Republicans could not match. What if the great Democratic coalition, put together by Roosevelt during the depression and held together during the war, had finally splintered? By 1948, Truman went on the offensive as he campaigned against the "Do-Nothing Eightieth Congress" that the Republicans controlled. Henry Wallace's fellow-traveling Progressive party siphoned off about a million disillusioned New Deal Democrats; Senator Strom Thurmond's Dixiecrats siphoned off a larger number of disgusted southern racists. But Governor Dewey's inability to hold even his own minority party together enabled President Truman to win an electoral college majority, though not a majority of the electorate itself. In repudiating both the Progressives and the Dixiecrats, Truman lost the votes of some extremists—both of the far left and of the far right—who had voted at least twice for Roosevelt, but won some middle-of-the-road voters who had drifted away from the Democrats in 1940 and 1944. No less important, the Democrats also regained control of the Congress by approximately the same margins they had lost it in 1946. Like the Republicans, two years before, they emerged with a working majority in the Senate (where only one third of the seats were at stake) and a landslide victory in the House, where all seats were contested. As a matter of fact, the Congressional Democrats ran ahead of the national Truman-Barkley ticket.

On July 1, 1947, after seven years' service in the State Department, Dean Acheson had returned to the practice of law with his Washington law firm as confident of the abilities of his old friend and successor, Robert A. Lovett, as he was of the abilities of their chief, General Marshall. Lovett had served as a naval aviator in the First World War, had become a successful New York banker during the years between the wars, and then served as assistant secretary of war for air under Colonel Stimson and General Marshall during the Second World War. But General Marshall, as he was rounding out his second year as secretary of state, had to undergo an operation for the removal of a kidney, and Truman pressed Acheson back into government service as Marshall's successor. Acheson took the oath of office on January 21, the day after Truman's inauguration and two years to the day after General Marshall had assumed office. James E. Webb, director of the budget, succeeded Lovett as undersecretary.

The shake-up seemed to confirm the hopes that the rising young Harvard historian Arthur Schlesinger, Jr., presently expressed in his short, topical book *The Vital Center*, setting forth the glowing prospects of a revitalized, modernized Democratic party. For the Democrats appeared to have succeeded where the Republicans had already failed in accommodating themselves not only to the accelerating events of the war but to the subsequent acceleration of the postwar economy. From

Republican Senator Robert A. Taft came the official confession of his party's intellectual and political bankruptcy: "I don't care how the thing is explained. It defies all common sense for the country to send that roughneck ward politician back to the White House."

If Taft had kept himself posted on the economic revolution taking place in his own backyard (not to mention the social and political revolutions in progress in foreign parts), he might have found it worth his while to try to explain the unexplainable. During the summer of 1948, employment in the United States reached an all-time peacetime high of 61,600,000. Industrial production rose three per cent for the year; so did employment in the service industries. The economy produced four per cent more goods in 1948 than in 1947. The United States had already entered the first stages of what the economists of the 1950's and 1960's called a postindustrial revolution based on automation and computers. While Stalin had again trapped himself in his own dialectic, Truman moved with the accelerating technology of his times and had begun to transform what Stalin mistook for the imperialism of a century ago into a high-energy North Atlantic community.

The roughneck ward politician's inaugural address then took as its theme: "The supreme need of our time is for men to learn to live together in peace and harmony." The President contrasted the "false philosophy of Communism," which assumes that man cannot govern himself "and therefore requires the rule of strong masters," with democracy "based on the conviction that man has the moral and intellectual capacity, as well as the inalienable right to govern himself with reason and justice." He based his hopes for the future on the United Nations, the European Recovery Program, "and other measures aimed at the betterment of life all about the world." Then came the heart of his message— "a bold new program" of continued support for the United Nations, continuing promotion of world recovery, "strengthening of the freedom-loving nations against the dangers of aggression," and his final "Point Four" that called upon the United States to feed the "children of starvation" and improve the lot of the "wretched of the earth." The President did not quote those phrases from the Communist *Internationale,* but he noted: "More than half the people of the world are living in conditions of misery," and this at a time when "For the first time in history humanity possesses the knowledge and the skill to relieve the sufferings of these people." Although the United States possessed only limited material resources, its "imponderable resources in technical knowledge are constantly growing and are inexhaustible."

The President then called upon the American people "to help the free peoples of the world, through their own efforts," to increase their production of food, clothing, housing, and mechanical power. He also invited other countries "to pool their technological resources" and to "work together through the United Nations and its specialized agencies wherever practicable." He urged American "business, private capital, agriculture, and labor" to co-operate. "The old imperialism—exploitation for private profit—has no place in the concepts of democratic fair dealing."

No doubt those concepts had no greater force than the rhetoric in which the President invoked them. But President Truman's rhetoric far surpassed his Point Four Program. Again, as during the closing months of 1945, his instincts told him that the devastation of the war had imposed global responsibilities on the United States. Hence the immediate priority he gave to the United Nations Relief and Rehabilitation program and the Hoover Emergency Famine Committee. In 1947 he followed up these emergency measures with the more ambitious Marshall Plan for the economic recovery of Europe only. And in September of that year General Marshall explained to a conference of American nations at Rio de Janeiro that the United States, because of its heavy European commitments, could offer no economic aid to Latin America. It was the same story at Bogotá in March 1948, when Marshall again refused to make any economic commitments to Latin America through the Organization of American States, as it drew up a charter affiliating it with the United Nations.

But while the Marshall Plan brought economic recovery to Europe, conditions in most of Asia went (as the Truman inaugural indicated) from bad to worse. The MacArthurization of Japan had, it is true, anticipated Germany's economic miracle by several years, several times over, but had little impact on the Asian mainland, where most eyes turned toward China, many Asian eyes being Chinese in the first place. In addition, more than two years before Mao Tse-tung proclaimed the People's Republic of China from Peking, Britain's Parliament passed the India Independence Act in June 1947, and on August 15 set up India and Pakistan as independent dominions. India then had a population of four hundred million, more than three hundred million of them Hindus; Pakistan, with a population of one hundred million, most of them Moslems, consisted of two zones (east and west), more than one thousand miles apart. Communal riots between Hindus and Moslems forced a hasty British withdrawal in August 1947. Lord Mountbatten remained as temporary viceroy of India, which, two years later, became a sovereign democratic republic, with Jawaharlal Nehru as its prime minister. Mohammed Ali Jinnah, president of the Moslem League, at once became Pakistan's governor general, but died in 1948.

On January 30 of that year a Hindu fanatic assassinated Mahatma Gandhi for having bowed to India's partition. But the violent death of this apostle of nonviolence had not been in vain. For one thing, it inspired a mood of expiation that cooled the ardor of India's Hindus and Pakistan's Moslems. For another, it had a salutary effect on the national independence movement throughout Asia. After all, Gandhi's nonviolent tactics might not appeal to Chinese Communists, Arab nationalists, and other freedom fighters from southeast Asia to Afghanistan's northwest frontier. Nor would other imperialist oppressors—Asian or non-Asian—have such respect for nonviolence as the British showed. Finally, could the living Gandhi have exerted so enduring an influence as patriot and politician as the murdered Gandhi did as saint and martyr?

·8·

THE DISTORTED VIEW of Soviet-American relations, spread far and wide by the cold-war myth, gave birth, almost at once, to the fantasy of the power vacuum which had few of the emotional overtones that sustained the cold-war myth. Japan, during the first two postwar years, and Germany, during the first four postwar years, qualified as temporary power vacuums because of the devastation the war had visited upon them. China's civil war and India's communal strife earned them power-vacuum status. But no other major power made any effort to assume the increasingly thankless task that the war-wearied British had performed in prewar India. Neither the United States nor the Soviet Union saw fit to intervene decisively in China's civil war.

For centuries, the Hapsburg, Ottoman, and Romanov empires had exploited the generally prevalent power-vacuum status among the smaller nations of the Balkan peninsula and of eastern and central Europe, but the First World War's aftermath had made that, too, an increasingly thankless and difficult task that only the anachronistic Stalin tried to undertake in those east-European nations which the Red army had occupied during the Second World War. The success of the Truman Doctrine, during the Second World War's aftermath, then suggested that the Middle East might prove as intractable as the Balkans while the solid achievements of the Marshall Plan doomed any hope

Stalin may have entertained of spreading Communism beyond the Stettin-Trieste line. On the other hand, Mao Tse-tung's victory in the Chinese civil war—coinciding as it did with the failure of the Berlin blockade—led Stalin to hope for new openings in Asia, if not in China itself, then in such peripheral regions as Korea and Indochina, both of which bore the earmarks of power vacuums, mid-twentieth-century style.

What is a twentieth-century power vacuum and what are its earmarks? Like the words "cold war," the words "power vacuum" contain an inherent contradiction. However, unlike the words "cold war," the words "power vacuum" have no absolute implications that lend themselves to such mythical purposes as the words "cold war" served. Nature abhors a vacuum; power corrupts and absolute power corrupts absolutely. A relative power vacuum exists when the wealth of a region so far exceeds its capacity for self-defense as to make it lie easy prey to foreign conquest. Thus, compared to prewar Germany, postwar France became a power vacuum. On the other hand, after Hitler made the mistake of treating the Soviet Union like a power vacuum, Stalin turned the tables on him and reduced Germany to power-vacuum status, not without considerable Anglo-American assistance. After the German surrender, Stalin assumed that the war had reduced all of eastern Europe to power-vacuum status and proceeded to treat it accordingly. He did not repeat the mistake Hitler made when he invaded the Soviet Union, but his victory looked more and more like a Pyrrhic one, as time went on.

For centuries the nations of eastern Europe had suffered from the conquests that their weakness had invited. The First World War then liberated most of that region from the rule of alien empires—Russian, Austro-Hungarian, German, and Turkish. But it had not delivered them from power-vacuum status. Franklin Roosevelt and the Second World War went on from where Woodrow Wilson and the First World War had left off. Although the intrusion of Stalin and the Red army marked a measurable improvement over the New Order that Hitler had tried to install there before and during the war, Tito's defection from the Soviet orbit in 1948 suggested that the wind had begun to blow in a new direction. Moscow's mid-twentieth-century commissars could not subdue and exploit their east-European neighbors as the kaisers, emperors, czars, and sultans had done in their simpler times.

President Truman saw himself as the inheritor of the Wilson and Roosevelt legacies. He also saw (perhaps more clearly than Stalin did) that the Second World War had made the power vacuum an anachronism in mid-twentieth-century Europe. By the end of 1949 Stalin had begun to learn that lesson the hard way at Berlin and in eastern Europe. But in the Chinese Revolution, Stalin thought he saw the opportunity to fill some of the new power vacuums that the Second World War had created in eastern Asia. This he did by persuading Mao Tse-tung to journey to Moscow, in November 1949, for prolonged discussions of Sino-Soviet relations in the light of Mao's proclamation of the Chinese People's Republic the month before. The talks began in December and continued until February, when the text of the new Sino-Soviet treaty was made public.

Here the Russians agreed to extend credits worth $300 million—at six per cent—over a five-year period to enable Sino-Soviet joint stock companies to exploit the resources of Sinkiang Province under the supervision of Soviet technicians. Subsequently, the Russians granted a five-year extension of the credits and cut China's repayment 20 per cent by devaluing the rubles in which repayment would be made by that amount. The Chinese Communists also persuaded the Russians to expand the treaty they had signed with Chiang Kai-shek and T. V. Soong into a "mutual assistance" pact under which the Russians would consult with them if Japan "or any other state" should join with it in threatening aggression. But the Chinese Communists got their greatest satisfaction from the Soviet promise to surrender, in 1952, the special rights in Dairen, Port Arthur, and the Manchurian railways that the Chinese Nationalists had virtually ceded to the Soviet Union under the revised terms of Roosevelt's Yalta deal with Stalin. Some power vacuum!

This evidence of closer co-operation between the Russian and Chinese Communists caused no pain at all among the frustrated Republican leaders in the United States. Still smarting from the surprise Democratic victories in the 1948 elections, the leaders of the Old Guard Republicans foresaw political advantage in charging the Democrats with playing Stalin's game in the Far East. Unable to charge the Democrats with softness toward Communism in Europe, they shifted their attack to the Administration's China policy, which had thrown Stalin and Mao Tse-tung into each other's arms, extending the supposed Communist monolith from the Stettin-Trieste line to the shores of the Pacific. Secretary Acheson, on the other hand, taking a longer look at both past and future, agreed with George Kennan that Stalin, having already run into trouble with Tito, was now headed for bigger trouble with Mao Tse-tung. While the oracles of the conventional Republican

wisdom on Communist affairs berated Truman and Acheson for betray-
ing China to Stalin's Communist stooges there, Acheson took his cue
from Kennan and began dropping hints in the State Department that
the "fraternal alliance" between Stalin and Mao might turn out to be
just the opposite of what it seemed.

Before a National Press Club luncheon in Washington, on January
13, 1950, Acheson recalled that Stalin had often blown hot and cold on
the Chinese Communists and described the Soviet drive to control
Outer and Inner Mongolia, Manchuria, and Sinkiang as "the single
most important, most significant fact" in contemporary Asia. Stressing
nationalism rather than Communism as the dominant tendency of the
postwar period, Acheson predicted that those Chinese who sought
"their own national independence" would turn to the United States, not
to the Soviet Union. But Acheson, like John Foster Dulles—the great
foreign-policy Panjandarum of the Republican party—had already succumbed to the cold-war myth that required all nations and peoples in
the postwar world to stand up and be counted as supporters of the
U.S. and the mythical free world or of the imaginary Sino-Soviet Communist monolith. Neither the existence of the Third World of developing nations nor the possible emergence of new and powerful third forces
entered into their calculations.

Nor did they enter into Stalin's. On the very day of Acheson's National Press Club speech Jacob Malik, Soviet delegate to the United
Nations Security Council, walked out of its deliberations, declaring that
he would not return until it ousted the Chinese Nationalist delegation
and replaced it with the Chinese Communists. Within another six
months, Malik and his Moscow masters found themselves whipsawed
by a new situation that they themselves had created and then aggravated. Two years before, in the spring of 1948, the United States and
Soviet governments had agreed, under United Nations auspices, to
withdraw their troops from their Korean occupation zones—the Russians to the north, the Americans to the south of the 38th parallel. Free
elections in South Korea resulted in the establishment of a Republic of
Korea, headed by Syngman Rhee, a lifelong fighter for Korean freedom
from Japanese rule. The Russians refused to hold free elections—even
as controlled as those which had resulted in Syngman Rhee's overwhelming South Korean triumph. Taking no chances, the Russians installed their own Democratic People's Republic of Korea, headed by
Kim Il Sung, a Moscow-trained North Korean Communist. Two years

later, in 1950, the Russians had equipped and trained a North Korean army of 135,000 men, whereas South Korea possessed only a lightly armed constabulary force half that size.

On the morning of Sunday, June 25, 1950—at the summer solstice of the mid-twentieth century—North Korean artillery, tanks, and infantry crossed the 38th parallel, invading South Korea at three points: the Onjin peninsula in the northwest, the city of Chunchon at the parallel's midpoint, and the capital city of Seoul in the west where the Han River flows into the Yellow Sea. Due to the time differential, the news reached Washington Saturday evening where three of Acheson's aides —Dean Rusk, Philip Jessup, and Ernest Gross—had already set the wheels in motion to request an immediate meeting of the United Nations Security Council to deal with this act of aggression against South Korea. Acheson approved their action and telephoned President Truman at his home in Independence, Missouri. The President applauded Acheson's quick response. The next day he flew to Washington.

The North Korean invasion of South Korea ended the Second World War's aftermath as sharply as the Munich conference had ended the First. In the case of Korea, quick headwork by Acheson and fast footwork by his three aides gave the sanction of Franklin Roosevelt's United Nations to the use of armed force against the North Korean invasion of South Korea. At Munich, Hitler had invoked the principle of national self-determination that Woodrow Wilson had enshrined in the League of Nations Covenant to justify the threat of force against Czechoslovakia. Hitler, in 1938, had no more respect for the League of Nations than Stalin, in 1950, had for the United Nations. But Hitler used Wilson's League of Nations for his own nefarious purposes, whereas Stalin's contempt for Roosevelt's United Nations led him to flout it to his own hurt.

As a result of Acheson's moves in Washington during the late evening hours of June 24, the United Nations Security Council voted 9–0 on the following day that "the armed attack on the Republic of Korea by forces from North Korea constituted a breach of the peace." Yugoslavia abstained, but it was Jacob Malik, leader of the Soviet delegation, whose obedience to Stalin's orders assured Truman and Acheson of United Nations support for the police action that they at once demanded. By boycotting the United Nations, Malik had deprived himself of the opportunity to wield his lethal veto. On Monday, June 26, with Yugoslavia dissenting, Egypt and India abstaining, and the Soviet Union absent, the Security Council approved a United States resolution calling upon United Nations members to restore peace to Korea. Again, no Jacob Malik stood in the breach.

On June 27, President Truman ordered United States "air and sea forces to give the Korean Government troops cover and support." He also ordered "the Seventh Fleet to prevent any attack on Formosa." To which he added, "As a corollary of this action, I am calling upon the Chinese Government on Formosa to cease all air and sea operations against the mainland. The Seventh Fleet will see that this is done." On June 28, General MacArthur flew to the Korean scene of the fighting, returning the next day to describe the South Korean retreat as a rout that only American combat troops could stop. Before the day was over, Truman accepted the unanimous recommendation of Acheson and the Chiefs of Staff to send two divisions from Japan to Korea. As Acheson put it in *Present at the Creation:* "We were then fully committed to Korea."

XXIX
Aftermath's Aftermath: Vietnam

·1·

THE NATO ALLIANCE to the west of the Stettin-Trieste line, the Peoples' Democracies to the east of it, and the overarching Soviet-American balance of nuclear terror had stabilized the division of Europe laid down at Potsdam by the victorious armies of the Anglo-Soviet-American coalition. The nations to which Japan surrendered the following month never arrived at so comprehensive or firm a settlement. For one thing, the Chinese Nationalists and the Chinese Communists had an unfinished civil war on their hands. For another, the Russians and Americans reached no such *de facto* agreement concerning the treatment of Japan as they had reached concerning the treatment of Germany. Finally, any Soviet-American settlement depended on the outcome of China's civil war.

Having driven Chiang Kai-shek to the island of Formosa in 1948 and proclaimed the Chinese People's Republic at Peking in October 1949, Mao Tse-tung hastened, the following month, to Moscow, where he and Stalin signed a pact in February 1950. What this pact might ultimately mean even the men who signed it could not know at the time, but in June 1950, Stalin made a more daring move than he had ever taken in Europe after Germany's surrender: he instructed North Korea's obedient Communist leaders to hurl their Russian-trained and Russian-equipped troops against South Korea and to drive all the American occupation troops stationed there into the sea within a month at the most. By expelling the Americans from South Korea, the North Koreans would not only bring all of Korea under their control. They would put Stalin in position to break the American hold on Japan, to force a new settlement there, and to check the further spread of American influence in other parts of east and southeast Asia. But everything hinged on the quick and complete success of the North Koreans' invasion of South Korea, and when they failed to dislodge the American Eighth Army from its Pusan beachhead at the southeast tip of Korea, Stalin lost his long-shot gamble.

As events presently revealed, Stalin never committed a single Red army soldier to fight in Korea. He had relied on his faithful North Korean allies to do all his fighting for him. Underestimating the strength of the United States and the resolution of the Truman administration, Stalin assumed that he could revise, by North Korean proxy, the settlement that the United States had imposed on the Japanese since their surrender. The inscrutable Mao Tse-tung, on the other hand, had made no firm commitment on his own behalf. He had no satellites to do his fighting for him. All he had was the largest, best equipped, and most throughly battle-hardened body of troops in the area. Whatever his intentions might be, his capabilities in his own immediate vicinity remained overwhelming.

In Stalin's case, his wide-ranging intentions far exceeded the limited capabilities he chose to bring to bear. Whereupon General MacArthur took what he described as one chance in five thousand, and won. On September 15, in a perfectly executed amphibious army-navy-marine corps operation, MacArthur began putting 70,000 troops of the U.S. Army's hastily assembled X Corps plus the First and Fifth Marine Divisions ashore at Inchon, just west of Seoul. They not only surprised the 20,000 North Korean defenders; they cut the North Korean supply line farther south, compelling the bulk of the North Korean invaders there to flee to their "privileged sanctuary"—as MacArthur later called it— beyond the 38th parallel. On October 1, Mao Tse-tung publicly declared: "The Chinese people will not tolerate foreign aggression and will not stand aside if the imperialists wantonly invade the territory of their neighbor." Three days later Foreign Minister Chou En-lai told the Indian ambassador to Peking: "If the United States or the United Nations forces cross the 38th parallel, the Chinese People's Republic will send troops to aid the People's Republic of Korea. We shall not take this action, however, if only South Korean troops cross the border."

On October 15, President Truman and General MacArthur conferred on Wake Island, where the general assured the President that neither the Russians nor the Chinese would enter the war, that all resistance would end by Thanksgiving, and that the Eighth Army would be back in Japan by Christmas. MacArthur could not have been more right about the Russians or more wrong about the Chinese, who, at the time of the Wake Island meeting, had already infiltrated 140,000 of their veteran guerrilla fighters into North Korea. On September 29, the Joint Chiefs had approved a plan, submitted by MacArthur, to hold all his troops except the South Koreans along the line of the 38th parallel. Not all the American units respected this restriction, but it remained for MacArthur himself to scrap it completely on October 24 when he ordered General Edward M. Almond's X Corps at the eastern end of the front and General Walton H. Walker's Eighth Army at its western end "to drive forward with all speed and full utilization of their forces."

General Walker at once noted with concern that his troops encountered no opposition as they made their way toward the Yalu River, which forms the natural North Korean-Chinese frontier. By early November the Joint Chiefs, increasingly concerned by reports of Chinese Communist infiltration, began suggesting that MacArthur take into account a new situation which his plan of September 29 had not considered. MacArthur replied with fulminations against the "Munich attitude" of the British and on November 17 informed the Joint Chiefs that he planned, in one week's time, to order a general offensive with the Yalu River as its objective. When cautioned to stop after reaching the high ground commanding the river, he replied, "Utterly impossible."

Right enough. But how wrong his reasoning and how disastrous its consequences. For the past month MacArthur had not only divided General Almond's X Corps from General Walker's Eighth Army, he had permitted the Chinese Communists to lure both the X Corps and the Eighth Army ever deeper into rough country where the Chinese Communists were stealthily infiltrating more than half a million troops. Night after night, they had crept and crawled unobserved, around, behind, and among the advancing Americans. On November 26 and 27, the Chinese struck from all directions. Not more than 60,000 of them clashed with the invaders, but they were able to cut one army division and one marine division to pieces in the worst American military disaster of the century—and the first major triumph of Chinese arms in many centuries. Early in December General Walker was killed when his jeep collided with another car on a dusty road. General Matthew B. Ridgway, already under secret orders to go to Korea, succeeded him.

Meanwhile General MacArthur charged the Chinese with having started that new war which he had insisted could never break out and demanded that the United Nations retaliate with a total response. For once, President Truman agreed with him—but not for long. On December 1 the President informed the press that the United Nations would use the atomic bomb, if necessary, in its fight for justice and peace. That sent Prime Minister Attlee scurrying to Washington and prompted Churchill to warn Britain's western allies against involvement in Asia at the expense of Europe. Thirteen Arab-Asian nations sponsored a resolution, which the United Nations General Assembly approved overwhelmingly on December 14, calling for a cease-fire in Korea. Truman had already taken Attlee's advice with the result that his relations with MacArthur became so strained that on April 11 he removed MacArthur from his command, replacing him with Ridgway, who soon found himself able to consolidate the Eighth Army's line along the 38th parallel. Two months later, the troubled Russians saw to it that their North Korean Communist clients opened armistice talks with the Americans, but not until four months after the death of Stalin, on March 6, 1953, did the armistice talks get off dead center and end with a negotiated settlement of the war, based on mutual troop withdrawals and restoration of the prewar boundary between North and South Korea.

·2·

ONE YEAR AFTER the Korean war had begun, and more than two years before it ended, Secretary of State Acheson and John Foster Dulles, soon to occupy the same post in the Eisenhower administration, combined forces to conclude a long-overdue peace treaty with Japan. The Soviet Union, Czechoslovakia, and Poland refused to sign it. The governments of the Philippines, Australia, and New Zealand felt it cheated them out of the reparations they deserved. But South Korea's President Syngman Rhee and Generalissimo Chiang Kai-shek welcomed the treaty, partly because it included a Japanese-American security pact, but mainly because it committed the United States to build a powerful military and political anti-Communist arsenal in the Far East. Japan also agreed to raise a 75,000-man national police reserve trained by American instructors and equipped with light United States artillery. Fully armed American occupation troops remained in Japan and at American bases on Japan's outlying islands.

The year 1951 also saw Winston Churchill and his fellow Conservatives return to power, as the Labour party fell exhausted by the wayside after the first six grueling postwar years. Two years later, the death of Stalin enabled Churchill to close his own political career on a note of stubborn hope. The man who had warned against Hitler in 1938 and against Stalin in 1945 now reversed himself one last time by welcoming the Soviet-American atomic breakthroughs as portents of a stabilized "balance of terror" peace. For the rest of his public life, which ended in 1955 with his retirement, Churchill repeatedly called for summit meetings with Stalin's successors and for an east-west détente.

While Churchill was executing the last political somersault of his versatile political career, Eisenhower began transforming himself from a professional soldier who had risen rapidly and recently to the top of his first chosen profession into an amateur politician who shot almost instantly to the top of another. Far from dehumanizing him, Eisenhower's military background depoliticized him, thus emphasizing the contrast between himself and the two highly professional politicians who had preceded him in the White House. But Eisenhower had more in common with the charismatic, intuitive Roosevelt than with the homespun Truman, the common man writ large. Indeed, Eisenhower displayed a thespian ability worthy of Roosevelt as he won the hearts of the American people in his role of grandfatherly, wide-eyed political novice whom a kindly fate had singled out to hold the highest political office in the land.

The contrast between America's two most successful and widely publicized military leaders during the Second World War reached its climax during that war's aftermath. In 1950 Eisenhower left the presidency of Columbia University to become NATO's first supreme commander, and in 1952 he left his NATO command to win the Republican party's presidential nomination and then to become the first Republican president in twenty years. Japan's surrender found MacArthur the biggest frog in the Pacific pond and Japan's first American mikado. But MacArthur's transcendent performance of that role inspired him with the delusion that he had thereby qualified himself to exercise similar authority in any and all parts of the Far East. Eisenhower, in Europe, bore down on learning much that he did not know. On his return to postwar America he applied the lessons he had learned from Churchill (of whom he never stood in awe) and from de Gaulle (whose genius he never underrated). MacArthur, on the other hand, ignored the advice and experience of all who did not tell him what he wanted to hear.

The repercussions of his retreat from the banks of the Yalu not only shook the walls of the Kremlin—after Stalin's death as well as before—

they redounded to the glory of Communist China among the emerging Afro-Asian nations on which both Moscow and Peking set great store. In the field of military strategy, MacArthur had repeated the error committed by General Claire Chennault during the 1940's while anticipating the mistakes the United States Air Forces made in Vietnam during the 1960's, when they, too, assumed that air power alone could overwhelm guerrilla fighters defending rough territory that they knew and loved. Finally, General MacArthur's example taught the North Korean Communists a political lesson that other Afro-Asians also learned: it had now become possible to play Moscow off against Peking.

But that was not the lesson that General MacArthur himself, on his return from Korea and Japan, expounded to a joint session of the two Houses of the Congress. There he took, as the theme of a magnificent oration: "There is no substitute for victory"—a theme, incidentally, more applicable to politics than to war. There is of course no substitute for victory—or for defeat either—though there are always ten thousand alternatives to each. But the issue never became a public one, because MacArthur got no chance to raise it. For the hearts of the Republican Old Guard belonged to Senator Taft, not to General MacArthur, whose resounding pomposities, as the Republican Convention's keynote speaker, torpedoed whatever chance he might have had as a compromise candidate. From the outset, the convention became a two-man race between Eisenhower and Taft, a race that Eisenhower won easily. Getting himself elected proved still easier. The campaign promise, "I shall go to Korea," did the trick, but it remained for Stalin to make the supreme sacrifice by obligingly dying six weeks after Eisenhower's inauguration.

·3·

WITH EISENHOWER INAUGURATED, John Foster Dulles ensconced as secretary of state, and peace restored to Korea, the new Administration thought it could relax. But not for long. Since 1950 Wisconsin's freshman Republican senator, Joseph R. McCarthy, had harried the anti-Communist Truman and the "Democrat party," as he called it, with charges of treason, based on the assertion—never proved, often refuted, constantly repeated—that hundreds of unidentified Communists had infiltrated the State Department and other branches of the United States government. Eisenhower had always despised but had never attacked McCarthy, reasoning that a gutter fight would do him and his office more harm than good and that McCarthy would bring himself down more rapidly and completely than anyone else could.

But the evil that men do lives after them. In 1954, McCarthy's fellow senators killed him politically with a vote of censure in which all the Democratic senators and half the Republicans voted to slap him down; three years later he died a natural death. By this time, however, Secretary Dulles had resumed and redoubled the anti-Communist crusade from where McCarthy had left off. Eschewing McCarthy's crude charges of treason, Dulles exploited the hysteria McCarthy had provoked to pursue personal, political, and ideological vendettas against such State Department officials as George F. Kennan, Charles E. Bohlen, John Paton Davies, John Carter Vincent, John Stewart Service, and other dissenters from Dulles' neo-McCarthyism—at the same time infiltrating the State Department with unreconstructed McCarthyites. Finally, Dulles favored the so-called "China Lobby," supported by such Republican worthies as Senator William Knowland of California, who equated criticism of Chiang Kai-shek with disloyalty to the United States.

On January 12, 1954, Dulles told the Council on Foreign Relations in New York that the National Security Council had decided "to depend primarily upon a greater capacity to retaliate instantly, by means and at places of our own choosing." Two months later came the first successful test explosion of an American H-bomb, of which the Russians were simultaneously developing their own equivalent. Whereas the original atomic arms race had raised Churchill's hopes for a "balance of terror" peace, Dulles now resumed his "brink of war" diplomacy with redoubled vigor. In January, 1954, the Big Four foreign ministers decided to hold their next quarterly meeting on April 26, at Geneva, to discuss the recently concluded Korean war and the prospects of bringing to a similar end the colonial war that the French had been fighting in Indochina for the past eight years at a cost to the United States that was now running at more than a billion dollars a year. On March 20 General Paul Ely, the French chief of staff, therefore flew to Washington to appeal to the United States to intervene, with atomic bombs, if need be, and thus to save the beleaguered French forces at Dien Bien Phu from annihilation.

Admiral Arthur W. Radford, chairman of the Joint Chiefs, and General Nathan B. Twining, air force chief of staff, favored granting the request; General Ridgway, army chief of staff, insisted that the Korean war had already proved the futility of American intervention in Indochina. On April 6, President Eisenhower propounded his so-called "falling dominos" theory to a press conference: "You have a row of dominos set up, knock over the first one, and what will happen to the last one is the certainty that it will go over very quickly. So you could have the beginning of a disintegration that would have the most profound influences." Moreover, as the President saw it, that last domino was Japan.

But he soon made it clear that he had no intention of playing falling dominos without any partners. Prime Minister Churchill at once dismissed the domino theory out of hand, as he had already rejected the parallel that Eisenhower had drawn, in a personal letter, comparing the Communist threat to Vietnam with Hirohito, Mussolini, and Hitler. Nothing daunted by these rejections, Dulles stopped off at London, on his way to Geneva, to make personal appeals to both Churchill and Eden, who brushed aside his eleventh-hour plea that the approaching conference made an air strike at Dien Bien Phu imperative. Vice President Richard M. Nixon had also associated himself, publicly, with this approach. But Ridgway's military objections to American intervention in Indochina and the President's own determination to make no move without full British and French support ruled out the military moves recommended by Radford, Twining, Dulles, and Nixon.

· 4 ·

HAVING TOLD OFF Field Marshals Brooke and Montgomery during the war, President Eisenhower stood in no awe of Admiral Radford or General Twining on matters of military strategy afterward. But when it came to postwar political strategy, the President had reason to respect Churchill and Eden more than Dulles and Nixon, especially when he had no way of compelling Britain's prime minister and foreign secretary to accept his. The showdown came at Geneva on May 7, 1954, with the arrival of word from Indochina that the French garrison at Dien Bien Phu had surrendered. Dulles, however, did not have to wait until then to recognize that he, too, had lost a battle, if not a war. For him the end came when Chou En-lai—the all-too-substantial foreign minister of a government that had no existence on the American tablets of international law—appeared at Geneva in response to invitations that Dulles had been unable to prevent the three other foreign ministers from extending. On May 4, Dulles therefore quit Geneva for his privileged Washington sanctuary, leaving as his replacement General Bedell Smith, Eisenhower's formidable wartime chief of staff, Harriman's hard-line replacement at the United States embassy in Moscow, and present undersecretary of state.

After leaving Geneva, Dulles at once began laying the groundwork for what became the South East Asia Treaty Organization (SEATO) consisting of three nonwhite Asian nations, Thailand, the Philippines, and Pakistan, and five white non-Asian nations, the United States, Great Britain, France, Australia, and New Zealand. On September 8, 1954, they signed a collective defense treaty at Manila, calling for "action" in the event of aggression in the "treaty area" and "consultation" in the event of a threat to its security. The "treaty area" embraced "the general area of southeast Asia, including also the entire territories of the Asian parties, and the general area of the southwest Pacific area north of 21 degrees 30 minutes north latitude," thus excluding the island of Formosa. On the other hand, the protocol of the treaty specifically covered Cambodia, Laos, and South Vietnam. In name, SEATO resembled NATO; in content, it included no such specific commitments. In theory SEATO invoked the United Nations Charter; in practice, it offended India and stirred more opposition than support in France.

Meanwhile, the Geneva Conference, which had continued by fits and starts since April 26, adjourned on July 21 after patching up a settlement of the Indochina war. The new French premier, Pierre Mendès-France—a wartime pilot in de Gaulle's Free French Air Force—had come to Geneva to make good on the promise that had won him a vote of confidence in the Chamber of Deputies to arrange an honorable cease-fire in Indochina. With the approval of the conference, Mendès-France agreed to turn North Vietnam over to the Communist Vietminh. Back in 1920, its leader, Ho Chi Minh, then a Socialist student in France, had become one of the founders of the French Communist party. He journeyed to Moscow, met Lenin, and devoted himself for the next twenty years to preaching Lenin's brand of nationalist, anti-imperialist Communism throughout Vietnam. As a result, the Vietminh movement had a wide popular appeal, especially when conducted by Ho, who had led the fight against the Japanese during the war and against the French Vichyites and Gaullists who joined forces afterward in seeking to reimpose French rule.

At the Geneva Conference on Indochina, Molotov and Mendès-France, Chou En-lai and Anthony Eden pulled themselves and most of the multinational peoples of Indochina together. Having conceded North Vietnam to Ho Chi Minh, who did not take orders from either Moscow or Peking, they granted shaky and provisional independence to the former kingdoms of Cambodia and Laos. The South Vietnamese, on the other hand, would not take orders from Moscow, Peking, Paris, or London. During the final stages of the Geneva Conference, a group of nationalists from South Vietnam hastily assembled an authoritarian, anti-Communist government, headed by Ngo Dinh Diem, scion of a well-to-do Roman Catholic family. His nationalistic views had not commended him to the French; his political and theological anti-Communism commended him to Dulles. To this government the conference extended its recognition, pending free elections to be held throughout both North and South Vietnam in July 1956. Because neither Diem nor Dulles signed the agreement, it bound neither of them. Nor had either man made any commitment to any of the other participants in the conference. But that noncommitment to the other powers bound them all the more tightly to each other—especially Dulles. For Diem represented nobody but himself and his family. He could eliminate himself at any time—or be eliminated. But Dulles represented more than himself. As secretary of state of the United States he had totally committed himself and his country to South Vietnam. From that moment on, he and his country assumed an obligation to South Vietnam such as no other official at Geneva had assumed toward any other part of Indochina or toward any other power with interests in that area.

In July 1955, Diem—in his own behalf and in his country's—filed his first claim on Washington. He announced that the election that the Geneva Agreement had called for in July 1956 would not be held—a stand that Dulles promptly and duly endorsed. So ended the closing chapter of the Korean war's aftermath. So began the opening chapter of the American commitment to South Vietnam. Dulles, the unreconstructed anti-Communist, had dissociated himself from the efforts of the British, French, Soviet, and Chinese governments to deal, jointly, with the new postwar myth of the Third World. The cold-war myth, which it replaced, had rested on the assumption that the sudden emergence of the two great super powers had reduced world politics to a life-and-death struggle between the United States and the Soviet Union. The Chinese Revolution then gave rise to the more gradual acceptance of a Third-World myth, based on the more gradual emergence of the newly liberated Afro-Asian nations.

·5·

LIKE THE COLD WAR, the Third World was born with a French name—
tiers monde, which originally described all those Afro-Asian nations
and peoples to whom the Second World War and its aftermath brought
political independence. Later, the *tiers monde* also included parts of
Latin America. But at no time did a third, fourth, fifth, or sixth world
exist—much less a first or a second. First, the Chinese Revolution split
the Communist monolith in two; then the Yugoslav, Italian, and Romanian Communists spread the theory and practice of Communist "polycentrism" more and more widely. The French might have had the
words for the Third World; Mao Tse-tung had the music—or at any
rate the political ideology and military strategy—tailored to Third
World conditions and needs, because those conditions and needs so
closely resembled China's own. As the most ancient, most populous,
and most centrally located of all Third World nations, China appeared
uniquely qualified (at least in Mao's revolutionary eyes) to lead and
unify them all.

And so it came to pass that within one year of the Geneva conference
on Indochina, the Chinese Communists made their first formal bid for
Third World leadership. Already, in 1954, China's Foreign Minister
Chou En-lai had conferred with India's Prime Minister Nehru and endorsed Nehru's Five Principles, the *Panch Sheela,* pledging themselves
to nonaggression and noninterference in each other's internal affairs. In
April 1955, delegates from twenty-five Afro-Asian nations gathered at
the Indonesian city of Bandung, under Nehru's chairmanship, to frame
principles of political conduct that conformed with Gandhi's political
doctrine of nonalignment, now labeled "positive neutralism" by Nehru.
Chou En-lai took advantage of the contacts he had established with
Nehru to have China represented at Bandung and—no less important—
to have the Soviet Union excluded. To Nehru the Bandung conference
meant the vindication of Gandhi; all the other twenty-four delegates
also interpreted it in their own, twenty-four different ways, Chou En-lai
taking it to mean whatever he chose to make it mean. But it was the
spirit, not the letter, that counted at this stage of the various games the
various participants at Bandung were playing from Indonesia's own Sukarno, to Egypt's Gamal Abdel Nasser, to Cambodia's Prince Sihanouk,
not to mention Yugoslavia's Afro-Asian President Tito. No wonder the

Soviet leaders, who regarded themselves as no less Asian than the Chinese, the Indians, and the Arabs, resented their exclusion—all the more so because they understood Chou En-lai's game as well as he understood theirs.

Chou En-lai's tactics at Bandung may have shaken up the men in the Kremlin, but Khrushchev had already set a counterstrategy in motion. From the moment of Stalin's death when Khrushchev vaulted into Stalin's post as first secretary of the Soviet Communist party, he recognized that the Soviet-American cold war was dying and that a new Third World of Afro-Asian nations was coming to birth. The death of Stalin had hastened the death of the cold war which in its turn portended the death of Stalinism. Premier Georgi Malenkov then celebrated New Year's Day, 1955, with the announcement that the Russians had their own H-bombs, which made peaceful coexistence with the West necessary as well as possible. But Malenkov had spoken out of turn and ahead of time. On February 8, Nikita Khrushchev demanded and got his resignation and had him replaced at once with Defense Minister Nikolai Bulganin, one of Stalin's political field marshals whom the surviving Stalinists preferred to Malenkov. But it was Khrushchev who had taken Bulganin into camp, thereby splitting the Stalinist Old Guard.

With Bulganin in his pocket, Khrushchev reversed course and reconciled himself with Stalin's old adversary, President Tito of Yugoslavia, who had attended the Bandung Conference in April and welcomed Khrushchev to Belgrade in May. The two men buried their hatchet in Stalin's grave, normalized Soviet-Yugoslav trade and diplomatic relations, thus putting Khrushchev in position to thrust programs of economic and military assistance upon Tito's fellow travelers at Bandung. Late in 1954, Khrushchev had even paid a flying visit to Peking, where he announced the return of Port Arthur, Dairen, and the Manchurian railways to full Chinese control. To Secretary Dulles, this gesture reaffirmed the permanence of the Sino-Soviet monolith.

In May 1955, Dulles ruefully informed Eisenhower (the adverb was the President's) that the Russians had suddenly agreed to sign the long-discussed state treaty with Austria, recognizing its independence and neutrality, and thus removing all occupation troops from the country. In one breath, Dulles declared that "an area of Europe is, in a very literal sense, liberated." In the next he warned against "a new set of dangers," owing to "the fact that the wolf has put on a new set of sheep's clothing, and while it is better to have a sheep's clothing on than a bear's clothing on, because the sheep don't have claws, I think the policy remains the same."

With Khrushchev, however, hardly anything ever remained the same for any length of time. On July 12, 1955, ten years almost to the day after Stalin, Churchill, and Truman had sat down together at Potsdam, Khrushchev and Bulganin sat down together at Geneva with the heads of the United States, British, and French governments—President Eisenhower, Premier Edgar Faure (who had replaced Mendès-France), and Prime Minister Eden (who had replaced Churchill). There they devoted several days to discussing European security and German reunification. The talk was more amiable but less gritty than it had been at Potsdam and they broke up congratulating themselves on having generated a new "Geneva Spirit," which Khrushchev at once displayed by arranging a deal—announced by Nasser on September 27—whereby Egypt procured from Czechoslovakia enough armaments to achieve its "revolutionary goals" in exchange for all its exports of long-staple cotton for the current year. This trumped an American offer to supply Nasser with arms on condition that he enter into "some kind of alliance"—whatever that might mean.

The announcement sent Dulles running to the British and to Eugene Black, president of the World Bank, to provide Egypt with credits of $1.3 billion toward building the long-projected High Dam at Aswan on the Nile River, capable of improving the fertility of its whole rich valley by fifty percent. But when Nasser, in May, 1956, recognized Mao's China and withdrew recognition from Chiang's Nationalist regime on Formosa, the howls from the China lobby panicked Dulles into canceling the Aswan offer. He had underrated the strength of Nasser's weakness as much as he had overrated the power of his own nuclear overkill. On July 26, 1956, Nasser celebrated the second anniversary of the revolution that had brought him and his young colonels to power by ordering Egyptian troops to occupy the Suez Canal and announcing the nationalization of the British company that operated it.

·6·

DURING AND IMMEDIATELY AFTER the Second World War horror at the Nazi holocaust of six million European Jews and admiration for the new state of Israel and its founders led the United States, the Soviet Union, and the United Nations to grant it full diplomatic recognition in

1947. By 1955, however, the Bandung Conference of Afro-Asian nations had swung full circle. The leaders of the newly emerging Third World now viewed the European neocolonialists and the American neo-imperialists as their enemies and the Russian and Chinese Communists as their friends, if not their allies, as their protectors, if not their masters. Specifically, they welcomed the Arab world to full membership in the Third World and treated the displaced Palestine Arabs as victims of imperialist aggression in the form of the state of Israel which, in its turn, had become the Middle Eastern bastion of the neoimperialist, neocolonial powers.

Neither President Eisenhower nor Premier Khrushchev viewed the world in such black and white terms. Eisenhower did not despair utterly of Britain, France, and the nations of western Europe which his armies had liberated from German occupation only ten years ago. But that did not mean that he fully supported the postwar policies of Britain and France in the Middle or Far East. As for Khrushchev, he had hopes that he and Eisenhower might use their joint nuclear monopoly to establish a new global balance of power. But Dulles' performance in July, 1954, at the Geneva Conference on Indochina undercut Khrushchev's whole strategy. For Dulles viewed the whole world as a single battlefield which an unbreakable and eternal Sino-Soviet monolith sought to bring under absolute control. Although neither Britain's Prime Minister Eden nor French Prime Minister Guy Mollet (who had recently replaced Faure) shared Dulles' apocalyptic vision, they, too, saw the Suez crisis in their own blacks and whites. Eden could not but regard Nasser as the reincarnation of Mussolini; Mollet saw in Nasser an Arab Hitler. Wartime memories died hard.

This muddle of conflicting theories led to a corresponding muddle of self-defeating actions. The arms that Nasser had received from Czechoslovakia supplied the Israelis with the incentive and justification they needed to throw 50,000 of their crack troops into a lightning invasion of the Sinai Peninsula on October 29, 1955. All went according to well-laid plans. British and French planes patrolled the air over Israel. French naval vessels patrolled Israel's coast. French planes dropped supplies to advancing Israeli troops. In a matter of hours the Israelis had occupied the bulk of the Sinai Peninsula where they destroyed and routed the bulk of the Egyptian army and captured all its Soviet arms and equipment. On October 30 Anglo-French ultimatums demanded that Israel and Egypt agree to a cease-fire and to troop withdrawals from the Suez Canal and Sinai. Israel accepted the offer; Egypt rejected it. On November 1, Nasser closed the Canal to traffic by sinking block ships along it.

The halting progress of the Anglo-French expeditionary force in the Suez Canal area offered a sorry contrast to the Israelis' lightning Sinai campaign. Not until November 4 did the Anglo-French troops, twenty-five thousand strong, begin to land on Egyptian soil, thus compelling Nasser to withdraw all his troops from the Canal area to defend Cairo. But the United Nations General Assembly had moved more rapidly than the Anglo-French military expedition. On November 4 at 2:15 A.M. (New York, not Cairo time) the Assembly voted 57 to nothing, with nine abstentions, to call upon Secretary General Hammarskjöld to produce, within forty-eight hours, a plan to set up "an emergency United Nations force to secure and supervise the cessation of hostilities." At 6 P.M. on November 6, Eden announced that a cease-fire would be ordered at midnight. The French cabinet let it be known that it had no choice but to do the same.

The brief, chaotic Suez War proved a fiasco for all concerned except the Israelis and three zealous peacemakers at the United Nations: the secretary general, Canada's foreign secretary, Lester Pearson, and Norway's ambassador to the United Nations, Hans Engen. Their combined efforts won the respect and support of a large majority of the entire United Nations membership for an unprecedented plan to dispatch a United Nations expeditionary force consisting of troops from various neutral nations to police the peace in the Sinai Peninsula and the Gaza Strip from which the Israelis withdrew all their forces. The British and French withdrew their troops from Egyptian soil and the Egyptians withdrew theirs from the Suez Canal area, as United Nations forces moved in to replace them. The Israelis accepted a United States guarantee of their freedom of navigation in the Gulf of Aqaba, but the Egyptians succeeded in continuing to bar Israeli shipping from the Canal.

President Eisenhower had kept his promise to keep America out of any kind of Suez war that might arise. On election day, November 6, he defeated Adlai Stevenson by an even bigger margin than he had four years before—but at what a price, both present and future. During the previous twelve months he had suffered a severe heart attack and undergone a successful ileitis operation on the lower portion of his small intestine. During the night of November 2–3 Secretary Dulles underwent an emergency cancer operation on his large intestine. Although he returned to his desk by mid-December, he had only two more years to live. The strain of the wartime years also took its toll of Anthony Eden, a victim of gall-bladder trouble which sent his temperature as high as 104 during much of the Suez crisis. A Caribbean vacation in December failed to restore his health, and he laid down his office on January 7, when Harold Macmillan succeeded him.

When Eden succeeded Churchill as prime minister and faced the prospect of having to deal again with Dulles—with whom he had clashed during the 1954 Geneva conference on Indochina—he groaned: "That terrible man. That terrible man." But when Macmillan, who had once served as Britain's minister of housing, first met Dulles, he confided, "I am just a child in these matters. I have been handling houses. You must teach me about foreign affairs." Dulles obliged by setting a series of horrible examples from which Macmillan—a loyal disciple of Churchill—learned what not to do as well as how not to do it. Nor was Macmillan the only statesman to benefit from the lessons of the Suez fiasco. De Gaulle—until that time an unreconstructed French colonialist—learned from Suez that the war in Algeria had become a criminal piece of folly from which he must extricate his country. Although Eisenhower had pulled Dulles back from the brink of war in Indochina and delivered a farewell address, in 1961, warning against the "military-industrial complex," he never saw as clearly as Macmillan and de Gaulle soon did the criminal folly of Vietnam. Nor—it should be added —did either Kennedy or Johnson when their turns came.

·7·

WHAT LESSONS did the Suez fiasco teach Nikita Khrushchev? From midsummer on, the gathering Suez crisis coincided with uprisings, first in Poland and then in Hungary, against those Stalinist policies from which Khrushchev had already begun to turn away. Between June 28 and October 19, 1956, strikes and riots by Polish workers compelled Khrushchev, Lazar Kaganovich, Anastas Mikoyan, and Vyacheslav Molotov to recognize the necessity of installing the anti-Stalinist Gomulka as first secretary of the Polish Communist party and dismissing Marshal Rokossovski—a Soviet officer of Polish birth—from that party's Politburo. But when the example of Poland's anti-Stalinists inspired Hungary's anti-Stalinists to stage mass uprisings in Budapest, things got out of hand. At first the Soviet leaders bowed to the demands of the demonstrators, replacing Hungary's Stalinist Premier Ernö Gerö, with the anti-Stalinist Imré Nagy, who announced Hungary's withdrawal from the

Warsaw pact while the Soviet leaders, on October 28, began withdrawing Soviet troops and tanks from Budapest. But on October 31, when Nasser rejected the Anglo-French ultimatum and Anglo-French planes began bombing Egyptian installations along the Suez Canal, the Soviet Politburo ordered its troops and tanks to double back on their tracks, crush the demonstrations, and arrest Nagy. As the Anglo-French expeditionary force crept toward Egypt Bulganin went so far as to hint at the possibility of bombarding London and Paris with long-range Soviet nuclear missiles. The threat, however, won Khrushchev and Bulganin few friends at the United Nations, especially when the Soviet delegate to the Security Council vetoed a resolution censuring the Russian attack on Hungary three hours after the General Assembly had approved the resolution that stopped the Suez War.

But Suez or no Suez, the Soviet leaders did not try to turn the hands of their Hungarian clock all the way back. They did not replace Nagy with Gerö or any other Stalinist. Instead, they installed the anti-Stalinist Janos Kadar whom the Hungarian Stalinists had jailed and tortured. It was one thing to exploit the Suez fiasco in a clumsy attempt to distract attention from their own troubles in Hungary. It was something else again when it came to reversing the anti-Stalinist line to which Khrushchev committed himself unequivocally the following February in his not-so-secret speech before the Twentieth Party Congress at which he described and denounced Stalin and his crimes. If the Suez fiasco had made it certain that nothing could ever be the same again in the Middle East, events in Poland and Hungary made it equally certain that nothing could ever be the same again in the Soviet Union either. But the postwar world embraced more than the Middle East and the Soviet Union. It embraced a Third World of developing nations of which the Arab world was only a part. It embraced a People's Republic of China with almost three times the population of the Soviet Union. And it embraced a United States of America which the Second World War and its aftermath had saddled with wider responsibilities than any other nation or people had to bear.

·8·

IN THE SUEZ FIASCO everybody had everybody else by the ears. Israel cut Nasser down to size, Nasser cut down Dulles, Dulles cut down Eden, Eden ran out on Mollet, Mollet built up Israel which the United Nations had tried and failed to restrict to its original meager dimensions.

Khrushchev built up Nasser with arms that fell into Israeli hands and used his own arms to crush an uprising in Hungary while threatening London and Paris with nuclear annihilation. Only the totally unarmed United Nations succeeded in restoring peace by demanding and obtaining concessions and co-operation from all. The permanent tinderbox of the Middle East became a temporary balance-of-power vacuum.

In the Middle East the Afro-Asian peoples and the peoples of the Mediterranean had mixed and mingled for thousands of years. In the Far East, for almost as many thousands of years, the peoples of Asia gravitated around China, which called itself the Middle Kingdom. Here, too, East and West had met, but with Japan's defeat, India's achievement of independence, the liberation of the smaller nations of southeast Asia, and China's revolution, the peoples of the Far East outnumbered and outweighed the peoples of the Middle East.

Although Mao Tse-tung had always scorned Stalin and rejected his advice to follow Russia's example and base China's revolution on the industrial proletariat, he viewed Khrushchev as a heretic from the Marxist-Leninist faith rather than a mere backslider. He also charged Liu Shao-ch'i and other moderate Chinese leaders with revisionist tendencies and inclinations to take the capitalist road. Specifically, he warned against the creation of a rigid bureaucracy along Stalinist lines.

By 1958 Liu Shao-ch'i had a firm hold on the Chinese Communist bureaucracy. To break that hold, Mao Tse-tung used his position as party chairman to foment a new revolution within his original revolution of 1949. Proclaiming a "Great Leap Forward," he called, among other things, for the construction of backyard blast furnaces which would enable Chinese industry to surpass British industry in five years' time. The horrified Khrushchev and his colleagues summoned home their technical experts who had helped China's nuclear program and other industrialization projects. Within less than a year Mao's "Great Leap Forward" set China's economy back a good five years, whereupon Mao followed through, in 1966, with his Great Proletarian Cultural Revolution in which twenty million semiliterate Red Guards in their late teens and early twenties ran amok through the land for the next two years, with such slogans as, "Without anarchy there can be no order!" "The revolution requires anarchy!" "Without anarchy there can be no revolution!"

At intervals during the Cultural Revolution, Mao's spokesmen suggested that he be judged by what he did, not by what he said. But no word came until April 24, 1969, when the Ninth Chinese Communist

Party Congress heard a beaming Mao Tse-tung break his three-year silence with assurances that this would be "known as the Congress of unity," and that his revolution had won still another victory. His words and actions left orthodox Communists and strict Marxists as confused as ever. As usual, Mao insisted that communism and socialism, like capitalism and imperialism, obeyed their own dialectics, which he called "contradictions among ourselves." His own *Thoughts*, which he circulated in millions of "Little Red Books," often ran on double tracks: "Bad things can turn into good things." "The waves that float the boat can also sink it." In one breath he predicted that Chinese industry would surpass British industry in five years' time; in the next he warned that it would take centuries for China to complete its revolution. He opposed Khrushchev's revisionist Communism as he had opposed Stalinism before it. His critics often conferred on him the supreme honor of quoting him against himself.

In 1959, the year after Mao's "Great Leap Forward" had come a cropper, Khrushchev executed a great transatlantic leap that included a junket across the United States and two days with President Eisenhower at the White House and Camp David. In 1957, barely a year after his anti-Stalin speech, Khrushchev had announced that a booster rocket of unprecedented power had put an 84-pound space vehicle into orbit around the earth at a speed of 16,000 miles an hour. He called it a *sputnik*, meaning "traveling companion." The United States still led the Soviet Union in the development of atomic and nuclear weapons; the Russians had put the German rocket experts who fell into their hands to quicker and more spectacular use, and Khrushchev made such effective propaganda use of *sputnik* on his American tour that he inspired his American hosts to close an imaginary "missile gap" and extend their lead in the arms race still further.

Nowhere did Khrushchev's American junket cause such anguish as in Peking, where the press and radio stepped up their charges of Soviet-American conspiracies. Mao Tse-tung therefore shed no tears on May 5, 1960, when a Soviet rocket shot down a U-2 American reconnaissance plane over Soviet territory. The pilot parachuted to safety. The plane crashed to earth. With it crashed the projected summit meeting, set for a few weeks later in Paris, where Khrushchev had hoped to confer with Eisenhower, Macmillan, and de Gaulle. Nor did the whole affair win any votes for Richard Nixon, six months later, when John F. Kennedy won the presidency by a whisker. His first hundred days included the Bay of Pigs fiasco in April 1961. Six weeks later, an arrogant, contemptuous Khrushchev gave him a rough, brief reception in Vienna. In August Khrushchev showed that he could out-Stalin Stalin by building the Berlin Wall, thus putting his personal seal of approval on the permanent partition of Germany. The following year, however, Khrushchev outreached and outsmarted himself by trying to sneak nuclear missiles into Cuba. This time, Kennedy won hands down by playing it cool. Between them, they had frozen the *status quo* in Germany while accepting the balance of nuclear terror as the best and perhaps the only insurance of peaceful Soviet-American coexistence.

, Nowhere did the settlement of the Cuban missile crisis cause such distress and anger as in Peking, where Chinese Communist propagandists denounced Khrushchev for combining capitulationism with adventurism. They had a point on which more and more of Khrushchev's associates in the Kremlin came to agree. In 1964, confused and exhausted by Khrushchev's zigzag approach to all problems, foreign and domestic, the Politburo put him out to grass on charges of "harebrained scheming" and pledged themselves to repair the damage he had done to Sino-Soviet relations. But they had reckoned without Mao's Cultural Revolution, which, in its turn, had reckoned without that Third World of emerging nations which Mao had aspired to lead. Between 1945 and 1960, more than eighty armed conflicts had taken place among the developing Afro-American nations. These outnumbered many times over all the other conflicts that had taken place elsewhere during this time. Moreover in only four of these more than eighty conflicts had any other nations than those of the Third World taken part.

Five years after the Bandung conference of 1955, the Chinese-Indian honeymoon had already run its course. In another five years the spirit of Bandung itself took bloody vengeance on its creators. Between 1955 and 1965 the Chinese Communists made dazzling progress in Indonesia, where the native party that they organized developed close ties with Indonesia's perpetual playboy President Sukarno. Having plotted during the summer of 1965 to murder Indonesia's general staff and to seize power in the subsequent disorder, the native Communists permitted the all-important but inconspicuous General Suharto (a Moslem Nationalist) to slip through their fingers and do to them and their fellow-traveling supporters what they had planned to do to him and to his anti-Communist supporters. Partly through direct action but more through deliberate nonaction, Suharto inaugurated a blood bath in which anti-Communist Moslems ran amok, killing an estimated three to four hundred thousand presumed Communists within the space of a few weeks. Thousands of other Indonesians of Chinese descent whose business acumen and industry had won them commanding positions in the national economy also met their deaths. Dead bodies and severed heads clogged the rivers, which ran red with blood. But Suharto and his supporters in and out of uniform gradually brought some order to the chaos that the crafty Communists and the supple Sukarno had spread throughout the land. Neither Communist dupe nor wily schemer, Sukarno possessed an instinct for survival that brought him safely through the holocaust with only a few of the trappings and none of the substance of the power he once enjoyed. The victorious anti-Communists attributed their quick victory and subsequent success to the Vietnam war, which, by that time, had so engrossed the Johnson administration that it had neither the resources nor the inclination to intervene in Indonesia's localized civil war—Third World style.

·9·

THE SECOND WORLD WAR, from its very beginning, offered repeated examples of the ironies, paradoxes, and contradictions that occur throughout history. But the accelerating progress of military technology since 1939 led to that corresponding speed-up of events which has given contemporary history a new dimension. Events now move at such a pace that history's ironies have become clichés, its paradoxes platitudes, its contradictions commonplaces. Can man's capacity to transcend himself keep pace with the challenges that now face him?

Without the First World War, there would have been no Russian Revolution, no Second World War. Without the Second World War, there would have been no Chinese Revolution, no emerging Third World nations with their wars and revolutions. And so it was that in August, 1964, Fritz René Allemann, Swiss editor of the West Berlin monthly *Der Monat*, devoted that month's entire issue of his magazine to a symposium in which a dozen European intellectuals developed the theme "Fifty Years of World Revolution." All these contributors had lived through most of those fifty years, and most had played active roles in some parts of the cycle of wars and revolutions that began with the First World War and ended with the Chinese Revolution and its aftermath. Whereupon President Johnson—all unwittingly—chose August 4, 1964, the fiftieth anniversary of Britain's declaration of war on imperial Germany, as the date on which to initiate a new cycle that at once departed from its forerunner in almost every direction.

The previous, fifty-year cycle began with war in Europe and ended with revolution in Asia. The new cycle began with President Johnson's request that Congress empower him to commit the armed forces of the United States to take action against the Communist Republic of North Vietnam because of an incident, on August 4, involving North Vietnamese gunboats and American destroyers in the Tonkin Gulf off the Vietnam coast.

The passage of the Tonkin Gulf resolution did not mark the dread outbreak of World War Three. Neither did it mark the spread of the Chinese Revolution to any region beyond China's own borders. It did, however, mark the unilateral intervention of the United States in a Third World civil war. Seven years later, in 1971, the *Pentagon Papers* laid bare the details of that intervention, before and after the Tonkin Gulf incident, in such profusion and scope as had never before been made public in connection with any comparable military operation still in full swing. Leslie H. Gelb, principal co-ordinator of the *Papers*, summed them up at the time in these pregnant words: "It was and is a Greek tragedy."

In Greek tragedy fate spins the plot; in Shakespearean tragedy, character holds the center of the stage. The satirical parody-drama *Mac-Bird* depicted Lyndon Johnson as a modern Macbeth, a flawed Shakespearean hero. In real life, however, Johnson found himself caught up in a Greek tragedy of fate, involving many characters—some of them flawed heroes, some mitigated villains, and one of them an Aristotelean "person of stature": Franklin D. Roosevelt. But blind, inexorable fate determined the destinies of them all. Events beyond human control, but not necessarily beyond human understanding, prevailed over the individual, great or small, flawed or flawless.

In describing the Vietnam war as a Greek tragedy, Leslie Gelb spoke on the basis of firsthand information compiled from the highest sources over a period of thirty years. This evidence not only traced the origins of the Vietnam war straight back to the Second World War itself. It showed that if any one figure can be said to have dominated that war, it was Roosevelt, head and shoulders. Indeed, the tragedy of the Vietnam war opened with Roosevelt's three outstanding personal contributions to the United Nations victory of 1945: his insistence on the unconditional surrender of Germany and Japan; the success of the Manhattan Project; the establishment of the postwar United Nations Organization before all hostilities had ceased. Although Roosevelt did not live to see events vindicate even one of his three great contributions to the victory of 1945, neither did he live to see the consequences of this vindication, a quarter of a century later, in Vietnam.

In the case of unconditional surrender, the defeated Germans and Japanese lived to see their acceptance of Roosevelt's terms yield them, within ten years, higher living standards, a faster rate of economic growth, and more peaceful conditions at home and abroad than they had ever known. General Marshall in Europe and General MacArthur in Japan, each in his own characteristic way, had followed guidelines laid down by Roosevelt. As to the successful Manhattan Project, the atomic bombs it developed not only enabled the Americans to compel Japan's unconditional surrender eighteen months ahead of schedule. America's postwar atomic monopoly excluded the Russians from the postwar occupation of Japan, but at the same time set off a Soviet-American atomic and nuclear arms race. Contrary to the expectations of many, this did not lead to a nuclear Soviet-American war, but to a Soviet-American balance of nuclear terror.

Roosevelt's third and final contribution to victory in the Second World War dominated the course and consequences of the Korean war. In 1950, the United Nations responded to the North Korean invasion of South Korea by endorsing the police action taken by the United States and fifteen other members of the United Nations. But it was also the last as well as the first time that the United Nations played any such role in any such dispute. Trygve Lie, Norway's prewar foreign minister, whom the United Nations had elected as its first secretary general, incurred the undying hostility of the Soviet Union by approving the American police action in Korea. By 1953, Soviet pressure forced Lie to resign, and it was only with some misgivings that the Russians approved of Sweden's uncompromisingly neutral Dag Hammarskjöld as Lie's successor. In December 1961, Hammarskjöld met his death in the former Belgian Congo, where he had gone to conduct an investigation of the brutal, political murder, almost a whole year before, of the native firebrand, Patrice Lumumba, whom the overeager Russians had rashly supported. By this time almost half the members of the United Nations could qualify as authentic Third Worlders, who therefore commanded the votes to elect as Hammarskjöld's successor the Burmese Buddhist U Thant, who fellow-traveled with Nehru and Nasser rather than with Khrushchev or Mao Tse-tung.

·10·

THE WORLD—and not the Third World only—had changed during the decade of the 1950's, and the weapons and strategies, the allies and adversaries had changed too. By the 1960's neither Khrushchev in Moscow nor Mao Tse-tung in Peking had been able to make puppets of Nasser or Nehru, Sukarno or Ho Chi Minh. How much less could Eisenhower, Kennedy, Johnson, or Nixon count on Macmillan, Wilson, or Heath, on de Gaulle or Pompidou, on Erhard, Kiesinger, or Brandt. Yet the habit of American command that dated back to Roosevelt and his era ran as strong as ever among his successors. For the United States, by virtue of the many strengths and wide experience it had developed in the prosecution of modern war, had proved itself first in peace as well.

Talk about "future shock." The shock of the *Pentagon Papers* came from a secret past which had produced neither villain nor hero but a steady process that Leslie Gelb dramatized in the words "Greek tragedy." Furthermore, Robert MacNamara, who conceived, sponsored, and supervised the whole project, had himself directed the innermost workings of the American military-industrial complex from his post as defense secretary in both the Kennedy and Johnson administrations. He therefore saw to it that the finished product spared nobody, least of all himself. In like manner, Daniel Ellsberg, who leaked the material to *The New York Times*, did so only because his years of devoted service in the Defense Department's prime and privately operated think-tank, the RAND Corporation, led to his final and complete disillusionment. He and MacNamara had known all along what the *Pentagon Papers* did not reveal until 1971—that every President since Eisenhower had publicly charged his predecessor with having assumed new obligations in Vietnam, while privately assuming still more obligations in his own behalf.

Thus Eisenhower and Dulles had embarked on a new and unilateral policy of support for Premier Diem such as Truman and Acheson had never undertaken in behalf of Korea's President Rhee. After President Eisenhower in his bold and widely ignored farewell address warned against the "military-industrial complex" with which he had worked closely for the past twenty years, along came President Kennedy, in his widely hailed inaugural, proclaiming: "Let every nation know, whether it wishes us well or ill, that we shall pay any price, bear any hardship, oppose any foe, to assure the survival and success of liberty." The Kennedy rhetoric went beyond the rhetoric of Woodrow Wilson, Franklin Roosevelt, or John Foster Dulles. Within another three months, however, the Kennedy record in the Bay of Pigs fiasco invited the most sinister conclusions as to what this rhetoric really meant. The following year, a contrite General MacArthur had the candor and courage to advise the new President in the light of his own sad experience: "Never commit American troops to a land war in Asia." All to no purpose. The Greek tragedy which had already entrapped Eisenhower and Kennedy presently claimed President Johnson and President Nixon in their turns.

Far from having betrayed Franklin Roosevelt, all his successors in the White House had remained stubbornly true to his legacy. It all went back to the Second World War and its aftermath: to the war because of the self-perpetuating, self-serving military-industrial complex it had spawned; to its aftermath because of the two postwar myths that reappraisal of the war only gradually dispelled. First came the cold-war myth that substituted an imaginary polarization between a nonexistent free world and a nonexistent Communist monolith for the real, wartime polarization between the United Nations coalition and the Axis powers. Then came the Third World myth and another exercise in polarization, this time with the United States attempting to save an imaginary, freedom-loving Third World from a chaotic coalition of warring Communist factions and an even looser alignment of new nationalist movements whose only common bond consisted of their nonalignment.

During most of the 1950's, nearly all the Republican leaders as well as most of those senior Democrats who considered themselves the inheritors of the Roosevelt tradition found it had committed them to the dubious assumption that the Chinese Revolution, far from having split and shattered the world Communist movement, had instead created a new and doubly dangerous Sino-Soviet monolith. Thus, by the time of the Tonkin Gulf incident, the Johnson administration—like the Kennedy and Eisenhower administrations before it—found itself committed to unleash the wrong kind of war machine against North Vietnam and then to justify that action with the wrong kind of war psychology and propaganda.

What next? The imperfectly known past still serves as a better guide than the unknown and unknowable future. "Westward the star of empire takes its way," orated the youthful John Quincy Adams in 1801. In 1876, George Bancroft, the historian who also served as secretary of the navy and founded the Naval Academy at Annapolis, used the same words as the epigraph to his ten-volume *History of the United States*. Roosevelt, in the mid-twentieth century, harked back to the man who had left the White House 104 years before he entered it and to the historian who had headed, a century before Roosevelt's time, the Navy Department in which Roosevelt had served during the First World War. To John Quincy Adams, as to some of his descendants, the West did not end at the Pacific coast any more than it did to Roosevelt or to his Delano ancestors who had engaged in the China trade. Like Bancroft (a Lincoln Democrat) and Adams before him, Roosevelt found himself caught up in the main currents of his time, currents that still flowed westward. That these currents, a quarter of a century after his death, swept the United States into war in Vietnam, suggests that such currents perhaps flow faster in the twentieth century than they did in the nineteenth and that Roosevelt was not the first President—nor is Nixon likely to be the last—to find himself enmeshed in the Greek tragedy to which the Second World and its aftermath consigned them.

Indeed, President Nixon's acceptance of Premier Chou En-lai's invitation to confer at Peking before May 1972 followed the release of the *Pentagon Papers* as day follows night. For those papers revealed that from the moment in October 1944, when Roosevelt recalled General Stilwell from China, America's star of empire took a westward course that favored Chiang Kai-shek's ailing and corrupt Chinese Nationalists rather than the red star of Mao Tse-tung's vigorous and victorious Communists. As a result, six successive American administrations, from Roosevelt's through Nixon's, found themselves ever more deeply involved waging a losing war against Vietnamese Communism in southeast Asia while continuing to support Chiang Kai-shek's lost Nationalist cause more than two decades after Mao had driven Chiang from the Chinese mainland to the island of Taiwan.

But it took the release of the *Pentagon Papers* in June 1971 to discredit the Vietnam war to such a point that even President Nixon, who had based his political career on anti-Communism (especially of the Chinese variety), deciphered the handwriting on the wall and responded accordingly. In this effort, moreover, he had the enthusiastic co-operation of Chou En-lai, who had reasons of his own, no less compelling than those of President Nixon, to seek a reversal of alliances somewhat similar to the Nazi-Soviet pact of 1939, but far more promising. For Russo-German relations had a long and stormy history and—for that matter—Russo-Chinese relations have an even longer, if not a stormier one. Between China and the United States, on the other hand, a history of primarily friendly relations has long prevailed. Both the Chinese and the Americans have also had more reason to mistrust the Japanese than they have to mistrust each other.

Where will it all end? The course of events, since Mao and Chou resorted to their ping-pong diplomacy in April 1971, has seen the American star of empire moving again in their direction. Both as Chinese and as Communists, they believe in the reconciliation of opposites and may therefore recognize in the anti-Communist Nixon their natural ally. Which makes sense even in the pragmatic terms of practical American politics. Have not Richard Nixon's efforts of the past quarter century at last flayed his spavined, anti-Communist battle charger to death? Has he not the capacity, in his own self-interest, to transcend his antiquated anti-Communism and deal with Chiang Kai-shek as relentlessly as he has dealt with Chiang's critics? Does the Greek tragedy of Vietnam have to end with the American star of empire setting over southeast Asia or can the men around Nixon and the men around Mao arrange for the American star of empire and China's red star to twinkle side by side over the Middle Kingdom?

To these questions, wrapped in the impenetrable mists of the immediate present in which statesmen and journalists must navigate as best they can, neither the irrevocable past nor the unknowable future can provide sure answers. But perhaps these words of the ex-Communist Polish philosopher, Leszek Kolakowski are not without hope: "Everybody can, if he wishes, interpret himself historically and discover the determinants to which he has been subject in the past. But he cannot deduce his own future development from the pronouncements of history in which he trusts. To work such a miracle would be to become the irrevocable past oneself; that is, to cross the river of death which, the poet says, no man ever sees twice."

Epilogue: Transcend or Perish

THE AGREEMENT reached in July 1971, between President Nixon and Premier Chou En-lai, to meet at Peking before May 1972, marked the beginning of the end of the Second World War's Asian aftermath. It also marked the first in a series of alliance reversals that spread at once to Europe. The next occurred on August 12 at Berlin, where the British, French, American, and Soviet ambassadors reached agreement on that city's future and the future of the two Germanys. No sooner had the People's Republic of China sought to normalize its relations with the United States and the United Nations than the Soviet Union sought to normalize its relations with the German Federal Republic and to encourage its European satellites to move in the same direction. The British, French, American, and West German governments had long favored the kind of agreement that the Soviet leaders had at last reached with the British, French, and Americans. Whereupon General Secretary Leonid Brezhnev of the Soviet Communist party and Chancellor Willy Brandt of the German Federal Republic concluded an agreement of their own along the same lines. In other words, the agreements reached in August among the British, French, Americans, Russians, and West Germans not only marked the beginning of the end of the Second World War's European aftermath, they also marked the beginning of the end of a cycle of east-European conflicts that two world wars had failed to abolish.

The ironies and accelerations of history continued throughout the Second World War and its aftermath. But not until the aftermath did the peoples of the world and their leaders enter a period during which their very existence began to depend more and more on their capacity for transcendence. Of the various wartime leaders only Churchill and de Gaulle lived to cope with postwar alliance reversals similar to those which the Second World War had brought forth from the Nazi-Soviet pact through the Russo-German war, and on to Japan's unconditional surrender. Churchill, having declared the cold war in 1946, undeclared it in 1953; de Gaulle, having pledged himself in 1958 to preserve French Algeria, presided in 1962 over its liquidation in order to preserve the Fifth French Republic, which he had established by making that very pledge, four years before. Emperor Hirohito's conduct of his country's unconditional surrender, during the second week of August 1945, remains the outstanding single act of wartime or postwar transcendence, ensuring as it did the instant and almost bloodless transition from war to peace. Yet it must never be forgotten that no leader—prewar, wartime, or postwar—could have begun to transcend himself if unknown, anonymous millions at Leningrad and Stalingrad, at London, Berlin, and Tokyo, and on Mao Tse-tung's Long March had not already chosen transcendence as a way of life as well as a way of death.

The quarter of a century that followed Japan's surrender then witnessed the emergence of such transcendent figures as Mao in China, Nehru in India, Sukarno in Indonesia, Tito in Yugoslavia, Ben Gurion in Israel, Nasser in Egypt, Adenauer in Germany, Khrushchev in Russia, Castro in Cuba. Had fate not consigned Kennedy to the tragic role of instant legend, he could have joined that company as surely as Johnson could not. When Nixon came along he displayed a genius for turning all his opportunities into corresponding crises which became for him the very breath of the anxious life that his dour temperament craved. Ever since the eight years of his vice presidency, the problems of foreign policy cast a growing spell on Nixon who, by the end of his second year in the White House, had persuaded himself that a complete reversal of his China policy could end the Vietnam war and win him re-election in 1972. At the same time, he foresaw that a deal with China could put him in position to wring concessions from the Soviet Union. No sooner had arrangements to meet Chou En-Lai in Peking been arranged, than he found it easy to arrange a subsequent Moscow meeting with Leonid Brezhnev.

Walter Lippmann applauded the "forward pass" that Nixon boasted of having thrown to Chou En-lai. But over whose heads had that forward pass gone—the Russians' or the Democrats'? As a football fan, Nixon had taken to using the words "game plan" to describe his various political strategies, both foreign and domestic, in the double assumption that the initiative always lay with him and that all his game plans would culminate in the grand political climax of the 1972 presidential election. But Chou En-lai and Brezhnev (like most other non-Americans) looked beyond the 1972 election that they regarded as little more than another prelude to the approaching end of the Second World War's Asian and European aftermaths.

But Nixon's infatuation with diplomatic game plans for Peking and Moscow had distracted his attention from economic game plans nearer home. On August 15, he suddenly put forward a New Economic Policy with a scope that he compared to Roosevelt's New Deal. The small print did not measure up to the headlines. Whereas the New Deal opened with the famous "Hundred Days" of drastic social and economic reform, the New Economic Policy began with a ninety-day wage-price freeze. Roosevelt had to deal with the impact of a worldwide deflation on the American economy; Nixon had to deal with the inflationary consequences of the Vietnam war which had not only brought forth a combination of inflation, unemployment, and recession in the United States but had also created an international monetary crisis of which the dollar seemed likely to become the chief and ultimate victim. To forestall that outcome, Nixon ordered a more abrupt and drastic suspension of the gold standard than Roosevelt had decreed but never undertook any such program of social and economic reform as the New Deal had set in motion. For the rest, Nixon's New Economic Policy consisted of a seven per cent tariff surtax on certain industrial imports, a seven per cent tax-cut incentive to certain industries, and the elimination of the seven per cent federal sales tax on new automobiles. His original, 1969-model, anti-inflation program had backfired from the start because its deflationary sponsors lacked the courage of their deflationary convictions. The President's halfhearted application of semi-inflationary remedies, coupled with a sadly inadequate wage-price freeze then left things about the way they had been when the ninety-day freeze set in.

Like the rooster in the fable of Chanticleer who believed that his crowing caused the sun to rise, President Nixon believed that his visits to Peking and Moscow could end the war in Vietnam and usher in a generation of peace. But Henry Kissinger's preliminary visits to Peking had yielded nothing of the sort. They had led to the triumphant admission of the People's Republic of China to the United Nations and to the summary expulsion of the Chinese Nationalists from that body. The voices of those China-watchers who had predicted irrepressible conflict between Moscow and Peking suddenly fell silent. It was the same story in eastern Europe. It did not require any Nixon visit to Moscow to dispel the mythical Soviet-American cold war as completely as his reversal of his China policy had dissipated the parallel fantasy of a war to the death between Russia and China.

In eastern Asia and in eastern Europe, President Nixon had dared to pluck the flower of safety from the nettle of danger. Transcend or perish. But southeast Asia required a different game plan. His Vietnamization policy led to political risks, his withdrawal of American ground combat troops led to military risks from which neither Chou En-lai nor Leonid Brezhnev could protect him—even should they desire to do so. But his greatest danger, which could also become his greatest opportunity, lay in his own hands: that New Economic Policy which he himself had put on a par with Roosevelt's New Deal. Nixon had dared to defy many Republican supporters and a smaller band of Democratic admirers in order to reverse American policy toward Peking and enter into new arrangements with Moscow. But when it came to committing himself, his party, and his country to a similar reversal in connection with economic and social reform at home, he had yet to recognize that only a new economic policy in fact as well as in name could underwrite the foreign-policy decisions to which his projected journeys in 1972 had committed him.

For all President Nixon's self-proclaimed expertise in foreign affairs, he had overlooked the American economy and its universal prestige as the greatest wonder of the modern world. Distance lends enchantment. Perhaps the American economy looms larger than life in non-American eyes. Perhaps foreign policy, in President Nixon's eyes, looms larger than the domestic economy. If so, so much the worse for his ability to see his country as other nations see it—and to see these other nations as they are. In any event, the same President Nixon who had transcended himself when it came to reversing his policy toward China (a nation of which he knew little) had yet to transcend himself when it came to reversing policy in connection with the one country he knew best and the one national political party to which he had always owed allegiance.

And so this account of the Second World War and its aftermath comes full circle, ending, as it began, with paradox. Roosevelt's New Deal, inaugurated to save the American economy from the gravest crisis in its history, wound up equipping that economy to ensure victory in history's greatest war. Some thirty years later, Roosevelt's closest associates, immediate successors, and truest disciples had all but wrecked their country's economy in the quagmire of Vietnam. By the end of the summer of 1971, President Nixon transcended himself to the extent of ditching Chiang Kai-shek and embracing Mao Tse-tung. The fulfillment of his promise to end the Vietnam war had begun with the reversal of his China policy. But he could not fulfill his larger promise of a generation of peace without ditching what he regarded as the American free-enterprise system and replacing it with what he regarded as a socialistic welfare state. The opening stages of his New Economic Policy amounted to no more than a halfhearted reversion to some of the lesser reforms of the New Deal.

Roosevelt in his time had only to follow his instincts and convictions, letting the chips fall where they might. Although he met and mastered the challenges that confronted him with a transcendent response, the final consequences backfired. How much more difficult are the challenges, and how much more dangerous the consequences, to the Nixon generation of Americans. Instead of following their instincts and convictions, they had to reverse them, not only in their policies toward eastern Asia and eastern Europe, but also in the administration of their own economy. The pace of events had accelerated since Roosevelt's day. In such times as these, the greater the acceleration the more transcendent must be the response of those who would survive.

One last, dangling paradox remains unresolved. How reconcile Goethe's admonition, quoted in the Prologue, "Die and transcend," with this Epilogue's subtitle, "Transcend or perish"? William James and Ralph Waldo Emerson supply the missing link. James' "twice-born man" meets Goethe's specifications, and James consigned Emerson to the ranks of "once-born men." But that did not prevent him from describing Emerson as having "electrified and emancipated his generation," nor Emerson from insisting that "dualism underlies the nature and condition of man." In his essay on Compensation, Emerson quoted the Apocryphal text "All things are double one against another," adding for good measure, "Every excess causes a defect, every defect an excess. Every sweet hath its sour, every evil its good." To Emerson "the deep today which all men scorn" remained the only reality. "The present hour is the decisive hour and every day is doomsday." To us too.

BIBLIOGRAPHY

Abel, Elie, *The Missile Crisis*. Lippincott, 1966.
Acheson, Dean G., *Present at the Creation*. Norton, 1969.
Alexander, Edgar, *Adenauer and the New Germany: The Chancellor of the Vanquished*. Farrar, Straus and Cudahy, 1957.
Alliluyeva, Svetlana, *Twenty Letters to a Friend*. Harper, 1967.
Alperovitz, Gar, *Atomic Diplomacy: Hiroshima and Potsdam*. Simon and Schuster, 1965.
Ambrose, Stephen E., *The Supreme Commander: The War Years of General Dwight D. Eisenhower*. Doubleday, 1970.
Amory, John Forth, *Around the Edge of War: A New Approach to the Problems of American Foreign Policy*. Clarkson N. Potter, 1961.
Arendt, Hannah, *The Human Condition*. University of Chicago Press, 1958.
———, *The Origins of Totalitarianism*. Harcourt, Brace, 1951.
Armstrong, Anne, *Unconditional Surrender: The Impact of the Casablanca Policy on World War Two*. Rutgers University Press, 1961.
Armstrong, Hamilton Fish, *Tito and Goliath*. Macmillan, 1951.
Aron, Raymond, *The Century of Total War*. Doubleday, 1954.
———, *Peace and War*. Doubleday, 1966.
Aron, Robert, *The Vichy Regime: 1940–1944*. Macmillan, 1958.
Baldwin, Hanson W., *Battles Lost and Won*. Harper and Row, 1966.
Barnett, A. Doak, *Communist China and Asia*. Harper, 1960.
Barraclough, Geoffrey, *An Introduction to Contemporary History*. Penguin, 1968.
Barrett, William, *Irrational Man: A Study in Existentialist Philosophy*. Doubleday, 1958.
Belden, Jack, *Retreat with Stillwell*. Knopf, 1943.
Bell, Daniel, *The End of Ideology*. Free Press of Glencoe, 1960.
Beloff, Max, *The Foreign Policy of Soviet Russia*, Vol. II, 1936–1941. Oxford University Press, 1948.
Benoist-Mechin, Jacques, *Sixty Days That Shook the West: The Fall of France, 1940*. Putnam, 1963.
Black, C. E., *The Dynamics of Modernization*. Harper, 1966.
Bolles, Blair, *The Big Change in Europe*. Norton, 1958.
Borsody, Stephen, *The Triumph of Tyranny*. Macmillan, 1960.
Bracher, Karl Dietrich, *The German Dictatorship*. Praeger, 1970.
Bradley, Omar N., *A Soldier's Story*. Holt, 1951.
Brooks, Lester J., *Behind Japan's Surrender*. Doubleday, 1968.
Brown, Cecil, *Suez to Singapore*. Random House, 1942.
Bruckberger, R. L., *Image of America*. Viking, 1959.

Bryant, Arthur, *Triumph in the West*. Doubleday,1959.
————, *The Turn of the Tide*. Doubleday, 1957.
Brzezinski, Zbigniew, *Between Two Ages: America's Role in the Technelectric Era*. Viking, 1970.
Bullock, Alan, *Hitler: A Study in Tyranny*. Harper, 1952.
Burns, James MacGregor, *Roosevelt, the Soldier of Freedom*. Harcourt, Brace and Jovanovich, 1970.
Byrnes, James F., *All in One Lifetime*. Harper, 1958.
————, *Speaking Frankly*. Harper, 1947.
Calvocoressi, Peter, assisted by Coral Bell, *Survey of International Affairs, 1953*. Oxford University Press, 1956.
Camus, Albert, *The Rebel*. Hamish Hamilton, 1953.
Catton, Bruce, *The War Lords of Washington*. Harcourt, Brace, 1948.
Chambers, Frank P., Christina Phelps Harris and Charles C. Bayley, *This Age of Conflict: A Contemporary World History, 1914 to the Present*. Harcourt, Brace, 1950.
Churchill, Winston S., *The Second World War*, Houghton Mifflin, Vol. I, *The Gathering Storm*, 1948; Vol. II, *Their Finest Hour*, 1949; Vol. III, *The Grand Alliance*, 1950; Vol. IV, *The Hinge of Fate*, 1950; Vol. V, *Closing the Ring*, 1951; Vol. VI, *Triumph and Tragedy*, 1953.
Clark, Alan, *Barbarossa: The Russian-German Conflict, 1941–45*. Morrow, 1965.
Clark, Mark W., *Calculated Risk: The Story of the War in the Mediterranean*. Harper, 1950.
————, *From the Danube to the Yalu*. Harper, 1954.
Clay, Lucius D., *Decision in Germany*. Doubleday, 1950.
Clemens, Diane Shaver, *Yalta*. Oxford University Press, 1970.
Clubb, O. Edmund, *Russia and China*. Columbia University Press, 1971.
————, *Twentieth-Century China*. Columbia University Press, 1966.
Connell, Brian, *A Watcher on the Rhine: An Appraisal of Germany Today*. Morrow, 1957.
Conquest, Robert, *The Great Terror: Stalin's Purges of the Thirties*. Macmillan, 1968.
Cook, Don, *Floodtide in Europe*. Putnam, 1965.
Craig, William, *The Fall of Japan*. Dial, 1967.
Crankshaw, Edward, *Khrushchev: A Career*. Viking, 1966.
Current, Richard N., *Secretary Stimson*. Rutgers University Press, 1954.
Dallin, David J., *Soviet Russia's Foreign Policy, 1939–1942*. Yale University Press, 1942.
Daniels, Jonathan, *Washington Quadrille*. Doubleday, 1968.
Davids, Jules, *America and the World of Our Time: U. S. Diplomacy in the 20th Century*. Random House, 1960.
Davies, Joseph E., *Mission to Moscow*. Simon and Schuster, 1941.
Davis, Forrest, and Ernest K. Lindley, *How War Came*. Simon and Schuster, 1942.
Deakin, F.W., *The Brutal Friendship: Mussolini, Hitler, and the Fall of Italian Fascism*. Harper and Row, 1962.
Deane, John R., *The Strange Alliance*. Viking, 1947.
de Gaulle, Charles, *War Memoirs*, Vol. I, *The Call to Honour*, Viking, 1955; Vol. II, *Unity*, Simon and Schuster, 1959.
Deutscher, Isaac, *Stalin: A Political Biography*. Oxford University Press, 1949.

Dill, Marshall, Jr., *Germany: A Modern History*. University of Michigan Press, 1961.
Divine, Robert A., editor, *Causes and Consequences of World War II*. Quadrangle Books, 1969.
———, *Roosevelt and World War II*. Johns Hopkins Press, 1969.
Djilas, Milovan, *Conversations with Stalin*. Harcourt, Brace & World, 1962.
———, *The New Class*. Praeger, 1957.
Donovan, Robert J., *Eisenhower: The Inside Story*. Harper, 1956.
Draper, Theodore, *The Abuse of Power*. Viking, 1967.
———, *Castroism, Theory and Practice*. Praeger, 1965.
Drucker, Peter, *The End of Economic Man*. John Day, 1939.
Drummond, Roscoe, and Gaston Coblenz, *Duel at the Brink: John Foster Dulles' Command of American Power*. Doubleday, 1960.
Dulles, Allen Welsh, *Germany's Underground*. Macmillan, 1947.
Eden, Anthony, *Full Circle*. Houghton Mifflin, 1960.
Eisenhower, Dwight D., *Crusade in Europe*. Garden City Books, 1948.
———, *Waging Peace*. Doubleday, 1965.
Elegant, Robert S., *Mao's Great Revolution*. World, 1971.
Fairbank, John K., *The United States and China*. Harvard University Press, 1948.
Fehrenbach, T. R., *This Kind of War: A Study in Unpreparedness*. Macmillan, 1963.
Feiling, Keith Grahame, *The Life of Neville Chamberlain*. Macmillan, 1946.
Feis, Herbert, *Between War and Peace: The Potsdam Conference*. Princeton University Press, 1960.
———, *The China Tangle*. Princeton University Press, 1950.
———, *Churchill-Roosevelt-Stalin: The War They Waged and the Peace They Sought*. Princeton University Press, 1957.
———, *From Trust to Terror: The Onset of the Cold War 1945–1950*. Norton, 1970.
Forrestal, James, *The Forrestal Diaries*, edited by Walter Millis. Viking, 1951.
Freidin, Seymour, and George Bailey, *The Experts*. Macmillan, 1968.
Fuller, Major General J.F.C., *The Second World War*. Duell, Sloan and Pearce, 1949.
Furniss, Edgar S., Jr., *France, Troubled Ally*. Harper, 1960.
Galbraith, John Kenneth, *American Capitalism: The Concept of Countervailing Power*. Houghton Mifflin, 1952.
———, *The New Industrial State*. Houghton Mifflin, 1967.
Gallagher, Matthew P., *The Soviet History of World War II: Myths, Memories, and Realities*. Praeger, 1963.
Gavin, James M., *War and Peace in the Space Age*. Harper, 1958.
Goebbels, Paul Joseph, *The Goebbels Diaries*, edited and translated by Louis P. Lochner. Doubleday, 1958.
Goerlitz, Walter, *History of the German General Staff, 1657–1950*. Praeger, 1954.
Goldman, Eric F., *The Crucial Decade: America 1945–1950*. Knopf, 1956.
———, *The Tragedy of Lyndon Johnson*. Harper and Row, 1969.
Greenfield, Kent Roberts, *American Strategy in World War II: A Reconsideration*. Johns Hopkins Press, 1963.
Grew, Joseph C., *Ten Years in Japan*. Simon and Schuster, 1944.
Griswold, A. Whitney, *The Far Eastern Policy of the United States*. Harcourt Brace, 1938.

Gunther, John, *Roosevelt in Retrospect*. Harper, 1950.
Hahn, Emily, *China Only Yesterday, 1850–1950: A Century of Change*. Doubleday, 1963.
Halle, Louis J., *The Cold War as History*. Harper, 1967.
Harris, Sir Arthur, *Bomber Offensive*. Macmillan, 1947.
von Hassell, Ulrich, *The von Hassell Diaries: 1938–1944*. Doubleday, 1947.
Hassett, William D., *Off the Record with F.D.R.* Rutgers University Press, 1958.
Herz, Martin F., *Beginnings of the Cold War*. Indiana University Press, 1966.
Hiscocks, Richard, *The Adenauer Era*. Lippincott, 1966.
Hitler, Adolf, *Mein Kampf*, complete and unabridged. Reynal and Hitchcock, 1939.
———, *My New Order*, edited by Raoul de Roussy de Sales, introduction by Raymond Gram Swing. Reynal and Hitchcock, 1941.
———, *Secret Conversations, 1941–1944*. Farrar, Straus and Young, 1953
Hughes, Emmet John, *The Ordeal of Power: A Political Memoir of the Eisenhower Years*. Atheneum, 1963.
Hughes, H. Stuart, *Consciousness and Society. The Re-orientation of European Social Thought, 1890–1930*. Knopf, 1958.
Hull, Cordell, *The Memoirs of Cordell Hull*, Vol. II. Macmillan, 1948.
Hunter, Guy, *South-East Asia—Race, Culture, and Nation*. Oxford University Press, 1966.
Isaacs, Harold R., *No Peace for Asia*. Macmillan, 1947.
Jackson, J. Hampden, *The World in the Postwar Decade 1945–1955*. Houghton Mifflin, 1956.
Jacobsen, Hans-Adolf, *Zur Konzeption einer Geschichte des Zweiten Weltkrieges 1939–1945* (On the Conception of a History of the Second World War 1939–1945). Bernard & Graefe, Frankfurt-am-Main, 1964.
Jones, F. C., Hugh Borton and B. R. Pearn, *Survey of International Affairs, 1939–1946: The Far East, 1942–1946*. Oxford University Press, 1955.
Jones, Joseph, *The Fifteen Weeks*. Viking, 1955.
Jordy, William H., *Henry Adams, Scientific Historian*. Yale University Press, 1952.
Kahler, Erich, *The Tower and the Abyss*. Braziller, 1957.
Kato, Masuo, *The Lost War: A Japanese Reporter's Inside Story*. Knopf, 1946.
Kaufman, Walter, *Hegel*. Doubleday, 1965.
Kennan, George F., *Memoirs, 1925–1950*. Little, Brown, 1967.
———, *Russia and the West Under Lenin and Stalin*. Little, Brown, 1961.
Khrushchev, Nikita S., *Khrushchev Remembers*. Viking, 1970.
Kirk, George, *Survey of International Affairs, 1939–1946: The Middle East in the War*. Oxford University Press, 1952.
Kissinger, Henry A., *Nuclear Weapons and Foreign Policy*. Harper, 1957.
Kleiman, Robert, *Atlantic Crisis*. Norton, 1964.
Klein, Burton, *Germany's Economic Preparations for War*. Harvard University Press, 1959.
Knapp, Wilfrid F., *A History of War and Peace 1939–1965*. Oxford University Press, 1967.
Kolko, Gabriel, *The Politics of War*. Random House, 1968.
Kuby, Erich, *The Russians and Berlin*. Hill and Wang, 1968.

Lacouture, Jean, *The Demigods: Charismatic Leadership in the Third World.* Knopf, 1970.

LaFeber, Walter, *America, Russia and the Cold War.* Wiley, 1968.

Laffan, R.G.D., *Survey of International Affairs, 1938.* Oxford University Press, Vol. II, *The Crisis over Czechoslovakia,* 1951; Vol. III, edited by Veronica Toynbee, 1953.

Laloy, Jean, *Entre Guerres et Paix.* Plon, 1966.

Langer, William L., *Our Vichy Gamble.* Knopf, 1947.

Langer, William L., and S. Everett Gleason, *The Challenge to Isolation, 1937–1942.* Harper, 1952.

——, *The Undeclared War.* Harper, 1953.

Laqueur, Walter Z., *Russia and Germany: A Century of Conflict.* Little, Brown, 1965.

Laqueur, Walter, and Leo Labedz, editors, *Polycentrism: The New Factor in International Communism.* Praeger, 1962.

Leahy, William D., *I Was There.* McGraw-Hill, 1950.

Liddell Hart, B. H., *History of the Second World War.* Putnam, 1971.

Lifton, Robert Jay, *Revolutionary Immortality.* Random House, 1968.

Linebarger, Paul M. A., *The China of Chiang Kai-shek.* World Peace Foundation, 1941.

Link, Arthur S., *The American Epoch.* Knopf, 1955.

Lippmann, Walter, *The Cold War.* Harper, 1947.

Luethy, Herbert, *France Against Herself.* Praeger, 1955.

Lukacs, John, *Historical Consciousness, or The Remembered Past.* Harper and Row, 1968.

MacArthur, Douglas, *Reminiscences.* McGraw-Hill, 1964.

MacDonald, Dwight, *Memoirs of a Revolutionist.* Farrar, Straus, 1957.

McGurn, Barrett, *Decade in Europe.* Dutton, 1959.

McInnis, Edgar, *The War, First Year,* 1940; *The War, Second Year,* 1941; *The War, Third Year,* 1942. Oxford University Press.

Macleod, Iain, *Neville Chamberlain.* Atheneum, 1961.

McLuhan, Marshall, *Understanding the Media: The Extensions of Man.* McGraw-Hill, 1964.

Macmillan, Harold, *The Blast of War.* Macmillan, 1967.

McNeill, William Hardy, *America, Britain & Russia: Their Co-operation and Conflict, 1941–1946.* Oxford University Press, 1953.

Maquet, Albert, *Albert Camus: The Invincible Summer.* Braziller, 1958.

Marchland, Bernard, *The Age of Alienation.* Random House, 1971.

Masur, Gerhard, *Prophets of Yesterday: Studies in European Culture 1890–1914.* Macmillan, 1961.

Matthiessen, F. O., *The James Family.* Knopf, 1948.

Maugeri, Admiral Franco, *From the Ashes of Disgrace: A Personal Memoir of Italy's Defeat and Rebirth.* Reynal and Hitchcock, 1943.

Maxwell, Neville, *India's China War.* Pantheon, 1971.

May, Arthur James, *Europe and Two World Wars.* Scribner, 1947.

Mehnert, Klaus, *Peking and Moscow.* New American Library, 1964.

Merkl, Peter H., *Germany: Yesterday and Tomorrow.* Oxford University Press, 1965.

Mikolajczyk, Stanislaw, *The Rape of Poland.* Whittlesey House, 1948.

Moley, Raymond, *After Seven Years.* Harper, 1939.

Montgomery, Field Marshal, the Viscount of Alamein, *Memoirs.* World, 1958.

Moran, Sir Charles Wilson, *Churchill: The Struggle for Survival, 1940–1965, Taken from the Diaries of Lord Moran.* Houghton Mifflin, 1966.
Morgenthau, Hans J., *Politics in the 20th Century.* University of Chicago Press, Vol. I, *The Decline of Democratic Politics,* 1958; Vol. II, *The Impasse of American Foreign Policy,* 1962; Vol. III, *The Restoration of American Politics,* 1962.
Morison, Samuel Eliot, *History of United Naval Operations in World War II.* Little, Brown, *The Battle of the Atlantic,* 1947; *Operations in North African Waters,* 1947; *The Rising Sun in the Pacific,* 1948; *Coral Sea, Midway, and Submarine Actions,* 1950; *The Invasion of France and Germany,* 1957.
———, *The Two-Ocean War.* Atlantic–Little, Brown, 1963.
Mosley, Leonard, *Hirohito, Emperor of Japan.* Prentice-Hall, 1966.
Murphy, Robert F., *Diplomat Among Warriors.* Doubleday, 1964.
Nelson, Donald M., *Arsenal of Democracy: The Story of American War Production.* Harcourt, Brace, 1946.
Niebuhr, Reinhold, *The Irony of American History.* Scribner's, 1952.
Perkins, Frances, *The Roosevelt I Knew.* Viking, 1946.
Pertinax, *The Gravediggers of France: Gamelin, Daladier, Reynaud, Pétain, and Laval. Military Defeat, Armistice, Counterrevolution.* Doubleday, Doran, 1944. ["Pertinax" is pseudonym of André Géraud.]
Pogue, Forrest C., *George C. Marshall,* Vol. II, *Ordeal and Hope.* Viking, 1966.
Reischauer, Edwin O., *Beyond Vietnam: The United States and Asia.* Knopf, 1963.
Revel, Jean-François, *Without Marx or Jesus.* Doubleday, 1971.
Ridgway, Matthew B., *The Korean War.* Doubleday, 1967.
Riencourt, Amaury de, *The Soul of China.* Coward-McCann, 1958.
Robertson, Terence, *Crisis: The Inside Story of the Suez Conspiracy.* Atheneum, 1965.
Robinson, E. E., *The Roosevelt Leadership.* Lippincott, 1955.
Roosevelt, Eleanor, *This I Remember.* Harper, 1949.
Roosevelt, Elliott, *As He Saw It.* Duell, Sloan, & Pearce, 1946.
Rosenberg, Arthur, *A History of Bolshevism. From Marx to the First Five Years' Plan.* Oxford University Press, 1934.
Rosenman, Samuel I., *Working with Roosevelt.* Harper, 1952.
Rostow, W. W., *The United States in the World Arena: An Essay in Recent History.* Harper, 1960.
Roszak, Theodore, *The Making of a Counter-Culture: Reflections on the Technocratic Society and Its Youthful Opposition.* Doubleday, 1969.
Rovere, Richard H., *Affairs of State: The Eisenhower Years.* Farrar, Straus, 1956.
———, *Senator Joe McCarthy.* Harcourt Brace, 1959.
Ryan, Cornelius, *The Last Battle.* Simon and Schuster, 1966.
———, *The Longest Day.* Simon and Schuster, 1959.
Salisbury, Harrison E., *The Nine Hundred Days: The Siege of Leningrad.* Harper, 1969.
Samuels, Ernest, *Henry Adams: The Major Phase.* Harvard University Press, 1964.
Schlesinger, Arthur M., Jr., *A Thousand Days.* Crest Books, 1967.
Schoenbrun, David, *The Three Lives of Charles de Gaulle.* Atheneum, 1966.

Schwartz, Benjamin I., *Chinese Communism and the Rise of Mao.* Harvard University Press, 1951.
Servan-Schreiber, J.-J., *The American Challenge.* Atheneum, 1968.
Seton-Watson, Hugh, *Neither War nor Peace.* Praeger, 1960.
Sheehan, Neil, and others, *The Pentagon Papers.* As published by *The New York Times.* Bantam Books, 1971.
Sherwood, Robert E., *Roosevelt and Hopkins.* Harper, 1948.
Shirer, William L., *Berlin Diary.* Knopf, 1941.
————, *The Rise and Fall of the Third Reich.* Simon and Schuster, 1960.
Shulman, Marshall D., *Beyond the Cold War.* Yale University Press, 1966.
Shwadran, Benjamin, *The Middle East, Oil, and the Great Powers.* Praeger, 1955.
Slim, William J., *Defeat into Victory.* McKay, 1961.
Smith, Gaddis, *American Diplomacy During the Second World War.* Wiley, 1965.
Smith, Walter Bedell, *My Three Years in Moscow.* Lippincott, 1950.
Snell, John L., *Illusion and Necessity.* Houghton Mifflin, 1963.
Snow, Edgar, *Red Star over China.* Modern Library, 1944.
Sorensen, Theodore S., *Kennedy.* Bantam Books, 1966.
Spanier, John W., *American Foreign Policy Since World War II.* Praeger, 1968.
Steel, Ronald, *The End of Alliance.* Delta Books, 1966.
————, *Pax Americana.* Viking, 1967.
Stettinius, Edward R., *Roosevelt and the Russians.* Doubleday, 1949.
Stillman, Edmund, and William Pfaff, *The New Politics: America and the End of the Postwar World.* Coward-McCann, 1961.
————, *The Politics of Hysteria: The Sources of Twentieth Century Conflict.* Harper, 1964.
Stilwell, Joseph W., *The Stilwell Papers,* edited by Theodore H. White. William Sloane, 1948.
Stimson, Henry L., and McGeorge Bundy, *On Active Service in Peace and War.* Harper, 1948.
Stowe, Leland, *They Shall Not Sleep.* Knopf, 1944.
Sulzberger, C. L., *The Big Thaw: A Personal Exploration of the "New" Russia and the Orbit Countries.* Harper, 1956.
Taylor, A. J. P., *English History 1914–1945.* Oxford University Press, 1965.
————, *Origins of the Second World War.* Atheneum, 1962.
Taylor, Maxwell D., *The Uncertain Trumpet.* Harper, 1960.
Taylor, Telford, *Grand Inquest: The Story of Congressional Investigations.* Simon and Schuster, 1955.
————, *Sword and Swastika: Generals and Nazis in the Third Reich.* Simon and Schuster, 1952.
Thompson, Lawrence, *1940.* Morrow, 1966.
Toland, John, *The Last Hundred Days.* Random House, 1966.
————, *The Rising Sun: The Decline and Fall of the Japanese Empire.* Random House, 1970.
Tompkins, Peter, *Italy Betrayed.* Simon and Schuster, 1966.
————, *The Murder of Admiral Darlan: A Study in Conspiracy.* Simon and Schuster, 1965.
Toynbee, Arnold and Veronica M., *Survey of International Affairs, 1939–1946: Hitler's Europe.* Oxford University Press, 1954.

————, *Survey of International Affairs, 1939–1946: The Re-alignment of Europe*. Oxford University Press, 1955.

Trevor-Roper, H. R., *The Last Days of Hitler*. Macmillan, 1947.

Truman, Harry S, *Memoirs*. Doubleday, Vol. I, *Year of Decision*, 1955; Vol. II, *Trial and Hope*, 1956.

Tsou, Tang, *America's Failure in China, 1941–1950*. University of Chicago Press, 1963.

Tuchman, Barbara W., *Stilwell and the American Experience in China, 1911–1945*. Macmillan, 1971.

Ulam, Adam B., *Expansion and Coexistence*. Praeger, 1968.

Van Sindern, Adrian, *Four Years: A Chronicle of the War by Months, September 1939–September 1943*. Yale University Press, 1944.

Wedemeyer, Albert C., *Wedemeyer Reports!* Holt, 1958.

Weller, George, *Singapore Is Silent*. Harcourt Brace, 1943.

Welles, Sumner, *The Time for Decision*. Harper, 1944.

Werth, Alexander, *Russia at War, 1941–1945*. Dutton, 1964.

White, Theodore H., *Fire in the Ashes*. William Sloane, 1953.

White, Theodore H., and Annalee Jacoby, *Thunder out of China*. William Sloane, 1946.

Williams, Francis, *Socialist Britain: Its Background, Its Present, and an Estimate of Its Future*. Viking, 1949.

Williams, William Appleman, *The Roots of Modern American Empire*. Random House, 1969.

Willkie, Wendell, *One World*. Simon and Schuster, 1943.

Wills, Garry, *Nixon Agonistes: The Crisis of the Self-Made Man*. Houghton Mifflin, 1970.

Wilmot, Chester, *The Struggle for Europe*. Harper, 1952.

Zinkin, Maurice, *Development for Free Asia*. Essential Books, 1956.

Index

Gandhi, Mohandas K., 175, 406,
480
assassinated, 464
Garner, John Nance, 107
Gauss, Clarence, U.S. ambassador
to Chungking, 307, 309
supports Stilwell against
Chiang, 304
resigns after Stilwell recall,
305
Gelb, Leslie H., 491, 493
General Federation of Labor
(French), 448
George VI, King of England, meets
Truman, 402
George, King of Greece, 292
German Federal Republic, 456
western allies begin organizing, 452–54
German General Staff, 134, 163
Gerö, Ernö, 486
ousted as Hungarian premier,
485
Gerow, General Leonard T., 306
Giraud, General Henri, 200
joins Torch, 201–5
placed in charge of French
affairs by Roosevelt, 206
prepares for Casablanca, 207
yields all power on Liberation
Committee to de Gaulle,
236
Goebbels, Dr. Joseph Paul, 29, 44,
59, 99, 226, 227, 230,
232, 266, 268, 351
views on Hess, 133
welcomes unconditional-surrender demand, 214
announces Stalingrad sur-
render, 221
on defeat in Tunisia, 229
announces July 20 plot, 283
hails Roosevelt death, 349
orders S.S. men execute him
and wife, 353
Goerdeler, Dr. Karl, anti-Hitler
plotter, 281

Goering, Hermann, 44, 64, 86, 282,
458
directs Luftwaffe in Battle of
Britain, 104
halts raids on British fighter-
plane bases, 105
directs air war at Stalingrad,
218
begins "final solution," 224
peace move fails, 351
suicide at Nuremberg, 353
Goerlitz, Walter, 235
Goethe, Johann Wolfgang von, 16,
17, 501
Gomulka, Wladyslaw, 360, 459
vice premier in Polish provisional government, 373
Gort, Lord, 55
Graf Spee, German pocket battleship, 69
Grant, General Ulysses S., 214
Gray, Thomas, 203
Graziani, Marshal Rodolfo, routed
by Wavell, 126
Great Artiste, Hiroshima instrument plane, 403
Great Leap Forward (Chinese),
259
Great Proletarian Cultural Revolution (Chinese), 259
Greater East Asia Co-Prosperity
Sphere (Japanese), 180,
195, 302
disintegrates, 248–49
disappears, 296
Greenwood, Arthur, 63
Greer, U.S. destroyer, encounter
with German submarine
off Iceland, 157, 158
Grew, Joseph C., U.S. ambassador
to Japan:
favors Roosevelt-Konoye meeting, 157
advises Lend-Lease cancellation, 365
praises Hopkins handling of
Stalin, 371

Marshall, General George C., 198,
201, 272, 296, 346, 347,
348, 354, 362, 426, 439,
449, 453, 463, 492
at Arcadia, 170
attends British inner-cabinet
meeting on second front,
186
at Casablanca, 208
sends Stimson to check on
Churchill and Alexander,
240
orders MacArthur to leapfrog
Pacific bases, 246
grand strategy includes China,
253
still presses for Overlord, 276
long-range strategy vindicated,
287
sustains Stilwell to end, 306
backs Eisenhower broad front,
338
backs Stimson's views on Russia, 366
again sides with Stimson
against alarmists, 363
replaces Hurley as U.S. ambassador to China, 438
named Secretary of State, 445
outlines his European recovery plan, 450
steps down as secretary of
state, 461
Marshall Plan, 450, 451, 452, 460,
463, 464
foreshadowed in 1945, 287,
339
Marx, Karl, 15, 112, 405, 406
Masaryk, Jan, murder of, 457
Masaryk, Thomas G., 26, 27, 37, 64
Mast, General Emmanuel, 201
Matsuoka, Yosuke, foreign minister
in Konoye cabinet, 121,
151, 391
meetings with Hitler and Stalin, 129–31

dismissed as foreign minister,
152
Maurras, Charles, 222
Maw, Ba, former Burmese premier
reinstated by Japan, 175
Mayo Clinic, 141, 329, 357
Meiji (Mutsuhito), Emperor of Japan, Hirohito's grand-
father, 410
Memel, forced "home to Reich," 46
Mendès-France, Pierre, as premier
takes France out of In-
dochina war, 475
Mers-el-Kebir, French naval base
near Algiers, 197
attacked by British, 102–3
Michael, King of Romania, 358
organizes anti-Axis government, 290
Midway, Battle of, 180, 181, 182,
184, 185, 350
Miklos, General Bela, Hungarian
commander in chief,
turns against Germany,
290
Mikolajczyk, Stanislaw, premier of
Polish exile government,
pleads for Warsaw up-
rising, 288
in Polish provisional government, 373
Mikoyan, Anastas, 485
Mindoro Island, Battle of, 323
Minin, Kozma, 148
Missouri, U.S. superbattleship,
scene of Japan's surren-
der, 415
Mitscher, Admiral Marc A., commands Fast Carrier
Force, 296, 300
Model, General Walter, appointed
aide to Rundstedt on
western front, 285–86
Mollet, Guy, successor to Faure
as French premier, 486
supports Israel against Egypt
in Suez War, 483

ABOUT THE AUTHOR

Quincy Howe was born in Boston, Massachusetts, in 1900, attended St. George's School at Newport, Rhode Island, and received his A.B. degree from Harvard in 1921. The next year he spent abroad, traveling in Europe and studying at Christ's College, Cambridge. From 1922 to 1929 he worked with the Atlantic Monthly Company in Boston, devoting more and more of his time to translating articles from the foreign press for The Living Age, *of which he became one of the editors in 1926. Two years later, the magazine was sold to a new owner in New York; a year later he followed and became its editor. His first book,* World Diary: 1929–1934, *appeared in 1934. The next year he became head of Simon and Schuster's editorial department. From 1939 to 1942 he also served as news commentator for radio station WQXR in New York. In 1942 he moved to the Columbia Broadcasting System in the same capacity, remaining until 1950, when he became an Associate Professor of Journalism at the University of Illinois and news commentator for the university's radio station, WILL. He also filled a number of news assignments for the American Broadcasting Company, to which he moved in 1954. In 1961, he became founding editor of* Atlas: The Magazine of the World Press, *where for the next five years he continued the same policies of selecting, translating, and reprinting material from the foreign press pioneered by* The Living Age *since 1844.*

For the past fifty years, Quincy Howe has followed the foreign press in the English, French, and German languages. From 1939 through 1970 he broadcast news commentaries over commercial and educational stations by AM, FM, and international short-wave radio and by television. In 1945 he embarked on his two-volume World History of Our Own Times *and since 1955 has worked on* Ashes of Victory, *which has claimed most of his time since 1966 and all of his time since 1970. He is the son of M. A. DeWolfe Howe, the biographer and literary historian, and of Fanny Quincy Howe, herself a novelist and essayist.*

He is the elder brother of novelist Helen Howe, author of The Gentle-
Americans, *and of the late Professor Mark DeWolfe Howe of the Harvard Law School, biographer of Justice Holmes and editor of the
Holmes-Pollock and Holmes-Laski letters. Quincy Howe married
Mary L. Post of Boston in 1932, and they are the parents of a son and
a daughter and the grandparents of four granddaughters and one
grandson.*